Robert J Shapiro
Oct 91

INFORMATION LITERACY

INFORMATION LITERACY

An Introduction to Information Systems

EILEEN M. TRAUTH
Northeastern University

BEVERLY K. KAHN
Suffolk University

FRANCENA WARDEN
Bank of New England

Macmillan Publishing Company
New York

Collier Macmillan Canada, Inc.
Toronto

Maxwell Macmillan International Publishing Group
New York   Oxford   Singapore   Sydney

Cover Art: Marko Spalatin
Executive Editor: Vernon R. Anthony
Production Editor: Constantina Geldis
Photo Editor: Gail Meese
Text Designer: Anne Daly
Cover Designer: Brian Deep

This book was set in Century Schoolbook.

Macmillan Publishing Company
866 Third Avenue, New York, New York 10022

Collier Macmillan Canada, Inc.

Library of Congress Catalog Card Number: 90-61944

International Standard Book Number: 0-675-20841-6

All photographs without specific credits following their captions are by Macmillan Pub-
lishing/Cobalt Productions, with the additional exceptions of: Figure 1.3 by Larry
Hamill; Figures 1.6, 4.2B, 5.9, 5.10, and 5.11 by Gail Meese/Macmillan Publishing; and
Figures A.11 and A.19 Courtesy of International Business Machines Corporation.

All screen representations of software used with permission of their respective copyright
owners: dBASE® and dBASE III PLUS® are registered trademarks of Ashton-Tate
Corporation. Copyright © 1984, 1985, 1986, Ashton-Tate Corporation. All rights re-
served. Reprinted by permission. Intellect™ software is a trademark of AI Corporation,
Inc. All rights reserved. Reprinted by permission. Lotus 1-2-3 is a trademark of Lotus
Development Corporation. All rights reserved. Reprinted by permission.

Printing: 1   2   3   4   5   6   7   8   9   Year: 1   2   3   4

To the people who provided moral support and understanding while this effort was coming to fruition—Kathy, Mike, Sarah, Bobby, David, and Michael.

PREFACE

It is a recognized fact that a complete business education requires a sound understanding of information processing and the role of information systems in supporting corporate goals. Not only must business students become proficient in using computers, they must also understand the management dimensions of information system use and the way in which information technology helps a company to achieve a competitive advantage. The knowledge that is required can be divided into three educational objectives. First, students should have some functional skills in the use of computer hardware and software relevant to their intended careers. This means that they should be comfortable using a computer and should be proficient in the use of such software as spreadsheets, word processing, statistical packages, and database management systems. Second, students should have a conceptual understanding of computer and communication technology. This includes an understanding of the terminology and the basic architecture of computers and communication devices. This knowledge is necessary to enable them to operate and perhaps manage computer operations, as well as to make informed decisions about the acquisition of information technology. Finally, and most important, students should have a firm understanding of the basic components of systems, the types of systems currently in use, the way in which they are planned and developed, and the management issues associated with their use.

The challenge facing educators today is to determine the best way to provide business students with this education. One major difficulty for colleges and universities is coping with the diversity in computing experience (computer literacy) among students. Increasingly, MBA students enter their programs already proficient in the use of spreadsheet and other software. To a lesser extent, undergraduate students enter college with a knowledge of computer software gained in high school or at home. As technological literature pervades the elementary and secondary curriculum, this trend will continue.

The problem facing the college instructor is to cope with this wide diversity in knowledge and experience. Schools which offer a "hands-on" type of course can simply exempt computer literate students from this course. Alternatively, functional skills can be taught in noncredit workshops.

In light of the increasing computer proficiency of business students, some might ask whether there is any longer a need for a required MIS course in the business curriculum. The perspective of this book is a resounding *yes*! Students who are computer literate have acquired only part of the knowledge that they need. They may have achieved the first educational objective—functional skills—and part of the second objective—an understanding of information technology. But the use of the computer alone will not provide them with an understanding of the role of information processing in a corporation or the issues associated with developing, planning, and managing information systems. Our view, which is reflected in this book, is that the required MIS course can now focus attention on this third objective—an understanding of system and management concepts. Experience tells us that while many students may have a functional knowledge of certain software packages and personal computers, what they lack is the "big picture." They lack an understanding of how a particular software package fits into the larger scheme of information system use for strategic benefit to a company. They also lack an appreciation for the significant behavioral and management issues that arise from increased and widespread use of computers in organizations. The purpose of this book is to facilitate a coherent and complete understanding of information systems for end users who have had some experience with computers.

MARKET

The intended market for this book is the MIS course required of non-MIS majors in business schools. This course has evolved over the years. Whereas previously it had focused primarily on the development of functional skills and an understanding of information technology, the trend now is toward separating computer literacy from the consideration of the strategic role of information systems in businesses today. The emphasis on functional skills is being replaced with an emphasis on the types of information systems used in business, the process of developing systems, and the planning and management issues related to system use. Functional skills are either assumed or provided in separate courses, whether for credit or as workshops. This book assumes some exposure to computers, yet the appendix provides all the technological background necessary for an understanding of the concepts being covered.

ORGANIZATION OF BOOK

This book is organized into four parts. Since it is oriented to the end user/manager, we begin with the contexts in which information systems exist. This includes understanding what an information system is, the various types of information systems found in organizations, and an introduction to the cases which will be used throughout the book to illustrate the concepts being covered. From this we move to the parts of an information system, including both the human and the technological components. The material covered in the first two parts of the book lays the foundation for the third part: developing the ability to acquire, plan, and manage information systems. The fourth part of the book is optional material—an appendix that presents a complete overview of information technology. At the beginning of many chapters, reference is made to those sections in the appendix which provide the appropriate technological background for the material being covered in the chapter.

Chapter 1: What Is Information Literacy?

This chapter introduces the thesis of this book: that business professionals need more than functional skills in the use of information technology. They also need to know why, when, and whether certain tools are appropriate. This is the essence of information literacy. This chapter also considers the different roles that an individual can play with regard to information systems—information systems professional, end user, or manager—and the knowledge requirements of these roles.

PART I: THE INFORMATION ENVIRONMENT

Part I of the book raises the reader's awareness about the role of information processing in organizations and the various forms that it can take.

Chapter 2: Information, Systems, and Information Systems

Chapter 2 lays the foundation for the material to be covered throughout the rest of the book. Using the principles of the Systems Approach, it answers such questions as: What is information? How does it differ from data? Where does it originate? What is an information system? How does it function to provide a user with valuable information? Two frameworks are presented in this chapter which provide a means of organizing the concepts presented in the rest of the book. The first framework is that an information system contains both technological and human resources. They are: hardware, software, data, procedures, and personnel. The second framework is that an information system functions through its activities of input, process, and output.

Chapter 3: Types of Information Systems

As information has exploded into many different forms and uses in our society, so too have the information systems developed to provide it. The different types of information systems discussed in this chapter reflect the purposes for which information is acquired and used in organizations today. These information systems are organized into three categories: access, analysis, and action. An access system focuses on the goal of efficient storage and retrieval of information. An analysis system extends an access system by providing a user with decision-making support. An action system uses an analysis system to carry out some activity on its own.

In order to demonstrate information system concepts in the context of their use, three organizations are studied throughout this book. These organizational settings are introduced in Chapter 3. A university is used because it is one organization with which every student is familiar. The second organization is a bank, an example of both a large organization and an information-intensive one. The third organization is a small, start-up company. This organization experiences all the growing pains of a small business, among which is the need to better organize and support its information processing activities.

PART II: THE COMPONENTS OF AN INFORMATION SYSTEM

While the first part of the book gives an appreciation for the existence of, need for, and uses of information, Part II focuses on the methods by which the transformation from data to information occurs.

Chapter 4: Computer-based Information Processing

Chapter 4 addresses the role of the computer in turning data into meaningful information. In so doing, it covers in detail the methods available for accomplishing the functions of input, processing, and output. Since the focus of this book is on the *use* of information, the focus of this chapter is on matching input, processing, and output methods to the type of information involved, the context in which it originates, and the way it is to be used.

Chapter 5: Human Information Processing

Since information systems contain both human and technological dimensions, the counterpart to computer-based information processing is human information processing. Chapter 5 considers the way in which people carry out the functions of input, processing, output, and storage. With an understanding of both computer-based and human information processing, it is then possible to consider the similarities and differences between the two. This leads naturally to a discussion of human-computer interfaces, the means by which a person's interaction with the computer is facilitated.

Chapter 6: Data Storage and Retrieval

One fact of human information processing is the limited capacity of the human brain for information storage. Storage is clearly an area in which the computer excels. Chapter 6 considers the various ways in which data can be stored in computers. Within the context of organizational uses, it considers the storage of data in both files and databases. The basics of data storage and retrieval methods are presented, but with the focus on the uses. The overall goal is to help the reader match intended uses of data with appropriate methods of storage and retrieval.

Chapter 7: Data Communication

The dramatic advances in telecommunications products and services in recent years have made data communication an integral part of data processing. The objective of Chapter 7 is to enable the reader to make intelligent decisions about the acquisition of data communication resources. The foundation of these decisions is an understanding of communication tools and concepts. This provides the reader with an understanding of what is possible and what to expect from a communication system. The remainder of the chapter addresses the satisfaction of communication needs. It does this by explaining how to identify communication requirements; by explaining the various technological, organizational, and regulatory constraints that exist; by describing the various options available for obtaining data communication resources; and by explaining how to make intelligent acquisition decisions in light of one's requirements and constraints.

PART III: INFORMATION MANAGEMENT

Following an awareness of the uses of information in Part I and an understanding of the tools available to provide it in Part II, Part III returns to the context of use. These chapters consider ways of ensuring that relevant information is available, accurate, and in a useful format. The objective is achieved by considering the ways in which the information system resources—hardware, software, data, procedures, and personnel—interact to produce information.

Chapter 8: Information Systems Development

With the growth of end-user computing, the role of the end user/manager in the systems development process has become more complex. In previous eras of computing, the user had little involvement in this process beyond commissioning a new system and accepting it at the end of the process. As users have become more actively involved in computing, their role in developing systems has grown as well. For this reason, an understanding of the systems development process has become a very pragmatic need for users.

There are now three basic roles that a user can play in the systems develoment process. The first is the traditional role in which information systems professionals develop the system for the user. In this setting, it is important for the user to be able to adequately convey his or her requirements and assess whether or not they have been achieved. At the other extreme, some end users are developing their own systems. This would occur in a small business, in some offices, and in the home. In this setting, the end user needs to know the basics of all phases of the development process, from identification of requirements to consideration of alternatives to methods of implementation. The third role is a combination of the first two. In many organizations, each department is responsible for developing and managing its own system in conjunction with the information systems department. In this setting, the end users need to know both how to develop information systems and how to relate their systems to the rest of the organization.

Chapter 9: Information Architecture

The decentralized nature of computing, along with the growth of data communication in large organizations, has led to the need to place greater emphasis on information systems planning from an overall corporate perspective. The goal is to ensure a fit between the activities of the organization and the information needed to carry them out. As explained in Chapter 9, an information architecture results from examining and analyzing the enterprise model or functions of a corporation in relation to the information model or structure of information processing resources. The benefit of an information architecture is that it provides a comprehensive, overall view of corporate information processing. It facilitates planning by enabling managers to see places where corporate functions are not adequately supported by information processing tools.

Chapter 10: Information Management

The previous chapters in the book provide the basis for Chapter 10: the consideration of procedures for directing an organization's hardware, software, data, and people toward the goal of producing and maintaining the types of information needed by its users. This means managing the data, the technology, and the people associated with information systems. Information management must be carried out at all levels of the organization. While information system professionals would probably be responsible for corporate information management, end users and managers are responsible for information management at the departmental and personal levels. Since the trend is toward each person in an organization having his or her own personal computer, each person must understand how to develop information management policies.

APPENDIX: INFORMATION TECHNOLOGY

To better accommodate the variation in technological proficiency among students, the material on computer technology is provided in a separate part of the book, the appendix. It is organized into five sections: computer hardware, communications hardware, software, programming languages, and information processing generations. The discussion of computer hardware explores the devices used for input, processing, output, and storage of data. The section on communication hardware describes the devices for sending and receiving messages and the channels available for doing so. The software section includes a discussion of system software used to manage computer operations, and the languages used to develop application software for business uses. The fourth section of the appendix discusses the five generations of programming languages. The final section on information processing generations describes the history of computing in terms of the hardware, software, data, and user generations.

The organization of this book is directed at the achievement of three objectives. The first objective is to demystify the technology. This is accomplished in two ways. One is by separating the technology from the systems based on it. By placing the discussion of technology in the appendix, the message is conveyed that the more important considerations for end users are the need for and uses of information. Then comes the consideration of appropriate technology. The second way to demystify the technology is by beginning the book with examples of types of information systems and the contexts in which they are used. Doing this helps to provide motivation to learn more about the technological considerations involved in developing these systems. In these ways the technology is put into an end user's perspective: it is a tool to be used in the acquisition, processing, and use of information within some business context.

The second objective is to provide a conceptual understanding of the kinds of support an information system can provide. This is accomplished by the careful categorization of information system types and by the use of three case studies throughout the book. They represent a range of organizational sizes, industries, and information needs. All examples used in the book relate to these organizations.

The third objective is to aid the development of informed consumers capable of articulating their information requirements to information systems personnel or vendors. It is accomplished by focusing the discussion of each information system topic on the decision-making process. Whether it is a discussion of input devices or data communication networks, the emphasis is on how to determine one's requirements, and the criteria to use in the acquisition of appropriate resources. Having knowledgeable consumers of information products and services is a necessity in light of the growth of end-user develoment and management of systems.

HOW TO USE THIS BOOK

While the chapters are intended to be used in sequential order, it is possible to rearrange some of them to suit an instructor's needs. The first four chapters should be covered first and in order, because they provide the necessary background for the other chapters. For students with little technological background, the appendix can be used in conjunction with Chapter 4. While Chapters 5 through 8 make reference to previous chapters, it is possible to cover these in a different order if desired. Chapters 9 and 10 should be covered last and in order, because they introduce the management considerations related to material covered in the earlier chapters.

Some detailed material in the chapters is presented in sections introduced by three colored rules. These sections can be omitted or covered later without interrupting the flow of the chapter. The instructor's manual accompanying this book provides further instructions regarding which sections of each chapter could be omitted if time or course orientation requires it.

Some business programs, particularly those at the MBA level, include the case approach in the MIS course. This book would be well suited for such a course. Strong emphasis has been placed on readability so that students can read and understand the material on their own as background to cases which would be considered in class.

Curriculum design for MIS courses requires planning for a moving target. Instructors must constantly monitor the changes occurring in industry and in society in order to provide responsive and relevant courses. This book, and the course it supports, is a response to the trend toward greater end-user involvement not only in computer use but in information systems planning, development, operation, and management as well.

ACKNOWLEDGMENTS

We would like to thank the following people who reviewed the manuscript and provided thoughtful and helpful suggestions for *Information Literacy*: David Anderson, Arthur Andersen & Co.; Gary Armstrong, Shippensburg University; Greg Baur, Western Illinois University; Charles Bilbrey, James Madison University; Glen Byerly, Pennsylvania State University; John Chandler, University of Illinois—Urbana; William Charlton, Villanova University; Mary Culnan, American University; Mohammed Dadashzedeh, Barton School of Business; Sasa Dekleva, De Paul University; Roger Flynn, University of Pittsburgh; Irene Hahn, University of Houston—Victoria; Tom Harris, Ball State University; Cary Hughes, North Texas State University; Dan Joseph, Rochester Institute of Technology; Lynn Markus, University of California—Los Angeles; Merle Martin, California State University—Sacramento; Lorne Olfman, Claremont Graduate School; Beverly Oswalt, University of Central Arkansas;

Ronald Schwartz, Wayne State University; Jim Trumbly, University of Oklahoma; and Kathy Brittian White, North Carolina—Greensboro.

We would also like to thank the students who provided assistance in developing this book: Christophe Deslandes, Chanapaul Akathaporn, and Carole Vitale; and colleagues Lynn DeNoia and Laura Bauman, who provided valuable feedback and assistance. Finally, we would like to thank the students at Suffolk University, Northeastern University, and Dublin City University who used drafts of this book and provided valuable input for refining and improving the text.

CONTENTS

CHAPTER 5
Human Information Processing

CHAPTER 10
Information Management

APPENDIX
Information Technology   437

CHAPTER 1

What Is Information Literacy?

CHAPTER OBJECTIVES

- To provide reasons for the increased emphasis on information processing in our society.
- To introduce the concept of information literacy.
- To explain why information literacy is an important part of a business education.
- To describe the way in which this book provides the reader with information literacy.

INTRODUCTION

One doesn't have to look very far these days to see evidence of the upheaval taking place in our society. "Computer revolution," "post-industrial age," "information economy," and "information age" are but a few of the labels used to describe the change that is occurring worldwide and especially in advanced industrial nations like the United States. This societal change is most evident in the shift in the makeup of the American labor force. Whereas in previous eras people made their living through agriculture or factory work, today most people work in an occupation which directly or indirectly involves the manipulation and movement of information, such as education and banking.

The 1980s witnessed a change in how we view the role of information processing in both organizations and society in general. During the 1980s there was a transition from *data* processing to *knowledge* processing, and with it a movement from computers which calculate and store data to systems that reason and inform.[1] Consequently, computer-based information processing in organizations moved from a "back room" activity that produced volumes of paper to a tool that can help a corporation gain a competitive advantage within an industry. Information systems are employed to produce information that is necessary for the ongoing operations and future success of a company.

In the 1990s information technology will play a key role in a company's success. It will help companies create new manufacturing methods, generate new classes of products and services, facilitate the worldwide operations of global corporations, and introduce new ways of buying and selling.[2] Information technology can shorten the product development process and help a manufacturer bring a new product to market more quickly and more profitably. It can enable a firm to sell not only its particular service but also information services. An example is American Airlines, which developed a reservation system now being used by other airlines as well. Communications technology can be used to coordinate work done in offices located in different countries. This would, for example, enable an American insurance company to have its claims processed at a site in Ireland. Suppliers such as American Hospital Supply have shown how they can gain a competitive advantage in an industry through the creative use of information technology — in American Hospital's case by linking its computer to hospital computers in purchasing departments.

Figures 1.1 through 1.4 show some of the ways information technology can be used in various professions.

As more and more people have engaged in the production and exchange of information, the value of information has grown and it has come to be seen as an important resource for society and organizations. Information has joined the ranks of other fundamental resources that organizations and society need in order to exist. When easily available, these resources are often taken for granted. But if they become scarce or more difficult to obtain, more attention is paid to their management. Two obvious examples are air and water. The

FIGURE 1.1
Information technology is used in the retailing industry to improve sales *(courtesy of Burroughs Corp.).*

early American settlers would have laughed at the idea of paying for water or passing laws governing air. But as the population grew and society became more interconnected, attention to the management of these fundamental resources became necessary. Today, we recognize that protecting the quality and

FIGURE 1.2
Computers are used to keep track of patient data and facilitate better utilization of hospital resources.

FIGURE 1.3
Robots are used in automated
manufacturing to increase efficiency of operations.

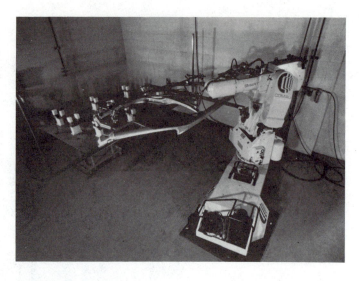

FIGURE 1.4
Portable computers enable managers to use their time more productively while
traveling (*photo courtesy of Radio Shack*).

availability of clean air and water requires serious planning, managing, and legislation. In similar fashion, corporations manage resources such as capital, personnel, and equipment. Today, information and information processing technology are included among the corporate resources which must receive planning and management attention.

At this point, one might ask, "Why has this issue become so important recently?" After all, people have always used information. (In fact, the ability to exchange information through the use of language is one of the primary distinctions between humans and animals.) There are four reasons why information processing has become so important in the last few decades of the twentieth century.

The first reason has been stated already: The kind of work people do has changed. Sociologist Daniel Bell has noted the shift in economies from those based on agriculture to those based on manufacturing to those based on knowledge.[3] This means that the focus of most people's work lives has changed from the production of food or goods to the provision of services. In an **information-intensive** or **post-industrial society**, since most people are concerned with the production and use of information or the production and use of information technology, it stands to reason that information would take on increased importance.

The second reason is that our society has become more complex. In the eighteenth and nineteenth centuries, business was conducted on a much smaller scale. The owner of a store probably knew all of his or her employees and most of the customers. A shopkeeper knew from direct experience which items sold well and how frequently they needed to be reordered. In addition, government made fewer demands on business. The tax laws were simpler and owners did not have to file reports to show compliance with laws. Competition was usually limited to another store in the same or a nearby town, so there was little need to know what was going on in a similar store across the state, much less on the other side of the country or in another part of the world. Today, enterprises need more and better information in order to be successful. As organizations have grown and the economy has become global, managers have less direct contact with each particular aspect of their businesses. They need mechanisms to provide them with information about internal operations, external competition, and governmental regulations which affect their industries.

The third reason information technology has become so important is that the pace of change has increased and along with it the need for information. In the past, life didn't change so much or so quickly. People didn't move about so often. Managers could rely on habit, custom, or direct experience for their information. Today, however, new information is always being required. A manager is less likely to be able to base decisions on the way they had been made previously. Such external factors as changing markets and new competition must continuously be considered in the decision-making process. In a sense, managers must make more first-time and one-time decisions, since circumstances are more likely to change and not allow them to use that same information again.

The final reason for the increased emphasis on information is that the growing need for information has been accompanied by the availability of sophisticated tools for providing it. The computers of the 1950s, 1960s, and 1970s were large, expensive, and difficult to operate. (See Figure 1.5.) Consequently, trained professionals were required to use them. In the 1980s computers became smaller, more affordable, and "user-friendly." (See Figure 1.6.) The result is that powerful computer technology is now accessible to the general public and is quickly permeating all aspects of everyday life.

This trend will undoubtedly continue in the 1990s. Robots and expert systems whose reasoning capabilities rival those of humans are the newest tools to become available. Our lives will depend more and more on information pro-

FIGURE 1.5
Early computers were large and too difficult for the business professional to use directly (*photo from U.S. Bureau of the Census*).

FIGURE 1.6
Today's business professionals make use of desktop computing technology to enhance their effectiveness.

FIGURE 1.7
Developing skills in the use of the computer often begins at an early age.

FIGURE 1.8
A college student uses a portable computer to research and write papers for class.

cessing tools, and at the same time we will need to have increased technical sophistication to benefit from this technology. Whether we like it or not, our lives have become technology-based. As a result, there has been a recognition of the need to instill a new "literacy" during the educational process, from elementary school (see Figure 1.7) through college (see Figure 1.8).

INFORMATION LITERACY

The first response by educators was the attempt to provide students with **computer literacy**. Computer literacy is defined as

> the ability to turn naturally to the computer for problem solving. It includes understanding the structure and operations of the computer as well as knowing how to use software packages.

The growing availability of personal computers in the early 1980s resulted in a wave of computer literacy courses in colleges and universities. The purpose of such a course was to provide students with a basic understanding of the computer and the functional skills needed to manipulate it. Therefore, the focus was on the ability to program computers in a language such as BASIC or the use of software packages for word processing, spreadsheet, and data management applications. This would enable students to utilize computers in their other courses and to possess the skills required of them in the workplace. Students today can expect to find computers as much a normal part of office equipment as telephones and photocopiers. And they can expect that their employers will assume they know how to use them!

While it is important to learn these functional skills, the reality is that this is not enough. Preparing for a career in an information-intensive society requires more than just knowing how to use the technology. One must also know *why* or *when* or *whether* the technology is appropriate. The term **information literacy** expresses the broader need: the ability to acquire, process, use, and communicate the *right* information. In a post-industrial society people need a level of literacy that will enable them to be effective consumers of information.

Information literacy is built on computer literacy in the same way that successful human communication is built on the ability to read, write, and speak. One must first understand the basics of the tools and how to use them. But one cannot stop there. Information literacy is defined as

> the ability to identify, gain access to, manipulate, and effectively use information within the context of one's personal and professional lives. This includes the ability to critically evaluate the quality of information, and knowing when information is incorrect, inaccurate, or incomplete. It is the ability to work with the information appropriate to one's task regardless of the form in which it arrives or the means by which it is processed.

Information Literacy Needs of Business Professionals

Given this general definition of information literacy, the next question is, "What specifically does a business person need to know?" To answer this question, it is first necessary to consider the ways in which an individual may interact with information and information technology in a company.

Information Systems Professionals

One category of persons consists of information systems professionals. These individuals develop and manage information systems for others. This involves working with all parts of an information system: the hardware (computer), the software, the data, the people who will use the system, and the procedures by which the system functions. However, working with information technology — the hardware and software — is the primary focus of their jobs. They may work for a computer vendor as a tool developer, in a company's data processing department as a system developer or manager, or in a functional area of a business as a liaison to the data processing department.

The educational preparation for such positions normally involves obtaining a degree in mathematics, computer science, engineering, computer information systems, or management information systems. Their knowledge requirements go beyond information literacy. The courses in these degree programs place heavy emphasis on knowledge of technology, computer programming, and the development and management of corporate information systems.

Information Systems Users

The second category of individuals is made up of the rest of the people in an organization. They may work in marketing, accounting, or finance departments, but they all rely on information systems in order to perform their jobs. When they interact directly with the technology to obtain or manipulate information, they are referred to as **end users**. End users may be managers, individual contributors, or clerical workers. At present, many business professionals are end users; in the future, most will be.

The end-user computing movement accompanied the proliferation of personal computers for three reasons. First, personal computers were smaller and much less expensive than the computers which had existed up to that point, meaning that a department could afford to purchase several, perhaps one for every office. Second, relevant business software was available to run on these computers, so the average business person could use a computer without having to learn computer programming first. These software packages were also "user-friendly," meaning that the instructions are easy to learn and the methods of interaction relatively simple. Third, the growing demand for information within corporations could not always be met by data processing personnel alone, so business people began to do some of this work themselves.

Today, business professionals carry out a range of activities involving information processing. As end users, they not only use but often develop, tailor, and manage their own **personal information systems**—those systems to be

FIGURE 1.9
Information literacy is needed to make sense out of the masses of data that daily invade our lives. Without it, we could be confronted with "data gridlock" (*photo courtesy of New York City Department of Transportation*).

used individually in their offices. As managers, they commission the development of information systems by others, make or approve decisions to invest in information technology, and consider the relationship between information systems and corporate goals. Increasingly, managing a department also includes managing a **departmental information system** — the information system used to support the operations of that department. These people, whether simply end users or managers who are also end users, need information literacy (see Figure 1.9).

This fact is supported by a recent study on the future of management education and development, commissioned by the American Assembly of Collegiate Schools of Business (AACSB). It emphasized the critical role that an understanding of information processing should play in a management education.[4] Managers need to know how to use information technology to support their own information-gathering and decision-making activities. They need to know how to effectively manage the information resource to its fullest advantage. Most important, they need to relate business objectives and organizational structures to the creative use of information technology. It is for such people that this book is written.

THE COMPONENTS OF INFORMATION LITERACY

The Information Environment

The first component of information literacy is an awareness of the importance of information to an organization. Related to this is an understanding of the various ways that information and its technology can be used. The first part of this book provides this background by considering what an information system is and the types of information systems that exist. The importance of information systems to an organization is demonstrated by the introduction of three case studies that will be used throughout the rest of the book. The organizations in the case studies are a bank, a university, and a small business.

The Components of an Information System

The second component of information literacy is an understanding of the methods by which data is transformed into useful information. This includes a conceptual understanding of the technology, and knowledge of the ways it is employed to produce and transfer information. Since information systems must be useful to people in order to be effective, one must also understand the difference between human and computer-based information processing. The second part of this book discusses the ways in which people and computers process information and the ways in which data is stored, retrieved, and communicated.

Because an adequate preparation for life and work in an information-intensive society must include both the ability to use information processing tools and the ability to make informed decisions about their acquisition, use, and management, one must also have a good understanding of what these tools can do. The Information Technology Appendix provides an overview of the computer hardware and software used to carry out the information processing functions of input, processing, output, storage, and communication.

Information Management

The final and most important component of information literacy for business professionals is the ability to manage the data and technology to ensure that relevant information is available, accurate, and in a useful format. Business people are not only end users, they are also managers of the tools being used. Therefore, they need to understand how to acquire and configure the appropriate technology, how to relate information systems to corporate strategy, and how to develop effective information management policies. The third part of this book relates information systems to the organizational setting by explaining the ways in which systems are developed, the methods for information systems planning, and the procedures for managing the technology, data, and people.

SUMMARY

This book has three goals, three intended outcomes, which should result from achieving information literacy. The first comes from having a better understanding of information processing tools. This goal is the demystification of the technology. While the computer is certainly a very sophisticated tool, it is still just a tool. A better understanding of computers, how they work, and how they can be used will help the reader understand that the real focus of attention should be the need for and uses of information. Technology exists to serve that end.

With a better understanding of the origins and uses of information and the systems that support them, the reader should achieve the second goal of this book: the ability to identify and articulate information needs to others, whether a salesperson in a computer store or a systems professional at a large corporation. In this way, the reader will be an informed consumer, able to know *why*, *when*, and *how* to use these tools to satisfy information needs.

The final goal of this book is the most important. People today constantly need new information. The information we have today may not satisfy tomorrow's need. What we learn in school won't suffice for the rest of our lives. The only way to successfully cope is to change our attitude about learning. It is not as important to have all the information that exists today as it is to know how to get that information when we need it. Therefore, we can say that the overall goal of this book is to help the reader *learn how to learn* about information processing. Rather than only focusing on what is known today, this book tries to help the reader develop strategies for learning what will need to be known tomorrow. If we remember that the reason we need information literacy is that we live in an information-intensive society, this goal seems to be both achievable and appropriate.

CHAPTER NOTES

1. Edward A. Feigenbaum and Pamela McCorduck, *The Fifth Generation: Artificial Intelligence and Japan's Computer Challenge to the World* (Reading, MA: Addison-Wesley Publishing Company, 1983): 1.
2. *The Landmark MIT Study: Management in the 1990s* (Arthur Young, 1989): 4.
3. Daniel Bell, *The Coming Post-Industrial Society* (New York: Basic Books, Inc., 1973).
4. Lyman W. Porter and Lawrence E. McKibbin, *Management Education and Development: Drift or Thrust into the 21st Century?* (New York: McGraw-Hill Book Company, 1988).

ADDITIONAL REFERENCES

Buckingham, R. A., R. A. Hirschheim, F. F. Land, and C. J. Tully, eds. *Information Systems Education: Recommendations and Implementation*. Cambridge, U.K.: Cambridge University Press, 1987.

Trauth, Eileen M. "A College Curriculum for Information Literacy." *Education and Computing* 2 (1986): 251–258.

Trauth, Eileen M., Kathleen F. Curley, and Stephen K. Kwan. "The Design of an Information Management Curriculum for Business Students." *Proceedings of the International Business Schools Computer Users Group and the Information Systems Association Joint European Meeting*, London, 1987.

KEY TERMS

computer literacy
departmental information system
end user

information-intensive society
information literacy

personal information system
post-industrial society

REVIEW QUESTIONS

1. What is meant by a post-industrial or information-intensive society?
2. How has computer-based information processing changed as the transition to knowledge processing occurred?
3. What are the main reasons for the current recognition of information as a key organizational resource?

4. What is meant by the term *information literacy*? How is it similar to computer literacy? How is it different?
5. Why is it necessary for non-information systems professionals to be information literate?
6. Why has end-user computing grown so rapidly?
7. Business professionals may use personal information systems and departmental information systems. Give examples of each.
8. What is information management?
9. Why is information management the most important dimension of information literacy?

PART I

The Information Environment

PART OUTLINE

CHAPTER 2

Information, Systems, and Information Systems

CHAPTER OUTLINE

WHAT IS INFORMATION?

WHAT IS A SYSTEM?

WHAT IS AN INFORMATION SYSTEM?

CHAPTER OBJECTIVES

- To present the Systems Approach as a useful framework for describing and understanding an information system.
- To explain the concepts of data, information, and system.
- To describe the properties of an information system, according to the Systems Approach.
- To describe the components or functions of an information system.
- To describe the resources or parts of an information system.

INTRODUCTION

The focus of attention in Chapter 1 was the increasing importance of information in our lives. The chapter pointed out that because of this fact, people need to acquire information literacy. In Chapter 2, we will examine information more closely, as well as some of the related concepts which lay the groundwork for the remainder of the book.

Three terms related to information processing are used quite frequently in our everyday lives: data, information, and information system. Rarely, though, are we called upon to critically examine them. Without a clear understanding of these fundamental concepts, however, we cannot use them to their fullest potential. The material presented in this chapter should be thought of as the foundation; what is presented in the remaining chapters are the building blocks from which information literacy is constructed.

To help you understand the concepts which are to be discussed, think of a setting in which you need information to help you accomplish some task. Suppose you are assigned a group research project in a marketing course. You need to incorporate data obtained from both library research and corporate interviews. Therefore, you need to construct an information system to help you. But what will this information system look like? What are its parts? How will it give you the information you require? The material presented in this chapter will provide you with the concepts needed to answer these questions.

WHAT IS INFORMATION?

So far in the book, the term *information* has been used as though everyone understood it in the same way. This is not the case, however. People generally agree that information is what makes up knowledge, that it is the basis for understanding, and that it answers our questions. Beyond that, there is no consensus on what it does mean or should mean, or whether this issue matters at all.

In one sense, a precise understanding of this term might not be required. In fact, some people who work in the information processing professions are more concerned with performing operations *on* information than having an exact definition of it. In general, people know when they have received information, and whether it is good information, even if they could not tell you unequivocally what they mean by the word. However, it is important to the achievement of information literacy to examine the notion of information a little more closely. If the goal of information literacy is the ability to acquire, process, and communicate appropriate information regardless of the technology involved, one must develop a clear understanding of this entity called information which has become so important in our lives.

Fundamental to a clearer understanding of information is an understanding of the distinctions among data, information, and knowledge. While this may seem fairly obvious, there is remarkably much confusion over the terms and any distinctions that might exist among them. A typical discussion about the meaning of the terms *data* and *information* might yield responses such as:

> Data is what you have when you use computers; information is what you have when people do the work.

or:

> You take information and put it into the computer and do things like statistics, and you get data as the output.

These responses suggest as much about our understanding of data and information as they do about the state of information processing systems today. That is, what is sometimes passed off as information (regardless of the method of processing) is, in fact, data. Just ask any user who has to spend many hours analyzing and interpreting the output from some "data processing" operation!

Data can be thought of as the raw material out of which information is formed. **Information** is processed data which is perceived to be meaningful or useful. **Knowledge** comes from the links established among related items of information. In your research project, *data* is the material that you read in the library and the notes you make from your interviews. You will have *information* when you relate this data to the problem you are researching and begin to find answers. The result of your research project will add to your *knowledge* of marketing.

The *Oxford English Dictionary* defines data as

> characters, or symbols on which operations are performed by computers and other automatic equipment, and which may be stored or transmitted in the form of electrical signals, records on magnetic tape or punched cards, etc.[1]

Data has objective, tangible existence; it is information *in potential*. But processed data does not necessarily result in information. Why? The answer lies with the recipient of the data. For the processed data to be considered information, the recipient must find it meaningful or useful. If the data is received by a user who is capable of understanding it or is motivated to use it for some purpose, the person can be said to have received information. An example might be a mathematical equation. To someone familiar with the language of mathematics, this equation, this data, when received (read) and contemplated (processed), conveys meaningful information. Someone unfamiliar with mathematical notation might read the same equation and, despite all attempts to do so, be unable to derive information from it. One important characteristic of information, then, is that it has *subjective*, not objective, existence. It is essentially an "individual" phenomenon; what is information for one person is not necessarily information for another. In fact, the growing popularity of end-user computing can be explained, in part, as stemming from a desire to "individualize" the process of acquiring information.

A given set of data can also result in different interpretations and therefore different information. For example, the statement "We had quite a snowfall last night" could be interpreted by someone in Florida to mean an inch of snow had fallen. To someone in New Jersey it might mean a foot of snow, while someone from Maine might take the statement to mean three feet of snow. Likewise, the same information can be produced from different sets of data which can, in turn, be processed in a variety of ways. One might learn that it is raining outside by hearing about it on the radio, seeing a person with an umbrella, or walking outside and getting wet. Despite the many forms, the same information results. Data has a tangible existence. Information, the result of a meaningful interpretation of that data, resides within the recipient. Its existence is *intangible*. Technically, it "resides" somewhere within the brain of the recipient. Because of this, information can be said to be the product of human intelligence.

A question still remains, however: How does someone determine that he or she has received information? At the most general level, we could say that information is data that is understood by and relevant to the individual. This suggests that we could define information as "data that is meaningful and potentially useful." A problem with this definition is that it is rather subjective; what is useful to one person may be of no use to another. For this reason, more specific definitions of information are used.

There are three general definitions of information. Depending upon the definition one uses, expectations about the information system developed to provide it will vary.

A Collection of Data

The broadest view of information defines it as the increase in knowledge that results from the acquisition of data. In other words,

> we have received information when we know something now which we did not know before.[2]

In other words, information is a collection of "new facts." According to this definition, a history book would contain information for many readers. This definition could be applied to the work of people in the marketing department of a company where market researchers are attempting to collect and understand "new facts" about potential customers. The information you will need for your research project would fit this definition.

Data for Decision Making

A second view concerns the amount of data needed to reduce uncertainty about a decision. It provides a more specific definition of information, based on a well-developed body of knowledge called **information theory**.[3] Information theory has had a significant influence on the field of information processing. In particular, it has influenced the definition of information used in most business contexts. The notion of uncertainty has been interpreted to mean *decision-making uncertainty,* and the amount of information has come to mean that amount of data needed for some decision-making process. Thus, a very popular definition of information, especially for managers, is "data that is of value in decision making."[4]

INFORMATION THEORY

This theory emerged from concern about the engineering aspects of communication. Claude Shannon and Warren Weaver, two leaders in this field, developed a mathematical representation of the uncertainty about the true message content in a communication event. Uncertainty, they said, arises because of extraneous signals being introduced. An example would be static that accompanies a radio signal. Because extraneous signals are present, it becomes difficult to separate the true signal from this extra data. A person who complains of **information overload** is describing the same phenomenon.

To improve the communication process in the presence of this "noise," Shannon and Weaver developed a way to calculate the number of message units (which they called "bits") needed to reduce the receiver's uncertainty about the true content of the message. This measure of the reduction of uncertainty was called "information," and the number of bits needed to accomplish it was referred to as the "amount of information." Part of the appeal of information theory is that it provides a tangible measure of something usually considered intangible.

Data Supporting Behavior

The third definition of information combines the two previous definitions. Information is thus seen as a collection of facts, but not just any facts. Information is defined as data that supports some behavior or is meaningful or useful for carrying out some activity including but not limited to decision making. An example of information according to this definition would be corporate procedures—the collection of data about tasks to be performed in accomplishing some corporate activity. This definition is a compromise. It is broader than the second definition, but not as general as the first.

From these three definitions, we can see that there are a number of ways to think about what information is and when it comes about. One definition is not necessarily better than the others. Each has its strengths and weaknesses. The important thing is that everyone working to acquire, manage, and/or evaluate the information should be using *the same* interpretation. This is crucial because the definition of information we use will shape our expectations about the technology and systems that are supposed to provide it.

For example, consider the development of an information system to help maintain inventory at a grocery store. Expectations of this system could range from keeping a simple count of the number of items on hand, to determining when it is time to order more stock, to automatically doing the ordering. If the person who designs the system uses the definition "a collection of data," the system is successful if it produces weekly reports showing the number of items in stock. But suppose the store manager wants to know on a daily basis which items are selling faster than others. To the manager, the reports must not only be a collection of facts, they must also help the manager decide when to reorder. These two individuals, then, will have different expectations about the system, because they are using two different definitions of information. It is very likely that the manager will not be satisfied with simple inventory counts, and the system designer will wonder why.

WHAT IS A SYSTEM?

The second important concept we need to define before discussing information systems is the term **system**, which has been used to describe everything from stereos (sound systems) to beauty parlors (hair cutting systems)! Perhaps it is more than accidental that this word is so popular. Perhaps it reflects a growing concern with wholes and the compatibility of their parts in the face of an increasingly specialized and complex society. Let us explore the notion of a system so we will be able to pair it with the word "information" to produce a meaningful and usable definition of an *information system.*

Several important theories have contributed to our present understanding of the concept of a system. These theories extend back many decades. In fact, some of the theories were developed before the computer. The notion of thinking about our modern world in terms of systems emerged at the end of World War II. **General Systems Theory**[5] was developed to help scientists consider the behavior of wholes. The intent of General Systems Theory was to focus on the *purpose* of the system, not just the observed behavior of its parts, with an eye to understanding the interaction of those parts.

Another important theory developed at the same time was **cybernetics**.[6] From the Greek word *kybernetes*, meaning "governor" or "pilot," cybernetics proposes that any entity (military aircraft, system, or organization) requires **feedback** on its progress as it moves toward its goal. In one of its earliest uses, the theory of cybernetics was applied to military command and control systems which governed the behavior of missiles. Today, however, the notion of feedback has been incorporated into organizational as well as physical systems.

The most significant contribution of the theory of cybernetics to the study of information systems is the notion that, in addition to having an overall goal, systems can adapt as they progress toward that goal. For our purposes, it means that an information system is not fixed for all time, but changes as user feedback is communicated back to its designer or manager. This notion will be discussed more fully in later chapters.

These two theories were incorporated into the **Systems Approach,**[7] which was developed during the 1960s. The purpose of the Systems Approach was to take the theories about systems that were used in engineering and the sciences and apply them to business settings and business problems. Thus, the intent of the Systems Approach is to give the *whole* as much attention as the parts. The Systems Approach provides a useful framework for describing the parts of an information system within a context. But before we describe an information system according to this perspective, let us consider the general properties of any system.

Purpose

A system must have a reason for existing. Therefore, one property of a system is its goal or **purpose.** Further, this purpose should be able to be articulated and should be achievable. For example, the purpose of one shoe manufacturer as an organizational *system* would be to take raw materials and produce certain kinds of athletic shoes within marketing and budgetary constraints. This purpose must be articulated in a way that can be understood by all personnel in the company, and it must be realistic in order to be achieved.

There can be two sets of purposes, *stated* and *real*. Sometimes the stated purpose is not the same as the real purpose. For example, the stated purpose of the shoe manufacturer (as expressed to employees and customers) might be to produce the highest-quality athletic shoes. To management, however, the real purpose might be to sell more shoes than the competition. Pursuing the real purpose might mean producing lower-cost shoes that are not of the highest quality. Since the purpose is the basis for evaluating the success of the system, a conflict can arise. The design and marketing departments, which are pursuing the stated purpose, believe the system is not successful if low-quality shoes are produced. But management thinks the system has failed if the shoes are not outselling the competition. It is for this reason that it is important to distinguish between stated and real system purposes.

Components

The **components** of the system are the *functions* or activities performed to achieve the system's goals. If we think of a bank as a system, the components are those activities associated with managing the flow of money into and out of the bank to achieve its goal of making money on that money.

One common way of describing a system is to think of it in terms of three primary functions: input, process, and output. **Outputs** are the products, services, or other effects produced by the system. **Inputs** are the materials and assets needed to produce the desired outputs. **Processes** are the activities by which inputs are transformed into outputs. According to the Systems Approach, all systems have these same components. Consider the human digestive system: Food is eaten (input), broken down into both usable and nonusable parts (process), and the result is energy, storage of calories, and waste (output).

Resources

The **resources** of the system are the means by which the purpose is achieved. Resources can be thought of as the *raw materials* of the system, or the inputs that are transformed into outputs. If we think of a business as a system, the primary resources would be personnel, machines, materials, and money.

Another way to think about resources is to say they are what is *inside* the system. That is, the system is composed of resources (parts) that work together to achieve its goal. For example, the resources of a manufacturing company are the raw materials, the manufacturing equipment, the product designs, and the personnel.

The individual resources can themselves be viewed as systems if they possess all the properties of a system. When this occurs, a resource is called a **subsystem** of the overall system. The goals of the individual subsystems, then, would be considered *subgoals* of the total system. For example, the design department of the shoe company, since it possesses all the properties of a system, can be viewed as a subsystem of the company. In situations like this, it is important to keep the overall system goal in mind and to make sure the goals of each subsystem are compatible with it. For example, the goals of the design department should be the same as those of the company as a whole.

This focus on the whole suggests the desire for synergy. **Synergy** is based on the belief that the whole is greater than the sum of its parts. For systems, synergy means that the effect of all subsystems working together is even greater than the combination of the individual effects of each subsystem. For the shoe manufacturer, this means that the variety and quality of shoes produced will be better if the design, marketing, and manufacturing departments all work together with a common goal in mind.

On the other hand, when the parts of a system do not work together, there is usually **suboptimization**, or the achievement of subsystem goals at the expense of the overall system goal. Suboptimization would occur if the manufacturing department compromised on the quality of shoes in order to save money and make its budget look better.

Environment

If the resources can be thought of as what is inside the system, the **environment** can be thought of as what is *outside* the system. What is outside the system is some context that must be taken into account when trying to understand the purpose and behavior of the system. Simply put, the environment is what *is not* the system.

For example, the environment of the shoe manufacturing company is the market for and suppliers of athletic shoes. What must be taken into account are: (1) kinds of athletic activities which are currently popular; (2) how serious people are about their sports; (3) the age of the people purchasing shoes; (4) design preferences; (5) the amount of money these people are willing to spend; and (6) the nature of competitors in this industry. All these characteristics of the environment must be taken into account in the design, manufacturing, and marketing of the shoes.

In order to define the environment, to be able to say what is and is not a part of the system, we must understand the system's boundaries. A **boundary** defines the scope of the system and specifies what is inside and what is outside the system. Boundaries can also change. That is, the definition of what is inside the system can change. Suppose the shoe manufacturer, observing the growing popularity of aerobic walking, decides to market a line of walking shoes. One option would be to acquire a company which already produces walking shoes. Such a company, previously considered part of the environment of the shoe manufacturer, would now be part of the system. In this example, the boundaries of the system are enlarged to include another manufacturing site. The decision regarding what *will* and *will not* be a part of the information system is a very important one.

The environment can also be viewed as the **constraints** on the system, what is "fixed," what the system cannot change. For example, one constraint on the shoe company is the nature of the industry: the number of competitors and the size of the market. Another constraint would be changes in consumer preferences, because as a sport becomes less popular, the demand for those shoes will diminish. The company must learn to work within these constraints.

Management

The final system property is the counterpart to purpose: **management**. There are three primary functions of management. First, if the goal is to be achieved, there must be a plan for achieving it. Second, there must also be a measure of performance or way of knowing whether the goal has been achieved. Finally, there must be a mechanism for providing feedback and altering the behavior of the system in light of this feedback.

A well-developed body of knowledge about the practice of management in organizations has evolved over the past seventy years. Since an organization is also a system, this view of management is applicable to our present discussion. Management is defined as:

> *Directing an enterprise through its human and material resources toward the achievement of a predetermined goal.*

The managerial activities that are involved in accomplishing this include:[8]

Planning—choosing goals, policies, and procedures from available alternatives.

Organizing—grouping tasks and establishing authority relationships to carry out these policies and procedures.

Staffing—selecting and training personnel who will carry out these tasks.

Coordinating—guiding and supervising personnel toward the achievement of the goal.

Controlling—measuring and correcting activities to make sure the plans are being accomplished.

Obviously, not all of these activities are carried out by each manager in an organization. Twenty-five years ago Robert Anthony developed a framework that describes three levels of management and the responsibilities associated with each.[9] The names of these levels reflect the kinds of decision making occurring in organizations and correspond to top, middle, and lower management, respectively. Figure 2.1 presents these levels.

Strategic Planning

Strategic planning is the process of decision making in four key areas:

1. the objectives of the organization
2. changes in these objectives
3. the resources used to attain these objectives

FIGURE 2.1
The levels of management

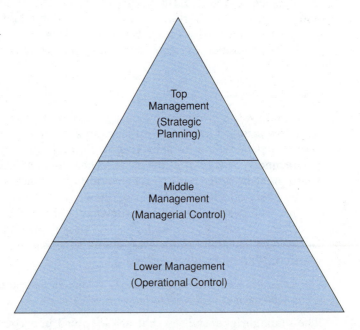

Top Management
(Strategic Planning)

Middle Management
(Managerial Control)

Lower Management
(Operational Control)

4. the policies that are to govern the acquisition, use, and disposition of these resources

Managerial Control

Managerial control is the process by which managers ensure that resources are obtained and used effectively and efficiently to accomplish the organization's objectives.

Operational Control

Operational control is the process of ensuring that specific tasks are carried out effectively and efficiently and communicating feedback about the success of doing so.

From this discussion of management, it becomes clear that there cannot be effective management of the system unless the purpose is clearly understood from the beginning. Complications arise when there is disagreement as to the real goals of the system or when the measure of performance is difficult to articulate.

The Systems Approach has made two very valuable contributions to our ability to understand information systems. First, it has provided a clear and usable definition of a system:

A collection of resources working together to achieve a goal.

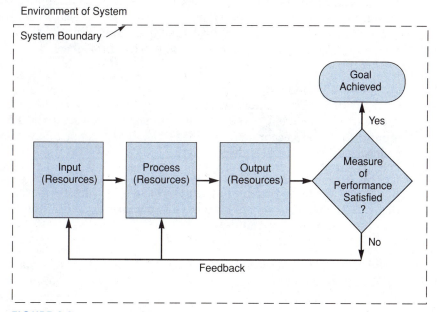

FIGURE 2.2
The properties of a system

Second, it has given us a useful way of thinking about systems. That is, we should focus on the interactions of the parts from the perspective of the whole and should incorporate feedback. For this reason, another term for the Systems Approach is Systems Thinking. To summarize this discussion of systems, Figure 2.2 shows the properties of a system and how they relate to one another.

WHAT IS AN INFORMATION SYSTEM?

The Systems Approach is a model that can help us understand the notion of an information system. Since an information system is one type of system, it should possess all the properties we described for any system. Let us now consider the properties of an information system according to the Systems Approach.

Information System Purpose

The ultimate purpose of an information system is to produce information from data. Therefore, identifying the purpose requires us to return to the definitions of information. Is the purpose to help someone maintain a collection of data? Is the purpose to enable a manager to make a better decision? Or is the purpose to help an engineer make better designs? What is the purpose of the information system you are using in your research project? From these simple questions, we can see that the first task in establishing the system goal is to determine why we want the information in the first place.

Information Properties

Once the definition of information is established, the properties of information can be used to articulate what the system should be able to do. The properties of information are accuracy, timeliness, reliability, consistency, completeness, conciseness, relevance, and integrity.

Accuracy **Accuracy** refers to the correctness of the information. For example, to achieve accuracy, a system that performs calculations must use the appropriate formulas and data.

Timeliness **Timeliness** means having the information in time to be able to use it. If the purpose of the system is to aid decision making, the information must be available in time to make the decision. Another aspect of timeliness is that the information must be up-to-date, or if it is not, the user should know whether the information was current as of today, last week, last month, or last year.

Reliability **Reliability** means that given the same data and procedures, the same result will always occur. For example, if the information is a procedure for carrying out some task, it should always result in the same outcome.

Consistency **Consistency** means that related groups of information are not contradictory. An information system to maintain inventory should not have some information indicating that an item is out of stock and other information indicating that there is plenty of that item on hand.

Completeness and Conciseness Completeness and conciseness are complementary properties. **Completeness** means having *enough* information to carry out a task; **conciseness** means having *no more* than what is needed. Having too much information is as bad as not having enough. Sometimes people respond to information overload by ignoring all of it, what is useful as well as what is not.

Relevance **Relevance** means that the information is meaningful and useful for the purposes for which it was produced. Since the users of the information system are the ones to determine relevance, we can see again that the user's opinion is important in establishing the goals of the system.

Integrity When information has all these properties, we say that it has **integrity**. Integrity means that the user can have confidence in the overall quality of the information.

One of the major problems with information systems stems from situations in which several different goals are set forth. As an example, consider the following scenario. A company has decided that it needs to have a computer-based information system. Suppose the goal as seen by the users is to provide better-quality information for decision making; this might be the *stated* goal. This goal is then articulated to those who will design and develop the system, and it should be the basis upon which both the users and designers will evaluate the system's performance. But suppose top management's *real* goal is to reduce the number of clerical staff in the company. When it comes time to evaluate the system to determine whether it is achieving its purpose, conflict could result. The system may have improved the quality of information available, but if there has not been a reduction in staff, top management will remain dissatisfied. To avoid such a conflict, it is necessary to be in as much agreement as possible about what all the goals are and how they are related *before* the system is developed.

Information System Components

Once the goals are agreed upon, how are they achieved? What are the operations performed on the data to turn it into the kind of information that is desired? The input-process-output model discussed earlier provides the description of how data is turned into information. Some data is collected from the environment; other data already exists within the information system. Once collected, this data is prepared, if necessary, and entered into the part of the system that will produce the information (INPUT). For example, if a purchase is made with a credit card, a form is filled out containing data that will later be entered into a billing system. This data comes from the environment—the context within which the data originates. Other data, such as account number, name, and credit limit, is already stored within the system. Next, manipulations such as calculating, classifying, organizing, and summarizing are performed on the data (PROCESS). For a billing system this will mean combining the data from the environment with that stored in the system to create a monthly bill. Finally, information in some usable form is produced (OUTPUT). Some of this output, such as the monthly statement sent to the customer, goes back into the environment. Other output, such as an updated record of current accounts, remains within the system.

We can observe, then, that the input and output functions sometimes interact with the environment and other times are concerned with data already in the system. Suppose the data for your research project comes from three sources: interviews, library sources, and course notes. In this case, data from interviews and the library comes from the environment; data from course notes is already part of your information system.

Because of the growing use of personal computers throughout organizations, these input, processing, and output functions are being carried out by many different departments in many different locations within a company. While this makes things easier for those using the information, it makes the task of managing the information system more difficult. This tradeoff must be kept in mind when the management of the system is being considered.

Information System Resources

An information system does not necessarily involve computer technology. One of the oldest types of information systems is the library, which existed long before computers. The information system you establish to support your research project may be a manual system. If this is the case, it would be made up of the data you collect, your notebooks, the people on your research team, the methods used to analyze the data, and the typewriter used to produce your final report. This book, however, is concerned with *computer-based information systems*. Therefore, when the term *information system* is used, it will be assumed that a computer is a part of it.

We know that resources are the parts of the system which carry out its functions. In an information system, resources are the parts that carry out the input, process, and output functions necessary to provide the kind of information specified in the goal. There are five resources or parts of a **computer-based information system** that work together to produce information: hardware, software, data, procedures, and people.

Hardware

Hardware refers to the computer itself, as well as to the technology used to acquire, store, and communicate data. Examples would be the computer terminal, printer, and communication devices. A complete overview of computer hardware is given in the appendix.

Software

Another term for **software** is *computer program*. The program tells the computer how to accept and manipulate the data in order to turn it into information. Computer programs can either be developed by people inside the organization or purchased from companies whose business is to develop software. The popularity of the personal computer has greatly increased the demand for software that can be purchased. Software is discussed in greater detail in Chapter 4 and in the appendix.

Data

As stated previously, data is the raw material from which information is obtained. Without it there can be no information. Data can therefore be thought of as the most basic of the information system resources. To ensure that appropriate data is available and in the correct format, methods for data collection, entry, storage, and retrieval are very important. Chapters 4 and 6 address these considerations.

Procedures

Just as software instructs the computer, **procedures** instruct the individual and the organization as to their roles in obtaining information. Examples of procedures are directions for how to operate the computer, training in the use of software, and decisions about who should have access to what data. As we can see, procedures range from very detailed statements to broad organizational policy.

People

There are three groups of people involved with the development, use, and management of information systems: the manager, the designer, and the client. The *manager* is responsible for establishing the goal of the information system. This also includes approving plans for achieving it. Sometimes the manager must alter the system if the goals are not being achieved; sometimes the goals themselves must be altered.

The **designer** is responsible for understanding the type of information system that is reflected in the goal. This person must then select and sometimes develop the appropriate hardware and software resources to accomplish this. He or she must also make sure the appropriate data resources are collected and stored in a fashion that will enable them to be transformed into information. To ensure that the system works properly, the designer must also establish procedures governing the use and maintenance of the system. In many cases the designer is an **information systems professional**.

The **client**, or **user**, is the person who is served by the information system. We know that the purpose of every information system is to provide information. We also know that there can be different expectations about the information provided. Therefore, it is the user who, through feedback, communicates to management whether the output from the system is actually useful information. When users also interact directly with the information system, they are called **end users**. In some cases, the end user is involved in the design and management of the information system as well. Sometimes the end user will play all three roles—that is, engage in the use, design, and management of the system. **End-user computing** refers to the direct use of computer-based technology by non-information systems personnel in the course of doing some other job.

People are the most critical resource of the system. Without the involvement of people, there can be no goal, no measure of performance, no feedback, and no way of determining if the system is successful in achieving its goal. Unfortunately, it is only recently that system designers have acknowledged this fact; some still haven't.

It is very much the case that each resource of the information system is itself a system. Consider the hardware resource. It is clearly a system in its own right: a computer system. It has parts that work together to achieve a goal, which is usually efficiency and accuracy of operations—or throughput. However, since the resource is a subsystem of the overall system—the information system—its own goals should not be pursued at the expense of those of the information system. If they are, suboptimization occurs. Sometimes the most effective way to provide information from the perspective of the information system as a whole is not the most efficient way from the perspective of the computer system. For example, a certain software package might be more efficient from a computer processing point of view, but it might be very difficult for the users to learn. The most effective choice from the total system perspective, therefore, might be less efficient software that is easier to use. This example is a reminder that the goals of the subsystem should always be sec-

FIGURE 2.3
Information resources and organizational resources

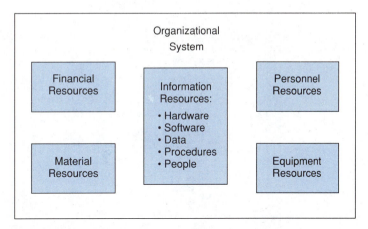

Organizational System

Financial Resources

Information Resources:
• Hardware
• Software
• Data
• Procedures
• People

Personnel Resources

Material Resources

Equipment Resources

ondary to the goals of the total system. Figure 2.3 displays the relationship between information system resources and organizational resources.

Information System Environment

The environment is the context within which the information need originates and in which the information system will operate. It is also the setting in which some of the data originates and from which it is collected for input into the system. For a billing system, the store where a purchase is made is part of the environment. For the information system you use to support your research project, the environment could be viewed as the marketing course in which you are enrolled. Sometimes the boundary between the environment and the information system is called the **interface**.

Our understanding of what should be included within the bounds of an information system has changed in recent years. In addition, we have come to see the implications of deciding what is to be part of the information system and what is not. The major change has been the inclusion of people within the system. For example, if the clients are considered to be part of the information system, their needs and viewpoints will be taken into account when the system is designed. It is precisely because users have not always been considered that many information systems have been ineffective in achieving their goals.

It is also important to note that an information system has more than one environment. For example, one environment for an information system would be the rest of the organization, while another environment would be the society outside the organization. Laws and industry competition exist outside the bounds of the organization, yet influence both the organization and its information system. Thus, we can say that there are both **local environments** (those within the organization) and **global environments** (those outside the organization). Your marketing course would be the local environment of your in-

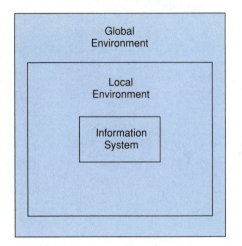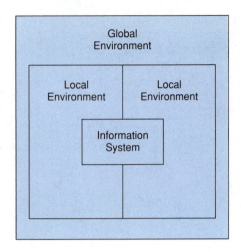

FIGURE 2.4
Global and local environments

formation system; the industry you are studying would be the global environment. There can also be more than one local environment. Figure 2.4 depicts these environments.

Information System Management

The management of an information system should include all the management activities that apply to systems in general. The system should have a goal. There should be a plan for producing the desired type of information. There should be criteria to determine whether this goal has been achieved. Finally, feedback on the operation of the information system should be collected so that it can be used to evaluate the success of the system. All the resources of the information system are important in this endeavor, but people are the most important resource. Feedback from users provides the ultimate measure of performance. Ideally, management should constantly collect feedback from users about the quality of the system and the information that is output. With this feedback, the system can be changed or improved to move it closer to the goal. Feedback can also be used to revise or redefine the goal itself as circumstances in the environment change. The information system users, designers, and managers should all work together to make productive use of this feedback throughout the process.

Just as there are three levels of management in organizations, there should be three levels of management of information systems. Chapters 9 and 10 will consider the dimensions of information system management in greater detail. A summary of the major activities is given here.

Strategic Planning for Information Systems

The strategic planning level is responsible for establishing the goal of the information system—that is, determining the type of information it will produce. It is also responsible for the overall policies governing the input, process, and output functions, and the time frame it works within is long-range. This level of management corresponds with the manager of the system.

Managerial Control of Information Systems

The managerial control level is responsible for the way in which the resources carry out the system functions. It coordinates the technology, data, and people so that the information system objectives can be achieved effectively and efficiently. The time frame for this function is short-term. This level corresponds with the role of the system designer.

Operational Control of Information Systems

The personnel working at the operational control level are those who actually use the information system. They include both computer professionals and end users, and their time frame is the immediate present.

Now that we have identified the properties of an **information system**, we can give it a formal definition:

> *An information system is a collection of resources which function together to produce information.*

Earlier in this chapter you were asked to think about a group research project as a setting in which you would need an information system. We can now identify the resources that make up this information system as the members of the research team; the data which you are collecting from the library and interviews and which is in your course notes; the notebooks used to record the data; the procedures used to evaluate the data; and the typewriter you use to produce the final report. These resources interact through the functions of input, processing, and output to produce the end result—your research paper.

Since a computer-based information system is one type of information system, it can be defined as

> *Data and hardware which are manipulated by software and procedures to produce information for people.*

The hardware, software, data, procedures, and people work together to carry out the input, process, and output functions on the data for the benefit of people. That is, data from both the environment and the system itself is input via the hardware, software, procedures, and people, then processed by means of the software, procedures, and hardware. Finally, information is output in a form that satisfies the goal as agreed upon by all the personnel in the system.

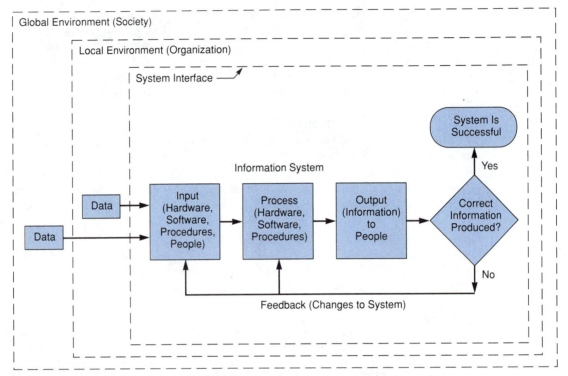

FIGURE 2.5
The properties of an information system

Figure 2.5 shows the relationship among these properties of an information system.

SUMMARY

Data is the raw material from which information is produced. Information is data that is meaningful and useful to the recipient. The major difference between data and information is that data has tangible existence, whereas information is the product of human intelligence. The same data can result in different interpretations and therefore different information. Likewise, the same information can result from different sets of data.

A system is a collection of resources that work together to achieve a goal. A system has five properties—purpose, components, resources, environment, and management. The purpose is the goal of the system. The components are the functions performed by the system in order to achieve the goal. The resources are the means by which the goal is achieved, the parts of the system. The environment is that which is outside the boundaries of the system. Management includes the plan for achieving the goal, the measures of performance, and a mechanism for incorporating feedback about the success of the system in achieving its goal.

Since an information system is a type of system, it too has five properties. The purpose of an information system is to produce information from data. The components are input, process, and output. There are five resources which work together to produce information: hardware, software, data, procedures, and people. The environment of an information system, whether local or global, is the context within which the information need originates and from which some of the data is obtained. The management of the information system involves establishing the goal, the criteria for evaluating it, and the mechanisms for collecting feedback about the success in satisfying the user's need for information.

CHAPTER NOTES

1. R. W. Burchfield, ed., *A Supplement to the Oxford English Dictionary*, vol. 1 (Oxford, U.K.: Clarendon Press, 1972), 737.
2. Donald M. MacKay, *Information, Mechanism, and Meaning* (Cambridge, MA: MIT Press, 1969).
3. Claude E. Shannon and Warren Weaver, *The Mathematical Theory of Information* (Urbana: University of Illinois Press, 1949).
4. Marshall C. Yovits and Bruce J. Whittemore, "A Generalized Concept for the Analysis of Information," in *Information Science: Search for Identity*, ed. Anthony Debons (New York: Marcel Dekker, 1974).
5. Ludwig von Bertalanffy, *General Systems Theory: Foundations, Development, and Applications* (New York: G. Braziller, 1968).
6. Norbert Weiner, *Cybernetics, or Control and Communication in the Animal and the Machine* (New York: John Wiley and Sons, 1948).
7. C. West Churchman, *The Systems Approach* (New York: Dell Publishing Co., 1968).
8. Harold Koontz, ed., *Toward a Unified Theory of Management* (New York: McGraw-Hill Book Co., 1964), xi.
9. Robert N. Anthony, *Planning and Control Systems: A Framework for Analysis* (Boston: Graduate School of Business Administration, Harvard University, 1965).

ADDITIONAL REFERENCES

Ackoff, Russell L. *A Concept of Corporate Planning*. New York: Wiley-Interscience, 1970.

_____. "Toward a System of System Concepts." *Management Science* (July 1971): 661–671.

Ackoff, Russell L., and Fred E. Emery. *On Purposeful Systems*. Chicago: Aldine and Atherton, 1972.

Boulding, Kenneth. "General Systems Theory—The Skeleton of Science." *Management Science* (April 1956): 197–208.

Churchman, C. West. *The Design of Inquiring Systems: Basic Concepts of Systems in Organizations*. New York: Basic Books, 1971.

Cyert, Richard M., and James G. March. *A Behavioral Theory of the Firm*. Englewood Cliffs, NJ: Prentice-Hall, 1963.

Emery, James C. *Organizational Planning and Control Systems*. New York: Macmillan, 1969.

Markus, M. Lynne. *Systems in Organizations: Bugs and Features*. Boston: Pitman, 1984.

Mason, R. O., and Ian I. Mitroff. *Challenging Strategic Planning Assumptions*. New York: John Wiley and Sons, 1981.

KEY TERMS

accuracy
boundary
client
completeness
components
computer-based information system
conciseness
consistency
constraints
cybernetics
data
designer
end user
end-user computing
environment
feedback

General Systems Theory
global environment
hardware
information
information overload
information system
information systems professional
information theory
input
integrity
interface
knowledge
local environment
management
managerial control
operational control

output
procedures
process
purpose
relevance
reliability
resources
software
strategic planning
suboptimization
subsystem
synergy
system
Systems Approach
timeliness
user

REVIEW QUESTIONS

1. What is the goal of information literacy?
2. What is the difference between data and information?
3. Does processed data always result in information? Explain.
4. What are the three definitions of information that are in use today?
5. What is a system? What are its properties?
6. What is a stated goal? a real goal? Give examples.
7. Explain the three primary functions of a system.
8. Explain subsystems and subgoals.
9. Explain the difference between synergy and suboptimization.
10. Compare the three levels of management.
11. What is an information system?
12. What is the purpose of an information system?
13. Discuss the properties of information and how they interrelate.

14. What are the components of an information system?
15. Why is it critical to clearly define all the goals of an information system?
16. What are the resources of an information system?
17. People are the most critical resources of an information system. Why?
18. What is the environment of an information system?
19. What are the management aspects of an information system?
20. List four managerial activities.

CASE   Mary Burke and Pat Broderick have decided to start an Irish import company. Their store will specialize in selling popular gift items to the sizable Irish-American population in their city. Since they are in the early stages of establishing this company, they know they need a considerable amount of information. The data to be obtained will come from a variety of sources. Marketing data is needed to decide which items to stock. Suppliers in Ireland must be identified. They must determine the best location for their store. Once the company is started, they must also establish procedures for the management of day-to-day operations such as inventory, billing, ordering, accounting, and general management. They are also aware that they need to organize this data so that it is usable and easy to obtain.

Mary and Pat have decided that the best approach is to establish information systems from the very beginning to support their efforts. These information systems should not only help to organize the data gathered from their initial research, but should also help with the ongoing management of their new business. They have decided to set up two information systems, one for research data and one for operations data.

DISCUSSION QUESTIONS

1. What is the purpose of each information system?
2. What is the scope and environment of each information system?
3. What resources will be needed for each information system to achieve its purpose?
4. How will they be able to determine whether the information systems have achieved their purposes?

CHAPTER 3

Types of Information Systems

CHAPTER OUTLINE

CASE STUDIES: THE USES OF INFORMATION SYSTEMS IN ORGANIZATIONS

TYPES OF INFORMATION SYSTEMS

INFORMATION SYSTEM PROPERTIES

CHAPTER OBJECTIVES

- To introduce the three information processing contexts which will be used throughout the rest of the book: a bank, a university, and a small business.
- To relate the purpose of an information system to the three major types of information systems: access, analysis, and action systems.
- To provide examples from the three case studies of the environment and management properties of an information system.

INTRODUCTION

Chapter 2 provided us with a useful definition of an information system. It also provided a way of thinking about the properties of information systems. In this chapter we will examine more closely the properties of purpose, environment, and management. In so doing, we will distinguish among the different kinds of computer-based information systems with which people come into contact in their work and personal lives.

It is crucial to an understanding of information systems to understand the contexts in which they are used. Understanding context is important for a number of reasons. First, the system properties remain abstract and irrelevant without a specific system to which they can be applied. For example, we know that one property of a system is its purpose, and the purpose of an information system is to "make information out of raw data." But what exactly does that mean? It is much easier to think about information in specific terms—maintaining an up-to-date listing of names, addresses, and phone numbers or projecting next year's budgetary needs based on this year's expenditures. Each of these is an example of a purpose of an information system. As we can see, it is easier to think about purposes of information systems if we have a concrete example in mind.

Another reason for studying specific contexts is that, just as there are different kinds of information, there are also different kinds of information systems. The choice of information system depends upon the kind of information needed and the way it will be used. In one type of system, facts will simply be stored for later retrieval, as in the case of an address book. In another type of system, information will be produced to answer a question, such as what next year's budget should be.

A final reason for studying contexts is that data becomes particularly meaningful when it is relevant. Thus, studying familiar systems makes it easier to understand the general concepts associated with information systems. Also, the knowledge we acquire is much more meaningful because of its potential usefulness.

CASE STUDIES: THE USES OF INFORMATION SYSTEMS IN ORGANIZATIONS

The kind of information an individual needs and the way it will be used should determine the kind of information system that is developed. The following section introduces three different kinds of organizations which will serve as case studies throughout the remainder of the book. In examining these organizations, we will learn about their information processing needs and how they have gone about satisfying them.

CASE 1: LAST NATIONAL BANK

The banking industry has undergone significant changes in recent years. Our increasingly complex society has created consumer demand for greater variety in financial services. Deregulation in the banking industry has resulted in numerous options for saving, investing, making payments, and obtaining loans. It has also resulted in increased acquisition of banks by other banks. All these factors have made the task of managing bank operations much more complicated. Last National Bank is located in a large Midwestern city. It is experiencing all the information processing and management problems of any bank wishing to increase its services and manage its operations more effectively. Let us consider a few of Last National's operations and the information processing tasks needed to support them.

Savings Accounts

First, imagine a typical retail (i.e., individual) customer at Last National Bank. This person would have a checking account to provide money for regular expenses and a savings account for special purchases, retirement, or emergencies. If the person decided to buy a house, he or she would obtain a home mortgage. Finally, this person would probably have at least one bank credit card, such as American Express, MasterCard, or Visa. To be managed properly, all of the services offered by a bank require the support of substantial record-keeping and analysis activities.

An individual utilizing all these services would have four different relationships with Last National Bank, each having its own record-keeping and information processing requirements. For the savings account, the bank keeps track of the amount of deposits and, at certain intervals, credits the account with an appropriate amount of interest. Banks also offer special savings accounts that pay interest according to the prime rate established by the Federal Reserve Board. Last National Bank must constantly monitor current interest rates and determine how much it should pay to these savings accounts. There are usually restrictions associated with these accounts, such as minimum balances required and limits on the number of withdrawals allowed in a given time period. Therefore, the bank must also carefully watch the activity of each account.

Checking Accounts

Basic checking accounts enable the client to write checks to be drawn on the bank. Additional services are also available. With some checking accounts the amount of an overdraft can be covered so that the check doesn't "bounce." In these cases, an automatic loan is made to the customer, usually with limits on the loan amount and how often such a loan can be made. Therefore, the bank must keep track of loans made to each checking account for these purposes. The bank also offers special, interest-bearing checking accounts, sometimes with limits on the number of checks that can be written. An account holder who exceeds that limit could incur a penalty in the form of a lower interest payment. Once again, Last National must carefully monitor the activity of these accounts.

Loans

In addition to house mortgages, other consumer loans commonly available at Last National Bank include car loans, school loans, home improvement loans, and commercial loans. When a person or company applies for a loan, information must be collected to determine the client's ability to pay. Typical information an applicant must supply includes current employer, current salary, rent payments, and outstanding loans or other debts. The bank must then verify this information and, using established rules, determine whether or not the applicant qualifies for the loan. If the loan is granted, the bank must then monitor the payments to make certain they are for the correct amount and made on time. If a loan such as a home mortgage is obtained during a time of high interest rates, when the interest rate drops some consumers will apply for a new mortgage at the lower interest rate. When interest rates drop significantly, banks can be deluged with requests for refinancing and be overwhelmed by the considerable extra paperwork these requests create.

Electronic Funds Transfer

Most of the banking services just described predate the use of the computer. But a number of services currently available are the direct result of computer and communications technology. **Electronic funds transfer (EFT)** refers to the transmission of *information* about money. **Automatic teller machines (ATMs)** enable a customer to obtain cash, make deposits, and transfer money without involving bank personnel. This greater flexibility in the time and location for conducting banking activities benefits both the consumer and the bank. In addition to credit cards, Last National also offers **debit cards**, which enable a cardholder to make a purchase and have the amount directly deducted from the account. This is a form of "electronic check writing." A final example of EFT is the automatic deposit or withdrawal of money from an account. With this service, paychecks can be directly deposited to one's bank account and insurance payments can be automatically deducted from the account.

CASE 2: STATE UNIVERSITY

State University is located in a small rural town in the Southwest. Just like any other business, a university must manage its organizational resources in order to provide a high-quality product (education) to its customers (students). Managing those resources requires a considerable degree of information processing. We describe a few types here.

Bookstore Inventory

The university bookstore is responsible for ensuring that the correct books are ordered and the correct number arrive so that all students can have the books they need for their courses. The bookstore personnel have two competing needs: to have enough books to support the courses offered but not to overstock any books. To accomplish this, they must maintain an *inventory system* which will keep track of data on the demand for books as well as the number in stock. Other information is needed as well. The bookstore must also know if a given textbook will be used again. If so, used books will be bought back from the students to be sold at a reduced price. The bookstore has to know too if a new edition of a book is coming out, so that the correct edition of the book will be ordered. Since these books must be available at the beginning of the semester, the bookstore manager will set certain deadlines for finding out which courses will be taught in the upcoming term, how many students are enrolled, and which textbooks will be used.

Library

The library is a significant resource of any university. In order for a library to operate smoothly, several information systems must be established. First, students doing research need to find out which books or articles contain information relevant to the topic. To assist in this process, the library maintains a *card catalog* of the books in its collection. By knowing the author's name or the subject of inquiry, the student can find out about available books. Historically, the card catalog has been a manual information system consisting of drawers containing cards, each of which contains data on a given book. However, since this information is now becoming available as part of computer-based systems, State University is considering switching to an *on-line catalog* when its new library is built.

Second, to make periodical articles easier to find, indexes are kept which contain references to journal and newspaper articles on certain subjects. For example, students doing a marketing project could consult the *Business Periodicals Index*. State University already has several of these indexes available in computer-based form. To use them, the student only has to enter the key words associated with the research topic and the computer will search for all relevant references. This greatly facilitates the task of researching a topic.

Finally, the library must have a *circulation system* to keep track of which books have been checked out or returned. Since faculty, graduate students, and undergraduate students have different time limits for borrowing, this data must be incorporated into the system as well so that overdue notices can be sent out when necessary.

Student Records

Certain information on students must be collected, stored, updated, and communicated. A record must be kept of the courses a student takes and the final grades assigned. This record becomes the transcript, a formal document that can be sent to employers or other schools. Each semester that record must be updated to include the final grades for the current term, a recalculation of the grade-point average, and a listing of the courses to be taken in the upcoming semester. Other data such as name and permanent address must be maintained so that students receive their bills and other important information. This record can also be used to determine whether the student is qualified to take a certain course in cases where a minimum grade-point average or a prerequisite course is necessary.

Scheduling

Several resources are required in order to ensure that the intended courses are offered in the right locations at the correct times to the appropriate students. Personnel resources — faculty — are needed to teach the courses. Physical resources — classrooms and laboratory equipment — are needed as well. It is the job of State University's *scheduling system* to match its available resources to the demand for courses and assign students to certain classes in certain rooms taught by certain professors. This system must keep track of the rooms that are used, the times that students have classes, and the times that faculty teach so that two classes aren't scheduled in the same room or a student or professor does not have two classes scheduled at the same time.

Accounting

Numerous accounting systems must be maintained in order to make any institution run smoothly. Two accounting systems at State University are discussed here.

Billing

State University must establish procedures for generating tuition bills and keeping track of payments. This can get very complicated, because tuition amounts vary. For example, state residents pay less than out-of-state students. In addition, some students have scholarships from outside sources. When this money is paid directly to the school, the *billing system* must keep track of the amount received, credit it to the proper student, and subtract that amount from the tuition bill. Some students receive scholarships or tuition waivers directly from the school. This means that no outside money comes in, but the amount of the credit must still be subtracted from the student's bill. Since the university has a limited amount of scholarship money available, it must keep track of how much has already been committed when determining how many new scholarships it can award.

Payroll

The university's *payroll system* must take into account three categories of employees: faculty, staff, and students. Faculty are normally paid over nine months. If they teach summer school, they are paid extra. Some professors who do not teach in the summer like to have their nine months' salary spread over twelve paychecks. Others wish to have their paychecks deposited directly into the bank. To fulfill all these requirements, the payroll system must keep track of how much each professor is paid, whether to pay in nine- or twelve-month increments, and whether to issue a check or send the amount directly to a specified bank. Other information, such as the amount withheld for taxes and retirement, must also be maintained by the system.

Staff members include secretaries, researchers, librarians, counselors, bookstore personnel, and others who provide services to the students. Some staff are paid weekly; others are paid monthly. Further, some are hourly and others are salaried workers. The information system must keep track of all these payroll variations in order to produce the correct paychecks in the appropriate time frames.

Students who have on-campus jobs can either receive their paychecks directly or have the amount deducted from their tuition bills. Some students are part of work-study programs; for these students, the university pays a portion of tuition and the government pays the rest. In addition, there are usually restrictions on the number of hours that students can work at these jobs, so the payroll system must also keep track of whether or not the students qualify and how many hours they are allowed to work.

CASE 3: WOODEN WONDERS

Paul Bunyan lives in a small town in southern New Hampshire. Until three years ago, he worked as an engineer for a large manufacturing company, where he designed tools used in the manufacturing process. His hobby was woodworking, and he liked to make small decorations out of odd pieces of wood he found on his property. Sometimes he would discover a rare piece with interesting lines in it and would create a new design to highlight the features of the wood. If he was happy with the result, he would save the design to use again. Paul decorated his house with these items and gave some to friends as gifts. Eventually he started displaying his wooden objects at local flea markets and art fairs.

Three years ago, because of a company reorganization, Paul was given the option of taking a position in another state or taking early retirement. He chose the latter, thinking it would give him time to spend on his hobbies—fishing, gardening, and woodworking. However, his friends encouraged him to become more serious about woodworking and sell his products commercially.

After giving it some thought, Paul decided to start a company— which he called Wooden Wonders—to produce, market, and sell wooden decorations. He started out small, continuing to exhibit at art fairs and taking special orders from friends or people who saw and admired his work. Some of the requests were for items he had made before; others required a new design. Since designing a new item was more time-consuming and therefore more costly, Paul decided to produce a catalog of designs from which customers could choose in ordering products. He distributed copies of the catalog at local fairs and at stores in town. He also began to produce some of his more popular items and sell them through the local stores.

Over the past three years business has grown dramatically. But this success presented Paul with a new set of problems. He found he was spending so much time managing orders, collecting payments, updating his catalog, and doing other paperwork that he didn't have enough time to do what he really wanted to do: make things out of wood.

Paul decided to hire someone to help him with these tasks, someone to manage all the business aspects of the company and allow him to spend his time being creative. He hired Mary Tyson, a recent business school graduate, for this position. She thought organizing Wooden Wonders would be an interesting challenge and set out to learn more about the company. After a short time she reported back to Paul about some areas that needed to be addressed.

Product Design

One significant aspect of the business was that of designing the products and keeping track of designs. Paul was not very organized, and his design sketches were sometimes misplaced. Further, it was quite a chore to put these designs in order when it was time to produce a new catalog. Mary suggested that a better means of storing and cataloging the designs was needed.

Advertising

The product designs formed the basis of the catalog of Wooden Wonders products. Until Mary was hired, Paul had used several people to help him produce the catalog. An artist redrew his rough sketches of new products.

Another person photographed products that had already been created. A third person typed the copy for the catalog. When these tasks were completed, Paul sent the catalog to a printer for production. With so many different people working on the catalog, the updating process was very tedious. Mary recommended that they should either produce the catalog themselves or hire a publishing company to produce it. They decided to revise the catalog twice a year, in the spring and in the fall. If the price or availability of an item changed between catalog runs, they would simply insert a notice into the catalogs.

Client List

The advertising considerations led Mary to determine that two sets of name and address lists were needed. A name and address list of current and prospective customers would be maintained so that copies of the catalog could be sent to them. The other list would contain the names and addresses of stores in which the products were sold. She also needed information about these stores for shipping and billing purposes.

Accounting

As Mary observed the company, she noted that better accounting procedures were badly needed. Such procedures would deal with managing the process of selling Wooden Wonders' products, purchasing supplies, and maintaining a budget.

Sales

Since items could be purchased in three ways—at fairs, through the catalog, or at local stores—different procedures had to be set up to manage each one. Purchases made at art fairs were cash-only. To evaluate the company's sales effectiveness at these fairs, Mary recommended setting up a system to track the number and kinds of products sold at each fair. She also thought they should consider enabling these customers to purchase goods with credit cards.

When products were purchased through the catalog, payments were made to Wooden Wonders in advance. Once an order was received, the payment was recorded and a receipt generated to send along with the item to the customer. Mary recommended conducting sales analysis in this area as well.

Items sold in local stores were ordered on a periodic basis by the store owners. Once the items were shipped, an invoice was typed up and sent along with the items. To support these activities, Wooden Wonders needed to set up billing and *accounts receivable systems* to generate, send, and record data about invoices and payments. In addition, they needed an inventory system to keep track of the kinds and quantity of items in stock.

Mary also recommended generating data to determine which items were in greatest demand and during which times of the year, to help Paul plan his work.

Supplies

To produce his wooden objects on schedule, Paul needed to have all the supplies on hand. These included wood, paint, glue, and various tools. His method had been to purchase supplies just before he ran out of them. Mary recommended that they analyze the use of these materials and set up a schedule for ordering and paying for them on a regular basis. To do so, they would need to establish an inventory of supplies and an *accounts payable system* to maintain a schedule for making payments.

Budget

The final accounting element that was needed was a budget. In Mary's view, Paul did not have a very clear picture of the company's financial situation. Income and expenses were not recorded in an organized fashion. Some purchases were recorded in his personal checkbook; others were written on the charge slip (if he used a credit card) or on the store receipt (if he paid cash). Other expenses that needed to be accounted for were catalog production and mailing. They also needed a better way to organize income from the different methods of sales.

At the time Mary was hired, all procedures were manual. Computers were not used for any of the record-keeping or analysis tasks. One of Mary's objectives was to determine where computers could help them work more efficiently and effectively.

As the previous examples have pointed out, every organization needs a great deal of information in order to operate. If the organization is in the *business* of producing information (as is the case with all three of these organizations), the information requirements are even greater. As long as organizations have existed, they have collected, stored, used, and communicated information. The role of the computer in this process is to facilitate these activities. With or without the computer, however, these activities would have to be carried out.

In the past forty years, there have been significant improvements in the techniques and technologies available for collecting, processing, and communicating information. At the center of these improvements is the computer. It is for this reason that the role of the computer is tied so closely to most discussions of information processing. The important thing to remember, however, is that the computer can play a variety of roles in information processing. It is the people — the system designers, users, and managers — who decide how the computer can best contribute to satisfying the information processing need.

TYPES OF INFORMATION SYSTEMS

We need information to serve many different purposes. For this reason, different types of computer-based information systems have emerged to support a variety of uses. Each type of system has its own advantages and disadvantages, costs and benefits. The best system is the one that fits the information need. It is very important to understand what kind of output is expected from the system. Is the system expected to produce data which will then be processed in someone's brain? Is the system supposed to do some of the decision making so that the output is in the form of a conclusion? Is the system expected to collect data, make an evaluation, then take some action? We have to know our expectations about the information so that we will have a basis for evaluating the system. This is what is meant by the *purpose* of the information system: the type of information it is expected to provide. The types of information and therefore the purposes of information systems fit into three general categories: access, analysis, and action. As Figure 3.1 shows, all information systems can be classified according to these categories.

Access Systems

The purpose of an **access system** is to facilitate the users' access to information. There are two kinds of access systems: record-keeping and transaction processing systems.

Record-Keeping Systems

The goal of a **record-keeping system** is the efficient storage and retrieval of data. These systems are often established to manage collections of documents such as letters, notes, journal articles, books, or graphics. Compared to data in other types of systems, data in record-keeping systems does not change very frequently.

FIGURE 3.1
Types of information systems

Purpose	Type of Information System
Access (Information storage and retrieval)	Record-keeping system Transaction processing system
Analysis (Access + Decision-making support)	Management information system Decision support system Expert system
Action (Access + Analysis + Behavior)	Automated business system Automated manufacturing system

The university library itself is an example of a record-keeping system. Books, periodicals, and other materials in the library are stored in such a way that patrons can easily locate them. So that the library can run smoothly, however, other record-keeping systems are also needed. A library is actually made up of several record-keeping subsystems. One is the card catalog, which contains a card for each book in the library. When a new book is added to the collection, a card containing the relevant information about that book is printed and added to the catalog. Likewise, when the library no longer owns a book, the corresponding card is removed. Each periodicals index is also a record-keeping system. These indexes are similar to the card catalog in that they contain references to published material, in this case newspaper or magazine articles. Since new articles are constantly being written, the indexes are updated periodically to include the most recent references.

Two record-keeping systems at Wooden Wonders are the *product catalog system* and the *product designs system*. The data for the product catalog includes sketches and photos of products, written descriptions, and price information. This data must be stored in such a way that Paul Bunyan can easily access it when he wants to change a price, add or drop a product, or produce a new catalog. In a manual system, data about each product could be stored in a file folder. A computer-based alternative would be to store the textual and graphic data in computerized form to facilitate retrieval. The product design system contains data about products which Paul has already designed or which he is currently designing. Like the catalog system, this system could employ either file folders or the computer to store designs. To facilitate the movement of new designs into the catalog system, these two systems could be linked so that the catalog system contains a reference to where a given design is located in the design system.

OFFICE INFORMATION SYSTEMS

Office information systems used by the personnel at Last National Bank are an example of common record-keeping systems used in business. The terms **office information system** and **office automation** refer to computer-based information systems established to facilitate the information processing activities which occur in offices. Such activities include:

1. Generation, storage, and retrieval of correspondence;
2. Production of reports;
3. Maintenance of calendar and scheduling data;
4. Communication of information; and
5. Manipulation of numeric data.

Such systems are developed and used by all levels of personnel in the office—clerical workers, business professionals, and executives.

In addition to making use of computers, record-keeping systems also utilize communication technology. Two examples of this type of record-keeping system are electronic mail and videotext.

ELECTRONIC MAIL

Electronic mail (email) systems facilitate the transfer of textual messages through the use of computer communications. Electronic mail systems are a key component of office information systems. Such systems can be organized in a variety of ways. Some email systems enable one person to send messages to another; this sort of communication is much like a telephone call or letter. Other systems enable one person to "broadcast" messages to a wide range of individuals; this is like circulating a memo. A third type of email system enables one to store some information in a way that many others will have access to it. This is similar to posting a notice on a bulletin board, and in fact this type of system is sometimes referred to as an **electronic bulletin board**. All of these electronic mail systems have one thing in common: they facilitate access to information. Electronic mail will be considered again in Chapter 7.

VIDEOTEXT

Having a current catalog of available products is a crucial component of a business like Wooden Wonders. Paul Bunyan decided that the company would produce and mail out an updated catalog twice a year. Changes that occurred in the meantime would be held until the next catalog. In a few cases, special inserts would be printed and included along with the catalog. Paul would have liked to produce the catalog more frequently, but the printing and mailing costs precluded it. There was a tradeoff between the benefits of having a more up-to-date catalog and the costs of producing and mailing it. He also noted that printing and mailing costs were always increasing.

Another alternative for giving his customers access to the catalog is to send it electronically through videotext. **Videotext** is an electronic means of producing and mailing documents by which pages of data are either sent over telephone lines or broadcast like television programs. Developed in the United Kingdom in the mid-1970s, videotext was first used to transmit pages from newspapers and mail-order catalogs. By having a specially adapted television set, consumers could receive this information in their homes. With the development of the home computer, television sets have been replaced by computers as the device used for receiving these electronic documents. Videotext is used in companies to provide information about job openings, products, and company procedures. The main advantage of videotext over conventional means of storing and retrieving data is that whole pages of text can be selected and sent at once, making retrieval much quicker. A disadvantage of videotext is that there is no single universal standard for delivery or presentation of the information.

Transaction Processing Systems

The second type of access system is based on some event that causes data which is already stored to be adjusted. This event is called a *transaction* and the information system that performs this task is called a **transaction processing system**. As in a card catalog, information is collected and stored in some organized fashion. However, unlike the data in the card catalog, some of the data in a transaction processing system is periodically changed. This was the first type of information system used in business and remains the basis for a company's information processing activities.

Last National Bank has a transaction processing system for each service it provides. Each time an account holder makes a deposit or withdrawal, whether through a teller or through an ATM, a transaction occurs. Following this transaction, the customer's balance will need to be debited or credited. Similarly, each time a payment is made on a loan, the customer's balance will be adjusted. If a customer has a bank credit card, each purchase is a transaction. At the end of the billing cycle, the purchase amounts must be totaled and added to the customer's balance, and any payments must be deducted from the balance. (See Figure 3.2.) In each of these situations an information system is needed to manage the process of collecting transaction data, entering it, and updating the existing data. These transaction processing systems are used to maintain an accurate accounting of customer data and to produce a statement and perhaps a bill to be sent to the customer.

Wooden Wonders has several transaction processing systems. A billing system will generate bills and manage data on items sold to local stores, and an accounts receivable system will keep track of the amounts due from these

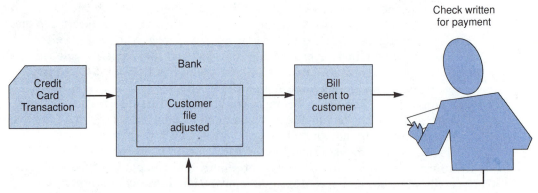

FIGURE 3.2
Flow of activity in bank's transaction processing system for credit card accounts

customers. When supplies are purchased, an accounts payable system will maintain data on supplies for which payment is owed. Such systems can also determine the appropriate time to make payments and can even write the checks.

The collection of student records at State University is part of a transaction processing system. When a student enrolls in the university, data on that student is collected and a student record is created. As each term is completed, that record is updated with the final grades for the courses taken, and the cumulative grade-point average is computed. When the student registers for the next term, those courses are entered into the record as well. Thus, recording final grades for courses completed, computing the cumulative grade-point average, and recording courses in which a student is enrolled are examples of transaction processing activities performed in this information system.

Related Systems Some information systems are closely connected to each other. That is, the output from one can be used as the input to another. This is what is meant by **coupled systems** or **related systems**. For example, consider the information needed and produced by the student registration process at State University. Before students can register for courses, certain data is needed. First, there must be a list of what courses are being offered, by whom, and when and where they are offered. Second, registration personnel need data on the students' history at the university. Students must maintain a certain grade-point average to continue in school. To enroll in certain courses they must have completed the prerequisite courses, and sometimes they must have earned a certain minimum grade in those courses. Finally, the system needs data on the courses in which the students are enrolling.

Not all the input data required for this process must come from the environment of the university's information system. Much of it already exists. The information about the courses to be offered, the instructors, and the times is the *output* of the scheduling system. Thus, the output of the scheduling system is one of the inputs to the registration system. Information about students' history already exists in the student records system. So the output from the student records system is another input to the registration system.

The final input needed for the registration system is the individual student request to take courses. This input *does* come from the environment. It can also be considered a transaction. When the three types of inputs are combined, the registration system can do the processing necessary to produce the desired output—an individual schedule for each student and faculty member and a master list of courses, enrollment, and locations. This process is illustrated in Figure 3.3.

Just as the output from the student records and scheduling systems provides input to the registration system, the output from the registration system provides input to the billing system. To generate tuition bills, that system needs to know if the student is graduate or undergraduate level, whether he or she will be part-time or full-time, and whether the base tuition should be

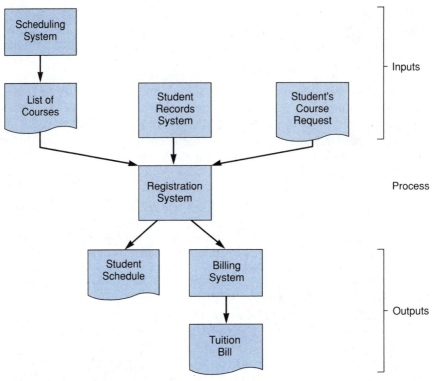

FIGURE 3.3
Related systems for registration process

changed (for a scholarship, because of a parent working there, or because the student is from out of state). All of this input data can come from the registration system.

Since there are many instances in which the output from one system can be the input to another, these connections must be taken into account when a system is being designed. If two systems are going to be connected, the form of the output from one system must be consistent with the format expected of the input for the other. This consistency applies to all the resources of the system. The data must be in a form that is useful for each system. If more than one computer is involved, each must be able to communicate with the others. Also, every person involved with the system must use the same terminology.

Each of the activities of operating and managing a business requires information systems to support it. Whether accomplished manually or through the use of a computer, each of these activities has an information system connected with it. Figure 3.4 shows some of the most common transaction processing systems associated with business activities.

FIGURE 3.4
Basic business operations and related systems

Basic Business Operations	Related Information Systems
Storing items	Inventory system
Selling products	Sales analysis system
Billing customers	Billing system
Collecting payments	Accounts receivable system
Purchasing materials	Purchasing system
Paying for goods	Accounts payable system
Paying employees	Payroll system

New Developments in Access Systems

Although access systems are the oldest type of information system, they are not necessarily the least sophisticated. In fact, conventional access systems are being enhanced by features which will serve to make retrieving and using information much easier for the end user. Two of these features are natural language and hypertext.

NATURAL LANGUAGE

One of the stumbling blocks in the use of access systems is the difficulty some people have in communicating with the computer. To retrieve stored information, the user must enter certain commands which instruct the computer to retrieve the data in a specific way. For those unfamiliar with the computer, this can be a very difficult process. Thanks to the growing use of **artificial intelligence (AI)** techniques, however, the goal of efficient storage and retrieval of information by all users has become easier to achieve. Artificial intelligence refers to activities which when carried out by people require human intelligence.

An AI technique employed by access systems is **natural language processing**. Natural language refers to the user's native language, such as English. An access system which incorporates natural language processing features would enable one to communicate with the computer by using English-like commands. These kinds of commands eliminate the need for complex commands and codes. Figure 3.5 shows a natural language request for information using a product called INTELLECT, which was developed by Artificial Intelligence Corporation.

HYPERTEXT

In 1945 Vannevar Bush[1] envisioned a text retrieval system that would store not only documents but also photos, graphs, and personal notes. This system would also enable a user to browse through documents and make associative links among related pieces of information. Memex, the machine

FIGURE 3.5
A dialogue using INTELLECT

SHOW ME THE AVERAGE SALARY FOR EACH JOB CATEGORY.

JOB CATEGORY	ANNUAL SALARY
MANAGER	$32,118.07
PROFESSIONAL	$24,123.49
TECHNICAL	$24,616.88
CLERICAL	$12,439.75
CRAFTSMAN	$16,435.16
AVERAGE	$21,946.67

NEXT REQUEST?

PUT IT IN A BAR GRAPH.

---

he designed, was limited by the technology available at the time. His vision, however, became the foundation for retrieval systems that take advantage of today's more sophisticated technology. These systems are called hypertext systems.

Hypertext is a type of access system in which the user can retrieve information out of the usual sequence. To understand how hypertext works, consider the uses a person normally has for a textbook. One use would be in conjunction with a course. In this case the instructor would assign certain chapters to certain lectures. If the structure of the class is the same as the structure of the book, the reader will move sequentially through the book. If not, the reader will have to read the chapters in a different order. This can create a problem if the textbook authors assume the student has read a previous chapter and refer to a concept explained earlier. In this case, the student would have to stop reading that chapter, go to the index to find where the concept was discussed, and read that discussion before continuing on with the chapter. Another use of a textbook would be for someone who wanted to learn about certain material but not in conjunction with a course. In this instance, the reader would have to use the table of contents and index and then leaf through the book to find the desired material. The hypertext format enables the reader to easily move to all locations in the "electronic document" where a given topic is discussed. This is possible because information is stored in discrete units which are then linked to other, related pieces of information.

Given the proliferation of information in our society, there are many contexts in which hypertext could be applied. One would be to help an individual better organize collections of data. Consider a research project which requires you to collect and organize a large body of facts. The problem is determining how to store this data so you can retrieve it in a useful fashion. One difficulty is that a certain note may be used in many different parts of the project. Hypertext systems store data so it can be retrieved in ways similar to the way we retrieve information from our brains. People are very good at making associations among data. For example, while working on your research project, you may suddenly remember a relevant piece of data to include. You then have to determine where that piece of data was stored. Perhaps in storing the data you did not think it would be relevant to the current task. Therefore, you will have to remember the planned use of that data before locating it. Hypertext "remembers" that location for you, so you don't have to spend time on that task. Commercial hypertext products are currently available on personal computers. Two of these are Guide, developed by OWL International, which runs on both Macintosh and IBM-AT-compatible computers; and HyperCard, which can be run on Macintosh computers.

"Electronic libraries," or large collections of information to which many individuals have access, are another context in which hypertext is applicable. Consider a person who is studying Shakespeare. While reading a certain play, he or she may come upon historical, geographical, or political references that are crucial to an understanding of the play. With hypertext, the reader can quickly and easily retrieve the relevant background information without having to stop and go to the library to look for books containing the information. This information can be displayed on the computer screen along with the text of the play, through the use of windows, which will be discussed in Chapter 5.

Hypertext has two key advantages over traditional means of storing and retrieving text. First, it personalizes the information storage and retrieval function. In some systems users can enter their own data and create their own links. In other systems which already provide the information and access to it, users can add notes and links. This is equivalent to being able to write comments in the margin of a text. The second major advantage of hypertext is that the information is stored in a way that is closer to the way people think. We do not use information sequentially; we use it associatively. One thought leads to another and takes us off on unplanned tangents. Hypertext, which is only in its infancy, promises to greatly enhance the benefits users will receive from access systems.

Analysis Systems

The use of information by business people, especially managers, is usually associated with decision-making activities. If decisions must be made based on output from an access system, further analysis by people is needed before a decision can be made. For this reason, a second type of information system exists, one which assists decision makers by analyzing data needed to support their decisions. This type of information system is an **analysis system**. The goal of an analysis system is to provide access to data and assistance in decision making. There are three types of analysis systems: management information systems, decision support systems, and expert systems.

Management Information Systems

The purpose of a **management information system (MIS)** is to provide information for management decision making by integrating and synthesizing data generated from business operations. An MIS is designed to collect and process data and to provide information in the form of regular and recurring reports to help all levels of management plan and control the activities of an organization. The main difference between a management information system and a transaction processing system is that an MIS is capable of supporting higher-level operations in the organization—decision making by middle and senior management—whereas a transaction processing system is usually geared to the operational control level.

For example, the inventory system for State University's bookstore can be arranged to do more than simply keep track of books that are ordered, sold, and returned. By using this data along with certain decision rules, the manager can also know how well certain books are selling and when it is time to reorder. University administrators responsible for scheduling classes can utilize an MIS that combines data on faculty, classrooms, and educational resources in order to support decisions about how to use resources most efficiently.

There are several management information systems in operation at Last National Bank. One is called the *Customer Information System (CIS)*. It is illustrated in Figure 3.6.

The purpose of this MIS is to provide bank managers with answers to questions about their customers. The data for this system comes from the various accounts a customer might have—checking account, savings account, car loan, and bank credit card, for example. Basic information such as name and address is collected and stored. In addition, with each transaction, such as writing a check or charging a purchase on the credit card, the record is updated to reflect the current balances.

The Customer Information System builds on and ties together the individual transaction processing systems. What makes it a management information system is the way the data is stored, retrieved, and processed and the kinds of answers that can be provided to managers. Suppose Last National Bank is planning to offer a new service: home equity loans. This kind of loan would enable homeowners to borrow money up to the amount of equity they have in their home. Suppose that, as a way of advertising this service, the bank would like to send out personal letters to certain bank customers. It wants to send letters to people who have had a relationship with the bank for at least five years, who already have a mortgage from the bank, and who do not overdraw on their checking accounts. Without the CIS, the manager would have to retrieve data on customers in each of the separate transaction processing

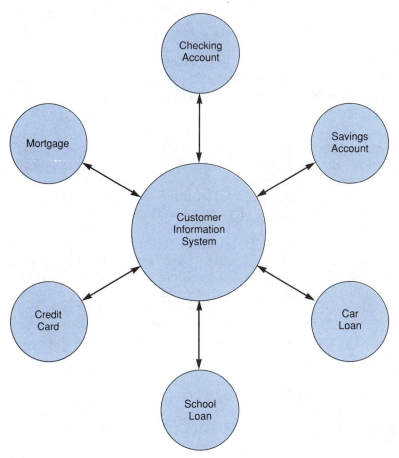

FIGURE 3.6
Customer Information System

systems and then cross-reference it to find those who meet all three criteria. So the manager would have to do quite a bit of work before the information need would be satisfied. With the use of an MIS like the Customer Information System, the data from the various transaction systems can be combined so that the computer can select those people who satisfy the criteria. By using an MIS, a manager has to do much less information processing to satisfy information needs. In this fashion, the system has aided in the decision-making process.

In Chapter 2 we discussed the three levels of management—strategic planning (senior or top management), managerial control (middle management), and operational control (lower management). Since the purpose of a management information system is to provide information for management decision making, it is very important to understand the types of decisions that managers will be making. This will tell us something about the type of information that will be needed to support those decisions. The higher the management level, the more wide-ranging the decisions. Conversely, the lower the level of management, the narrower the scope of the decisions. These different decision-making characteristics in turn result in different information needs. Figure 3.7 shows the relationship between the different levels of management and the related information needs.

Strategic Planning   Those individuals at the strategic planning or senior management level are responsible for establishing the long-range plans for the organization. The policies they establish will then be translated into specific objectives to be achieved by the lower levels of management in the organization. Examples of personnel at this level are the president and vice-presidents of Last National Bank, the president and vice-presidents of State University, and Paul Bunyan at Wooden Wonders. These people deal with forces in the environment (the industry, the government, the society) that will have an impact on the organization. They are concerned with internal operations only in a general sense. Decision makers at this level therefore need information primarily to support the planning process. In addition to highly summarized and integrated internal information, the strategic management level requires information from external sources as well.

Operational Control   At the other extreme are decision makers at the operational control level. These managers are primarily concerned with carrying out the policies on a day-to-day basis and providing feedback or control information to senior managers about their success in doing so. Examples of

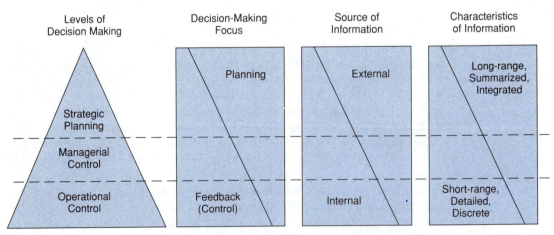

FIGURE 3.7
Levels of management and management information needs

personnel at this level would be department chairs in a university, department managers in a bank, and Mary Tyson at Wooden Wonders. The source of their information is primarily internal, and since they are concerned with management of daily activities, they work with very detailed information.

Managerial Control Between these two levels of management are the middle managers at the managerial control level. Division managers at Last National Bank would be an example of decision makers at this level. While a department manager would be responsible for one service, such as one type of commercial loan, a division manager would be responsible for an entire category of services, such as all commercial lending. Deans of the various colleges at State University would also be decision makers at this level. Their role in the university is primarily to move information between the two other levels of management. They take long-range policies from the strategic planners and translate them into medium-range plans before disseminating them to the lower-level managers. Likewise, they receive control or feedback information from the operational control level and summarize it before passing it on to the strategic planning level. Since their information needs are therefore a combination of those required by the other two levels, they need both planning and control information from both internal and external sources. This information must be more general than that used at the operational control level, but not as general as that used by senior managers.

Decision Support Systems

Management decision making is supported by management information systems through the provision of integrated and summarized reports tailored to the needs of the various levels of management. Such systems are appropriate when the kind of information needed is known in advance. These systems also tend to provide the same information on a periodic basis. However, for decision-making situations in which the information needs vary or the decision process is not completely understood, a different kind of analysis system is needed: a decision support system. The purpose of a **decision support system (DSS)** is to help someone with the analysis of alternative courses of action in a decision-making setting. To understand more about these decision-making situations, let us consider the differences between two classifications of decisions: structured and unstructured.[2]

Structured Decisions **Structured decisions** are those which occur when all the components of a decision are understood and all the necessary information is available for carrying it out. They also tend to be routine decisions which are frequently repeated. In these situations, specific decision rules can be established in advance. An example would be an inventory reorder formula at State University's bookstore. From data on past usage and the timing of demand, a procedure can be established such that when the stock level of a book gets to a certain point, and when the time is right (i.e., before the beginning of a term), it is *automatically* time to reorder. In situations such as this, the MIS can assist in the decision-making process by incorporating the appropriate decision rules.

Unstructured Decisions   In contrast, **unstructured decisions** are those which have no preestablished decision procedures. This could be the case for two reasons: either the decision is so infrequent that it was not worth the organization's effort to establish decision-making rules, or the decision-making process is not understood well enough for clear and precise rules to be established. Two examples would be the decision to introduce a new service at Last National Bank or the decision to make changes in the budget at Wooden Wonders. It is in situations such as these that a decision support system could be used to help decision making. It would do so by enabling the user to enter data, retrieve selected portions of it, and systematically examine alternative courses of action and their consequences.

Gorry and Scott Morton[3] related this classification of decisions to the different levels of management in the grid shown in Figure 3.8.

There are several differences between an MIS and a DSS. First, as pointed out earlier, an MIS is used to support structured decision making, whereas a DSS is used for unstructured decision making. Second, management information systems are typically bigger systems which encompass a large part of the organization and support a class of users such as strategic manage-

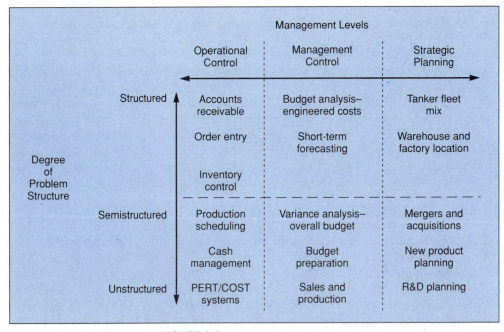

FIGURE 3.8
The Gorry and Scott Morton framework

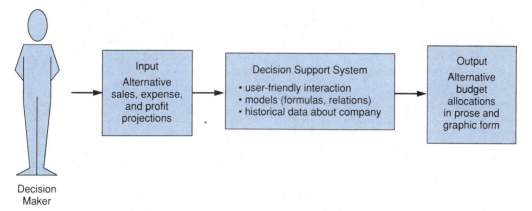

FIGURE 3.9

A decision support system for budget analysis at Wooden Wonders

ment. Decision support systems, on the other hand, tend to be much smaller, usually supporting an individual decision maker. Third, the output from an MIS is in the form of regular and recurring reports; a DSS may produce output for a one-time decision. Fourth, the method of interacting with the computer can be different. An MIS would be designed and developed by information system professionals, and the users may or may not directly use the computer. They may simply receive periodic reports from the MIS. The users of a DSS, on the other hand, generally work with the computer in an interactive mode. That is, they retrieve data and give instructions for testing out various alternatives in a decision-making situation. This is commonly referred to as conducting "what if" analyses. The users may also develop the DSS themselves. Finally, the software used in developing these two systems is different. An MIS is typically developed in a third-generation language such as COBOL, whereas a DSS is developed using languages specially designed for these "what if" analyses. An example would be Lotus 1-2-3. Decision support systems are sometimes a component of an office information system. Figure 3.9 illustrates the components of a decision support system for budget analysis at Wooden Wonders.

EXECUTIVE INFORMATION SYSTEMS

Decision support systems represent the attempt to respond on a more personal level to the information requirements of managers. This trend was continued in the 1980s by **executive information systems (EIS)**, which were developed to support the information needs of the most senior executives in a company. An EIS contains features of both decision support systems and management information systems, yet differs from each of them.

Both a DSS and an EIS are used to respond to the individual information needs of managers. However, a DSS is used to *analyze* problems and opportunities to help a manager make specific decisions. An EIS, on the other hand, is used to *identify* problems or opportunities. Its purpose is to monitor the status of the company rather than to conduct "what if" analyses of alternative courses of action in specific areas. Therefore, its purpose is broader than that of a DSS: it is designed to help top executives structure and articulate strategic issues and then to track and monitor changes in the dimensions of these issues.

Both an MIS and an EIS are presentation tools. That is, their main function is to provide managers with information about the status of the firm. An MIS does this by providing periodic reports about various aspects of the company. The assumption here is that the information requirements are known and can be satisfied by the content of the reports and the format in which they are presented. While management information systems are important to a company, it has also become clear that they are not sufficient. Senior executives who are concerned with planning the strategic direction of a firm do not always know in advance the information they need. Executive information systems provide them with the ability to satisfy both anticipated and *unanticipated* information requirements.

An EIS accomplishes this through several features. First, it facilitates direct access to very large stores of data both within and outside the company. Second, since this data appears immediately on the computer screen, it is much more current than output from an MIS produced in paper form and distributed to people within the organization. Third, the data can be presented in a variety of forms: textual, numeric, and graphic. For example, a high-level manager could monitor sales performance through written data, statistics, or graphs comparing performance of this year and last. Finally, an EIS is designed to be very easy to use. A senior executive does not have time to sift through volumes of documentation to determine how to request and examine certain data; so this data must be accessible and retrievable in a timely fashion to be useful. Some of the features which facilitate the use of executive information systems are considered in Chapter 5 in the discussion of the human-computer interface.

An executive information system could be used at Last National Bank by the president or senior vice-presidents. It might help them track the success of financial services, such as new types of loans, or monitor the effects of certain types of investments. Alternatively, it might be used to examine features of the environment which will impact the strategic goals of the bank.

Expert Systems

Like decision support systems, **expert systems** also assist with unstructured decision making by guiding the behavior of an individual in a decision-making task which normally requires considerable experience and knowledge in some subject. This is accomplished by the use of artificial intelligence techniques to provide expert advice. These systems are also called **knowledge-based systems**, because they translate the knowledge of one or more individuals into rules which can then be used by others making similar decisions.

MYCIN, one of the earliest expert systems, was developed to assist medical diagnoses. Another, called PROSPECTOR, was developed to serve as a consultant to geologists in explorations for different kinds of mineral deposits such as copper, nickel, and uranium. Expert systems have also been developed to assist decision makers in business. American Express has developed an expert system to assist in the credit authorization process. Digital Equipment Corporation developed XCON (e_xpert _configurator) to assist computer sales personnel in configuring large computer systems for clients.

Expert systems differ from management information and decision support systems both in the kind of data involved and in the way it is processed. Since expert systems assist decision makers working in a particular domain, all the data relevant to this domain must be captured by knowledge engineers and placed in a **knowledge base**. A **knowledge engineer** is a person who works with the expert to identify the way decisions are reached and the knowledge needed to do so. Since these are ill-structured decisions, the knowledge engineer must extract the reasoning process used by the expert to arrive at a conclusion. People make decisions in such circumstances using **heuristics**, or "rules of thumb." That is, they do not carefully and logically compute all the alternatives, but rather, rely upon their considerable knowledge of the subject matter, judgment, and experience. It is the task of the knowledge engineer to translate these heuristics into rules which can then be incorporated into the expert system. This component of the expert system is called the **inference engine**.

Since this type of system is to be used by an end user, it is also important for a person to be able to interact with it easily. For this reason, expert systems often include a natural language facility. That is, the user's input to the system is provided in the form of answers to questions posed by the expert system in English or some other human language.

The output from an expert system can take several forms. First, it can be a decision. Second, it can be a recommendation. Finally, once a decision or recommendation is given, an expert system is capable of explaining its reasoning process to the user. The input to an expert system comes at several points in the system's use. When it is being developed, the expertise is entered into the knowledge base. When the system is being used, it accepts input from the end user. However, it is also able to "learn"—that is, it can incorporate changes in its knowledge base and rules based on feedback from previous decisions.

Such features as heuristic reasoning, learning, and natural language are the artificial intelligence techniques employed in the development of expert systems. The main advantage of expert systems is that they enable non-experts to make decisions in domains which previously required one to be an expert. They can be valuable to an organization that desires to capture the knowledge and expertise an individual has developed over a number of years to make it easily available to others in the company. This can be invaluable in the training of new employees or when this expertise is in great demand. It is also a useful way of retaining the expertise of someone after he or she leaves the company. Expert systems are the newest type of analysis system, and considerable research is currently under way to determine the most appropriate applications for expert systems and the efficient methods for developing them. Figure 3.10 is an illustration of the components of an expert system.

Action Systems

Once a business decision has been made, some action usually results. It may be producing a new product on the assembly line, processing a withdrawal from a checking account, ordering more inventory, or generating a bill for materials ordered. In certain circumstances, these actions can be accomplished by computer-based information systems. Such systems are called **action systems**.

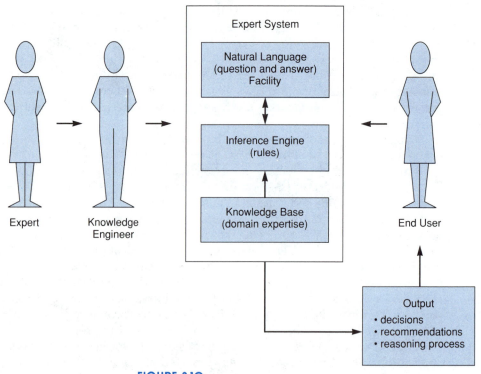

FIGURE 3.10
The components of an expert system

The goal of an action system is to access some data, analyze it to reach a decision, and then carry out some activity. It builds on access and analysis systems and extends them by carrying out some behavior. There are two types of action systems: **automated manufacturing** systems and **automated business systems**.

Automated Manufacturing Systems

The most common applications of action systems today are in manufacturing. Engineers use computer-based action systems to convert general product designs into detailed manufacturing specifications. Scheduling systems are used to automatically schedule the resources needed to manufacture a certain product. **Process control systems** are used to monitor the manufacturing process and adjust it as circumstances require.

Probably the best-known example of an action system is a **robot**. A robot is a computer-based tool which combines artificial intelligence with physical mobility. It is a programmable computer designed to move material, parts, tools, or specialized devices through a series of motions to perform a variety of tasks. Robots are used on assembly lines, in hazardous manufacturing such as steel production, and in space flights. The main advantages of robots are that they can do repetitive work without getting bored, they can do very detailed work without making mistakes, and they can perform tasks which would be hazardous for humans. Figure 1.3 in Chapter 1 showed a robot involved in manufacturing.

Automated Business Systems

The newest examples of action systems can be found in management rather than in the engineering or manufacturing parts of a business. These systems will collect, store, retrieve, and analyze data, then make a business decision and act on it.

One example of an automated business system is a **program trading** system used in the stock market. These systems store data on the behavior of certain stocks. Based on programmed rules, they will make a decision about buying or selling stocks and then execute that buy/sell decision. Another example is an automatic teller machine at a bank. When a client wishes to withdraw money from a checking account, the system collects data such as the account password and the amount of the transaction. It then accesses other data to determine whether the transaction can be completed. Based on that data and certain rules, it makes a decision. If the transaction can be completed, the system takes an action: it disburses the money. The decision-making processes supporting these actions have a range of sophistication. Some, such as those used in ATMs, are based on relatively simple rules. Others, such as those used in program trading systems, rely on expert systems.

In certain situations, the action taken by the system involves interacting with the information system of another company. In such cases, the action system is part of an **interorganizational system**. Consider the bookstore inventory system. At a minimum, the system must keep an accurate account of the books in stock. When books are added to or removed from inventory, the system must be able to update the list of books. In this case the inventory system would be an example of an *access system* because its goal is simply storage and retrieval of the information. If the system could also monitor sales and returns and had rules so that it could advise the manager when to reorder a book, it would be an *analysis system* because it would actually participate in the decision-making process. Now suppose that, instead of signaling the bookstore manager that it was time to reorder a book, the system went ahead and actually placed the order automatically. In this case, the inventory system would be an *action system*, because it would take some action automatically. Since the bookstore's system would be communicating with the order entry system of a publisher, it would also be considered an interorganizational system. This interorganizational system could be further expanded if the publisher's order entry system automatically sent the book order to the shipping department and produced and sent a bill in electronic form back to the bookstore. The term *electronic data interchange (EDI)* is also used to describe this process. EDI will be discussed further in Chapter 7. Automated business systems, particularly those which are part of interorganizational systems, promise to increase the efficiency of normal business transactions.

INFORMATION SYSTEM PROPERTIES

Chapter 2 discussed the properties that all systems, including information systems, possess—purpose, environment, components, resources, and management. The purpose of the information system determines the type of system—access, analysis, or action—that will result. The components (input, process, and output) together with the resources (hardware, software, data, procedures, and personnel) describe the way the information is actually produced. The environment explains the context in which the information need originates and the constraints on the system to be developed. Finally, management is the mechanism for determining whether the purpose has been achieved.

Our discussion of types of information systems demonstrated the different purposes of information systems. The components and resources of computer-based information processing are considered in more depth in Chapter 4. The following section examines the two remaining properties of information systems: environment and management.

Environment

By understanding the context of the information need and use, we can better understand how the information system can satisfy that need. We can also understand the role each of the resources should play. Context is another word for environment. Environment means the setting within which the information need originates and in which the information system will function to satisfy those needs. The features of this setting will have some influence on the information system. This is why it is impossible to separate the context from the consideration of the system itself.

When an information system is being developed, certain factors must be taken into consideration. A significant one is money. The financial condition of an organization looking to acquire computers will certainly affect its choice. The organization's current competition will also influence its decisions; for example, one reason for purchasing personal computers for office workers might be that a rival organization has them. Financial constraints and competition within the industry are both aspects of the environment as well. Therefore, in addition to being defined as the context for information use, the environment can be defined as the constraints imposed upon the information system. Constraints such as budgetary limitations represent forces that are outside the control of the information system yet influence the system in some way. The financial constraint, for example, will influence the kind of computer that can be purchased and the amount of software that can be bought.

Since the environment is what is outside the information system, a key issue for organizations today has to do with the people who use computers. Which people should be considered part of the computer-based information system? The answer will influence the way the system is designed.

The Context of the Information Need and Use

The context for Last National Bank's MIS which monitors customers' accounts is a business fact of life: time is money. Therefore, timeliness of information access will influence the way its information systems are designed. The bank wants to know very quickly when an account is overdrawn so that no more checks can be written on that account. It also wants checks to be processed as quickly as possible.

If a decision support system to help State University administrators plan for future resource needs is being developed, an important part of that context is the people who will be using this system. If the users are very knowledgeable about computer technology, certain options will be possible. On the other hand, if none of them has ever used a computer before, a different approach would be called for. This might include purchasing software that is very easy to use and establishing training classes as part of the system development process.

Constraints Imposed upon the Information System

All human endeavors have limits imposed upon them from the outside. The design of information systems is no exception. When computer-based information processing is being considered, external constraints have to be taken into account. Although Mary Tyson might like to utilize computer software for all aspects of producing product designs and company catalogs for Wooden

Wonders, no such software might be commercially available. She might not possess the technological knowledge to develop it herself, and the company might not have the money to hire someone to develop it for her. Therefore, she might have to settle for a less sophisticated alternative.

State University might like to have an information system that integrates registration, billing, and accounts receivable information. Given the university budget, however, this might not be possible. This could result in the development of each system separately or in phases, with the objective of linking them together at some later date.

There are other constraints besides financial ones. One environment of Last National Bank is the rest of the banking industry. Competitors may have introduced certain services which Last National, in order to be competitive, must offer as well. An example would be interest-bearing checking accounts. Adding a new service like this will result in the need for an information system to support it. In addition to the rest of the industry, society represents another environment for a bank. Laws governing the amount of time it can take to clear a check will also impose constraints on the development of a system to handle this activity.

Computer hardware already in place in an organization represents a potential technical constraint on the acquisition of new hardware and software. Not all software runs on all hardware. If an organization wishes to acquire software for a new system, it may be limited to the kind of software that runs with the existing hardware.

Local and Global Environments

Usually, the boundaries of an information system—the lines between what is and is not part of the system—are conceptual rather than physical boundaries. That is, they include or exclude what one *chooses* to put inside or outside the system. The process of establishing boundaries results in the local and global environments of a system. The local environment is the rest of the organization; the global environment is the rest of the society. The most immediate local environment of State University's library card catalog system is the rest of the library. Another local environment is the rest of the university. In both cases, what goes on in these environments will influence the activities of the card catalog system. The library's technological resources will influence the extent to which the catalog can be automated. The type of library patrons and the financial resources of the university will influence the contents and size of the library and therefore the card catalog.

The local environment of Last National Bank's information systems could be thought of as all the departments in the bank other than the information systems department. If the bounds around the system were drawn this way, the only *people* who are a part of the system would be the system designers, managers, and computer programmers. The users of the information would not be considered a part of the system. The implication of drawing the bounds this way is that the users might not have any involvement in decisions about the system and their views might not be taken into account when the system is developed and changed.

The emergence of management information systems was, in part, an acknowledgment that the decision-making needs of managers had not been sufficiently taken into account in system design. One improvement management information systems provide is that managers are considered a part of these systems. Therefore, their satisfaction with the information which the system provides is built into the design and evaluation of the information system.

The introduction of personal computers and the emergence of end-user computing are an extension of this perspective. With end-user computing, the needs not only of managers, but of *all* users of information, are taken into account. If computers are used by personnel throughout the organization, the scope of the information system might include the entire organization! One practical implication of drawing the bounds in this way might be that the sophistication of all users would be taken into account when computer software was purchased, so that one would not have to be a computer expert to use the computer. If the system bounds are drawn more narrowly to include only data processing personnel, however, one probably would have to know considerably more about a computer to be able to use it.

Subsystems

The term *system* is used frequently in discussions of information processing. It can have many different meanings. Up to this point it has been used to mean *information* system; that is, it has been used to refer to the combination of all five resources. However, in conversations with information systems personnel and in literature you may encounter the word in reference to the computer or software only. This is not a contradiction, because each of the resources is itself a system: a subsystem of the information system. We defined a system as a collection of parts that work together to achieve a goal. Therefore, a computer can also be viewed as a system. It has numerous mechanical and electronic parts that function together. The goal of a computer system is to take data, transform it into electronic form, process it, and produce a result. It is both a complete system in itself and a subsystem of the information system. Subsystems are created by the way the boundaries are drawn. In the case of the computer subsystem, only the hardware is included within the boundaries. Other subsystems may contain all five resources but address only a part of the organization's overall information processing needs.

Some people who work with information systems concern themselves with only one or two of these subsystems. Computer programmers, for example, are concerned primarily with the hardware and software subsystems. This is not a problem as long as someone else in the organization is concerned with the other three resources. It is important not to give too much attention to one subsystem at the expense of the others.

For example, suppose the goal of a new information system at Last National Bank is to enable mortgage department personnel to be more efficient in doing their jobs. But suppose the software subsystem is given all the attention and, as a result, a very sophisticated but difficult-to-use software package is purchased. Now suppose the people who are to use that software aren't very computer literate. Since the knowledge level of the end users was not sufficiently considered, they could end up being less efficient at their jobs because of the time and effort required to learn the new system. This is an example of suboptimization. An information system is not as effective as it could be if one or a few resources are suboptimized. For a truly successful information system, the goals of all the subsystems must be achieved. The bank has some alternatives. It can acquire less sophisticated but easier-to-use software. Or it can draw upon other personnel resources and develop education and support procedures. When all the subsystems work both individually and together to achieve a common goal, the result is synergy. This is the ultimate goal of any information system.

Just as whole information systems can be categorized by type, subsystems can be categorized as well. It is useful to understand these different categorizations because the term "system" is used so frequently in discussions of information processing and many different meanings are assigned to it. Since an information system can be viewed as a collection of subsystems, each having its own purpose and properties, the use of the term "system" can be confusing. One person could be using the term to refer to the entire information system, while another person could be using it to refer only to a part of the system such as hardware or software. The following is a discussion of the most common types of information system subsystems.

Software Subsystem The software subsystem refers to the computer programs designed to carry out a particular task, such as billing. Another term for software subsystem is **application**. Thus, a *billing application* refers to the software subsystem that will collect transaction data, manipulate it, store some of the results, and produce bills. Information systems are commonly categorized according to their applications. For example, if one were to combine the billing application with the related hardware, personnel, procedures, and data, one would have a billing information system. The term **applications portfolio** is used to refer to the complete set of applications that exist in an organization. Understanding the applications portfolio of a business is important for information system managers who are concerned with the sum of information processing activities for planning purposes.

Content Systems can also be grouped according to content or the kind of information being processed. This is a useful way of categorizing subsystems when associating them with the various units of an organization. Examples would be marketing information systems, human resources information systems, and accounting information systems. In a university there are information systems associated with students and the management of the services provided to them. One that has been discussed is the student records system. Another is the scheduling system. A third is the bookstore's inventory system.

It is especially important to make the distinction between accounting and non-accounting systems. An *accounting system* is one which stores, retrieves, and manipulates a firm's financial data. **Non-accounting systems** are those which are not involved with financial data. The reason for maintaining a distinction is that procedures governing the design and operation of the two types of systems should be different. To prevent computer crime, organizations should have procedures that prohibit those who design accounting systems from operating them as well. This procedure is referred to as *separation of duties*. Just imagine for a moment what could happen if the person who designed a company's payroll system were also responsible for producing the monthly paychecks.

Scope A third way of categorizing subsystems is by scope or how the boundaries are drawn. This will determine the portion of the organization it serves. Some information systems have a very narrow scope; for others it may be very broad. Scope can be used to organize information systems into three categories: personal information systems, departmental information systems, and organizational information systems.

Personal information systems are designed to serve an individual. An individual office information system is one type of personal information system. The data in these systems is often temporary, such as that in an individual's personal calendar and activities management systems. An information system set up to assist the loan department of a bank is an example of a **departmental information system**. The scope of this information system would be broader than that of a personal information system. It would include the activities of those in a given department, perhaps ten or twenty people. A corporate planning information system designed to assist all the managers in the bank would be an example of an **organizational information system**. Since departmental and organizational information systems are not directly tied to an individual, they could exist long after those who originally designed and used them have gone. As a result, the procedures governing their use must be more formal.

The Role of the User Systems can also be categorized by the intended role of the information system user. In some cases the user may have little or no direct interaction with the system. This might occur for a management information system which produces periodic reports for personnel at various levels of management. In contrast, a bank's ATM system is based on the assumption of direct end-user interaction with it. One benefit of categorizing systems in this way is that it facilitates the task of determining the type of procedures that are necessary. For an MIS with little direct end-user involvement, procedures relate primarily to the operations of information system professionals who are familiar with computers. In some cases, training might also be included. Bank customers, on the other hand, cannot be required to attend classes before using ATMs, yet they must be able to operate the machine. The bank system, therefore, will need different kinds of procedures. It will need to provide very explicit and easy-to-understand instructions for operating the system, and it will have to provide these instructions when and where the ATM is in use.

Figure 3.11 relates this discussion of subsystem categories to the previous discussion of types of information systems.

Management

If an information system has a purpose, there must be some way of determining if that purpose has been achieved. This is the role of the system property called management. The purpose of any information system is to provide a certain type of information. One role of management is to ensure that feedback is provided which reveals whether this goal is being reached. The clearer and more explicit the purpose, the easier the task of management. Based on feedback about the system's performance, adjustments can then be made to the system so it can better achieve its goal.

The purpose of an access information system is efficient storage and retrieval of information. What becomes important in achieving this goal is the accurate capturing of transaction data and the timely updating of information already in the system. The kind of feedback about this system's performance that would result in alterations might be that the output is not timely, accurate, or in the format desired by the user. Based on this feedback, changes to the input, process, and/or output functions can be made. For example, if the scheduling system's output—room assignments, faculty assignments, and stu-

FIGURE 3.11

Summary of types of information systems

Purpose	Subsystem	Content	Scope	Role of End User
Access	Accounts Receivable Application (Software Subsystem)	Library	University Registration System (Organizational System)	Automated Teller Machine (End-User Involvement)
Analysis	Customer Information System (Data Subsystem)	Market Research System	DSS (Personal System)	MIS (Some End-User Involvement)
Action	Robot (Hardware and Software Subsystems)	Automated Inventory System	Product Design System (Departmental System)	Office Security System (No End-User Involvement)

dent lists—is not ready in time for the first day of class, the purpose of that system has not been achieved. Changes in when and how the data is input might be required. There might also have to be changes in the way the output information is distributed to students and faculty.

The purpose of an analysis information system, on the other hand, is a bit more complex. The purpose of a management information system is to go one step beyond the collection and storage of transaction data. Such a system also intends to integrate and synthesize this data to help managers make better decisions. An MIS to support the loan department of a bank would capture data about applicants for loans, those who were rejected, and those who received loans. This data would later be useful, for example, in determining to whom advertising of commercial loan services should be directed. If the output from this MIS fails to give satisfactory information to those managers who will use it, adjustments must be made. The important thing to remember is that the ultimate test of the system is how useful the information provided is to those who need it, not how well the hardware and software perform. The system may be producing output very quickly and efficiently, but if it is the wrong information, changes have to be made.

The purpose of a decision support system is to help its user structure and manipulate data which will assist in the analysis of alternative courses of action. To create a useful DSS, one must start with the decision to be made. Based on that, one can identify the information needed to reach the decision. Then one must identify the input data needed to generate the required output. Since each person makes decisions in different ways, DSSs are usually individual systems. Standard software such as Lotus 1-2-3 might be used, but the way the software is adapted for a DSS will vary from user to user. A DSS can therefore be evaluated according to the help it gives a specific user in evaluating alternatives.

One way in which feedback can influence the system was just described: it can change the approach to achieving the information system's goal. Another effect of feedback, however, is that the goal itself might have to be altered. For example, one of the goals of the university's scheduling system is to have an accurate list of students enrolled in each class on the first day of the term. Suppose the feedback showed that this was not happening. Upon further investigation, it was determined that it would be impossible to have an accurate class list on the first day, because students drop and add classes in the first two weeks of the term. Thus, the system goal might be altered to state that by the end of the second week of the term a complete class list would be compiled. People who design systems spend considerable time dealing with these kinds of issues. Nevertheless, some adjustments are inevitably needed. The plan for the information system must therefore include provisions for making changes.

Another problem in achieving information system goals occurs when the people associated with the system have different goals. This most often occurs when the designers and programmers have one understanding of the goal and the users have another. If the designers of the bank's information system think they are designing an access system, the integration of output data with that from other systems will not be part of their goal. If the bank's managers, on the other hand, want to use the output for long-range planning, they will be frustrated if none of the information produced by these separate systems has been integrated.

At the very earliest stages of developing an information system, the goal of the system should be identified and agreed upon by all. As we can see, it is not sufficient simply to have a goal of using a computer to help with work. The goal must also specify the way the computer will be used and the kind of information it is expected to produce. Just as establishing a clear goal should be part of designing the system, so too should there be a mechanism for continuously collecting feedback and making changes to the system based on that feedback. An information system is not a static entity; it is dynamic.

SUMMARY

Three different kinds of organizations and their information needs were introduced in this chapter—in case studies that will be used throughout the rest of the book. The purpose of these cases is to provide common contexts for discussing the concepts presented in the book. These organizations reflect the activities businesses carry out and the decisions they have to make. Therefore, they need information in order to support those activities and decisions.

Of the five properties an information system possesses, it is the property called purpose by which information systems are categorized. An information system can have one of three purposes. This purpose will, in turn, influence the other properties of the system—its components, resources, environment, and management. An access system has the purpose of information storage and retrieval. An analysis system has the purpose of information storage and retrieval plus decision support. An action system has the purpose of information storage and retrieval, decision support, and automatic behavior.

Information systems can also be categorized by subsystem. Subsystems are created by the drawing of boundaries. One type of subsystem is the software subsystem or application. A second type (such as an accounting system) is associated with a functional area of the business and the content it includes. A third type of subsystem is created by its scope, or how broadly the boundaries around the system are drawn; this would result in personal, departmental, or organizational systems. Finally, information systems can be categorized by the intended role of the end user.

The counterpart to determining the appropriate type of information system is the management of that system. This involves collecting feedback about the behavior of the system in achieving its goals. If the goals are not being met, changes must be made. In some cases, this means changing features of the system. In other cases, the goal itself must be changed. In still other cases, the personnel associated with the system may have to come to an agreement on what the goal actually is.

CHAPTER NOTES

1. Vannevar Bush, "As We May Think," *Atlantic Monthly* (July 1945): 101–108.
2. H. A. Simon, *The New Science of Management Decision* (New York: Harper & Row, 1960).
3. G. A. Gorry and M. S. Scott Morton, "A Framework for Management Information Systems," *Sloan Management Review* (Fall 1971): 55–70.

ADDITIONAL REFERENCES

Anthony, Robert N. *Planning and Control Systems: A Framework for Analysis.* Boston: Graduate School of Business Administration, Harvard University, 1965.

Conklin, Jeff. "Hypertext: An Introduction and Survey." *IEEE Computer* (September 1987): 17–41.

Davis, Gordon B., and Margrethe H. Olson. *Management Information Systems: Conceptual Foundations, Structure, and Development.* 2d ed. New York: McGraw-Hill, 1985.

El Sawy, O. "How to Make DSS 'EIS-Ready'." *DSS-89 Transactions*, ed. G. Widmeyer. Providence: The Institute of Management Sciences (June 1989): 57–59.

Feigenbaum, Edward A., and Pamela McCorduck. *The Fifth Generation: Artificial Intelligence and Japan's Computer Challenge to the World.* Reading, MA: Addison-Wesley, 1983.

Fiderio, Janet. "A Grand Vision." *Byte* (October 1988): 237–244.

Frisse, Mark. "From Text to Hypertext." *Byte* (October 1988): 247–253.

Guterl, Fred V. "Computer Think for Business." *Dun's Business Month* (October 1986): 30–37.

Halasz, Frank. "Reflections on Notecards: Seven Issues for the Next Generation of Hypermedia Systems." *Communications of the ACM* 31, No. 7 (July 1988): 836–852.

McFarlan, F. Warren. "Portfolio Approach to Information Systems." In *Catching Up with the Computer Revolution*, ed. Lynn Salerno, 178–193. New York: John Wiley and Sons, 1983.

Rockart, J. F. *Executive Information Systems.* Homewood, IL: Dow Jones-Irwin, 1988.

Rockart, J. F., and M. E. Treacy. "The CEO Goes On-Line." *Harvard Business Review* (January-February 1982): 82–88.

Scott Morton, M. S. *Management Decision Systems.* Boston: Harvard University Graduate School of Business Administration, 1971.

Scown, Susan. *The Artificial Intelligence Experience: An Introduction.* Maynard, MA: Digital Equipment Corporation, 1985.

Smith, John B., and Stephen F. Weiss. "An Overview of Hypertext." *Communications of the ACM* 31, No. 7 (July 1988): 816–819.

Soelberg, P. O. "Unprogrammed Decision Making." *Industrial Management Review* 8, No. 2 (Spring 1967): 19–30.

Spiegler, Israel, and Eileen M. Trauth. "A Framework for Office Automation Education." *Journal of Computer Information Systems* 28, No. 2 (Winter 1987–88): 32–38.

Sprague, Ralph H., Jr., and Barbara C. McNurlin, eds. *Information Systems in Practice*. Englewood Cliffs, NJ: Prentice-Hall, 1986.

Turban, E., and D. Schaeffer. "A Comparative Study of Executive Information Systems." *DSS-87 Transactions*, ed. O. El Sawy. Providence: The Institute of Management Sciences (1987): 139–148.

KEY TERMS

access system
action system
analysis system
application
applications portfolio
artificial intelligence
automated business
  system
automated manufactur-
  ing system
automatic teller machine
  (ATM)
coupled systems
debit cards
decision support system
  (DSS)
departmental informa-
  tion system
electronic bulletin board

electronic funds transfer
  (EFT)
electronic mail
executive information
  system (EIS)
expert system
heuristics
hypertext
inference engine
interorganizational
  system
knowledge base
knowledge-based
  systems
knowledge engineer
management information
  system (MIS)
natural language pro-
  cessing

non-accounting systems
office automation
office information
  system
organizational informa-
  tion system
personal information
  system
process control systems
program trading
record-keeping system
related systems
robot
structured decisions
transaction processing
  system
unstructured decisions
videotext

REVIEW QUESTIONS

1. An information system may have one of three purposes. List the three categories of information systems and give an example of each.
2. What is the purpose of an access system? What kinds of access systems exist?
3. What is the main difference between a record-keeping system and a transaction processing system?
4. What are related or coupled systems?
5. What is the purpose of an analysis system?
6. Discuss the difference between a management information system and a transaction processing system.
7. What are the differences among management information systems, decision support systems, executive information systems, and expert systems?
8. How do information requirements vary at different management levels?
9. What is the purpose of a decision support system?
10. Explain the difference between structured and unstructured decision making.
11. Explain the following concepts related to expert systems:
    knowledge based
    heuristic
    inference engine

12. What is the advantage of an expert system?
13. What is the purpose of an action system? What types of action systems exist?
14. Explain process control systems.
15. Discuss local and global environments. How are the boundaries determined?
16. What are some of the subsystems of an information system?
17. Why is it important to have content subsystems?
18. What is the function of system management?
19. Discuss the importance of feedback in fulfilling a system management role.
20. Why is goal setting important?

CASE

Last National Bank would like to improve the process of managing consumer loans for home mortgages. The current information system to support this activity is a transaction processing system. Once a mortgage loan is approved by bank personnel, the system maintains data on the client and keeps a record of payments and current balances. This data is then combined with other data in the bank's consumer loan management information system.

The problem is that there has recently been a sharp increase in both new mortgage and remortgage applications. Bank management would like to cut down on the amount of human resources devoted to the approval process. Since there are certain rules used in the approval process, it seems appropriate to employ the computer to reduce human effort. The issue confronting management is determining what type of system to use: a decision support system, an expert system, or an automated business system.

DISCUSSION QUESTIONS

1. What are the purposes and features of each of these systems? How do they differ?
2. Who would be the users of each type of system? Why?
3. What are the strengths and weaknesses of each system?

PART II

The Components of an Information System

PART OUTLINE

CHAPTER 4

Computer-based Information Processing

CHAPTER OUTLINE

INFORMATION PROCESSING TOOLS

RESOURCES OF A COMPUTER-BASED INFORMATION SYSTEM

COMPONENTS OF A COMPUTER-BASED INFORMATION SYSTEM

PROCESS

INPUT

OUTPUT

CHAPTER OBJECTIVES

- To explain how the computer hardware and software interact to provide useful information.
- To describe the basic input, process, and output tasks that are involved when the computer processes data into information.
- To list the differences among the generations of programming languages.
- To show how to determine which input and output methods and devices are appropriate for what circumstances.
- To follow the process of developing a computer-based information processing system through the example of developing an application system for a budget.

INTRODUCTION

Part I of this book, The Information Environment, provided the necessary background for the development of information literacy. Chapter 2 explained the concept of a system and the properties of an information system, and Chapter 3 extended this discussion by considering particular types of information systems and the contexts in which they might be found. With that as background, we are now able in Part II to explore the specific dimensions of an information system in greater depth. Chapters 4, 5, 6, and 7 discuss the specific functions an information system carries out to transform data into information. Chapters 4 and 5 examine the input, process, and output functions carried out by the two most common information processors: computers and people. Chapter 4 considers how computers process data; Chapter 5 considers how people process data into information.

There are two reasons why one should have a basic understanding of how the computer processes data into information. One reason is that this knowledge will be useful in making decisions about acquiring computer-based tools. If a person understands something of what is going on inside the "black box," he or she will be better able to make sure that the appropriate equipment is being acquired. The other reason is that one must have some understanding of the operations of the computer to be able to use it effectively. Information literacy means not only knowing *how* to use the equipment, but also knowing *when* and *whether* certain technology should be used and the implications of those decisions.

The material covered in this chapter is closely related to Sections I and III in the Technology Appendix, which discuss computer hardware and software. Therefore, before reading this chapter, the reader should become familiar with the computer hardware used for input, process, and output discussed in Section I, the discussion of programming languages and generations of programming languages in Section IV, and the history of information processing discussed in Section V of the appendix.

INFORMATION PROCESSING TOOLS

Information is so fundamental to our lives that we are not always consciously aware of its importance. In general, we use information to guide our behavior. Sometimes the information is in the form of knowledge needed to perform some task. We use information found in a cookbook to prepare a meal. We use information found in an address book to contact people in writing or by telephone. A very common reason for wanting information is to help make a decision. For example, when someone wakes up in the morning, he or she might like to know if it is raining, to decide whether to carry an umbrella. A person consults a television guide to help decide what to watch that evening. A teacher needs information about students' test scores and homework to assign a final grade.

Information processing is the act of transforming data (**input**) into information (meaningful **output**). Over the years, techniques and technologies have been developed for assisting with the collection, processing, and storage of data and the dissemination of information. Notebooks, typewriters, adding machines, mathematical formulas, and alphabetical ordering are some examples of these aids. Long before the computer was invented, information systems existed to facilitate information processing, and they have been used to carry out the functions of input, process, output, storage, and communication. These functions can be accomplished entirely by a person, by a person with the assistance of a machine, or entirely by a machine. These three methods of information processing are referred to as manual, machine-assisted, and computer-based information processing. Regardless of the method used, there are nine activities involved when data is processed into information:

Recording/Originating — collecting relevant data or recording the new or corrected value of data

Classifying — arranging data according to like characteristics

Sorting — arranging data in some sequential order

Calculating — performing arithmetic operations on numeric data

Summarizing — reducing masses of data into concise and usable form

Storing — setting data aside in some organized fashion for future reference

Retrieving — obtaining stored data when needed

Reproducing — making copies when needed

Communicating — transferring information to another person or to a machine for further processing

However, there are two primary advantages the computer has over other techniques and technologies used for information processing. The first is that it can usually manipulate the data to produce information faster, more accurately, and more efficiently. The second is that the computer can do things that none of the other techniques or technologies can do. Not only can it assist us with storing and retrieving information and making decisions, but in some cases it can actually make the decision for us and carry it out. A computer-based information system, therefore, is capable of providing us with a wider range of information processing services. Figure 4.1 shows the various ways in which these functions have been carried out, and the types of devices which have been employed to do so.

Manual Information Processing

Manual information processing, the oldest type, involves a person and some tool usually for recording and writing. An example of manual information pro-

FIGURE 4.1
Types of data processing activities with examples

	Processing Methods		
	Manual Methods	**Manual with Machine Assistance**	**Computer-based Methods**
Originating/ Recording	Human observation, handwritten records, pegboards	Typewriter, cash register	Magnetic tape encoder, magnetic and optical character readers, card and tape punches, on-line terminals, key-to-disk encoding
Classifying	Hand posting, pegboards	Cash register, bookkeeping machine	Determined by systems design computer
Sorting	Hand posting, pegboards, edge-notched cards	Mechanical collators	Computer sorting
Calculating	Human brain	Adding machines, calculators, cash registers	Computer
Summarizing	Pegboards, hand calculations	Accounting machines, adding machines, cash registers	Computer
Storing	Paper in files, journals, ledgers, etc.	Motorized rotary files, microfilm	Magnetizable media and devices, punched media, computer, microfilm
Retrieving	File clerk, bookkeeper	Motorized rotary files, microfilm	On-line inquiry with direct-access devices; movement of storage media to computer
Reproducing	Clerical, carbon paper	Xerox machines, duplicators, addressing machines	Multiple copies from printers; microfilm copies
Communicating	Written reports, hand-carried messages, telephone	Documents prepared by machines, message conveyors	On-line data transmission for printed output, visual display, or voice output

cessing would be a student listening to a lecture and taking notes. The student listens to the speaker, determines the important information, and writes the information down so it can be referred to later. The student is using the data processing activities of recording, storing, and retrieving. When the notes are used for studying, the student will summarize, sort, and classify the data in the notes. If there is a study group, data will be reproduced and communicated, and perhaps changed if discrepancies are found among students' notes.

The primary advantage of manual information processing is that, since no machine is involved, the additional costs of acquiring and taking care of one are not incurred. In addition, changing the way information is processed is simply a matter of learning a new procedure. For example, a change in the tax law will change the way income taxes are calculated. In a manual system, while the new procedures are being learned, the task may be performed less efficiently. But after the learning process is completed, the new procedures will be performed as efficiently as the old. This is called a high degree of procedural flexibility.

Manual information processing has some obvious disadvantages, however. Some information processing tasks can be very labor-intensive if done manually, and a considerable amount of processing by several people may be required. An example would be a task that involves performing many calculations, such as payroll production. Moreover, labor costs are generally higher than machine costs.

A second disadvantage is that people are likely to commit errors during repetitive tasks. Therefore, in activities which require many calculations, there may be an unacceptably high rate of errors. No one would want to do business with a bank that could not keep an accurate balance.

A third disadvantage of manual information processing is that for certain time-consuming activities, the information may not be available in a timely manner. For example, if a report needed Tuesday morning is not completed until Wednesday morning, its value is greatly diminished.

Machine-assisted Information Processing

Machine-assisted information processing overcomes some of the disadvantages of the manual method. The first types of machines assisted people in information processing by improving accuracy and increasing the speed of calculating. Some of these machines, such as the abacus, have been around for a very long time. Others, such as the calculator, are a product of the twentieth century and have undergone significant changes in recent decades. An abacus and a calculator are shown in Figure 4.2.

Other machines focus on improving such data-handling tasks as storage, retrieval, and communication. An example is the typewriter. Because handwritten notes may be difficult to read, a typewriter is used to facilitate the retrieval and communication of that data. Mimeograph machines and photocopiers provide multiple copies of a document and facilitate communication.

Some machines are used to carry out a sequence of information processing tasks. The machines associated with punched cards are one example. Before the computer was invented, punched cards were used to store data. Data was recorded on a card by the use of a *keypunch machine*. These cards could be arranged in a variety of orders with a device called a *sorter*.

FIGURE 4.2
Abacus and calculator

Another example is a cash register. A cash register determines the amount of the sale by summing the prices of the items and calculating the amount of tax due. These machines can also calculate a daily summary of the amount of gross sales, which might be categorized by department. In addition, it might keep track of the sales tax collected and the items sold for inventory purposes.

The main advantage of machine-assisted information processing is that it can improve the speed and accuracy of information processing tasks. This will result in information that is useful and produced in a timely fashion. With machines to assist information processing, less human labor is usually required. This means a savings in personnel costs.

The disadvantages of machine-assisted processing include the cost of purchasing and maintaining the machine, the decrease in procedural flexibility, and the fact that the individuals hired to operate the machine may be more costly to employ than those who performed the task manually. The machine may need to be changed when the procedure or rules change, resulting in a decrease in procedural flexibility. For example, if a state decides that food is no longer subject to sales tax, all cash registers in that state which automatically calculated sales tax will need to be changed. This requires time and money.

Computer-based Information Processing

Computer-based information processing is fast becoming the most common means of processing data. The use of the computer overcomes many of the disadvantages of manual methods. By being more sophisticated, it overcomes many of the disadvantages of the machine-assisted method as well.

Computer-based information processing has two main disadvantages. One is that currently computers are generally more expensive than other data processing machines, although the costs of computer-based tools are decreasing. Nevertheless, the total costs associated with computer processing can still be high, so careful thought must be given to the information processing needs and how the computer can meet them.

The other disadvantage is that computers are more complicated than other data processing tools. For this reason, people who intend to use computer-based tools should have some understanding of how they work. We devote the rest of this chapter to a detailed discussion of computer-based information processing tools.

RESOURCES OF A COMPUTER-BASED INFORMATION SYSTEM

Resources are the parts of a computer-based information system which are needed to turn data into information; that is, they are what is *inside* the system. The resources of an information system are hardware, software, data, procedures, and personnel. The features of these resources will vary depending on the type of system being designed. An example of a computer-based information system is shown in Figure 4.3.

Hardware

Hardware refers to the computer and other technology needed to acquire, store, process, and communicate data and information. State University uses

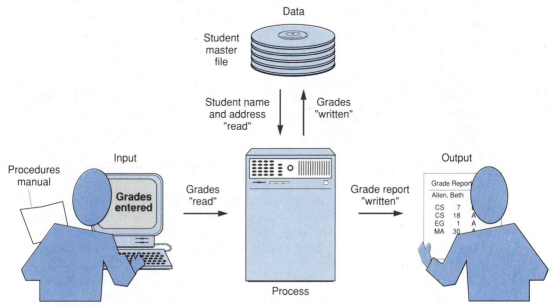

FIGURE 4.3
Computer-based information system

a large mainframe computer for registration, scheduling, billing, and payroll applications. The bookstore has its own minicomputer for inventory and book ordering. The individual schools and departments have minicomputers and personal computers to handle their administrative needs.

Last National Bank has one large mainframe computer at its main office and smaller computers at branch offices. These computers are connected to the main office through communication hardware. Also in use at the bank is automated teller machine (ATM) equipment. ATMs are actually **terminals** connected to one of the bank's computers.

Software

Another term for **software** is computer program. The program instructs the computer to collect the data and tells it how to turn that data into information. More detail about the kinds of software that exist and how these instructions are actually carried out is given later in this chapter.

The software for an access system would be concerned primarily with the efficient collection and storage of data. At Wooden Wonders, this might mean maintaining a customer list. For word processing applications in an office information system, the software would help the writer enter and save text, make it easy to make changes, and facilitate moving text about in the document. The software for a transaction processing system at Last National would handle the creation and changes made to customer accounts.

Software for an analysis system at the bank would need to combine data from a number of sources. For example, when a customer applies for a loan, the system would have to pull together all the information the bank has about the person. If the person has several accounts, all this data would need to be combined. Outside information about the applicant's employment and debts would have to be collected as well.

The software for action systems such as robots in a manufacturing setting has to be very sophisticated. It would incorporate features of artificial intelligence. The robot may have to be programmed to "see" items on the assembly line and "know" how to add parts to them.

Data

Data is the raw material from which we get information. Sometimes all the computer does is store this data, as in an action system. In this case, the act of turning the data into information is done entirely by the user. For example, the bookstore's inventory system might simply keep track of the number of books in stock and adjust this number to reflect books sold and returned. It is then up to the manager to read this data and determine how many of which books to order and when.

But if the inventory system is also able to make projections about demand based on past sales, projected enrollment, and courses to be offered, the system has some decision-making capability and the output from the computer will require less human processing.

If the bookstore's information system can communicate with the computers of the various publishers, and the system can not only determine what books need to be ordered and when but can actually do the ordering, then even less processing is required by humans. In this case, the bookstore's information need is completely satisfied by the information system.

Procedures

Software refers to instructions governing the computer's role in information processing. **Procedures** refer to instructions governing the person's role in this process. Both are necessary if the desired information is to be produced. Users have not always been considered an integral part of information systems. An information system designed twenty years ago would probably have placed the user outside the system's boundaries. But since it is a person who has the information need, it is a person who is the ultimate judge of the value of the information system. For this reason procedures related to the user's interaction with the computer are a necessary part of a system.

Procedures refer to both individuals and groups within the organization. In reference to actions taken by individuals, the term *procedures* is used. In reference to activities of groups within the organization or those of the entire organization, the term *policy* is often used. Instructions for using the computer or directions for running a certain program are examples of procedures. Rules regarding who has access to corporate data and under what circumstances are an example of organization-wide procedures—that is, policy.

Many first-time users of personal computers are unaware of the importance of procedures. One very important procedure is keeping a backup or extra copy of the programs and data. This protects the user in case something happens to the original. Most manuals accompanying computer software include instructions for making backup copies.

In large organizations with many computer users, procedures need to be rather formal. These organizations have people whose entire job is to see that procedures are carried out. These procedures ensure that the computers are used properly and that the data is accurate and up-to-date. If Last National Bank has inadequate procedures, it may have customers with overdrawn accounts. It could also be in violation of laws which specify the proper use of certain financial information.

The more sophisticated the information system, the more important it is to have adequate procedures. If it does not have good procedures for entering current data into its automated inventory and ordering system on a timely basis, the bookstore could end up with too many or not enough books.

Personnel

Three main groups of personnel are associated with information systems. The first group is made up of information processing professionals. These people must be very knowledgeable about computer technology and programming.

They design information systems, write computer programs, and help other people use computers more effectively. They are usually part of the MIS or data processing group in the company. The second group is made up of management personnel. Some are managers of information systems; others are managers of departments for which the information system is designed. An example would be the manager of the loan department at Last National Bank. The third group consists of end users—people who actually use the computer to help them do their jobs. A professor who uses the computer to do research is one example. The bank teller who uses it to check account information is another. Since each of these groups has a different relationship with the information system, the group's actions will be governed by different procedures. Also, since each group will have a different level of knowledge about computer technology, each will use the computer in a different way.

COMPONENTS OF A COMPUTER-BASED INFORMATION SYSTEM

The **components** of an information system are the functions that the various resources perform in acquiring data and turning it into information. In other words, the resources are the *what*; the components are the *how*. It is the resources—the technology, the computer programs, data, and people—which carry out the functions of the system. These functions are input, process, and output.

The input function involves collecting data from the environment, putting it into a form understandable to the system, and entering it into the system. What is usually considered the main activity of an information system is the second function, processing. This function includes the operations which the computer and personnel perform on the data to turn it into the information needed by some user. The last function, output, is the communication of the results of that processing in a format understandable to the person using that information. Since the process component is the main activity of the system, we will begin our consideration of system functions with process.

PROCESS

End users and managers are primarily involved with the input and output functions. They first decide what output is desired, and based on that decision, they decide what data to collect and how it should be entered into the information system. The processing function is mostly carried out by the computer and information systems professionals. Their role is to make sure that the appropriate computer programs are being used and that they operate correctly.

The processing activities are carried out by the **central processing unit (CPU)**—the processing hardware—of the computer. The processing activity consists of developing an algorithm, documenting the steps in this process for future reference, and converting the algorithm into computer-understandable form.

Algorithm Development

An **algorithm** is a set of steps to be followed in order to solve a problem or accomplish a task. It is like an outline that one would develop before writing an essay. It is important to remember that the computer will only do what it is told; it can only follow a sequence of instructions, step by step. The only "knowledge" it has is what it has been told. Even a sophisticated computer such as a robot must be told exactly what steps to follow. If a robot is told to leave a room, it will go *through* the door unless instructed to open it first.

The algorithm is carried out in the computer by means of the software. Since different software is developed to satisfy the different purposes of an information system, before any software can be developed, its objective must be known. In this section we will examine the process of algorithm development for a payroll system. The objective of this system is to produce paychecks and budgetary and tax information. One major subsystem is the part that handles the paychecks.

The first step in developing an algorithm is to specify the outputs from the proposed processing activity—that is, to clearly identify the desired result of the information processing activity. For example, there are two outputs from a payroll application: a paycheck for each employee and a summary report showing the amount of funds expended in salaries. These outputs are shown in Figure 4.4.

The second step is to identify the input data required to produce the outputs. Two types of data are required for this activity. One type of input—the number of hours worked (regular and overtime)—comes from the environment or from outside the system. The other type of input, which is internal to the system, includes the employee's hourly rate, tax information, and year-to-date totals. These inputs are shown in Figure 4.5. The summary reports are a by-product of the check-producing activity. No additional inputs are needed to produce this output.

The third step in developing an algorithm is to identify the processes involved in transforming the inputs into the outputs. For payroll this includes (1) verifying that the employee number is valid, and (2) specifying the formula for calculating gross salary based on hours worked. Thus, the basic formula for paycheck production for hourly workers would be

Gross Pay = Hours Worked × Pay Rate

For employees paid time-and-a-half for overtime hours, the formula would be

Gross Pay = (Regular Hours Worked × Pay Rate)

+ (Overtime Hours Worked × Pay Rate) × 1.5

FIGURE 4.4

Outputs of payroll application

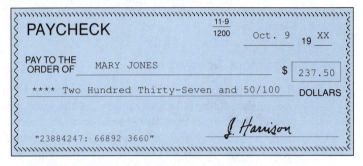

(1) Paycheck with Stub

(2) Personnel Funds Expended Report

Also, if one knows that overtime hours are those exceeding 37.5 hours per week, the formula for employees who work overtime is

$$\text{Gross Pay} = 37.5 \times \text{Pay Rate}$$
$$+ (\text{Hours Worked} - 37.5) \times \text{Pay Rate} \times 1.5$$

Documenting the Steps in the Algorithm

Documenting the steps in an algorithm means expressing the logic for solving the problem in a form that people can understand. One may wonder why it is necessary to do this. There are several good reasons. The first is that this documentation is a form of written communication among the various individuals involved in the process of developing the software. As we will discuss in

FIGURE 4.5

Inputs to payroll application

(1) Time Card

Name	Mary Jones
ID	1234567
Regular Hours	40
Overtime Hours	9
Signature	

(2) Employee File

Name	ID	Pay Rate	Year-to-Date Salary	Deduction Information
Mary Jones	1234567	12.50	15000.00	2
John Smith	2223334	10.00	12000.00	1

greater detail in Chapter 8, some of them focus on identifying the inputs and outputs; these are the systems analysts. Others focus on turning the algorithm into a form the computer can read; these are the **programmers**. Since there are usually several different people involved in the process of developing software, it is crucial that the process be written down. This documentation records the consensus reached by the individuals involved. Documentation also serves as a reminder if some time has elapsed and one has forgotten how a certain process works.

Documentation can also provide for control or feedback. This occurs when documentation serves as the basis of an audit trail. An **audit trail** is a list of events that have occurred. This list can be reviewed later to show what has occurred and when it has occurred, thus allowing others to verify the events that have transpired. For example, a bank would maintain an audit trail of the events that occur from the time a check is presented for payment until it is processed and the cancelled check is returned to the client.

There are several techniques used to document the algorithm. Some, such as pseudocode and program flowcharts, document the complete algorithm. Others, such as a decision table, document only portions of the algorithm.

Pseudocode

Pseudocode literally means "false code." It is a prose-oriented technique using structured natural language (such as English) to outline the steps involved in carrying out the algorithm. This structured language resembles a real programming language in form, but it cannot be processed by the computer. This is why it is called *pseudo*code. The advantage of pseudocode is that the logic of the entire algorithm (program) is outlined in a convenient and formal manner, easily read and understood by nontechnical people. A second advantage is that it is compatible with a top-down design approach. In a top-down design, the general design of the program—the "what"—is understood first, followed by successively more detail—the "how." The steps involved in carrying out the algorithm are presented in ordered form.

A disadvantage of pseudocode comes from the fact that the logic is expressed in words and not graphically. Therefore, when a decision could result in one of several choices, it may be more difficult for the user to see this represented. Figure 4.6 shows the pseudocode for the payroll example.

Program Flowchart

A **program flowchart** is a graphical presentation of the logic or procedures required to carry out the algorithm. Rather than express the logic in words, as with pseudocode, a **flowchart** expresses it through the arrangement of symbols which stand for certain types of activities. These symbols are shown in Figure 4.7.

As we will learn later in this book, flowcharts are used to document other information system activities as well. *System* flowcharts are discussed in Chapter 8. Program flowcharts can also be used to document manual activities. This can be useful if some process is being converted from manual to computer-based methods. As an example of flowcharting a manual process, consider the flowchart of the activities involved in getting ready for work, shown in Figure 4.8.

To make sure that everyone can understand a flowchart, there are some rules to follow. The first rule is to use the standard symbols. Second, the logic should flow from top left to bottom right. The third rule is not to cross flow

FIGURE 4.6
Pseudocode for payroll program

```
BEGIN PAYCHECK PRODUCTION
INITIALIZE VARIABLES
DOWHILE THERE ARE MORE EMPLOYEE TIME CARDS
    READ EMPLOYEE'S TIME CARD
    FIND EMPLOYEE'S RECORD
    IF EMPLOYEE DOES NOT EXIST THEN PROCESS NEXT EMPLOYEE'S
      TIME CARD AND GO BACK TO READ
    CALCULATE EMPLOYEE'S GROSS PAY
    CALCULATE EMPLOYEE'S TAXES
    DETERMINE EMPLOYEE'S DEDUCTIONS
    CALCULATE EMPLOYEE'S NET PAY
    UPDATE EMPLOYEE'S YEAR-TO-DATE INFORMATION
    UPDATE SALARY SUMMARY AMOUNT
    PRINT EMPLOYEE'S PAYCHECK
END-DO
PRINT SALARY SUMMARY INFORMATION
STOP
```

FIGURE 4.7
Flowchart symbols

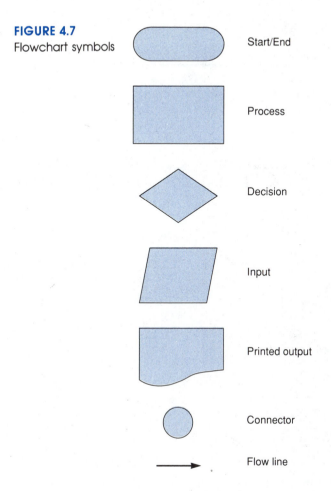

Start/End

Process

Decision

Input

Printed output

Connector

Flow line

lines connecting activities. Fourth, a process should have one entry point and one exit point so it is clear what comes before and what comes after that process. Finally, for each decision there should be two options, and these should be clearly labeled. Figure 4.9 shows examples of correct and incorrect program flowcharts.

There are several advantages of using flowcharts to reflect the logic of the algorithm. The main advantage is that, since the logic is represented graphically, it is often easier to understand the overall logic of some process. Developing a flowchart is similar to drawing a map instead of giving written directions. Because of their graphic form, flowcharts can more easily show the interrelationships among the various components of the algorithm. The logic can also be expressed in less space than if it were written out.

Another advantage is that flowcharts facilitate standardization and consistency. As Figure 4.7 showed, there are standard symbols used in developing program flowcharts to represent such activities as input, output, a

FIGURE 4.8
Getting ready for work

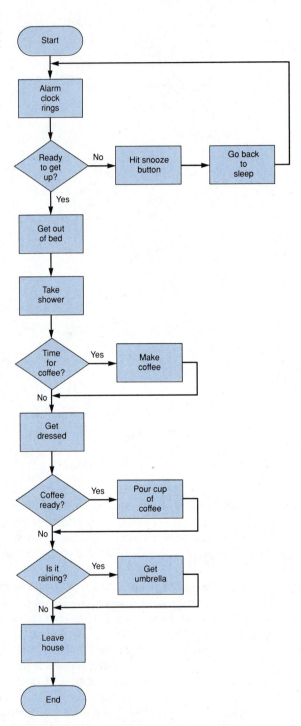

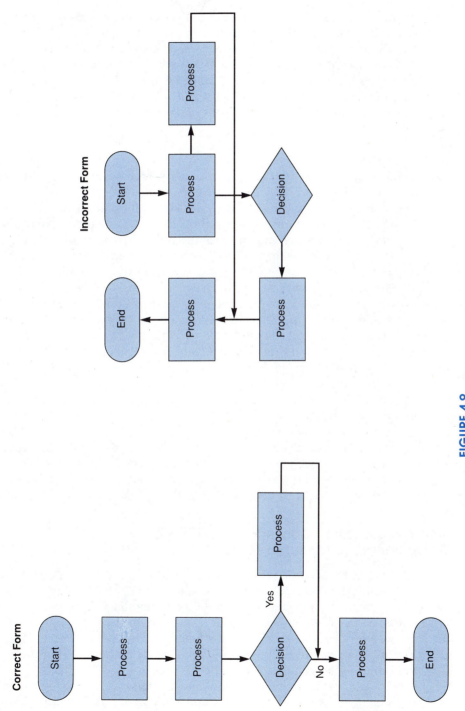

FIGURE 4.9
Correct and incorrect flowcharts

decision, or a process. Therefore, the use of these symbols leads to a standard "language" for representing the logic of some activity.

The disadvantage of using a program flowchart is that it is a formal method of documenting the algorithm. Because there are specific rules to follow, flowcharts can be time-consuming to draw and difficult to change. However, there is software available which facilitates creating and maintaining flowcharts. A program flowchart for the payroll algorithm is shown in Figure 4.10.

Decision Table

Pseudocode and flowcharts reflect not only the processes but the inputs and outputs as well. However, there are other documentation methods which focus specifically on the process component. A **decision table** is one example. It represents the decision points in the algorithm. Decision tables are used to outline a set of conditions which may be encountered and to indicate what actions should be performed for each condition. A decision table has two parts. The condition part identifies the possible conditions from which a decision must be made. In the payroll algorithm, conditions would include whether an employee worked overtime and, if so, whether the person qualifies for overtime pay. The action part indicates the possible actions that can be taken. Figure 4.11 shows a decision table for payroll calculation. As we can see, Y (yes) or N (no) is indicated for each of the conditions, and a resulting action is indicated by an X in the action part of the table. In this way, all possible decisions and resulting actions are described.

An advantage of decision tables is that they help one to precisely specify the logic in situations in which a number of conditions exist and, consequently, a range of possible actions could be taken. A disadvantage of using decision tables is that, although all the decisions are laid out, the order in which one should consider the conditions is not. Therefore, before the logic represented in a decision table can be converted into computer software, some further processing is needed to determine the order of checking conditions.

Writing a Program — Converting the Algorithm to Computer-Understandable Form

Once the logic of the algorithm is understood and expressed in understandable form, the final step is to express this logic in some form that is understandable to the computer. This is what is meant by programming. A **program** is a series of detailed instructions which must be carried out by the computer in order to solve a problem. These steps must be described precisely, in a language that the computer can understand. The actual set of statements in the particular programming language is referred to as the *code*.

A successful program has two requirements. One is that the logic of solving the problem is expressed accurately and completely. The other is that the

FIGURE 4.1O

Program flowchart of payroll algorithm

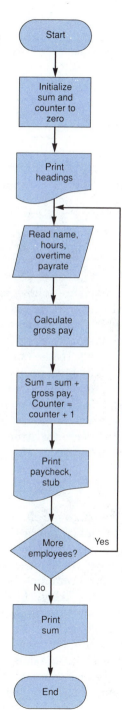

FIGURE 4.11

Decision table for payroll calculation

Conditions				
Worked regular time	Y	Y	Y	Y
Worked overtime	N	Y	N	Y
Overtime-exempt	N	N	Y	Y
Actions				
Gross Pay = Regular Hours × Pay Rate	X		X	
Gross Pay = (Regular Hours × Pay Rate) + (Overtime Hours × Pay Rate)		X		
Gross Pay = (Regular Hours + Overtime Hours) × Pay Rate				X

rules of the programming language are followed. This is analogous to following the rules of grammar in the use of some natural language like English.

A good program is one which communicates effectively to the computer as well as to the programmers and other people who may use the program. If it does not communicate effectively to the computer, it cannot be executed. If it does not communicate effectively to people, there will be problems when another person tries to run or change the program. Documentation techniques like pseudocode, flowcharts, and decision tables help make the program understandable to other people. There are also features of programming languages called *comments* which allow the person writing the program to include notes about the program within the program itself.

Programming Languages

A **programming language** is the language that is used to express the instructions to the computer. As in human languages, a specific vocabulary must be used. There are also specific rules of grammar that must be followed, referred to as the **syntax** of the language. Great precision of expression is required when expressing something in a programming language. There are several generations of programming languages. Today, third-, fourth-, and fifth-generation languages are most often used to develop programs. Figure 4.12 compares the generations of programming languages.

In deciding which programming language to use, the type of problem to be solved is the most important consideration; but there are other factors to take into account as well. One is the technical competence of the people who will be developing and maintaining the programs. Whether or not these people have extensive knowledge about programming will influence the type of language that is most appropriate to use. Some languages are easier to learn

FIGURE 4.12
Programming languages

First-Generation: Machine-dependent and difficult to learn
　　Example: Binary languages

Second-Generation: Symbolic versions of first generation
　　Example: Assembly languages

Third-Generation: Procedural languages; algorithm represented by structured
　　　　　　　　procedure
　　Examples: FORTRAN – used for scientific applications
　　　　　　　　COBOL – used for business applications
　　　　　　　　BASIC – for use by unsophisticated end users
　　　　　　　　PASCAL – requires extensive programming skill

Fourth-Generation: Nonprocedural languages; allow users to concentrate on
　　　　　　　　problem to be solved rather than syntax
　　Examples: Lotus 1-2-3 (menu-oriented 4GL)
　　　　　　　　dBASE (command- and menu-oriented 4GL)

Fifth-Generation: Uses artificial intelligence features such as natural language
　　　　　　　　processing capabilities
　　Example: INTELLECT, which allows questions to be asked in everyday
　　　　　　　　conversational language

and use than others. The tradeoff, however, is that the languages which are easier for people to learn and use generally require more hardware and software resources. For example, a language that is easier to use may take longer to execute, so speed of program execution must be traded off against the ease of using the language and developing the program. However, a language that is more difficult to learn and use may be an acceptable alternative if there are people available who can provide support to those who are developing and using programs. Some of these support features are discussed in Chapter 5.

Another factor to take into consideration in choosing a programming language is the ease of modifying the program to accommodate changing requirements. Some programming languages lend themselves to the creation of modular, well-structured programs which are more easily modified. What also affects the ease of program modification is the readability and understandability of the program code by other people. Often the programmer who initially designs and develops the program is not the same person who makes the changes. A program that is easily understood by the programmer will be modified more easily and therefore will facilitate the entire process.

Software that processes a program written in a programming language must be purchased. This software is called a *program translator*. The cost of the software depends on the hardware and the sophistication of the programming language. Some program translators cost less than a hundred dollars, while others cost over a thousand dollars. In addition, some program translators can only be acquired through a perpetual lease.

Early generations of programming languages are machine-dependent and difficult to use. Binary languages are the first generation of programming languages. The second-generation languages are symbolic versions of the first and are called assembly languages. Neither generation is appropriate for the development of information systems, however, so we will discuss the generations that are appropriate for this task.

To demonstrate some of the features of programming languages, let us consider converting the payroll algorithm into computer-understandable form using representative third-, fourth-, and fifth-generation languages.

Third-Generation Languages

A *third-generation language (3GL)* is a programming language that requires the algorithm to be represented in the form of a structured procedure. For this reason, these languages are also referred to as *procedural languages*. There are many different third-generation languages. Some are best suited to scientific applications (e.g., FORTRAN); others were developed for business purposes (e.g., COBOL). Some are intended for use by the unsophisticated end user (e.g., BASIC); others require extensive programming skill (e.g., PASCAL). To demonstrate these differences, let us consider the same application developed in two different third-generation languages.

BASIC (Beginners All-purpose Symbolic Instruction Code) was originally developed to teach students the concepts of programming. It allows the person to concentrate on the programming logic without having to worry about complex input and output commands and other "overhead" statements. BASIC is also the third-generation language most frequently used with microcomputers. For this reason, it is now used for business as well as instructional purposes. A BASIC program for producing paychecks is shown in Figure 4.13. It is based on the flowchart shown in Figure 4.10 and the decision table shown in Figure 4.11.

This program was developed by first identifying the output: paychecks and a summary of personnel funds expended. Next, the inputs were identified. Finally, the procedures for converting the inputs into outputs were developed. The input is entered into the computer using the READ command. The output is accomplished using the PRINT statement. The other statements relate to the processes involved in converting the input into the desired output. Documentation within the program is accomplished by the REMark statement.

A slightly more elaborate BASIC program is shown in Figure 4.14. This program will find the employee with the most recent pay raise. To accomplish this task, both the current date and each employee's "raise date" must be considered. In addition, these dates must be represented in the form "year-month-day" so that the largest number can be selected by comparing the current date to each employee's raise date.

COBOL (COmmon Business Oriented Language) is a programming language that was designed for business applications. To enhance readability, the

FIGURE 4.13

BASIC program to produce paychecks with its output

```
100 REM THIS PROGRAM GENERATES PAYCHECKS FOR 5 EMPLOYEES
110 REM INITIALIZATION
120 SUM=0
130 COUNTER=0
135 PRINT "NAME", "REG. HOURS", "OVERTIME", "PAYRATE",
    "GROSSPAY"
137 REM BEGIN PROCESS
140 READ ENAME$, REGHOURS, OTHOURS, PAYRATE
150 GROSSPAY=REGHOURS*PAYRATE+OTHOURS*PAYRATE*1.5
160 SUM=SUM+GROSSPAY
170 COUNTER=COUNTER+1
175 PRINT ENAME$, REGHOURS, OTHOURS, PAYRATE, GROSSPAY
180 IF COUNTER<5 THEN GOTO 140
190 PRINT
200 PRINT "TOTAL AMOUNT SPENT ON SALARIES IS: ";SUM
210 END
215 REM END OF PROGRAM
216 REM DATA FOLLOWS
220 DATA JOHN SMITH, 40,7,10.5
230 DATA MARY JONES, 37.5,10,12.5
240 DATA GLORIA BLUSH, 30,0,12
250 DATA CHUCKY CHEESE, 40,10,9
260 DATA HULK HOGAN, 25,0,15
EXECUTING THE PROGRAM
RUN
```

NAME	REG. HOURS	OVERTIME	PAYRATE	GROSSPAY
JOHN SMITH	40	7	10.5	530.25
MARY JONES	37.5	10	12.5	656.25
GLORIA BLUSH	30	0	12	360
CHUCKY CHEESE	40	10	9	495
HULK HOGAN	25	0	15	375

```
TOTAL AMOUNT SPENT ON SALARIES IS: 2416.5
```

structure of the commands resembles English grammar. Figure 4.15 shows a COBOL program to find the employee with the most recent raise.

In comparing the COBOL program with the BASIC program, we can see that the input and output parts of the COBOL program are much more elaborate. Since COBOL is more difficult to learn and use than BASIC, it is normally used only by professional programmers.

To facilitate the development of programs in languages like COBOL, software has been developed which will enable the user to generate the program directly from pseudocode. This software is referred to as a **program generator**. The advantage of program generators is that they greatly speed up the process of program development and produce consistent code. The disadvantage

FIGURE 4.14
BASIC program to find employee with most recent pay raise

Program	14:58

```
10 REM***FIND THE MOST RECENT PAY RAISE***
20 CLS
30 FOR I=1 TO 5
40 READ ENO,ENAME$,PAY,YPAY,RDATE
50 IF I=1 THEN RAIS=RDATE
60 IF RAIS < RDATE THEN RAIS=RDATE
70 NEXT I
80 PRINT "THE LAST PAY RAISE WAS ON "RAIS;" FOR "ENAME$
90 DATA 1234,STEVE MARKEY,7.50,12357.67,861231
100 DATA 1235,DEV PELLANI,8.60,15667.35,870628
110 DATA 1236,PATRICIA MORGAN,7.50,67898.45,861211
120 DATA 1237,LISA LITCHMAN,6.50,14895.50,871130
130 DATA 1238,ROGER SMITH,8.30,23525.47,860112
```

Output
```
THE LAST PAY RAISE WAS ON 871130 FOR ROGER SMITH    14:59
Ok
```

is that, in order for this to work, the pseudocode must be very structured and detailed to the point where the pseudocode begins to resemble a programming language.

Fourth-Generation Languages

A *fourth-generation language (4GL)* allows the user to concentrate more on the problem to be solved and less on syntax. In contrast with third-generation languages, 4GLs are referred to as *nonprocedural* or *problem-oriented languages*. Program development using 4GLs is much faster than with third-generation languages. Fourth-generation languages can be command-oriented, menu-oriented, or both. Working in a command-oriented mode is similar to using a program developed in a 3GL. This mode is more powerful than the menu-oriented mode, but it is also more complicated and normally requires a certain amount of programming skill. In the menu-oriented mode, the user is presented with a set of options from which to select. Lotus 1-2-3 and other spreadsheet packages are examples of menu-oriented 4GLs.

After word processing, spreadsheets are the most common application of personal computers. Spreadsheets allow users to develop budgets, project sales and profits, and accomplish other types of financial analysis. Solutions to financial problems are simplified through the application of a spreadsheet. A student's personal budget represented in a spreadsheet is shown in Figure 4.16. Spreadsheet programs allow the user to set up data in rows and columns. Data in these rows and columns can be manipulated in any way desired through

FIGURE 4.15
COBOL program to find employee with most recent pay raise

```
IDENTIFICATION DIVISION.
PROGRAM-ID.    PAYRAIS.
AUTHOR.        RAM RAMANAN.
ENVIRONMENT DIVISION.
CONFIGURATION SECTION.
    SOURCE-COMPUTER.   PRIME-750.
    OBJECT COMPUTER.   PRIME-750.
INPUT-OUTPUT SECTION.
FILE-CONTROL.
    SELECT EMP-DAT ASSIGN TO PFMS
    ORGANIZATION IS INDEXED
    ACCESS MODE IS SEQUENTIAL
    RECORD KEY IS EMP-NO.
DATA DIVISION.
FILE SECTION.
FD   EMP-DAT
    LABEL RECORD IS OMITTED
    VALUE OF FILE-ID IS 'EMPLOY'.
01   EMP-REC.
    02   EMP-NO   PIC 9(4).
    02   E-NAM    PIC X(20).
    02   HR-PAY   PIC 9(2)V99.
    02   YER-PAY  PIC 9(5)V99.
    02   L-RAIS   PIC 9(6).
WORKING-STORAGE SECTION.
77   CHEK    PIC 9(6) VALUE 0.
77   F-STAT  PIC X VALUE 'N'.
77   NAM     PIC X(20) VALUE IS SPACE.
PROCEDURE DIVISION.
OPEN-PARA.
   OPEN INPUT EMP-DAT.
   PERFORM READ-PARA UNTIL F-STAT = 'Y'.
   IF F-STAT = 'Y' PERFORM END-PARA.
READ-PARA.
   READ EMP-DAT  RECORD AT END MOVE 'Y' TO F-STAT.
   IF CHEK = 0 MOVE L-RAIS TO CHEK   MOVE E-NAM TO NAM ELSE
      IF L-RAIS > CHEK MOVE L-RAIS TO CHEK   MOVE E-NAM TO NAM.
END-PARA.
DISPLAY 'THE LAST PAY RAISE WAS ON ' CHEK.
DISPLAY 'EMPLOYEE NAME IS ' NAM.
CLOSE EMP-DAT.
STOP RUN.
```

Output from the COBOL Program (on Prime 750)
```
THE LAST PAY RAISE WAS ON    891110
EMPLOYEE NAME IS MARC CAPANO
```

FIGURE 4.16

Student's personal budget

STUDENT'S PERSONAL BUDGET

QUARTER	1	2	3	4
BEGINNING BALANCE	$10,000.00	$8,720.00	$11,786.00	$10,835.68
INCOME				
Salary	$6,000.00	$6,600.00	$6,600.00	$6,600.00
Interest	$120.00	$132.00	$132.00	$132.00
Dividends	$0.00	$0.00	$0.00	$541.78
Tuition reimbursement	$0.00	$1,250.00	$0.00	$1,250.00
Scholarship	$0.00	$0.00	$0.00	$0.00
Misc./Loan	$0.00	$0.00	$0.00	$0.00
TOTAL	$6,120.00	$7,982.00	$6,732.00	$8,523.78
EXPENSES				
Mortgage/Rent	$2,500.00	$2,500.00	$2,750.00	$2,750.00
Food and Utilities	$800.00	$816.00	$832.32	$848.97
Transportation	$350.00	$350.00	$350.00	$350.00
Tuition and fees	$2,500.00	$0.00	$2,500.00	$0.00
Car Payment	$500.00	$500.00	$500.00	$500.00
Misc.	$750.00	$750.00	$750.00	$750.00
TOTAL	$7,400.00	$4,916.00	$7,682.32	$5,198.97
ENDING BALANCE	$8,720.00	$11,786.00	$10,835.68	$14,160.50

the use of different formulas. In Figure 4.16, note that the TOTAL row under INCOME has the sum of the previous six rows (e.g., Salary to Misc./Loan). Spreadsheets also have the ability to support "what if" analysis. A student could use a spreadsheet to determine the impact of a ten percent tuition increase. The computer screen acts as a window to view part of the data, since the computer can store more data than can readily be seen on the screen. The user can view desired data by scanning up and down (e.g., to view different rows) or across (e.g., to view different columns) portions of the spreadsheet.

Fourth-generation languages allow for increased programming productivity, because they require less attention to the code than third-generation languages. In addition, less programming knowledge is needed to use a 4GL than to use a language like COBOL. Therefore, end users can use fourth-generation languages rather easily, whereas extensive training is usually required before one can use a third-generation language. Since the resulting applications are more easily developed, maintained, and changed, the user's information needs can be more easily and quickly satisfied. The fourth-generation language dBASE can be used in menu-oriented mode as well as in a more powerful command mode. Figure 4.17 shows the data and associated program in dBASE which will find the employee with the most recent raise.

Fifth-Generation Languages

A *fifth-generation language (5GL)* is the most advanced type of programming language. Fifth-generation languages involve the use of artificial intelligence

FIGURE 4.17
dBASE

Employee Database

```
DISPLAY ALL TO PRINT
Record#  ENO   ENAME               PAY   ANNUALPAY  RAISEDATE
      1  1234  STEVE MARKEY        7.50  12357.67   12/31/86
      2  1235  DEV PELLANI         8.60  15667.35   06/28/87
      3  1236  PATRICIA MORGAN     7.50  67898.45   12/11/86
      4  1237  LISA LITCHMAN       6.50  14895.50   11/30/87
      5  1238  ROGER SMITH         8.30  23525.47   12/01/86
```

Database Definition

```
. DISPLAY STRUCTURE TO PRINT
Structure for database: C:EMPLOYEE.dbf
Number of data records:      5
Date of last update   : 12/14/87
Field Field Name  Type       Width   Dec
    1 ENO         Character     5
    2 ENAME       Character    30
    3 PAY         Numeric      10     2
    4 ANNUALPAY   Numeric      10     2
    5 RAISEDATE   Date          8
** Total **                    64
```

Program to Find Employee with Most Recent Raise

```
. USE EMPLOYEE
. SORT ON RAISEDATE /A TO EMPSORT
EMPSORT.dbf already exists, overwrite it? (Y/N) Yes
  100% Sorted        5 Records sorted
. USE EMPSORT
. DISPLAY
```

Output

```
Record#  ENO   ENAME               PAY   ANNUALPAY  RAISEDATE
      1  1238  ROGER SMITH         8.30  23525.47   12/01/86
```

---

features, one of which is the natural language processing capability. This capability enables the user to communicate with the computer in the same language used for human communication. An example of a fifth-generation language is INTELLECT, whose users can ask questions in everyday, conversational dialogue, phrased the way the user wants. Unlike third- and fourth-generation languages, a language like INTELLECT has minimal or no requirements regarding the structure of code, syntax, punctuation, data definitions, or key words. INTELLECT does require a lexicon or dictionary which contains terms with synonyms, in order to understand the user's natural language. The lexicon must be developed by the organization which will use the software.

The major advantage of a 5GL is the ease of learning and the power of each command. It may take a year or more to be proficient in a third-generation language, or several months to be proficient in a fourth-generation language; but one can use a fifth-generation language almost immediately. A single statement in a fifth-generation language would require several statements in a fourth-generation language or traveling through several menus. It would probably require an entire page of code in a third-generation language. As with fourth-generation languages, the output of 5GLs is structured for the user. In most third-generation languages, the programmer must spend considerable time designing the form of the output and developing the instructions for carrying it out.

Fifth-generation languages have some disadvantages, however. One is that considerable computer resources are needed to take input expressed in natural language and translate it into commands for the computer. Further, for the computer to understand these natural language commands, a dictionary of terms must be created and constantly updated, and this is a time-consuming task. Finally, these languages are generally more expensive than third- or fourth-generation languages. Fifth-generation programming language translators are expensive to acquire and require a lot of machine resources to process a program.

To learn which employee has received the most recent pay raise, the user would query INTELLECT in a form similar to the following two examples:

```
GIVE ME THE EMPLOYEE WITH THE MOST RECENT RAISE
```

or

```
PRINT THE NAME OF THE EMPLOYEE WITH THE MOST RECENT RAISE
```

Programming Quality Control

Providing the user with the type of information needed is the objective of an information system. Providing output of the appropriate quality requires that similar quality exist in the input and processing activities as well. Therefore, an important aspect of the programming process is the development of procedures to ensure program quality control. Maintaining quality control means that the programs produced will be error-free. It also means having a program development environment which will facilitate the production of error-free programs that are easy to maintain and use. Finally, it means that resources will be used wisely in the development and operation of programs.

Regardless of the quality of programs, as circumstances and user needs change, programs need to be modified. Some programs are easier to modify than others. A well-structured program is much easier to change than one in which the instructions are less properly organized. Programs which are readable by people other than the initial programmer are also easier to maintain.

Types of Errors

One way to provide error-free programs is to do adequate testing. This means trying out the program to make sure it works properly. Errors should be detected and corrected as early as possible in the programming process. Program errors are sometimes called *bugs*, and the process of correcting the errors is called **debugging**. There are three types of errors: syntax, execution, and logic errors.

Syntax errors occur when the program is not written according to the rules of the programming language. An example would be mistyping the name of the command, such as typing PRNT for PRINT. Another example would be omitting or misusing a statement of the language. In BASIC, when an IF statement is used, it must be accompanied by a THEN statement. The computer checks for these errors first. In most languages, a program with syntax errors will not run, and the computer will provide a list of errors that must be corrected.

Some errors are not detected until the program runs (i.e., is executed). In this case, the program has been successfully translated into machine code from a higher-level programming language. However, while the program is running (executing), some problem arises. This is what is meant by an **execution error**. An example of an execution error is the attempt to process character data as though it were a numeric value, such as trying to perform a calculation on a person's name.

A **logic error** occurs when the program runs but does not produce the correct results. Logic errors result when either the wrong algorithm was used to solve the problem or the correct algorithm was converted into computer-readable form incorrectly. Examples would be using the wrong formula or using logic that does not enable the program to handle all situations or all types of data that could be input. It is primarily because of logic errors that thorough program testing should be done.

Programming Teams

One way of creating a program development environment which will promote error-free programs that are easily maintained and used is to use a team approach to developing programs. A team approach involves a group of programmers, each of whom has responsibility for a portion of the program and who conduct formal sessions to review the logic of the program.

Team Approach and Modular Programming   Large system projects are usually implemented by more than one team. Using a "top-down" approach, a system is broken down into a collection of subsystems. A team is then assigned to develop and implement one or more subsystems. For large programming projects with complex subsystems, the programming tasks are further broken down into a series of **program modules**. Programming teams are then created and assigned responsibility for one or more of these **modules**. Each team is composed of a chief programmer, several programmers, and a librarian. The *chief programmer* is responsible for making sure the program logic is correct and supervising and assisting the other programmers. The *program librarian* is responsible for documenting the program modules. Since the program modules are the result of a team rather than an individual effort, this method is sometimes referred to as **egoless programming**. This approach facilitates the sharing of ideas by promoting a cooperative atmosphere and capitalizes on the different strengths of the programmers. In addition, it enables the organization to cope more easily with changes in personnel. If one of the programmers leaves in the middle of the project, there are others who can take that person's place.

Structured Walkthrough   A **structured walkthrough** is a review of the developers' work by a small group of interested individuals, such as members of the programming team, members of other related teams, and representative users. It is like a dress rehearsal for a play or a concert. The purpose is to identify errors and potential problems. The walkthrough must occur early enough in the development process to identify and correct problems before they become expensive to fix or delay progress on the project. It is the task of the librarian to see that all the pertinent documentation is distributed to those who will be involved in the session. A walkthrough can also promote a feeling of team responsibility for the project. The major disadvantage is the amount of time devoted to preparing and performing a walkthrough, as this is time that could be spent on programming.

Methods of Evaluation

The final aspect of quality control concerns the efficiency and effectiveness with which the programs are developed. Before a programming project is undertaken and after it is completed, the efficiency and the effectiveness of the project should be evaluated.

Efficiency refers to the use of the hardware and software resources and the time and energy of the personnel developing the software. An efficient computer program is one which minimizes the consumption of the hardware resources, such as the time it takes to execute the program or the computer memory required. As pointed out in the discussion of computer languages, there is usually a tradeoff between the efficiency of the programmer and the efficiency of the computer. Programming languages that are easier for the programmer to use are usually less efficient for the computer to use. A compromise should be reached in the selection of the programming language so that both technological and personnel resources are used wisely. Often there are limits on the computer resources available. Care must be taken to achieve a level of efficiency so that the software can operate within the resource constraints.

Effectiveness refers to the quality of the output produced by the program. An effective program is one which accomplishes what was intended. Programming teams and structured walkthroughs contribute to effectiveness because they help to identify and remedy potential problems early in the process. An important aspect of effectiveness is ensuring that the program can handle *all* kinds of data. That is, the program should not only be able to accept and process the intended input, it should also be able to identify and respond to incorrect input. This is particularly important in situations in which there is a likelihood that incorrect data will be entered, such as when large volumes of data are being entered or when inexperienced personnel are using the program.

INPUT

In order to process the data and provide the desired output, the appropriate data must be collected from the environment. There are two requirements for having appropriate data. One is that the *correct* data must be collected. Since data is the raw material for information, the wrong data will result in the wrong information. Correct data possesses such properties as accuracy, timeliness, and completeness. The second requirement is that the input data be in the form needed to process it. An example of this is the social security number, which sometimes includes dashes and sometimes does not. If the software is expecting to process the social security number without dashes, but it is input with them, there will be problems. The input function can be enhanced by both the devices used and the procedures established to govern the activity.

The objective of the input component is the collection and entering of data into the computer for processing. Three activities are part of the input function: origination, preparation, and data entry.

Origination

Origination is the task of identifying and sometimes gathering the data which will be entered into the computer. An example of origination for a word processing system would be writing the text of a letter. Very often origination is the result of some event or transaction. In a transaction processing system or management information system, a transaction would be an event such as the purchase of an item with a credit card. Typically, a paper document which contains the data from this transaction is created, such as a receipt from a credit card purchase. This document is called a **source document**.

Preparation

Preparation is the act of taking the data from the source document and converting it to machine-readable form so that it is suitable for entry into the computer. An example of preparation when punched cards are used for data entry is transferring the data from the source document onto the punched cards. Other examples of preparation are entering the data onto a diskette or magnetic tape for later entry into the computer. Preparation is not always a separate activity, however. Sometimes the data is entered directly into the computer, such as would occur at a point-of-sale terminal in a bookstore which transmits information to the inventory system at the time of each purchase. When there are many source documents to be entered at one time, there is the potential for errors in entering this data. Therefore, procedures have to be established to reduce the likelihood of these kinds of errors.

Data Entry

The final input activity is called *data entry*. This means the actual entering of the data into the computer. There are two basic methods of data entry: off-line and on-line. Each form of input is suitable for certain contexts. Therefore, after considering the advantages and disadvantages of each method, we will consider criteria for determining situations in which each would be the appropriate choice.

Off-line Data Entry

When a device is **off-line**, it is not connected to the computer. Some devices, such as a keypunch machine, are always off-line. Other devices, such as a terminal, may be off-line until contact with the computer is established. Off-line data entry means that the data is prepared off-line and entered into the computer later. This shortens the computer time dedicated to data entry but increases the time between data origination and data entry. If Last National Bank processes credit card purchases for hundreds of clients, the process of entering in the data from all those source documents will be very time-consuming and prone to error. If someone were to enter this data into the computer directly from a terminal, the CPU would be engaged in this task for quite a while. One way for the bank to speed up the process and reduce the likelihood of errors would be to have some data entry personnel enter this data onto diskettes before it is entered into the computer. This will enable someone else to check the data for accuracy. It will also speed up the process of actually entering the data, since data can be read from a disk drive into a computer much faster than it can be entered at a terminal keyboard. This method will use the CPU more efficiently, since that device will not remain idle waiting for someone to type in the data (although in a multiprogramming environment, the computer can be doing something else while it is waiting for input).

The example of off-line data entry which was just given is also an example of **batch processing**. In batch processing, a group of data is collected and then entered into the computer at once, in a *batch*. With off-line data entry, the data from many source documents can be batched together and processed at the same time. Batch processing is also used in certain methods of storing and retrieving data.

In addition to determining what devices to use, procedures regarding the input function are needed. Procedures must be established to determine what data will be collected on the source document and how the data will be prepared for entry. A very important procedure is the verification and validation of the data. This is usually done by having a second person examine the data to be sure it is accurate. If punched cards are used, a second person will key in the same data from the source document using a machine called a *verifier*.

The advantage of the off-line method is that it speeds up the process of actual data entry, because the data is transferred to a device which will enter the data into the computer much more quickly than a person can type it at a terminal. This saves processing time because the computer is not idle while it is waiting for the data. The disadvantage is that it takes time to prepare the data before entering it into the computer, making off-line data entry very labor-intensive. There is also a delay between when the transaction occurs and when the data is finally entered into the computer. It is more difficult to locate the source of an error when the error is detected at processing, not at entry. The tradeoff is computer time versus human time. This method is most appropriate when there are large volumes of data to be entered and some delay before processing is acceptable.

On-line Data Entry

An **on-line** device is one which *is* in direct contact with the computer. A terminal which is communicating with a CPU is an example of an on-line device. On-line data entry means that the data is taken from the source document and entered directly into the computer. In the credit card example, if a restaurant transmits the charge information directly to Last National Bank when a credit card is used, it is using on-line data entry. In this case, the data is being sent as soon as the transaction occurs.

Since the preparation activity is combined with data entry for on-line input, the same methods of verification to reduce errors are not applicable. Therefore, different procedures must be established to reduce errors during data entry. If there is a source document, it can be designed so that it is easy for the person entering the data to read. Other procedures are implemented through software. Verification procedures are especially critical when there is no source document. An example of on-line data entry without a source document would be the use of a bank's ATM. The user enters the transaction data, such as a deposit or withdrawal request, and then enters the amount of the transaction immediately.

To protect against errors, certain features should be incorporated into the software. One feature is the design of the screen itself. The screen should be easily readable and not confusing to the person entering the data. Features can also be built into the software to identify errors. These are referred to as *edit checks*. For example, the social security number has nine digits. To guard against the mistake of entering a ten-digit number, the software can be designed to determine that an error was made and request the user to reenter the number. Another way to reduce errors is to provide feedback to users and ask them to verify that the transaction data is correct. This occurs at ATMs. After the amount of the transaction has been entered, the software asks if the amount entered is indeed the amount to be withdrawn or deposited and to confirm its accuracy.

The main advantage of the on-line method is that the data entry task is shortened because the preparation stage is combined with data entry. Entering the data directly from the source document or when the transaction occurs saves time. When it is important to record the transaction immediately, the on-line method is the more appropriate method. In addition, input errors can be detected at input and be immediately corrected. The main disadvantage is that more computer resources are devoted to on-line data entry. The tradeoff, then, is less preparation time for the person but a greater burden on the technology: more complicated software is required to check errors and to make the system more user-friendly. Consequently, the CPU is not used as efficiently. Another drawback of the on-line method is that the data cannot be entered if there is a malfunction of the computer and it is not working.

Machine-readable Data Entry

An alternative which combines the best features of off-line and on-line data entry is to create a source document which is **machine-readable**. This means that the source document is understandable to both people and computers. Account numbers on checks printed using magnetic ink are one example. The account number can be read by a person, and it can also be read by a magnetic-ink character recognition device.

Another example is mark-sense forms, consisting of a series of bubbles. Bubbles are filled in to denote input data. If a student records the answers to test questions using a mark-sense form, the test—the source document—can be read by the student and teacher as well as by the computer. A third example is the use of optical character recognition (OCR) devices, which can read printed or handwritten data. In some cases, a special set of characters is used. Business use optical character recognition to read data from price tags by connecting an OCR reader to a point-of-sale terminal.

Other OCR devices can read whole pages containing both textual and graphic data. Some insurance companies are using this technology to enter claim forms. The Kurzweil scanner can scan book pages and produce output using a synthetic voice. This provides a great service to the blind.

Machine-readable input can be done either in batch form or as each transaction occurs. Processing bank checks is an example of batch data entry. Entering product information from the bar code at a grocery store checkout is an example of entering each transaction as it occurs. The advantage of using this method for data entry is that it has the speed of the off-line method and the immediacy of the on-line method. Not all situations lend themselves to this method of data entry, however.

Other Methods

In addition to these input methods, there are other methods in use which are less common. One such method is **voice input**. With a **voice recognition** input device, the computer is able to accept spoken natural language as input. Users for whom this input method would be desirable would include handicapped persons who do not have the use of their eyes or hands.

Another application would be for people who are engaged in some activity which requires the use of their hands but who need to communicate with the computer. One example would be a doctor using a computer in an operating room while performing surgery. Another example would be a person who is engaged in some manufacturing task which uses his or her hands but who needs to enter some data into the computer. There are two major obstacles to be overcome in developing voice recognition systems. One is that the computer must be able to understand a very large vocabulary, since people have many different ways of saying the same thing. The other, even more difficult obstacle to overcome is the considerable variation in the way different people say the same words.

Criteria for Choosing a Data Entry Method

Since there are advantages and disadvantages to each data entry method, how does one decide which to choose? The answer is to consider the context. How and where does the data originate? Will there be large volumes of data to be entered at regular intervals, such as for calculating monthly credit card bills? Or does the data need to be entered as soon as the transaction occurs? The answers to these questions will help determine the best input method. The context and the type of data involved should determine which input method and input devices are most appropriate. Three criteria can be used to help determine which input method will be most effective.

Speed

Whose time is more valuable, the person's or the computer's? If people are available and a delay can be tolerated, the off-line method is a good choice. If there are no people available to prepare the data off-line, if the data must be entered right after the transaction occurs, or if the data must be updated immediately, the on-line method is the better choice.

Accuracy

While the off-line method enables checking for typing errors, the on-line method is capable of more sophisticated error checking. Many current on-line data entry systems have software which checks whether the input from the transaction "makes sense." This increase in accuracy may allow for other capabilities. For example, if a clerk is entering a clothing order and gives the code for the desired color, the software will check to see whether the item is actually available in that color. The on-line system allows the clerk to offer the item to the customer in an available color. This capability improves customer satisfaction and is *not* possible with off-line data entry. The off-line method, on the other hand, results in fewer typing errors because the data is checked by another person before it is entered into the computer. Therefore, it is appropriate for entering large volumes of data. An alternative method for entering large amounts of data, if the circumstances allow, would be to use machine-readable source documents.

Context

Sometimes it is not possible to enter the data directly into the computer at the time or the location of the transaction. An example is processing credit card transactions. Restaurants may not be able to communicate immediately with the bank that issued the credit card. Therefore, the restaurant personnel would have to prepare this data off-line and send it in batches to the bank for processing. Machine-readable input is a nice option, but not all situations lend themselves to it. For example, a teacher would be able to use mark-sense forms for multiple-choice and true-false questions but not for essay questions.

OUTPUT

The purpose of the output component is to display the results of the information processing activity in a form that is relevant to the way the information will be used. Although output is the final function in the flow of activity within the system, it really should be considered first, because the type of information desired and the form in which it is needed will govern the activities of the input and process components.

There are two primary ways that computer output is presented: on paper and on the computer screen. Output can also be stored in a file, produced in computer-readable form, and rendered in photographic form, such as microfiche or film.

Output on Paper

When the output of the computer processing is printed on paper, it is referred to as **hardcopy output**. If a tangible form of the output is needed, either as a "permanent" copy or as a draft to work from, hardcopy output should be the choice. In determining which hardcopy device is the most appropriate, the user should consider how the output is going to be used. Let us consider some of the options and how we would go about deciding among them.

Criteria for Choosing Among Hardcopy Devices

Which hardcopy device will be the best choice depends on several factors, including how the output will be used, what type of data will be required, and in what context the device will operate.

Uses of Output Since there are several levels in the quality of printed output, the user needs to know the intended uses of the information. Is the output just a draft that no one else will see? A dot matrix printer can produce varying quality of output. It can operate in draft mode or in near-letter-quality (NLQ) mode. For example, Wooden Wonders has many alternatives for preparing its catalog. One is to produce a draft and have it professionally typeset. This draft could be produced using a dot matrix printer. This printer could also be used to generate packing lists and management reports, and output in near-letter-quality (NLQ) mode would be sufficient for correspondence. Another option is to prepare the catalog text directly, using a laser printer which produces letter-quality and good graphic output. With a laser printer, one could use desktop publishing software to prepare the catalog. *Desktop publishing* refers to the use of personal computer software to produce output of similar quality to that of professional typesetters.

Type of Data Besides knowing the uses of the data, one must also understand something about the form in which it is to appear. Data output from a computer commonly comes in three forms: numeric, textual, and graphic. All printers can print numbers and text, but not all printers can produce graphics. Therefore, if one desires to produce the output in graphic form, a printer with this capability must be selected. An additional consideration would be the quality of the graphics that is desired, since graphics appropriate for desktop publishing would require a much different—and more expensive—printer than graphics for in-house use.

Contextual Considerations In addition to the type of data and the intended uses of the output, there are other considerations having to do with the context within which the output is produced. One of these considerations is speed. How quickly does the output have to be produced? If the output is needed very quickly, a laser printer which prints a page at a time would be a better choice than a printer which prints only a character at a time. Laser printers are more expensive, however. Another consideration associated with the context is what noise level is acceptable. An impact printer such as a dot matrix printer makes a certain amount of noise. Therefore, if producing output quietly is an important consideration, a nonimpact printer might be a better solution.

Advantages and Disadvantages of Hardcopy Output

The main advantage of hardcopy output is that it provides a tangible copy of the output. This means that the output can be read in any location because a computer is not needed to view it, and multiple copies can be produced and disseminated. One disadvantage of hardcopy output is that there is often a delay between when the output is actually created and when it is available from the printer. This is especially a problem when many users share a common printer. In addition, the value of data presented is correct at the time generated and may have changed between the time the output was generated and the time the user received it. Another disadvantage is that the data is static. That is, it cannot be moved about as it can on the screen. This is a definite drawback for applications such as word processing. Also, users often keep hardcopy output in case it may be useful in the future. There is a cost associated with storage of this output, since it can take up a lot of space if produced in large quantities.

Output on the Computer Screen

When the computer output is displayed on the screen or CRT, it is referred to as **softcopy output**. There are several reasons why one would want to produce the output on the screen rather than on paper. One is to produce temporary output. If the output is needed only temporarily, there is no need to print it on paper. An example would be a bank executive using a spreadsheet on the screen to view possible impacts of an expected budget change. Another example would be a student wishing to review a program before running it. In this case, the softcopy output provides a means of reviewing the data prior to producing the hardcopy output.

Other reasons for using screen output are printer availability, time, and flexibility. If not all users have easy access to a printer, softcopy output may be an appropriate alternative for many situations. If speed is a consideration, output is printed on a screen faster than on a printer. CRTs provide greater flexibility because the same information can be presented on multiple screens simultaneously and because they allow users to selectively review portions of a document. The user can then decide which portions of the document to print and the type of printer required.

Criteria for Choosing Among Types of Terminals

As with the choice among hardcopy devices, there are certain factors to consider in choosing among terminals. As with hardcopy output, the type of data to be displayed will influence the type of terminal that is needed. Like printers, terminals are not all capable of representing graphics. Therefore, if graphic output is a desired feature, it is important to have a graphics terminal. Further, this data can be presented either in a single color (usually green or amber) or in several colors. If color would enhance the presentation of the data, a color terminal might be desirable. If color is not important, a less expensive monochrome terminal might be suitable. Finally, the resolution of the terminal should be considered; the higher the resolution, the clearer the image. A larger screen (diagonally measured) is usually needed to accompany high resolution.

Advantages and Disadvantages of Softcopy Output

The main advantage of softcopy is that the output is available immediately. This is especially valuable when the purpose of the output is to review a draft prior to printing it out in final form. Other advantages of softcopy output are that the output is produced quietly and the terminals are generally less expensive than printers. The main disadvantage is that a computer is required in order to view the data. Softcopy output is therefore most appropriate for reviewing data prior to printing a final copy or in some setting in which all the users have access to a terminal. An example of the latter case would be a travel agency, where agents view scheduling data from an airline reservation system.

The temporary nature of softcopy—having no updated record produced—can also be a disadvantage in some cases. For example, suppose the bookstore manager at State University is preparing an inventory report and gathers information from a spreadsheet shown on a screen. A few days later, when proofreading the report, the manager is perplexed about the content of the report. The manager is unable to duplicate the results obtained a few days ago because there is no record of the exact operations that were performed.

Other Methods of Output

In addition to the most common methods of output we have described, there are some alternatives which are appropriate for circumstances with special output requirements.

Film

One option is to output the data onto film. A common method of doing this is to transfer the output to microfilm or microfiche (sheets of microfilm). This is done for *archival storage*—long-term storage of material that will not be accessed very frequently. This method, referred to as *computer output microform*, is used in libraries. Computers are also being used to generate animation for movies. In this case, the output is transferred to celluloid or videotape.

Voice

Another alternative form of output is **voice output**. Voice output is much easier to achieve than voice input. To produce voice output, the data is converted by a *voice synthesizer* into human speech. This method of output has applications for the blind as well as for those who are not free to look at a computer screen. Some examples in use today are telephone directory assistance and devices in automobiles which communicate messages to the driver.

Criteria for Choosing an Output Method

As with the choice among input methods, the type of data and the characteristics of its use should be the basis for determining the most appropriate form of output. Unlike the input methods, however, the hardcopy and softcopy output methods are not mutually exclusive. In the case of input, one does either off-line or on-line data entry. In the case of output, one generally has both hardcopy and softcopy devices available. The issue then becomes one of determining which aspects of a task lend themselves to each of the output methods.

Timing of Output

One consideration is the intervals at which the data is output. If it is produced at regular intervals, printed output might be the most appropriate. If the data is provided only on demand—that is, when a specific user requests it—providing this data on the screen might be the best alternative.

Volume of Output

The size of the document will also influence the choice of output medium. If Mary Tyson at Wooden Wonders wanted to review the status of certain customers, she could do so on the CRT and print data of interest. This method would be much more efficient than printing out the entire customer list on paper in order to examine it. In other circumstances, the size of the document would suggest that printed output is the most appropriate choice. An example would be a listing of a computer program. If the program is too long to fit on one screen and the programmer needs to look at different parts of it simultaneously, he or she might prefer to work with hardcopy output.

EXAMPLE: DEVELOPING A BUDGET AT WOODEN WONDERS

Introduction

A significant management problem which Paul Bunyan encountered soon after Wooden Wonders was established was how to control the cash flow. When he thought about it, Paul Bunyan realized he did not have a clear idea of what it cost to run his business. When he sold products primarily as a hobby, before he retired from his engineering position, costs were not that important to him. He never carefully analyzed the cost of producing the items when he determined their prices because he did not depend on the income from their sales. The situation changed when he began to work at Wooden Wonders full-time and when he hired Mary Tyson. Not only did he have to recover the cost of producing the items and the catalog, but he also had to pay himself and Mary. Paul felt that one of Mary's first assignments should be to develop a quarterly budget.

The purpose of this budget would be to show how money was being spent. It also would enable Paul to make projections about expected new costs. This information would help him make better decisions about managing the financial affairs of Wooden Wonders. Mary recognized that Paul needed a decision support system. She decided to use a fourth-generation language to develop the software resource of the system—a computer-based spreadsheet so that projections and "what if" questions could be explored. In developing an application system for the budget, she proceeded by analyzing and then developing each of the components of the spreadsheet: input, process, and output. The following is a description of the activities carried out by Mary Tyson in developing a budget for Wooden Wonders.

Developing the Budget Application

Input

The first task in developing any application is to understand the kind of data it is to contain. For a budget application, this meant examining the expenses and revenues for the past year, which she termed "Year 1." She talked to Paul to learn about the kinds of expenses he currently has or expects to have in operating Wooden Wonders. Among those identified were:

- catalog preparation
- postage for catalog and product shipping
- wood
- supplies such as nails, screws, and wooden wheels for toys
- paint
- contractors to assist with tasks such as painting
- supplies
- taxes

These expenses were determined by looking at Wooden Wonders' checkbook, cash receipts, and tax forms. No taxes were due in Year 1 since expenses exceeded revenues.

This process of gathering the data to be entered into the system was the origination activity. But before the data could actually be entered, some preparation was required. The data was related to specific transactions such as writing a check. However, for the quarterly budget Mary needed to have totals for each category of expenses for each three-month period. Therefore she had to add up the expenses in each category for each quarter in order to have the data in the form required for processing. The use of spreadsheet software to develop the budget application facilitated on-line data entry.

Process

Once the data was ready for input, Mary began to work on the process component of her system. The first task was to design the spreadsheet or determine its layout. This involved determining what data and formulas would be placed in which rows and columns. Six columns were needed in all. Since she was creating a *quarterly* budget, four columns were needed to hold data for each quarter. A fifth column was needed to hold labels or descriptions of the different kinds of expenses. The last column would show the totals—the sum of all four quarters. Finally, a descriptive heading was placed at the top of the spreadsheet and each column was labeled. The layout of her spreadsheet is shown in Figure 4.18.

Once the spreadsheet was designed, Mary began to enter the data she had prepared. Since the data represented money, she used the currency option of the spreadsheet so that the dollar sign ($) would appear. In addition to numeric data, she also needed to enter formulas that would enable her to perform the calculations necessary to analyze data and prepare the budget. The formulas Mary created and entered, along with the data manipulation features of the spreadsheet software, constituted the process component of her application.

She developed her formulas or algorithms by observing patterns or interrelationships among the data items in the spreadsheet. For example, the pattern for catalog expenses was that two catalogs are prepared each year, in spring and fall. She also observed that the bulk of the catalog production costs were related to reproduction. The only costs incurred between catalog runs were for preparing inserts which contained price changes and sale notifications.

A second example is postage. The majority of postage costs were related to the number of catalogs produced. The number of catalogs was stored in cell A6 of the spreadsheet. Since customers are required to send advance payment for both item and mailing costs, the postage entry in the budget did not need to take into account mailing invoices or items

FIGURE 4.18
Layout of spreadsheet for Wooden Wonders

```
     EXPENSES INCURRED BY WOODEN WONDERS - YEAR 1

EXPENSES             QUARTER 1 QUARTER 2 QUARTER 3 QUARTER 4    TOTAL
-------------------------------------------------------------------------
CATALOG PRODUCTION

POSTAGE
WOOD
WOOD SUPPLIES
PAINT
CONTRACTORS
MISC. EXPENSES
-------------------------------------------------------------------------
  TOTAL EXPENSES
```

purchased. The following formula was used to calculate postage costs in the spreadsheet:

$$.25 \times \text{Number of Catalogs} + \text{Other Postage Costs}$$

Other postage costs were related to sending invoices to stores and miscellaneous correspondence; she estimated these costs at $125.00. In the spreadsheet this was entered as

$$\$A\$6 * .25 + 125$$

Cell A6 contained the number of catalogs produced. Since this value would be copied to other cells using the COPY command, absolute addressing had to be used. (This is why A6 was used to represent cell A6.) The cost of mailing a catalog was $.25, and the amount spent on miscellaneous postage was $125.00.

To produce a sum of the expenses in each column—that is, for each quarter—the function @SUM was used. The statement @SUM(B5..B12) means to add together the values in cells B5 through B12, which is equivalent to

$$B5 + B6 + B7 + B8 + B9 + B10 + B11 + B12$$

Figure 4.19 shows the raw data entered into the spreadsheet and the formulas used for the first quarter. Figure 4.20 shows the completed spreadsheet that resulted.

Output

The purpose of creating the spreadsheet was to have data on expenses in a form that facilitated its analysis while preparing a budget for Year 2. One thing Paul wanted to know was how the various expense categories

FIGURE 4.19

Data and formulas in spreadsheet

```
    EXPENSES INCURRED BY WOODEN WONDERS - YEAR 1

EXPENSES             QUARTER 1 QUARTER 2 QUARTER 3 QUARTER 4    TOTAL
-----------------------------------------------------------------------------
CATALOG PRODUCTION  0.5*$A$6
            1000
POSTAGE             +$A$6*0.25+125
WOOD                    200
WOOD SUPPLIES       0.2*B28
PAINT                   75
CONTRACTORS             80
MISC. EXPENSES          200
-----------------------------------------------------------------------------
  TOTAL EXPENSES     @SUM(B25..B32)
```

FIGURE 4.20
Completed spreadsheet

EXPENSES INCURRED BY WOODEN WONDERS - YEAR 1

EXPENSES	QUARTER 1	QUARTER 2	QUARTER 3	QUARTER 4	TOTAL
CATALOG PRODUCTION	1000				
POSTAGE	$125.00	$125.00	$125.00	$125.00	$500.00
WOOD	$200.00	$300.00	$200.00	$500.00	$1,200.00
WOOD SUPPLIES	$40.00	$60.00	$40.00	$100.00	$240.00
PAINT	$75.00	$35.00	$88.00	$125.00	$323.00
CONTRACTORS	$80.00	$50.00	$120.00	$180.00	$430.00
MISC. EXPENSES	$200.00	$125.00	$225.00	$300.00	$850.00
TOTAL EXPENSES	$720.00	$695.00	$798.00	$1,330.00	$3,543.00

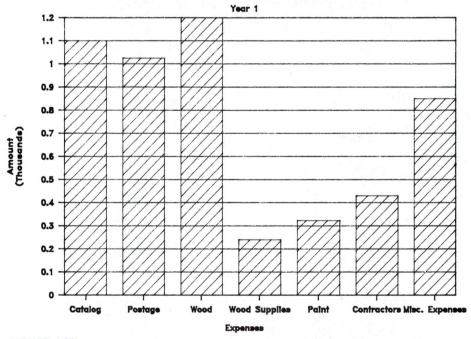

FIGURE 4.21
Bar chart of expenses (actual output from near-letter-quality dot matrix printer)

contributed to the overall expenses of the company. Mary's spreadsheet software provided considerable flexibility in presenting this information. In addition to the tabular format, it could also display information in pie charts, bar charts, and graphs. Mary felt that Paul would be most satisfied seeing the data in graphic rather than numeric form. She represented this information in two formats to let Paul see which one he liked better. First, she developed a bar chart showing the actual amount spent in each expense category in Year 1; this is shown in Figure 4.21. Then she developed a pie chart showing the percentage that each expense category contributed to the overall expenses of Wooden Wonders; this is shown in Figure 4.22.

The pie chart enabled Mary to see that the bulk of Wooden Wonders' expenses (almost 70 percent) were due to wood, catalog production, and postage. Since most of the postage was for mailing catalogs, catalog-related expenses dominated. Mary was aware that there were several alternatives for producing paper or hardcopy output. Wooden Wonders required a device that could be used for correspondence as well as business graphics. Cost was a major factor, so a laser printer with the capability to produce

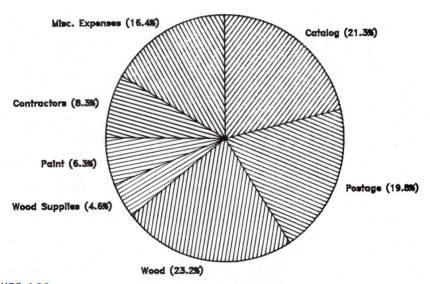

EXPENSES of WOODEN WONDERS

Year 1

Misc. Expenses (16.4%)

Catalog (21.3%)

Contractors (8.3%)

Paint (6.3%)

Postage (19.8%)

Wood Supplies (4.6%)

Wood (23.2%)

FIGURE 4.22
Pie chart of expense categories for Year 1 (actual output from near-letter-quality dot matrix printer)

high-quality output was considered too expensive. A dot matrix printer was judged to be acceptable. Mary thought that when Wooden Wonders' financial situation improved, however, they should purchase a laser printer.

Using the Budget Application System

The reason for preparing a budget for last year (Year 1) was to use it as a basis for the upcoming year (Year 2). Mary began to estimate expenses for Year 2 using the data in last year's spreadsheet as input. She made the assumption that overall expenses would increase as the business grew. For Year 2 she projected that Wooden Wonders would have a catalog run of 2,500. Mary felt that since catalogs should also be available for distribution at fairs, only 80 percent of the catalogs printed would be mailed. Therefore, a different formula for postage for Year 2 was used:

$$.8 \times \$A\$6 \times .25 + 125$$

A major expense at Wooden Wonders is wood. Wood prices are volatile and difficult to estimate because of the wide variation in prices of different types of wood. In addition, prices of wood and related supplies continually increase. Mary decided to assume that wood expenses would be 25 percent higher in Year 2. This was denoted in the spreadsheet by multiplying the current wood costs in cell C5 by 1.25. The resulting formula was

$$1.25 * C5$$

Since expenses of wood supplies were 20 percent of the cost of wood, these expenses would automatically increase as well. The cost of paint was assumed to increase 20 percent from Year 1 to Year 2. Contractor and miscellaneous expenses were not expected to change.

In addition to the expense categories present in Year 1, several new expenses needed to be incorporated into the budget for Year 2. These included Mary's salary and the cost of computer hardware, software, and related supplies. Therefore, rows for these expenses needed to be added to the spreadsheet.

Mary wanted to take all these expenses into account in analyzing the cost of the items they produced in order to determine the best price for their products. Prices needed to recover the costs of producing the items, support business activities, and still be affordable to customers. The estimated expenses for Year 2 are shown in Figure 4.23.

One area of interest to Mary was noting changes in expenses from Year 1 to Year 2. At first Mary had included all expenses in the chart, but this made it look too busy. Because there was so much data, it was difficult to quickly identify the relevant information. She thought Paul would experience information overload when looking at it. To simplify the graph,

FIGURE 4.23
Spreadsheet of expenses for Year 2

WOODEN WONDERS - YEAR 2

EXPENSES	QUARTER 1	QUARTER 2	QUARTER 3	QUARTER 4	TOTAL
CATALOG PRODUCTION	$1,250.00	$62.50	$1,250.00	$62.50	$2,625.00
2500*					
POSTAGE	$500.00	$140.63	$500.00	$140.63	$1,281.25
WOOD	$250.00	$375.00	$250.00	$625.00	$1,500.00
WOOD SUPPLIES	$50.00	$75.00	$50.00	$125.00	$300.00
PAINT	$90.00	$42.00	$105.60	$150.00	$387.60
CONTRACTORS	$80.00	$50.00	$120.00	$80.00	$330.00
MISC. EXPENSES	$200.00	$125.00	$225.00	$300.00	$850.00
NEW EXPENSES - YEAR 2					
SALARIES	$750.00	$750.00	$750.00	$750.00	$3,000.00
COMPUTER HARDWARE	$1,500.00	$0.00	$0.00	$0.00	$1,500.00
COMPUTER SOFTWARE	$500.00	$0.00	$0.00	$250.00	$750.00
MISC. COMPUTER EXP.	$125.00	$50.00	$125.00	$56.00	$356.00
TOTAL NEW EXPENSES	$2,875.00	$800.00	$875.00	$1,056.00	$5,606.00
TOTAL EXPENSES	$5,295.00	$1,670.13	$3,375.60	$2,539.13	$12,879.85

*Number of catalogs produced. With this spreadsheet software, character fields are left-justified and numeric fields are right-justified in their respective columns.

she decided not to include any expenses that were new to Year 2. To represent this output she developed the bar chart shown in Figure 4.24. From this graph Mary and Paul could easily see that all expenses except those of contractors would be higher in Year 2. The final output Mary wanted was a breakdown of the various expense components. For this she used a pie chart for Year 2, as shown in Figure 4.25.

Conclusion

When this budget was completed, Wooden Wonders had a computer-based tool which enabled Mary and Paul to examine current expenses, project future costs, and see the relationships among expense categories. The spreadsheet software facilitated the development of the budget and was easy for a nonsophisticated user like Paul Bunyan to use. The various options for representing output enabled Mary to choose formats which best suited the type of information being output. In the end, Wooden Wonders had a valuable decision support tool.

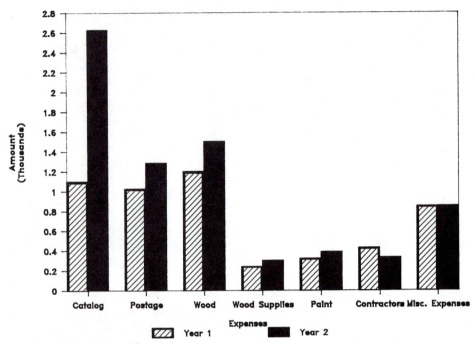

FIGURE 4.24

Bar chart of expense comparisons (actual output from near-letter-quality dot matrix printer)

SUMMARY

The process of transforming data into information can be achieved in a variety of ways. It can be performed manually and has been for centuries. Devices such as typewriters exemplify machine-assisted information processing. The current availability of computer technology has led to the development of a range of computer-based information processing tools. This method relies upon five resources—hardware, software, data, procedures, and personnel—to transform data into information.

The activities involved in computer-based information processing involve three functions: input, processing, and output. The input function involves the activities of origination, preparation, and data entry. The primary options for data entry are off-line and on-line data entry. In the off-line method, the source documents are transferred to a computer-readable medium, reviewed for accuracy, and then entered into the computer in batches. In the on-line method, the data is entered through a terminal directly from the source document or at the point of transaction. Other means of input include the use of machine-readable source documents and voice input.

EXPENSES of WOODEN WONDERS
YEAR 2

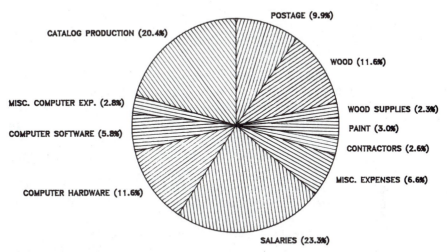

FIGURE 4.25
Pie chart of expense categories for Year 2 (actual output from near-letter-quality dot matrix printer)

    The purpose of the process function is to develop the computer program which will process the input data to produce information. This involves developing and documenting the algorithm, converting it into computer-understandable form, and maintaining program quality control. Developing the algorithm means understanding the purpose of the program and identifying the steps to be taken to solve the problem or accomplish the task. The purpose of documenting the algorithm is to have an expression of the logic of the program that can be understood by a person. There are several options available for documenting the algorithm. Pseudocode is a written form of the steps to be undertaken, while program flowcharts are a graphic representation of the program logic. Decision tables show the various possible conditions which could occur in the program and the appropriate action to be taken in each case.

    A variety of programming languages exist for converting the algorithm into computer-understandable form. Third-generation languages focus on the logic as well as the syntax of the commands. More skill, in general, is required for writing programs in a third-generation language than for writing programs in a fourth-generation language, which is less procedural. The emphasis in fourth-generation languages is on the problem to be solved rather than the syntax. Some fourth-generation languages are available in menu-mode, which requires very little programming skill on the part of the user. Fifth-generation languages employ the artificial intelligence feature of natural language. The user is not required to learn a new vocabulary in order to use them. In deciding among the types of languages, the tradeoff is between human and computer resources. Those languages which are the easiest for people to learn and use require the greatest amount of computer resources. Those languages which use the least amount of computer resources require the user to have considerable skill before they can be used proficiently. It is therefore important to know the personnel and hardware resources available when deciding among programming languages to be used in a system development project.

Program quality control is achieved through developing error-free programs in an environment which will ensure that the programs can be successfully used and easily maintained. Testing for all types of errors—syntax, execution, and logic—should be done early in program development. Programming teams, modular programming, and structured walkthroughs help create a programming environment which will result in efficient and effective programs.

The purpose of the output function is to display the results of the processing in a form that is relevant to the way the information will be used. The two primary forms of output are hardcopy and softcopy. In choosing an output method, one should consider the type of data and the way it will be used. Other forms of output include computer output microform and voice output.

KEY TERMS

algorithm
audit trail
BASIC
batch processing
central processing unit
  (CPU)
COBOL
components
data
debugging
decision table
effectiveness
efficiency
egoless programming
execution error

flowchart, program flow-
  chart
hardcopy output
hardware
input
logic error
machine-readable
module
off-line
on-line
origination
output
preparation
procedures
program

program generator
programmer
programming language
program modules
pseudocode
softcopy output
software
source document
structured walkthrough
syntax
syntax error
terminal
voice input, output, and
  recognition

REVIEW QUESTIONS

1. Discuss the two major advantages computers have over other techniques for information processing. Using examples, relate the advantages to the nine steps of information processing.
2. When would it be appropriate to use a manual information system? What are the disadvantages of this approach? Give two examples of manual information systems and defend your choice.

3. Describe the resources of a computer-based information system.
4. Discuss in general terms the steps in algorithm development.
5. Discuss the importance of an audit trail in the documentation process.
6. Compare and contrast algorithm documentation methods.
7. Consider payroll processing and draw an input-process-output–oriented chart of the system. Should payroll be implemented as a computer-based information system? What are the advantages and disadvantages of this approach?
8. Develop an algorithm for getting to school in the morning. Document the decision of what to wear as a decision table considering the temperature and whether or not it is raining.
9. Identify an application system that should be developed using a third-generation programming language. Defend your choice.
10. Identify an application system that should be developed using a fourth-generation programming language. Defend your choice.
11. What criteria should one use in selecting a programming language? Review your criteria with respect to your answers to questions 9 and 10.
12. What are the advantages and disadvantages of fifth-generation languages?
13. Explain the three types of programming errors. From a management viewpoint, which type of error is most critical? Illustrate your choice with an example.
14. Discuss each role in the team programming approach.
15. What is the difference between efficiency and effectiveness? Give an example of an efficient process and an effective one.
16. Describe the three activities associated with the data input function.
17. When would one use on-line data entry versus off-line data entry? Give an example of a system which requires on-line entry and one which would use off-line entry.
18. How is a verifier similar to an edit check?
19. How does machine-readable data entry combine features of off-line and on-line data entry?
20. What criteria should be used in selecting a data-entry method?
21. What criteria should be used to select an output method? Select three different output methods and give an example of when each is appropriate. Defend your choices.
22. Learn how to use a spreadsheet package and develop an application. For example, develop a personal budget on a quarterly basis. List all your expenses and sources of income.

CASE

The bookstore at State University decided to open a video department to rent videotapes and sell related items. This new department was to be a self-contained business and was provided with the manual cash register that book operations had discarded. Tamara Petersen was hired as head of the video department and reports to the manager of the bookstore. Currently she is using the manual cash register and keeps track of transactions and inventory using a manual system. Each time a customer rents a videotape, she records the customer's name, address, and license number, the name of the movie, the rental amount, and the date. Tamara's boss had recently asked that she start summarizing the sales information and determine which videos were not renting and should be removed from the shelves. It was difficult and very time-consuming to summarize any useful information by hand. Her boss also wanted to identify good customers so promotional and discount information could be sent to them.

Tamara decided to approach her boss with a request for a computer system to automate the task of data gathering and information processing. Her boss was not very familiar or comfortable with computers and asked her to provide written answers to the following questions. Put yourself in Tamara's position and answer these questions.

DISCUSSION QUESTIONS

1. Support why a computer-based information system is needed. List the advantages and disadvantages of computerizing the manual system.
2. Outline the resources that would be required to support the computer-based information system.
3. Describe the functions that these resources perform in gathering data and turning it into information.

CHAPTER 5

Human Information Processing

CHAPTER OUTLINE

CHAPTER OBJECTIVES

- To describe how humans acquire data, process it into information, and put it to some use.
- To consider the different ways that humans process and use information.
- To note some of the differences between human and computer-based information processing.
- To consider the ways in which these differences can be minimized or overcome through the design of human-computer interfaces.
- To explain the purpose of three types of interfaces: hardware, software, and organizational.

INTRODUCTION

There are a number of reasons for including human information processing in the study of information literacy. One is that understanding how humans process information can help us better understand how the computer works, since there are several *similarities* between human and machine information processing. We will also be able to appreciate the *differences* between the way people think and computers "think," so that we can better identify difficulties people might have in working with computers, as well as anticipate when users will need extra support. We will also be able to see the strengths and limitations of computer processing. With this knowledge we will be in a better position to know how the computer can be most appropriately used. If computers are used inappropriately or if sufficient support is not provided, it should be no surprise if computer use is ineffective or creates resistance on the part of users. To appreciate the differences in the ways computers and humans process data, the reader should be familiar with the material in Sections I and III of the appendix, which discuss computer hardware and software.

HUMAN INFORMATION PROCESSING

Some information processing concepts are applicable to both humans and computers. One is the input-process-output model of information processing. Just as this model was used in Chapter 4 to describe how the parts of the computer

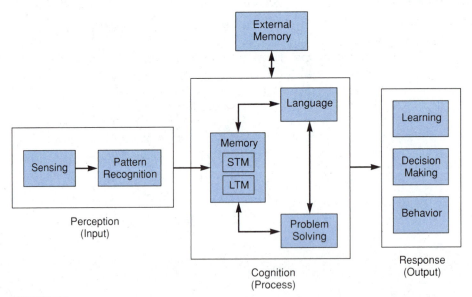

FIGURE 5.1
The components of human information processing

work together to process data, it can also be used to describe the activities involved when a person acquires data from the environment and processes it into information which is then stored and put to some use.

The **human information processing** activities which carry out these input, process, and output activities are perception, cognition, and response. Perception involves the sensing and pattern-recognition activities performed on the input data. Memory, language use, and problem solving are the cognitive activities involved in processing data into information. Human output from this processing activity—the response—can take the form of an action, a decision, or an addition to memory. Figure 5.1 illustrates the way in which these components of human information processing fit together.

To describe the human activities involved in acquiring and processing data and using the resulting information, let us use the example of human speech. A person hears something, interprets the sounds, gives them meaning according to the language being used and the social context, relates them to some information already in memory, and, finally, does something as a result. What are the components of human information processing which are necessary to accomplish these tasks?

Perception

To perceive means to become aware of something through one's senses. Thus, **perception** is analogous to the input component of an information system.

Sensing

In our example of speech, sensing means the reception of auditory signals by the ear. Consider for a moment what happens when one person speaks and another person listens. The speaker says a few words aloud, causing sound waves to travel through the air. Eventually they are heard by the other person. These sound waves have caused the listener's eardrum to vibrate. Sensory signals in the form of vibrations are then transmitted through the various parts of the ear and eventually create neural impulses which carry this acoustic data to the brain. In the process, the signals are interpreted and organized so that meaning can be extracted from them.

Pattern Recognition

The purpose of **pattern recognition** is to take the auditory input which arrived at the ear and convert it into a recognizable message. Accomplishing this, however, means overcoming a number of barriers. The signal could come in a variety of forms because of the influence of accents or volume, it could be distorted by other sounds in the environment, or it could be incomplete.

Feature Analysis The first step in the process of pattern recognition is **feature analysis**. This is the task of identifying and classifying the important features of the signal into a recognizable pattern—in this case, a sequence of words. **Speech analysis** is the particular form of feature analysis in this example. Speech analysis is a very complicated process. Those working to develop voice input to the computer have learned that there are some formidable difficulties to overcome. The problems with speech analysis derive from the variability in spoken language and the fact that speech is communicated as a continuous stream of sounds. This continuous signal makes it more difficult to extract and identify the parts of the signal.

The basic unit of speech is the **phoneme**. Phonemes are the unique sounds in a language which, when combined in certain ways, result in meaningful spoken words. Examples of phonemes are "a," "e," "i," and "oo." One problem of feature analysis is that people don't use the same phonemes to say the same word. In parts of New England, for example, a person will pronounce the phrase "pierced ears" as "pea-ess dee-ess"!

Unlike written language, which has discrete features—letters, words, and sentences separated by spaces and punctuation—spoken language does not have consistent and clear distinctions between speech units. Think about a time when you heard someone speaking in a language you did not understand. It probably sounded like a continuous stream of sounds. Even if someone is speaking in a language you do understand, the same sequence of sounds can have two different meanings depending upon how the speech units are segmented. Therefore, a second problem in speech analysis is that the same phonemes are used for different words. Consider the phrases "I scream" and "ice cream." Both are made up of the same phonemes.

Contextual Cues   Because of these difficulties, context is also necessary to understand the spoken word. **Contextual cues** enable the listener to piece together what the signal probably means even if a clear pattern cannot be recognized. Recall for a moment what it is like to listen to a two-year-old child speak. The child may mispronounce certain words or leave out some of the syllables, yet an adult can usually figure out what the child is trying to say. Contextual cues also help if there is distortion due to other sounds in the environment. If the listener cannot correctly hear a certain word in the sentence, he or she can usually guess what the word should be, based on the words that preceded and followed it. This is possible because what has been said up to that point establishes expectations and plausible interpretations of the auditory signals and thereby limits the possibilities of what should be heard next.

Redundancy   By its nature, human language also contains a built-in aid for helping with the analysis of features: **redundancy**, or repetition. Repetition exists in language so that if some words are missed, the listener has other chances to figure out what the sentence means. For example, the first sentence in this paragraph expresses the same idea twice: "an aid" and "for helping with." If one of these phrases were missing, the general idea of the sentence would still come across.

Perception, then, is the process of taking signals received by the sense organs and eliciting the features necessary to create a meaningful pattern. For this to be done successfully, sensory data must also be compared with information already in memory. For example, sensory data that has been received incorrectly may be recognized as a valid pattern (e.g., a word) but might not be meaningful in the context of the other words that have been heard. When this happens, past experience and expectations which are in memory are used to revise the interpretation of the incoming signal so that a meaningful pattern results.

Cognition

Cognition is the act of knowing something. This act of knowing is analogous to the process component of an information system. The ability to know includes both awareness and judgment. Just as the central processing unit of the computer relies upon its input devices, cognition builds upon perception. If the input activity (perception) is not successfully accomplished, the processing activity (cognition) will be incomplete or inaccurate.

Memory

Computers utilize both primary and secondary storage devices to process data. Likewise, human information processing involves the use of both a short-term memory (STM) and a long-term memory (LTM). Unlike computer memories, however, these two memories have automatic and constant interaction between them.

Short-Term Memory In the case of human speech, when a meaningful representation of the auditory signals is achieved it is placed in **short-term memory**. This memory is very limited, however. Data stays there for a very short time (about thirty seconds). The capacity of the short-term memory is also limited. Experimental studies of a human's capacity to distinguish signals received by the various senses have shown that the capacity of the short-term memory is limited to roughly seven items or groups of data.[1]

During the brief span of time that data stays in STM, if it is to be retained, it must be transferred to long-term memory. Through concentration, attention, and placement of the data into a context, the content of the words is sent to long-term memory, where it is incorporated into the existing store of information.

Long-Term Memory **Long-term memory** stores the concept or meaning behind the words that were heard, not the sounds of the words themselves. This means that a person who understands both French and English will form the same concept whether the word was heard as "mother" or "mère."

Despite great advances in the development of computer-based information storage and retrieval systems, we are not yet able to replicate in machines the way information is stored in long-term memory. This is partially due to our incomplete understanding of long-term memory.

We do know some things about long-term memory, however. We know that its capacity is much greater than that of short-term memory. We also know that memory is not localized. That is, the memory of a certain event is not stored in a single physical "place" in the brain.

In addition, we know there are two major activities involved in remembering. The first is the actual storage of information—the addition to the memory structure. This activity includes the encoding and remembering of concepts, events, and their interrelationships, which are built up by past experiences. We can think of the memory system as a collection of pathways or possible routes for storing and gaining access to the information stored there. In Chapter 6 we will consider the creation and use of files and databases, which are the analogous storage components in computer-based information systems.

The second activity of remembering includes the interpretive processes involved in using and altering the basic store of information. Information in STM that is to be remembered must be evaluated and incorporated into the existing collection of information. This means that pathways must be established between information already there and this new information. Information is also constantly being retrieved to answer questions, solve problems, speak, think, and engage in daily actions. Long-term memory's ability to rapidly locate and retrieve all the relevant information is the most distinctive feature of human memory.

The act of retrieval involves the use of rules to analyze stored information. Remembering, then, requires two things: a memory structure and an analysis function. To understand the kind of analysis that is involved, consider for a moment what happens when you are asked a question.

First, you must determine whether or not the question is answerable. This involves analyzing the meaning of the question as well as knowing what is in your memory. In carrying out these tasks, humans have the ability to quickly disregard nonsense questions. Consider the following two questions: "When did your grandfather bear a child?" and "When did your grandfather get gray hair?" In both cases, you may not be able to answer the question, but for different reasons. The first question is unanswerable because an answer does not exist: men do not bear children. An answer to the second question might reasonably exist, but it could be unanswerable because you do not have the relevant information—information that would answer the question—in your memory structure. The vehicle used for the movement of concepts into and out of human memory is language.

EXTERNAL MEMORY

Although long-term memory has much greater capacity than short-term memory, it has limits as well. With increased amounts of information to be remembered and processed, a strain is put on the human memory system.

For this reason, people make use of **external memory** to assist them. Pencil and paper is the simplest example of external memory. In the past century, a succession of memory-aid tools have been invented, the most recent being the computer. A computer-based information system, then, not only produces information in much the same way as humans do, it can also be viewed as a part of human information processing.

Language

There is a tremendous interplay between language and memory. **Language** provides the labels necessary to turn experiences and events into concepts so that they can be stored in memory. Incoming data is encoded according to language labels before being stored in memory. For this reason, the words in a language affect the way experiences are remembered. Consider the following example. The Eskimo language has many more synonyms for snow than the English language. In Alaska, for example, snow plays a much more influential role in the lives of the people than it does in Ohio. For this reason, the Eskimo language is able to provide many more labels which, in turn, allow for finer discriminations in the storage of concepts related to snow. If you live in Ohio, however, you don't make such fine distinctions; you only distinguish among hail, sleet, snow, and slush. Therefore, the concept of frozen precipitation would have fewer memory labels if stored by someone who speaks English than by someone who speaks the Eskimo language.

What has been described so far is the contribution that language makes to the operation of memory. In similar fashion, memory is necessary for the operation of language. We said earlier that the words in a language provide the basis for the labels used to organize concepts in memory. Given this fact, we can then say that language is really a method of communicating the memory structure of the speaker to the memory structure of the listener. The process of learning a language, then, becomes the process of learning labels for concepts, and the rules according to which these labels are combined. Since language use involves the application of rules for combining concepts in memory, we can also say that learning a language is a form of problem solving.

Problem Solving

A problem can be defined as the difference between the present state and some desired state. Solving a problem is the act of moving from the first state to the second. For example, for a laboratory rat placed in a maze, "solving the problem" means finding and following the route which will lead it out of the maze. If you are hungry, your present state is one of hunger. The desired state is one of satiation. "Solving the problem" in this case would involve acquiring and eating food. The desired state can also be called the goal. Thus, **problem solving** can be defined as behavior directed toward the achievement of a goal.

In the course of solving a problem, a series of tasks must be accomplished. The first is problem identification. Identifying the problem is not always as easy as it might seem. Implied in this task is the ability to identify the goal and the ability to understand the present state relative to that goal.

The next step is to break the goal down into subgoals. In solving the problem of a person's hunger, several subgoals must be achieved before the ultimate goal of satisfying hunger can be reached. First, food must be acquired. This can be done in a variety of ways, such as by going to a restaurant, by purchasing the groceries needed to prepare a meal, or by going to a fast-food establishment and buying food that is ready to eat. Depending upon the route that is chosen, other tasks must be accomplished. If the choice is made to cook a meal, there are activities involved in cooking. The choice to go to a restaurant might imply wearing certain clothes. Finally, the subgoal of eating the food must be accomplished. If all these subgoals have been achieved, the main goal of satisfying hunger will have been accomplished. These activities are depicted in Figure 5.2.

Through experience, memory, the development of rules, and trial and error, people refine their ability to solve problems. In choosing a method of satisfying hunger, the person may remember a bad experience at a certain restaurant and therefore reject that option. Suppose the person chooses to cook a meal at home. In this case, certain subproblems must then be solved, such as determining what dish to prepare and how to go about preparing it. Deciding what to prepare may be based on experience: a certain dish may have been very tasty the last time it was eaten. The decision may also be based on memory: remembering what food is in the refrigerator might determine what to cook.

Once it is decided *what* to cook, the next problem is *how* to cook it. The two basic approaches to cooking demonstrate the two different methods by which humans solve problems: **algorithms** and **heuristics**. Some people cook "by the book"; that is, they always use recipes and follow them carefully, never deviating from the instructions. This is an example of using an algorithm to solve a problem. In Chapter 4 we defined an algorithm as a step-by-step rule or procedure for solving a problem. By following the algorithm, the same solution to the problem should always be achieved in the same way. An alternative is to use a combination of experiences, analogies, common sense, and trial and error. This is an example of using heuristic, or "rule of thumb," reasoning to solve problems. It is heuristic problem-solving ability which would enable one to decide to substitute chicken for turkey in a recipe because he or she knows that these two meats have very similar properties.

Solving problems requires the use of memory. As the problem-solving process gets more complex, external memory is needed. For example, one may be able to remember three items to purchase at the grocery store. But if one is shopping for the entire week, some memory aid such as a written shopping list would probably be needed. Today, the computer plays an increasing role in assisting human problem solving. Cognition, then, can be thought of as a joint endeavor, in which the computer is used to enhance the memory and problem-solving skills of the human.

FIGURE 5.2

Solving the problem of hunger

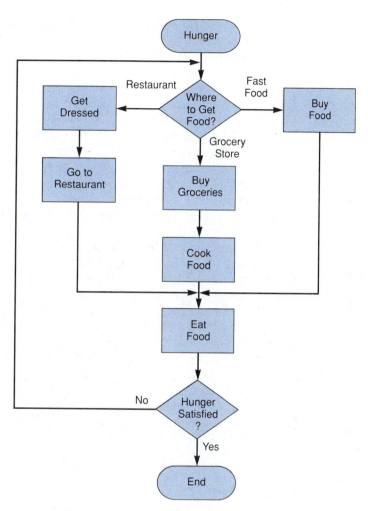

Response

After the acquisition of data from the environment and the act of processing it into information, some form of response occurs. The forms of human response parallel the purposes of information systems which were described in Chapters 2 and 3. We should expect this to be the case, since computer-based information systems are meant to be extensions of human information processing functions. The three purposes of human information processing are learning (access), decision making (analysis), and informed behavior (action).

Learning

Learning is based on the activities involved in memory and problem solving. It can be defined as the accumulation of concepts and the establishment of connections among them. These connections are constantly being made and revised, so that the memory structure becomes continuously more elaborate. This helps to explain how different people learn material at different levels of depth. For example, to a child of six a snowfall is associated with pleasure: perhaps a day off from school and an opportunity for sled riding. By the age of fourteen that person has learned that, in addition to pleasure, a snowfall means work: perhaps shoveling the driveway. By adulthood, the person has learned that, in addition to pleasure and work, a snowfall also means anxiety: worrying about driving conditions. Thus, the more someone understands something, the more connections there are to other concepts in memory.

In the early stages of human development, learning is primarily the process of acquiring and storing concepts. This is what is meant by rote learning. As one gets older, the learning process shifts emphasis from the accumulation of concepts to the establishment of more connections among those already in memory. Another way to think about these connections is to view them as relationships within the memory structures. Learning, then, is establishing relationships among concepts. These concepts are derived from words, which have in turn been perceived through the senses.

When something is learned, the new information is integrated into the existing memory structure. This means that something is added to the store of information and that connections are made between that new information and existing concepts. **Knowledge**, the outcome of learning, results from the increasingly complex network built up through the assimilation of information.

Knowledge is not necessarily acquired for any immediate purpose. Consider some of the subjects you have studied in school. Some of what you have learned was simply received, processed, and stored. Perhaps you have used it since, perhaps you haven't. Most effective learning occurs, however, when what you learn can be found to have some actual or potential usefulness in your life.

Decision Making

A very common purpose for acquiring information is for decision making. **Decision making** is the application of problem-solving skills to the analysis of alternative courses of action and to the ultimate choice among them. When one has to make a decision, the first task is to identify the situation as a problem-solving situation. That is, one must identify the goal and his or her state relative to the attainment of that goal.

The next step is to identify the available methods for achieving that goal. In our earlier discussion of problem solving, the goal was to satisfy hunger. A series of decisions were involved in solving this problem. First, the person had to decide among three alternatives for obtaining a meal: (1) going to a restaurant, (2) cooking a meal at home, and (3) purchasing already-prepared fast food. Second, the person had to assess the relative merits of these three alternatives. In other words, the implications associated with each course of action had to be identified and examined. Choice one – going to a restaurant – might result in a medium amount of effort and the best-tasting meal, but at the greatest expense. Choice two—cooking a meal at home—might result in a satisfactory-tasting meal at the least cost, but at the greatest expense of time and effort. Choice three—getting fast food—might be cheaper than going to a conventional restaurant and less time-consuming than cooking, but the meal might be the least appetizing. How will the person decide?

After the goal has been identified and the alternative courses of action have been examined, the final step in decision making is to assign values to the various courses of action and their implications. Perhaps the person loves to eat, and the taste of the food is the most important consideration. In that case, the choice will probably be going to a restaurant or cooking the meal at home. The choice between these two alternatives will depend on yet another set of values—the value of the person's own time and energy. If they are important considerations, the choice will probably be the restaurant.

What is the role of information in all this? In order to evaluate the various alternatives and their implications, the person needs information. First, the person needs information about the existence of the alternatives. There must be at least one restaurant, fast-food establishment, and grocery store within a reasonable distance, or that alternative will not exist for this decision-making situation.

In the scenario we just described, three criteria were used to evaluate the alternatives: cost, taste, and effort. To consider the implications of choosing each of the alternatives, information must be available about each of these criteria. Figure 5.3 describes the information that would be needed.

The example we have used is rather simple; many people could evaluate the alternatives and make a decision without collecting any new information. Unfortunately, decision making in other parts of our lives is not that simple. As the number of alternatives increases, the burden of establishing criteria, valuing them, and assessing the implications of a choice becomes greater. Because of the human's *limited* memory and the computer's *unlimited* storage capacity, the computer is especially suited to assist people in decision-making settings. It is for this reason that computers have become so invaluable and that analysis-type information systems are needed.

FIGURE 5.3
Information for decision making

Criteria	Available Alternatives		
	Restaurant	Home Cooking	Fast Food
Cost	Most	Least	In between
Taste	Best	In between	Worst
Effort (Personal time and energy)	In between	Most	Least

Informed Behavior

The third reason for acquiring and processing information is to have assistance in carrying out some action. Consider the process of getting dressed in the morning. After the alarm clock has been shut off, some information that has already been learned about the days of the week—such as the difference between Saturday morning and Monday morning—must be retrieved. Assuming it is Monday morning, some other information is needed to select the appropriate clothes to wear that day. If it is January, alternatives will be considered that would not be considered if it were June. This information will also be retrieved from long-term memory. If it *is* January, perhaps some new information will be collected, by turning on the radio to hear the weather report or looking out the window to see if it is snowing.

Once the relevant alternatives have been evaluated and a decision among them has been made, the next step is to put the clothes on. The type of information needed here is to guide the actions of the various parts of the body. This is an example of feedback information. If the eyes are watching the hand as it attempts to button a sleeve, feedback about the success of that attempt is being sent back to the brain. If the brain determines that the fingers are going about it all wrong, it will signal them to start over or to revise their approach.

A COMPARISON OF HUMAN AND COMPUTER-BASED INFORMATION PROCESSING

With some understanding of what is involved in both human and computer-based information processing, we can draw comparisons and contrasts between the two. There are two reasons to do this. First, if we understand the differences between humans and computers, we will better understand some of the areas in which people might have difficulty using a computer. Second, we will be able to appreciate the difficulties involved in getting the computer to mimic certain aspects of human information processing behavior.

Before probing the differences, however, let us first consider what they have in common. The major similarity is that the information processing model (input-process-output) can be used to describe both types of information processing. During both input phases, data from the environment is received, encoded, and transmitted to the memory. Both types of information processing use two kinds of memory: internal memory and external memory. Problem solving can be accomplished either by following an established procedure (algorithm) or by using trial-and-error (heuristic) techniques. Human learning is the process of establishing connections among facts stored in long-term memory. Likewise, when data is stored on the computer's devices, links are set up so that similar data can be retrieved. Data collected from the environment is processed into information by both people and computers for three primary purposes: to add to the existing store of information, to help in the decision-making process, or to guide some behavior. Now, in what ways do humans differ from computers with regard to processing information?

Perception

The computer receives data primarily by means of written words and codes. There are other means, such as voice input, in existence, but these are not currently in widespread use. Humans, on the other hand, can receive input through their five senses: sight (seeing words and images), sound (hearing words), smell, touch, and taste. In addition, humans quite frequently receive data from more than one source simultaneously. An example is what happens during a conversation. Besides hearing the words that are spoken, the listener is also receiving signals in the form of **nonverbal communication** such as tone of voice and "body language" (gestures, posture, and eye movements). In fact, during a typical conversation, much of the data that is exchanged does not come from the words that are spoken but from the way they are spoken and other nonverbal communication. In contrast, the computer receives input from a single source at a given point in time and does not receive nonverbal communication.

Memory

While it is true that computer processing usually involves considerable interaction between primary and secondary storage, there are three significant differences between the operation of human memory and that of computer storage. First, data used by a computer must be deliberately moved from one storage device to the other, whereas with humans there is an automatic and constant interaction between short-term memory and long-term memory. Second, use of the computer's secondary storage is not absolutely necessary to process data. Data can be input, processed, and output from the computer without the involvement of secondary storage. Human information processing, on the other hand, requires that data be moved from STM to LTM before it can be successfully processed. Finally, there are no physical limits to the capacity of a computer's primary memory. There are only memory limits for certain types of computers. With humans there are definite limits to short-term memory. For this reason, long-term memory is an integral part of human information processing. In fact, data only becomes *information* when meaning is assigned to the data, and meaning is a function of the connections made among items stored in long-term memory.

As noted in the discussion of human memory, the way humans store information and establish connections is not completely understood and so far cannot be replicated in a computer. Part of the difficulty arises from the individual nature of remembering. All people do not make connections in the same ways. Two people who have received the same data will not necessarily integrate this information in the same way. How that new information is connected to the existing store will depend on what is already in memory and the individual style of the person. Some people automatically make more connections than others. Consider what happens in a classroom. If there are fifty students in a room listening to the same lecture, there will be many different ways in which this same information will be remembered. This occurs because the connections or meaning is based on the relevance of the data to the listener, and relevance is a very individual phenomenon.

Language

Both computers and humans make use of language as a vehicle for input and output. The major difference is that computer language is very precise and human language is not. Human language is highly redundant: many different words can be used to refer to the same concept. Consider the concept of love. Think of all the ways this concept can be communicated in words. To help you out, think of the numerous kinds of Valentine cards that are available every February! Human language is also ambiguous: the same words can be used to convey different meanings, depending on context, past experience, and nonverbal cues which accompany the communication. The sentence "I was so embarrassed *I nearly died*" has a very different meaning from the sentence "The accident was so serious *I nearly died.*"

All of this is complicated by the existence of many different human languages. An individual who knows several languages can receive and process input using more than one language at once. Have you ever listened to a conversation between two people who speak two languages, such as English and Spanish? They may talk for a while in English and then lapse into Spanish to express certain words or phrases. While a computer has the capability of processing data using more than one programming language, a single language must be used for a given information processing task. Through the use of natural language processing software, interaction between humans and computers has become more like dialogue between humans, but there is still a long way to go before such software can accommodate the degree of ambiguity and redundancy which is second nature to humans.

Problem-Solving Behavior

Solving a problem or attaining a goal can be accomplished either by means of an algorithm or by the use of heuristics. Computers and humans have very different strengths in this regard. Computers perform best with algorithms, while humans excel in the use of heuristics. The major challenge to artificial intelligence is to develop better heuristic problem-solving techniques. Humans, on the other hand, often have difficulty breaking a problem down into the discrete steps necessary to execute an algorithm for solving it. This is why some people have difficulty developing computer programs: programming requires the development of algorithms. These differences demonstrate the fact that humans and computers have complementary strengths and weaknesses in the area of problem solving.

Individual Differences in Human Information Processing Behavior

Not only are people different from computers, but they are also different from each other. Because people are not all alike, there is considerable variation in the way the input, process, and output activities of human information processing are carried out. A term used to describe this human trait is **cognitive style**. Numerous models have been developed to explain these differences, ranging from physiological explanations — the dominance of the right or left hemisphere of the brain — to psychological categorizations of personality types, to astrological explanations based on the time of year a person was born. Given all these different explanations, what is important is to appreciate the fact that people acquire and process information differently, whatever the reason. This appreciation will make us more sensitive to the different manifestations of information processing behavior that we encounter, especially when they are different from our own.

As a way of learning a little more about individual differences in information processing behavior, let us consider one framework which describes these differences — the Jungian typology of personalities. Carl Jung was a psychologist who identified four basic factors that influence one's personality. The two that are relevant to the present discussion are those which characterize the way people acquire data and the way they process it into information.

According to Jung's model, a person's data-gathering style falls along the continuum from extreme sensing to extreme intuition. Likewise, the method of processing that data into information ranges from complete emphasis on thinking to complete emphasis on feeling. Figure 5.4 presents this framework.

FIGURE 5.4
Jungian framework of information processing

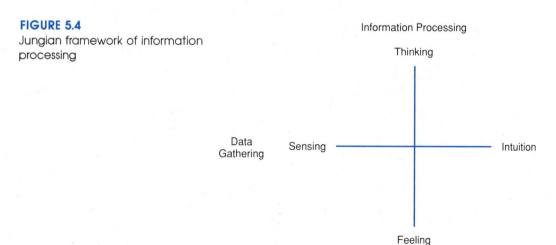

Most people use a combination of these methods, but psychological tests have been developed to identify a person's dominant data-gathering and information processing methods. A commonly used psychological test for categorizing people according to their cognitive style is the Myers-Briggs Type Indicator.[2]

Data Gathering

According to this theory, a person whose behavior suggests the **sensing type** is very detail-oriented in data gathering. Attention during input tends to be focused on a single source, such as spoken words only. This approach tends to emphasize literal interpretation. In contrast, a person reflecting the **intuitive type** would tend to be holistic or global in gathering data. Data gathering according to this approach would involve receiving input from several sources at once and would place heavy emphasis on the influence of context in the interpretation of the input data. One way of distinguishing these two approaches is to say that the intuitive type "sees the forest" while the sensing type "sees the trees."

As an example of how this theory could be employed to interpret the differences in human information processing behavior, consider the following scenario. One afternoon, three people are in a room, and one of them comments on the weather and the recent severe snowfall. Suppose one of the listeners is labeled as a sensing type (S) and the other listener as an intuiting type (N). The speaker looks out the window, then turns to the other two and says, "That *really* was quite a snowstorm we had yesterday." The S-type responds by saying, "It sure was. I bet a foot of snow fell!" The N-type then says, "I don't agree. He *could* have come if he had really *wanted* to." What just happened? Why do the two responses appear to be so unrelated?

To understand what just transpired, we need a little background to this scenario. These three people work for a company which is in the process of hiring new personnel. A job applicant who was scheduled to come in for an interview that morning failed to appear. In the course of discussing why this person did not show up, the possibility was raised that he couldn't make it because of the snow.

After lunch, when the speaker made the comments about the recent snowstorm, the two listeners reacted very differently. Why? The reason is that each of them had received different input data even though both had heard the same words. Person S reacted only to the content of the words that were spoken. She took the words at face value. To her, the context of the conversation was the weather. Person N, on the other hand, was processing input data from other sources as well. One source of input was the memory of what had happened that morning: the discussion about whether the snow had prohibited the job candidate from appearing. The other input was the nonverbal communication: the sympathetic tone of voice that was used as the speaker emphasized the word "really." From these three sources of data, N inferred that the speaker thought the snow probably *did* keep the candidate from showing up for the interview. Since he was not in favor of the applicant, person N voiced his disagreement about the candidate; hence the comment that was made.

How did the speaker react to these two different responses to her comment about the snow? It probably depended on her own cognitive style. If she is also an S-type, she was probably very confused by N's comment. Her reaction to N would have, in turn, confused him. On the other hand, if the speaker is a type N herself, she probably would have embarked on a discussion of the merits of the job applicant. If this had happened, S would have been totally perplexed. If this kind of confusion can occur in communication among people, just think of the confusion that can arise in communication between a person and a computer! Computers do not exhibit such individual differences in information processing behavior.

Information Processing

Once the input data has been received, the thinking-feeling dimension is used to describe the way this data is processed into information. A **thinking type** (T) uses logical analysis to form a conclusion. Thinking types are more impersonal and unemotional in their information processing. A **feeling type** (F), on the other hand, would tend to personalize the situation and base conclusions on feelings and personal values.

In a business setting, a thinking type would make a decision based on a logical assessment of the available information. A feeling type would consider the people involved and how they would be affected by the decision.

In the job-applicant scenario just described, a thinking type's evaluation of the applicant's behavior would be based on logical reasoning. If there were sufficient evidence to suggest that the snow was an important factor in his failure to appear, a T-type might be inclined to give the applicant the benefit of the doubt. A feeling type would assess the situation based on affective criteria: What would be the applicant's motivation for behaving in this fashion? What would be the impact on the company of rescheduling the interview? What would be the impact of refusing to see the applicant? The objective facts about the amount of snowfall would probably have less to do with an F-type's assessment of the data.

By combining the ways people acquire data with the ways they process it, we arrive at the four different types of information processing behavior: sense-thinking (ST), sense-feeling (SF), intuitive-thinking (NT), and intuitive-feeling (NF). The Jungian typology has been used to describe the personality characteristics associated with certain tasks and hence the professions to which certain types would gravitate. While all of Jung's types can be found in all lines of work, certain types have been associated with certain lines of work. Figure 5.5 lists some professions which are typically associated with each of the four types of information processing behavior.

Decision-Making Strategies

During the discussion of problem solving and decision making earlier in this chapter, we pointed out that people solve problems and make decisions based on the identification of a goal and the choice of a strategy for achieving it. While this is generally the case, we should point out that there are a variety

FIGURE 5.5

Professions associated with Jungian types

Sensing Thinker	Sensing Feeler	Intuiting Feeler	Intuiting Thinker
Applied science	Patient care	Behavioral science	Physical science
Business	Community service	Research	Research
Production	Sales	Literature and art	Management
Construction	Teaching	Teaching	Forecasts and analysis

of ways in which people can carry out these activities. There are four general strategies people employ to make decisions: the rational approach, the political approach, the adaptive approach, and the nonrational approach.

Rational Approach   The **rational approach** views decision making as a logical sequence of steps. It makes three important assumptions. First, it assumes that the goal can be clearly identified. Second, it assumes that sufficient information exists to enable one to select the most appropriate strategy for attaining that goal; this is sometimes referred to as **perfect information**. Third, it assumes that, given the goal and the strategy, the decision maker will automatically follow that strategy. For certain decision-making situations, this is an accurate description of what happens. An example would be a bookstore's inventory system. In some cases the desired amount of stock can be determined and rules regarding when and how much to reorder can be set. If certain circumstances, such as time of year, must be considered, they can be incorporated into the rules as well. As we can see, this is a very logical process and the label "rational" is appropriately applied.

Political Approach   But the rational model is not an accurate description of all types of decision-making behavior. The **political approach** describes decision making in circumstances in which the goal might be identified but **imperfect information** exists. That is, not all of the information needed to support the choice of a strategy is available.

Suppose State University's bookstore has the goal of having enough textbooks on hand for every class being taught in a given term. But suppose the bookstore is cramped for space and does not have enough room to hold all the books that are needed. The manager of the bookstore must therefore decide how many books to order for which classes. Some information is available, however. It is known that not all the books ordered by the bookstore will actually be purchased. Not as many students may enroll in the class as the instructor projected. Or perhaps something will happen and certain classes will be cancelled. Or some students will purchase used books from their friends instead of from the bookstore. The problem is that the manager does not know in which courses these circumstances will apply. A decision must be made regarding how many books to purchase, and regardless of what is decided, the possibility will exist that there may not be enough textbooks for one class and too many for another. In essence, there are tradeoffs that must be considered. This is why the term "political" is applied to this approach; certain interests may be served better than others.

Adaptive Approach The **adaptive approach** describes decision making in circumstances of even more uncertainty. This approach is used in settings in which neither the goal nor the strategies are completely understood.[3] The decision maker must therefore constantly collect feedback about actions taken and make alterations in behavior as a result. Suppose the bookstore has plenty of room and wants to use it to stock other books besides textbooks. How does the manager decide what kinds of books the students, staff, and professors will purchase? Will they come to the bookstore to purchase the current bestsellers, or will they come to the bookstore to find the kinds of books that aren't normally sold in other bookstores?

The bookstore manager could send out a survey asking people what they would buy. But that doesn't mean that these people will actually purchase those books. One strategy would be for the manager to purchase a limited number of several categories of books and see how well they sell. Based on this feedback, an adjustment to the goal and the strategy for achieving it can be made. Because changes are continually being made to the goal and the method for achieving it, this method of decision making is called "adaptive."

Nonrational Approach Besides these "classic" approaches to decision making, there is one final approach that is particularly characteristic of human decision making. This model can be called the **nonrational approach**. People do not always behave in a logical, rational fashion. A person might choose a goal (make a decision) and then change it, not according to logically processed data, but based on impulse or emotion or in reaction to something. In addition, once a goal has been identified and a strategy chosen, there is no guarantee that the decision maker will actually *follow* that strategy.

Figure 5.6 illustrates how these four models of decision making differ with respect to the understanding of the goal and the amount of information used to select a strategy for achieving it.

Human Versus Computer-based Decision Making Information systems designed to support decision making are better at employing certain models of decision making than others. The computer is best at structured decision making, which is reflected in the rational model. These are situations in which complete information and well-defined decision-making rules exist. An example would be a management information system for inventory control.

However, many of the decisions made in a company are described by the political model. These are circumstances of unstructured decision making in which tradeoffs must be considered and not all of the information is available.

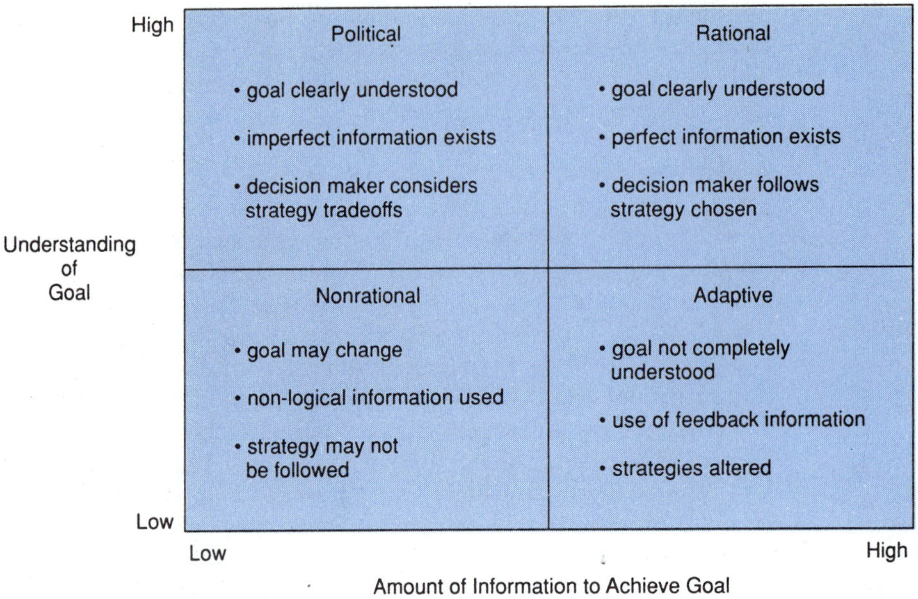

FIGURE 5.6
Models of decision making

Such decisions are those made by some tactical and all strategic levels of management.[4] Decision support systems have been designed for these decision-making situations. They help the user examine alternative strategies and their consequences. An example would be a decision support system to help a bank decide whether to offer a new service to its clients.

A more difficult decision-making approach for the computer to support is the adaptive approach. This approach is more difficult because the information system must not only be capable of processing information and examining alternative strategies, but must also be able to incorporate feedback and change strategies as needed. Expert systems can support this type of decision making because they incorporate the learning features of artificial intelligence. An example would be an expert system designed to assist in medical diagnosis.

The nonrational model is the most dramatic example of the differences between human and computer-based decision making. People do not always base judgments on logic and often change their minds about decisions. In addition, a person may use different decision-making approaches in different circumstances or may even switch methods in midstream. For example, a person may start with the rational model and then switch to the political, adaptive, or nonrational model later in the process. The challenge for information systems professionals is to acknowledge these human traits and attempt to account for them in the design of information systems. Computers are easier to change than people.

Figure 5.7 summarizes the differences between human and computer-based information processing.

FIGURE 5.7

Differences between humans and computers

Information Processing Activities	Humans	Computers
Input	Perception through more than one sense simultaneously Verbal and nonverbal input Redundancy in input	Input primarily through written words in highly structured language Precision in input
Memory	Limited Automatic interaction between STM and LTM	Unlimited Secondary storage not required for processing
Language	Ability to use more than one language at a time Ambiguity and redundancy	One language at a time Precision, no redundancy
Problem Solving	Best at heuristics Make connections easily Individual differences	Best at algorithms Fixed relationships among data Consistent approach
Communication Style	Politeness	Impersonal

HUMAN-COMPUTER INTERACTION

Human-Computer Communication

Once we have an understanding of the differences in the ways humans and computers process information, we come naturally to the next set of considerations. In an information-intensive society, people have a growing need to *communicate* with the computer because it is increasingly needed to support their intellectual work. Further, this mode of interaction is different from *operating* other machines such as an automobile or a videocassette recorder. Since people already know how to communicate—with other people—the challenge for effective human-computer interaction is to determine those features of human communication that should be present in human-computer dialogue. Once we know what should be present in this dialogue, the next task is to ensure that these features are incorporated into the design of information systems. While this is being done, special attention needs to be given to the potential trouble spots in the dialogue which are a byproduct of the differences in the way that computers and humans process information. The goal of human-computer communication, then, is to enhance communication between humans and computers, given the differences in the way each processes and uses data.

Human-Computer Interfaces

We know from Chapter 2 that systems are made up of other systems which function as subsystems. We also know that an information system is composed of both a technological subsystem (hardware and software) and a human subsystem (personnel and procedures). Further, we know that a system is defined by the boundaries which separate it from its environment. At the boundary between two systems is the interface. The **human-computer interface**, then, is at the common boundary of the technological and the human subsystems. When employed successfully, this interface joins these two subsystems together to create an information system like that shown in Figure 5.8. Our purpose in this section is to consider the features that should be incorporated into these interfaces which would take into account the characteristics of human information processing and the way that humans communicate.

Successfully joining the human and technological subsystems together is the overall goal of interface design: to ensure that the output from the computer is usable input for the person and that input to the computer is something that is convenient for the user to provide.[5] Human-computer interfaces are designed to take into account the characteristics of human information processing and to overcome the differences in how humans and computers process information. Some specific goals of interface design are the following:

1. **Minimize memory load.** Given the limitations of human memory, the interface should be designed to minimize the amount that the user has to memorize. One way to accomplish this is to provide all the necessary information on the screen. Allowing the user to select the desired activity eliminates the need to learn many new commands. Another way of accomplishing this is to have consistency across interfaces. For example, always using the F1 function key to indicate the same activ-

FIGURE 5.8

An interface to an information system

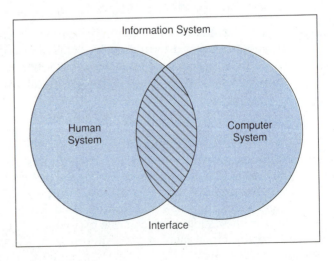

ity (such as help) eliminates the need to relearn the role of every function key each time a new piece of software is encountered.

2. **Ease of use.** The interface should facilitate the user's interaction with the computer. This includes increasing the speed with which a user can enter and retrieve data. The use of function keys to execute a command facilitates interaction by enabling the user to depress one key rather than type in a complete phrase. The use of a mouse to point to commands on a screen eliminates the need to use the arrow keys and type in commands. Another aspect of ease of use is reducing the likelihood that a user will make errors. An example would be requiring the user to confirm a command such as to delete information. In the event that the user entered such a command by mistake, this verification process would allow the user to recover from the error before catastrophic consequences occurred. Ease of use also relates to the arrangement of equipment and furniture so that they can be manipulated without difficulty.

3. **User-friendliness.** The term "user-friendly" was first used to describe interfaces that enabled a person with little computer expertise to successfully use a computer. Since then the term has been used quite frequently in advertising, and as a result it has taken on many different interpretations. Here we use the term to describe the quality of the dialogue between the person and the computer. In human communication there are certain conventions governing discourse, such as that people are expected to be polite to each other. Since people *communicate with* rather than *operate* computers, the dialogue should have some of the features that people have come to expect in human communication. Error messages that are cryptic and use obscure terminology are not user-friendly. When a user has made an error, the message should be understandable. It should indicate what the user did wrong and what should be done to correct the error. An example would be to point out in clear language that the user entered the wrong data rather than to respond with "fatal error."

There are three types of human-computer interfaces: hardware, software, and organizational interfaces.

Hardware Interfaces

The term **hardware interface** refers to those characteristics of the input and output devices which interact with the human sensorimotor system. For example, a keyboard interacts with the eyes, hands, and fingers. The CRT display interacts with the eyes. The goal of hardware interface design is to reduce eye fatigue, neck strain, backaches, and other discomforts, as well as to enhance the ease with which the user can interact with the hardware components such as the keyboard.

One problem with input and output devices derives from the different rates of speed at which humans and computers can function. Computers can accept and output data much faster than humans can either enter or assimilate it. Another difficulty is directly related to the nature of human communication. Humans can communicate using several methods simultaneously. For example, in conversation, people use nonverbal communication in the form of tone of voice and gestures to enhance verbal communication. This use of multiple modes of communication helps to overcome the ambiguity in human language. While significant advances have been made, the computer is still not able to accept information in the manner in which humans are used to communicating it.

Two approaches to interface design can be taken in response to these issues. One approach is to constrain the individual to the use of structured techniques for human input into the computer—that is, give the individual a limited set of choices or responses during interaction with the computer. Examples would be the use of function keys which carry out a prespecified activity, or alternatives to the keyboard such as the mouse, touch screens, and optical readers. This approach reduces or eliminates the human tendency toward ambiguity.

The second alternative is to try to make the computer adapt to the range of ways that humans communicate. This is accomplished primarily through the use of natural language. Rather than forcing the person to use a structured vocabulary, natural language employs artificial intelligence to allow the person to communicate with the computer using a very large vocabulary. Natural language input can be accomplished in several ways, the most common form being to type in commands at the keyboard. Another method of natural language input is voice input, which is much more difficult to accomplish because there is another factor to take into account besides the words themselves. To accept voice input, the computer must be able to associate a variety of different sounds with the words they form, since different people say the same words differently.

Another possibility would be to have individualized interface design—to "train" the computer to understand the way a certain user thinks and communicates. The computer would then be customized to receiving input according to that person's particular style of information processing and communication. Research is currently being conducted in this area, but such methods of input are not yet commercially available.

Software Interfaces

The **software interface** refers to the features incorporated into the software that enable users to interact with the computer. These features are intended to facilitate the use of the input and output devices in order to enhance the dialogue between the user and the computer. The main problems of software interface design arise from our incomplete understanding of human information processing. We know much more about the capabilities and limitations of machines than we do about those of humans. However, as computer-based tools become more pervasive, it is the cognitive aspects of matching technology to users that become the most critical aspects of human-computer interaction.

It is the task of the software interface to acknowledge the often invisible factors inherent in effective communication. A good software interface must be built on a good hardware interface. The hardware interface should ensure that the cognitive requirements of the user can be met. For example, a software interface with desirable features such as a menu will not be very effective if the display screen has flickering lights which bother the user's eyes.

Some hardware interfaces are more involved with the software interface than others. For example, the only cognitive aspect taken into account in a keyboard is the layout of the keys. In general, it resembles the layout of a typewriter so that people who already know how to type do not have to learn a new arrangement of keys. As pointed out later, the design of a menu or command language must incorporate numerous cognitive features such as the choice of words that will be used and the amount of data that will appear on the screen.

The need for the software interface becomes apparent if one remembers that human-computer interaction is really an interaction between two different kinds of information processing systems. As pointed out earlier in this chapter, these two information processing systems differ in the way they acquire, store, process, and communicate information. Choosing an appropriate type of human-computer dialogue is the first step in the design of a software interface. The following paragraphs describe the most common types of dialogue and what one must know to utilize them.

Programming Languages The earliest mechanism for facilitating human-computer interaction was the **programming language**. As explained in Chapter 4, a programming language is a highly structured method of communication with the computer. Using the proper vocabulary and syntax is crucial to successful interaction. In other words, the human is expected to adapt to the computer's method of processing. Thus, to have a successful dialogue in a programming language, the user must have an extensive understanding of computer operations in addition to an understanding of the information that is needed.

Command Languages Somewhat easier to use than programming languages are **command languages**. They also use a specific vocabulary and syntax for expressing an information need, but require a less detailed expression. This type of interface is commonly employed for gaining access to large stores of data in the computer. The primary advantages are more flexibility in retrieving information and greater control over the process. There are tradeoffs, however. The user must spend some time learning to use a command language. Thus, this type also requires the user to have some understanding of computer operations in addition to an understanding of the information need.

Menus In contrast with programming and command languages, which give the user considerable control over the process of obtaining the data, menus are rather limiting. By presenting the user with a set of options from which to choose, **menus** help to minimize the long-term memory load associated with remembering many commands. The main advantage of a menu is also its main disadvantage: It is a constrained dialogue. This makes it a good communication technique for inexperienced or infrequent users. But experienced users can get frustrated at having to move through several layers of menus to execute a command. Another disadvantage of menus is that if a user makes a wrong choice three layers into the process, he or she might have to start all over again. The primary advantage of menus is that the users need to know very little about how the computer has stored the data. They just need to have an understanding of their information need.

Question and Answer In the **question-and-answer** approach, as with menus, the user is not required to know much about the computer. Rather, the user need only understand the information processing task at hand. Typically, the user is presented with a question that appears on the screen, and responds using either a regular keyboard or function keys. **Form filling** is one type of question-and-answer interaction, in which the user is presented with a display screen and is instructed to provide the necessary information. Generally, the user need only know about admissible entries, since even the placement of data on the display is taken care of by the computer (by means of a cursor showing the proper position for the data to be entered). Figure 5.9 shows an interface that employs the question-and-answer method.

Icons Although words have traditionally been the basis for interfaces, the popularity of graphic representation of data has led to the development of interfaces based on symbols. The Apple Macintosh computer, for example, enables the user to execute a command by means of an **icon** as an alternative to typing it in from a keyboard. Icons are symbols which represent an activity to be carried out by the computer. An example is a picture of a trash can to indicate the "delete" command. Rather than typing in a command to delete some data, the person uses a **mouse** to move the cursor to the desired icon and then presses a button on the mouse to execute the command for "delete." The advantage of using icons is that users are able to communicate commands to the computer using a "language" that is familiar to them. By eliminating the requirement that users learn a new vocabulary, this type of interface places the burden of communication more heavily on the computer. Users can therefore focus on the task at hand rather than on learning commands like "load," "delete," or "store." Figure 5.10 shows icons on a computer screen.

After the type of dialogue is determined, other decisions have to be made. Certain features can be added to increase the user-friendliness and usability of

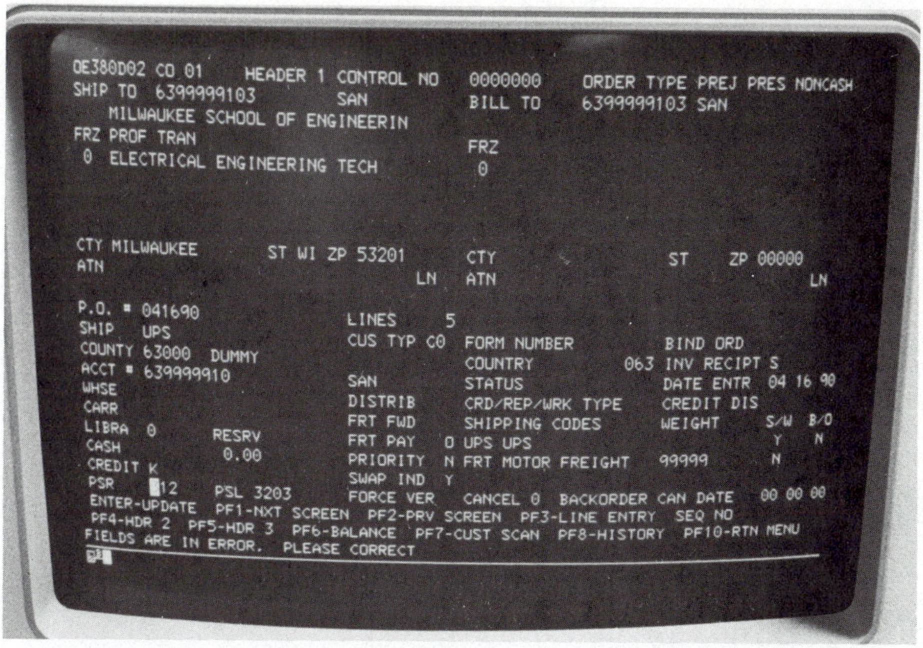

FIGURE 5.9
A question-and-answer interface

the software. These features improve the quality of the interaction and reduce the probability of catastrophic mistakes. The following is an overview of such features.

Command Changes Since a user might hit the wrong key by mistake, he or she should be able to change the command before a catastrophe hits (such as deleting data). One way to do this is to ask for confirmation that the user really wanted to execute that command. Another way is to have an "undo" or "cancel" command—a "panic button" users can press whenever they are in trouble. A more sophisticated interface would be able to determine that the user misspelled a command. It might deduce what the user meant to say and ask for confirmation before executing it.

Prompts In human communication, nonverbal signals are used to indicate that it is the other person's turn to speak. These signals might be a pause, a look, a nod, or an inflection (such as when someone asks a question). This is what is meant by a **prompt**. In human-computer communication, there is no built-in signal to indicate that it is the other's turn to communicate. Therefore, a good interface will provide these cues. Prompts from the computer system can come in the form of a word, a symbol, or a flashing cursor. For example, in the BASIC programming language, the prompt "Ready" is

FIGURE 5.10
A screen showing icons

used while a person is writing a program. During the execution of the program, when the user should enter some data, the prompt is a question mark. A flashing cursor is often used as a prompt in form-filling interfaces. This tells the user that it is time to enter some data and also indicates the position on the screen where the data should be entered.

Stopping In addition to being able to cancel a command that has been entered, the user should be able to stop execution of a process that is under way. Suppose you gave a command to print a ten-page document, then for some reason decided not to print it. The interface should have some way of allowing you to stop the printing process.

Help A very basic aspect of the interface is the **help** facility. In contrast with the more specific aids we have described, this facility should be capable of responding to a wide range of user questions. The help facility is like a smaller version of the written documentation that accompanies the particular computer software being used. Sometimes a complete version of the written documentation is available through help. This is called **on-line documentation**.

Windows As more and more automated support for data-handling tasks has become available, users have begun to need the computer to execute more than one program at the same time. For example, consider the activities involved in producing an updated product catalog for Wooden Wonders. The text of the new catalog would be produced using word processing software. Suppose Paul Bunyan developed the drawings of products with the help of graphics software. If he can only run one computer program at a time, he would have to exit the word processing program and enter the graphics program to find the appropriate illustration. **Windows** enable a user to work with more than one process at the same time. This is accomplished by partitioning the computer screen into a series of boxed-in areas referred to as windows. Therefore, if Paul needs to refer to an illustration while writing copy for the new catalog, he can have his word processing program in one window and his illustrations in another window. If he wants to know how to execute some command, he can get help from a third window. Figure 5.11 shows a computer screen with windows on it.

In the design of software interfaces, it is crucial that the characteristics of the intended user be in the forefront. Are these frequent or infrequent users? Do they already know much about the computer? Have they used similar software before? Obviously, the designers of commercial software packages that will be used by a range of users cannot have definitive answers to these questions. That is why there is the need for a third type of human-computer interface.

Organizational Interfaces

Unlike the hardware and software interfaces which are features of the technology (the computer subsystem), the **organizational interface** is part of the context in which the computer system will be used (the human subsystem). An organizational interface refers to people, procedures, or data positioned between the user and the technology to facilitate the interaction between the two.[6] Some common types of organizational interface features are shown in Figure 5.12.

Two of the most common types of organizational interfaces are education and support. Education means teaching the user how to communicate with the computer system. Education in this context normally refers to classes that users attend to learn how to use certain hardware or software. The information provided in these classes can be tailored to the specific users more than the help facilities provided in the software interface can. Support means having people in the organization whose job it is to help users when they have questions, problems, or special needs. Once the formal education is completed, the

FIGURE 5.11
Windows on a screen

informal education provided by support personnel should be ongoing. The support function can take several forms. One is to have an organizational unit — called an **Information Center** or Micro Center — where users can go to use certain software or to get help. Another way that support can be provided is by having a telephone "hot line." ATMs in some banks make use of this method. If some problem arises during a banking transaction, the customer, using a phone available near the terminal, can call and ask for assistance. Both education and support make use of the personnel and procedures resources of the information system.

Another type of organizational interface that utilizes personnel and procedures is a staff of people whose job is to retrieve data from the computer. Suppose a command language is the available mechanism for retrieving data from an organization's computer system. For those unfamiliar with the operations of a computer, using this command language could prove very difficult and time-consuming. An alternative to providing classes or buying user-friendly software — neither of which might be practical or affordable — would be

FIGURE 5.12

Features of an organizational interface

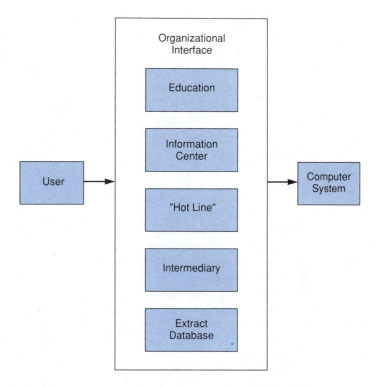

to employ an **intermediary**, an expert in the use of the command language and the information stored in the computer. This person could then do the searches for other people. Intermediaries are commonly used in libraries to retrieve computerized bibliographic data for patrons.

The data itself can also be a feature of an organizational interface. Suppose a number of people in an organization need access to the company's sales data, and suppose some of these people are not very knowledgeable about the computer. They need to use the computer in their work, but an inexperienced user could inadvertently damage the data. What should the company do? One alternative would be to have an intermediary retrieve the data; but this might take more time than the user can afford. If the only way the users can get the information in a timely fashion is to retrieve it themselves, how does the organization ensure that they won't accidentally damage the data? One way would be to provide a *copy* of the data. This could be either a copy of the entire set of data or a copy of that portion of the data the particular user needs to obtain. In this way, if a user accidentally damages the data, only the copy is affected, not the actual data. This feature of an organizational interface is referred to as an **extract database**.

The need for an organizational interface may exist for several reasons. First, there may be financial constraints. The existing software interface may be difficult to use, but the organization may not wish to purchase a more sophisticated one. Second, there may be a time constraint. A person might be under pressure to produce some output using the computer without having the time to read through the manuals and learn to use the software interface without assistance. Third, users in most organizations vary in skill level from the very knowledgeable to the very inexperienced, so it would be both expensive and difficult to provide a software interface to suit every type of user. Fourth, a commercial software package cannot be tailored to the specific needs of every individual in an organization. The software may have some features such as a help facility and menus, but it would be impossible to build in a response to every kind of difficulty every user might have. Fifth, infrequent users, no matter how much education they receive, will forget how to accomplish certain tasks because they will not be using the software often enough. Therefore, they will need to have support available to them. A final reason to have an organizational interface is that it is human nature to go to another person when one has a question or problem.

The ultimate goal in the design of any type of interface should be effective use. Computer system **usability** has been defined as the capability, in terms of human functioning, of being used easily and effectively by a specified group of users to accomplish a specified range of tasks within a specific context.[7] From this definition we can note that usability should take into account the user, the task to be performed, the technology available for performing it, and the context within which the task is to be carried out. The organizational interface has two goals. One is to enhance the hardware and software interfaces by providing a form of assistance tailored to the specific needs of a given individual in a particular context. The second is to fill in any gaps left by the hardware and software interfaces. True usability occurs through the interaction of the hardware, software, and organizational interfaces.

For example, consider an organization with two different kinds of end users—those who use the computer frequently and are comfortable with it, and those who are either new or infrequent users. Suppose the organization purchased a word processing package whose software interface employs a menu. For the novice or infrequent user, such a device reduces memory load. But for the experienced user, it can cause delays. For this reason, the software also allows for the use of shortcuts—keystrokes which enable one to accomplish tasks more quickly. This is provided by the use of function keys. Here, we can see how the hardware interface (the keyboard) contributes to an improved software interface by the availability of function keys. However, despite the existence of menu items from which to choose, management is also aware that some users will probably have difficulty using the software without some additional help. Therefore, two organizational interfaces also exist. Education sessions are provided for new users of the software package, and consultants are available to help users. These consultants might assist infrequent users who have forgotten some of what they learned in the classes, as well as experienced users who want to accomplish more difficult and less common tasks with the software. Through the combination of all three types of human-computer interface, the special characteristics of the user, the task, and the context are taken into account.

The need for all three types of interfaces—hardware, software, and organizational—reinforces the fact that all five resources of the information system—hardware, software, data, procedures, and personnel—are needed in order to have an effective and usable information system. It is also a reminder that information systems do not exist in a vacuum. They exist in a specific context with specific individuals using them. Unless all three types of interfaces are provided, the information system will probably not be as effective as it could be.

SUMMARY

There are both similarities and differences in the ways in which humans and computers process information. Through perception, cognition, and response, humans carry out the functions analogous to the input, process, and output functions carried out by the computer. The response, or output, of human information processing could be learning, decision making, or some informed behavior. The major difference between human and computer-based information processing is that there is much greater variability in the way humans accomplish information processing tasks. Computer-based information processing systems are predictable; humans are not. Human information processing activities are also characterized by degrees of ambiguity, redundancy, and imprecision. This becomes evident when we consider the different decision-making strategies people use. The four models of decision making—rational, political, adaptive, and nonrational—represent a continuum of strategies ranging from the most to the least logical. Not only do humans differ from computers in decision making, they also differ among themselves.

Since people *communicate* with computers rather than *operate* them, the challenge for effective human-computer interaction is to incorporate some of the features people expect in human dialogue. This is the purpose of the human-computer interface. There are three types of interfaces. The hardware interface is concerned with facilitating the person's use of computer hardware, primarily the input and output devices. The software interface is concerned with facilitating the person's interaction with the software and data. Increasingly, software is being designed to adapt to the person rather than requiring the person to adjust to the technology. The organizational interface includes those features of the context of use which can fill in the gaps left by the hardware and software interfaces. Education and support are the most common types of organizational interfaces.

As the use of computer-based support for tasks becomes widespread, the design of an appropriate interface becomes a key requirement for effective information system use.

CHAPTER NOTES

1. George Miller, "The Magical Number Seven, Plus or Minus Two: Some Limits on Our Capacity for Processing Information," *Psychological Review* 63, No. 2 (1956): 81–96.

2. Isabel Briggs Myers, *The Myers-Briggs Type Indicator* (Palo Alto, CA: Consulting Psychologist Press, Inc., 1962).

3. Eileen M. Trauth, *An Adaptive Model of Information Policy* (Ph.D. Dissertation, University of Pittsburgh, 1979).

4. G. A. Gorry and M. S. Scott Morton, "A Framework for Management Information Systems," *Sloan Management Review* 13, No. 1 (Fall 1971): 55–70.

5. Raymond S. Nickerson, *Using Computers: Human Factors in Information Systems* (Cambridge, MA: MIT Press, 1986), 89.

6. Eileen M. Trauth and Elliot Cole, "The Design of Organizational Interfaces," *Proceedings of the Second International Conference on Human-Computer Interaction*, August 1987.

7. B. Shackel, "The Concept of Usability," *Proceedings of the IBM Software and Information Usability Symposium*, September 1981: 5.

ADDITIONAL REFERENCES

Benbasat, I., and A. S. Dexter. "Individual Differences in the Use of Decision Support Systems." *Journal of Accounting Research* 20 (Spring 1982): 1–11.

Card, Stuart K., Thomas P. Moran, and Allen Newell. *The Psychology of Human-Computer Interaction*. Hillsdale, NJ: Lawrence Erlbaum Associates, 1983.

Fried, Louis. "Nine Principles for Ergonomic Software." *Datamation* (November 1982): 163, 165–166.

Henderson, J. C., and P. C. Nutt. "Influence of Decision Style on Decision Making Behavior." *Management Science* 26, No. 4 (April 1980): 371–386.

Huber, G. P. "The Nature of Organizational Decision Making and the Design of Decision Support Systems." *MIS Quarterly* 5, No. 2 (June 1981): 1–10.

———. "Cognitive Style as a Basis for MIS and DSS Designs: Much Ado about Nothing?" *Management Science* 29, No. 5 (May 1983): 567–579.

Jung, Carl G. *Psychological Types*. New York: Harcourt, Brace and Company, Inc., 1924.

King, W. R., and D. I. Clelland. "Decision and Information Systems for Strategic Planning." *Business Horizons* (April 1973): 29–36.

Lindsay, Peter H., and Donald A. Norman. *Human Information Processing: An Introduction to Psychology*. 2d ed. New York: Academic Press, 1977.

Mintzberg, H., D. Raisinghani, and A. Theoret. "The Structure of 'Unstructured' Decision Processes." *Administrative Science Quarterly* 21, No. 2 (June 1976): 246–275.

Robey, D., and W. Taggart. "Human Information Processing in Information and Decision Support Systems." *MIS Quarterly* 6, No. 2 (June 1982): 61–73.

———. "Measuring Manager's Minds: The Assessment of Style in Human Information Processing." *Academy of Management Review* 6, No. 2 (July 1981): 375–383.

Schneiderman, Ben. *Designing the User Interface: Strategies for Effective Human-Computer Interaction*. Reading, MA: Addison-Wesley, 1987.

Sprague, Ralph H., Jr., and Hugh J. Watson, eds. *Decision Support Systems: Putting Theory into Practice*. Englewood Cliffs, NJ: Prentice-Hall, 1986.

Stewart, Tom. "Software Ergonomics: Making Systems Friendly." *Information Resource Management* 1 (April 1983): 40–43.

Trudgill, Peter. *Sociolinguistics: An Introduction*. Baltimore, MD: Penguin Books, 1975.

Waltz, D. L. "Helping Computers Understand Natural Language." *IEEE Spectrum* (November 1984): 81–84.

Winograd, Terry. "Computer Software for Working With Language." *Scientific American* 251, No. 3 (September 1984): 130–145.

KEY TERMS

adaptive approach
algorithm
cognition
cognitive style
command language
contextual cues
decision making
external memory
extract database
feature analysis
feeling type
form filling
hardware interface
help
heuristics
human-computer interface
human information processing

icon
imperfect information
information center
intermediary
intuitive type
knowledge
language
learning
long-term memory
menu
mouse
nonrational approach
nonverbal communication
on-line documentation
organizational interface
pattern recognition
perception

perfect information
phoneme
political approach
problem solving
programming language
prompt
question and answer
rational approach
redundancy
sensing type
short-term memory
software interface
speech analysis
thinking type
usability
window

REVIEW QUESTIONS

1. What are the components of human information processing? What are their functions?
2. Explain the steps in the pattern recognition process.
3. Discuss the memory, language, and problem-solving aspects of cognition.
4. Discuss the three purposes of human information processing.
5. How is human information processing similar to computer-based information processing? How is it different?
6. Describe the four different modes of data gathering/information processing according to the Jungian framework.
7. Describe the different decision-making strategies employed in human decision making.
8. A computer is best suited for which type of decision making? Why?
9. What is the purpose of a human-computer interface?

10. Discuss the goals of successful interface design.
11. What is the purpose of a hardware interface? Give some examples.
12. What is a problem of hardware interface design?
13. What is the purpose of the software interface? Give some examples.
14. Explain one of the difficulties in software interface design.
15. Discuss several of the common types of human-computer dialogue.
16. What is the purpose of the organizational interface? Give some examples.
17. Why are organizational interfaces necessary?

CASE

The Computer Services Department at State University has been confronted with a dilemma. People are complaining about the word processing package currently in use. It is the policy of the department that only one word processing package will be supported. If some schools and departments choose to use a different package, the department will not supply answers to questions or contact vendors on their behalf. Five years ago, when word processing was less pervasive than it is now, the university purchased a package at a very reasonable price. The software interface was comparable to those of other word processing packages available at that time.

The problem is that today newer packages are available with much better software interfaces than the one currently in use. Consequently, some students and faculty have been requesting that the university change to a new package. Since the current package was purchased at a very reasonable price, the Computer Services Department knows that purchasing a new one will involve considerably more expense. Therefore, ease of use has to be balanced against cost. In the view of Computer Services, the current package contains all the functionality that is needed and the software interface is good enough. Besides, those recommending a change don't agree on which package they should purchase.

DISCUSSION QUESTIONS

1. How important should the software interface be in the decision regarding which word processing package to have at the university?
2. What organizational interface features can be employed to enhance the usability of the current word processing package?
3. If the university decides to purchase a new word processing package, what criteria should it use to evaluate the software interfaces of the candidate packages?

CHAPTER 6

Data Storage and Retrieval

CHAPTER OUTLINE

DATA

FILES

DATABASES

DATABASE MANAGEMENT SYSTEMS

CHAPTER OBJECTIVES

- To describe the activities of data storage and retrieval.
- To explain the impact of inadequate or inappropriate data storage and retrieval.
- To explain how the selection of storage media impacts the alternatives for data storage and retrieval.
- To define the components of the hierarchy of data.
- To describe how data can be organized and processed.
- To explain how to select the most appropriate technique for data storage and retrieval.
- To describe database and database management system concepts and when to use them.

INTRODUCTION

In Chapter 4 we considered the techniques associated with the components of a computer-based information system: input, process, and output. In Chapter 5 we considered the ways in which humans carry out these same functions and the differences between human and machine information processing. This chapter is concerned with methods of storing data so that it is available for later use. Since the purpose of an information system is to use data to produce high-quality information, that data must be available to the system. This chapter describes the various techniques used by an information system for the storage and retrieval of data. There are two reasons why it is appropriate for an end user to know this material. One is to have realistic expectations concerning his or her data storage and retrieval requirements. The second is that data storage and retrieval software packages available for use on personal computers are among the most commonly used applications by end users.

This chapter builds on the material presented in Chapters 2 and 4 and the appendix. Readers should be familiar with the systems concepts presented in Chapter 2. They should also be familiar with Section I of the appendix, which discusses primary and secondary storage, and Sections III and IV, which consider systems and application software and programming languages.

DATA

Data Characteristics

For a computer-based information system to operate effectively, the data required for the production of information must be available to that system. The characteristics that facilitate this availability are the existence, correctness, locatability, manipulation, provision, and presentation of the data.

Data Existence

For data to be usable by a computer, it must be in a suitable form. A computer cannot directly read a document or memo written by an individual. These are examples of data in user-readable form. Data in this form must be transformed into computer-readable form before it can be used directly by a computer. *Data existence* in a computerized information system means that the data to be processed exists in computer-readable form. Therefore, appropriate data entry procedures must be followed to ensure that this is the case. These procedures were discussed in Chapter 4.

Data Correctness

Data correctness or **integrity** describes the criteria used to determine that data is correct, consistent, and accurate. An example would be the following rules defining data integrity at Last National Bank: (1) a bank account number has six digits; and (2) the first two digits indicate the branch at which the account was opened.

Data Locatability

Data is only useful if it can be found when it is needed. For example, suppose some signs on a major road are missing. There are signs indicating the cross-roads but not the road being traveled. With this level of information available, it would be difficult to locate one's position on a map. Similarly, if files are misplaced in an office, data may not be able to be located when it is needed. If the correct data is not available, decision making may be delayed or based on incomplete data.

In a computer-based information system, once the data is found, it must be transferred from secondary storage to primary memory, where it can be processed. The **secondary storage device** can be either magnetic tape or disk. The technique used to locate the desired data depends, in part, on the storage device being used. *Data location techniques* are described later in this chapter.

Data Manipulation

After the data is retrieved, it usually needs to be manipulated in order to be transformed into information. In Chapter 4, various types of operations for processing data were described. For example, an application system may need to *calculate* revenues as profit minus cost or do *summarization* to determine annual profit as the sum of all monthly profits/losses.

Data Presentation

Once all the required data has been retrieved and processed into usable information, it must be presented in a form that is compatible with the use for which it was produced. The concern in *data presentation* is to maintain a balance between providing too little and too much information. A user should receive a sufficient amount of information to accomplish the task at hand, but not so much that attention is diverted from the really valuable information being presented. A manager with too many facts to consider may not be able to isolate the relevant and important facts from those that are not. Such a manager is being subjected to *information overload* and as a result might ignore all of the output from the system or consider the wrong data. To remedy information overload, the information system should be able to filter data so as to present only the relevant information to the user.

The data storage and retrieval portion of an information system is concerned with four main activities. First is data storage. Data should be checked for correctness and then stored in a form that facilitates its retrieval. Second is data retrieval—searching and locating the desired data and then moving it to where it can be processed. The third activity is data modification, in which data is updated to maintain its correctness. The fourth is data reporting, which means presenting data in a form that enhances its usefulness and facilitates decision making.

Data Hierarchy

Data, whether it exists in human-readable or machine-readable form, is organized into units which can be further broken down into subunits. For example, a book is composed of chapters which are made up of paragraphs which contain sentences made up of words. Similarly, data which will be used by an information system is also arranged into levels of organization. This is referred to as a data hierarchy. Figure 6.1 shows the data hierarchy with an example of each level.

Data Item

A **data item** is the smallest meaningful unit of data which is used by a computer. A data item is made up of characters or bytes which, in turn, are made up of bits. A checking account balance and the amount of interest paid to date

FIGURE 6.1
Data hierarchy

BINARY DIGIT (BIT)	0, 1		
CHARACTER (BYTE)	A & , 5		
DATA ITEM	NAME - Mary Smith		
RECORD	STUDENT_NAME Mary Smith	ID 123456	GPA 3.5
FILE	Sally Adams John Bets	1111231 1245636	3.0 2.8

DATABASE

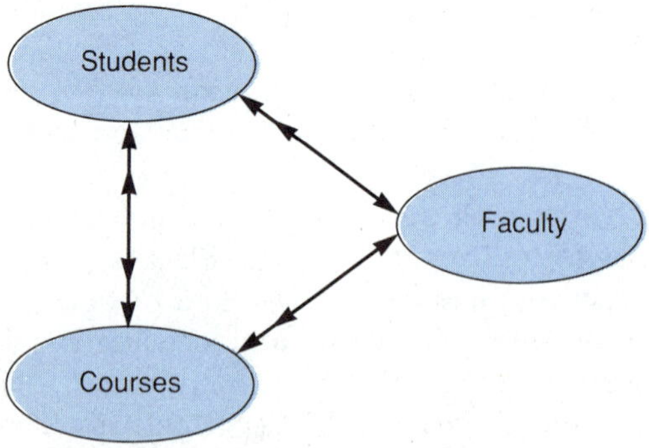

are examples of data items. Most often, a user is concerned with data at the data item level. Data items are also referred to as **data elements** or **fields**.

A data item can be described in terms of its name and value. The *name* of a data item refers to the type of data it will contain. For example, a data item with the name "account number" will contain a customer's account number. The *value* of a data item refers to its actual contents. At a bank, the data item named "account number" will have many different values, one for each customer. Thus, the value of data item "account number" for one customer might be 12-34567 and the value of the corresponding data item "account balance" might be $534.67.

Record

The next level in the data hierarchy is a record. A **record** is a collection of related data items which describe a single entity. For example, State University needs to store and retrieve data about students, faculty, courses, and departments. The relevant data about each student, faculty member, course, and department is stored in a different type of record.

A record can be described in terms of type and occurrence. A **record type** defines the data items that make up the record. For example, the student record type contains the following data items: student's name, student's identification number, student's address, and student's telephone number. A record about a specific student, or a **record occurrence**, contains the values for each of that student's data items that have been collected and stored. An example of a student record type and occurrence is as follows:

Name	ID	Address	Phone no.	Type
MARY SMITH	123456	22 OAK STREET BOSTON MA 02121	(617) 555-1234	occurrence

When end users refer to the term "record," generally no distinction is made between type and occurrence. Instead of record type, users refer to "defining a record"; instead of record occurrence, users refer to the "contents" of a specific record.

Each data item in the record has characteristics such as type, length, and valid values it can contain. For example, "account number" is numeric since its value contains only numbers, whereas "customer address" is alphanumeric since it can include numbers, letters, and special characters.

File

A *file* is a collection of record occurrences of the same type. For example, a student file contains data about students. Data files can exist in manual as well as computer-readable form. An example of a student file in manual form is a folder containing a separate sheet of paper (record occurrence) for each student.

A sample checking account form is shown in Figure 6.2. This form contains the relevant information about a bank customer such as account number, customer name and address, social security number, and account balance. Each entry is a different data item. The entire form is a record about a single cus-

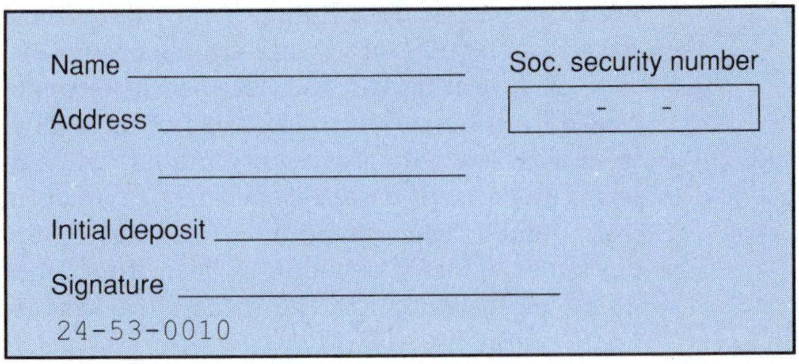

FIGURE 6.2

Form used to open a checking account

Name _____   Soc. security number

Address _____   [___ - ___ - ___]

_____

Initial deposit _____

Signature _____

24-53-0010

tomer. A checking account file, therefore, would contain a set of completed checking account forms. A computerized version of the checking account file would contain the data for all the checking accounts that existed at the bank. Each line in this file would describe a different checking account. Thus, the checking account file contains a number of checking account records, each of which describes a different account.

Database

Sometimes files are grouped into yet another level of organization. When this occurs, a database is created. A *database* is a collection of interrelated and integrated sets of files that are used by many applications. Databases are valuable when different record types need to be used together. A bank's database would consist of many files such as customer, checking account, savings account, credit card account, and loan files. A database at a bank would enable it to produce an integrated statement for a customer which contains information from checking account, savings account, and loan files. Databases will be discussed in greater detail later in this chapter.

Views of Data

Data which is to be retrieved for use by an information system can be viewed from several different perspectives. One is the perspective of the person who will be using that data. Another is the perspective of the software which will store and retrieve that data. The third is the perspective of the storage media which actually contain the data. The three perspectives vary in the technical detail that must be taken into account when considering the issue of data storage and retrieval. These views are referred to as the **user view**, **logical view**, and **physical view** of the data, respectively.

These views can be explained by analogy with a house. There are different views of a house when it is being built, just as there are different views of the data. The owners are like the users. They are concerned with the construction of the house from the perspective of how it will be used. Similarly, the users of data are concerned with the data items that are needed to enable them to do their jobs. They are most concerned with such things as what data will appear in a report or on a screen. The users are least concerned about the order in which the data items are stored in the file or how the data is located on a storage device.

The architect's plans for a house form a conceptual or logical view of the building. Likewise, the view of data from the software perspective is a logical representation of how the data is stored. This view contains sufficient detail so that the data in the files can be stored, retrieved, and used. This is achieved by the inclusion of a description of the files in the software. The amount of detail depends on the programming language. For example, a language like COBOL requires more detailed information than one like BASIC.

The view of the data from the perspective of the device relates to where and how the data is physically stored. This is analogous to the builder, whose concern is the actual construction of a house. The characteristics of the storage device, such as magnetic disk or tape, influence the way the data is stored and retrieved in the same way that the characteristics of the property, such as the type of soil and contours of the land, influence the way the house will be built. These three views of data are shown in Figure 6.3.

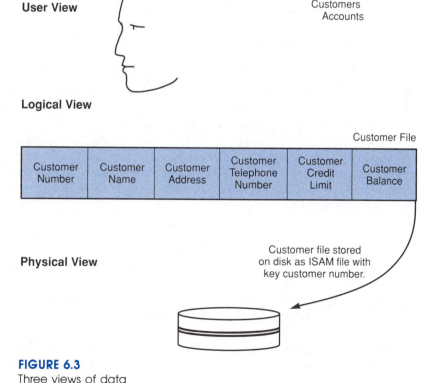

FIGURE 6.3
Three views of data

FILES

File Processing Concepts

There are three types of file organizations: sequential, direct, and indexed sequential. A sequential file can be stored on either magnetic tape or disk; direct and indexed sequential files can only be stored on a disk. A user should know two key things about files: (1) how the data is stored and retrieved according to each of these methods; and (2) circumstances in which each type of file organization is appropriate. From a user's perspective, it is critical that the file organization be suited to the way the data will be used, because the method of storage will determine the kind of retrieval possible within time constraints and the efficiency or costs of file processing. In this section we discuss the important concepts to take into consideration in making a decision about file organizations.

Key

A file usually has one special set of data, called a **key**, which is used to arrange the records in some order and to locate a specific record. The key may be either a single data item or a collection of data items. A key used for ordering is often called a *sort key*, while a key used to locate records is referred to as a *search key*. The sort key is *generally* a unique value, which means that no other record will contain this same value. Often, to achieve uniqueness, more than one data item is required to create the key. For example, the course file at a university has the following data items: course number, section number, current enrollment, location, and time. In this file no single data item in these records is unique. For example, course number is not unique since there may be multiple sections of a course. However, if course number and section number are used together they will comprise a unique key for ordering the records. In order to use the key to locate a specific record, it *must* have a unique value. For example, since more than one student at a university could have the same name, a better record key to use for locating records would be the social security number. A key whose value is unique and whose value is always known is called a **primary key**.

Master File

A **master file** is a file containing the complete and current data about some person or entity. For example, a bank maintains a master file of customer accounts. This file would contain the name, telephone number, permanent address, and current account balances of each customer account. All data updates are made to this file. To facilitate processing, the master file is often arranged in a certain order. In some file organizations, the master file must be completely rewritten when it is updated. When this happens, the original file is referred to as the *old master file* and the updated version is referred to as the *new master file.* For security, organizations usually keep the two most recent versions of the master file as backup.

Transaction File

A *transaction* is an event which will cause a change in the master file. An example is a withdrawal from a checking account. A **transaction file** contains the data from these transactions which will then be used to update the records in a master file. To facilitate processing the transaction file, it is sorted into the same order as the master file. This means that the same sort key is used for both files. **Transaction processing** refers to using the data in the transaction file to update the master file or database.

Batch Processing

Transactions can be processed (i.e., used as the basis for an update) when the transaction occurs or at a later time. When these transactions are not processed as they occur, there is some time delay and information in the master file is not always current. For example, a customer's order could be processed when it is received and the items committed to that order at that time, or the order could be collected with others and processed at the end of the day. This delay enables the organization to process a collection of transactions at once. This approach is referred to as **batch processing**. Transaction data is held until there are a large number of transactions to be processed or until a designated time period such as a day has elapsed. Batch processing is usually done to reduce the cost of processing transactions and to manage the computer's processing load. With batch processing, a large number of transactions are processed and the cost per transaction is low.

Response Time

Response time is the amount of time that elapses between a user's request for information and the receipt of that information. Regardless of file organization, the answer to an information request can eventually be obtained. The issue, therefore, is whether the response time for a given file organization is acceptable. To be acceptable, the answer must be received in time for it to be useful. Usually, a very fast response time is accompanied by high operating costs.

File Activity

An important aspect of choosing the most appropriate file organization is knowing the number of records in the file to be used by the application. The number of records can range from only a few to most or all of the file. For example, when a bank customer inquires about his or her current checking account balance, the application will retrieve a single record: the specific checking account record. On the other hand, all checking account records in the file are processed when checking account statements are generated. The percentage of the file processed by an application is referred to as the *activity* of the file. High activity means that a large portion of the file is used, while low activity means that very few records are processed. The number of records being processed out of the total number of records in the file is referred to as the *activity ratio*.

File Reorganization

Sometimes a file organization may be deemed inappropriate. When this occurs, the file may be reorganized into a different file structure. This reorganization is usually accompanied by program maintenance tasks which are needed to make the existing software compatible with the new file structure. Because the costs of changing the programs are even higher than the data reorganization costs, considerable attention should be given to understanding how the data will be used so that the most appropriate file structure is chosen in the first place.

Sequential Files

Sequential File Concepts

A **sequential file** is one in which each record is arranged in sequence according to its key, in either ascending or descending order. Sequential files can be stored on either magnetic tape or disk. The key is used to determine both the logical ordering of the records in the file and the physical ordering of the records on the storage device.

In sequential file organization, records can only be accessed in sequence. Direct access to a single record is not possible. All previous records in the file must be examined in order to find the desired record. In a sequential checking account file, the records would be ordered by account number, such as 111111, 222222, 343433, 444444, 888888, and 909090. Since it is necessary to examine all preceding records, to reach account 343433, accounts 111111 and 222222 would have to be examined first. This is like using the fast-forward button on a tape recorder to find a certain song.

If a new record with account number 555555 is to be added to this file, it would have to be inserted between records 444444 and 888888. Since the records are physically in order on the storage device, there is no room to insert this record. Therefore, the whole data file must be rewritten with record 555555 inserted in the proper place. Figure 6.4 shows the sequential file of checking accounts before and after a new account is added. Note that after the update the file is longer and the records have been moved.

Because all preceding records must be examined before the desired record can be located, sequential processing is most appropriately used when the file has high activity. That is, sequential file structure is most efficient when a large portion of the file is to be processed.

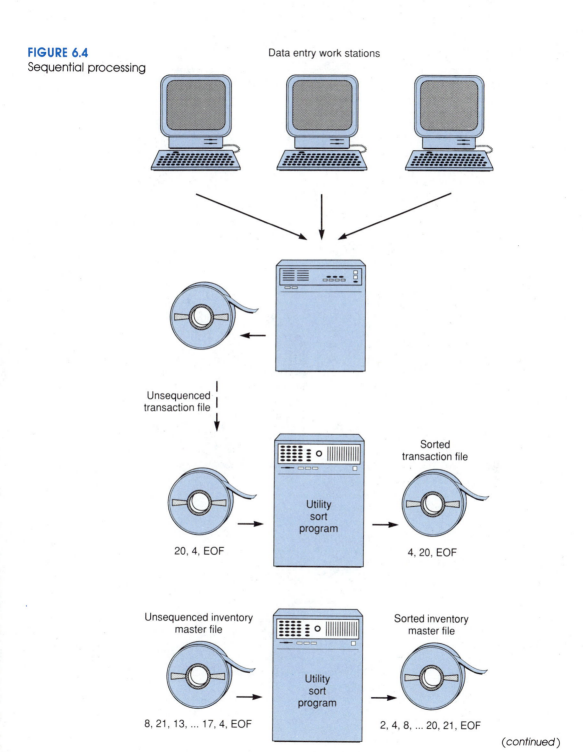

FIGURE 6.4
Sequential processing

Data entry work stations

Unsequenced transaction file

Sorted transaction file

Utility sort program

20, 4, EOF

4, 20, EOF

Unsequenced inventory master file

Sorted inventory master file

Utility sort program

8, 21, 13, ... 17, 4, EOF

2, 4, 8, ... 20, 21, EOF

(*continued*)

FIGURE 6.4 *(continued)*

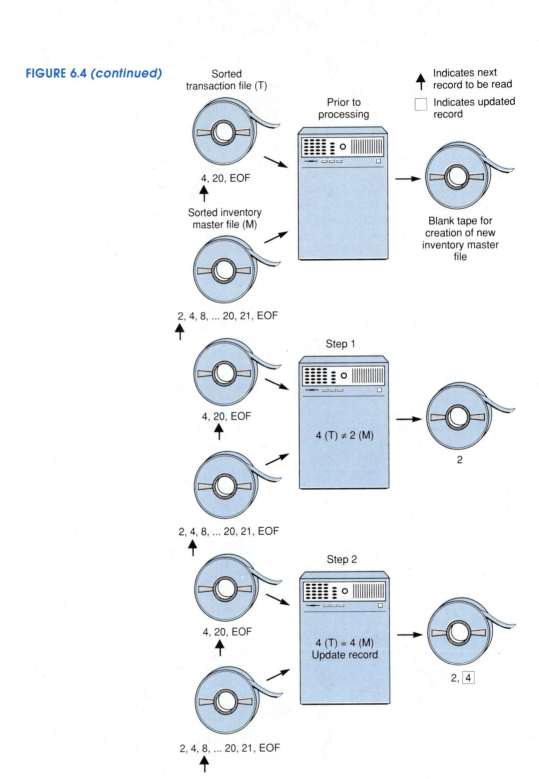

Sorted
transaction file (T)

4, 20, EOF

Sorted inventory
master file (M)

2, 4, 8, ... 20, 21, EOF

Prior to
processing

Indicates next
record to be read

Indicates updated
record

Blank tape for
creation of new
inventory master
file

Step 1

4, 20, EOF

4 (T) ≠ 2 (M)

2, 4, 8, ... 20, 21, EOF

2

Step 2

4, 20, EOF

4 (T) = 4 (M)
Update record

2, 4, 8, ... 20, 21, EOF

2, 4

FIGURE 6.4 (continued)

Indicates next record to be read

Indicates updated record

Step 3

4, 20, EOF

2, 4, 8, ... 20, 21, EOF

20 (T) ≠ 8 (M)

2, 4, 8

Step 4

2, 4, 8, ... 20, 21, EOF

4, 20, EOF

20 (T) = 20 (M)
Update record

2, 4, 8, ... 20

2, 4, 8, ... 20, 21, EOF

Backup

Step 5

4, 20, EOF

New Master
File

EOF (T)
EOF (M)

2, 4, 8, ... 20, 21, EOF

2, 4, 8, ... 20, 21, EOF

Using Sequential Files

Using a sequential file includes four different types of activities:

1. Adding new records or file population
2. Updating the contents of specific data items in the records
3. Deleting obsolete records
4. Generating reports from the file

Three files are involved in the process of adding new records or updating the contents of existing ones: the old master file, the transaction file, and the new master file. The transactions, after they are batched together, make up the transaction file. This file is then sorted according to the record key to facilitate processing. The file being updated is called the old master file. The file which results from the updating process is called the new master file.

The process of updating the master file is one of taking the data in the transaction file and combining it with the data in the master file. For example, the customer master file for a bank credit card would be updated by adding the amount of new charges to the current balance data item and subtracting the amount paid. In this way, the entire master file is updated, one record at a time. This updating occurs in the following way. The record key of the first record in the transaction file is compared with the key for the first record in the master file. If they match, the data from that transaction record is combined with the data from the master record and a new master record for that account is stored. If they do not match, the next master record is read, and so on. At the end of the file processing activity, three files exist: the old master file, the transaction file, and the new master file. The existence of all these files provides built-in file backup. If something happens to the most recent master file, it can be recreated by reprocessing the old master and transaction files. The steps involved in batch processing are summarized in Figure 6.5.

In sequential processing, the more records that are processed, the lower the cost per transaction since many transactions are processed at one time.

FIGURE 6.5
Steps in batch processing

1. Collect the transactions to form the batch.
2. Sort the transactions on the same key and in the same order as the master file being updated, creating the transaction file.
3. Match the transaction file to the master file.
4. Copy non-matched records directly to the new master file, then update and write the matched records.
5. Continue processing until all records in the transaction file have been read and processed and all non-matched records from the master file have been recorded on the new master file.

The cost of creating the new master file is the largest component of sequential processing costs. However, the time required to locate a specific record is very long and is usually unacceptable. For example, if one wanted to know the current balance of a specific checking account, the checking account file would have to be read record by record until the account is located.

Advantages and Disadvantages of Sequential Files
Historically, arranging files sequentially was the first method of organizing files. The first media employed — punched cards and magnetic tape — are both sequential storage media. It remains an appropriate file structure for certain circumstances. Like any method of organization, however, it has advantages and disadvantages.

Advantages A sequential file can be stored using any type of secondary storage, thereby creating flexibility in the selection of secondary storage devices. Since most sequential files are stored on magnetic tape, an inexpensive storage medium, sequential files can be less costly than other options. In addition, the cost of updating a transaction is low when the activity rate is high, thus lowering the overall cost of processing.

Sequential files also have the advantage of built-in backup because of the way the files are processed. If the old master file and transaction file are saved, the current master file can be recreated if necessary.

Disadvantages The main disadvantage of sequential files is that it is both difficult and costly to process a single record or just a small percentage of the records in the file. To locate a single record, the preceding part of the file must be read. To update a record, a complete new master file must be created. This is a very costly process, since updating a file requires that a new file be completely rewritten. As a result, there is usually a delay between a transaction and the incorporation of that transaction data into the master file.

In addition, a sequential file can only be organized according to a single key. For example, a student file can be organized by student identification number or student name but not both. This allows for efficient processing according to the data chosen as the key, but inefficient processing with regard to any non-key data.

Direct Files

Direct File Concepts
A **direct file** is one in which records can be accessed directly by use of the record key. A direct file is also called a *random file*. Direct files are used when there is a need for fast access to individual records. For example, an airline reservation system needs to provide fast access to records based on flight

source and destination and passengers on a specific flight. A person requesting information about specific flights from Boston to San Francisco does not
want to wait a long time to learn about flight and fare availability. The secondary storage device is on-line, or directly connected to the computer.

In contrast with those in sequential files, records in direct files can be located without examining any preceding ones. A direct file must be stored on
a direct-access storage device so that each record in the file will have a unique
address. The most common *direct-access storage devices* are floppy disks, hard
disks, and optical disks. System software is employed to place each record on
the disk so that it can be rapidly retrieved according to its key. The key is used
to determine a unique location (and accompanying address) for each record.

A direct file can be created in one of two ways. The first method is called
hashing. This process inserts the key into a mathematical function, the result
of which is a number representing the record's physical address. Hashing results in very fast access. However, only one key can be used for this type of
direct access. An alternative method is called *indexed* or *table look-up*. Often
files based on this method are called *indexed files*. A table is created which contains each record key and the accompanying physical address for each record.
The table is then searched to find the physical location of a record. Searching
the table based on key can be accomplished fairly rapidly. Once the record's address is determined it can then be retrieved. In contrast with sequential files,
direct files may have more than one key. When this is desired, multiple tables
are created, one for each type of key. The key used the most is called a **primary
key** and the others are referred to as **secondary keys**. Accessing a record according to the primary key generally involves the hashing method, while the
secondary keys involve the use of a table look-up.

Using Direct Files

In a direct file, once the record's key is known, its physical location can be rapidly determined and the record immediately retrieved. If a checking account
file is organized as a direct file, the user can rapidly retrieve an account by entering the account number, the primary key. In addition, one can designate the
customer's social security number as a secondary key and retrieve records that
way as well. Therefore, a checking account record could be retrieved if either
the account number or social security number were known.

There are several significant differences between direct files and sequential files. When a record in a direct file is updated, the new data simply replaces
the old. Unlike sequential files, the master file does not need to be copied when
additions and modifications are made to it. However, this means that there is
no built-in backup. Also, since the retrieval of records is based on the physical address provided by the key, records are not stored in any particular order.
Therefore, there is no advantage to processing several records at one time as
there is with sequential files. The cost of retrieving or updating a record is always the same. As a result, direct files are most appropriately used when only

single records need to be accessed. These would be circumstances of low activity, such as responding to individual customer inquiries.

Advantages and Disadvantages of Direct Files

Direct files became possible with the advent of direct-access storage devices, namely magnetic disk. This file organization is most useful when direct access to records is needed. It too has advantages and disadvantages.

Advantages The main advantage of using direct files is that a specific record can be accessed quickly at an acceptable cost. This means that a single record can be updated as soon as a transaction occurs; there is no cost savings in waiting to process several transactions at once. In addition, since a record can be updated or inserted directly, there is no need to rewrite the entire file when records are changed, added, or deleted.

Disadvantages The disadvantages of direct files arise in situations of high activity — that is, when most of the file is to be processed. Updating a large number of records is more expensive with direct processing than with sequential processing because the cost per transaction does not decrease with increased volume: there is a uniform cost per transaction. There is also no built-in backup of files since updates are done in place. As a result, backup procedures must be developed. Users of large systems must be encouraged to create their own backups periodically because most automatic system backups are only performed once a day. In the PC environment, there are generally no automatic backups, except in the case of some software packages which have this feature built in. An example is Word Perfect, which does automatic, periodic backups of the file being edited. Finally, direct files permit less flexibility in the choice of secondary storage device than sequential files because a direct file must be stored on disk.

Indexed Sequential Files

Indexed Sequential File Concepts

There are many circumstances in business when a user would want to have the capability of both direct and sequential access to files. An example would be the checking account file. At the end of the month when statements are prepared, the activity would be high because all records in the file would be processed. This type of processing would lend itself to the use of sequential files. However, during the month, the bank would like to have the capability of responding to customer inquiries by accessing an account directly. This situation of low activity would lend itself to the use of direct files. Indexed sequential files were developed to respond to both situations. An **indexed sequential file** is one in which records can be accessed either sequentially or directly.

The records in this type of file are stored sequentially by record key. In addition, an index table like the one described in the discussion of direct files is also created. This index is used to indicate the physical location of each record or of selected records. For example, the index table will have the location of the first record whose last name begins with "A," with "B," and so on down the alphabet. The records themselves are stored sequentially. There are two components of these files: the index table and the sequential data file. Indexed sequential files are also referred to as **I**ndexed **S**equential **A**ccess **M**ethod (**ISAM**) files or are named after a specific vendor's version of the file, such as IBM's VSAM (**V**irtual **S**equential **A**ccess **M**ethod) file.

Using Indexed Sequential Files

When records are to be processed sequentially, the method is the same as it is for sequential files. That is, a transaction file is created and used to update the master file. In the course of doing so, a new master file is created and the transaction and old master files are saved for backup. In this case, only the data file is used; the indexes are ignored. To access a record directly, the record key is used to search the index table to determine the record's address. If the direct-access capability is to be used, indexed files must be stored on a disk. As with direct files, there is no built-in backup when these records are processed individually. Adding new data to the file requires updating both the data file and the indexes. Therefore, updating an indexed sequential file is more complicated and time-consuming than updating either a direct or a sequential file.

Advantages and Disadvantages of Indexed Sequential Files

Indexed sequential files provide the user with a range of file processing options. Because they combine the capabilities of both direct and sequential methods, indexed sequential files are the most common type of files used in business. Like the other file types, however, indexed sequential files have their advantages and disadvantages.

Advantages   The major advantage of indexed sequential files is that they allow records to be processed either sequentially or directly. Both types of access can be accomplished at reasonable costs with an acceptable response time. Sequential processing can be used for applications with high activity, while direct processing can be used for those with low activity. In addition, multiple keys are available for direct access to records. These can be added gradually as an organization's need for the data changes. As a result, this file structure provides the greatest flexibility.

Disadvantages   The key disadvantages of indexed sequential files are increased overhead, greater complexity, and less efficiency in processing records. Overhead occurs both in storage requirements and in response time, although the slight increase in response time is usually imperceptible to the user. While indexed sequential files provide more file processing options, they bring with them greater hardware and software overhead because of the added complexity of the file. More secondary storage is required because of the need to hold the index as well as the data file. This method is also less efficient for a single type of processing than either of the other two methods. A record is not accessed as quickly by its key as it would be in a direct file, because there are two steps involved. First, the index must be searched to find the address, then the file must be searched to find the desired record. For the sequential processing capability, the cost of creating and maintaining the file is higher than for a plain sequential file since the index table must be stored and maintained. As a result, it is more expensive to do direct access than with a direct file and more expensive to do sequential processing than with a sequential file. There is also a higher level of file complexity because of the need to create and maintain the index table.

In addition to these disadvantages, indexed sequential files also have disadvantages similar to those of direct files: there is no built-in backup; users must take care to verify that adequate backup procedures are employed; and only disks can be used as the secondary storage media.

Selection of File Processing Techniques

The selection of a file processing technique depends on several factors—namely, the storage media available, the characteristics of the file, and the way the file is to be processed. If magnetic tape is used, the only option is sequential processing. If magnetic disks are available, any one of the three file organizations is possible. File characteristics include the size of the file, the average number of records (occurrences), and the size of the average record. The characteristics of processing include:

- The desired response time for an answer to an inquiry;
- How often the data must be updated to provide an acceptable level of timeliness;
- Types of file processing operations (i.e., primarily update, primarily retrieval, or a combination);
- The activity of the file.

Since each file organization has its advantages and disadvantages, selection of the most appropriate file organization will result from a good understanding of how the data is to be used. A comparison of the techniques just described is given in Figure 6.6.

The Use of Files in Information Systems

Over the years, there have been different types of relationships between applications and data. Historically, the characteristics of the application have determined the method used to organize the data required to support it.

FIGURE 6.6

Comparison of file processing techniques

	Sequential	Direct	ISAM	Comparison
Cost per Transaction				
Low activity rate	High (H)	Medium (M)	Medium Plus (P)	H > P > M
High activity rate	Low (L)	Medium (M)	Low Plus (LP)	M > LP > L
Time for a Random Record	Long (L)	Fast (F)	Fast Plus (FP)	L > FP > F

Similarly, it was the growing sophistication of the applications required to support users that accounted for the progression from simple single-application data files to shared data files to integrated databases.

Single-Application Systems

When computer-based information processing was first introduced into organizations, the type of application usually implemented was a single-application system. A *single-application system* deals with only one application area, such as checking accounts or credit cards. In this setting, the software resource of an information system consists of a single application. These systems usually represent the automation of existing and well-defined manual activities. In such situations, manual procedures are converted into a collection of application-specific programs which perform all the activities of data storage and retrieval. The data is organized and stored in application-specific data files as well. This means that the data is arranged in such a way that it is only useful for that specific application. Therefore, every time a new application is required, new programs and data must be created.

Each system has its own programs and associated data. For example, the checking account application would include programs to set up new accounts, process transactions such as deposits and checks, and generate statements. This system would also have its own master file of customer checking accounts. The data items are defined within the programs using a traditional third-generation programming language such as COBOL. If the data file is changed, the program must be changed as well. This situation is called **data dependence**. The types of data file changes which could occur include the addition or deletion of a data item, or changing the item's characteristics such as type and length. For example, if the checking account system needs to accommodate a new type of checking account such as an interest-bearing checking account, new data items will need to be added to the customer file. These new items might be "interest paid to date" and "interest accrued since the last statement." Because of data dependence, all programs using this customer file would have to be changed as well.

In a single-application system, data is not shared among applications because the files are usually organized sequentially for batch processing.

Single-application systems are still in use today. For example, a personal computer may be employed for information processing and each application may use its own floppy disk files. In this approach, little thought is given to the relationship among applications. As a result, the application portfolio of an organization is not viewed as a whole, but rather is viewed on an application-by-application basis. Systems are evaluated in terms of their individual efficiency using a measure such as the cost of processing a single transaction. Consequently, there is little opportunity for synergy to develop among applications.

There are certain benefits of using the single-application approach to information processing. The scope of control is narrow; it is limited to a single organizational unit. Data protection is easy to achieve because the application is used by a single organizational unit which is also responsible for the data. Therefore, security procedures need only take into account a single system. Also, the programs are usually well defined and easy to maintain, so the data file design is tailored to be efficient for this particular use. For example, when the checking account system's customer file is changed, only the programs comprising this system are affected. Finally, the impact of a hardware or software failure can be less severe because it is localized to a single application.

However, the drawbacks of this approach tend to overshadow its benefits. As more organizational units implement single-application systems, a proliferation of redundant files results. **Redundancy** occurs when the same piece of data is stored in more than one file. For example, each system requiring customer data will create its own customer file and store its own data. For a bank, redundancy occurs when both the checking account and savings account applications have their own customer files. Both files will contain some of the same data items such as name, address, telephone number, and social security number. Further, since files are controlled by separate applications and organizations, no single application is concerned with or responsible for keeping all occurrences of the redundant data identically valued. For example, if a customer moves and only gives the bank the checking account number with the new address and telephone number, the customer may end up with current data in the checking account file and old data in the savings account file. The impact of such inconsistencies is felt when incorrect data appears in reports or when statements are mailed to the wrong address. This is an example of *asynchronous data*. Asynchronous data occurs when the same piece of data is stored redundantly and has different values.

Redundant data causes excessive storage costs, inconsistent reporting, and, perhaps, inappropriate management actions. For these reasons, an organization using this approach will eventually recognize the need for an alternative method of information processing.

Multiple-Application Systems

The shortcomings of the single-application approach served to diminish the usefulness of an organization's applications portfolio. To counter this, a new approach was developed that redefined the relationship between an application and its data. In the multiple-application system approach, data is designed to satisfy, as much as possible, the requirements of a collection of applications. A single data file stored on disk, not on tape, is available for use by many applications. Thus, the information system contains more than one application. For this approach to work, each application must have the same view of the data file. That is, the same data items must be used in the same order and be accessed according to the same keys.

The resulting data file represents a compromise. While it will serve the needs of all the applications, it is not necessarily the most efficient way to process an individual application. For example, the checking and savings account applications could use a single customer file as shown in Figure 6.7. The data items in this customer file represent the union of the customer-related data items needed by both applications. In creating this combined file, name inconsistencies (most of names of data items) had to be resolved. Suppose both of the customer files had a data item named "account number," one referring to the savings account number and the other to the checking account number. This is an example of a *homonym*, which is the term for an identical name given to two different pieces of data. These two data items would have to be

View 1: Customer File (Savings Account System)

Savings Account Number	Customer SSN	Customer Name	Customer Address	Customer Telephone Number	Account Type	Balance	Year-to-Date Interest

View 2: Customer File (Checking Account System)

Checking Account Number	Customer SSN	Customer Name	Customer Address	Customer Telephone Number	Account Type	Balance	Year-to-Date Interest

Consolidated View
Customer File

Customer SSN	Customer Name	Customer Address	Customer Telephone Number

Account File

Account Number	Customer SSN	Account Type	Year-to-Date Interest	Balance

FIGURE 6.7
Multiple views of customer file (integrated for savings and checking)

renamed to denote the type of account number: "Checking-acctno" might be used for the checking system and "Savings-acctno" for the savings system. This renaming, then, resulted in two new data items: "savings account number" and "checking account number."

The benefit of using this combined file is that both applications can have access to data that was not previously available. For example, during an inquiry about the checking account, the customer can also be provided with data about the status of the savings account. In addition, rules for a "free" checking account can be based on a minimum balance in a savings or checking account. Access to this file can be through either the primary key or the secondary keys.

The process of creating the data file, modifying it, and retrieving data from it is achieved by a collection of application programs. However, since data is still defined in the programs, data dependence still exists. In fact, its impact is greater than in single-application systems. In the multiple-application system environment, data file structure modifications can be requested from more than one application. Therefore, the number of modifications will be more numerous than in a single-application environment. In addition, more programs would be affected by a change in the data file. If the checking account application needs new data items in order to accommodate checking accounts that pay interest, programs in both the checking and savings account applications would have to be changed since both use the same customer file.

Data protection is provided by the computer's operating system. A program will have either access to the complete data file or no access at all. A program can update anything or nothing in a data file. As a consequence, the checking account application could inadvertently change a customer's address since it has the ability to update any of the data items in the customer file. This ability to change any data items makes the implementation of security and privacy procedures more difficult.

The multiple-application approach has many advantages over the single-application approach. Because of the ability to share files among applications, data redundancy is reduced. A related benefit is that fewer files exist, making their management and control easier. Also, there is less asynchronous data since there is less redundancy and inconsistency. Finally, there is improved data control from a corporate perspective since there are fewer distinct files to manage and control.

However, there are also many problems with the multiple-application approach. First is that of data dependence. A change in a file will necessitate a corresponding program change. With several applications consisting of many programs, each sharing a single file, the decision to change a file has the potential to affect many programs. The modification of all of these programs is quite costly and time-consuming.

Second, the process used to design a file to serve one application is simpler and less time-consuming than the process used for multiple applications. The process of achieving consensus requires give-and-take among the people in the organization. Sometimes people find it difficult to compromise. Also, the resulting compromise can lead to a design which is not very efficient. The need to compromise in order to create a file that allows all applications to work may lead to applications with poor performance.

Third, a file may be shared and used by several programs across many parts of the organizations. Because of the limited controls provided by the computer's operating system, there is the likelihood of an individual inadvertently changing data and ruining a data file. When this happens, each part of the organization with an application that uses that file is affected.

Because of these drawbacks and because of the increased availability of large-capacity secondary storage devices, an alternative to the multiple-application system approach exists in the form of databases. In addition, software to operate on databases is available, and today's computers possess sufficient primary memory speed to provide good performance with this software.

DATABASES

Database Concepts

The database approach is an alternative to the file management techniques described earlier in this chapter. It is a technique for the management and control of an organization's data resources. There are two aspects to this approach. One is the development of an integrated database. The other is the acquisition and use of system software that facilitates the use of data items in the database. This software is commonly called a database management system (DBMS).

A **database** is one or more files which are organized in an integrated, controlled, and standardized manner in order to serve more than one application. Because of the direct-access nature of a database, these files *must* be stored on disk, not on magnetic tape. A *corporate database* refers to all the databases which taken together satisfy the information requirements of the whole organization. In this case, all the data is defined in a standardized manner.

Standardization is the development of consistent names for all pieces of data, the identification of a list of synonyms and abbreviations for data, and the assignment of organizationally defined values for data items. To achieve this the organization may define rules for naming. For example, a bank could decide that all data items describing accounts would be named with the prefix "type of account-" followed by the data item name. Thus, the savings account would be named "savings account-number" and the checking account would be named "checking account-number."

Name standardization also ensures that all data of the same type is identified by the same data item and that a given data item actually holds the same type of data. That is, standardization must cope with synonyms and homonyms. *Synonyms* are different names given to the same piece of data; a homonym is the same name given to different pieces of data. An example of a synonym would be the name of the data item holding the customer's address. In the checking account file it may be called "customer address," while in the savings account file it may be called simply "address." In this situation, one is designated as the primary name and the other as a synonym. Synonyms may result from the integration process. For example, the bank's checking account system may refer to the key of the customer file as "Customer-number" and define it as a six-character field, while the savings account system may call it "Custno" and define it as a seven-character field. In the database describing customers, the key will be named "Customer-number" with a synonym of "Custno," and a consistent seven-character coding scheme will be developed. Similarly, name standardization would involve the identification of homonyms.

Finally, the possible values for each data item should be defined. For example, it could be determined that all values of the checking account data item would be six-digit numbers with the first digit denoting the number of the branch office in which the account was opened.

A database can be more complex than a file and describe more than one type of information. A sample database for a bank's retail operations is shown in Figure 6.8.

The database shown in Figure 6.8 supports the bank's retail banking activities and represents inherent facts about the bank's operations. For example, a customer may have several different types of accounts, such as a checking account, a savings account, and a credit card account. Also, a customer may have more than one account of a certain type, such as more than one checking account. The diagram representing the bank's database in Figure 6.8 is called an *entity relationship diagram*. (See highlight on the following page.) Such a diagram describes facts about the interrelationships between the components of the database. For example, at State University the facts may include: (1) a course is taken by many students; (2) a student may enroll

FIGURE 6.8
A bank's database as a data structure diagram

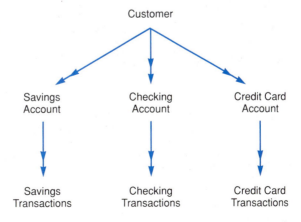

**Entity
Relationship
Highlight**

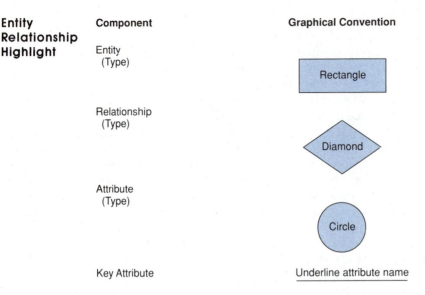

Component	Graphical Convention
Entity (Type)	Rectangle
Relationship (Type)	Diamond
Attribute (Type)	Circle
Key Attribute	Underline attribute name

Example: There are two related entities, Customer and Savings-Account. The Customer may potentially have many Savings-Accounts. This is denoted by the numbers on either side of the relationship – Has. This represents the cardinality of the relationship. The component attributes of Customer are Customer-Name and Social-Security-Number, plus others.

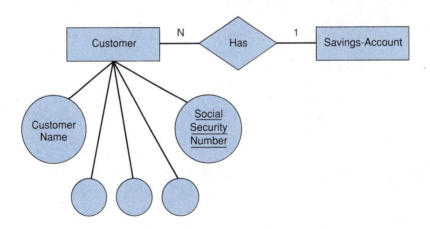

in many courses; and (3) an instructor teaches many courses. These facts describing mappings between records are shown in Figure 6.9.

There are three types of mappings: one-to-one, or 1:1; one-to-many, or 1:N; and many-to-many, or M:N. To form the record CUSTOMER, there is a one-to-one mapping between CUST-NO and SAVINGS-ACCT-NO, which means for a given CUST-NO there is only one or zero SAVINGS-ACCT-NO's and

FIGURE 6.9
Facts about the bank

1. A customer can have several accounts across many types.
2. A customer can have many checking accounts.
3. There can be many transactions for each account.

---

there is only one CUST-NO for a given SAVINGS-ACCT-NO. There is also a one-to-many mapping between SAVINGS-ACCOUNT and SAVINGS-ACCOUNT-TRANSACTIONS; a given SAVINGS-ACCOUNT has one or more SAVINGS-ACCOUNT-TRANSACTIONS and a given SAVINGS-ACCOUNT-TRANSACTION is related to only one SAVINGS-ACCOUNT. On the other hand, there is a many-to-many mapping between STUDENT and COURSE since a STUDENT can enroll in many COURSES and a given COURSE has many STUDENTS enrolled in it. A graphic depiction of the types of mappings is shown in Figure 6.10.

Database Philosophy

Before an organization can switch from the use of files to the use of a database, it must evaluate its current data management practices. The decision to employ a database is really two separate and independent decisions. One is the decision to integrate and control its data. This is often called *adopting a database philosophy*. It occurs when an organization makes a conscious decision to have a database instead of a collection of files which will be used by more than one system. The term database philosophy is used because a database is implemented as a result of organizational policies rather than the acquisition of software. The other decision relates to determining and acquiring the most appropriate database management system to access and manage the organization's data resources. A **database management system (DBMS)** is system software used to create, manipulate, manage, and protect databases. The status of an organization with respect to these two decisions will be one of four states:

1. Non-integrated data without a DBMS
2. Integrated data (database philosophy) without a DBMS
3. Non-integrated data with a DBMS
4. Integrated data with a DBMS

The first state is the same as a single-application system, in which each application uses and maintains its own files. The second state is equivalent to

1. One-to-One (1:1) Mapping

Owner   1   Member

Example:

Employee

Manages

Department

- An employee can manage only *one* department.
- A department can have only *one* manager.

2. One-to-Many (1:N) Mapping

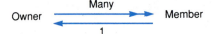

Owner   Many   Member

Example:

Department

Assigned

Employee

- A department has *many* employees assigned to it.
- An employee can be assigned to only one department.

3. Many-to-Many (M:N) Mapping

Owner   Many   Member

Example:

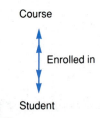

Course

Enrolled in

Student

- A course has *many* students enrolled in it.
- A student is enrolled in *many* courses.

FIGURE 6.10
Types of mappings

the multiple-application system but with more care and attention directed to maintaining data quality and control. The last two states deal with the acquisition of a database management system. The third state is a situation in which the DBMS is used without having integrated data. This is the way PC-based DBMSs such as dBASE IV and R:base are used by most end users. The fourth state contributes the greatest amount of data management. The data is integrated and controlled in the organization's database(s) and is manipulated via a DBMS. These four states are shown in Figure 6.11. Often, different parts of an organization will be in different states at the same time. An organization may even have examples of all four states. In this case, the organization must decide which is the preferred state for most of its data and should plan for migration and conversion to this desired state.

There are several costs associated with the adoption of a database philosophy. An organization can measure the costs of database development in terms of both direct labor costs and opportunity costs. Opportunity costs are the costs of dedicating resources to this endeavor rather than to other activities. First, a data inventory must be compiled. This process is begun by the identification of the organization's data resources, usually starting with computerized data. Considerable personnel time may need to be devoted to this activity. Second, if the organization has a standards development organization, its work is now expanded. If one doesn't exist, it may need to be formed. In addition, there now exists a need to develop organizational standards for data naming, data use, and data definition. A related issue is that the organization's system development practices may need to be changed. All of the tasks are labor-intensive. Third, comprehensive database design is more time-consuming than a less centralized approach to data management, because the resulting database must cope with naming problems such as synonyms and homonyms and the development of consistent data element values. These tasks are people- and labor-intensive. Finally, because of the effort required, it is sometimes difficult to get organizational consensus on important database issues.

The benefits of using a database are more difficult to measure in financial terms. Nevertheless, the benefits clearly outweigh the costs. First, redundancy is controlled. This will result in lower storage costs, less asynchronous (i.e., more consistent) data, and more consistent reporting. Second, a greater degree of data integrity is possible since the organization will be making a conscious effort to determine and document its criteria for data correctness. De-

FIGURE 6.11

Approaches to databases

	No DBMS	DBMS
Non-integrated Data	Single-application system	PC single-user systems
Integrated Data	Multiple-application system	Multiple-user DBMS

termining and documenting the rules for data correctness is an inherent part of the database approach. Third, organization-wide knowledge about the data resource is one of the objectives of a database approach. For this reason, databases facilitate better communication about data.

For an organization to manage a database and get the most out of its use, the database must be easy to use and maintain. This can be accomplished by a software package that is designed to facilitate its use. Such software exists in the form of database management systems.

DATABASE MANAGEMENT SYSTEMS

The software which makes up a database management system is available on all types of computers. In the case of some large computer configurations, the database management system may include hardware as well. Such a system is referred to as a *database machine* or *back-end*. Using a specialized computer for such database operations as access and manipulation relieves the main computer of those tasks and gives it more time for other activities. The role of a DBMS in an information system is depicted in Figure 6.12.

A database management system provides data access, manipulation, reporting, privacy/security, and backup capabilities. It augments the capabilities of the operating system by providing data security at the record or data item level instead of at the file level. Additional features provided by DBMSs differ among the commercially available packages depending upon the size of the computer on which it will be used. As discussed previously, the data to be processed by a DBMS may be in either a conventional file or a database format. Therefore, the use of a DBMS does not necessarily mean that the data is integrated, standardized, or controlled.

Multiple Views of Data

Earlier in this chapter, multiple views of data were described (Figure 6.3.) For database management systems, these levels have been formalized and additional levels are incorporated. This multiple view and leveled approach to data

FIGURE 6.12
Role of a DBMS in an information system

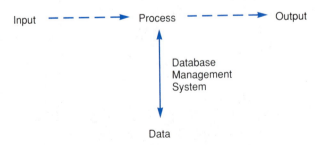

is called the **ANSI/SPARC Model** (since it was developed by the American National Standards Institute/Standards Planning And Requirements Committee). The terminology used in this model has been adopted for general use in describing the aspects of database management systems. This standard is depicted in Figure 6.13.

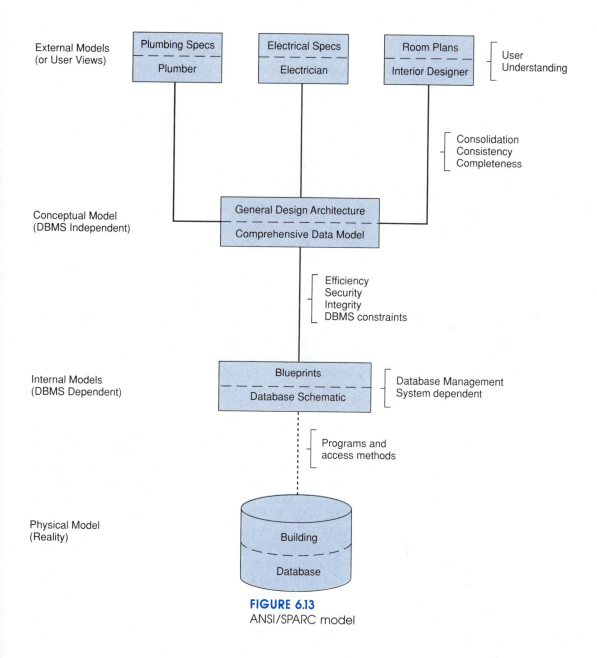

FIGURE 6.13
ANSI/SPARC model

As shown in this model, there are four different views present in a DBMS. The first is the **external view**, which is the user's view of the database. Second is the **conceptual view**, which refers to the total data environment. This view is independent of a given DBMS as well. The third view, the **internal view**, is the conceptual view constrained by a specific DBMS. It is also sometimes called the physical database structure. As such, the internal model is a representation of the conceptual view which can be processed via some specific DBMS. The translation of the conceptual view into the internal view is carried out by the DBMS according to the rules supplied by the database designer. Taken together, the conceptual and internal views of the database make up the **logical view**. The final view is the **physical view**. It depicts the actual storage of the data on the secondary storage device. These four views are also represented by their own data models, which are described later in this chapter.

The existence of multiple views of the data eliminates the need for users to be concerned with the physical aspects of data storage such as where the records are located, how the records are arranged, and how they will be accessed. In this way, the user is able to use the DBMS without being concerned with the physical details of data storage. Multiple levels also make changes at the lower levels *transparent* to the user. Thus, a user would not have to be concerned about the use of a new secondary storage device or the creation of a different blocking factor for the records in the database. The user could still expect that the DBMS would be able to operate on his or her database.

Since a DBMS provides data independence, the logical and physical views of data remain separate, thereby allowing for different user views to exist. There are two levels of **data independence**, physical and logical. *Physical data independence* exists when the physical or internal view can be changed without requiring a corresponding change in the conceptual view. When physical data independence exists, reprogramming is not necessary when changes occur in the internal and physical views. The major cost of database reorganization is in the reprogramming, not in the reformatting of the database and its repopulation. Most DBMSs provide physical data independence.

Logical data independence occurs when the conceptual view is changed and the external views are still valid. Logical data independence is very important to users since it protects them from any changes. Most DBMSs provide limited logical data independence. The DBMS decides the best way to store and access the data, and the user can concentrate on what to do with the data and how to logically organize it. The DBMS handles all transformations required to bridge the gaps between the external and physical views of data.

All mainframe and some PC database management systems provide for multiple individual views (or external views) of the database. Each of these views is consistent with the complete database, which is called the **schema**. Each external view is called a **subschema**, or simply *view*. A subschema may be a subset of the schema or comprise the complete schema. Figure 6.14 depicts multiple external views of a bank's database. (The notation used in this figure is called an entity relationship diagram.)

FIGURE 6.14
Multiple external views

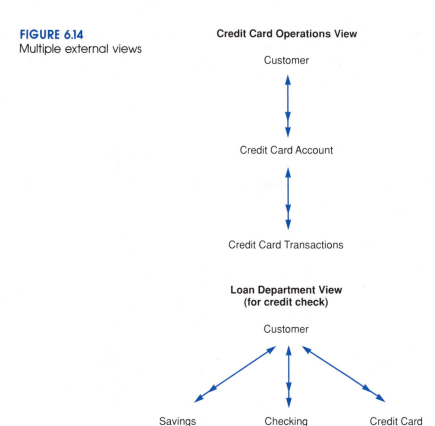

Credit Card Operations View

Customer

Credit Card Account

Credit Card Transactions

**Loan Department View
(for credit check)**

Customer

Savings Account   Checking Account   Credit Card Account

The external view of data focuses the user's attention on the characteristics of data rather than how it is stored or accessed. Because each user knows only about the data defined in his or her external view, increased data security is provided. In addition, it is easier to gain organizational consensus when each group can have its own view as long as it is consistent with the global, conceptual one. These local views are the users' personal views of the data and facilitate their ability to understand and use the database and DBMS.

Database Management Systems in Detail

Features of a DBMS

The capabilities of a database management system are related to the type of computer to be used and the number of different users to be supported. Many of the PC-based DBMSs are intended to be used by a single user and have less functionality than those designed for multiple users on a mainframe computer. The general capabilities of DBMSs are described in this section, followed by a consideration of the characteristics specific to PC-based DBMSs.

Data Definition One task a database management system must accomplish is describing the contents of the database. This is referred to as **data definition**. It must also provide the user with the means for creating and changing these data definitions. A language which facilitates this activity is

FIGURE 6.15

External view for Savings Account System is identical to the conceptual view.

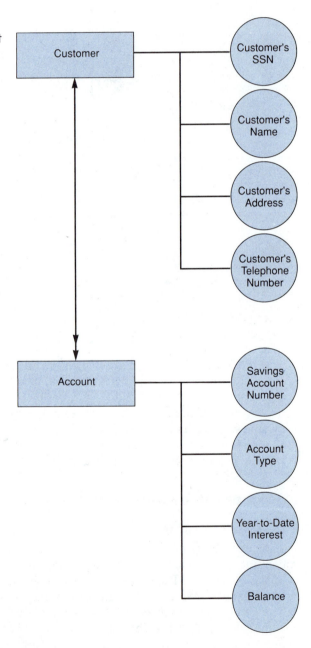

referred to as a **data definition language** or **data description language** (DDL). The DDL is used to describe the way the data is stored in the database. In microcomputer-based DBMSs, data definitions are usually provided through a series of menus. In mainframe systems, there is a structured language for defining the database.

The data is defined from two different levels (see Figure 6.13). First, there is the view of the complete database, called the conceptual view. Second is the individual user's view, called the external view. An external view must be consistent with the conceptual view. A conceptual view and external view for a bank are shown in Figure 6.15.

In addition to describing the content of the database, it is also necessary to define the semantics and integrity constraints on the data. *Integrity constraints* are a formal definition of when data is correct. These aid in ensuring a high quality of data in the database. When data is added to the database or modified, its compliance to these constraints is evaluated and all data that does not conform to them is rejected by the DBMS. In its simplest form an integrity check would give a data item a type (such as numeric) and a length (such as seven characters). Example constraints in a bank customer database are the definition that Checking-acctno is a numeric data item eight characters long, the value for this data item is unique and is different from all Savings-acctno's, and the first two digits denote the branch in which the account was opened. An example definition of the Checking-account in the DDL of a mainframe-oriented DBMS is shown in Figure 6.16.

Data Manipulation   Since data in a DBMS is independent of any particular computer program, traditional programming language statements cannot be used to access and store data in the database. Instead, a data manipulation language is used. A **data manipulation language (DML)** is a component of a DBMS which provides the capabilities for locating, retrieving, storing, and reporting the data in the database. It provides a simple means for allowing users to specify the data of interest, then it locates, retrieves, and presents that data. In addition, the DBMS facilitates the data entry process by providing a method for prompting the user for data entry.

There are two types of data manipulation languages. One type, called **host language DML**, is used by professional programmers and consists of

FIGURE 6.16

Checking account defined as a record in a CODASYL data definition language

```
RECORD NAME IS CHECKING-ACCT
    LOCATION MODE IS CALC USING ACCT-NO
    WITHIN SC-ACCT AREA

1    ACCT-NO; PICTURE X(9).
1    ACCT-BAL; TYPE DECIMAL 10,2.
1    YTD-INT; TYPE DECIMAL 6,2.
1    ACCT-TYPE; PICTURE X(2).
```

statements used to augment an existing programming language like COBOL, FORTRAN, or PL/1. In fact, the first DBMSs were developed to extend the data manipulation capabilities of COBOL. Thus, all data manipulation was accomplished by adding new statements to COBOL. In this setting, the DML is used to find or store the data in the database. Changes to the data and calculations are accomplished through statements in the programming language. This type of DML often employs a step-by-step approach to accomplishing activities. Some examples are as follows:

FIND – to locate a record in a database

GET – to transfer the data into the program

STORE – to add a new record to the database

MODIFY – to change the data values in an existing record

In addition, there are commands which enable the programmer to create the structure of the database, to define transactions to be accomplished, and to aid in data protection. An example of a DML is given in Figure 6.17.

The other type of data manipulation language is commonly called a **query language** and is intended for end users. A query language is a separate, self-contained language which provides retrieval, modification, and presentation capabilities. It can be used to define the contents of a database, enter the data, and modify its contents in addition to providing the traditional retrieval and reporting capabilities. It is either in English-like or menu-driven form so it can easily be used by the novice.

FIGURE 6.17

CODASYL DML for finding all checking accounts for customer with social security number = 123456789

```
/* Find the desired CUSTOMER record*/
MOVE '123456789' TO SSN IN CUSTOMER
FIND ANY CUSTOMER USING SSN
GET CUSTOMER
IF ERROR-STATUS = 0 THEN FOUND CUSTOMER
     ELSE ...Error Routine
Display or Print desired CUSTOMER data
FOUND CUSTOMER


/*Find the Checking Account for this Customer*/
FIND FIRST CHECKING-ACCT WITHIN HAS-CACCT.
IF ERROR-STATUS = 0 THEN NEXT SENTENCE
     ELSE ...print message "no checking account"
DO WHILE DB-STATUS = 0
     GET CHECKING-ACCT
     [process to display desired information]
     FIND NEXT CHECKING-ACCT WITHIN HAS-CACCT.
END-DO
```

In 1986, the American National Standards Institute (ANSI) accepted **SQL** (pronounced "sequel") as the national **standard query language** for relational databases. SQL is a comprehensive database language; it has statements for data definition, query, and update. Hence, it is both a DDL and a DML. Many DBMSs have adopted this standard, although many have not fully implemented all aspects. ORACLE supports a full implementation, whereas R:base has a partial implementation and is considered SQL-like. The number of DBMSs fully implementing the SQL standard is continually increasing. This provides portability for database applications from one SQL to another.

Many DBMSs offer more than one mode of interaction with the database. For example, dBASE has an ASSIST mode which is menu-oriented and a command mode which allows the user to issue commands by typing them in directly. The ASSIST mode provides the user with a menu of commands from which to choose. Most but not all of the dBASE commands are available in this mode. Some DBMSs have a host-language interface, in order to provide the ability to define procedures, as well as the self-contained (query) language. In this way, a single database can be used by both programmers and end users because they are using different data manipulation facilities developed specifically for their type of use. To enhance the capabilities of those without the host-language interface, the query language has the facility to define procedures. Procedures may be defined in a separate application development facility (such as in ORACLE) or in a "programming language" (such as the programming language used in dBASE).

Data Protection Features A DBMS provides data protection features beyond those provided by the operating system of the computer. Since many people working in different departments in an organization may use the same database, they will be adversely impacted if the database is damaged or destroyed. The data protection features are intended to prevent or minimize database destruction and misuse.

One feature limits the ability of a user to access and change data to that which is defined in his or her view. This facilitates privacy by restricting access to those with a legitimate need to know. In this way, users only know about the existence of the data in their own view and do not know about data to which they do not have access. Other types of controls include requiring passwords for access to certain views, and requiring a different password for updating the data.

The data protection methods described so far are intended to prevent unauthorized access to data. However, additional controls are needed in the event that unauthorized access does occur. *Encryption* is used to prevent an unauthorized user from using or damaging the data. Encryption is a technique for coding data so that the stored data is meaningless unless it is decoded. To decode the data, the user needs to know the coding/decoding algorithm and a key value used in this algorithm. Data encryption has been used by the military as the means of ensuring that an intercepted message will not be understood by the enemy. Many DBMSs, including PC-based DBMSs, provide the feature of optional data encryption.

When multiple users can access and update the same database concurrently, controls must be in place to maintain data accuracy. Consider a client who is withdrawing cash at the same time that someone at the bank is transferring money into that customer's account. The resulting balance should reflect both transactions: the amount debited with the withdrawal and the amount added by the transfer. Without proper **concurrency control**, the balance may only reflect one of these transactions.

If the database is destroyed or put into an inoperative state, it needs to be made operational as soon as possible. The DBMS provides backup features to facilitate this task and to allow the organization to recover in an orderly and predictable manner. Backup facilities include the ability to periodically copy the database, the ability to log all update transactions (called *journaling*), and the utilities that bring the database back into a usable state, called a **restart/recovery** feature.

Report Writer A DBMS includes a facility that simplifies and expedites the presentation of the data from the database. This is called a **report writer**. Many DBMSs provide the capability of presenting data in graphic as well as tabular form. The report writer will allow users to define headings for the whole report or for specific portions of it. The reporting facilities can be an extension of the DML. These would include a collection of predefined reports and a simple manner for developing user-specific reports. An example report is shown in the Wooden Wonders case (see Figure 6.31).

Data Dictionaries A large organization will have a considerable amount of data stored in traditional files or in databases. If databases are used, an organization will want to control data redundancy. In order to do this, the organization needs to know what data it has; it needs to have an inventory of its data. This data inventory will describe the data in terms of data item names, synonyms for that data item, the kind of data stored in that data item, its location, applications which use it, and the organizational unit responsible for it. This data about data is called *meta-data*. The collection of all the organization's meta-data is compiled in a **data dictionary (DD)**. To facilitate access and maintenance, this data dictionary is stored in computer-readable form. In fact, a computerized data dictionary is actually another kind of database. A software system that operates on a data dictionary is called a **data dictionary system (DDS)** (see Figure 6.18).

A data dictionary system performs many functions. However, there is some variation in the features available in the different commercial products. The DDS provides many of the same features for the data dictionary that a DBMS provides for a database. These include security features governing access to the data dictionary; a report generator with a collection of standard reports; the ability to generate the data definition language of specific DBMSs;

FIGURE 6.18

The relationship between
DDSs and DBMSs

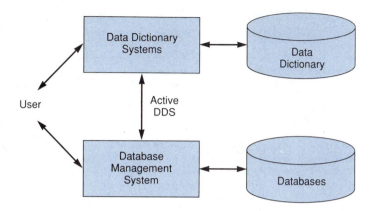

and utilities which facilitate building the data dictionary. The most frequently used features are those which produce reports and those which facilitate the production of the data definition language. Since the data definition language may be cumbersome to use, alternatives to preparing the DDL can improve productivity.

There are two types of data dictionary systems: passive and active. The first DDSs were passive and distinctly separate from a DBMS. A *passive data dictionary* may provide reports that are then used as input to a DBMS. One report contains the database definition expressed in a data definition language. These DDSs can be used to generate reports containing data definition language for more than one DBMS. The data definitions defined in the DDS and DBMS may not be consistent, since the analyst must manually maintain the data definitions which are stored in two different places. DataManager and UCC10 are examples of passive DDSs.

To eliminate this two-stage approach to data definition, the active data dictionary alternative was developed. An *active data dictionary* is an inherent part of the DBMS. The same data definition is used for both data dictionary functions and by the DBMS for executing applications. In this case, the easiest-to-use data entry facilities of the DDS can be employed instead of those of the more cumbersome DDL. While running an application, the user can inquire about the database. For example, the user can ask the questions about the contents of the database, such as "What are the data items which describe Customer?"

In addition to facilitating the use of a DBMS, the data dictionary system provides other benefits to an organization. It provides the ability to determine the impact of a data change on programs which use that data. A DDS can also facilitate system development by providing some of the documentation required by the process. This documentation facilitates communication between users, analysts, and designers and provides a location for the storage and a means of retrieval and maintenance of the information collected about data during system development.

Mainframe-based Versus PC-based DBMSs

A DBMS on a personal computer — often called a *PC-DBMS* — has most of the features of its mainframe counterparts. The features which are not present can be attributed to the fact that most PCs have a single user, to the characteristics of PC-based operating systems, and to the historical simplicity of end-user applications. However, the capabilities of the PC-based products are continually being enlarged and are beginning to deal with multiple-user-oriented features.

The PC-DBMSs usually, but do not always, include the following features:

- A data definition facility for the data definition and retrieval functions.
- A report writer for specifying customized printed reports and a collection of standard functions for statistical and financial analysis. These might include functions such as average, standard deviation, mortgage payment, and internal rate of return.
- A programming language for building command files, user interfaces to applications, and custom reporting beyond the capability of the report writer. These features would include control logic such as IF-THEN-ELSE, subroutine calls, and other functions.
- A menu-driven front end that uses menus to prompt the user in carrying out the commands associated with data definition, retrieval, and modification.
- A query language for data retrieval which may be augmented by a natural-language processor.

Despite these features, PC-DBMSs differ from those on mainframes in several other respects. First, they do not provide comprehensive restart and recovery support, data protection procedures, and concurrency control. Second, PC-DBMSs use a single data model, the relational model, to structure the data (although PC-Focus supports multiple-data models). Third, many PC-DBMSs do not have the ability to define multiple external views; the external view and the conceptual view are one and the same. In dBASE III, for example, the database has only one definition or view, although multiple views do exist in dBASE III Plus and IV. The user's view is therefore both the conceptual and the external view. However, the emergence of external views as a PC-DBMS feature is evidenced in products such as ORACLE. Fourth, backup is considerably different. In a PC-DBMS package, it would refer to the occasional backup copy made. For example, dBASE III Plus does not log transactions (i.e., database change commands), or maintain an audit trail, but it does automatically create an occasional backup copy. If a user inadvertently creates a database file with a name which already exists, the original file is destroyed by the DBMS and can only be restored if the user has maintained a personal backup copy. For these reasons, the trend is toward including more of the security and recovery features of the mainframe DBMS in PC versions. Both

R:base and ORACLE have some of these facilities. Finally, the maximum size of the database that the PC-DBMS can effectively process is also much smaller than that on a mainframe DBMS. As with their mainframe counterparts, the relational DBMSs attempt to support the SQL standard used as the basis for the data manipulation language.

PC/DBMS Approaches

There are four different approaches to using database management systems on personal computers. These approaches differ with respect to the number of users, the type of equipment involved, and the intended use of the DBMS.

Single-User Approach A DBMS intended for a single user on a stand-alone personal computer is the most common PC-DBMS environment. Each user's database is considered personal. Because of this, data redundancy and inconsistency between user's databases are quite common. Example products are Paradox and dBASE III.

Multi-User Approach In this environment, individual computers share a common database. This is accomplished by the use of communication technology, usually a local area network. The database in stored on a common hard disk. There is usually little concurrency control and few data protection features. As with the single-user approach, PC databases are kept separate from the mainframe databases. Paradox does include strong multi-user capabilities. Another example product is dBASE III Plus Network Administrator.

Linked Mainframe/PC Approach With this approach, the same DBMS is used on both PCs and the mainframe computer. This provides a means of sharing data or databases between these two computing environments. The communication link is usually included in the PC version of the DBMS. Users familiar with one version can easily and quickly use the other. The PC version can be used for inquiring purposes while the mainframe concentrates on transaction processing activities. ORACLE, Focus, and Cullinet Personal Computer Software are examples of DBMSs used for this approach.

Multifunction Approach Some PC-DBMS packages provide integrated, multifunction capabilities. In addition to a DBMS, they might provide spreadsheet, graphics, and word processing capability. Symphony, Framework, and ENABLE are examples of such products.

PC-DBMSs extend the potential capabilities and sophistication of end-user applications. These products can greatly aid organizations in solving their data management problems. However, accompanying this increased power is increased organizational risk. End users must be adequately trained in the use of these packages and in ways of designing sound databases. In addition, procedures need to be developed for proper backup and recovery practices and appropriate data security measures. Finally, management procedures need to be established governing such activities as naming conventions and the maintenance of a consistent organization-wide view of data.

Benefits and Costs of a DBMS

Benefits

The features of a database management system provide several benefits to both the end user and the personnel on the MIS staff. First, by providing data independence, a DBMS allows information systems personnel to properly address technical issues and minimize the impact of changes on users. Second, the ability to define and maintain multiple external (user) views enables users to maintain their own individual views that are easy to understand. This makes it easier to achieve organization-wide consensus on the global view of the database (e.g., conceptual model). As a result, the MIS staff's task of controlling and standardizing data is made easier. Third, a DBMS augments the capabilities of the operating systems by providing better security, privacy, and backup. This maximizes the likelihood that the database will be available to the entire user community. Fourth, the requirement of a conceptual model of the database ensures that a global view of the data will exist in the organization. A global/organization-wide view of the data enhances the potential benefit to upper-level managers and increases their potential use of the database. It also improves communication among users and between users, MIS, and technical personnel. Fifth, the amount of time required for application development can be shortened, although there will be some initial loss in productivity while personnel are becoming proficient at using these new tools. Finally, most DBMSs include a query language which facilitates the use of the DBMS and database by the nontechnical user.

Costs

To achieve the benefits of database use, the organization must be willing to pay certain costs. First, the database management system software must be purchased. The costs vary depending on the hardware environment. DBMSs for PCs cost several hundred dollars. Mainframe systems cost several thousand dollars per month on a perpetual lease or more than a hundred thousand dollars to purchase. In some cases, a monthly maintenance fee must also be paid.

The second cost is that of converting existing files into databases. Both computer and personnel resources are required since the programs that operated correctly in the file environment will have to be changed to operate on the database. The third cost is associated with learning. Both users and programmers must receive training, and the programmers will be less productive while this is occurring. Fourth, hardware changes are often required in order to operate the DBMS effectively. The changes to the computer system may include increased primary memory, enlarged secondary storage, and improved input/output and communication capacity. Fifth, DBMSs bring an increase in operating system overhead because data is now accessed through the DBMS in addition to the operating system and programming languages. Finally, new personnel may need to be hired. Both technical expertise and knowledge of control and data management will be required if a database is to be used effectively. Data and database administration functions are discussed in more detail later in this chapter and again in Chapter 10.

Data Models

Database management systems are classified according to ways in which the elements of the database can be represented. A **data model** defines these rules for linking the data items together. There are three different types of data models: hierarchical, network, and relational. These models differ with respect to the underlying rules used in the data definition language of the database management system. Some DBMSs require the same data model to be used for both the conceptual and external views, while others allow more flexibility. Most of the data models have their own vocabulary. The vocabularies of the various data models are shown in Figure 6.19.

Hierarchical Model

The **hierarchical model** is the oldest of the three data models. In this model the data items are linked in similar fashion to the branches of a tree. An example of arranging the data at Last National Bank according to the hierarchical rules is shown in Figure 6.20.

The hierarchical data model has an inherent genealogy which naturally organizes the data through levels. The top of the hierarchy is called the "root." Any data items or records at the same level are "siblings." If the two are at different adjacent levels, one is the "parent" and the other is the "child." At a bank, Savings Account, Checking Account, and Credit Card Account are sibling record types since they have a common parent, Customer.

FIGURE 6.19
Vocabulary used in data models

Data Model	Data Item	Record Type	Relationship Occurrence
Hierarchical (IMS)	*Field*	*Segment*	No term
Network (IDMS)	*Item*	*Record*	*Set*
Relational (SQL)	*Attribute*	*Relation, N-tuple*	No term

FIGURE 6.20

Bank's database as a hierarchy

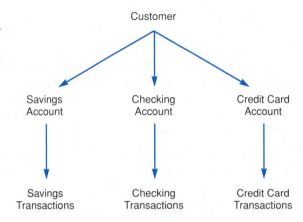

The hierarchical model has many rules. The parent-child relationship is a one-to-many relationship because one parent can have many children but a child can have only one parent. This is true at both the type and instance level. For example, a Customer has many different types of Accounts, but all the Accounts have only one parent, Customer. Further, a given Customer such as Mary Smith can have more than one savings account, but that savings account belongs to only one Customer, Mary Smith. Since some users' structures do not naturally conform to a hierarchy, redundancy and multiple hierarchies must be introduced to represent these structures. Consider the relationship between the two records Student and Course. A Student is enrolled in many Courses and a given Course has many Students. Therefore, two different hierarchies must be established to show these relationships. Because the records of concern and the relationships among them are explicitly defined, no name is given to the relationship that exists. Consequently, it is difficult to represent two relationships between the same two record types such as relationships ENROLLED-IN and HAS-TAKEN between the records Student and Courses.

The major database management system based on the hierarchical model is International Business Machine's IMS, which was initially released in the late 1960s. Several versions of IMS have evolved to respond to more powerful hardware and the increasing sophistication of operating systems. IMS is no longer undergoing further development because IBM is concentrating its efforts on its mainframe relational system, called DB2.

The hierarchical model provides for a well-organized database and an efficient DBMS. Because it is most appropriate for well-structured and routine tasks, it is typically used for transaction processing. Since the data manipulation language can be quite complex, the expertise of a professional programmer is usually required. The data manipulation language requires knowledge of the retrieval path. Consequently, it provides a low level of data independence because a path change will usually require reprogramming. Finally, the data manipulation language has the characteristics of third-generation programming languages (3GLs). Most often it is used in conjunction with a 3GL, usually COBOL.

Network Model

The **network model** was developed as an alternative to the hierarchical model to represent data that does not lend itself to being organized as a hierarchy. A network model allows for the definition of associations between records that may be one-to-one, one-to-many, or many-to-many. In a network model, there are no restrictions on the number of relationships that can exist among data record types. However, as in the hierarchical model, both records and relationships are explicitly defined.

The specifications for DBMSs based on the network model were developed by a committee of the National Bureau of Standards. The objective of this committee, called the **CODASYL** (COmmon DAta SYstems Language) Committee, was to extend the data manipulation capability of COBOL. The general specifications of DBMSs based on the network model have been implemented by various hardware and software vendors. Often the network-based DBMSs are called CODASYL DBMSs. Commercial products are summarized in Figure 6.21. The list in this figure is not exhaustive and is intended only to show the breadth of CODASYL products. There are CODASYL DBMSs for all types of computers: mainframes, superminis, minis, and micros.

The data definition and data manipulation languages of the CODASYL DBMSs are similar but not identical, and therefore there is not portability among these systems. The initial data manipulation language was host-language-oriented with COBOL as the host. It consists of a collection of verbs or subroutine calls. A special precompiler is required to produce object code from the COBOL programs which incorporate the CODASYL data manipulation verbs. Various query languages and report writers have subsequently been added by vendors. For example, IDMS includes OnLine English, an English-language query language, and CULPRIT, a report writer. The level of user sophistication that is required varies widely among the CODASYL DBMSs.

FIGURE 6.21

CODASYL systems

Vendor	Product	Hardware
Cullinet Software	IDMS/R	IBM mainframes, DEC VAX/VMS
Bull	IDS II	Bull mainframes
Prime	PRIME DBMS	Prime minis and superminis
DEC	DBMS, DBMS 10	VAX, PDP 10
Micro Data Base Systems	MDBS III	PCs under CP/M and MS-DOS

IDMS/R, developed by Cullinet Corporation in the early 1980s, is a CODASYL system that has been extended to incorporate features of the relational model. IDMS/R is essentially a CODASYL system which gives the appearance of being a relational DBMS.

An example data definition for Customer and Account and the relationships between them, named Customer's Checking Account, is shown in Figure 6.22 using the CODASYL standard.

The advantages and disadvantages of the network and hierarchical models are similar. Both provide efficient processing and are normally used for transaction processing systems developed by MIS professionals. These systems are used to process routine, well-structured tasks. Because access paths must be prespecified and known by the programmer, they allow for little flexibility. Because of the complexity of mainframe DBMS software, most organizations using it require a large support staff of MIS professionals. For network systems, there is usually a self-contained language to support the less sophisticated user. This is not usually the case with the hierarchical systems.

For the most part, these systems are used on mainframe and superminicomputers and accommodate multiple users. There are sophisticated

FIGURE 6.22
CODASYL data definition

```
RECORD NAME IS CUSTOMER.
     LOCATION MODE IS CALC USING SSN
     WITHIN ACCT-AREA.


1    SSN; PICTURE X(9).
1    CUSTOMER-NAME; PICTURE X(50).


RECORD NAME IS ACCOUNT.
     LOCATION MODE IS CALC USING ACCT#
     WITHIN ACCT-AREA.


1    ACCT#; PICTURE X(9).
1    ACCTBAL; TYPE DECIMAL 10,2.
          .
          .
          .


SET NAME IS CUSTOMER-CHECK-ACCT.
     OWNER IS CUSTOMER.
     ORDER IS SORTED BY DEFINED KEYS.
     MEMBER IS ACCOUNT.
     INSERTION IS AUTOMATIC.
     RETENTION IS FIXED.
     SET SELECTION IS BY VALUE OF SSN.
     KEY IS ACCT#.
```

backup features including journaling, periodic database backup copying, and recovery software. They also provide concurrency control and an elaborate security system.

Relational Model

The **relational model** is built on basic files called tables. The file structure is simple. The bank's database represented graphically and in the relational model is shown in Figure 6.23. Data from other data models can be transformed into this model through a process called normalization, which was developed by E. F. Codd, the father of the relational model. Most PC-DBMSs are based on this model. Examples are dBASE IV, Paradox, and R:base. DB2, a product from IBM, is an example of a mainframe relational DBMS. IBM's hierarchical IMS databases are also accessible through DB2.

The two-dimensional table consists of both columns and rows. Each row is a **tuple**, or record occurrence, and is unique. Each column is an attribute or data item. An entry in the table can only be a single value.

A standardized version of the data manipulation language called *Structured Query Language*, or *SQL*, has been developed. There are three basic operations involved in the relational model: (1) SELECT, to locate tuples (record occurrences) that satisfy a specified criteria; (2) PROJECT, to create a new ta-

FIGURE 6.23
Relational view

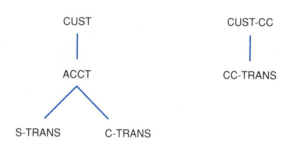

CUST
  SSNO, NAME, ADDRESS, PHONE

ACCT
  SSNO, ACCTNO, ACCTTYPE, ACCTBAL, YTD-INT

S-TRANS
  ACCTNO, TRANSNO, DATA, TRANSTYPE, AMOUNT

C-TRANS
  ACCTNO, TRANSNO, DATA, TRANSTYPE, AMOUNT

CUST-CC
  ACCTNO, NAME, ADDRESS, SSNO, BAL, AMT-DUE, LMT, YTD-INT

CC-TRANS
  ACCTNO, TRANSNO, DATE, TRANSTYPE, WHO, AMOUNT

ble containing the subset of the columns of another table; and (3) JOIN, to combine two tables and form a third. Examples of these operations are shown in Figure 6.24.

Different tables are connected through common data. Most of the DMLs are self-contained, although a host-language interface does exist in a few systems such as ORACLE.

The relational model provides a great deal of flexibility and allows for easy implementation of ad hoc requests. The systems do not require the sophistication of professional programmers and can be successfully used by end users. In contrast to those in the network and hierarchical models, access paths in these systems do not have to be predefined. The main disadvantage of the relational DBMS is its processing efficiency. Although the efficiency of these systems is continually improving, most do not have the ability to produce a machine code/object program version of their programs/applications. This requires that each "program" must be converted into machine code each time it is used. The vendors of these systems are working to make them more efficient, however. Many of these systems are not currently suited for transaction processing systems or others that process a large amount of data and

FIGURE 6.24
SQL example (relational operations)

```
SELECT ACCTNO, SSN, ACCTBAL
   FROM ACCT WHERE ACCT_TYPE = 'CH'
```

Takes 3 columns ACCTNO, SSN, ACCTBAL from the ACCT relation for checking accounts.

ACCT

SSN	ACCTNO	ACCTTYPE	ACCTBAL	YTD-INT
123456789	123422	CH	1200.50	50.50
234567901	221331	SA	2500.00	110.05
234567901	232124	CH	500.00	25.60
.				
.				
.				

Extract

ACCTNO	SSN	ACCTBAL
123422	123456789	1200.50
23212	234567901	500.00
.		
.		
.		

operate on large databases, although ORACLE and DB2 are used for transaction processing.

Other Data Management Issues

Distributed Databases

When an application or user operates on a database, this is the logical database. The *physical database* may actually be located in one or more locations. A situation in which the logical database is stored in a central physical location is referred to as a *centralized database* environment. In this case, the database(s) may be accessed through remote terminals. This is the traditional mode of operation. In a *distributed database* environment, a single logical database may be located in multiple physical locations connected by a data communication network. The fact that the database does not reside in a single location, however, is transparent to the user. A user's request for data is automatically forwarded and processed at the correct location. These two types of databases are shown in Figure 6.25.

The major objective of a distributed database is to provide easy access to data for users who are at different locations. The users need not know the location of the desired data. This feature is called *locational transparency*. The data at the separate locations is integrated to maintain consistency and integrity among locations. Local control of the data, hardware, and software employed allows for modular growth. In addition, the data communication costs are lower than those of a central database accessed by remote terminals.

There are several ways of distributing a database. The database structure employed depends on the structure of the network. Four strategies can be used for distributing databases. The relational table will be used to exemplify these strategies. The first, *replication*, occurs when data is redundantly stored at more than one site. The second, *horizontal partitioning*, puts selected rows of a relation at different sites. For example, the student database of a university having a number of colleges might be partitioned so that data about students enrolled in a given college would be located in that college's computer. That is, the School of Management's computer would store data on business students, and the computer for the School of Law would store data on its students. The information about a single student is stored in only one place, since a student can only be enrolled in one college at a time. The third, *vertical partitioning*, stores selected columns of the relation at different locations. For example, the STUDENT table has personal information about students as well as course and billing information. The personal and course information is stored in the registrar's computer, whereas the billing-related information is stored in the accounting department's computer. Finally, a common method of distributing a database is to use a combination of the other three strategies.

In considering the possible use of distributed databases, the disadvantages should be considered along with the benefits. For one thing, there is more

FIGURE 6.25
Single centralized database and
distributed database

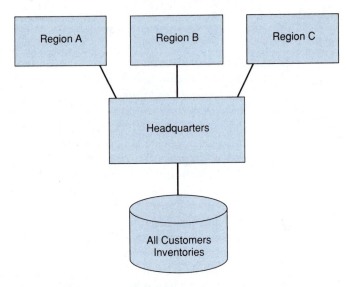

Single Centralized Database

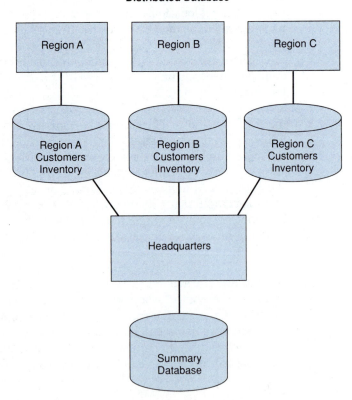

Distributed Database

software complexity in a distributed DBMS environment than in a centralized one. In addition, processing overhead is greater because of message switching among locations and the time needed to collect the required data. Also, when the database design is not sound, the response time may be slow. Because of the limitations of current distributed DBMSs, there are potential data integrity problems as well. Finally, since a distributed database assumes a data communication network, the DBMS is only as good as the network it uses. That is, data quality depends on high-quality data communication lines, and data security depends on the level of security provided by the network. Besides these aspects of dependence, the additional costs of implementing, maintaining, and operating a network must also be considered.

Organizational Functions for the Database Environment

To have a successful database environment, appropriate support personnel and associated organizational functions are required. The functions include database administration and data administration. **Database administration (DBA)** is a technical function which performs database design and development, provides education on database technology, provides support to users in operational data-management-related activities, and may provide technical support for data administration. Database administration is only concerned with computerized data; management efforts are directed toward databases and files used by multiple users and applications. This usually means mainframe computers or networks rather than PCs. **Data administration (DA)** is the organization which establishes and enforces the policies and procedures for managing the company's data as a corporate resource. It involves the collection, storage, and dissemination of data as a globally administered and standardized resource. Data administration is often called information resource management.

There is no single prescription for organizing these two functions. A corporation may have one or many organizational units concerned with data administration. The same is true of database administration. Finally, both data and database administration may or may not be in the same organizational unit.

EXAMPLE: DEVELOPING A CUSTOMER INFORMATION SYSTEM FOR WOODEN WONDERS

When Paul Bunyan started Wooden Wonders, he sold wooden objects at local fairs and to customers who contacted him directly. These customers found out about the company through word of mouth. To attract more customers, Paul decided to produce a catalog of his products.

Over the past few years, the business has grown dramatically, but this success has presented new problems. Paul found he was spending too much time managing orders, collecting payments, updating his catalog, and doing other forms of paperwork (i.e., manual data processing). He wasn't finding enough time to do what he really wanted to do: make things out of wood.

When Paul thought that he could use a computer to manage the paperwork, he hired Mary Tyson to help in the business and computer activities. One of her first projects was to start working on a Customer Information System which could later be combined with order entry and inventory systems. Mary decided to use dBASE, because it is a popular PC-based relational DBMS and one with which she was familiar.

First, she identified the objects of concern and the outputs the system would be expected to provide. Wooden Wonders is concerned about customers, catalogs, products, and orders. She noted the following inherent facts about these objects:

- A customer can be sent many catalogs;
- A customer can place many orders and an order can be for many products; and
- A catalog describes many products.

This information is presented in a **data structure** diagram in Figure 6.26.

Mary then identified the key outputs and activities of the Customer Information System. These include

- Generating mailing labels to be included in mass mailings;
- Generating mailing labels for those requesting catalogs;
- Producing sales information reports such as which products have been sold; and
- Producing other reports Paul might request.

Mary decided not to address the preparation of catalogs at this time. Later on, she would consider catalog production, which would involve producing and formatting text and images. However, she would produce the current price list, which would appear in the catalog.

The first thing she had to do was develop the structure of the database. Since a relational database management works the best when operating on normalized relations, Mary normalized Wooden Wonders data. This resulted in six normalized relations: Customer, Customer's Orders, Products Ordered, Product, Catalog, and Catalog's Product. These normalized relations are shown in Figure 6.27.

However, the normalized relations are in a form that is independent of dBASE, the database management system chosen for this application. Therefore, to be consistent with dBASE conventions, Mary had to make some adjustments. She had to determine the location of data items in the record, as well as the data item length and type. To add efficiency in data retrieval, certain data items were selected as an index (e.g., direct access key). For example, the Product database was redefined in Figure 6.28.

Like most DBMSs, dBASE has its own vocabulary. The relations (i.e., record types) are called databases, and the tuples (i.e., record occurrences) are called records. All of the dBASE database definitions produced by

(1)   Customer information required includes:
```
LAST NAME
FIRST NAME
CUSTOMER NUMBER          KEY
CUSTOMER ADDRESS (STREET ADDRESS, CITY/STATE/ZIP)
PHONE NUMBER
DATE CATALOG WAS SENT
NUMBER OF CATALOG SENT
```

(2)   Customer's products ordered:
```
ORDER NUMBER        KEY
CUSTOMER NUMBER
PRODUCT NUMBER      REPEATS FOR EACH PRODUCT ORDERED
QUANTITY ORDERED    REPEATS FOR EACH PRODUCT ORDERED
ORDER DATE
SHIP DATE
```

(3)   Product information:
```
PRODUCT NUMBER      KEY
PRODUCT NAME
PRODUCT TYPE
NUMBER ON HAND
PRODUCT COST
```

(4)   Catalog information:
```
CATALOG NUMBER      KEY
EFFECTIVE DATE
LAST DATE
NUMBER SENT
PRODUCT NUMBER      REPEATS FOR EACH PRODUCT IN CATALOG
```

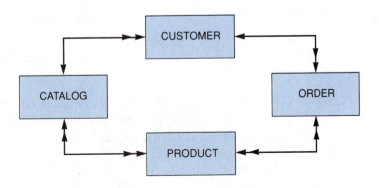

FIGURE 6.27
Normalized relations for Wooden Wonders

CUSTOMER
    CUSTOMER NUMBER, CUSTOMER'S NAME, CUSTOMER'S ADDRESS, CUSTOMER's PHONE#,
    DATE CATALOG SENT, CATALOG NUMBER, NUMBER OF CATALOGS SENT, YTD PURCHASES
CUSTOMER'S ORDERS
    ORDER NUMBER, CUSTOMER NUMBER, ORDER DATE, SHIP DATE, ORDER AMOUNT
PRODUCTS ORDERED
    PRODUCT NUMBER, ORDER NUMBER, QUANTITY ORDERED
PRODUCT
    PRODUCT NUMBER, PRODUCT NAME, PRODUCT DESCRIPTION, NUMBER ON HAND,
    PRODUCT COST
CATALOG
    CATALOG NUMBER, EFFECTIVE DATE, LAST DATE, NUMBER SENT
CATALOG'S PRODUCT
    CATALOG NUMBER, PRODUCT NUMBER

FIGURE 6.28
Definition of product

Old Name	dBASE Name	Type	Length (Decimal Places)	Index
PRODUCT NUMBER	PROD_NUM	Numeric	6 (0)	Yes
PRODUCT NAME	PROD_NAME	Character	32	No
NUMBER ON HAND	NOH	Numeric	3 (0)	No
PRODUCT COST	PROD_COST	Numeric	6 (2)	No

FIGURE 6.29
dBASE definition of product

Field	Field Name	Type	Width	Dec	Index
1	PRO_NUM	Numeric	6		Y
2	PRO_NAME	Character	32		N
3	NOH	Numeric	3		N
4	PROD_COST	Numeric	6	2	N
** Total **			48		

Mary using the Create Database command are shown in Figure 6.29. (These were generated using the Display Structure command.)

Once a database has been defined, it can be populated. That is, the data can be entered and stored in the database. Mary has several options for populating her databases. One would be to write a program. She decided that this would be too time-consuming. Another option would be to use dBASE commands, such as Append, which allows a record to be entered one data item per line, or Browse, which allows the record to be entered on a single line. Mary decided to use Browse for databases whose record size would fit on the screen in a single line (e.g., where the record length is 72 characters or less) and Append for the others. To verify that the data would be correct after entry, Mary printed the whole database using the List command and then corrected typing errors using the Browse command. The contents of the Product database are shown in Figure 6.30.

After completing the Product database, Mary repeated the tasks for the Customer, Order, and Prodord databases. Once these databases were created, she began to generate some reports before dealing with the catalog-related databases. To produce a report, she first had to create the structure of the report. This meant instructing dBASE as to the contents of the report and how they would be displayed. This was done using the Create Report command. The report itself was generated using the Report command. Before beginning report generation, however, Mary realized that an important piece of information about Product was missing: the year-to-date units sold. To remedy this problem, Mary used the Modify Database Structure command to add another numeric data item, Amtsold.

The first report that she generated summarized information concerning the products sold. It had two parts. The first part listed all products which were not sold, using the following commands:

```
USE PRODUCT
LIST ALL FOR AMTSOLD<1 TO PRINT
```

The second part summarized the products sold by customer. Because this report requires information from more than one database, a temporary database had to be created using the Join command. The resulting database, named Temp, contained data from the Customer, Custprod, and Product databases. The specific data items included were Prodno, Prodname, Custno, Custname, Orderno, Orderdate, and Qtyorder. Mary selected Temp as the active database and then entered the Create Report command menu. In creating the report Mary had several formatting decisions to make. She had to select the report heading, the column headings, the data items to include in the report, and the grouping criteria of Prodno and Custno. A copy of this report is shown in Figure 6.31.

FIGURE 6.30
Product DB contents

Record#	PRO_NUM	PRONAME	NOH	PROD_COST
1	124068	DRESSER 5 DRAW	31	320.45
2	379106	BUNK BED	7	408.29
3	244813	TABLE	12	124.38
4	219424	CHAIR	64	59.48
5	136645	DRESSER 8 DRAW	27	413.32

FIGURE 6.31
dBASE report

```
                          PRODUCT LIST

 Product           Product              Number      Product
 Number              Name               on Hand       Cost
 124068      DRESSER 5 DRAW                 31       320.45
 379106      BUNK BED                        7       408.29
 244813      TABLE                          12       124.38
 219424      CHAIR                          64        59.48
 136645      DRESSER 8 DRAW                 27       413.32

                                 Total     141      1325.92
```

These reports enabled Paul Bunyan to make several important management decisions. He was able to determine which items to eliminate from his next catalog. He could also see that one of his products, an alphabet puzzle, was a big seller, so he decided to make more of these puzzles as soon as he had some time. Paul then met with Mary to talk about the next set of reports to develop. He was convinced that the computer, and the database software in particular, was going to improve his decision-making ability.

SUMMARY

The objective of an information system is to produce high-quality information. There are two techniques for information storage and retrieval which can aid in providing the user with this information. Information can be stored as either a file or a database. Three file organizations are available: sequential, direct, and indexed sequential. The choice of file organization influences the amount of time it takes to retrieve information and the cost of this retrieval. A sequential file is best used when there is high activity, because it results in a low cost per transaction. A typical setting would be transaction processing. A direct file is used when access to a single record at a time based on its key is desired; this is because the cost of processing each transaction remains the same. An indexed sequential file can be used for both sequential and direct-access applications. This is possible because it provides low-cost transaction processing as well as instantaneous retrieval of a single record.

There are several problems associated with the file-oriented approach to information storage and retrieval that are overcome with the use of databases. The use of individual files inhibits data sharing. There is no data integration. Consequently, management cannot be provided with a global view of the organization's data. Since security is provided by the operating system, the use of files also requires the organization to provide its own backup and privacy at the individual file level. In contrast, the database is a central pool of data controlled by the organization which serves one or more applications. The shared database is most effective when it is used in conjunction with a database management system. A DBMS provides for the definition, population, retrieval, and modification of the database, along with security, privacy, backup, and report generation. One of the greatest advantages of using a database management system is more data independence. That is, programs do not have to be altered every time there is a change in the database.

There are several ways to view a database. One of these is the ANSI/SPARC model. It reflects the external model (user's view), the conceptual model (DBMS-independent global view), the internal model (DBMS-dependent global view), and the physical model (where data actually exists on a secondary storage device). In addition, there are three ways to organize data in a database — hierarchical, network, and relational — and each of these has its advantages and disadvantages. The DBMSs for transaction processing are primarily hierarchical and network-oriented, whereas those for end users and PCs are based on the relational model.

Besides creating a database and using a database management system, an organization can do other things to improve its information storage and retrieval. A data dictionary system can provide a central repository for the definitions of the organization's data (called meta-data) as well as reports on and access to this meta-data. The organization can institute the data administration and database administration functions to support its data management activities. These functions can provide policies, procedures, and education/consultation as well as being a focal point for data management efforts.

REFERENCES

Ackoff, R. L. "Management Misinformation Systems." *Management Science* 14, No. 4 (December 1967): B140–B156.

Chen, P-S. "The Entity-Relationship Model — Toward a Unified View of Data." *ACM-TODS* (March 1976): 9–36.

Database Architecture Framework Task Group (DAFTG) of the ANSI/x3/SPARC Database System Study Group. "Reference Model of DBMS Standardization." *SIGMOD RECORD* 15, No. 1 (March 1986): 19–58.

Elmasri, R., and Shamkant B. Navathe. "Examples of Relational, Hierarchical, Network, and Other Systems." In *Fundamentals of Database Systems*, 663–729. Menlo Park, CA: Benjamin-Cummings, 1989.

Harrington, Jan L. *Relational Database Management for Microcomputers: Design and Implementation*. New York: Holt, Rinehart and Winston, 1988.

Kahn, Beverly K. "Some Realities of Data Administration." *Communications of the ACM* 26 (October 1983): 794–799.

_____. "An Environmentally Dependent Framework for Data Dictionary Systems." *MIS Quarterly* (September 1985): 199–220.

Kahn, Beverly K., and Linda Garceau. "The Database Administration Function." *Journal of Management Information Systems* (Spring 1985): 87–101.

McFadden, F. R., and J. A. Hoffer. *Data Base Management*, 2d ed. Menlo Park, CA: Benjamin-Cummings, 1988.

Potter, W. D., and R. B. Trueblood. "Traditional, Semantic, and Hyper-Semantic Approaches to Data Modeling." *Computer* (June 1988): 53–63.

KEY TERMS

ANSI/SPARC data model	data independence–logical, physical	network data model
batch processing	data manipulation language (DML)	physical view
CODASYL	data model	record (type)
conceptual view	data structure	record occurrence
concurrency control	direct file	redundancy
data administration	external view	relational data model
database	hierarchical data model	report writer
database administration	host language	restart/recovery
database management system (DBMS)	indexed sequential access method (ISAM)	schema
data definition/description language (DDL)	indexed sequential file	secondary storage device
data dependence	integrity	sequential file
data dictionary	internal view	SQL
data dictionary system (DDS)	key–primary, secondary	subschema
data element, item, field	logical view	transaction file
	master file	transaction processing (system)
		tuple
		user view

REVIEW QUESTIONS

1. Discuss the five data characteristics to be concerned with in determining data availability for a computer-based information system.
2. What is the hierarchy of data? What are the major components? Give a definition and example of each component.
3. What factors must be considered when selecting a file organization system?
4. When would an organization select to organize its data in a sequential file? What are the disadvantages of this approach? Give two examples of information systems that require a sequential file and defend your choices.
5. What are the advantages and disadvantages of selecting a direct file for an information system? Give examples of two information systems that can best be served by a direct file and defend your choices.
6. What are the advantages and disadvantages of selecting an indexed sequential file for an information system? Give examples of two information systems that can best be served by an indexed sequential file and defend your choices.
7. Compare the similarities and differences between single-application and multiple-application systems using an information systems example.
8. Discuss the importance of standardization to the database concept.

9. What is the difference between a database philosophy and acquiring a database management system (DBMS)?
10. Discuss the costs and benefits to consider prior to adopting a database philosophy.
11. What is the purpose of the ANSI/SPARC data model? Define its constituent levels—external view, conceptual view, internal view, and physical view.
12. What are the major features of a database management system?
13. Explain physical and logical data independence.
14. Why should integrity constraints be considered in data definition?
15. Identify and describe two types of data manipulation language.
16. Why are data protection features necessary? Explain encryption.
17. Compare active and passive data dictionaries.
18. Compare and contrast a mainframe-based DBMS and a PC-based DBMS.
19. What are the benefits and costs of a DBMS?
20. What is the data model? What is the purpose of data models?
21. Compare and contrast the three major types of data models—hierarchical, network, and relational.
22. Discuss several ways of distributing databases.
23. What is the function of database administration?

CASE State University is having registration problems. Students are registering for courses for which they have not yet met prerequisites. A record of the courses that each student has taken is stored in computer-readable form. The administration wants to implement an on-line registration system that will automatically check student prerequisites and course availability. The administration still wants to generate a course schedule for each student two weeks before the term and a course roster for each faculty member several times over the term. This system should also be used to record grades at the end of the term and generate grade reports for students. Over time, the university would like some management reports to be used to detect students having academic difficulties and to plan future course offerings.

DISCUSSION QUESTIONS

1. Does this system require a database or DBMS? Are both needed, or could the system just have a database using non-DBMS access or a DBMS without a database? (Be sure to provide the definitions of database and database management system.) How does the database or DBMS relate to the organization's MIS? Does an MIS require a database? a DBMS?
2. What are the advantages and disadvantages of using a database management system?
3. Describe several (at least four) key features of a DBMS that are pertinent in the university's decision. Explain what they are and why they are important to the university.
4. What is the difference between batch, on-line, and real-time applications? Categorize four of the university's applications and defend your choice.

5. Can the university use PCs to support registration or other DBMS-based operations? How do PC-based DBMSs differ from their mainframe counterparts?

6. Given your knowledge of registration at your own university, develop several external views. First draw the forms and then normalize them. Represent the external views in an entity relationship model. Integrate the external views to form a conceptual model. Graphically present the conceptual and external views in an entity relationship diagram (i.e., use boxes and arrows with arrow heads denoting the type of connectivity, 1:1, 1:N, M:N). Show the data items and underline the key.

7. Data models define the interrelationships between the components of data. They capture the meaning of data (i.e., data semantics). The major types of data models are relational, network, and hierarchical. Consider the conceptual model defined in question 6, and represent an external view in each of the three data models. The external view may be different from the one used in question 6 and you may use a different external view for each of the data models. The external model(s) used must have the equivalent of three record types. Which data model does the conceptual view satisfy?

CHAPTER 7

Data Communication

CHAPTER OUTLINE

COMMUNICATION TOOLS AND CONCEPTS

DATA COMMUNICATION REQUIREMENTS

CONSTRAINTS ON COMMUNICATION SERVICES

DATA COMMUNICATION OPTIONS

CHAPTER OBJECTIVES

- To provide an understanding of communication tools and concepts.
- To explain how to identify data communication requirements.
- To describe the kinds of technical, organizational, and regulatory constraints that can be imposed upon communication decisions.
- To explain how to go about making communication decisions given one's requirements and constraints.

INTRODUCTION

We have learned that a system is composed of resources which function together to achieve some goal. The resources of an information system can be grouped into three subsystems: a technological subsystem (the hardware and software), a human subsystem (the personnel and procedures), and a data subsystem. We have also learned that the way these subsystems work together to produce information—that is, achieve the goal—is by carrying out the functions of input, process, storage, and output. In other words, an information system's resources move data into, through, and out of the information system. This process of moving data is called communication. **Communication** is the act of sending a message from a source to a destination.

We can think of communication as the glue that binds the components of the information system together. The input component brings the data into the system. That is, data from the environment is communicated to the system via input devices and procedures. It is then transmitted to the process and storage components, which manipulate this data into meaningful information. Finally, the output component transfers the information out of the system and back into the environment. As we can see, communication is an integral part of any information system.

Since the objective of an information system is to process data into information, and the objective of communication is to move data and information, an understanding of communication becomes a necessary part of a complete understanding of an information system. Just as communication is a part of data collection and processing, learning about communication should be a part of information literacy. Remember, the goal of information literacy is the ability to articulate needs and then to acquire, store, process, and communicate information.

Communication is as basic a human activity as breathing. In fact, a society can be defined as "people in communication."[1] The ability to communicate effectively, with or without technological assistance, is crucial to the operations of human organizations. After all, what is the point of having good information if you can't communicate it in an effective, efficient, and timely fashion?

The study of communication involves several bodies of knowledge, including human communication, communication disorders, mass communication, telephone communication, and data communication. The intent of this chapter is to concentrate on data communication, or communication with a computer. **Data communication** is the transmission of data between computer systems and terminals (used for sending and/or receiving). However, as we move through our consideration of data communication, it will also become clear that data, video, and voice messages are increasingly integrated in today's communication systems. Figure 7.1 shows the relationships that exist among the different forms of communication.

In addition to the fact that communication activities are closely related to the activities of an information system, there are two other reasons why it

FIGURE 7.1
The various forms of communication

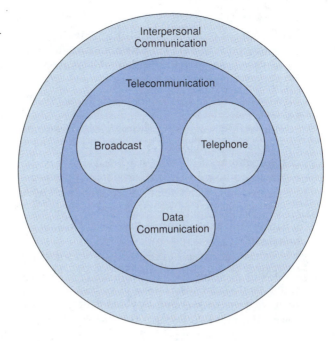

is more important than ever to understand data communication tools and the implications of using them. One reason is that these tools, like all kinds of information technology, are increasingly available and affordable. As more and more people use computers, they begin to see the benefits of connecting their own individual computers to other computers. As a result, data communication is becoming an increasingly important part of end-user computing. Therefore, an important aspect of information literacy is the ability to assess one's communication needs and options in order to acquire the most appropriate technology.

The other reason is related to the recent changes in public policy in the United States regarding the manufacture, use, and sale of communication technology. The communication industry used to be highly regulated. That is, there were strict rules governing companies involved in providing communication goods and services. In 1984, this situation changed. The communication industry became less regulated and much more competitive. This increased competition has resulted in many more options for the consumer. It is therefore in the consumer's interest to know something about such products as local area networks and electronic mail so that informed decisions can be made regarding them.

To make informed decisions and to make effective use of communication technology, it is first necessary to know what is involved in the process. Therefore, one purpose of this chapter is to provide a basic understanding of communication technology and how it is used.

With this general knowledge of data communication and the role it plays in the operation of information systems, we are in a position to achieve the other purpose of this chapter: to provide an understanding of the process of making communication decisions. The first requirement here is to know one's communication needs. But knowing the technology is not enough. One must also know which options are *realistic*, given the constraints present in the context of use.

Part of this process involves understanding the implications of choosing one technological option over another. Some of the implications are financial; a given choice, especially a wrong choice, can be very expensive. Other implications are human. A certain choice may enhance or degrade human communications. In the choice of communication tools, we want to be sure that we are consistent with the principles of human-computer interaction discussed in Chapter 5. Based on an assessment of implications, then, we encounter some constraints.

Other constraints are simply imposed upon us from the current technological environment. Tools that are to be a part of a communication system must be compatible. These devices must be able to "talk" to each other. To achieve this, the technology must conform to certain standards. These standards therefore represent another form of constraint. We need to know what standards are involved in the communication industry and how they influence the options that are available. The final type of constraint imposed from the environment is communication regulation. Changes in communication policy and the effect that they have and are likely to have on communication decisions are another consideration in the decision-making process.

COMMUNICATION TOOLS AND CONCEPTS

Data communication tools can be associated with the five major parts of the communication process: source, destination, channel, message, and feedback. The technology used to facilitate data communication is discussed in Section II of the appendix. You should become familiar with this material as you read this chapter.

The Basic Communication Model

Any communication event, including data communication events, can be expressed in terms of the communication model shown in Figure 7.2. Before considering what is involved in communicating with a computer, let us first consider what occurs in human communication.

The most basic type of communication is between two people engaged in a conversation. This is an example of interpersonal communication, specifically, *one-to-one communication*. The messages sent are the content of the

FIGURE 7.2

The basic model of communication

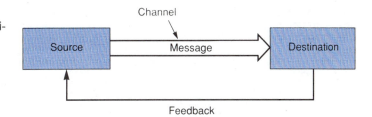

conversation — words spoken between the two participants. A **message** is data that travels between the source and the destination. The message can be thought of in terms of both its meaning and its form. In physical terms, a message is a **signal**. When two people are having a conversation, the one who is speaking is the source, and the one who is listening is the destination. The **source** originates the message and the **destination** receives the message. Those involved in a conversation will take turns acting the roles of source and destination. It is for this reason that we can describe the conversation as *two-way communication*.

Consider a conversation between John and Mary. John asks the question, "Are you free for lunch?" In this situation John is the source and Mary is the destination. Mary replies, "Yes, at 12:30." Mary is now the source and John has become the destination. The channel is the means used to move the message between the source and destination. A **communication channel**, like a road for cars or a pipe for water, is the route along which the message, the data, is transmitted. In a face-to-face conversation, air is the channel. Now suppose that when John asked the question, there was loud music being played and Mary could not hear him. She probably would have said something like, "I can't hear you. Could you please repeat what you just said?" In this case, Mary's request constituted feedback to John. **Feedback** is a verification that the message was received. Mary was sending feedback to the effect that she couldn't hear the message. Often it is necessary to verify that the message sent by the source is the one actually received by the destination. In the conversation between John and Mary, this kind of feedback would be for John to reply, "A 12:30 lunch would be great," to confirm the engagement. Sending an RSVP in response to a dinner invitation is another example of feedback. This communication process is depicted in Figure 7.3.

Many times feedback is needed because there is noise or interference. **Noise** refers to variations introduced into a signal from some source other than the sender. The music which prohibited Mary from hearing John is an example of noise. Noise distorts and therefore interferes with the clarity of the message. While an instructor is lecturing in a classroom, there are often many side conversations occurring among the students in the class. These student-to-student conversations are noise if they interfere with the message from instructor to student and make it difficult for students in the back of the room (i.e., far away from the instructor) to accurately hear the complete message.

FIGURE 7.3
Human communication

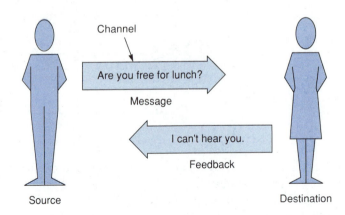

To improve the communication between instructor and student, there are two options available: the noise can be reduced or the message can be improved or enhanced. **Enhancement** is the process of improving the signal or the physical form of the message. Enhancing a message is often accomplished by making the message louder, such as by using a microphone for amplification.

There are also examples of communication between machines other than computers. Consider communication between the local television station and the television set in your house. The source is a transmitter located at the television station. The physical form of the message is the broadcast signal. The content of the message is the television program you are watching. The receiver, then, is your television set. In this example, both the source and destination are machines.

In the case of data communication, a computer can be the source, the destination, or both. For example, think of using your computer at home to contact another computer with a request to receive data from some database. When you send in the request for data, your computer is acting as the source. When the requested data is sent to you, your computer is acting as the destination.

Data Communication Systems

Like information processing, data communication can also be viewed as a system. In fact, its resources are the same as those for an information system. The difference between these two systems is in the goal. Whereas the goal of an information system is to *produce* information, the goal of a communication system is to effectively *transmit* that information. Both, however, utilize hardware, software, data, procedures, and personnel to accomplish their respective goals.

Communication *hardware* includes the technology used to generate, transmit, receive, and decode messages. Two types of *software* are used in a data communication system. One type of communication software assists the hardware in transmitting the message. It manages the process of routing the message through the maze of communication channels. If one route is too congested, the software will direct the message to use another route. Its function is much like that of the radio announcer who reports on traffic conditions from a helicopter. If one road is too congested, the reporter will advise listeners to take another route. The other type of communication software performs coordination and control functions, such as sending feedback to the source that the message was received. The message that is sent is *data* which, when interpreted by some human receiver, will result in information.

Procedures deal with how to make the other resources interact effectively. For example, in the conversation between John and Mary, if both were to speak at the same time, each would be simultaneously acting as the source. Since this would interfere with effective communication, human communication has certain conventions, such as waiting to speak until the other person has finished. This is an example of procedures for the human communication system. Data communication systems have similar procedures. *People* are the ultimate receivers of the message. Personnel are also needed to design, install, and maintain the data communication system. The remainder of this chapter will be concerned with the procedures involved in identifying the communication needs of individuals and organizations, understanding about the data to be transmitted, and determining the appropriate type of data communication configuration.

Data Communication Networks

A network can be defined as an interconnected or interrelated set of items. Sociologists talk about society as a "social network" and individuals talk about their "network of friends." **Telecommunication networks** are concerned with transmitting data over a distance. There are three types of telecommunication networks: broadcast networks, telephone networks, and data communication networks. A broadcast network is a group of radio or television stations linked by channels such as wire or radio relay. A telephone network refers to locations connected by devices such as telephone lines, microwave, or satellite. A *data communication network* is a collection of hardware and software—computers, terminals, and the interconnecting links, plus the communication software— which enables the data to be communicated through the network. Another term for computer-to-computer communication is **computer network**. Throughout the rest of this chapter, when the term *network* is used, it will refer to a data communication network.

The computers in a network can be all of the same size or a variety of sizes. That is, an organization may choose to have only personal computers in the network, or to have personal computers which are connected to a mainframe or minicomputer. A network can be composed of computers from a single hardware vendor or from multiple vendors. All the points in the network which can send or receive data and which can do local processing are called

FIGURE 7.4
A data communication network

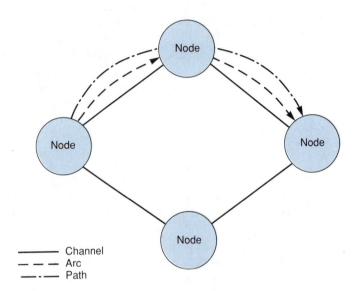

Channel
———— Arc
——·—— Path

nodes. The nodes in the network are linked together by channels. A variety of media are available to form the channel. The movement of data from one node to another is referred to as an **arc**. The **path** of a message through a network is achieved by a series of arcs. Figure 7.4 is a depiction of a data communication network.

The relationship among the computers in the network can take one of two basic forms: either the computers are equals or one computer dominates the others. There are two **topologies**, or network structures, which will support a network in which one computer dominates and the others are subordinate: a star network and a hierarchical network. Likewise, there are two topologies which will support a network in which all computers are equals: a ring network and a bus network. Figure 7.5 shows these four different topologies.

Networks with a Central Node

Star Networks In a **star network**, all data is sent directly to the dominant computer, which either processes it or acts as a message switch by accepting a message from the sending node and forwarding it to the destination node. There is no direct communication between the subordinate nodes; the central computer acts as an intermediary in the routing of all messages. A star network is shown in Figure 7.5(a).

The star topology has three main advantages. First, the path from sender to receiver is relatively short. The message has only two arcs: from the sender to the central node, and from the central node to the receiver. When the route is short, there is less of an opportunity for noise and interference. Second, the central computer can maintain a considerable amount of network control since

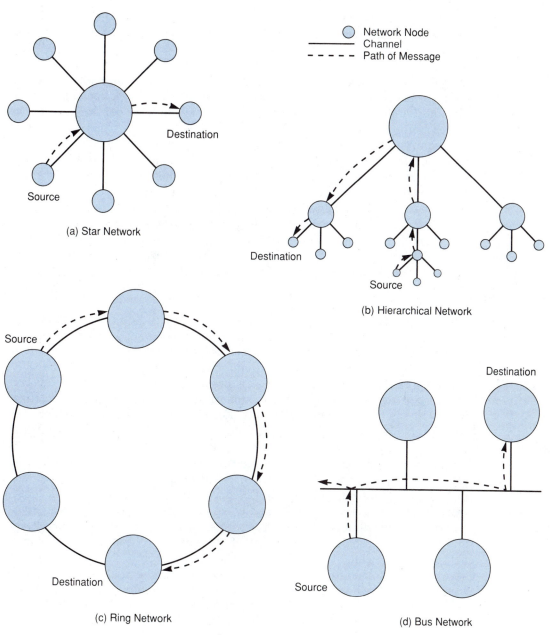

Network Node
Channel
Path of Message

Destination

Source

(a) Star Network

Destination

Source

(b) Hierarchical Network

Source

Destination

(c) Ring Network

Destination

Source

(d) Bus Network

FIGURE 7.5
Network topologies

it has contact with every message. Finally, expanding the network by adding new nodes is relatively easy, because only the central node of the existing network is affected.

Among the disadvantages of the star network structure is the possibility of network congestion, since all messages must go through the central node. Second, the network is vulnerable. The entire network depends on a single node, so if something happens to the central node, the entire network becomes nonfunctional. Third, in the case of a geographically dispersed network, the requirement to send all messages through the central node could greatly increase communication costs. In light of these disadvantages, this topology would be appropriate when it is important that all nodes communicate with the central computer. One reason for choosing this network structure would be that the organization is geographically dispersed yet its computer processing is done on one central computer. The computer processing site would be the central node of a star network. The other sites from which the computers or terminals send data to the central site to be processed are the subordinate nodes. This centralized method of interactive information processing is called *time sharing*.

Hierarchical Networks A **hierarchical network** is structured like a company's organization chart. In fact, the structure and paths of the network should mirror the structure of the organization and the information flows within it. At the top of the hierarchy is the dominant computer, which would service the home office or corporate headquarters of an organization. The node containing the dominant computer is sometimes referred to as the **root** from which all the other nodes *branch* off. For this reason, the hierarchical network is also referred to as a *tree* structure. All subordinate nodes eventually communicate to the root, as shown in Figure 7.5(b).

For example, consider the network structure of an organization with offices throughout the United States, as shown in Figure 7.6.

Suppose the home office is in Chicago. This is where the network root is located. The next level in the hierarchy would be the computers servicing the five regional headquarters, in the Northwest, Southwest, Midwest, Northeast, and Southeast. The computer at each of these regional headquarters would be able to communicate directly with the central computer in Chicago. If there are several sites in each region, these would constitute the next level of nodes in the hierarchy. Each level would, in turn, have subordinate computers that support an even lower level in the organization. Normally, the lower the level of the node in the hierarchy, the smaller the computer and the lower the level of the organization it serves.

Corporate reports from a given site in one of the regions would be consolidated at the regional level and then passed up to the top or corporate level. If a regional site in the Southwest wanted to communicate with one in the Northeast, the message would have to take a path traversing four arcs: from the source site to the Southwest regional headquarters, then to Chicago, then to

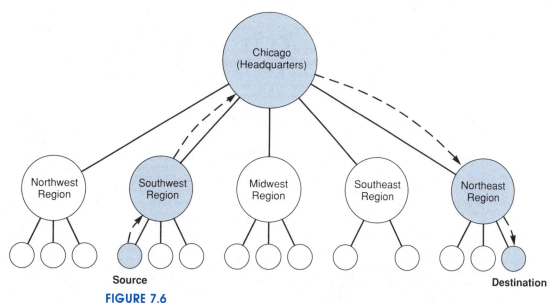

FIGURE 7.6

Hierarchical network for a national company with regional offices

the Northeast regional headquarters, and finally to the destination site in the Northeast region.

Obviously, there are some disadvantages to this network structure. The nodes in the network depend upon the nodes above them in the hierarchy. In the example just given, if something happens to the computer in Chicago, messages can only be passed among the nodes within one region. If something happens to one of the computers at a regional headquarters, none of the computers in that region can communicate with each other. Another problem would occur if the organizational structure changed. If another regional headquarters were established or if two regions were consolidated into one, the communication paths would have to be reconfigured.

The main advantage of the hierarchical network structure is that it supports the "chain of command" in the organization. That is, the paths in the network reflect the flow of information in the organization. An advantage this structure has over the star network is that, since much of the information in a company flows between the regional sites and the regional headquarters, there is rarely a need to involve the central computer. The star network requires that *all messages* go through the central computer.

Networks with No Central Node

In a network with no central node, all nodes are considered to be equals. This does not mean that all computers are of equal size. Messages are often "broadcast" throughout the network. Each node, then, checks the message to see if it is the intended receiver. Two topologies are used for this type of network:

ring and bus. They are also the most common topologies for local area networks, which will be discussed later in the chapter. It is the task of the communication software to make sure that **collisions** are avoided or overcome. Avoiding collisions means keeping the messages from bumping into each other. Overcoming collisions means retransmitting until the message gets through the network.

Ring Networks The nodes in a **ring network** are arranged in a circle, as shown in Figure 7.5(c). The data flows among nodes by moving in one direction around the ring. A ring network allows the computers to share resources such as files, software, and hardware. It is often used in distributed data processing. **Distributed data processing** means that a number of computers are involved in the information processing function. This would contrast with a star network, in which all data is usually sent to one central computer to be processed. Since it has no one dominant computer, a ring network permits less central control than a hierarchical or star network. People at the local sites have more control over their own resources since they are actually doing the processing. Depending on one's perspective, this may be either an advantage or a disadvantage.

The main advantage of a ring network is that information system resources can be shared more easily. For example, all the nodes in a ring network could share a common printer and thereby save on hardware expenses. Another advantage is that the network is specifically designed to overcome node failures, so the reliability of the network remains high. This means that if one node is malfunctioning, the message is automatically routed to the next node. Only the failed node is lost and the rest of the network can communicate as usual. Ring networks are also easy to expand. Finally, since networks using this topology are generally kept small in scope and involve small computers, costs are lower than those associated with star networks and hierarchical networks.

However, because there is no central computer, organization-wide control over the network's activities is more difficult to achieve. This, in turn, makes it is more difficult to control access to the data in the network. As a result, data security can become an issue. In addition, if each node will be doing its own information processing, computer operators and programmers may be required at each node, and this can lead to higher personnel costs.

Bus Networks A **bus network** is like a ring but without the ends connected. This topology is shown in Figure 7.5(d). A *bus* is a channel to which devices such as computers or terminals can be connected. A message is propagated throughout the network in two directions and the intended receiver picks it out. All nodes are equal and control is commonly distributed among them when baseband transmission is used. This topology is only applicable to networks which cover a small geographical area.

Like that of the ring network, the reliability of a bus network is high; the loss of one node has no effect on the others. It is also often inexpensive to implement.

The bus topology has two major drawbacks. The first is that it is limited to networks covering a small geographical area. The second is that in the case of high volume it can become overloaded. High volume can come from a few users sending a large amount of data, from many users sending a small amount of data, or from noise forcing retransmissions. Collisions between messages can occur since data travels in two directions. In addition, messages may be sent multiple times as a result of the collisions.

The Open Systems Interconnection Reference Model for Data Communications

A data communication network consists of many hardware and software products as well as procedures governing how they will be used in the transmission of data. As a result, a variety of considerations must be taken into account, ranging from physical issues to organizational concerns. Because data communication resources are produced by a variety of vendors and because new technology becomes available at a rapid pace, ensuring that all the parts of the network are compatible is a significant concern in network design. In an effort to make data communication products more "compatible," standards have been developed by the standard-setting bodies. These standards are an example of technological constraints which influence an organization's decision-making process in the acquisition of telecommunication products.

An example of the kind of standards in use today is the Open Systems Interconnection (OSI) standard, which was developed by the International Standards Organization (ISO). It describes the interactions required of systems that wish to communicate with other systems. It is referred to as the **OSI model**.

The OSI model is based on the recognition that there are several levels of communication in a network and therefore several levels of compatibility that must exist. For example, consider the levels required to support telephone service at your home. A household may have a portable telephone or a telephone answering machine which is "plugged into" the local telephone service. One level of communication provides the means to connect different devices. Another level of communication routes a phone call to the appropriate location. A third level transports the message from sender to receiver. Therefore, a successful telephone conversation between two people requires successful communication both within and between all these different levels.

In order to have successful communication at each level, a person who is designing a network must understand the requirements within and between levels as well as the types of interfaces that are needed. This is the purpose of the OSI reference model. It defines each level of communication and the appropriate interfaces. The OSI model is a functional description of the layers of services required for the interconnection of systems. It describes the external interactions required of systems wishing to be "open" for communication with other systems in order to be compatible. It also promotes the formulation and adoption of standard "rules of communication."

Standards are developed in three ways. Some are established by standard-setting bodies such as the National Institute for Standards and Technology (NIST), the American National Standards Institute (ANSI), and ISO. In addition, industry groups such as the Institute for Electrical and Electronic Engineers (IEEE) develop standards. Finally, vendors such as International Business Machines (IBM) and Digital Equipment Corporation (DEC) set standards; this happens when a vendor's approach is in widespread use and, therefore, becomes a "de facto" standard. Ethernet has become a de facto standard for certain types of local area networks.

The OSI model consists of seven layers of functions that every network should fulfill. This layered model includes the definition of protocols and interfaces. **Protocols** are the "rules of communication." They describe how communication is carried out within a layer and must be agreed upon by the participants in order for communication to succeed. An interface is the point of intersection between two subsystems. In this case, the layers are the subsystems and the interface is concerned with communication between two adjacent layers. These seven layers can be divided into two groups. The first four are concerned with the physical aspects of communication; the last three are concerned with communication from an organizational or people perspective. The seven layers of the OSI model, from the most physical to the most organizational, are shown in Figure 7.7.

Physical

The *physical layer* specifies the electrical connection between the transmission medium, the communication circuit, and the computer system. An example would be standards for voltages on telephone wires and pulses of light in fiber

FIGURE 7.7
The seven layers of the OSI model

Physical	Electrical connections
Data Link	The physical path
Network	Routing messages
Transport	Reliable transmission
Session	Connection between user and network
Presentation	Generalized formatting of data and code conversion
Application	Formatting data to suit specific application

optics. Another would be defining how many and which wires (or pins) are required to carry a signal according to a standard such as RS-232C or RS-449.

Data Link

The *data link layer* establishes and controls the interpretation of the signals over the physical link. Its tasks include detecting and correcting errors, defining the beginning and end of the character being sent, resolving competing requests for a circuit, and ensuring that all forms of data can be transmitted. For example, this level checks parity and, if necessary, sends an appropriate error message to the sender. The error checking is often done at the receiver's end.

Network

The *network layer* is responsible for selecting the next link along the way in the delivery of a message from a source to a destination, and for collecting accounting data. For example, in a telephone conversation, the message will not directly travel between the two parties involved. It will go to intermediate points along the way, in order to find the least congested path between the source and the destination. Therefore, if someone in Boston is calling someone in Miami, the message travels to several intermediate points before reaching its final destination. This coordination and routing is the responsibility of the network layer.

Transport

The *transport layer* is the highest of the physical-communication-oriented levels. It is responsible for the reliable, efficient transportation of data from one end to the other, and for adding any functions necessary to improve the quality of service provided by the network layer. This would include further error checking, as well as features such as multiplexing which would enhance the sharing of network facilities. The issues addressed in this layer are independent of the communication media involved. In a telephone conversation, the transport connection is not established until the intended recipient picks up the phone and speaks. The physical movement of the message is then handled by the network layer.

Session

The *session layer* is responsible for establishing the connection between applications—that is, the interaction between the user and a network resource. It is also responsible for maintaining this connection in the event of a network problem. A session maintains continuity over the period of time during which a connection is established between the source and the destination. Establishing this connection is referred to as "logging in." Breaking the connection is referred to as "logging out." This layer is responsible for such tasks as checking user identification and allowing the user to log in. It is concerned with guaranteeing that once activities are begun they will be completed properly. For example, an application may send a large amount of data to a printer which has a limited output *buffer*. For the printer to be able to print the complete document correctly, it must be broken into small pieces. This capability is provided by the session layer.

Presentation

The *presentation layer* accepts the data from the application layer and provides generalized formatting of the data that is commonly useful to many applications. These functions may include data encryption for privacy, data compression for efficient transfers, and terminal screen formatting. It also carries out conversion from one transmission code to another, such as from the EBCDIC code to the ASCII code. For example, if the President of the United States is making a sensitive telephone call from Air Force One, it is necessary to guarantee that the contents of the message are known only to the intended receiver. The presentation layer encrypts the call so that, even if the transmission is intercepted by someone else, its meaning cannot be determined.

Application

The *application layer* is the most user-oriented of the seven layers. It is functionally defined by the user. This means that the content and format of the data are dictated by the application or information need to be satisfied. The protocols and standards at this level are defined according to the specific requirements of the information processing task at hand. Such tasks may include accessing a remote database, accessing a bank from an ATM, or communicating with an airline reservation system from a travel agent's terminal.

The relationships among the layers of communication are exemplified in the task of placing an order by telephone, as shown in Figure 7.8.

DATA COMMUNICATION REQUIREMENTS

With a general understanding of what is involved in data communication, we now turn to the most important issue from a user's perspective: determining one's communication requirements and identifying options for satisfying them. Three factors must be taken into account: the communication requirements, constraints imposed by the environment, and realistic options given those requirements and constraints. This process is another example of problem solving, which was discussed in Chapter 5.

Data communication requirements come from the organizational context of the communication. For example, an organization might want to automate some communication process through the use of data communication. Or an organization with an existing network structure might want to change or expand it in some way.

The point of departure in determining data communication requirements should be the existing structure of organizational communication. Just as an

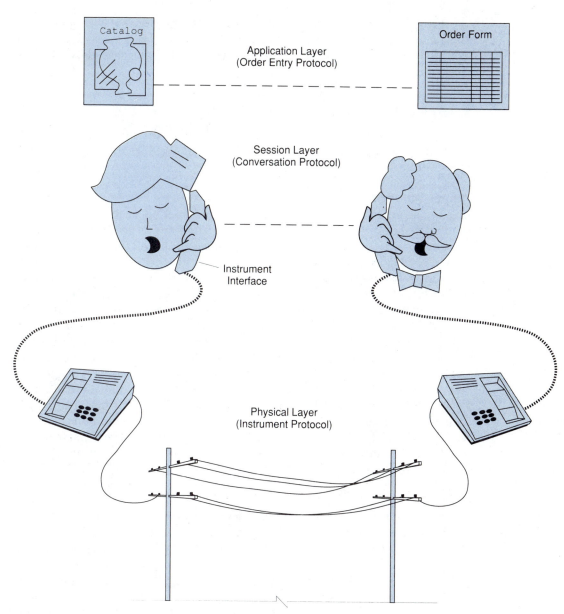

FIGURE 7.8
Protocol layers in human communication

information system is developed to provide support for decisions and activities that are carried out in an organization, a communication system should be developed to support the communication of the people in it. Supporting organizational communication activities requires an understanding of the information flows, the nature of the information, and the physical location of the people involved. Our discussion of communication requirements will center on a consideration of the physical location of the people to be served by the data communication system.

Communication Between Organizations

Data communication exists both between and within organizations. There are a number of examples of data communication between organizations. We will discuss three of them.

External Databases

Some of the information an organization needs to support its functions does not exist within the organization. This information must therefore be obtained from outside sources. As we learned in Chapter 6, there is an entire industry of people called **information providers** who provide access to vast databases. For example, suppose State University wants to do long-range planning regarding future student enrollment. To accomplish this, it would need certain demographic data on trends in college attendance, population shifts, and the birth rate. This data is available through commercial databases, and numerous companies provide it to them through subscription to their database services. Examples of commercial databases are the New York Times Information Bank and the Dow Jones Retrieval Service. Some libraries also have access to these databases. But an organization might decide it would be more efficient to enable its employees to have access from their offices. In this case, a communication structure must be developed to enable them to communicate with these information providers. They would need a computer or terminal, perhaps a printer and communication software, a modem, and access to some communication channel, such as a telephone line.

Service Bureaus

An organization may choose to have someone else handle its computer-based information processing tasks, perhaps because it does not have sufficient technical expertise or because it does not have a computer. Even if an organization does have a computer, in certain circumstances it may desire to have an outside entity do some of the information processing. Perhaps the organization collects sales data and produces periodic reports. But suppose once a year it would like to have a detailed market study done. If no personnel in the organization are qualified to do such market analysis tasks, the company might have this work done by another company specializing in market research. These are all examples of **service bureaus**, companies which specialize in doing data processing for others. During the 1950s and 1960s and into the 1970s, many organizations had all or part of their data processing done by service bureaus.

Electronic Data Interchange

Electronic Data Interchange (EDI) is a form of communication between organizations which enables the automatic exchange of business information between a company and its suppliers, customers, partners, or others outside the company. Organizations generally implement EDI for two reasons: efficiency and competitive advantage.

EDI contributes to greater efficiency because it enables a company to send a purchase order directly to a supplier's computer, which can then produce and send back an invoice. When it is done without human intervention, EDI is an example of an action type of information system.

Some providers of goods and services have found that one way to gain competitive advantage within an industry and increase sales is to use technology to facilitate customer ordering. If customers have computer terminals which can be used to access the provider's computer, they can order goods and services electronically. This eliminates the delay associated with contacting the sales representative and waiting until the sales request is processed.

Electronic data interchange can benefit both suppliers and customers. A supplier might offer this direct method of ordering to attract new customers and increase the likelihood of retaining existing customers. It would also save on the personnel costs associated with receiving and processing customer orders. The customer would benefit from being able to obtain products or services faster.

Communication Within Organizations

The kind of facilities an organization chooses for internal data communication will depend to a large extent on the physical location of its offices. An organization has different options depending upon whether it has wide geographic dispersion, different physical sites within the same general area, or all offices in a single location or building.

Geographical Dispersion of Offices

An overriding consideration when offices are far apart is that the nodes of the network will be geographically dispersed. As a result communication costs can be very high. This is the case for the company we discussed earlier, with the home office in Chicago and five regional offices spread across the country. If this organization were interested in developing a data communication network, it would be very important for it to study the volume and frequency of data transmissions.

A starting point would be to understand the current flows of information. For example, what kind of data is sent from the regions to the regional offices and from the regional offices to the home office? How much data is sent? How often is this data sent? Since the distance between the individual sites within a region and the regional office is probably much less than the distance between the regional sites and the home office, different options would be appropriate. It is also likely that the sites in a given region would need to communicate with the regional office more frequently than the regional offices would need to communicate with the home office.

It would also be important to understand something about the data itself. For example, is the data output from some computer, or is it in the form of memos and reports? Does the data need to be shared throughout the company, or do other regions and the home office need this data in summarized form only? Does the data need to be sent from the source to the destination very quickly? Is it hard to predict who will need data from a given regional site? The answers to these questions will help the network designers determine the most appropriate communication structure. For example, if most of the data communication occurs within a region, there may be no need to have a data communication link with the home office. On the other hand, if there has to be frequent communication with the home office and if the data being sent is time-sensitive, some form of data communication probably will be needed.

Offices in the Same General Area

Organizations whose offices are located in the same general area, such as a bank with one main office downtown and several branch offices in the suburbs, have a different set of issues to address. Because the distance between the nodes is not as great, one might think that the communication costs would be much lower; but that is not always the case. Often, as the distance between source and destination increases, the cost per mile of sending that message decreases. Also, even if the message is being sent a relatively short distance, if it is outside the local calling area, higher rates might be charged. For this reason, it is very important for the organization to know how rates are determined by the companies which might be providing the communication service.

This bank also needs to understand its information flows and organization structure. For example, does it do all of its decision making and record keeping centrally, or is this work distributed? How much communication must go on between the bank's branches and the central office? More data communication facilities would be needed if all record keeping is done at the main office than if some of the processing is done at the branches.

The type of data that is communicated will also influence the type of network that is needed. Suppose many phone calls are made among the branch offices throughout the day. Electronic mail is an option that can reduce wasted time associated with making and receiving telephone calls. The person sending the message can do so at his or her convenience, and the person receiving the message does not have to be interrupted. The response can be made at the receiver's convenience. Electronic mail also helps to eliminate wasted time due to "telephone tag"—that is, the "game" that results when you try unsuccessfully to reach someone who then tries unsuccessfully to reach you. If an organization has offices throughout a metropolitan area but the employees must communicate frequently with people in other locations, electronic mail might be a very good option. Electronic mail will be considered in more detail later in the chapter.

Offices in a Single Location or Building

Before the development of the personal computer, the technical structure for computing consisted of a single computer to which the users had access through terminals. This centralized method of information processing has its drawbacks, but it has one big advantage. Since everyone communicates with the same computer, it is easy to share data. With the growing use of personal computers has come the desire to have the benefits of both forms of computing. Users like the autonomy of using a computer located in their offices, but they also want the ability to share data. The desire to share data among users of personal computers or between the mainframe computer and the personal computers has resulted in a growing demand for data communication networks.

Since the computers are located physically close together, more technical options are available. The costs are also much lower than those for networks which cover great distances. The kind of data which could be communicated in this type of network would be data which is currently distributed manually as well as output from computer processing. Examples of manual communication which could be accomplished though a network would include electronic mail, memos, and reports. Computer data might be files, portions of a database, or software. Sometimes networks are used to make better use of technology. For example, if several personal computers are connected together, they can share a common storage device (such as a magnetic or optical disk) and a common printer. As we can see, these networks enable an organization to share such information resources as data, hardware, and software. In determining which of the system resources should be shared, the organization needs to consider who uses them, how they are used, and how frequently they are used.

CONSTRAINTS ON COMMUNICATION SERVICES

Once the communication requirements are understood, the focus shifts to environmental factors that limit the choices. We have said that constraints are factors in the environment which influence the system. Since data communication is a type of system, it too has constraints imposed upon it from the environment. These constraints are found in both the local environment (the rest of the organization) and the global environment (the society). Three types of constraints will influence decisions regarding the choice of data communication products and services: technological, organizational, and regulatory constraints.

Technological Constraints

One type of constraint is imposed by the technology. Because the essence of communication is the movement of a message between the sender and the receiver, when computers are involved in this process, it is crucial that the computers involved can "talk" to each other. The term **compatibility** refers to the ability of different devices to communicate with each other. Therefore, any changes to an existing communication structure require that the technology be compatible. This may limit the choices available to an organization.

There are three types of technological constraints. The first is related to the capabilities of the technology. An organization may not be able to find available or affordable technology to suit its purposes. For example, transmission media that would enable an organization to send data in a variety of forms (e.g., voice, data, and video) may not be available or affordable. A second type of technological constraint is the technology that already exists in the organization. Suppose a certain type of network structure is already in use. If the organization wants to expand that network, it may be too expensive to change the topology. Therefore, the optimal network structure from a technological point of view might not be the most practical. The final type of technological constraint is related to the previous two. Because the essence of communication is compatibility, the need to conform to certain network standards may limit the available choices as well.

Organizational Constraints

Another type of constraint is imposed by the organization or the context in which the communication system will be used. Organizational constraints are related to the nature of the information and the type of information flows that exist in the organization. Therefore, organizational constraints represent factors such as the type of information, the organizational structure, and the type of individuals to be taken into account.

The Type of Information

The type of information and the uses to which it will be put should influence decisions regarding data communication tools. Suppose an organization is interested in implementing an electronic mail system. Management has determined that instead of making so many phone calls and using expensive paper for sending memos, electronic mail is a more cost-effective choice. One question that should be asked is whether all communication should be handled through electronic mail. Upon closer examination, management might find that certain communication such as personnel matters would be better handled face to face. On the other hand, it might find that straightforward, factual information is well suited to electronic mail. Thus, the type of information being communicated will have an effect on decisions regarding how and whether communication activities will be automated.

The Organizational Structure

Since data communication systems should support an organization's information flows, the existing organizational structure must be well understood before any attempt is made to alter an existing data communication system or to implement a new one. Not only should the direction of the information flows be understood, but the intended senders and receivers should be understood as well. For example, is this a one-to-one, a one-to-many, or a many-to-many communication? Depending upon the answer, different data communication structures will be suggested. This is an example of an organizational constraint: the nature of the organizational communication influences the options to be considered.

Another type of organizational constraint arises when certain data communication options which are very appealing from a technological perspective just might not be realistic from an organizational perspective. For example, suppose the computer experts in an organization determine that considerable time and money would be saved by the implementation of electronic mail. Time would be saved by the elimination of "telephone tag," and the ever-increasing paper costs would be lowered. While the logic of this suggestion is very appealing, the reality might be that there are many individuals who do not sign onto the computer on a regular basis. Therefore, forcing these people to get their "mail" in electronic form would be seen as an extra burden. The computer experts might not have thought of this because they are signed onto the computer constantly. If data communication is to support organizational objectives, it must be able to reflect the current type of organizational communication and must be consistent with the organizational culture.

The Type of Individuals

Some constraints brought about by the type of individuals involved with the communication system were suggested earlier. That is, the intended users' knowledge about and comfort with new modes of communication must be taken into account. Suppose the objective of the data communication system is to automate a communication process which is currently being accomplished by the telephone or face-to-face communication. For the system to be effective, certain human factors must be taken into account. The users must feel comfortable with this method of communication and must support the goal of organizational units working together. Therefore, the most desirable choice from a technological perspective might not be the best choice from the perspective of human communication.

Regulatory Constraints

A final type of constraint which has an impact on communication decisions comes from the global environment, specifically, public policy. Unlike other aspects of information processing, government regulations influence the way private-sector data communication activities are carried out. As a result, decisions about communication services must also take into account the regulatory implications of these choices. Two aspects of public policy should be understood in order that regulatory constraints can be incorporated into the decision-making process: deregulation of telecommunications and transborder data flow.

Telecommunications Deregulation

Monopolies and Regulation Monopolistic control has been a part of the American telecommunications industry from its beginning. Monopolies existed because of technological and capital constraints: a huge investment in equipment is necessary to set up a telephone, radio, or television network. In the case of broadcasting, there was another reason for the existence of monopolies. The airwaves are a limited resource. Therefore, to prevent interference with the sending of signals, only a single user in a certain geographical area could be allowed to use a given frequency.

The limited radio spectrum was the original rationale for bringing telecommunications under governmental control. Some entity was needed to allocate spectrum space and oversee the distribution of licenses to use that space. A related rationale for regulation derived from the fact that since the airwaves are "public," some governmental agency should oversee this form of communication to make certain that the public interest was served. The government agency set up for this purpose was the Federal Communications Commission (FCC).

Gradually, nearly all aspects of telecommunications were brought under governmental control. The rationale for regulating the telephone industry was that the country would benefit from the economies of scale which would result from having a single telephone carrier, called a "common carrier." However, since the common carrier would be a monopoly, some agency was needed to oversee its operations. The monopoly in this case was American Telephone and Telegraph Company (AT&T) and its local operating companies. When cable television first became available, it was also regulated by the FCC. Despite the fact that the rationale of a limited number of channels didn't exist for cable television, the FCC attempted to regulate it in the same fashion that it regulated broadcast television.

The only part of telecommunications not regulated by government agencies was data communication. Of course, when computer output was sent over telephone lines, it was treated the same as voice and was therefore regulated in that sense, but the providers of equipment for data communication were not regulated as such.

The structure of the telecommunications industry was radically altered in 1984 when the industry became deregulated. The key events were that AT&T divested itself from its local operating companies, and that other long distance carriers were allowed to compete with AT&T on an equal basis. As a result, a much more competitive industry began to emerge. We have already started to see the effects of this new policy; other effects are more long-term in nature. Some effects have been obvious to the average citizen; one has been **divestiture**. One result of divestiture has been that the local telephone companies, called local operating companies, are no longer owned by AT&T. Another effect has been **equal access**, which means that all long distance carriers have an equal chance to attract and serve customers. That is why citizens are now required to choose a primary long distance carrier. A person can now choose AT&T, MCI, US Sprint, or any of a number of long distance providers.

In exchange for agreeing to these terms, the long-standing antitrust suit against AT&T was dropped. Further, AT&T became free to enter the unregulated data processing segment of the industry, which it did by establishing AT&T Information Systems. It is this company which is able to manufacture and market computers.

The Effects of Deregulation[2] Some of the effects of this policy change are less easily observed than others; some have yet to be felt. We have just entered a newly competitive environment that contains many alternatives and even more unknowns. The challenge for informed consumers of telecommunications technology is to develop some appreciation for the possible implications of this new environment on their decisions.

Probably the most evident impact is the increase in the number of communication products and services that have become available. Because communication companies may now enter computer markets and computer vendors can now offer communication services, many companies are trying to establish a position in this industry. This push to be more competitive is driven by the desire to establish a secure market position. The introduction by AT&T of a line of personal computers is just one example. With many more products available on the market, the consumer must be sure that all of this equipment can work together.

In addition to new devices for performing existing functions, there are also more options for performing totally new functions. One example is the option of **bypass**, which is now available to companies that wish to set up their own communication networks. Bypass means that an organization does not have to be connected to the local operating company: it can be its own telephone company.

One of the problems associated with so many players in the industry is that not all of them will survive. This is what is meant by a "shakeout." In decisions about the acquisition of computer and communication equipment, the long-term viability of the vendor and the product is an important consideration. The consumer wants to be sure the vendor will be around in case there are any problems.

Another effect being felt in organizations is the gradual shift toward the integration of information types. Organizations have the choice of delivering all types of information—voice, video, and computer data—through the same device. This opens up whole new vistas for the effective communication of information. But it also makes for a much more complicated situation. Many more factors must be taken into consideration. The financial risks are also greater. If an integrated system breaks down, all forms of communication are affected. The human risks are greater as well. The use of technology can be employed to effectively enhance human communication, but it can also work against it. It is important that human considerations remain in the forefront when these kinds of decisions are being made.

Finally, given this more complex operating and decision-making environment, it stands to reason that new expertise will be needed. While there will still be the need for people with expertise in specific aspects of information processing and communication, two new types of expertise are needed. First, people are needed who have an "integrated perspective" on the data that an organization must communicate. These people understand that sometimes it is not necessary to make distinctions among data, voice, and video communication. The other kind of person that is needed is one who is capable of doing "technology assessment"—that is, one whose job it is to study new technologies and consider their potential benefit to an organization.

All of this points to the requirement that knowledge about telecommunications is an important component of one's overall information literacy. With this knowledge it will be easier to answer some of the important questions an organization must ask in determining its most appropriate type of communication structure.

THE HISTORY OF DEREGULATION

Prior to the growth of data communication, communication channels were only used for a single purpose: the telephone was only used to transmit voice; the airwaves were only used to transmit audio and video; and coaxial cable was only used to transmit televisions shows.

The growing use of data communication in conjunction with computer processing presented two problems for regulators. One problem was that this one sector of the communication industry was not regulated, while other sectors, which might conceivably want to offer the same product or service, were. For example, if AT&T wanted to provide a new data communication service, it would have to get permission from the FCC. But if IBM wanted to provide the same service, it wouldn't have to. On the other hand, if IBM wanted to develop a certain product which was considered to be a "communication device," AT&T was able to impose strict guidelines on the production, sale, and use of this device in its network. This became an issue as data communication became more popular and companies started to produce equipment such as modems.

The other problem had to do with an evolving understanding of communication technology and the uses to which it could be put. People learned that the airwaves could be used to transmit not only audio and video, but text as well. An example of this is videotext, which was discussed in Chapter 3. It was observed that coaxial cable, which was used for cable television, had a huge transmission capacity. With the ability to carry 150 channels simultaneously, coaxial cable could theoretically be used to deliver all kinds of information to the home or office: not just television, but radio, telephone, and computer data. The problem was that the existing regulation was not set up to accommodate these innovative uses of the technology. There were regulations, for example, which precluded cable TV operators from providing telephone services, even though it was technologically possible.

Throughout the 1960s and 1970s, attempts were made to change telecommunications regulations to be consistent with technological innovations. The problem was that as soon as a new set of regulations was disseminated, it was outdated. The FCC held two Computer Inquiries during this time. That is, the commission solicited comments from members of the telecommunications industry regarding recommended changes to current regulations. The First Computer Inquiry was held in the late 1960s.[3] During this time, remote access to computers and time sharing were becoming popular. This inquiry concluded that data processing should remain unregulated but that communications should still be regulated. That is, services which were primarily data processing would be unregulated and services which were primarily data communication would be regulated. Since this inquiry was held before the advent of intelligent terminals and personal computers, such a distinction was easier to make.

By the time this report was published, however, the assumptions guiding it were being challenged. Computers had become a vital part of communications and communications had become an important part of data processing. In addition, the presence of distributed processing, which combined both computing and communicating, made it nearly impossible to make a clear distinction between the two. It was obvious by then that regulation could not be based on the technology itself. The Second Computer Inquiry, completed in the late 1970s, concluded that regulation would be based on the type of service provided rather than the technology involved.[4]

Three types of communication service were identified: voice, basic non-voice, and enhanced non-voice. **Voice service** referred to the transmission of the human voice — human telephone conversations. **Basic non-voice services** were those which involved the use of a computer but only to assist in the transmission of the communication signal. Examples were message switching and signal conversion from digital to analog and vice versa. Both of these services could be offered by the regulated common carriers such as AT&T. The third type of service, *enhanced non-voice*, or **enhanced services**, referred to services in which the computer was used to change the data in some way. If common carriers wanted to provide this service, they had to do it through a totally separate organizational unit of their company.

In addition to the work of the FCC in the two Computer Inquiries, there were also several attempts made to revise the Communications Act of

1934. During the late 1970s a number of bills were introduced in Congress. But there was still another regulatory issue to be settled.

As a result of an antitrust suit settled in 1956, AT&T was prohibited from engaging in the unregulated areas of telecommunications, such as the manufacture and marketing of equipment. In 1974, AT&T was sued again for violating this consent decree. AT&T was charged with abusing its monopoly status by keeping competitors out of the markets for equipment and long distance telephone services.

In January 1982 the Justice Department proposed a settlement with AT&T. The major thrust of this settlement was that the case against AT&T would be dropped in exchange for AT&T divesting itself of some of its holdings. Following several modifications, the results of this settlement went into effect in January 1984. Under the terms of this settlement, greater competition would be allowed in the telecommunications industry. This is what is meant by "deregulation of telecommunications." The new environment is one of less governmental regulation of telecommunications and more competition within the industry. This new "industry" is one in which computing and communicating are integrally related. The effect of this settlement was to introduce a new era of telecommunications policy.

Transborder Data Flow

While telecommunications policy is the most pervasive form of regulatory constraint on data communication decisions, there are other types of regulatory constraints which influence our choices. In the case of transborder data flow, it is not so much U.S. law as it is laws in other countries which influence the data communication decisions of multinational companies operating in those countries.

Until the technical capability for data communication existed, international communication was conducted via telex, telephone, and mail. With the advent of remote access to computing and computer networks, these methods of communication have been gradually replaced by electronic methods. The term **transborder data flow (TDF)** refers to data which is sent through transnational communication networks for the purpose of storage, processing, and retrieval by a computer. Another term for TDF, then, would be international data networks. Although the literal interpretation of the phrase simply refers to a type of communication, TDF is normally used in conjunction with public policy governing the flow this of data.

The impact of transborder data flow legislation on U.S. corporations is the potential for increased cost of operations and a decrease in the efficiency of data communication. Costs associated with these laws come from licensing, registering of databases, compliance reporting, and response to inquiries about the existence of personal files and their content. Other costs come from government inspection and disclosure of information, taxes, and the requirement to use less economical methods of data transmission.

Multinational corporations with highly centralized information systems feel the effect the most. Those corporations required to use a government-owned network will probably have to pay higher communication costs. Companies which store a considerable amount of personal information in their databases are subject to scrutiny and possible restrictions on use. A recent policy adopted by some European countries requires that personal data may only be exported to countries which have reciprocal data protection laws. For a country such as the United States which does not have a comprehensive privacy law, this has the potential to be a severe restriction on the movement of data.

At a minimum, TDF laws are requiring U.S. corporations to be more accountable for their use of data. In some cases, multinational corporations are being required to support the development of infant information infrastructures. These laws can also be seen as a form of trade protectionism. In this information age, countries have recognized that information is a valuable national resource and that they are in a position to exert influence over its use and export.

THE HISTORY OF TRANSBORDER DATA FLOW

In the early 1970s some countries in Europe and the Americas began to recognize the potential negative consequences of transborder data flow for both the individual citizen and their national well-being. They voiced the concern that it might not be in their nations' best interests to allow the free flow of information when the direction was nearly always out of their countries and into the United States.

The ostensible issue that is raised is that of balancing two competing interests. On one side is the benefit to be derived from the free flow of information. On the other side is the potential impact of the unrestricted flow of information on a nation's economy, society, and defense. The background to this issue is that there are many databases owned and operated by agencies in the United States which contain information about citizens from other countries. These are either databases owned by multinational corporations or bibliographic databases owned and operated by information providers based in the United States. The establishment of transborder data flow legislation is an outgrowth of a series of recognitions on the part of foreign nations.

In the early days of the transborder data flow controversy, the issues centered on personal privacy and the right of access to information. Over the years, the emphasis has shifted to national sovereignty issues and the protection of fledgling information industries in the face of competition from foreign multinational corporations.

Issues associated with the invasion of privacy present perhaps the most concrete example of the negative side of transborder data flow. Of concern to some nations is the fact that information which has moved out of the host country (the country in which it originated) is no longer controllable by that country. Other nations are concerned about the security and confidentiality of data about its citizens which flows across national boundaries (and usually ends up in the United States). For example, Sweden found that information about its citizens appeared in more than 2,000 data banks outside Sweden. A Canadian study found that 48 percent of its record-keeping organizations furnished data to U.S. organizations such as credit bureaus, law enforcement agencies, and insurance companies. A concern these countries have is that this data, if stored by U.S. corporations, is at the mercy of U.S. laws. If there is a discrepancy between U.S. laws and those of the host country, the rights guaranteed to its citizens are not being upheld. Since there is wide variation in the type of privacy protection that is afforded by different nations, this is a very real concern.

Another issue is the threat to national sovereignty. Just as no company would want to rely on a competitor to provide its vital information, sovereign nations do not want to be in the position of depending on another nation for the safekeeping of their information. When databases and computer services which are vital to the functioning of government or business are physically or technically under the control of foreign authorities, the host nation becomes vulnerable to whatever happens in that foreign country. In the extreme case, if two countries who are allies become enemies, one of those countries could be cut off from vital information sources. The motivation for transborder data flow regulation in this context is to extend the notion of "national sovereignty" beyond the geographical bounds of a country to apply to its information as well.

A closely related but perhaps more subtle issue is the fear of cultural inundation. Cultural encroachment can exist in the form of information brought into a country which uses a different language and mode of thinking and reflects a different value system from that of the country receiving it. If much of the information a host nation receives has been collected, processed, stored, and disseminated by another nation, that other nation can be viewed as exerting a form of "electronic colonization" or "electronic imperialism" over the host nation.

A final issue that falls within the domain of transborder data flow is the fate of fledgling information industries and a nation's emerging information infrastructure. Some countries just beginning to develop wide-scale information processing and data communication services must compete with large and well-developed international networks used and owned by multinational corporations. In response, some governments, through the postal, telegraph, and telephone (PTT) organizations, have developed their own national networks. Another route has been the banding together of several nations to develop and use one common network. EURONET is an example of such a network.

Some multinational corporations make use of communication services provided by private organizations. Large corporations may have their own networks. Others use network services purchased from companies which provide access to a communications medium owned or leased from a communications common carrier. (This option is explained in more detail later in the chapter.) When these options are chosen, the multinational company is not technically dependent upon the host country. This presents two potential problems. If these companies do not use the host country's network, the host country has lost a mechanism for control over what is done with the information. In addition, large multinational companies represent a major source of revenue for these fledgling national networks. If they use private networks, this will pose a real threat to the economic vitality of national data communication networks.

All of these issues point to the fact that the United States is perceived as being an "information-rich" nation capable of exploiting the world's information. The response on the part of other nations has been to enact laws which serve to restrict the flow of information out of host countries and at the same time support the development of emerging industries. Controlling U.S. corporations' access to and use of foreign information is viewed by some nations as a way of exerting control over the United States.

The first piece of transborder data flow legislation was the Swedish Data Act of 1973, which required the licensing of both public and private organizations that maintained personal registers (that is, databases about people). It became the model for similar laws that were enacted in other countries. These laws typically apply to citizens of the country (as opposed to business enterprises) and relate to the use of name-linked data and personal identifiers (the equivalent of the social security number in the United States). These laws exercise control in the form of requiring the registration of personal databases, requiring a license to export data, and/or monitoring data transfers. The right of access to information is protected by giving citizens the right to know who has information about them and the nature of this information, and giving them the right to challenge its accuracy.

Protecting the development of the infant information industries in these nations has been carried out in several ways. In some cases, corporations are required to use the national networks. Tariffs and export taxes are also levied against multinational corporations. These laws carry with them various sanctions, including loss of licenses, requirement to compensate victims, data confiscation, fines, and imprisonment.

DATA COMMUNICATION OPTIONS

As our discussion of telecommunications deregulation has made clear, the decision-making process has become much more complex in recent years. In addition, because of the connectivity issues related to data communication, the consequences of decisions are more far-reaching than those of decisions regarding other information technology/systems, such as the purchase of a single personal computer. For this reason, vendors, consultants, and other specialists are available to help in the evaluation of data communication tools and in the development of data communication networks.

An organization has several alternatives available to enhance its communication environment. It could choose to acquire the technological and personnel resources and develop its own data communication network. Or it could engage the services of data communication specialists. Some specialists act as consultants to organizations that want to develop their own systems. In this way, an organization has access to the kind of expertise it needs to evaluate the alternatives without having to permanently hire such a person. Another option is to purchase or lease the network services from a telecommunications supplier. With this option the organization will not have to deal with maintaining the equipment.

Constructing a data communication network involves two major decisions: determining the scope of the network and deciding how to acquire the necessary technical and personnel resources. Having already discussed the kinds of communication requirements an organization might have and the types of constraints that must be taken into account, we will now consider the options available for meeting an organization's communication requirements.

The Scope of the Network

The scope of the data communication network derives from the context of the communication requirements. The network scope can be divided into four categories: external communications, wide area networks, metropolitan area networks, and local area networks. The first category refers to communication between organizations; the others refer to various types of communication within organizations.

Communication Between Organizations

Generally, an organization requires data communication with another organization because some component of information processing is to be accomplished by an outside source. In our discussion of data communication requirements, three examples of shared processing were given. First, an organization might require access to data stored in another's database. In this case, the provider of the database is performing the *information storage and retrieval* function. Second, an organization might need to have a service bureau do its computer-based information processing. Here, the *processing* component is accomplished by the service bureau. Finally, a client organization might want to directly *input* requests for goods or services into the supplier's information system, which will, in turn, *output* an invoice for those goods or services.

These examples are all instances of a star network structure, in which the customer organization communicates to a central computer in order to access data or send data to be processed. The customer organization may or may not have its own computer. Within the boundaries of these networks are two organizations: the consumer organization, and the provider of the data or the information processing capability. Figure 7.9 shows these three network structures.

The technical requirements for this type of network are minimal. An organization needs a terminal, a modem, and access to a telephone line. If an organization chooses to access these companies from a computer, the computer must be adapted to include the necessary communication hardware and software. The organization may also want to have a printer. There are several ways that the communication channel can be provided. They will be discussed in a later section which considers options for acquiring communication resources.

Wide Area Networks

A **wide area network (WAN)** is one that connects parts of an organization which are spread across a wide geographical area, such as a company with offices throughout the United States. WANs can be expanded to cover more

FIGURE 7.9
Star networks for communication between organizations

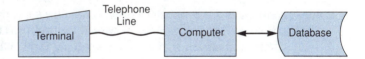

(a) Gaining access to information provider's database

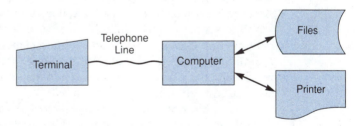

(b) Using a service bureau for information processing

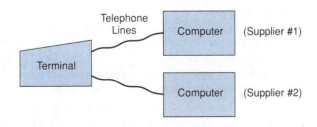

(c) Electronic data interchange between customer and supplier

than one country if a company has offices abroad. In this case the network is also referred to as an international network. International networks are subject to regulatory constraints in the form of both telecommunications regulations and transborder data flow regulations. An organization interested in developing an international network should learn about the data access and communication laws in the countries which would be involved.

A hierarchical network structure might be appropriate for this type of network, for two reasons. First, it probably isn't necessary to process all of the data in a single location. Much of the data could be processed at the location where the data originates. The purpose of the network would be to communicate reports and messages. The second reason for using a hierarchical structure is to save on communication costs. Given the long distances involved, an organization might want to process as much as it can locally. Figure 7.6 was an example of a wide area network.

The technical requirements for a wide area network are considerable. Each site would have a computer called a **host computer**. This computer would have the technical capability to transmit data through the network. In addition, each site would have peripheral devices such as terminals, printers, and storage devices. A variety of media are used to provide the communication channels for these networks, including satellites, microwave relays, and wire. To develop a wide area network, an organization must acquire long distance communication services. This can be done either by leasing a communication channel such as a telephone line or by utilizing complete data communication services such as those provided by a public data network vendor (e.g., Telenet).

Metropolitan Area Networks

A **metropolitan area network (MAN)** is smaller in scope. It might be developed for an organization which has offices at different sites within a city or metropolitan area. If this network spans more than one communications area (known by area codes—e.g., 617 or 212) as designated by the state communications regulatory body or involves more than one state, the network activities will be subject to regulatory constraints.

Star, hierarchical, and ring network structures can be used for a MAN. A bank, for example, might do all of its processing at one central location. This would be an example of a star topology. However, if some of the processing needed to be done at each of the bank's branches and some at the home office, a hierarchical structure would be appropriate. Figure 7.10 shows a metropolitan area network.

Each node or office in the network would need at least a terminal, a modem, and a communication channel. If a hierarchical structure is chosen, other resources such as a computer, a printer, and storage devices would be needed as well. Data in a metropolitan area network can be transmitted using microwaves, cables/wires, cellular radio, and optical fibers. Typically, the communication channel is supplied by the local telephone company. However, an organization may choose to supply the channel itself, in which case it may set up microwave links among the different sites.

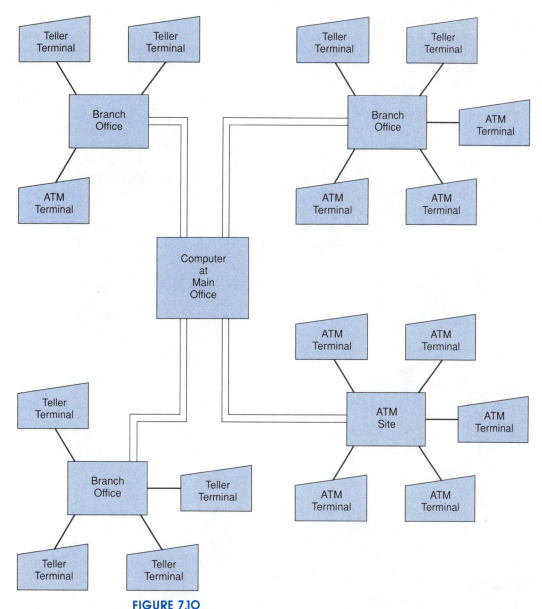

FIGURE 7.10
A metropolitan area network for a bank (star topology)

Local Area Networks

In a **local area network (LAN)**, the geographical scope is limited to a single building or cluster of buildings which are close together, such as those on a college campus. In addition to data communication, LANs can also support internal communication of voice and video. Local area networks are used to facilitate the sharing of reports, data, software, storage disks, and printers, as well as to enhance human communication through features such as electronic mail. In addition, several LANs can be connected together to create a metropolitan area network. Of the four types of networks, local area networks are the type an end user is most likely to encounter, so we will consider LANs in greater detail than the other types of networks.

A local area network provides decentralized access in a network. Therefore, either a ring or a bus topology would usually be used in developing a LAN. Figure 7.11 shows a local area network using a ring topology.

The technical requirements for a LAN include computers (usually personal computers), a communication channel, network software, and peripheral devices such as printers and storage devices. The media used for the communication channel are usually twisted pair wires or coaxial cables. Sometimes microwave relays and fiber optics are used as well.

The most popular media for LANs are twisted pair wires, those used for telephones. Since buildings are already wired for telephones, any excess capac-

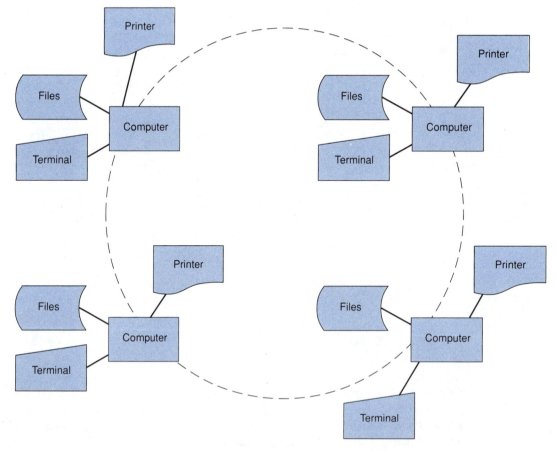

FIGURE 7.11

A ring topology for a local area network

ity can be adapted to other uses. The decision to use twisted pair wires for a LAN because the building is already wired that way is an example of working within a technical constraint in choosing among options.

Coaxial cable is the second most popular transmission medium. It has a number of advantages over twisted pairs, including greater carrying capacity, wider bandwidth, and less susceptibility to noise. In an organization without existing telephone lines, coaxial cable networks can cost significantly less for installation and for continuing maintenance. Some new office buildings are being "wired" for local area networks in much the same way that buildings have traditionally been wired for electricity and telephones.

Fiber-optic and microwave links are other alternatives for transmission, but there are technical constraints regarding these options. Fiber-optic wiring is not available everywhere. In addition, connections between fiber-optic wires are difficult and costly to make. Since microwave transmission uses the airwaves, this option might not work in locations which have physical barriers between sites such as tall buildings or large hills. A regulatory constraint on the use of microwave is that the organization must obtain a radio license in order to operate it.

The oldest type of LAN is a network which was originally used for voice communication. This is the **private branch exchange (PBX)**. PBXs have been providing circuit switching for offices for years. PBXs were initially only provided by telephone companies. Today numerous companies are providing them. A PBX is an inexpensive alternative for integrated voice and data communication. It can use standard telephone wires as a single transmission medium for both voice and data. In addition, the existing wiring in the building can be used to support the PBX. When high data transmission rates are required, however, coaxial cable may be required and digital rather than analog transmission may be desired.

There are two signaling alternatives for transmission in a LAN, regardless of whether the medium is twisted pairs, coaxial cable, microwave, or fiber optics: **baseband transmission** and **broadband transmission**. In baseband transmission, all data is transmitted at the same frequency. Transmission of multiple messages across this channel is provided by some method of sharing. In this way, a single cable can be used for data as well as voice and video transmission. A popular baseband option which uses coaxial cable is Ethernet, which was developed by Xerox in 1972, and later Digital Equipment Corporation and Intel joined in its further development. The environments for which this type of network is well suited are those in which continuous transmission is rare and messages are smaller than 1,000 characters. Ethernet has become the industry standard for baseband LAN transmission. One technical constraint on the Ethernet option is that there are limits to how far the messages can be sent, although multiple LANs can be interconnected for greater distance. This is to make certain that collisions are consistently detected throughout the network. Ethernet uses the CSMA/CD (carrier sense multiple access with collision detection) protocol, which is prone to performance problems under heavy loads.

Broadband transmission overcomes some of the limitations of baseband transmission. The bandwidth of the coaxial cable is divided into a distinct number of communication channels, each of which will support a particular function. For example, the total bandwidth may be divided into a series of channels such as a voice channel, a video channel, a low-speed data channel, and a high-speed data channel. Each channel is assigned its own frequency. Community antenna cable (CATV) systems have used broadband transmission over coaxial cable for many years.

The main advantages of broadband transmission are that it can accommodate a large number of channels in a single cable and the signal can be sent great distances without becoming degraded. The main disadvantage of broadband networks is that they are more technically complex and therefore more expensive to implement and maintain than baseband networks.

Acquiring Data Communication Resources

A data communication network requires both technological and personnel resources. There are three options available to those in the process of acquiring these resources. First, an organization can purchase communications capability from a variety of companies now providing access to communication channels. Second, it can engage the services of a company that not only provides access to the communication channel, but also provides additional services such as the use of an established network. Finally, the network can be developed "in house" using the organization's own resources or by employing a telecommunications company to help it develop a network. The choice among these options should be based on the type of network desired, the size of the organization, and the technological and personnel resources within the company. Along with these considerations is one overriding consideration: cost.

Common Carriers

A **common carrier** is a regulated entity which provides its users with access to communication channels. The rates a common carrier can charge are regulated by state and federal agencies. Sometimes this can work to a user's advantage; other times it means the rates are higher than other alternatives. Examples of common carriers are the various local operating companies, such as New England Telephone, and long distance carriers, such as AT&T and MCI. Prior to the deregulation of telecommunications, common carriers provided a few basic services. In this newly competitive environment, however, the number of services common carriers are permitted to provide has grown considerably. They are now able to offer both regulated and unregulated services.

Switched Lines   Probably the most common method of acquiring data communication capability is to use **switched** (regular telephone) **lines** in conjunction with a modem. The advantage of this option is that when the line is not being used for data communication it can be used for voice. This might be the case for an organization wanting to gain access to an external database on an infrequent basis. But if there is need for more frequent data communication, a separate line might be needed. This line could also be a switched line.

Very few constraints will affect this decision. Unless one of the database providers requires the use of a certain kind of terminal, the organization is free to choose the type of terminal which best suits its needs. While modems may be chosen from any vendor, the technical characteristics must match those of the database provider. However, one organizational constraint must be taken into account. If a switched line is to be used for both voice communication and access to an external database, procedures may need to be established regarding when the line can be used for each purpose. Perhaps the line has to be available for voice communication during certain times of the day. This might limit the times when the external databases can be accessed. Switched lines might also be an option for a metropolitan area network which has a hierarchical structure. If much of the processing is done locally and only summary reports and messages need to be sent to the other offices, a switched line might be adequate.

Leased Lines   If an organization has a large volume of data communication, it may decide to have a *dedicated line*, or **leased line**, for this purpose. These lines are leased from a common carrier, and no one else uses them. The main advantages are the capacity to transmit large volumes of data; less chance of interference which could result if other users are on the line; and greater speed of data transmission. Some of these lines are capable of direct digital transmission, so the data entered at a terminal would not have to be translated from analog to digital form by a modem as it must be with switched lines. Digital transmission speeds the data communication process, but digital lines are not available in all locations. This is an example of a technical constraint. An organization which uses a service bureau for all or most of its data processing might choose to have a leased line. If a considerable amount of data is to be transmitted within an organization through a wide area or metropolitan area network, leased lines might be the appropriate choice there as well.

Enhanced Services

Companies providing enhanced services provide more than just the communication channel. They provide network services such as access to an established network, and enhancements to a communication channel which will provide better protection for the data. They also provide specific applications such as electronic mail, teleconferencing, and access to commercial databases. These companies are less regulated than common carriers. For this reason, these services are sometimes referred to as "unregulated services." Common carriers may also provide enhanced services; however, the revenues must be kept separate from those derived from its regulated services. To accomplish this, a separate organizational unit has to be established by the common carrier. The following are examples of some of the unregulated services which an organization can acquire to satisfy its data communication requirements.

Data Network Services An organization can have the benefit of a data communication network by purchasing network services to cover any geographical scope. As the geographical distance grows, so does the likely cost effectiveness of purchasing these services rather than developing them. Therefore, this is a common option for wide area networks. The provider of a **data network** gives its customers access to the hardware, software, and protocols required to support the desired *network activities*. The transmission line is provided by a common carrier. The data network vendor provides the communications expertise, technical support, and security. There is no need for the customer to develop in-house expertise in the design, installation, and operation of a network. Just as there are service bureaus which can provide all the resources necessary to support an organization's information processing requirements, these network vendors provide all the resources required to support an organization's data communication requirements. The main advantage is that an organization does not have to get involved in hiring communication personnel and in acquiring, installing, and maintaining the technology. An example of a data network vendor is Satellite Business Systems (SBS).

Value-Added Services In a **value-added network (VAN)**, a vendor provides all the related hardware, software, and protocols as well as the transmission line. Transmission lines are leased to the vendor by a common carrier, and these leasing costs are included in the costs to the organization purchasing the value-added network service. The vendor enhances the communication lines by providing such additional or value-added features as error detection, a faster response time, and security. Access to a VAN can be acquired by an organization for a small initial investment. Since the design, installation, and operation of the network are the responsibility of the vendor, the organization only needs to have a minimal internal network support staff. An example of a value-added network service is TYMNET. VANs might be appropriate for communication between organizations or for a wide area network.

   The constraints related to this data communication option are primarily organizational. While the initial investment is low, the recurring costs can be quite high if there is a high volume of usage. In addition, the customer organization has little control over the network itself. Since the network is shared by many organizations, security problems could arise. The use of a value-added network is an appropriate data communication option for an organization that is not large enough to support its own network or does not have sufficient data communication volume to warrant it.

Electronic Mail **Electronic mail (email)** is a computerized system for the electronic delivery of textual messages. It is an electronic alternative to both the telephone and the mail. Email messages are routed to the appropriate destination, where they are stored until the destination site is able to receive the message. Sometimes these messages are stored at an intermediate location. This form of transmission is referred to as **store-and-forward**.

Electronic mail is becoming a popular form of data communication within all types of networks. An electronic mail service provided by a vendor could be utilized for communication between organizations. For example, an organization which does direct ordering from a supplier located in a different time zone might want to have electronic mail to send and receive messages at a time that is most convenient to both. It could also be part of a wide area network. BITNET and INTERNET are electronic mail services available to academic institutions, allowing faculty around the world to communicate. This is especially useful in communication with people in time zones that may differ by many hours.

Teleconferencing An alternative to face-to-face meetings is **teleconferencing**. If a meeting needs to be scheduled for participants who must travel a considerable distance, the costs to an organization can be very high. An alternative is to utilize communication technology that will enable people to hold meetings electronically. The oldest type of teleconferencing is computer conferencing. It is much like electronic mail. Rather than meeting in person to share ideas, participants can circulate messages throughout the computer network for viewing by all parties. A common type of teleconferencing today is video conferencing. With this mode, people can see and hear each other as they share ideas.

In-house Development of Data Communication Networks

There are several reasons for choosing to develop a data communication network rather than using the services provided by a vendor. One reason is that the organization may be so geographically dispersed and the volume of data so large that it would be more economical to have one's own network. An example of this would be a multinational company developing its own wide area network. Another reason would be that the scope of the network may be small enough that an organization could cost effectively acquire the necessary technical and personnel resources. An example of this would be the development of a local area network. A final reason would be that the recent changes in telecommunications policy have resulted in alternatives to the use of common carriers. An example of this would be an organization which *bypasses* the local common carrier and acquires its own communication channels for its metropolitan area network.

If an organization chooses to develop its own network, it needs to have access to telecommunications specialists. This can be accomplished either by hiring the necessary staff or by engaging the services of a telecommunications consultant. The choice between these two options depends on the organization's ongoing need for expertise.

If an organization intends to develop its own wide area network or to bypass the local common carrier and develop its own metropolitan area network, it would need to have data communications experts on its staff. These people would design and develop the initial network and would be available to make further enhancements and respond to problems that arise.

On the other hand, many companies can help an organization develop its own local area network. They will do the planning and design for the network and help the organization choose the most appropriate technology. It may not be necessary for the organization to retain a staff of data communications experts. However, it is necessary to have personnel who have sufficient knowledge to communicate with the consultants while the LAN is being developed and who can spot problems after it is implemented.

Criteria for Choosing Among Options

There are many criteria for an organization to consider in deciding which data communication option to choose. Since a data communication network is composed of technology, data, and people, all three should be considered in evaluating the available options and making a choice among them.

Technology

In addition to determining which data communication system can accomplish the designated tasks, the organization must also be concerned with the system's performance. Response time is a common performance criterion. *Response time* refers to the amount of time it takes to transmit a message. In the context of computers, it is the elapsed time between pressing the ENTER key and receiving either feedback that the message was sent or the results of the process that was requested. A related performance measure is the availability of the resources when they are needed. When resources are not available, response time is adversely affected. Another performance measure is reliability. If individuals depend on the correct operation of the network, it is important for there to be quick recovery from technical failures. To a large extent, the degree to which a system is available and reliable depends on the amount of money the organization is willing to pay. To ensure availability, the system must be able to detect and remove a failed component, substitute a working one, and compensate for the change. Reliability is enhanced though redundancy, internal diagnostics, and backup capabilities. All of these cost money.

Data

Users of a system in which data is shared need to have confidence beyond the assurance of reliability. They must also be sure the data will not get into the wrong hands. Therefore, the network must have an adequate level of security and privacy. Users are concerned with the security and privacy of their data whether it resides in a single computer or travels throughout a data communication network. They should be able to assume that messages are private and are protected against interception and alteration, whether intentional or accidental. Security and privacy procedures are discussed in greater detail in Chapter 10.

The distance to be covered by the data communication network will also influence the alternatives available. Earlier in the chapter we described the types of networks available to serve data communication needs between and within organizations.

In addition to network scope (i.e., the distance covered by the network), the type of data contained in the messages must be taken into account. Some networks will only support a single type of message, while others may support multiple types. For example, an organization's decision whether to transmit data only or data and voice will affect its selection of transmission equipment and the sophistication of the technology employed.

The volume of data to be transmitted in the network is another factor which must be taken into account. Two dimensions of message volume must be considered. One is the size of the messages. A message being transported from the central office to a regional office could range from a large portion of a computerized database to a short memo. The organization must know the size of the messages to be sent and verify that the network can accommodate such messages. The other dimension is the number of messages per unit time to be processed by the network. A heavy volume of short messages can be more of a burden on the network than a small number of large messages. A related consideration is the peak times of communication activity. If a given network cannot support the message volume, there are two alternatives. The technical alternative is to change the network structure. The organizational alternative is to establish procedures regarding when certain types of messages may be sent.

People

An organization must have enough qualified personnel available for the data communication tools it is using. Personnel are required for the design, installation, operational support, and maintenance of the data communication systems. Data communication specialists are expensive and in short supply. An organization must decide whether it wants to have its own staff or would prefer to purchase the services of personnel, either as consultants or as part of data communication services such as vendors or value-added networks.

Data communication costs are a major concern to most organizations. Some initial or one-time costs include the costs of determining the data communication requirements, acquiring the data communication system, and installing the system. There is a cost associated with each of the resources of the data communication system: hardware, software, data, procedures, and personnel. In addition, the recurring costs associated with maintaining each resource must be taken into account.

EXAMPLE: DEVELOPING A DATA COMMUNICATION NETWORK AT STATE UNIVERSITY

To see how an organization might develop a data communication network, let us consider how State University went about it.

Background

State University is located in a small town in a rural part of the Southwest. As the university grew, so did the surrounding area. Today the university is part of a small community and is the main employer in the area. There is also a state hospital in the town. While it is not officially part of the university, the hospital collaborates with the university on a considerable amount of research. Many of the doctors who work at the hospital are also on faculty at the university's medical school, and patient data collected by the hospital is used by sociology faculty in their research.

There are currently three levels of computer use among the faculty. The first level consists of departments such as computer science and biomedical engineering which receive outside funds in the form of research grants to be used primarily for purchasing computing equipment. Each has its own local area network. The second level consists of departments like the sociology department. They use the university's mainframe computer but must pay for terminals and communication services out of their own budgets. Since they receive less outside funding, they do not have the money to provide the computing support their faculty needs. The final level consists of departments such as the English department which receive little or no outside funding and cannot afford to purchase terminals and communication services in order to have access to the mainframe. They would like to have access to the campus computer, but they don't have the budget to allow it.

Communication Requirements

The impetus for a change in the current status of telecommunication service came from two sources. University administrators, noting that current telephone costs were too high, wanted to consider cost-cutting measures. They were thinking of setting up their own internal telephone network which could be used by university personnel (mostly during the day) as well as by students (mostly at night). Since most of the computer access was achieved through telephone lines, it seemed natural to include a consideration of data communication needs as well.

At the same time there was a growing demand for access to computing facilities. At the time of the data communication study, departments were paying for any computing or data communication equipment out of their own budgets, and many of the departments did not have enough money. Concurrently, the Academic Computing Department realized that it did not have the money to support the increasing demand for computing on campus. The Computing Center also had communication issues. Most users gained access to the mainframe computer through telephone lines. The sociology department leased dedicated lines from the local telephone company to connect its terminals to the mainframe. The few users in the English department had to use their voice telephone lines if they wanted to gain access. This posed the problem that voice lines could be tied up for long periods of time.

An outside consulting firm was brought in to study the situation. The first thing the consultants did was to survey the university personnel, asking about their use of both voice and data communications. They asked what data communication resources were currently available and how these resources were used. The purpose of this survey was to learn more about both the technological needs and the functional or job-related needs that a new network should be able to support.

As a result of their survey, the consultants learned several things about the functional requirements of a new network. First, they learned that it would have to accommodate three classes of users. Departments such as computer science were being served very well; they had the funds to support their computing needs. Departments such as sociology had limited access to computing but did not have the funds to meet the level of faculty demand for computing resources. Departments such as English were barely served at all, because they did not have the funds to support even the most basic level of computer use. Second, they learned that many faculty had terminals in their homes and gained access to the mainframe computer through switched telephone lines. Finally, they learned that those physicians who were also on faculty at the university maintained two offices and wanted to be able to access the same software and data from either place.

From a technological perspective, a new network would need to support three types of data communication. First, it would have to support communication between terminals and mainframe or minicomputers. Second, it would need to support communication among computers. Examples would be communication among personal computers or between an engineering work station and another computer. Third, it would have to support communication between personal computers and **network servers**. A network server is one computer in a local area network which serves management functions. Often the network server holds a single copy of some software or database to which the other computers have access. In this way the network server can exert some managerial control over the other personal computers. Sometimes the server has a shared disk on which all the data in the local area network is stored. This facilitates procedures such as making regular backups of the software and data.

Thus the requirements of the new network were: (1) to improve the cost effectiveness of voice communication services; (2) to enhance the current data communication network so that all personnel in the university could afford access to the computer; (3) to enable hospital personnel to have easier access to the university's facilities; and (4) to facilitate faculty access to the university's computers from their homes in the surrounding community.

Constraints

Technological

Before any options could be considered, however, an important technical constraint had to be taken into account: the university already had a small data communication network on campus. Several years earlier, the computer science, radiology, and biomedical engineering departments had joined together to develop a bus network that would connect each of their individual local area networks, which were Ethernets. Figure 7.12 shows this data communication configuration.

This network was a broadband network using coaxial cable. It had three channels on it: an Ethernet channel to connect the three local area networks, a terminal channel to connect terminals to the mainframe, and an educational video channel. Thus, an issue confronting the university administrators was whether to extend this network throughout the campus or develop a totally new one. A related issue was whether to have two separate networks—one for voice and one for data—or to have a single integrated network.

Organizational

There were also several organizational considerations. The university administrators acknowledged that having three classes of users among the faculty was not in their best interests. There were those who had the money to pay for the computing services they needed. These users understood what a data communication network could do for them. Then there were the users who were currently being underserved; they had little experience with data communication. They only knew that they were not receiving an adequate level of computing support. Finally, there were those who were not served at all; they had no experience with data communication and were therefore unable to say what data communication could do for them. The university decided that in order to compete effectively with other universities, it had to make access to the computing resource—just like the library—available to all members of the university. Therefore, the

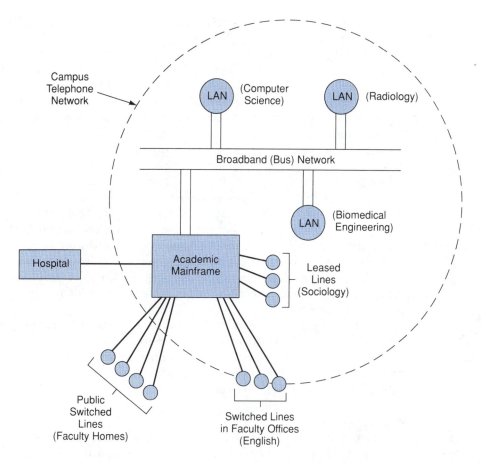

FIGURE 7.12
Existing data communication facilities at State University

requirement of providing a basic level of computing support became an important organizational constraint.

Another organizational consideration was related to the reporting structure of those involved in providing computing and voice and data communication services. Three offices in the university shared these responsibilities, and they didn't get along with each other. The Telecommunications Office was responsible for maintaining the broadband network and the telephone service which was provided by the local telephone company. The telecommunications personnel installed telephone wires and cables and understood electronic circuitry but knew very little about data communication. This office reported to the Vice-President for Business and Finance. The second office, the Office of Administrative Computing, was responsible for maintaining the mainframe computer used by university administrators. These personnel also reported to the Vice-President for Business and Finance.

The Office of Academic Computing was responsible for providing computing resources to the faculty. This office reported to the provost of the university. Many of the people in this office had degrees in computer science and taught part-time at the university. They considered themselves to be the most knowledgeable computer people on campus. When the issue of a new data communication network surfaced, they assumed that they should be the ones in charge of it. A power struggle arose between the Academic Computing people and the Telecommunications people. Telecommunications thought it should control any new data communication network since it had been responsible for *voice* networks in the past. Academic Computing, however, did not have confidence in the Telecommunications people because they were inexperienced in the area of *data* networks. In fact, the main reason consultants were brought in to analyze the data communication requirements and identify options was that neither of these groups would cooperate with the other. The need to overcome this organizational infighting, then, became another important organizational constraint.

The final organizational constraint was financial in nature. The Academic Computing Office did not currently have the budget to support the level of computing service that the university administration had decided all faculty should have. Therefore, they had to find a way to subsidize this increased level of use.

Regulatory

Two regulatory issues also had to be taken into account. Because the university wanted to facilitate access to its computing resources from the hospital and from faculty homes in the surrounding community, this new network would have to have features of a metropolitan area network. In the case of the hospital, the solution was easy. Since the hospital was adjacent to the university, cable or wires could be used to connect the physicians' terminals to the university's computers. Providing better access to faculty from their homes was another matter. Because of the recent changes in telecommunications regulation, the university thought it could perhaps bypass the local operating company and enable faculty to communicate with the university's computers through its own network. After this possibility was discussed with the consultants, however, it did not seem like a good idea. Since faculty homes were not adjacent to the university, right-of-way permission would have to be obtained to string wires across all the intervening properties between a given home and the university. This did not seem realistic. Another alternative would be the use of microwave transmission. This, too, was not realistic because it would require each faculty member to have a microwave transmitter and to obtain a radio operator's license from the Federal Communications Commission.

The second regulatory constraint was associated with the university's desire to establish its own telephone network for voice communication and sell these services to the students. The problem was that there were state laws governing how a nonprofit institution like a university could engage in profit-making activities such as becoming its own telephone company. The consultants agreed to explore the state laws in this regard.

The Options That Were Considered

Common Carrier

The consultants recommended two courses of action. Given the regulatory constraints associated with the metropolitan area network and the organizational constraints in the form of infighting, one option was to go to the local operating company. Since the university was the major contributor to the area's economy, and the major user of the telephone system, it was in a position to ask for services that other organizations could not. The consultants suggested that the local operating company be asked to install new telephone wires throughout the community that could accommodate both voice and data transmission at the same time. This would provide the faculty with access to computing from their homes without tying up their telephone lines. This type of service is referred to as an **Integrated Services Digital Network**, or ISDN. ISDNs have two main advantages. First, both voice and data messages are sent in digital form, eliminating the need for a modem and increasing the transmission speed. Second, having both voice and data sent at the same time makes it unnecessary to have two telephone lines in one's home.

Having the on-campus communication needs provided by the local telephone company could also eliminate one of the organizational constraints. If the local operating company developed and installed the data communication network on campus as well, the power struggle between Academic Computing and Telecommunications could be resolved by putting an objective third party in charge of it.

Private Network

The other option was for the university to establish its own private voice and data networks. If it were able to sell telephone services to the students, it could use the proceeds to provide increased computing and data communication resources to parts of the university which were currently underserved or unserved.

When the current technology to support on-campus integrated voice and data communication was considered, the consultants recommended that the university keep two separate networks. They felt this was necessary because the current technology could not support the level of high-speed data communication needed for communication between mainframe computers. The existing telephone network could be upgraded so that all students could have telephones in their dorm rooms. The data communication network could be developed by extending the existing broadband network.

To fund the acquisition of these new facilities, the university was advised to establish its own long distance communication network as well. The university was currently receiving long distance service from the state, which functioned as a network vendor for state institutions. The consultants advised that it could save money by leasing long distance lines directly from a carrier like AT&T or MCI.

The Choice and Its Justification

After reviewing the proposal submitted by the local common carrier, the consultants advised the university administrators that the private network option would be more cost effective. To overcome some of the organizational constraints, a new organizational unit was established to manage these two networks. The three existing offices—Telecommunications, Administrative Computing, and Academic Computing—would all report to the new Vice-President for Information Resources. This person would also be responsible for the campus library. Some of the personnel from Academic Computing who were knowledgeable about data communication were moved over to the Telecommunications Office. In addition, several of the people in Telecommunications enrolled in classes to become more familiar with data communication. The following network design was then developed by the consultants.

Voice Communication

The state law governing the sale of telephone services to students was unclear. Since a ruling could go either way, the university reached an agreement with the state regulatory commission with authority in these matters. State University agreed to remain in the state-operated long distance network in exchange for being permitted to own and operate an on-campus telephone network. The regulatory commission agreed to this because State University was the biggest client of the long distance network. If State University left the network, it probably could not afford to stay in business. The university also agreed to use all revenue from this telephone service for enhancing and maintaining voice and data communication services.

Data Communication

State University decided to use the income from the telephone network to pay for the development and installation of an expanded data network. Figure 7.13 shows the plan for the new communication network.

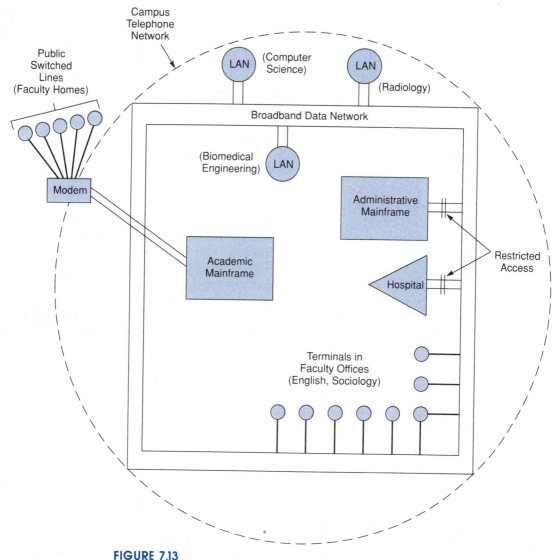

FIGURE 7.13

Design of new data communication network at State University

All buildings on campus and at the hospital would be connected to the broadband network with coaxial cable. Departments such as English and sociology would have access to the academic mainframe through terminals. There would no longer be a need for switched or leased lines. The data communication facilities would be installed and maintained by the Office of Telecommunications. The departments would share the costs of terminals with the office. Local area networks such as those in the computer science, radiology, and biomedical engineering departments would be connected to this campus-wide network since the new network was an extension of the existing one. In addition, the hospital would be connected to the network but would implement certain hardware, software, and procedural restrictions so that access to hospital data could be controlled. The administrative mainframe was also connected to the network. Again, security procedures were to be put in place.

Because of regulatory constraints, the university was unable to provide faculty with integrated voice and data transmission from their homes. But it was able to simplify the process of gaining remote access to computers by providing a single link from their telephones to the network. This way, faculty members would only have to dial one telephone number no matter which computer they wanted to reach.

The resulting network design was a combination of local and metropolitan area networks. Both voice and data communication resources would be enhanced. The requirement that all members of the university have access to computing resources was satisfied. By owning its telephone network, the university was able to upgrade telephone service and at the same time raise the funds necessary to finance the upgraded data communication facilities. When the project was completed, the consultants left feeling that an enormous task had been accomplished and that both they and the university were satisfied with the result.

SUMMARY

Acquiring data communication services requires a combination of technological, organizational, and regulatory knowledge. One must know about existing technology to serve as the source and destination as well as know which channels are appropriate for which types of messages. Data networks can be configured using a variety of topologies. The choice among star, hierarchical, bus, and ring network structures will depend upon the distance between network nodes and how much and how often data is transmitted.

In developing or enhancing a data communication network, the starting point should be the answers to the following two questions: How does the organization use the data, and with whom does it communicate? Depending upon whether the communication is between organizations or within the organization in the form of a wide area, metropolitan area, or local area network, the requirements of the network will differ.

Once the requirements have been determined they must be reviewed in light of technological, organizational, and regulatory constraints. Data communication facilities can be provided by common carriers, supplied by enhanced services providers, or developed by the organization itself. The options that result will be a compromise between what is desired and what is realistically available. The selection process should take into account not only the technology and data but also the people in the organization who will be using the data communication network.

CHAPTER NOTES

1. Colin Cherry, *On Human Communication*, 2d ed. (Cambridge, MA: The MIT Press, 1966), 4.
2. Eileen M. Trauth, "Telecommunications in an Era of Deregulation" (Information Systems Research Center Working Paper, Boston University, 1985).
3. 28 FCC 2d 267 (1971).
4. 77 FCC 2d 384 (1980).

ADDITIONAL REFERENCES

Buss, M. "Legislative Threat to Transborder Data Flow." *Harvard Business Review* 62 (1984): 111–118.

De Noia, Lynn A. *Data Communication: Fundamentals and Applications*. Columbus, OH: Merrill Publishing Co., 1987.

General Accounting Office. *Telephone Bypass — Selected Information on Bypass of Local Telephone Companies*. GAO/RCED-68-100 (February 1986).

General Accounting Office. *Telephone Communications — Bell Operating Company Entry into New Lines of Business*. GAO/RCED-86-138 (April 1986).

General Accounting Office. *Telephone Communications — Bypass of the Local Telephone Companies*. GAO/RCED-86-66 (August 1986).

Kalin, Martin J. *Telecommunications Policies in Ten Countries: Prospects for Future Competitive Access*. U.S. Department of Commerce — National Telecommunications and Information Administration, NTIA-CR 85-33 (March 1985).

Palmer, Janet, and Andria Page Dukes. "Transborder Data Flow: A Corporate Problem." *Proceedings of the National Computer Conference*, 1986: 29–33.

Stamper, David A. *Business Data Communications*. 2d ed. Menlo Park, CA: Benjamin-Cummings, 1989.

Trauth, Eileen M., Denise M. Trauth, and John L. Huffman. "Impact of Deregulation on Marketplace Diversity in the USA." *Telecommunications Policy* 7 (June 1983): 111–120.

Turn, Rein, ed. *Transborder Data Flows: Concerns in Privacy Protection and Free Flow of Information*, Volumes 1 and 2. Arlington, VA: American Federation of Information Processing Societies, 1979.

Wigand, Rolf T., Carrie Shipley, and Dwayne Shipley. "Transborder Data Flow, Informatics and National Policies: A Comparison Among 22 Nations." Paper presented at the International Communication Association Annual Meeting, May 28, 1983.

KEY TERMS

arc
baseband transmission
basic non-voice services
broadband transmission
bus network
bypass
collisions
common carrier
communication

communication channel
compatibility
computer network
data communication
data communication network
data network
destination

distributed data processing
divestiture
electronic data interchange (EDI)
electronic mail (email)
enhanced services
enhancement
equal access

Ethernet
feedback
hierarchical network
host computer
information provider
integrated services digi-
  tal network (ISDN)
leased lines
local area network (LAN)
message
metropolitan area net-
  work (MAN)
network server
node

noise
Open Systems Intercon-
  nection (OSI) model
path
private branch exchange
  (PBX)
protocol
ring network
root
service bureau
signal
source
star network

store-and-forward
switched lines
telecommunication
  network
teleconferencing
topology
transborder data flow
  (TDF)
value-added network
  (VAN)
voice services
wide area network
  (WAN)

REVIEW QUESTIONS

1. Define the basic components of the communication process. Give some examples of data communication.
2. Explain the difference between a communication system and an information system.
3. Describe the four topologies that are used to construct data communication networks.
4. What is the main difference between a star network and a ring network?
5. Explain time sharing and why it is important.
6. Identify an obstacle in a network with no central node.
7. What is the OSI model? What is its purpose?
8. Discuss the several layers of the OSI model.
9. The layers of the OSI model are divided into two groups. Describe the groups.
10. What factors must be taken into consideration when determining communication requirements?
11. Explain the function of a service bureau.
12. Why do organizations implement EDI?
13. Data communication exists both between and within organizations. Describe the four types of networks which relate to these different types of communication requirements.
14. Give an example of each of the three types of constraints—technological, organizational, and regulatory.
15. Describe the three types of technological constraints on communication services.
16. Discuss the effects of deregulation on the communications industry.
17. Explain the impact of transborder data flow.
18. Compare LAN, MAN, and WAN.
19. Explain the difference between baseband and broadband transmission.
20. Describe the three options an organization has for acquiring data communication resources.
21. Common carriers may provide two types of lines. Discuss each, comparing advantages and disadvantages.

22. What are the criteria for selecting a data communication system?
23. What are the advantages of developing an in-house data communication network?

CASE

Last National Bank has recently acquired two banks in Ohio. One is located in a small farming town and consists of a single office. The other, in a moderate-size city, has a main office in the center of town and several branch offices in the suburbs. These two banks are a hundred miles apart and both are approximately three hundred miles from Last National's main office (which is also in a different state). The computer-based processing of customer accounts in the smaller bank is done through a service bureau, and the bank's only computer equipment consists of terminals and modems. Manual records are kept on hand to answer account inquiries. The larger bank has a computer at the main office and at each branch office. However, these computers are not networked together. Consequently, customers cannot check the status of their accounts from a branch other than their own.

Last National currently has a wide area network incorporating all of its banks. Some processing is done locally and some—mostly management processing—is done at the bank's headquarters. Since Last National would like to incorporate these two new banks both organizationally and technologically into its method of operations, it must make some important data communication decisions.

DISCUSSION QUESTIONS

1. What are some of the data communication requirements the bank must take into account in planning to incorporate these two banks into its network?
2. What are some of the technological, organizational, and regulatory constraints which need to be considered?
3. What type of network recommendations would you make?

PART III

Information Management

PART OUTLINE

CHAPTER 8

Information Systems Development

CHAPTER OBJECTIVES

- To explain the circumstances that would cause an organization to want to acquire a new information system.
- To describe the phases of the systems development life cycle: perception of need; feasibility; analysis; design; development; implementation; and operation, evaluation, and maintenance.
- To explain how the life cycle would be used in a typical systems development project.
- To describe new approaches to systems development: the active involvement of the end user; iterative development; and the use of software development tools.
- To explain the circumstances which would call for a new approach to systems development.
- To identify the issues associated with end-user-developed systems.
- To understand the issues associated with co-developed systems.

INTRODUCTION

In Part I of this book we examined information systems—both information systems in general (Chapter 2) and specific types of information systems (Chapter 3). In Part II we examined in more detail the components and resources which make up an information system. In Part III we consider systems in general: how the appropriate information resources are identified and acquired (Chapter 8); how information systems are planned and related to organizational objectives (Chapter 9); and how the resulting product—the information systems—are managed (Chapter 10). In this chapter, we will draw upon our detailed understanding of an information system to consider why and how computer-based information systems are developed. Some major changes in the classic approach to systems development have occurred in recent years. However, to appreciate the significance of these changes, we will start with the traditional approach to systems development and then proceed to consider recent adaptations of this approach.

The systems development process is really just an application of the problem-solving approach that was considered in Chapters 4 and 5. That is, it is a standard approach for moving from a current state to a desired state in some logical fashion. As we examine the process of systems development and consider some examples, we will see this problem-solving approach carried out over and over again.

There are two reasons why an information-literate person needs to know about the systems development process. One is that when a system is being developed in a large organization by the MIS department, selected users are asked to be involved. They may be asked to be part of a committee which will review the work the MIS department is doing, or they may be interviewed regarding the information need. Therefore, the more the users understand about the process, the more they are able to contribute to the process, and the greater the likelihood that the system being developed will be the system they really want.

The second reason for knowing about the systems development process is that end users are increasingly developing systems *themselves*, either alone or in conjunction with the MIS department. Therefore, it is very likely that you will be developing an information system yourself (if you haven't already). This chapter won't teach you everything you need to know, but it will give you an overview and a basis for further learning.

TRADITIONAL SYSTEMS DEVELOPMENT

The Systems Development Life Cycle Concept

During the 1980s there were several significant changes in our conception of information processing. One of these was in the area of information systems development. To fully understand these changes, however, we must understand what these systems changed *from*. We must therefore start our discussion of information systems development with a look at the way systems were developed during the 1960s and 1970s and, in some cases, are still being developed today.

In those earlier decades, information systems were thought of primarily in terms of hardware and software. Consequently, information systems *development* focused on those two aspects as well. The software for these systems was usually developed "in house" by programmers in the data processing department. Systems were developed using a third-generation programming language such as COBOL which required detailed program specifications to ensure that the system would meet the needs of users and solve the specific problem. To effectively develop these systems, a concept called the **systems development life cycle** was formalized. A formal systems development life cycle is a methodology for decomposing the systems development process into a series of phases. The methodology defines each phase with respect to its tools and techniques; its inputs and outputs, including required documentation; quality control and review criteria; and the role of personnel (e.g., users, designers, analysts, and programmers) involved in the process. In addition, it describes the interfaces that exist between the different steps.

While the activities are the same, descriptions of the various life cycles vary in the number of steps involved in this decomposition process. Most descriptions of the process have between four and nine steps. Despite the labels used, all systems are described as passing through the same universal life cycle: birth, development, maturity, decline, and death. Birth is the recognition that there is a need for a new system. Development is the process of building the new system. Maturity is the operation and maintenance of the system. Decline occurs when the existing system can no longer satisfy a majority of the users' requirements. Death occurs when the system is replaced by a new one. The formal systems life cycle deals with the first three phases of the universal life cycle. The fourth and fifth steps are really a return to the beginning of the systems development process. The life cycle approach to information systems development is depicted in Figure 8.1.

The formal systems life cycle approach is often called "prespecified systems development." This label is used because the assumption underlying this approach to systems development is that a complete requirements document describing in detail what the ensuing system *should do* can be prepared and followed.

In this chapter, the life cycle will be discussed in terms of seven phases:

1. Perception of need
2. Feasibility
3. Analysis
4. Design
5. Development

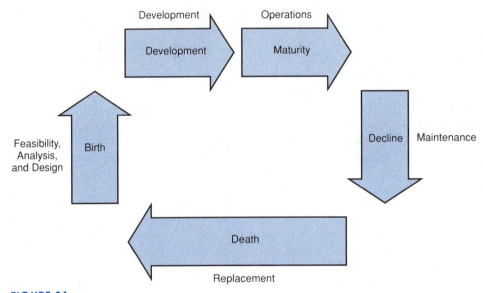

FIGURE 8.1
Life cycle approach with steps of the systems development life cycle

6. Implementation
7. Operation, evaluation, and maintenance

Figure 8.2 presents the objectives of each of these phases.

The major reason for using the formal systems life cycle approach to systems development is that it is a *formal*, well-defined process that can be applied over and over again so that the systems development process in an organization is conducted in a consistent fashion. Therefore, responsibilities, review points, and definition of the final system output can all be well defined.

The users of the intended system play a consultative role in the systems development effort. Often the request for a new system or a system change comes from the users. They should be involved in developing the criteria for evaluating the system's success. Users provide the basis for the new system requirements by identifying problems with the existing system and suggesting features the new system must have to overcome them. In addition, each phase of the systems development life cycle is subject to review by users.

Users carry out these activities in their capacity as members of two advisory committees, the steering committee and the project team. The **steering committee** is a high-level committee which authorizes the systems development effort to get under way and conducts the final evaluation which concludes the project. The members of the steering committee include some intended users, information systems professionals, and senior managers of the organization. They are responsible for evaluating the feasibility study, authorizing the project to go forward, and conducting the post-implementation audit once the system has been developed and implemented.

FIGURE 8.2

Objectives of the systems development life cycle

Perception of Need

Objective:
- To determine what is not working and to identify the need for a new system
- To form a feasibility team

Feasibility

Objective:
- To determine the major system objectives
- To determine if the system is technically, operational, and economically feasible
- Organizational steering committee assigns project a priority.

Analysis

Objectives:
- To study and document the current system and delineate the problems with it
- To collect the requirements for the new system
- To integrate the requirements, forming a model of the new system

Design

Objectives:
- To develop a conceptual model for the entire system
- To evaluate the decision whether to develop a system in-house or to buy a package
- To describe the system in detail

Development

Objectives:
- To build/produce a correct operating version of the system

Implementation

Objectives:
- To convert from the old/existing system to the new system
- To train users to use the new system effectively
- To have a successful completion of an organizational acceptance test

Operation, Evaluation, and Maintenance

Objectives:
- To evaluate the performance of the new system and its compliance with the requirements
- To document all changes to the system

Once the project is under way, users on the **project team** are directly involved in the system project by providing input during each phase of development. The project team is made up of representative users and the systems professionals responsible for developing the system. Sometimes the membership of the project team changes as the project moves from one phase to the next. That is, some users might only work on the analysis phase. Likewise, some members of the data processing team might work on feasibility and analysis and others might work on design and development. Users are most involved in the feasibility, analysis, and implementation phases, and least involved in the design and development phases. At the conclusion of each phase, the project team gives the authorization to move on to the next phase of the project.

Perception of Need

All system projects begin because there is an information need in the organization that is not currently being met. This need can arise for several reasons.

New Information Requirements

Sometimes events occur in the environment of the organization which cause it to change its existing method of information processing. The federal government may impose a new law or reporting requirement with which an organization must comply. An example is the requirement that large cash transactions at banks be reported to the Internal Revenue Service. To be able to comply, banks must keep records about any large cash transactions. If the existing information system cannot provide that information, the system may have to be altered, or even abandoned altogether and replaced with a new one.

Another external motivation for a new information system is competition in the industry. For example, if Last National Bank's major competitor is providing a certain type of service, Last National may be forced to offer this service as well in order to remain competitive. A good example of this motivation for a new system is the introduction of automatic teller machines (ATMs). Once one bank in a city offers this service to its customers, other banks will probably need to follow suit or else risk losing customers to the bank which has ATMs.

New information requirements may also be the result of some organizational change. Suppose Last National Bank merged with another bank. If the two banks had different types of information systems set up to support check processing, a new information system would be needed—one that supported the check processing activities of the new conglomerate bank. This new system could come about in several ways: one check processing system could be scrapped in favor of the other; both could be scrapped and an entirely new one developed; or one system could be the dominant system and salvageable parts from the other added to it. In any event, the organizational change brought about by the merger of the two banks would result in new information requirements that neither system is able to adequately satisfy. Consequently, there would be a need for a new system.

Emergence of New Technology

Sometimes the problem is not with the information but with the technology. An information system developed ten or fifteen years ago would probably not have the features of a system developed more recently, because certain technology was not available then. Information systems using older technology may not be suited to today's information needs, or may not be as efficient as systems incorporating newer technology.

Consider, for a moment, the technology available to small businesses in 1975. Computers were *much* more expensive then. Personal computers were not available, and most small businesses could not afford a minicomputer. The only option was to use the computer services offered by a service bureau. Today, however, because of the availability of personal computers and packaged software, virtually every small business can afford a computer-based information system. In this case, the movement from the existing system to the new one is from a manual to a computer-based system.

In the early 1980s, point-of-sale terminals at grocery stores just recorded sales and tax totals. The availability of inexpensive and reliable scanners with point-of-sale terminals enlarged the potential scope of systems. Now grocery stores use scanners to move customers through the checkout lines more quickly and to support systems for inventory control and sales management.

Problems with the Existing System

Perhaps the most common reason for wanting a new information system is that there is a problem with the current one. As we stated before, a problem is the difference between a current state and a desired state. Therefore, if there is a problem with the existing system, the information currently provided is lacking in some way. Sometimes the problem is related to the response time, processing speed, or storage capacity of the technology currently being used. If the existing information system is manual, the problem might be the timeliness of the information that is provided. Sometimes the system does not adequately respond to users' needs. And sometimes, after using a system for a while, users discover new things they would like the system to do for them.

Because information exists in some organizational context, it is often difficult to separate organizational problems from information problems. At times it may look as though the information system is not providing the necessary information to support a task. In reality, however, some organizational problem may be preventing the right people from getting the information they need. One of the important benefits of the systems development process, then, is the examination and possible solution of organizational problems.

Regardless of how it comes about, once the system need is recognized, certain individuals in the user community are selected to formally describe it in a document called a *Request for a New System*.

Feasibility

Before a new system project is undertaken, it must be determined whether it is realistic to develop a new system. That is, the project proposal must be evaluated for technical, economic, and operational feasibility.

Technical Feasibility

A project is technically feasible if hardware and software necessary to satisfy the information need are available to the organization. For example, an information system based on automatic teller machines requires communication capabilities so that information can be accessed from a remote computer. It also requires that multiple ATMs have access to a central database so that transactions can be processed as they occur. The system must also be able to handle multiple transactions at the same time. The successful operation of ATMs thus requires certain types of technology, and so any organization wishing to have a network of ATMs must have or be able to acquire such technology.

Economic Feasibility

The evaluation of economic feasibility usually requires the organization to conduct a cost-benefit analysis of the system project. Two types of costs must be considered:

One-time costs associated with the development of the system

Recurring costs associated with its operation and maintenance

Many organizations are able to estimate these costs. Costs associated with systems development include those which affect all the resources of the system: personnel, such as the time of the users and systems personnel devoted to the development project; procedures, such as changes in work design; computer hardware and software needed for developing and implementing the system; and finally, data collection, preparation, and input.

The recurring costs are related to the five resources as well. They include the time of personnel needed to operate and manage the system; hardware and software acquisition costs, if new technology must be obtained; maintenance costs associated with keeping the hardware, software, and data in usable form; and costs associated with ongoing operating procedures. These projected costs are then compared to the costs of operating the existing system.

Once the costs are determined, they are weighed against the expected benefits. It is often difficult to assign monetary values to the potential benefits of an information system, because many of the benefits are intangible. Benefits such as increased management productivity or greater effectiveness are hard to measure in dollars and cents. However, certain direct benefits can be measured, including decreases in personnel, increased data accuracy (which will avoid costly reruns), and faster response time. For example, a manual system for payroll is usually labor-intensive and prone to error because of the large number of calculations involved. Automating such a system would result in the direct benefits of reducing personnel costs and improving data quality. Of the three types of systems we discussed in Chapter 3, access systems are the most likely to have direct benefits, whereas measurable benefits deriving from analysis and action systems may not be as easy to demonstrate. Analysis and action systems are usually implemented to provide indirect benefits such as increased efficiency, better decision making, and improved customer satisfaction and services. These indirect benefits are much more difficult to measure in dollars.

Operational Feasibility

In evaluating the operational feasibility of a system, an organization examines how the system will fit into the organizational structure during its operation. For this reason, operational feasibility is connected most closely with organizational issues. One issue of concern is the ability of the system to perform within the existing organization environment given the current personnel and procedures. A second issue is whether the development schedule is feasible based on how long development will take and when the system is needed. The third issue is whether or not the proposed system fits into the long- and short-range plans of the organization. The last issue is whether the organization has sufficient resources to complete this system project. The evaluation of operational feasibility is based on a project schedule with the tentative assignment of personnel to the project. The project schedule is a major output of this systems development phase.

Once the feasibility study is completed, the project team which conducted the feasibility study submits a recommendation to the steering committee for its evaluation and approval. The response will be one of the following:

- STOP – the project will not proceed beyond this phase
- WAIT – the project is not assigned a sufficiently high priority to proceed at this time
- MODIFY – the project scope or proposal must be modified and then reevaluated
- PROCEED – the project has authorization to proceed to the next phases and is assigned an organizational priority. Included here are any conditions that may result in the reevaluation or discontinuation of this project.

Upon completion of the feasibility phase, a feasibility report is written containing the results of the committee evaluation. If the project has been approved, a project team is formed and a project schedule is developed which will include the following: a project budget; a schedule for project completion; and appropriate approval mechanisms which will be detailed for subsequent phases and deliverables. Finally, a proposal to conduct a systems analysis is prepared. It will include such things as the approved objective and scope of the proposed system; constraints, assumptions, or potential problems that may arise; and the type and source of information to be collected during the next phase — analysis.

Analysis

The analysis phase is often called "systems analysis" or "requirements specification and analysis." The task of this phase is to specify in a detailed and consistent manner *what* the new system should do. The objectives of this phase are:

- To study and describe the existing system;
- To identify the problems with the existing system(s) and the requirements for the new system;
- To integrate the list of problems and requirements into a document which serves as a model of the new system;
- To produce a requirements document and system plan.

This task is crucial to the success of the intended system because the failure to determine and specify requirements accurately and completely is a major cause of new system failures, as Figure 8.3 shows.

The task of the project team during this phase is to develop the new system requirements. This project team will consist of systems analysts from the data processing staff and selected users who will be available for consultation on the project. Additional users involved will be those interviewed about the existing system and requirements for the new one. After these interviews have been conducted, the users on the project team will verify that the analyst's interpretation of the requirements is accurate.

Describing the Existing System

Since a system is made up of resources and components, describing the existing system means identifying and describing in detail the hardware, software, data, procedures, and personnel in the system as well as the inputs, processes, and outputs. This description is accomplished by a combination of methods such as reviewing the documentation about the existing system, observing the current system in operation, and interviewing representative users.

Certain techniques have been developed to assist the systems personnel in describing the current system and presenting the specifications for the new one. The analysis can be conducted in either **top-down** or **bottom-up** fashion. The top-down approach begins with the organizational unit under study and the relationship of the existing information system to it. We begin to describe the system resources at the level of the whole system and then proceed to describe it in successive layers of detail. Bottom-up design, on the other hand, means that we start with the subsystems. The lowest level of system resources is identified first, followed by successive layers of aggregation until the whole system is described. The choice of approaches depends on the degree of emphasis being placed on the whole and on the parts. The top-down approach places most emphasis on the whole, while the bottom-up approach places most emphasis on the parts. Because our orientation in this book is grounded in the systems approach, which emphasizes the whole, we will use the top-down approach to demonstrate how to analyze the existing system and design the new system.

In addition to the system resources, the system components must also be described. This description can be either *process-driven* or *data-driven*. In

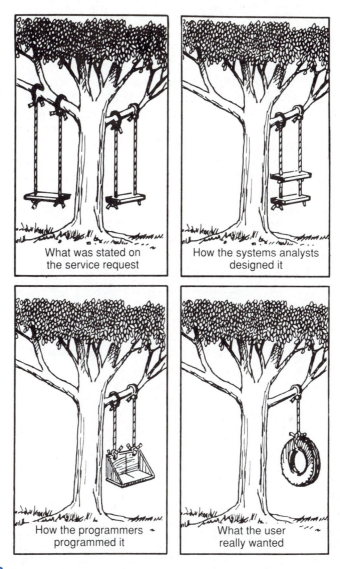

FIGURE 8.3
The result of failure to determine and specify system requirements. From Larry Long, *Introduction to Computers and Information Processing*, © 1984, p. 4O8. Reprinted by permission of Prentice-Hall, Inc., Englewood Cliffs, New Jersey.

process-driven analysis, the processes of concern are identified first. Then the input data that is required to support those processes and the output data that results must be identified. The input data either comes to the system from the environment or is internal data already stored in the system. Likewise, the output data either leaves the system and enters the environment or remains inside the system and is used to update some internal data. In data-driven analysis, the data produced by the system is the point of departure. Once it is identified, the processes needed to produce that data are then identified.

Structured Systems Analysis   One of the most popular techniques for systems analysis is **structured systems analysis (SSA)**. This top-down technique is "structured" in that the system is systematically partitioned into a collection of subsystems which are in turn hierarchically decomposed into their resources and components. Hierarchical decomposition means breaking something down into its component parts. An example of hierarchical decomposition is an organization chart of a bank shown in Figure 8.4.

A **structure chart** is used to graphically represent this decomposition. In the course of developing such a chart, the interfaces or links between the resources and components are described as well. The advantages of representing the system in this way are that it enables the system developers to focus on specific tasks that must be completed and enables them to keep track of which tasks have been completed. The benefits of developing an overview of information processes and information flows before actually developing the system will be discussed again in Chapter 9.

Data Flow Diagrams   A common technique used in structured systems analysis is the development of **data flow diagrams (DFDs)**. A data flow diagram is like the system flowchart discussed in Chapter 4 in that it is a graphical representation of the activities of a system. Unlike a system flowchart, however, a DFD enables the analyst to identify the different categories of data

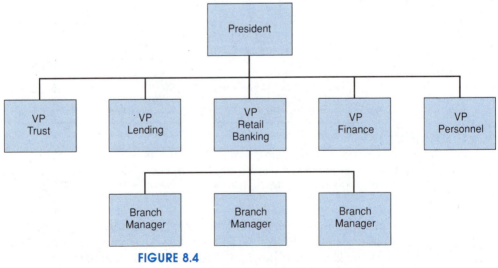

FIGURE 8.4
Functional organizational chart for a bank

that are involved in the system. A separate data flow diagram is created for each process in the structure chart, beginning with the top system process. The data going into and out of each process is identified and labeled.

Four symbols are used to develop a data flow diagram. Figure 8.5 shows these symbols.

A **process** is some activity which transforms the data. An example would be updating the current balance on a credit account. The data going into and out of each process is identified and labeled as **data flows**. The source and destination of each data flow are either an **external entity** or a **data store**. An *external entity* is some person or organizational unit in the environment of the information system which either provides input data or receives output information. A bank client using an ATM is an example of an external entity which both provides input data and receives output information. A *data store* is a repository for the data which is a part of the system. An example of a data

FIGURE 8.5
Symbols used for data flow diagrams

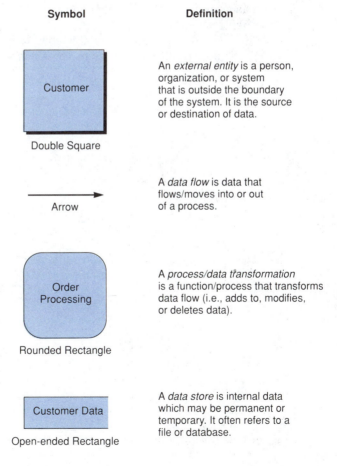

Symbol	Definition
Customer Double Square	An *external entity* is a person, organization, or system that is outside the boundary of the system. It is the source or destination of data.
Arrow	A *data flow* is data that flows/moves into or out of a process.
Order Processing Rounded Rectangle	A *process/data transformation* is a function/process that transforms data flow (i.e., adds to, modifies, or deletes data).
Customer Data Open-ended Rectangle	A *data store* is internal data which may be permanent or temporary. It often refers to a file or database.

store is a customer file. A data flow diagram of the inventory system for State University's bookstore is shown in Figure 8.6.

Data Dictionary Another source of documentation about the existing system is information about the content and form of the data in the system. This information is collected and stored at the same time that the data flow diagrams are being developed. A data dictionary can be used for this purpose. A data dictionary was described in Chapter 6 as a repository for information describing the data and the processes involved in the information system. A data dictionary ensures that information about the data manipulated by the system is available to analysts, designers, and users in an organized fashion. An example of an entry in a data dictionary is that the social security number is stored without dashes separating the numbers—that is, in the form 123456789 rather than 123-45-6789. A data dictionary is especially useful when more than one information system will be using the data. In addition, the data dictionary will contain abbreviations such as SSN, definition as a unique identifier of the employee, and a list of systems and programs using the data.

The amount of documentation needed to describe the existing system is directly related to the complexity of the existing system. To be complete, the

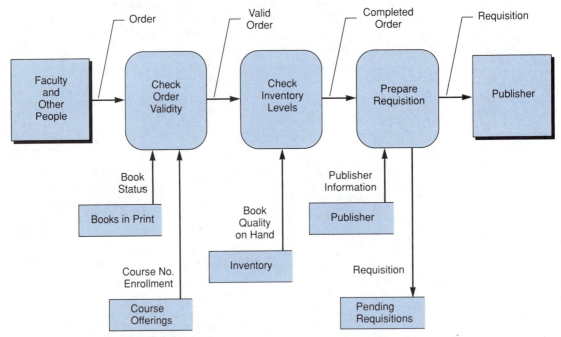

FIGURE 8.6
Data flow diagram of the order subsystem (bookstore's inventory system)

documentation must cover all components of the system—hardware, software, data, people, and procedures.

The New System Requirements

The counterpart to describing the existing system is describing the new system. This process involves identifying the problems with the existing system and the changes that must be made to achieve the information system's goal. These new system features are called the **system requirements**.

Once there is a clear representation of the existing system, it is much easier to pinpoint the problems with the existing system which brought about the request for a new system. The description of the new system is accomplished using the same techniques as those used to describe the existing system. That is, the processes and data flows can be represented utilizing such techniques as structure charts, data flow diagrams, and data dictionaries.

The System Proposal

The final activity of the analysis phase is producing a formal document which states the plan for moving from the present state to the desired state. This report is called the **system proposal**. Included in the system proposal are the necessary changes to all the system resources: the hardware, software, data, people, and procedures. For example, a change to the existing hardware might be the acquisition of computer terminals. A change in personnel might be the hiring of a communications specialist.

Design

In the design phase, the requirements stated in the system proposal are translated into the information system design. The system proposal states *what* the system should do; the design describes *how* those requirements can be satisfied. There are two levels of design:

1. Conceptual or logical design, and
2. Detailed or physical design.

These two phases are followed in sequence for major portions of the system. That is, a complete logical design is not required before the physical design can be undertaken. Usually, a high-level conceptual design is conducted for the whole system in order to identify major subsystems. Then the conceptual design of each subsystem is followed by its corresponding detailed design.

Conceptual Design

The objective of **conceptual design** is to translate the requirements into an overall model of the system. This model must be in a form that is understandable to the system users as well as the systems analysts and designers. It provides the basis for the subsequent phases of the life cycle. While the conceptual design is being developed, the feasibility, economic constraints, and requirements must all be taken into account. At the conclusion of this activity the plan for the remaining phases of the life cycle is reviewed and revised if necessary. During the conceptual design a decision regarding the manner of acquiring the software will also be decided. As discussed in Chapter 4, there are three options: an "off-the-shelf" software package can be purchased; software tools can be purchased which will then have to be tailored to the specific system requirements; or the programmers in the organization can develop the software themselves. This decision is referred to as a *make or buy* decision.

Detailed Design

During the **detailed design**, the model developed during conceptual design is expanded and more details are added. The activities carried out here are those which specify exactly how the hardware, software, and data will work together to provide the desired information. The tasks carried out include the following:

- Program specification
- Layouts for inputs and outputs
- Database and file designs
- Required system controls and operating procedures
- Details of the hardware and software required for system operation

We can examine these tasks in further detail by considering the inventory system at State University's bookstore.

Program Specification **Program specification** refers to the logic of the computer software, or what it is that the programs are supposed to do. Each function to be carried out by the new system should be described in terms of the information processing logic involved. For example, let us consider what happens when a book is sold. Information about the book such as title, author, publisher, and course for which it was purchased must be collected. The correct file containing the information about that book must be located. Next, the file must be updated to reflect the fact that one item from that collection has been sold. These are the activities that must be described during program specification. Several techniques can be used to specify the program logic, including pseudocode, structured diagrams, decision trees, and decision tables. These techniques were described in Chapter 4.

Layouts for Inputs and Outputs In the conceptual design phase, the contents of each input and output were identified. In the detailed design phase, the layout of forms or computer screens which will be used to collect and show this data are developed. Suppose the instructor's book-order form was described during conceptual design as containing the following data: instructor's name, address, and phone number; course number and name; expected course enrollment; book's title and author; and whether the book is required or recommended reading. In detailed design, then, the form that instructors will use to order books is developed and the screens that bookstore personnel will use to input this data are designed.

Database and File Designs   In conceptual design, the contents of the files or database that the system will use are identified. As discussed in Chapter 6, there are several ways of storing and retrieving data. In detailed design, the decision is made regarding how the data will be stored and which data items will serve as access keys to that data. For example, the inventory file might be organized as a direct file with course number serving as the access key.

System Controls and Operating Procedures   Certain procedures must be developed and implemented to ensure that the system is used in the proper fashion. These procedures include decisions about who will have access to the data, methods to keep unauthorized personnel from gaining access, and procedures for backup of the data.

Details of the Hardware and Software   If the bookstore personnel are going to be able to enter book orders through a terminal, a decision must be made regarding the kind of terminals and software that will be used to accomplish this. If the software is to be developed by the university staff, they must decide what computer language to use. Usually there is a policy stating what language will be used. COBOL is a popular language for developing information systems in business. (See the appendix for a complete discussion of the various computer languages.) If the bookstore is going to use the central computer of the university, the telecommunications equipment and software that will be needed must also be specified.

If structured systems analysis was used during the analysis phase, structured systems design should be used as well. This means that a top-down, detailed specification of each resource and component must be developed. When this process is completed, one way of making sure each resource and component has been addressed is to conduct a **design walkthrough**. A design walkthrough is a type of structured walkthrough that addresses the evaluation of the design, whereas a structured walkthrough more commonly addresses requirements. It is a step-by-step review of the input and output layouts, the processing logic, and the procedures regarding the use of the system. The major reason to conduct a design walkthrough is to verify that all of the parts of the system work together. If there are gaps, they can be addressed before the project moves to the actual development phase.

A detailed model of the whole system is the major product of the design phase. This model includes the hardware, software, data, and procedures and outlines the role of the people who will use the system. While several alternatives may be considered, only one design is presented to the project team for review. There are several reasons for doing this. One is to ensure that users have been informed about the system and are satisfied with the development plans. Another is to verify that the system goals and constraints are being met. One constraint that must be met is a technical one: the planned system must fit with any existing technology standards that exist in the organization. The final purposes are to make certain that the initial assumptions are still true and that the system will be easy to use from a human perspective.

Development

The objective of the development phase is to produce a system that conforms to the model developed in the design phase. This includes verifying that all the requirements specified in the previous phases have been satisfied. Another term for development is "resource acquisition," since not only must software be purchased or written, but any additions to the other four system resources that may be needed must also be made during this phase.

Hardware

Any new hardware that is needed for the system is purchased at this time. If the organization is moving from a manual to an automated system, this purchase can involve a considerable amount of work. In other cases, hardware acquisition may be nothing more than purchasing additional computer terminals or printers.

Software

During the design phase a decision was made regarding the acquisition of the software resources for the system. If the software is to be purchased from an outside vendor, the task of development is considerably easier. But if the organization decides to develop the software itself, this phase involves much more work. In this case, the program specifications must be turned into computer programs. During design, a computer language was selected; during development the computer programs are actually written. This means that the code is written and tested. To assist in representing the logic of the programs, flowcharts are used. The way flowcharts are developed and used was explained in Chapter 4.

Before this phase has been completed, the software must be completely tested and determined to be error-free. The software must be tested on a piece-by-piece basis following a bottom-up approach—first the modules, then the interrelating modules forming a subsystem, and then the interrelating subsystems.

Data

The data to be processed by the system must be collected and translated into computer-readable form. Some of this data must be available to the computer *before* the system is operational. Other data will be entered *as a part* of the operation of the system. Consider the bookstore inventory system. The file of books currently in the inventory must be created before the inventory system can work. Therefore, as part of the development phase, someone must input the relevant information about each book into a computer file. Book orders from professors, on the other hand, will be input into the system as part of its operation.

Procedures

The procedures associated with using the system should be completely developed by the end of this phase. One procedure that is very important to the entire systems development project is documentation. Documentation is a written description of the activities and parts of the information system. The role of documentation in the analysis phase was already discussed. The conceptual and detailed models of the system that are produced in the design phase are another example of documentation. In the development phase, the form of documentation is primarily program documentation. This is the most detailed form of documentation. An exact account of what goes on in each program must be clearly recorded. Without this documentation it becomes very difficult to make later changes in the software, especially if the person who originally wrote the program is no longer around. Documentation of programs should be an ongoing task. Anytime the programs are changed, the documentation should be revised as well.

Other procedures to develop would be those regarding security. Security procedures would specify who has legitimate access to the data and under what circumstances. Security also includes procedures for backup of the data. In addition, there are procedures for data entry and the generation and distribution of outputs.

People

In some cases, new personnel must be hired to help operate the system. If this is the case, the hiring process should be carried out during development. In some instances, an individual's job function will change as a result of the system. When this happens, the changes in the job description should be carried out in this phase. In general, any effects of the new system in terms of personnel should be identified and planned for during this phase.

Implementation

The objective of the implementation phase is to begin to use the new system. There are both technical and organizational considerations which must be taken into account. Also, there must be a procedure for switching from the existing system to the new one. Users must be educated and prepared to use the new system effectively. Documentation such as user manuals should be available to the personnel who will be associated with the system. Finally, a user/organizational acceptance test must be carried out. Many systems fail because of poor implementation even when technically sound.

System Conversion

The major task during implementation is system conversion. This is the process of moving from the existing to the new system. Different circumstances require different approaches to accomplishing this. For this reason, four major conversion techniques are used for system implementation. One technique is not necessarily better than another. It is up to those responsible for the implementation phase to determine the technique that is most appropriate. These four techniques are shown in Figure 8.7.

Parallel Conversion This method of conversion involves duplication. In **parallel conversion,** *both* the existing system and the new system are operating at the same time. This allows time for users to get accustomed to the new system and for any unforeseen errors with the new system to be corrected. Once it has been determined that the new system can operate effectively, operation of the existing system ceases. Parallel conversion is a conservative method of conversion. If some problem with the new system arises, the organization still has the existing system to fall back on. There is automatic backup since each process is being done twice. Parallel conversion, however, is also expensive. Since two systems are in operation, there may be duplicate personnel and files, and the organization may be supporting two separate computers. In addition, the resources for the two systems must be available, and this too is very costly. For parallel conversion to be an appropriate choice, it must be important to the organization to have the system operational at all times.

Direct Conversion **Direct conversion** takes the opposite approach. Once the new system is operational, the existing system is no longer used. Since the backup that exists with parallel conversion does not exist here, this method can be very risky. With no other system to rely on, it is crucial that the new system be as error-free as possible. On the other hand, it is a less expensive method of conversion since it requires only one system to be operating at a time. Direct conversion is used when it is not possible to have two systems operating at once, such as when the organization lacks the hardware resources required to operate the existing and the new system in parallel.

Pilot Conversion Both parallel conversion and direct conversion are methods of converting the *entire* system. An alternative is to convert to the new system *in parts.* With **pilot conversion,** a system is implemented for one group of users at a time. For example, if State University's library wants to convert to a new book-circulation system, and there are three library facilities on campus, one option would be to convert one facility at a time. An advantage of pilot conversion is that the effects of system failure are minimized. For example, if something happens with the new circulation system, only one library is affected.

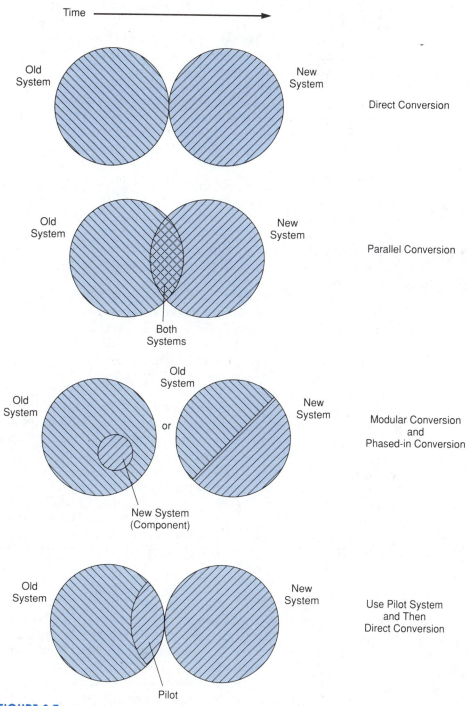

FIGURE 8.7
Conversion techniques

Phased-in Conversion **Phased-in conversion** is an alternative method to convert to the new hardware and software gradually. The advantages of this approach are that the change is very gradual and that the impact of this change on the organization is minimized. The disadvantages are that it is a lengthy process and can be costly as well. Suppose Last National Bank is changing its method of storing customer information from using individual files to using a database. The goal would be to have all customer information stored in this database. With the phased-in method, perhaps the processing of customer checking and savings account data would be converted first. At some later date, the processing of customer loan data would be converted.

Preparation and Education of Users As we know, an information system is more than computers, programs, and data; it is also the people who will use it and the procedures by which they will do so. The implementation process must therefore have both technological and organizational aspects. Conversion refers mainly to the technological aspects of system implementation. Preparation and education of users addresses the people and procedures resources of the information system.

It stands to reason that the more the intended users of the new system are involved in the development process, the more likely they are to accept this new system. If they are part of the decision-making process, they are less likely to resist any changes in their work routine. This is an important reason for having users on the steering committee and project team. Therefore, an important rule in systems development is to be certain to have user involvement throughout the process.

But there are two organizational issues beyond user involvement that must be addressed during the implementation phase. First, if the new system will change the way the users normally work, they must be informed about these changes and new work procedures may have to be established. Second, users must be taught how to use the new system. User education can be a major feature of implementation depending upon the computer skills the users already have. If they are already familiar with using a computer, user education may be as simple as explaining the new procedures. If the change is from manual to automated methods, however, quite a bit more education will be required. Users may even have to take formal classes to learn how to use the new system.

Acceptance Test

During an **acceptance test**, the new system is operated in test mode. During development, system resources such as software were tested individually. During the acceptance test, all parts of the system are tested together. In this way, certain features such as the interfaces or links between subsystems and other systems can be tested. The users interact with the system and evaluate it with respect to usability and consistency with the requirements document.

After a successful acceptance test, the system is ready for operation. Someone from the user population must then certify that the new system is acceptable. This is referred to as a "final sign-off."

Operation, Evaluation, and Maintenance

Operation is the actual use of the new system in the organization. That is, it begins once the conversion process is completed and the users have "accepted" the system. However, this does not mean the *evaluation* process is over. After the system has been in operation for a period of time, such as six months, the system is evaluated by the steering committee with respect to properties such as timeliness, response time, and quality of output. Minor modifications may have to be made to fine-tune the system's technical performance or ease of use. This evaluation is sometimes referred to as a **post-implementation audit**. Since the functional and technical environment of the system is not static, the system will change as well. As new laws, regulations, reporting requirements, and industry competition appear, the system will be adapted to suit these new requirements. This is what is meant by system **maintenance**.

EXAMPLE: DEVELOPING A REGISTRATION SYSTEM AT STATE UNIVERSITY ═══

Now let us consider how these phases of the systems development life cycle would be carried out in an actual setting.

Perception of Need: A Problem with the Existing System

The administrators at State University were having difficulties with the preregistration process for an upcoming term and the course registration and drop/add process that occurs at the start of each term. During the beginning of one term the schedule of classes for the next one must be developed. This is a difficult task for two reasons. First, because State University has a large number of part-time students, it is difficult to predict the number of students who will actually be taking classes and how many they will take. Second, since there is a continuing turnover of faculty, it is difficult to know whether there will be enough professors to teach the courses in which students will enroll.

Students register for the upcoming term during the middle of the current one. Students select their courses from a course schedule which shows course offerings and the time and place they will be offered. They are asked to provide an alternative selection in case the desired course section is not available when the enrollment form is processed. Students do not know which courses they will actually be taking until just before the term begins, when the course schedules are mailed out. These schedules are a combination of first- and second-choice course selections and usually bear little resemblance to the schedules they desired. It is therefore difficult for students to schedule work and other activities.

Currently, students' criteria for course selection are not part of the course assignment process. The criteria used by students to choose course sections include a desire for back-to-back classes, a preference for a specific instructor, and a dislike of very early or late classes. State University would like the students to be more active participants in the registration process so they are happy at the institution. With declining student enrollments, the university does not want to lose students because of dissatisfaction with course scheduling.

The registrar identified the following specific problems:

- Course offerings published in the course schedule do not satisfy students' requirements. The university is constrained by the availability of faculty and classrooms. There is no planning data available.
- Students are passively involved in the enrollment process. The registration system is unable to inform students at the time of registration when course sections are not available so that students can make substitutions based on their personal criteria. This is because the current system uses off-line data entry and delayed transaction processing in batch mode.
- Course offerings are static. There is no way to add and delete course sections based on student demand and resource availability.
- There is no checking of prerequisites for course selections. As a result, students can be enrolled in courses they are not qualified to take.

Feasibility Study

One day the registrar paid a visit to the manager of the school's MIS Department to talk about these problems. At the end of the conversation, both the registrar and the MIS manager concluded that it would be a good idea to consider developing a new registration system, one which could do on-line processing of registration forms using a database.

Before the systems development effort could proceed, however, a project proposal had to be prepared and the proposed system had to be evaluated with respect to technical, economic, and operational feasibility. If developing this new system were deemed feasible, the systems development project would be assigned a priority by the university's central steering committee. This committee determines the schedule for carrying out system projects.

The steering committee determined that a new registration system was feasible. Technical feasibility was no issue since hardware and software already existed to support a centralized database that could be accessed and updated at remote terminals. The project was economically feasible because the increased revenue from maintaining enrollment levels would offset the systems development costs. Since the university already had personnel in the MIS Department who were responsible for operating and maintaining the existing registration system, operational feasibility presented no difficulties either.

Based on the results of the feasibility study, the steering committee authorized the project to proceed. Because of the university's desire to increase student satisfaction and quality of life as a means of maintaining enrollment, the proposed registration system was given a high organizational priority. Along with assigning this priority, the committee allocated the funds and staff that would be necessary to carry out this project.

Analysis

The Project Team
The project was now ready to be launched. A team of analysts and users was formed to describe the current system in detail, to determine the scope of the new system, and to specify its requirements.

Describing the Existing System
Once the project team was formed, it could begin to specify the requirements for the new system. Before it could do this, however, it had to describe the current system in detail. Fortunately, State University has a well-run MIS Department, and all existing systems have been completely and precisely documented. This documentation has constantly been updated to keep the information current.

The New System Requirements
With a complete picture of the existing system, the next tasks were to identify the problems with the existing system and begin to identify the requirements for the new system. In addition to a review of documentation, a number of interviews would also be conducted. First, pertinent users had to be identified. They included the registrar, a clerk involved in processing registration forms, a student counselor who helps students prepare registration forms and who has used the existing system, and several students and faculty members. These individuals were interviewed by members of the project team to determine problems with the existing system and the users' views about what a new system should contain.

Since the point of view of each of the interviewees was somewhat different, it was expected that each would have his or her own list of problems and suggestions. For example, the registrar's problems were stated as follows:

- Too many students complain about the schedule generated by the system.
- The process of producing the schedule of class offerings is cumbersome and unscientific.
- No data for future planning is available.

On the other hand, a list of problems from a typical student included the following:

- The class schedule generated by the system does not allow me to work in four-hour blocks.
- The final schedule isn't available until just before the beginning of the term. This is too late for me to plan a work schedule.
- The courses offered do not satisfy my needs. Not all the courses that I need to fulfill graduation requirements are being offered, and there are often time conflicts with the other courses I need to take.

After the pertinent users were interviewed, a composite list of problems that the new system would have to solve was developed and stated in terms of requirements for the new system:

- Students should be involved during the registration process so that their personal priorities can be satisfied.
- Final student schedules should be available at time of registration.
- Planning data should be generated that can be used to automate the process of producing the schedule of course offerings.
- Verification that course prerequisites have been satisfied should be available before a student can enroll in a course.

Structured systems analysis was used to describe the new system. The system was first documented in a high-level (level 1) data flow diagram with one process: registration. The components of such a diagram were discussed earlier in this chapter. Data coming into (i.e., inputs) and going out of (i.e., outputs) this process is identified as high-level data aggregates. The source of each piece of data is identified, as is its destination. This is shown in Figure 8.8.

The processes involved are the following. A student brings in a completed registration form. The student and the form are validated before the form is processed. Each course selection on the form is processed independently. First, the course's prerequisites are determined and a check is made to ensure that the student satisfies them. Then a check is made to determine if the course section that the student desires is open. If the section is available, the student is enrolled. If not, open sections are identified until one is chosen that satisfies the student's needs. This process uses many different types of internal data:

- General student information used in validation to determine whether the student can be enrolled at this time
- Course information used to document the course's prerequisites

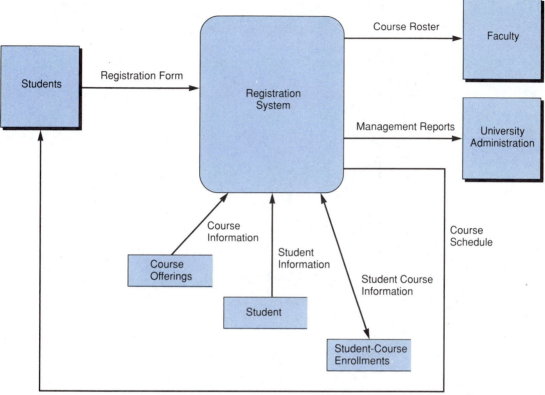

FIGURE 8.8
High-level data flow diagram of the registration system

■ Student's transcript, used to determine if the student can enroll in a specific course and the number of courses that can be elected
■ Course schedule, including all the course section offerings, their time, location, instructor, and maximum and current enrollment

After the top-level diagram was documented and agreed to by the project team, lower-level diagrams were prepared. Before this could be done, the registration system had to be decomposed into its constituent parts or subsystems. The registration system consists of the following subsystems: (1) registration form validation, (2) course section enrollment, (3) generation of student schedules and course rosters, (4) database population and update, and (5) generation of planning and other administrative data. Next, a data flow diagram was produced for each of these subsystems. A diagram for the course enrollment subsystem is shown in Figure 8.9.

Each subsystem was decomposed into its major functions, which were then decomposed until the lowest level of functions was derived. As the system was decomposed into a hierarchy of processes, more detailed data

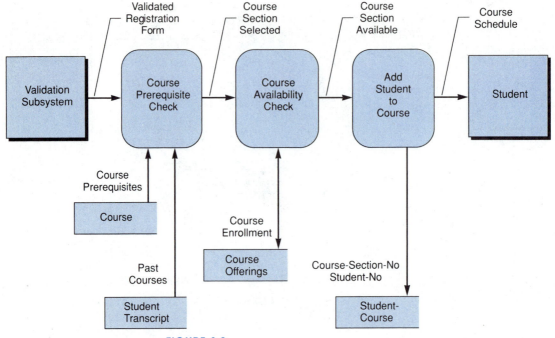

FIGURE 8.9
Data flow diagram for course enrollment

flow diagrams were drawn, which aided in subdividing the system further and in presenting each level of system flow.

In addition, the data items that must exist for each type of input and output had to be determined. For example, the registration form included a student identification number and the unique identifier for each course section.

Other requirements determined during the analysis process were as follows:

■ The system must be on-line and process registration forms in real time, while the student is present, as well as be able to generate a schedule at this time.
■ Students should have the option of dropping off forms and picking up schedules the next day.
■ There is a high volume of registration lasting for two weeks, twice every term: at the beginning of the term and during the preregistration period.
■ Multiple registration terminals must be used during these peak periods.
■ The processing of other university information systems may be delayed during peak registration processing in order to provide additional computer capacity that might be needed.

The System Proposal

All of this information was used in the preparation of the system proposal. But before the system proposal was presented to the steering committee for review, the project librarian had to verify that it was complete. That is, he had to make sure that the proposal outlined the scope of the new system, that it described all five resources (hardware, software, data, procedures, and personnel), and that it included a plan for the rest of the systems development project in terms of schedule and resource requirements. After the relevant documents were approved by the project team and the users involved in the process, the steering committee reviewed the material and gave the go-ahead for continuing with the design phase.

Design

Conceptual Design

The first phase of the design process was conceptual design. Each of the resources of the system was designed. In the case of the software resource, the project team considered both in-house software development and purchasing a software package. At first it was thought that the current registration requirements at State University might be satisfied by a software package that was commercially available. However, the package they considered did not include planning data and a student database. Further, the package was not available in source code and therefore could not be altered or extended. For these reasons, the software package was not considered to be a viable alternative. The alternative that was chosen was in-house software development.

Next, a conceptual model of the system was created. That is, the configuration of the hardware, software, and data resources that would be part of the new system was developed. Plans regarding personnel and operating procedures were also established. After the users approved the model of the new system, more details were developed.

Detailed Design

The members of the project team were assigned different tasks with regard to detailed design. A team was assigned to each subsystem of the registration system. Each team was responsible for developing the input and output layouts, the database contents, and the operating procedures. Technical specialists such as telecommunications and database experts were made available so that the teams could consult with them on complex or difficult design issues.

A structure chart for the new registration system is shown in Figure 8.10. This structure chart provided the basis for determining the inputs and outputs associated with each process. In the conceptual design, the contents of each input and output were identified. For example, the

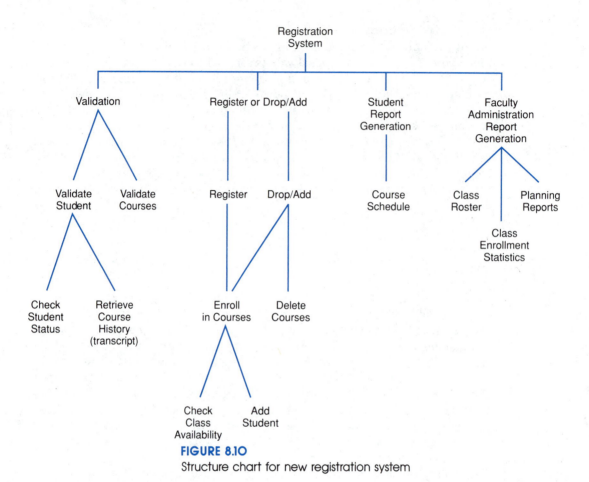

FIGURE 8.10

Structure chart for new registration system

contents of the new registration form are as follows: student name, student ID number, term to which the registration applies, and desired courses (designated by course and section number). In the detailed design phase, the layout of the registration form and the design of the input screen were developed.

The validity of the conceptual design was evaluated in the detailed design phase by using a series of structured walkthroughs. For example, the designers of the course enrollment subsystem presented their design to the other members of the project team, two users—a student and the assistant registrar—one of the programmers assigned to that subsystem, and the telecommunications specialist. The project librarian took notes as people commented on the design. For the walkthrough, mockups of forms were developed to demonstrate the use and layout of the registration forms and input screens. This demonstration allowed the users to verify that human-computer interfaces such as the screen design were adequate.

The student representative wondered if a form was necessary since a student's course selections would be directly entered at a terminal. The other attendees felt a registration form would make certain that students came to the registration process with all the necessary information, thereby avoiding possible delays. The users and other designers felt that the new forms would be easy to use and that their layout was consistent with the designs.

Since the software for the registration was to be developed by programmers at the university, considerable attention was given to program specification. Sufficient detail had to be given to guide the programmers in developing the code. It was also necessary to specify any links that would occur between the various programs that would make up the system. These detailed program specifications were expressed in pseudocode. (Pseudocode was discussed in Chapter 4.)

At the end of the design phase, the new configuration of system resources was specified in sufficient detail to enable their development and implementation.

Development

The programmers in the university MIS Department were the personnel involved in this phase of the project. The software was developed using the COBOL language and a database management system. The programs that were written were based on the program specifications developed during detailed design. Once program modules were developed, they were tested, first with test data and then with real data. At the same time, student data for the database was collected and entered into the database. Since the existing computer was able to support the new system, hardware acquisition consisted of purchasing more terminals and linking them to the existing local area network.

Once the hardware, software, and data resources were acquired, the users were provided with documentation and given a demonstration of the system to verify that it satisfied the requirements specified in the system proposal. Finally, the plan for user education was reviewed and approved.

Implementation

Parallel conversion was the method chosen for implementing the new registration system. Since registration is such an important function of a university, it was decided that, for the first term, the new system should be operated in parallel with the existing one. This would provide the necessary backup in the event of some unforeseen problem. While the old system was still operational, users were provided with documentation and given instruction in the use of the new system. The acceptance test revealed that students were very satisfied with this new method of scheduling courses and administrators were pleased with the planning data the new system provided.

Operation, Evaluation, and Maintenance

Since no difficulties were encountered during the period of parallel operation, the new system was used alone the following term. The MIS Department kept a log of system performance. It noted that delays in student scheduling were greatly reduced. Students were asked to fill out an evaluation form after completing the registration process. The results indicated that they were much happier with their schedules, although some did comment that the enforcement of prerequisites reduced their flexibility in enrolling in courses.

Some slight operational problems did occur, however. For example, when one of the printers broke down for a day, students had to wait for a copy of their schedules. The MIS staff evaluated the registration period with respect to the system plan, the new system's performance, and its impact on the operation of other university systems. This post-implementation audit indicated that the system was successful, and therefore no plans were made to modify it in the near future.

NEW METHODS OF SYSTEMS DEVELOPMENT

While the systems life cycle approach to systems development continues to be in widespread use, some other approaches are currently being taken which represent a departure from tradition. These new approaches are a direct result of the increasing demand for computer-based systems in business, the popularity of the personal computer, the availability of user-friendly software, and the growth of end-user computing.

Insofar as these approaches to systems development depart from the way the life cycle has traditionally been applied, they represent "nontraditional" approaches to the systems development process. In this section we will consider three new approaches which have become popular in recent years:

1. The active involvement of end users in the design and development as well as analysis and implementation phases
2. Iterative rather than linear enactment of the life cycle phases
3. The use of software packages and software development tools over in-house programming by the MIS staff

Let us first learn a little more about these new approaches and then consider why these techniques have become popular.

New Approaches to Systems Development

The Active Involvement of End Users in the Entire Process

In the traditional systems development approach, the user's role is primarily consultative. That is, the user's views are taken into account, but someone else makes the decisions regarding the development of the system. In this approach to systems development the user is primarily involved in the feasibility, analysis, and implementation phases. The user's role is limited to expressing the need for the system, helping state the requirements of the system, and accepting the system.

In organizations today, however, end users are getting more involved in the entire development process. Some end users do the entire development themselves. This might occur in a small business in which no systems personnel are available, or in a large organization in which one needs to develop a personal system such as a customer tickler file. Many medium-size and large organizations have a functional area designated to aid end users in their systems development efforts. This area is usually called an **information center**. An information center is a resource area usually consisting of hardware, assorted software, and personnel acting as internal consultants. Users utilize the information center as a place to develop systems (either at initial phases or continually), to get advice, or to sound out ideas.

Some large organizations have developed procedures whereby the end-user department develops systems in conjunction with the MIS department. In this situation, the end-user department takes the lead and the systems professional plays the consultative role.

Iterative Systems Development

The traditional systems development life cycle approach to systems development is a linear approach. That is, the tasks to be carried out in the development project are known in the beginning of the process. Both the content of these tasks and the order in which they will be completed is supposed to be known. In many cases, a given task cannot be undertaken until another task has been completed.

This approach has two major drawbacks. First, because this process is so structured, obtaining approval before moving to the next stage often takes time. Sometimes, however, those who need a new or enhanced system cannot afford to wait for it. As a result, both users and systems professionals have looked for shortcuts to speed up the systems development process.

The second drawback is that sometimes the earlier stages cannot be completely defined in the beginning. This is especially true in the case of systems with which the user is not familiar. Suppose the system being designed is an office automation system which will include electronic mail, an electronic calendar, and a database for personal use. An end user unfamiliar with these applications would find it very difficult to state unequivocally in the very beginning of the process what his or her requirements are.

What is needed to overcome both these drawbacks is a way of moving more quickly into the design and development phases and then backing up to the analysis phase to make adjustments where necessary. A development tool that has become very useful in this regard is the prototype. A **prototype** is a model or representation of the system used to help one "visualize" what the system will be like. In some cases, only a part of the system is prototyped — for example, to demonstrate input and output formats. In other cases, a miniature version of the entire system is developed as the prototype.

The use of prototyping overcomes the drawbacks just described. With a prototype we can move into the design stage more quickly. By having the ability to test out the implications of a certain specification, an organization does not have to be as careful in the way it expresses the requirements because it will have a chance to revise them upon seeing the prototype. For new systems with which users may be unfamiliar, a prototype can be used as a learning device by helping them "see" what the system can do. They will then be better able to articulate their requirements after having some experience using this model of the real system.

The use of prototyping represents a significant modification in the life cycle concept. Rather than limiting development to a linear process, the use of a prototype enables the development process to evolve through a series of iterations. Another way of thinking about a prototype is to think of it as a way of collecting feedback about the system before it is completed. In this way, modifications can be made throughout the process. Therefore, rather than executing each phase only once, by using a prototype, the phases can be repeated incorporating the feedback that has been collected. Figure 8.11 shows this process.

The Use of Software Packages and Software Development Tools

The development phase of the systems life cycle has historically taken up the major portion of the project time and effort. The reason is that the systems professionals had to write the programs themselves using a third-generation language such as COBOL. Today, however, a variety of options are available for developing the software. As was discussed in Chapter 4, computer software can be acquired in several ways. Having the ability to purchase "ready-made" software or to develop software using fourth-generation language tools makes the software-acquisition part of the development phase much easier to accomplish. Because systems can be developed with "off-the-shelf" software or easy-to-use tools, individuals who do not have formal training in computers and information systems — the end users — can now be engaged in this process.

For those organizations which choose to develop their own software, new tools have become available to significantly improve programmer productivity. **Computer-aided software engineering (CASE)** refers to a collection of tools which facilitate accomplishing the spectrum of tasks involved in the systems life cycle, from systems analysis through development to maintenance. CASE tools include a central repository of the information collected during the life cy-

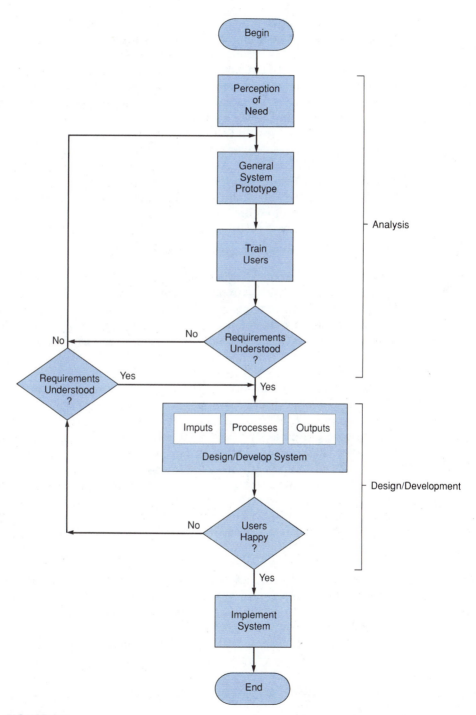

FIGURE 8.11
Use of prototyping in systems development

cle phases, a graphics interface for collecting and documenting this information, and a report generator. CASE tools provide assistance in the analysis phase by determining errors and inconsistencies in requirements so that they are corrected prior to development. Since humans are prone to errors in dealing with detail, complexity, and extensive cross-checking, CASE, with its database and associated software, can help improve efficiency and accuracy. Because the later in the life cycle an error is detected the more expensive it is to correct, CASE improves productivity in systems development and decreases the time spent in developing new applications. The learning process for CASE is usually short. For CASE to be effective, it should be used with structured techniques. CASE tools incorporate methodologies such as structured analysis and data flow diagrams, and they guide the analyst or designer through steps which result in a sound design.

Circumstances Calling for New Approaches

Now that we have considered some of the new approaches to systems development that are being taken, let us consider *why* these changes are occurring. Four factors are pushing the trend toward different approaches to systems development: the user-friendliness of the technology, the growth of end-user computing, the increasing demand for computer-based systems, and user dissatisfaction with existing systems.

The User-Friendliness of the Technology

Since the microcomputer (personal computer) is much more affordable than larger computers, its introduction in the early 1980s sparked a great increase in computer use. Besides price, what has helped make the personal computer so popular is the availability of software packages. This means that one does not have to write programs in order to use the computer. In addition, commercially available software is geared to the end user. For example, the setup instructions do not assume extensive knowledge of computers, and "help" routines are built into the software to assist users who get stuck. Often, all the commands are presented through menus so that the user doesn't have to remember a lot of commands. All these features serve to make the software user-friendly and to encourage its use.

The personal computer has helped to produce a growing population of very computer-literate users. While many of those who would like to benefit from computers do not understand very much about them, the population of those who do is growing. It stands to reason, then, that as their knowledge and experience grows, users would want to be more involved in the process of developing the systems that are intended for their use.

The Growth of End-User Computing

Because personal computers have become so easy to use, more and more clients of information systems are becoming end users. That is, instead of requesting that the MIS department produce a report for them, they are the ones who are actually interacting with the computer to produce the output. The term *end user* has come to denote those who are actually involved in developing the system they will use. In contrast, the term *user* has come to denote one who will use a system developed by the MIS department of an organization. It is increasingly the end users who originate the idea for a new or enhanced information system, in part because of their increased knowledge about computers. This is also the result of their experience in using computers. While users may not have had much knowledge when computer-based information systems came into being, their experiences in using systems have now given them insight into what kinds of features they should expect from these systems.

Demand for Computer-based Systems

With the increased popularity of computers, there is an increased demand for the development or enhancement of computer-based systems in organizations today. As a result, many users have become dissatisfied with the process whereby systems are developed for them. MIS departments are having a difficult time keeping up with this demand, and there is often a long wait. Sometimes users are told they will have to wait for months, sometimes even years! In addition to the inconvenience of waiting so long, there is the possibility that by the time the system is developed, the information need will have changed and the system developed will no longer be relevant. This situation is referred to as the **applications development backlog**.

To cope with this backlog, some organizations have developed policies specifying when the MIS department will develop the system and when the end-user department will develop it. An organization may have a policy which states that systems involving more than one department or the use of corporate-wide data will be developed by the MIS department, and that others will be developed by the end-user department. Systems developed by the user departments might be small or personal systems, such as those found in one's office. These organizations can be said to have a corporate culture which encourages end-user computing and end-user involvement in the systems development process.

Dissatisfaction with Systems

In addition to the development backlog, there is the problem of the failure of systems to meet the user's needs. This problem usually arises because the requirements were not expressed adequately. Sometimes a better job at requirements specification could have been done; sometimes it is not possible. Nevertheless, both of these situations suggest that making some changes in the systems development process would improve the chances of minimizing this problem. In the first case, the problem usually arises because the systems analyst is not the one who has the information need. The user often must communicate the need to the analyst. No matter how capable he or she is, the systems analyst will never know the requirements of the system the way the user does. There is always the potential for misinterpretation of the requirements, which would result in a system that does not satisfy all of the user's expectations. Because of this problem, both users and systems professionals are recognizing the benefits of having users express their requirements to the system directly rather than through an intermediary. The other problem with requirements specifications results from systems with which the user is not familiar. If the user has no experience with the type of system under consideration, it is often difficult to state exactly what the requirements should be. As discussed earlier, prototyping is very useful in these kinds of situations.

COMPLETE END-USER DEVELOPMENT

Certain circumstances require the end user to carry out the complete systems development effort alone. These circumstances are usually associated with systems development for home use or in a small business where there is no systems professional on the staff. In these situations the end user cannot rely on the expertise of technical experts. As a result, the end user must either retain the services of a consultant or incorporate a certain amount of learning into the systems development effort. To observe how this process would be carried out, let us consider the case of systems development at Wooden Wonders.

EXAMPLE: SYSTEMS DEVELOPMENT AT WOODEN WONDERS

Step One: Investigation

Not long after Wooden Wonders was established, Paul Bunyan decided that he should have a computer to help with the administrative aspects of the business. Since he knew little about computers, he really had no idea what he would need to buy or what alternatives were available. After talking to some friends, Paul decided to visit a local computer store. What happened at the first store pretty much sums up his experience in general.

When the salesperson approached him, he told her he wanted to buy a personal computer to support his new business. She then asked Paul what he wanted it to do, and Paul said that he had not thought about the specifics but was interested in learning what personal computers could do and what they cost. He asked her how one should go about selecting a PC. She said that cost is one important consideration and that prices range from under a thousand to several thousand dollars. She asked him how much he wanted to spend. Paul knew that he would spend whatever was necessary to get the kind of help that he wanted, but he didn't tell her this.

They went on to other topics. Looking at some of the computers, Paul saw some brands that sounded familiar and others he had never heard of. When he asked if there were other considerations besides cost to help a person make a decision, she told him that it also depends on what software you want to run on the computer.

While he knew generally what he wanted—the computer should support his business activities to allow him more time to spend on woodworking—he did not seem to be able to communicate with her. He thought he had told her plainly enough what he wanted, yet they seemed to be talking in circles. He decided that he needed to get more specific about his needs so that he could have more concrete criteria for evaluating his options. Thanking her, he drove home with a headache. All that Paul learned from this visit is that the process of selecting a computer is more complicated than he had thought. Paul decided that Mary Tyson, whom he had recently hired to manage business operations, should be involved in this effort. Mary had recently graduated from business school and had taken a course in information systems. She suggested to Paul that he should write down his requirements and then they could go on from there.

Step Two: Determining the System Requirements

Paul sat down with a paper and pencil and tried to make a list of what he wanted the computer to do for Wooden Wonders. He had some difficulty, however, because he wasn't quite sure what a computer *could* do for him. He had some ideas based on how people he knew were using computers. This knowledge led him to make two lists. One was a list of things that his information system had to do. Then he made a list of other tasks that needed to be performed in the course of doing his job. If it would be possible to do these things on the computer, it would be even better. However, he didn't know whether these things were technically possible, at least with the kind of personal computer he could afford.

Paul started with the system features he felt were absolutely necessary for supporting Wooden Wonders. First, the software had to be able to keep track of customer information in order to send them catalogs and other mailings. Also, Paul wanted to keep track of his expenses and income, to make a budget, and to keep track of inventory. He also wanted help in preparing his catalog, invoices, and correspondence. These tasks also required him to have a printer. Paul then jotted down questions to which he wanted answers:

- Which products sell well and which do not?
- Do I use any supplies more than others, so that I may purchase supplies in larger quantities to save money?
- Where do I sell the most products?
- How much money am I spending? When will I make a profit?
- Do I need to borrow money to keep my business going?

Paul felt he could go on forever writing down questions, but he still did not know what exactly a computer could do for him. All he wanted it to do was to enable him to spend more time on woodworking and make enough money to support his business, including Mary and himself. Paul asked Mary to work on identifying their requirements before they paid a second visit to the computer stores.

Step Three: Considering the System Alternatives

In developing an information system for Wooden Wonders, Mary knew that all five resources had to be taken into consideration. She first thought about personnel and procedures. Mary observed that Paul had no experience with computers, and she knew the basics from courses she had taken in college. This led her to make three decisions: (1) they should acquire either software with which she was already familiar or that would be easy to learn; (2) the hardware should be purchased from a company which would also provide a service/support contract; and (3) they might have to invest in some training.

Next she considered data and software. In order to determine the data to be included in the system, Mary noted the tasks involved in the different aspects of managing the business. She then identified the types of software which could support them. The following list of requirements and alternatives resulted:

Task	*Appropriate Software*
Budget	Spreadsheet
Maintaining client list	Database management (DBMS)
Generating mailing labels	DBMS or word processing
Correspondence	Word processing
Invoices	DBMS and/or word processing
Inventory control	DBMS
Answer "what if" questions	DBMS or spreadsheet

Mary and Paul then established a priority of Wooden Wonders' requirements and decided that managing the budget and client list were the top priorities.

Mary summarized the needs of Wooden Wonders in terms of both software and hardware. First, system software in the form of an operating system was needed. The operating system chosen would depend on the type of computer purchased. Second, the application software would need to be able to support data management, spreadsheet, and word processing activities. It could be in the form of three separate software packages or in the form of an integrated package with all three functions.

For the hardware resource, Mary suggested that they should purchase an IBM-compatible computer because of the software they desired. The hardware features that they needed included a CPU; a hard disk for secondary storage; floppy disk drive and disks for software loading and backup; a controller for the secondary storage devices; a monitor with its associated controller; and a printer. Mary wanted hardware that would not be obsolete in the near future, would be expandable, and would have good vendor support. She then made a list of these hardware features and the associated alternatives:

Hardware Features	*Alternatives*
CPU	IBM-PC family clones: PC(8088), AT(286), 386, or PS/2
Primary memory (RAM)	640KB or more
Floppy disk drive	3-1/2-inch or 5-1/4-inch format, high or regular density
Hard disk	20 to 80 MB or more
Monitor	Monochrome or color
Monitor controller	Compatible with monitor (Hercules, EGA, or VGA)
Keyboard	Standard with twelve function keys and a numeric pad
Printer	Dot matrix with near-letter-quality option or a higher-quality laser printer
Ports	One parallel for the printer and two serial for devices such as a mouse

Step Four: Acquiring the System Resources

While Mary knew that Paul could save money by purchasing the computer through a mail-order company, she believed Wooden Wonders would do better with the support available from a local computer store. Therefore, they visited several computer stores with their list of requirements. They investigated alternative software packages which would satisfy their needs. They evaluated the various options on the basis of suitability to their needs, cost, ease of learning and use, and support provided by the vendor.

After reviewing the requirements of Wooden Wonders, Paul and Mary decided on the following configuration:

- IBM-compatible computer with a 286-based processor (called an AT machine) with 1 MB of primary memory, a standard keyboard, 1 or 2 serial ports, and parallel port
- 12-inch monochrome monitor with an EGA controller
- Two secondary storage devices: an 80-MB hard disk drive, and a 1.2-MB 5-1/4-inch floppy drive which can also handle 360-KB diskettes. The device controller must be able to handle two additional devices such as a 3-1/2-inch floppy and tape backup unit.
- A near-letter-quality (NLQ) printer such as an Epson LQ printer
- System software—disk operating system (DOS), which is the standard for IBM-compatible PCs

▪ Application software – an integrated package with word processing, spreadsheet, and database management system. They determined that buying an integrated package is less expensive than purchasing these packages separately. Paul decided to choose between Lotus's Symphony and Aston-Tate's Framework.

The next decision is to determine where to make the purchase. Paul and Mary had two alternatives: a computer store or a mail-order firm. The price from the mail-order company was lower than from the local computer store, but the level of support was not as good. With the mail-order firm, if the computer required any repairs it would have to be shipped back, and Wooden Wonders could be without its system for several weeks. Also, the mail-order company offers no training. The local store provides on-site repair and, as part of the service contract, a loaner when the computer cannot be repaired within twenty-four hours. Repairs for the first twelve months are free. In addition, training is provided at a reduced fee for those who purchase a computer at the store.

Step Five: Implementation and Operation

Since Paul and Mary decided to assemble the computer themselves, they departed from the store with a collection of boxes and cables. They also purchased a printer stand and furniture to hold the computer. To put the computer together, the only tools that were required were some screwdrivers. Paul was ready to demonstrate his mechanical expertise as he uncrated the computer components. Assembling the computer involved installing the monitor controller in one of the computer's slots, and connecting the monitor to the computer with its cable. The printer was connected by attaching the printer cable to the parallel port of the computer.

Once the hardware was assembled, Mary began to install the software. Installation is the process of moving the software from the floppy disks to the hard disk where the programs will be used on a daily basis. The first software package to be installed was the operating system, DOS. Mary put the DOS setup diskette into the drive, turned on the computer, and followed the instructions which appeared on the screen for completing the installation of DOS. When this was completed she began to install the other software packages.

Once the computer and software were set up, the next task was to begin operating it. Mary decided to help Paul feel at ease with the computer by demonstrating how to use it. She started by showing him one of the sample spreadsheets that came with the software. This example involved the development of a budget for human resource expenses. Mary decided to interact directly with the computer and ask Paul to supply the input.

First, Mary showed Paul how to turn on the computer and load the spreadsheet program. She showed him how the cursor could be moved around the spreadsheet using the cursor keys and how the commands of the spreadsheet could be executed through the software's menu. She then showed him how the spreadsheet could be moved from the floppy disk to the primary memory in order to be displayed on the screen and how it could be moved to the disk for storage.

When the demonstration was completed, Paul shook his head in disbelief. While he saw how powerful spreadsheet software could be, he felt he could never do it himself. Since Paul needed to be able to use the computer when she was not around, Mary suggested he take some courses on using the software they had purchased. One of the reasons for choosing the store at which they purchased their equipment was that it provided end-user training at a reduced cost to its customers. When Paul completed his training, he not only felt comfortable using the system they had acquired, he also had ideas about additional computer-based support for Wooden Wonders in the future.

A Summary of the End-User Development Process

Before we consider how the life cycle steps were carried out in this systems development example, let us consider why complete end-user development was used. The primary reason was that, since Wooden Wonders is a small company, it did not have the need to employ any systems professionals. While Paul could have hired a consultant to help him, there are several reasons why he chose not to. First, based on Mary's experience with computers in college, she had some idea of what computers could do for her. Second, because of advertising about personal computers and user-friendly software, Paul thought the process would be simple enough for Mary and him to manage. Finally, as he realized during his first conversation with salespeople at the computer store, he was the one who best knew his information requirements. Therefore, he should be the ultimate judge of the system that would be most useful.

Despite Mary's prior experience and the claims of vendors, the process was a little more difficult than Paul had originally envisioned. Nevertheless, in the end, they were successful in getting an information system that satisfied their needs. However, the way they went about it was different from the traditional approach to systems development. Let's see how the systems development life cycle applied to this case.

Perception of Need

Their primary motivation was that suitable technology was available. Based on her exposure to computers, Mary knew that using a computer to support business operations would be more efficient than doing these things manually.

Paul just had a general sense that using computers would give him more time to spend on woodworking. *In this case, the perception of need was more vague than that expected in the traditional life cycle.*

Feasibility

This phase was addressed during step one, Paul's first visit to the computer store. Technical feasibility was no issue. It was clear that technology existed to satisfy his needs. The real considerations were economic and operational feasibility. However, he found that he was unable to determine these types of feasibility without more information. Paul found he needed to know more about the products that were available and which ones would be suitable for the system at Wooden Wonders. *Therefore, education and requirements analysis became a prerequisite to completing the feasibility phase of the process.* This is another departure from the traditional approach, in which a feasibility study is completed before the requirements are determined.

Analysis

Determining the scope of the existing system was relatively simple for Paul. He could easily describe the tools, procedures, and data used in the current method of managing operations at Wooden Wonders. Determining the scope of the desired system was another matter. Because of his incomplete knowledge of what was available, he was unable to state exactly what the requirements of his new system should be. *He found that further information gathering was also necessary before he could clearly state his requirements.* In the traditional approach, the user, in conjunction with the systems analyst, is expected to clearly state the requirements of the new system. *Without the aid of a systems professional, education about available options is necessary during the analysis phase.* Mary proved helpful to Paul in this regard.

Design

While the feasibility and analysis phases seem to have grown in this case, the design and development phases were shortened. The design consisted of a description of the hardware and software capabilities needed to satisfy the requirements that Paul and Mary identified. Primarily because they were purchasing products that would all fit together, there was no need for the detailed design activities typically involved in the traditional approach. *Design became a more detailed form of requirements analysis: specifying requirements in terms of hardware and software capabilities.*

Development

Because they were purchasing software packages, the typical tasks of the development phase of the life cycle were not relevant. *Rather than involving the writing of computer programs, the development phase became the process of selecting the software that best fit the specified criteria.*

Implementation

Since Wooden Wonders was moving from a manual system to an automated one, conversion was less of an issue than it might have been. *A more significant issue was that of having the expertise to physically install the computer system.* Fortunately, Mary knew enough from her previous courses and Paul was mechanically adept enough to enable them to accomplish this task. Installation is less of an issue in organizations having technical personnel available for such tasks. Another significant issue was training and support. Neither is automatically provided. They acquired the former by purchasing their equipment from a company that provided support. Paul acquired training by enrolling in special classes provided by the computer store. *This is one example of a task that needs to be approached in a similar fashion regardless of the method of systems development being used.* In both cases, training and support need to be consciously incorporated into the implementation process.

Operation, Evaluation, and Maintenance

After using the system and completing the training, Paul discovered other features that he wanted the system to have. *The operation and evaluation tasks are therefore similar in both approaches to systems development. Maintenance, however, is not automatic. By purchasing equipment from a store which also provided service, Paul was able to provide for maintenance.*

In analyzing the process that Paul Bunyan and Mary Tyson at Wooden Wonders went through, we can see that the major difference between their approach and the traditional approach is not in *what* is done. Rather, the difference lies in the emphasis placed on the various phases and the iterative way in which the phases were carried out. A greater percentage of Paul and Mary's time was spent on the feasibility and analysis phases than on design and development. Rather than completing one phase before moving on to the next, they sometimes found they had to go to the next phase in order to complete the current one.

CO-DEVELOPED INFORMATION SYSTEMS

In this approach to systems development, the end-user department develops the information system in conjunction with the MIS department of the organization. Therefore, we can say that it is **co-developed**. There are a number of reasons this approach is attractive to large organizations. Let's start by reviewing the problems that Paul had in attempting to do systems development by himself.

The problems Paul encountered during his systems development effort were due to a lack of technical expertise. Technical expertise is knowledge of available technological solutions to information problems. Part of this expertise is understanding the hardware implications of software decisions. Throughout the process Paul encountered situations which required him to get more information before he could move ahead. Since he did not possess this expertise, he had to rely on Mary's knowledge and information from friends, sales personnel, other users, and computer magazines. The lack of technical expertise on the part of the end user is probably the major drawback of complete end-user-developed systems.

In a large organization with an established MIS department, it would be an inefficient use of personnel resources if the end user did not have access to the technical expertise in the company. The MIS department could provide technical support not only during the systems development process, but throughout the entire "life" of the system.

There is another reason for the MIS department to be involved in systems development. In Chapter 3, information systems were categorized according to scope into organizational, departmental, and individual systems. While end users may have a good understanding of the information requirements associated with their specific activities, they would have less opportunity to see the interactions involved in systems that are organization-wide or affect more than one department. In systems which cross departmental boundaries, there is also the issue of hardware and software compatibility, which is required for successful data communications. Therefore, when the end user desires to develop a system which would involve more than one department in the organization, the MIS department should probably oversee this development. Many organizations have policies in this regard stating when the end user may develop a system alone and when it must be done in conjunction with the MIS department. Such a policy might be stated as follows: Organizational systems should be developed by the MIS department, departmental systems should be co-developed, and personal systems may be developed by the end user.

EXAMPLE: A CO-DEVELOPED SYSTEM AT LAST NATIONAL BANK

A mortgage tracking system is to be developed for Last National Bank. The purpose of this information system is to keep track of the data that is collected, stored, and processed in the course of processing and approving an application for a home mortgage. When customers apply for a mortgage, they have to prove their ability to make the payments on the loan. To do this, they submit certain information such as salary, other sources of income, other debts, years of employment, and total net worth. The bank then has to collect and organize this data and determine, based on established rules, whether or not the applicants qualify.

Last National Bank recently acquired two smaller banks. Each of these banks had existing mortgage tracking programs running on minicomputers. When these smaller banks were acquired, a consolidated mortgage department was created with the two banks still performing the mortgage approval function at their locations. Since there were now three sites that comprised the mortgage department, the bank's management determined that a single system should be developed which would utilize the central mainframe computer. The mortgage department requested that they develop the system themselves. As a result of negotiations with the MIS department, it was decided that this system would be a good candidate for co-development. Let us consider how this decision was reached and then examine how the systems development process was carried out.

Rationale for Complete End-User Development

1. *It is a non-accounting, departmental system.* Since this system was not keeping track of the flow of money in the bank, it did not affect the accounting function. Therefore, if end users developed it, the bank would not be violating any computer security policies. (Auditing policy requires that those who develop a system not be the same people who use it if accounting-type data is involved. This is to limit the potential of someone committing a crime.) Further, the intended system was a departmental system that did not need to interface with other systems or business units in the bank. Finally, it was noted that the end users, the mortgage personnel, were the *experts* when it came to the information. They were the ones who best understood the information needs involved in approving a mortgage application. The MIS department realized that there would be much less likelihood of a misinterpretation of requirements if the users were the ones directly translating those requirements into information system features.

2. *The bank had a systems development backlog.* The systems personnel at Last National Bank already had a huge backlog of development projects. If the MIS people were going to develop the system, the mortgage department would be in for a long wait. The mortgage department did not want to wait. They also did not want to get involved in arguing the case that their system should be given a higher priority than other development projects.

3. *The cost would be lower.* Cost was another consideration. The bank had a *chargeback* policy whereby user departments were charged for the time systems personnel spent on developing systems for them. The mortgage people figured it would be much cheaper if they developed and operated the system using their own personnel.

4. *The mortgage department had experience with end-user computing.* The mortgage department already had people with computer expertise who had been managing the old mortgage systems on minicomputers. Since there were experienced people within the department, they saw no reason to give control of development and operations over to the MIS people.

5. *Software packages and development tools were available.* The mortgage department already had a certain software product in mind for their new system. They had already concluded that most of their processing needs could be satisfied by this software. The remaining

programs and modifications could be easily accomplished through the use of the software development tools that were also included in this product. Some of the tools that were part of the product included the ability to easily design on-line screens, the ability to generate COBOL programs from the input of pseudocode, and the ability to quickly and easily generate reports through a report-writer feature.

The Rationale for Co-development

The case for complete end-user development appears to be a strong one. But the bank decided upon co-development. Why? There are two reasons this systems development effort had to involve the MIS department.

1. *The system had organizational aspects and involved data communications.* The first reason has to do with the scope of the system. While it is true that this is a departmental system in the sense that it only involves the mortgage personnel, it is organizational in the sense that the mortgage department is located in three separate facilities located in three different states. To be available to all three sites, therefore, the system needed to be implemented on the central mainframe computer and have certain data communication capabilities. The computer experts in the mortgage department only had experience managing a minicomputer and had no experience with data communications. Therefore, it was decided that the expertise of the MIS department would be needed to ensure that the system would function on the mainframe and that all three sites would have access to it.

2. *The MIS department had responsibility for maintaining mainframe applications.* Because the system would be on the mainframe, the MIS department *had* to be involved, because it was responsible for the operations of the central computer. The systems personnel were responsible for any software that ran on the mainframe. They would be the persons contacted if something malfunctioned. Therefore, the MIS department had to be sure that the mortgage department was not developing something that would cause problems later on.

The New Approach to Systems Development

Based on the preceding rationale, the MIS department agreed to allow the personnel in the mortgage department to develop the system under their oversight. Next came the issue of how the system would be developed. The MIS department of Last National Bank had always used the traditional life cycle approach to developing information systems. Almost all of the software in use had been developed by the programmers at the bank. The mortgage department, however, wanted to alter this approach. They wanted to use an iterative approach to systems development that focused on the business activities, and they wanted to use packaged software and software development tools. After much negotiating, the mortgage department eventually convinced the MIS department that this was a valid way of developing their system. The following is a description of how they went about developing their information system.

1. *Iterative development.* As the mortgage department saw it, the traditional systems development approach would involve a lot of "red tape," because each phase had to be completed before moving on to the next. In addition, because of the number of development projects the MIS department was involved in, the mortgage people thought this approval procedure would slow up the systems development process. Besides, they saw no reason to get approval from MIS for their project since it was a departmental system which would only affect their area. Since the system developers and users would all be part of the mortgage department, informal communication seemed to be sufficient.

Since the people in the mortgage department viewed the system from the perspective of business functions, they had difficulty with the idea of doing all of the analysis first, before moving on to the design. They saw the traditional life cycle approach as a linear process, depicted in Figure 8.12.

Instead, they decided to organize the development activities around the business functions involved in the mortgage tracking process. They wanted to apply the analysis, design, development, and implementation activities, in turn, to each of the tasks associated with the mortgage approval process. In this way, the development approach would be more

FIGURE 8.12

The systems development life cycle as a linear process

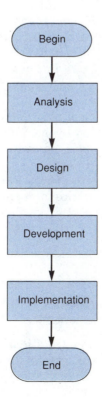

circular. In addition, mortgage personnel could be assigned responsibility based on their business expertise in certain aspects of the approval process.

First, an application is "opened" or the approval process is begun. They analyzed their needs, and then designed, developed, and implemented the input, process, and output functions that would take place in this business function. For example, since the data would be entered on-line, they had to design screens for collecting input. CASE tools were used to design the screens and to give users an option to practice with the mockup screens. They implemented those features of the software product that enabled them to do this before moving on to other business functions.

After a mortgage application is opened, it is "tracked." That is, mortgage personnel monitor the process of collecting information, such as current employer, which is needed to complete the approval of the mortgage application. If certain data has not been provided, the applicant must be contacted. One feature of this new system was to be the generation of letters to be sent out to applicants. This and other features of the "tracking" function were designed, developed, and implemented before moving on to the next business function.

Once all the necessary data has been collected, a decision is made as to whether the loan application is approved. If the loan has been approved, all this data is sent to the mortgage accounting office, which will manage the payments made on the loan. If the loan has not been approved, the applicant must be notified and provided with reasons. As with the previous two business functions, the analysis, design, development, and implementation phases were carried out here.

We should note that what was nontraditional about this approach is not *what* phases were carried out, but *how* they were carried out. The mortgage department's approach is depicted in Figure 8.13.

2. *The use of a software package and software development tools*. The fact that the mortgage personnel were using a software package minimized the need for a linear application of the life cycle phases. Since they were not writing programs themselves, an overall analysis of the data processing needs was not required prior to entering the design and development phases. They could simply install those features that applied to the business function they were working on and then make modifications as needed. Since this was how the mortgage personnel best understood the information processing activity, they were much more comfortable with the process.

Differences Between Co-development and Traditional Systems Development

Co-development is different from traditional systems development in that the respective roles of the user and systems professional are reversed. The user

FIGURE 8.13
Iterative development of mortgage system

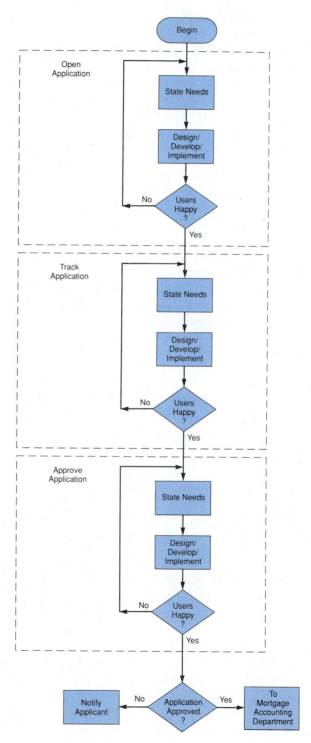

plays an active role while the MIS department plays the consultative role. Since the end user is probably not proficient in programming, co-development usually means that software will be purchased rather than developed in-house. In some cases, software development tools are purchased which enable the end user to develop programs quickly and easily, as was done in this example. Because the software already exists, it is much easier to move through the life cycle phases. This means that the end user can become involved in the design and development phases without a complete statement of requirements. This is especially valuable if the end users are developing a new kind of system, the capabilities of which may not be completely known at the beginning.

The co-development approach falls in between the two extremes: complete development by the MIS department and complete end-user development. Being a form of compromise, it incorporates the benefits while overcoming the drawbacks of each. By developing the system in conjunction with the MIS department, the end user has access to expertise when needed. From the perspective of senior management, co-development also provides a form of control. Since the MIS department is involved, even if only as a consultant, it will be aware of systems that are being produced. This will enable it to anticipate potential compatibility problems if there are plans to integrate this system with others in the future.

But if the responsibility for systems development is placed on the shoulders of the end user, many of the problems currently experienced in traditional systems development can be overcome. Systems can be developed more quickly and more cheaply. In addition, there is less chance of dissatisfaction due to misinterpretation of requirements or the perception of being controlled by the MIS department.

SUMMARY

Whether it is carried out traditionally or nontraditionally, the systems development life cycle is an application of general problem solving that is appropriate for developing information systems. Since the definition of information is to provide data that supports some business activity or is of value for decision making in some organizational context, the systems development process should start with the activities and decisions that the system is supposed to support. Next, the information needed to make those decisions should be identified. After the role of the current system in providing that information is understood, problems and improvements should be noted. These will then be translated into new system requirements. The design and development of the system will depend upon whether software will be purchased or developed. It is important that the implementation process include sufficient training and support for the system's users. Feedback mechanisms should exist that can be utilized both during the systems development process and after the system is in operation.

There are three options regarding who does the systems development. For large, organization-wide systems or those with accounting/control considerations, the MIS department will normally manage the systems development effort. When the system is small and not too complex, or when it will be a departmental system, co-development is often a good approach. For small, personal systems in an organization or in a small business without systems personnel on staff, complete end-user development may be a viable option. It is important to remember, however, that these are merely guidelines. All three approaches are points on a continuum of involvement by computer experts and end users. In the end, both groups are vital to the successful development of an information system.

REFERENCES

Bachman, Charlie. "A CASE for Reverse Engineering." *Datamation* (July 1, 1988): 49–56.

De Marco, Tom. *Structured Analysis and System Specification.* Yourdon, Inc., 1978.

Gane, C., and T. Sarson. *Structured Systems Analysis: Tools and Techniques.* IST, Inc., 1977.

Gibson, Michael L. "A Guide to Selecting CASE Tools." *Datamation* (July 1, 1988): 65–66.

Kahn, Beverly K. "Requirement Specification Techniques." Chapter 1 in *Principles of Database Design,* ed. S. Bing Yao. Englewood Cliffs, NJ: Prentice-Hall (1985).

Martin, James, and Carma McClure. *Structured Techniques: The Basis for CASE.* Englewood Cliffs, NJ: Prentice-Hall, 1988.

"The Software Trap: Automate—or Else." *Business Week: Special Report* (May 9, 1988): 142–154.

KEY TERMS

acceptance test
application development
bottom-up design
co-development
computer-aided software engineering (CASE)
conceptual design
conversion – direct, parallel, pilot, and phased-in
data flow
data flow diagram (DFD)

data store
design walkthrough
detailed design
end-user computing (EUC)
external entity
maintenance
post-implementation audit
programming language
program specification

project team
steering committee
structure chart
structured systems analysis (SSA)
systems analyst
systems development life cycle
systems proposal
systems requirements
top-down design

REVIEW QUESTIONS

1. What are the benefits and disadvantages of a formal systems development life cycle?

2. List the phases of a formal systems development life cycle with the objective of each phase.
3. Discuss several factors to consider when evaluating the perception of need.
4. Discuss the factors included in the feasibility report.
5. Why is the systems analysis phase crucial to the success or failure of a project? Give examples.
6. What are data flow diagrams? What are the major components and their purpose? Develop a data flow diagram for payroll processing.
7. How are data flow diagrams and structured systems analysis related?
8. Discuss the task completed during the design phase.
9. What resource additions are made in the development phase?
10. How are users involved in each phase of the systems development life cycle?
11. There are four techniques for system conversion. Discuss each.
12. Consider the systems at your university. Sketch out the development process for one system such as billing, student recruiting, and application processing using the formal systems development life cycle.
13. Why is a post-implementation audit necessary?
14. What are the benefits and disadvantages of a nontraditional systems development process?
15. Explain the importance of end-user involvement in nontraditional systems development.
16. Discuss the major disadvantages of iterative systems development.
17. Give examples of two systems that should be developed in a nontraditional manner. Defend your choices.
18. Explain the factors which have led to the changes in the systems development process.
19. When should an organization select to develop a system without a formal life cycle?
20. Compare and contrast end-user development and co-development.

CASE

Carlton Industries is a medium-sized company whose MIS department has followed the traditional systems development life cycle approach for developing new information systems. User departments have always complained about the delay between the initial request and completion of a project. It often takes more than a year before a finished product is received. Many of the projects requested are small and cater to the needs of individual users or small groups of users. These requests are not given a high priority, and the users are forced to wait while the programming staff works on higher-priority projects. User needs and expectations often change during the long delay between request and receipt of the information system. As a result the information systems often need much modification when received by the user. In addition, users complain that their input is not solicited during the course of system development. It is often difficult, if not impossible, for them to state their needs to the systems analyst at the beginning of a project, especially when the analyst is unfamiliar with the applications being computerized.

DISCUSSION QUESTIONS

1. Should Carlton change its approach to information systems development? What would this change involve? Should this approach be changed for all types of information systems developed?
2. What approach could Carlton take to speed up the development process and assist users in visualizing their needs to help ensure that the information systems developed will satisfy those needs?

CHAPTER 9

Information Architecture

CHAPTER OUTLINE

CHAPTER OBJECTIVES

- To explain what is meant by the term *information architecture*.
- To discuss the relationship between the information architecture concepts and information storage and retrieval, communication, information system development, and information management.
- To describe the activities involved in creating an information architecture.
- To show the application of an information architecture to a real situation.

INTRODUCTION

As we saw in Chapter 8, part of information literacy is understanding what is involved in developing an information system. A related aspect of information literacy is understanding what is involved in creating an information processing environment which will enable the efficient and effective functioning of one or more systems. The environment should not only respond to current needs but should also anticipate future needs. That is the purpose of this chapter and that is what is meant by the term *information architecture*.

Creating an information architecture involves identifying, analyzing, and planning for all five resources of the information system (hardware, software, data, people, and procedures). Therefore, an organization must have an understanding of both the technological and organizational resources which are in place. This chapter builds upon the concepts developed in Chapters 6, 7, and 8 and lays the foundation for Chapter 10. Chapter 6 was concerned with methods for storing and retrieving data and procedures for efficient data administration. Chapter 7 addressed the technological mechanisms needed to facilitate data communication, both inside and outside an organization. It pointed out that in making data communication decisions, the technology should be configured to support organizational information flows. Our concern in Chapter 8 was the process of developing an individual system. The process is one of identifying the type of system required and then carrying out a set of activities. In doing so, the system structure and functions are identified first, and then the technology to support such functions is acquired and configured. Finally, Chapter 10 discusses mechanisms to ensure that the information in an organization is of high quality and is available to those who require it.

The present chapter is an extension of the ideas presented in the previous chapter. Chapter 8 was concerned with the current and desired state of a *single* information system. This chapter, on the other hand, is concerned with the current and future state of *all* information processing systems in an organization so as to ensure that they will operate in a consistent, controlled environment. This global perspective on information processing also enables an organization to develop a plan or blueprint for the future development and use of systems in the organization. This blueprint is developed by identifying the hardware, software, and data involved in the organization's information systems and by depicting the flow of data among organizational units.

This chapter will make references to terms associated with computer and communication technology. Therefore, the reader should be familiar with Sections I, II, and III of the appendix.

THE INFORMATION ARCHITECTURE CONCEPT

An **information architecture** is an overall plan for computer-based information processing in an organization. The term *architecture* is used because the *struc-*

ture of the systems and the *flow* of data among them are represented in a form of blueprint similar to that used in the design and construction of a building. The term *information* rather than data is used for the same reason that the term *information system* rather than *data system* is used: While it is data that actually flows and is processed, the goal of the system or the architecture is to enable users to have the kind of information they need to carry out their functions in the organization.

Having a blueprint or overall plan for information processing helps to ensure that the technology will be compatible and that the information flows are consistent with the organizational hierarchy and the functions which are carried out. An overall plan for information processing is important in any setting, but the growth of end-user computing has made this need even greater. With the trend toward every office having its own information processing capability, the lack of an overview perspective on information processing could result in both redundant data and redundant processing.

Architecture

To better understand the concept of an information architecture and its relationship to information system development, let us consider the role of the architect in relation to that of the construction engineer.

Architecture Versus Construction

An architecture helps to put things into both a physical and a conceptual structure. One definition of architecture is "the art and science of designing and erecting buildings." This definition emphasizes the fact that architecture is concerned with more than physical structure. The use of the term *design* indicates a concern with the use of the building as well. An architect is therefore a designer.

The work of an architect results in blueprints or graphic representations of the plans for constructing the new edifice. They are like road maps: they show the current position, the destination, and the means for moving from one to the other.

In contrast, construction is "the act or process of building, erecting, or forming by assembling parts." The relationship between architecture and construction is the following: The architect designs the structure, and the construction engineer carries out the actual building tasks. The architect is a *designer*, whereas the construction engineer is a *developer*.

Once the blueprint or plan is developed, the process of construction becomes one of physically implementing the plans. This involves acquiring the appropriate materials and configuring them in such a way that they conform to the design developed by the architect. We can think of the construction process as a set of detailed procedures for following the road map developed by the architect.

Remodeling a House

The concept of architecture can be further illustrated by considering what is involved in remodeling a house. First, the architect needs to get an understanding of the existing structure. A detailed examination will result in a blueprint of the house as it currently exists. Next, the architect will need an understanding of the lifestyle of the owners. Questions such as the following would be asked: How many children live in the house? Does one of the adults do office work at home? Do the owners entertain frequently? By asking these kinds of questions, the architect is attempting to determine any mismatch between the current structure of the house and the lifestyle of the people living in it.

Once these mismatches have been identified, the architect can go about developing a revised architecture of the house, one whose structure will be compatible with the functions carried out by the people who live in it. This architecture serves as the plan which will guide the construction effort—the physical implementation of the plan.

Information Architecture

The concept of an information architecture is subject to different interpretations. Some see it as a form of strategic planning. Others view it as an inventory of an organization's technical facilities. The definition of information architecture presented in this chapter is a composite of these two views.

Strategic Information Planning

This view sees an information architecture as a way of planning for the development of information systems. The term **strategic information planning** is used because it emphasizes long-range planning, the integration of systems, the flows of data among them, and the use of information systems to gain competitive advantage for the organization. As such, it is proactive rather than reactive planning.

Reactive planning means developing systems piecemeal without an overall view of what the end product—the information processing environment—will look like. This is similar to building a house without a vision of the complete set of alterations to be done later. As a consequence, additions are made here and there without an overall plan.

Proactive planning means having a comprehensive view of the end product so that even if the systems are developed in piecemeal fashion, they will end up being compatible. This is especially important if the information processing environment is widely distributed, with a heavy emphasis on data communication and the sharing of software and data among systems. An example of this would be an environment which contains local area networks and departmental minicomputers. Proactive planning is similar to designing one's dream house even if the house is not all built at once. It allows an organization to plan now for the growth, flexibility, size, and life cycles of its systems.

A Description of Technical Facilities

The other interpretation of an information architecture is that it represents the *technical facilities* of an organization. This view focuses on the establishment and maintenance of an up-to-date inventory of the information technology. It sees the architecture as a set of rules for the implementation of technology. These rules would govern the introduction and use of computer and communication hardware and application and operating system software. The goal of an information architecture, then, would be to have an overall design for the use of information technology by the organization.

The Composite View: Structure and Flow

The combination of both perspectives on information architecture results in a richer view, one which incorporates both strategic planning and an understanding of the technical facilities. This is done by relating the information systems to the objectives of the organization. The structure of the systems and the flows of information among them are compared to the structure of the organization and the functions to be carried out. The resulting information architecture is a graphical representation or blueprint to guide the organization in altering the information processing environment so that the structure of the resultant information systems is consistent with that of the organization.

Specific information systems are viewed in the context of the strategic plan for information processing. This plan is a map which will guide the development of the individual systems. Therefore, when a new system is proposed or major modifications to existing systems are required, they can be compared to the information architecture to see how they fit into the overall plan. This process is an extension of the notion of related systems discussed in Chapter 3.

The important aspect of this view is that the organization or enterprise drives the information architecture. Creating an information architecture can then be defined as

> the process of building a high-level map of the information requirements of an organization to provide a guide for applications development and the deployment of technology and people, and to facilitate the integration and sharing of data.

There are several reasons why an organization might want to develop an information architecture. First, it can be used to document the current functions of the information systems and the flows of data among them. Second, it can be useful in planning for future system expansion or reduction by helping the organization to see the areas in which there are too few or too many resources. Finally, if there is an understanding of how the information systems relate to the organizational structure, when organizational or system changes are contemplated an impact analysis can be conducted. During an impact analysis, the information architecture will be useful in showing whether the planned changes will result in any incompatibilities between the structure of the organization and the structure of the systems.

In order to view the process of developing an information architecture in some context, we will consider the development of an information architecture at Last National Bank. The example will be highlighted after appropriate sections instead of appearing at the end of the chapter.

DEVELOPING AN INFORMATION ARCHITECTURE AT LAST NATIONAL BANK

Last National Bank decided to develop an information architecture because it had recently acquired several smaller banks. There was a general feeling among senior management of the combined organization that there was redundancy in several areas. The information processing environment was chosen for analysis because information systems support all major functions of the organization. It was thought that the resulting documentation of systems would be useful in ferreting out redundant processing and in planning for future economies of scale. The systems personnel at Last National Bank are very supportive of the concept of distributed processing, but only when it is carefully controlled and can be shown to be effective. Systems management reasoned that the architecture or blueprint would demonstrate to senior management where it would be conceivable to distribute functions and processing to particular organizational entities.

An information architecture is composed of two parts: an analysis of the business enterprise and an analysis of the existing information systems. In order to conduct these analyses, a detailed description of each is needed. These two descriptions are referred to as the enterprise model and the information model. The **enterprise model** is a description of the organization or environment within which the information systems exist. The **information model** is a description of the information system resources in the organization. Since information systems exist to serve the organization, the enterprise model should

FIGURE 9.1

The major features of an information architecture

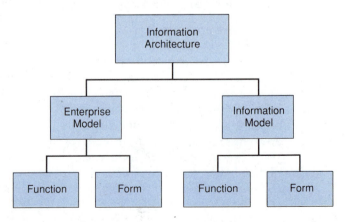

be the standard against which the information model is evaluated. The major features of an information architecture are shown in Figure 9.1.

Both the enterprise model and the information model are described in terms of their functions and form. **Function** refers to the *flow* of information or work. **Form** refers to the *structure* of the organization or system. That is, the form or structure defines *what* the organization or system is about, while the function or flow defines *how* it accomplishes its goals. If we relate these terms to systems concepts, the structure refers to the system resources (hardware, software, data, people, and procedures) and the flow refers to the system components (inputs, processes, and outputs). It is also important to define the boundary or scope of the endeavor.

The steps involved in developing an information architecture and the order in which they should be carried out are outlined as follows:

I. Develop the enterprise model.
   A. Identify and document the business *functions*.
   B. Identify and document the organizational *form*.
   C. *Analyze* the matches or mismatches between the function and form and present in an enterprise document.
II. Develop the information model.
   A. Identify and document the *structure* of the information systems.
   B. Identify and document the *flow* of information among those systems.
   C. *Analyze* the match or mismatch between the flow and structure and present in an information document.
III. Develop the information architecture.
   A. Analyze the match or mismatch between the enterprise model and the information model; determine the ramifications of the match or mismatch; and make recommendations for change in one or the other.
   B. Formalize the results in a new information architecture document.
   C. Develop a plan for the future based on the recommendations which were accepted.

These steps represent an ideal order in which the activities should be carried out; however, the most important thing is to fit this process to the context within which the architecture is being developed. Just as the system development process can be adapted to the special considerations of the context of use, the information architecture process should be adapted to the organizational culture within which it will exist.

All companies, large or small, can benefit from the expert advice that results from the development of an information architecture. How much time, effort, and money should be invested in the project is a decision that each company must make for itself. It is not necessary to spend enormous amounts of time, energy, and money on this project. There is a connection between the size of the company and the complexity of its business and technological architectures. Smaller companies can accomplish the project faster, with fewer people involved. Automated tools such as data dictionaries, data flow diagrammers, graphics software, and personal computers are useful but not absolutely necessary.

One of the first considerations should be to set the project boundary and depth. It is important to determine at the outset whether the goal should be a narrow, deep analysis or a wide, shallow review. Either can be effective in the right circumstances. If the project is well conceived and controlled, it is possible to get at the important issues quickly and to get the right people involved to address them. As with any large project, it is easy to be pulled into areas outside the boundary initially set. This must be carefully monitored. In some cases, what appears to be a tangent may turn out to be a major area that was mistakenly omitted from the original plan. In most cases, this new area should be documented for future consideration. To stay on target, it is important that the team members be carefully chosen, and that each understands his or her role. A synergy develops as each member works from his or her strength. It is often a good idea to use project management software to control the project. Many such systems are available for use on personal computers.

If necessary, outside consultants can be assigned to the team, to lend expertise in the mechanics of developing an information architecture, to act as facilitators to keep the project on target, or to act as a resource for documenting results. However, the ultimate decisions must be made and supported by management of the company.

DEVELOPING THE ENTERPRISE MODEL

Business Functions

A benefit of clearly identifying the business functions is acquiring a better understanding of the mission and goals of the organization or unit. Everything else is put into perspective. This top-down approach shows the "big picture" first. It also helps the systems analysts, who are working with the business analysts, to understand the business.

This effort is normally carried out by a team. Two groups of personnel should be involved: the systems analysts in the systems department and the business analysts or liaisons in the user departments. The involvement of both groups contributes to the creation of synergy because each group has strengths which can complement the other's.

One reason for beginning with the enterprise model is that it allows users to be involved from the start. Another reason is that the activities of the business should drive the information systems. In the creation of the enterprise model the *functions* of the enterprise are considered first, because it is usually more meaningful to identify the mission and goals of the enterprise and then decide if an appropriate organizational structure is in place to support them. This perspective reflects the strategic planning view of an information architecture. In the creation of the information model, however, the order is reversed: the form or structure is considered first, then the function or flow. Since information systems have tangible properties, it is easier to first identify the discrete parts of the systems and then consider how the information flows among them. This perspective reflects the technical facilities view of information architecture.

THE BANK'S ENTERPRISE MODEL

Business Functions

The first step in developing the enterprise model was to determine the bank's business functions or lines of business. This was done by identifying the services provided and the support functions that were necessary to carry them out.

Last National Bank began by identifying the major services which it provides. These include offering various types of loans and deposit accounts as well as services such as those provided at automatic teller machines (ATMs) and at the branch offices. Figure 9.2 shows a sample of the services provided by the bank.

Once the services were identified, they were then grouped into three major categories. Loan services included home mortgages, car loans, and credit cards. Deposit services included savings accounts, checking accounts, and certificates of deposit. Other services included providing traveler's checks, foreign currency, and cashier checks. Figure 9.3 shows the bank's services organized by major categories.

The team working on the enterprise model soon realized that the services could also be grouped by market or type of customer. The two

FIGURE 9.2
Services provided by Last National Bank

Savings accounts	Cash withdrawal
Checking accounts	Money transfer (wire)
Car loans	Cash management
Mortgages	Payroll services
Cashier's checks	ATM cards
Commercial loans	Real estate (construction) loans
Leases	Asset-based lending
Credit cards	Traveler's checks
Certificates of deposit	Foreign currency
Safe deposit boxes	

FIGURE 9.3
Last National Bank's services by major categories

Deposits	Savings accounts
	Checking accounts
	Certificates of deposit
Loans	Car loans
	Mortgages
	Commercial loans
	Credit cards
	Real estate loans
	Leases
	Asset-based lending
Other Services	Cashier's checks
	Money transfer (wire)
	Cash withdrawal
	Safe deposit boxes
	Cash management
	Payroll services
	ATM cards
	Traveler's checks
	Foreign currency

major types of customers at the bank were commercial customers (i.e., large companies) and retail customers (i.e., individuals). Some services such as cash management and payroll services are provided for commercial customers but not for retail customers. Other services such as automobile loans and ATM cards are only provided for retail customers. Figure 9.4 shows the bank's services organized by type of customer.

Early in the process, a distinction was made between "front office" functions—those which involved dealing directly with the customers—and "back office" functions—those which involved supporting the bank itself. It was important to make this distinction since one type of possible mismatch could occur between the front and back offices. For example, sales personnel could be selling services that might not be easily provided by the production staff. Conversely, the back office could be planning services that the customers do not want. The major back-office functions of the bank are shown in Figure 9.5.

As the functions were being identified and categorized, the team began to see the connections between the different units of the bank. The amount of interaction between back-office functions and front-office or customer services is one example. Another was the cross-selling of services to the same type of customer. The team noted that some customers who held commercial loans with the bank also had deposit accounts and used the bank's cash management service. Likewise, the retail customers often

FIGURE 9.4
Last National Bank's services by customer (market)

Retail Services	
Deposits	Savings accounts
	Checking accounts
	Certificates of deposit
Loans	Car loans
	Mortgages
	Credit cards
Other Services	Safe deposit boxes
	Cashier's checks
	Cash withdrawal
	ATM cards
	Traveler's checks
	Foreign currency
Commercial Services	
Deposits	Checking accounts
	Jumbo certificates
Loans	Commercial loans
	Real estate loans
	Leases
	Asset-based lending
Other Services	Money transfer (wire)
	Cash management
	Payroll services
	Foreign currency

had several services such as a car loan, a home mortgage, and a checking account. The team also noted places where there was no interaction between units. For instance, there was no interaction between the personnel and customer services functions.

Organizational Form

Once the functions have been documented, attention is turned to identifying the form or structure of the company. This is accomplished by examining the company's organization charts, starting with the most general chart and then proceeding with successively more detailed ones.

It is important to remember that while the financial services (banking) industry is different from many other industries, the concepts described here are not. Examples exist in other industries as well. A fairly recent example is International Business Machines and the changes it made in the structure of its

FIGURE 9.5
Back-office (support) functions by category
at Last National Bank

Employee Services	Payroll
	Benefits
Financial Services	General ledger
	Accounts payable
	Accounts receivable
	Tax
	Investments
General Services	Purchasing
	Inventory control
	Property management
	Security
	Mail service
Operations	Credit verification
	Loan payment processing
	Check processing
	Customer files
Systems	Analysis/Programming
	Computer operations

sales force. IBM had traditionally been organized by product—large main-frames, minicomputers (system 36/38), and personal computers. However, as personal computers became more of a presence in large companies, there was no one person responsible for the range of IBM equipment at a particular company. IBM now has its sales force more aligned to the customer or market, with one salesperson covering a particular company (perhaps in a particular geographic region) for all products.

At Last National Bank, a problem the team encountered was that organization charts are typically used to show the people in the organization and who reports to whom. However, the purpose of examining organization charts for the enterprise model is to document the structure of the bank from a business function point of view. Therefore, the team had to rework some of the organization charts so that the end result reflected the functions rather than the names of the people carrying them out. Figure 9.6 shows a high-level organization chart which reflects the business functions.

By examining these charts, the team was able to see the relative emphasis being put on various functions. The analysis demonstrated what expertise was needed to sell/manage/perform various services. This could be seen from the types of people and resources needed. It also became obvious

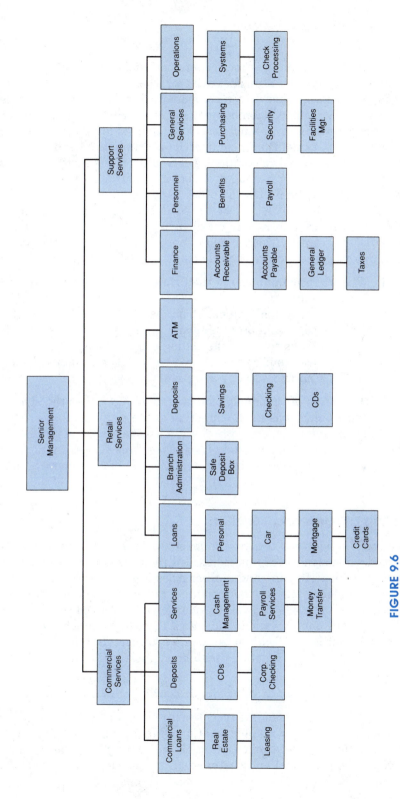

FIGURE 9.6
High-level organization chart of Last National Bank, categorized by function

that the current thinking is more customer-oriented than product/service-oriented. This makes it a market-driven rather than a product-driven type of company. In a market-driven company, it is more important to segregate the support according to commercial and retail customers rather than to segregate according to products/services (such as loans and deposits).

At Last National Bank, commercial accounts are handled by account officers, who call on large companies. The officers attempt to cross-sell other services, offering packages of services that benefit both the customers and the bank. On the other hand, retail customers go into the branches or to an ATM when they need to deal with the bank directly. Although there are many more retail customers (in numbers) than commercial customers, there is more money in the commercial accounts. Given this fact, the factors that the bank needed to consider are:

1. Whether the emphasis in the future would be on retail or commercial;
2. The kind of organizational structure that needs to be in place (e.g., whether to have more ATMs and branch locations or distributed remote offices to serve the calling officers); and
3. The services that can be offered to both types of customers (such as checking and savings accounts).

In the course of this analysis it was discovered that the strength of the combined banks was in the direction of the retail customer. The smaller, community banks had brought with them a large number of retail accounts, and a support system of branches. This served to increase the geographic distribution and influence of the combined organization.

Analysis of Form and Function

Once the functions and organizational structure of a company have been documented, an analysis is conducted to identify any matches or mismatches. The intent is to identify gaps and inefficiencies in the functions. For example, if there is too much structure supporting a given function, it would be evident in the number of people or levels of management assigned to that function. Alternatively, the analysis would indicate if there is too much function for some structure. That is, there might be too many diverse services being supported by one group or some functions with no support structure at all.

The bank discovered that the recent mergers had resulted in too many branches in several geographic locations. Management decided to close some of them after determining that the remaining branches would be able to absorb the personnel and customers from the closed branches. On the other hand, two branch buildings were scheduled to be enlarged to allow for a "remote" office for commercial calling officers. In addition, new territories were defined for these officers.

In analyzing the customer base, a new category was identified: the mid-size company and professional individuals such as doctors, lawyers, and accountants. Before the mergers, neither Last National Bank nor the smaller banks had directed their marketing efforts toward this class of customer. Last National had directed its marketing mostly toward large companies, and the smaller banks had not been able to offer all the services this type of customer needed. The combined bank, however, was in a position to service this new customer with only a minimum of reorganization.

This analysis also had to take into account the influence of the environment, especially regulatory constraints. Although the bank was prohibited by law from operating branches in most other states, it was possible to generate business such as commercial loans and leases from remote offices. However, the team noted that a support structure would be needed if the bank were to move in this direction. Some means of communication among these offices and between them and the head office would be needed as well.

Another result of the analysis was the discovery that payroll, a function the organization was providing for itself, could be marketed outside the bank as well. Most small companies cannot afford to do their own payroll processing, in part because of the regulations which must be followed. By offering a payroll service, the bank saw that it could recoup some of the system and support expenses it incurred in doing its own payroll. The newly identified category of customers—mid-size companies and professionals—was seen as a perfect market for such a service.

DEVELOPING THE INFORMATION MODEL

The team that developed the enterprise model was composed primarily of representatives from the various departments of the company with a few members from the Systems Department. The team which will develop the information model will have a different composition. Most of the members of this team will be from the Systems Department, with additional representatives from the various user departments. The role of the user representatives is primarily to help in the analysis of the form and function of the information model. They will also gain an appreciation for the existence and functions of the information systems in the company.

When documenting the information model, the team starts with the structure of the information systems. They start by compiling an inventory of the information system resources at the company.

Information System Structure

Software Inventory

An inventory of all software is accomplished by gathering together existing documentation about the company's applications. The software is then categorized by criteria which include the language in which it was written, whether it was developed in-house or was purchased, and whether it is an on-line or a batch processing system. Most of this information is available from the programmers and computer operations personnel.

External data processing services utilized by the company are documented as well, including time-sharing services and service bureaus.

An example of Last National Bank's software inventory matrix is shown in Figure 9.7.

Hardware Inventory

The information for the hardware inventory exists in a variety of forms and comes from a number of sources. For example, a description of on-line networks, developed to assist in solving network problems, would be available from the telecommunications department. This inventory shows all the relevant communication hardware such as terminals, modems, and communication lines. The computer operations department would have an inventory of all the mainframe computers and minicomputers in operation. The Information Center would have information about all the local area networks and personal computers that are in use. This data is then organized according to such categories as vendor; whether it is owned, rented, or leased; model numbers and types; and quantity.

Last National Bank's hardware inventory matrix is shown in Figure 9.8.

The next step is to relate the software to the hardware. This is done to determine on which computer(s) the software is being executed. A column is added to the software matrix to show the hardware on which the software runs.

Last National Bank's matrix is shown in Figure 9.9.

Data Inventory

Finally, a data inventory is conducted. Without a data dictionary, this task can be relatively difficult. As described in Chapter 6, a data dictionary is a tool that enables one to describe the data which exists in an organization. Starting at the highest level, the team gathers data at successive levels of detail, by working on one application at a time. Each application contains a number of files, which in turn consist of records and fields or data elements. An inventory of each of these files is then created. Much of this information exists in the documentation accompanying the applications, but in some cases more elaboration is required.

Each file, categorized by purpose, such as transaction file or master file, is then analyzed to learn what types of data it contains. These types of data

FIGURE 9.7

Software inventory matrix

Application	Developed by	Maintained by	Version	Language	Batch vs. On-line	Year Installed	Comments
Commercial Loan	In-house	In-house	–	COBOL	Both	1982	
Demand Deposit	In-house	In-house	–	COBOL ADPAC	Batch	1981	
Customer Reference	UCCEL	In-house	5	Assembler COBOL	Both	1979	RDAM access method
ATM	XYZ Corp.	XYZ Corp.	1.3	Assembler COBOL	On-line	1985	No source code in-house
Payroll	Payrolla Co.	In-house	2	–	Batch	1978	In-house support except last revision
General Ledger	UCCEL		4.5	Assembler COBOL	Batch	1979	RDAM access method
Installment Loan	L & M	In-house	3.5	COBOL	Batch	1983	
Credit Cards	ABC Service Bureau	ABC Service Bureau	–	–	On-line	–	
Mortgage	Home Mortgage System	In-house	1	COBOL	Both	1984	
Check Processing	IBM	IBM	–	Assembler	Both	1975	

FIGURE 9.8
Hardware inventory matrix

Device	Manufacturer	Model	Quantity	Lease	Rent	Own
CPUs	IBM	3090	1	X		
	IBM	3081-KX	1	X		
	IBM	4341-MZ	1			X
	DEC	PDP 11/70	3			X
	DEC	PDP 11/44	1			X
	DEC	VAX 11/780	1			X
	Wang	VS-65	1			X
	Wang	VS-80	1			X
	Wang	OIS	1			X
	IBM	PC	500			X
	IBM	PS/2	250			X
	Apple	Macintosh	100			X
Disk Drives	IBM	3380	52	X		X
	IBM	3350	12	X		
	STC	4305	1			X
	DEC	RA80	1			X
	DEC	RM05	13	X		
Tape Drives	STC	3430	2	X		
	STC	3650	20	X		
	DEC	TE16	4			X
Printers	IBM	3800	3	X		X
	IBM	1403	1			X
	Troy	200	1			X
	Kodak	200	1			X
Sorters	IBM	3890	3	X		
Terminals	IBM	3278	144			X
	IBM	3279	19			X
	IBM	3287	115			X
	IBM	3268	3			X
	IBM	3604	232			X
	IBM	3624	62			X
	IBM	3178	224	X		
	IBM	3179	23	X		
	IBM	3180	144			X
	DEC	VT220	10			X
	DEC	LA120	53			X
Communication Control Units	IBM	3272	2			X
	IBM	3274	70	X		
	IBM	3791	3	X		
	IBM	3880	9	X		X
	DEC	RM05	2	X		
Modems	IBM	3603	97			X
	IBM	3863	31		X	
	RACAL-M	COMLINK3	24	X		
	NETEL	DDS9600	13	X		
	Paradyne	T-96	18			X

FIGURE 9.9
Software/hardware matrix

Application	Developed by	Maintained by	Version	Language	Batch vs. On-line	Year Installed	Hardware
Commercial Loan	In-house	In-house	—	COBOL	Both	1982	IBM 3090
Demand Deposit	In-house	In-house	—	COBOL ADPAC	Batch	1981	IBM 3090
Customer Reference	UCCEL	In-house	5	Assembler COBOL	Both	1979	IBM 3090
ATM	XYZ Corp.	XYZ Corp.	1.3	Assembler COBOL	On-line	1985	IBM 88
Payroll	Payrolla Co.	In-house	2	—	Batch	1978	IBM 3090
General Ledger	UCCEL	UCCEL	4.5	Assembler COBOL	Batch	1979	IBM 3090
Installment Loan	L & M	In-house	3.5	COBOL	Batch	1983	DEC VAX
Credit Cards	ABC Service Bureau	ABC Service Bureau	—	—	On-line	—	—
Mortgage	Home Mortgage System	In-house	1	COBOL	Both	1984	DEC PDP/44
Check Processing	IBM	IBM	—	Assembler	Both	1975	IBM 3090

include dates, balances, demographic data, and codes. The purpose of this analysis is to see where multiple systems are storing the same data. Decisions can then be made as to whether this redundancy is necessary or acceptable.

A portion of Last National Bank's data inventory is shown in Figure 9.10.

The detail of each field was compiled from program documentation and stored in one place. The team, with the concurrence of the bank's management, decided that a data dictionary would be very useful in documenting and analyzing the organization's data resource. Therefore, a task force was created to evaluate alternative dictionary products and make a recommendation. All of the gathered material was subsequently entered into the dictionary.

Compiling the data matrix provided several benefits. It enabled the bank to gain a better understanding of the data being created and stored by the various applications. By documenting the data, both systems analysts and users would be able to make better use of the data. It was important that the end users understand the underlying data so that they could create ad hoc reports and develop decision support systems based on it.

A second benefit was facilitating data protection and security planning. Last National Bank had an automated security system that defined different levels of access to data and other resources (such as

FIGURE 9.10

An example of a data inventory

Application	Files	Records	Types of Data
Commercial Loan	Master	Customer Account	Name Account number Account type Balances Account codes Dates
	Transaction	Account	Balances Dates
Customer Reference File (CRF)	Customer	Customer	Name Address Social security number
		Account	Customer key Account number

terminals). This system monitored and controlled who had access to what data and who could update or delete it.

A third benefit to the bank was more effective data sharing. Data sharing may involve granting access to files, or it may involve setting up an interface file to be transferred on some regular basis to another application. Sharing data reduces the amount of redundant data. One method of sharing data is to pull out the common data and place it in a separate file to which multiple applications would have access. An example of this at the bank was the Customer Reference File, which contained information about the customer such as name, address, and social security number. This had been implemented because it was found that several applications used the same information. Storing this data in a single place meant that additions and changes would only have to be input once. It is possible to obtain a customer profile so that the bank would know what services it provided to each customer. This information would provide for more effective cross-selling of banking services. However, not all applications were taking advantage of this capability.

The final benefit of the analysis was the ability to see how applications could be distributed. Information about the existence of data and where it was used would now be available in an organized form. Where data was used by only one application, that application could possibly be moved to other hardware such as a departmental computer or a personal computer.

As this discussion of benefits points out, an information architecture is an important component in the development of effective information management policies. These are discussed in greater detail in Chapter 10.

Information Flow

Having identified, documented, and analyzed the structure of the systems, the team next must look at the flows among the system resources. Just as an inventory of hardware, software, and data was developed, a depiction of the integration of applications, the hardware connections, and data flows is also developed. To document the flow, diagrams rather than matrices are used. Again, high-level diagrams are developed first, then successively more detail is included.

The flow among applications at Last National Bank is shown in Figure 9.11.

In a similar fashion, a hardware diagram is developed to show how all the computer and communication equipment is tied together. This diagram is based on the hardware inventory matrix shown in Figure 9.8. The process of creating the hardware diagram is facilitated by the telecommunications dia-

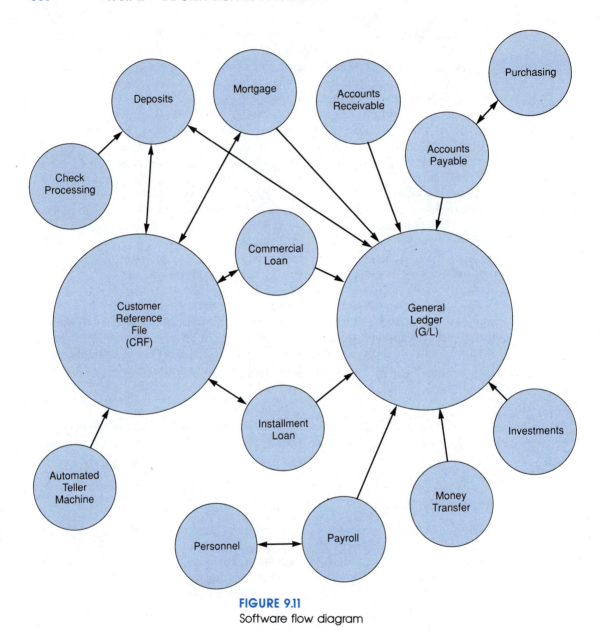

FIGURE 9.11
Software flow diagram

grams that already exist at the company. These diagrams show how the various types of equipment work together.

Figure 9.12 shows the hardware flow diagram at Last National Bank.

Finally, data flow diagrams are used to demonstrate the flows of data. The data flow diagrams are developed from the data inventory taken when the

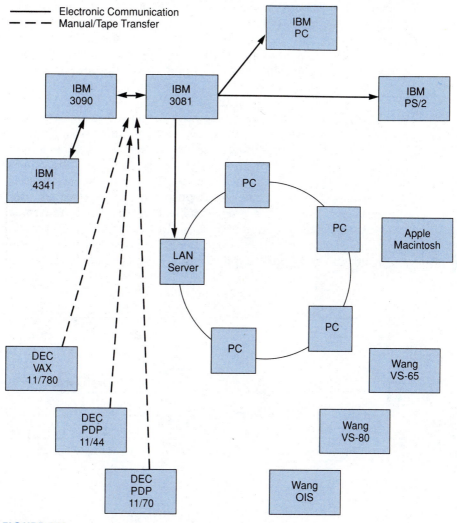

FIGURE 9.12
Hardware flow diagram

information system structure is defined. Analysis of the data flow diagrams may identify data redundancy and data location inefficiency.

The bank did not have any computer-aided system development tools with features for automated creation of data flow diagrams. It learned, however, that many such tools were currently available for use on personal computers. Therefore, after a short evaluation, the bank purchased one of these tools for use in creating the data flow diagrams. As described in Chapter 8, such tools can also be used in the design and development of new systems. An example of the data flow diagrams that were created is the data flow diagram shown in Figure 9.13. It shows the flows between the Deposit application and the Customer Reference File (CRF).

Upon closer examination of this data flow diagram, the team was able to consider data and processing redundancies and logistics issues. For example, the CRF stores all of the customer information such as name, address, and social security number. The deposit subfile on the CRF stores certain deposit account information. In addition, it stores the customer's name for reporting purposes and the CRF customer key used to directly access the CRF file. Since the Deposit application does not store the customer's address, the program that creates Deposit statements must also access the CRF to obtain that data. In the current configuration, the CRF provides some rudimentary account data and points to the appropriate account in the Deposit application by using the account number as the key.

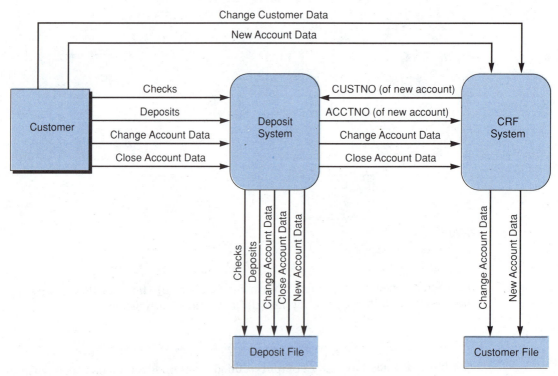

FIGURE 9.13

Data flow diagram of Deposit application

After examining the flows of data between the Deposit application and the CRF, the team discussed the advantages and disadvantages of redundancy. One disadvantage of redundancy is that the data in the two files can be in conflict if the two files are not updated consistently. Another disadvantage of redundancy is inefficiency in producing deposit statements since it is necessary to access two files. On the other hand, greater efficiency in answering customer inquiries might result if deposit data were stored in the CRF as well as the Deposit master file. Customer balance information could be provided by going to a single source. For this reason, some thought was given to adding deposit balances in the CRF. However, this would require that the CRF be updated on a much more frequent basis so that up-to-date balance information would be available. After considering the pros and cons, the team decided that greater accuracy and consistency of account data would result if that data were stored in a single place. They therefore decided not to add the deposit balance data to the CRF. Instead, customer inquiries would be answered by going first to the CRF and then to the Deposit master file.

An Analysis of Structure and Flow

As with the enterprise model, an analysis of the structure and flow of the information systems can show gaps and mismatches. Hardware processing inefficiency may be identified as a result of under- or over-utilization. For example, some current PC applications may be better suited to larger mainframes, or vice versa. Reports may exist that duplicate information several times as individual departments create ad hoc reporting mechanisms.

Last National Bank found that two systems, Demand Deposit and Savings, were carrying out similar functions. The major difference between Demand Deposit and Savings is the method of withdrawal. Demand Deposit accounts are usually debited by check, whereas Savings accounts require the customer to initiate a specific withdrawal. In the past, there was another difference: Demand Deposit accounts did not pay interest. After analyzing these two systems, the team decided that the processing for Savings accounts could be combined with the Demand Deposit system. Since that application had been written in-house, there was adequate staff knowledge to make this change.

They also saw that there was one old language being supported. Some of the modules of the Demand Deposit system were written in ADPAC, a language no longer in use elsewhere in the bank. The team observed that if this language could be replaced by one of the languages in common use, such as COBOL, the systems department could save valuable time, energy, and money that was currently devoted to supporting this language.

It was also noted that some applications were run too frequently. For example, the Leasing application was run daily, yet the transactions only took effect at month end. Therefore, they decided that storing the transactions daily and posting them monthly would save computer processing time every day.

On the hardware side, the team saw opportunities to move some applications to smaller hardware such as departmental minicomputers, local area networks, and personal computers. An example is Purchasing. Purchasing of all items for the bank, from paper clips to desks, is controlled through an automated system. Since this application does not need to interact with any others, they decided to move it to a departmental local area network. Since the Purchasing Department was also the owner of the Inventory Control system, it too was to be moved to the LAN. Moving these applications to personal computers provided an additional benefit. Since both of these systems had been developed in batch processing mode, data entry and access were difficult tasks to achieve. By moving them to a personal computer on a LAN, they would be operating in an on-line and multi-user environment which would eliminate the drawbacks of the batch method.

Conversely, it was noted that some applications currently on several small machines could be combined and run on one larger machine. While reviewing some systems which were running on older equipment from Digital Equipment Corporation (DEC), the team noted that these systems should either be rewritten to run on one of DEC's more powerful VAX machines or else moved to the IBM mainframe. The reasoning was that it was no longer economical to operate the small machines from the computer room since they take up floor space, must have special operators, and require periodic maintenance.

THE INFORMATION ARCHITECTURE

Once the analysis of the information model has been completed, it is then time to combine both models to create the information architecture.

The previous steps in the architecture process involve breaking the organization and the information systems down into their component parts for purposes of identification and analysis. The final step, developing the information architecture, involves bringing together the components of each model so that an analysis of the fit between the enterprise model and the information model can be conducted. As the analysis is being carried out, the team notes the possible ramifications of matches or mismatches between the models and makes recommendations. Following the analysis, and a review of the recommendations, a formal information architecture document can then be prepared. This represents the blueprint for changes in the information processing environment.

Enterprise and Information Model Analysis

At this point, the team is now ready to compare and contrast the two models that have been documented. The enterprise model identified the business functions and the organizational form; the information model identified the information systems structure and flow. By overlaying the information model onto the enterprise model, from both a logical and a physical point of view, the team will be able to isolate potential or actual areas of concern. The degree of resemblance will provide insight into the organization's structure and the effectiveness of its information systems in supporting the goals of the organization. Important things to look for are similarities and differences in the structure and flow of the models. Once the areas of concern are identified, the ramifications of the match or mismatch can be considered. Finally, recommendations for change can be made.

A beneficial byproduct of conducting this analysis is a better understanding of the organization structure and information processing environment. By having people from different areas of the organization work together on this project, the organization can create a synergy as each member of the team brings a strength to the process and gains a better understanding of and appreciation for other parts of the organization. As a result, not only does this analysis produce more thorough results, but it helps create an ongoing relationship to ensure more efficiency and effectiveness in the future. This is where an outside consultant can be very helpful by providing insights about what other industries, organizations, and systems departments are doing. They have experience with many different environments and can see opportunities for change. Let us consider some of the issues that should be taken into account as this analysis is being carried out.

Reasons for Lack of Fit

A lack of fit between the enterprise model and the information model is often a result of the changes that occur naturally in an organization. The structure of the organization might have changed because of recent reorganization, geographical growth, or vertical or horizontal integration within the organization or its industry. The company can be radically affected by new management, external regulation (or deregulation), and market/product mix. The introduction of a new line of business can also add new functions that need to be supported. In such situations, the information model may not have kept pace with these changes.

Similarly, technology introduces changes into the structure and flow of system resources. However, while the information systems will change with the technology, the organization itself is not always able to assimilate change at the same pace.

Organizational Goals

A part of this analysis should include an examination of the relationship between the functions carried out and the organization's goals. For instance, if most of the effort is going into the least profitable area of the business, it would be a good idea to look a little closer to find out why. The amount of information available and the ease of getting to it are other important factors. It is possible that too little information is available in the most important areas of the organization.

Corporate Culture

Every organization has a corporate culture or informal rules and ways of doing things. This culture will often influence both models. For example, the degree of communication between layers of management (vertical) and across structural boundaries (horizontal) will have a direct bearing on information flow. If the culture of a company discourages open communication, there may be no point in trying to force sharing of information, no matter how efficient it might be. On the other hand, in an organization that encourages communication, it is possible to gain economies by sharing reports, terminals, and data.

Another aspect of corporate culture is authority and responsibility. Some organizations are very structured in this regard. An important issue for these companies is the structure and ownership of data. Information systems and the data they process will probably tend to be very structured also. Ownership of the data, and the information derived from it, may be jealously guarded, even if this creates inefficiencies. Conversely, a less structured company may have problems assigning ownership of the data for purposes of initial definition, integrity, and security.

A related issue is the sensitivity of the data. Security procedures that define who can access and update information will influence the amount and kind of data sharing that can exist. Privacy may be an issue as well. Some information may be so sensitive that only certain people should be able to see it. This must be factored into the information system plans.

Centralization/Decentralization

The degree of centralization in an organization is another factor to be considered. It should be revealed in the documents produced from the enterprise and information model analyses. In a centralized environment, the major components will tend to be at a central location. This may be the headquarters in a geographically distributed company. Major business decisions and policies usually emanate from this central office. If there is a match between the enterprise and information models, information will also flow into and out of this central source.

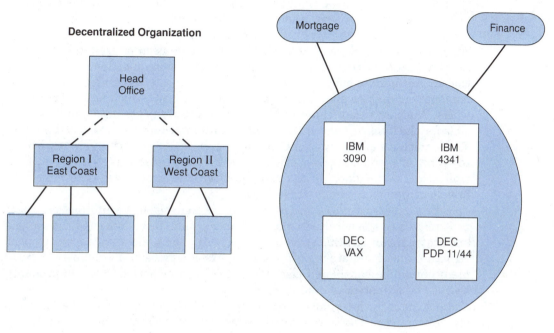

FIGURE 9.14

Decentralized organization with centralized information systems

A mismatch would occur if the corporate culture is centralized and the information processing structure is decentralized. It would be difficult to aggregate information at headquarters level.

On the other hand, if the corporate culture is decentralized and the information processing environment is highly centralized, the information processing environment would not adequately meet the needs of the organization. The most appropriate solution would be to change the information processing structure to fit the organization structure. Figure 9.14 shows an example of a decentralized organization and a centralized information environment.

Acquisition of Information System Resources

Closely related to the centralization issue is the degree to which individual departments are allowed to purchase outside computer services. Outside time-sharing services are very prevalent in some industries and provide a vital service that is not available internally. Access to external services may also be provided by service bureaus that will process the organization's data. In both these cases, it is the processing service that is being purchased. It is also possible to access external data to be processed internally.

With the advent of personal computers, many small departments throughout an organization have the opportunity to purchase their own computer power. Since this situation brings the potential to radically affect the information flow, it is important to plan and manage so as to be in sync with the corporate culture. Several of the issues that have been presented in this section are pertinent to personal computer usage. Communication issues involve the amount of data sharing it is reasonable to expect. To be effective, users of personal computers should not have to reenter data which is available elsewhere. Authority and responsibility dictate who owns the data and is responsible for the integrity and accuracy of the information wherever it is produced. The sensitivity of the information may affect access policies such as whether read-only or read-and-update privileges are to be available at a local level. Centralization, particularly of the computer services group, will determine how prevalent personal computers will be.

Being aware of these issues helps in the analysis of the information model as it relates to the enterprise model. Various time frames change the models and may explain any mismatches. For instance, an understanding of the past structure may facilitate updating it to reflect the present environment. Future plans should be considered also. Work and/or information flow will probably have to be adjusted as well.

Changes in the organization necessitate changes in the information models. As stated in the last section, there are many reasons for organizational changes. Changes on the technical side may dictate that information systems need to be redesigned for efficiency and/or effectiveness; to accommodate new products, services, or markets; or to keep pace with growth of the organization. The introduction of new technology can create opportunities for the organization. The use of personal computers can radically change the information model by bringing technology closer to the end user. Input (data entry) as well as output (on-line systems and user-friendly query languages) are obvious areas to analyze.

New information systems will be called for in some cases. These may be replacement systems or first systems. In the creation of a new system, considerations should include the structure and flow, the interfaces to current automated systems as well as manual systems, and the effect it will have on the current organization structure. Automation of manual functions usually causes the most radical changes and must be carefully designed so as not to disrupt the corporate culture.

To sum up, the analysis should point out inconsistencies in the two models. Does one system support one business function? Should it? Are there clusters of systems by market or by product/service? Are there duplicate systems company-wide? Should there be? Chapter 7 considered various types of networks. The enterprise can be viewed as a network as well: groups of people and departments interacting to perform functions. Does the organization look more like a star, with one central node controlling everything? Or does it resemble a ring, with all nodes being equal?

Numerous benefits are derived from having the enterprise and information models synchronized. We have discussed the more common ones, such as cutting costs, automating functions, distributing systems, and gaining efficiencies and economies of scale, but there are others. Using information as a competitive weapon is being acknowledged as a strategic goal in many companies today. This does not mean that the information model drives the enterprise model. However, it does mean that having the right information available at the right time in the right format can give any organization an advantage over the competition.

In the following section we discuss some of the results of the analysis of the enterprise and information models at Last National Bank.

Market

As was stated earlier, Last National Bank became a larger, more complex organization as a result of several mergers. Consequently, the market served by the bank had changed, both in the size of companies served and in their geographic distribution. A strategic opportunity to serve these new customers was discovered in the analysis of the enterprise model. By analyzing the information model, however, the bank could see that the strength in information systems and the staff to support them was on the commercial side, not the retail side. A task force, consisting of senior management and appropriate systems department management, was formed to study the issue in more detail, using the documentation now available, and to set goals for the bank. A decision had already been made to combine the Demand Deposit and Savings applications; a bigger issue was whether the same system could serve both commercial and retail customers.

Mortgage

Another system that needed more attention was the Mortgage system. Up to this point, it was not considered to be an application of strategic importance to the bank. But with more emphasis being placed on retail customers, it was now seen as an important service. The Mortgage system currently ran on a dedicated DEC machine. Although it could handle the existing number of accounts, it would not be able to handle additional volume. A decision was made to move the Mortgage system to the IBM mainframe and add the mortgage customers to the Customer Reference File. They had not been included in the past for several reasons. First, since the bank sold all of its mortgages to the secondary market, the people applying for mortgages were not considered to be customers of the bank in the traditional sense. Second, it had previously been difficult to link the DEC and IBM machines together. Third, the Mortgage system carried all of the customer information normally stored on the CRF. By putting the mortgage customers on the customer file, it would save the effort of entering and storing the information twice, and would allow cross-selling opportunities. Many people applying for mortgages are new to the geographical area and need other banking services as well, such as checking and savings accounts and ATM cards. In addition, as these customers build equity in their homes, they become excellent potential customers for other bank services.

Other Results

The bank considered several new strategic opportunities in light of its new market, which consisted of small and mid-size companies and professional individuals. One which was mentioned previously was offering them payroll processing services. Since the bank had to perform this service for itself anyway, it would be able to process other companies' payrolls as well with only minor modifications to the payroll system. Because additional resources would be required to do so, another task force was formed to address such issues as staffing, marketing this service, and pricing.

Another issue that was raised was the amount of decentralization possible and desirable. As previously stated, the Purchasing and Inventory applications were to be distributed to local hardware, under the control of the primary user department. The bank saw this as a relatively new direction and something to be carefully monitored. The new emphasis on end-user computing required some organizational changes as well. The Human Resources Department, along with representatives from each major division, was asked to research changes in staff composition and job descriptions. The Systems Department was asked to create a new group to support end-user computing from a technical point of view. Policies, staffing, and software tools as well as hardware issues needed to be researched also.

The New Information Architecture Document

After the results of the analyses and decisions are reviewed, recommendations from the various task forces should be considered. At this point, it is necessary to step back from the details of the current environment to gain a broader per-spective and consider what form a new information processing environment could take. Up to this point the effort has focused on documenting and ana-lyzing the past and current environments. Now decisions must be made about the future, and in particular, the information architecture to support that fu-ture. The activities involved in step I—developing the enterprise model—and step II — developing the information model — were directed toward representing the existing architecture. The objective of step III — developing the information architecture — is to develop a representation of the new architecture.

The new enterprise model will address organizational structure changes such as new subsidiaries, divisions, and geographic locations. It will also outline new or deleted products/services and lines of business. The new information model will demonstrate how the identified changes such as removing or adding hardware, rewriting or combining applications, or sharing data are to be implemented. It will also show redeployment of resources such as systems professionals, hardware capacity, and money for new systems.

The results of this project should be formalized into a document to be approved by senior management and to be shared with management at various levels throughout the company. The document will show the existing enterprise and information models, with an appropriate description of matches and mismatches, levels of importance, and recommendations. A new information architecture should be presented as the final recommendations. This new architecture incorporates the changes that are needed and represents the desired information processing environment for the company. After securing senior management approval, a plan can then be developed for moving from the old to the new environment.

Let us now consider what occurred at Last National Bank. The most salient result of the project was a realization and acknowledgment of the need for reorganization throughout the company. The bank had grown tremendously over the last few years, without the necessary adjustments in the support structure. Also, because of several mergers, there was considerable duplication of effort. Several options were available to the bank.

One option was to completely centralize all functions. This would mean developing a strict management reporting structure as well as consolidating all data processing. Another alternative was to completely decentralize into logical functions, probably along product or customer lines. While this option raised the possibility of more duplication of effort, it would be controlled at the local level. The bank saw advantages and disadvantages associated with each of these options. Upon further consideration, it decided on a compromise: to centralize the control and policy making and distribute the operational support functions.

The key to the success of this option is to understand the difference between *distributed* and *decentralized*. The bank realized that there must be a strong central core to the organization, in order to make the necessary strategic policy decisions. This core includes a small cadre of functionally oriented executives, such as those in the Human Resources, Finance, and Systems Planning Departments. Policies emanate from this core to the distributed units, which have local resources and the ability to set shorter-term priorities and controls.

In order to succeed with this structure, both human and technological communication channels are necessary, because both the enterprise structure and the information resources are being distributed. An example of this is the decision about the amount of hardware and processing power to be distributed to local entities. The advent of personal computers, local area networks, and high-speed, high-capacity telecommunications links makes it possible to distribute many functions. It is important to decide what functions will need to interact with the central mainframes and what functions can operate independently. Examples of applications that could be distributed are Purchasing and Inventory Control. Just as some hardware and applications were distributed, others were consolidated, such as by installing the Mortgage application on the mainframe. Figure 9.15 shows those applications to be centralized and those to be distributed in the new architecture.

Another decision regarding information resources was to distribute certain systems professionals to local entities. Systems analysts and application programmers were to be transferred to the business units they

FIGURE 9.15
Centralized and distributed applications
in new information architecture

Distributed Applications

Mortgage
Installment Loan
Commercial Loans
Real Estate Loans
Credit Cards
Safe Deposit
Inventory Control
Purchasing
Leasing
Asset-based Lending

Centralized Applications

Payroll/Personnel
General Ledger
Accounts Payable
Accounts Receivable
Customer Reference File
Investments
Deposits (combined)

supported. This would allow managers of these units to have better control over all resources for purposes of setting priorities and budgeting. In conjunction with this decision it was acknowledged that careful career planning was necessary to ensure a viable career path for systems professionals working in the functional areas. At the same time, it was acknowledged that there needed to be a strong core group responsible for the systems and hardware deemed central to the organization. Support of the mainframes, their operating systems, on-line monitors, and large database management systems would all remain centralized under the responsibility of this core systems group. Those individuals who were or wanted to be more technical were assigned to this central support group.

Finally, it was recognized that a strong information processing presence was needed at the highest level in the organization. A chief information officer position at the senior vice-president level was created. The responsibility of this person would be to work with other business executives on strategic issues.

The existence of an information architecture was crucial to the changes that were planned. It is not possible to distribute some information processing functions and resources without an overall understanding of how they will ultimately work together. The architecture allows for distribution without undue duplication and redundancy.

Plans for the Future

The plans for the future are a combination of immediate and long-term solutions, based on the information architecture document. Some recommendations can be enacted immediately. Others, which involve capital expenditures or staff reorganization, may require more time. The analysis team serves as the initial catalyst for change. The members of this team tend to view the information architecture from the perspective of the enterprise. But to carry out the specific recommendations that result from this study, ad hoc task forces are usually needed to study specific issues in more depth. In these cases as well, changes would take longer to implement. An example would be combining certain applications. Implementing a new information architecture requires both an overall awareness of the architecture and specific expertise which can be brought to bear on particular issues. The role of the architecture is to provide a framework for these specific changes so as to ensure future consistency.

Each action should be assigned a priority to make sure that it receives the appropriate attention. Because the goal of the architecture is to develop a coherent and integrated plan for information processing, there will be dependencies among the actions that will dictate the order in which they are addressed. As the plan is being carried out, minor modifications might be needed in order to adjust to changes in either business or technology related issues. However, if the original analysis was thorough, there should be no need for major modifications to the plan. If changes are needed, a full review of the original plan should be undertaken to understand the ramifications of these modifications and to secure management approval. One note of caution: the longer the plan takes to implement, the greater the likelihood that there will be changes in the original plan.

Considerable changes are ahead for Last National Bank. Many of the changes outlined in Figure 9.16 will be implemented immediately. Several of the enterprise model changes will be implemented without delay. New territories will be assigned to the lending officers in conjunction with establishing new lending offices and closing existing branches. As branches are closed, personnel will be relocated to the newly established lending offices. Developing new markets and emphasizing the retail business will also begin immediately. Accommodating additional retail business should be quite simple, as the current retail business is well within constraints on system capacity. Providing payroll services will require a longer development time because of information system requirements. Proposed changes to the information model will take longer than those to the enterprise model, though a few will be started immediately. Because ADPAC has required considerable time and resources, effective immediately, ADPAC will no longer be supported. ADPAC procedures will be converted to other languages used at Last National. Resources previously dedicated to supporting ADPAC will then be redirected to other information model changes. The Mortgage application will be moved to the mainframe as the Inventory and Purchasing systems move to the LAN. The changes will continue at Last National Bank, and the enterprise and information models will be reevaluated as the business evolves.

SUMMARY

The analogy of remodeling a house was used to explain the notion of architecture and its relationship to the new structure that results. While architects are often employed to design *new* structures such as houses and office buildings, they are also needed to analyze and design changes to *existing* structures. This is the view of architecture that is used in the concept of information architecture.

There are three steps required in the creation of an information architecture. Step I, developing the enterprise model, involves identifying and documenting the business functions and structures and analyzing them for matches and mismatches. Step II, developing the information model, involves documenting the resources and functions of the information processing environment. Following that, the structure of the systems and the flows or interconnections among them are analyzed to determine redundancies and in-

FIGURE 9.16

Changes in information and enterprise models
in new information architecture

Changes in Information Model

Distribute information system resources.

Establish group within centralized systems to support
   end-user computing.

Strengthen telecommunications.

Acquire new software tools (data dictionary, CASE tools,
   project management software).

Move Purchasing and Inventory Control systems to
   LAN.

Expand Customer Reference File to include Mortgage.

Eliminate use of ADPAC language.

Move Mortgage application to the mainframe.

Eliminate use of dedicated DEC equipment.

Change Leasing processing schedule.

Place greater emphasis on retail systems.

Combine the following applications:

> Demand Deposit and Savings
> Cash Management and Wire Transfer
> Leasing and Asset-based Lending
> Commercial Loan and Real Estate Loan
> Purchasing and Inventory Control
> Mortgage and Installment Loan

Changes in Enterprise Model

Place greater emphasis on retail business.

Develop newly identified market: mid-size companies and
   professional individuals.

Provide payroll processing service to outside customers.

Close some branches of the bank.

Establish remote lending offices.

Assign new territories to lending officers.

---

efficiencies. Steps I and II result in the documentation of the existing information architecture. Step III, developing the information architecture, results in the new architecture. It first involves analyzing the fit between the enterprise model and the information model. Based on this analysis, recommendations are formalized into a new information architecture document. While some recommendations can be enacted immediately, others will take more time. These latter changes are incorporated into the plans for the future.

If done correctly, this project will be viewed as vital to the success of the company. It will be seen as a plan which will ensure that the business is adequately supported by its information systems. Furthermore, it not only provides the blueprint of current support, but also facilitates movement in future directions.

The plan should be reviewed every year to be sure it is still being followed. Not all issues that were originally raised will be addressed or resolved immediately. This is sometimes a long-term process. Every three years the plan should be reviewed in depth to verify its components. Organizations do not stand still, and neither does technology. The plan must be a living document. Just as it is important to protect their investments in other assets, companies have found that information processing has become a critical protection for their investment in organizational success.

REFERENCES

Ashmore, Michael G. "Keeping the Future in Perspective." Pp. 57–60.

The Dooley Group. "Linking Business and Information System Planning." *Society for Information Management Spectrum* 3, No. 3 (June 1986).

Forsythe, Jason, and Bruce Page. "Banking Heavily on Information Systems." *Information Week* (August 3, 1987): 26–32.

Johnson, James R. "Enterprise Analysis." *Datamation* (December 15, 1984): 97–103.

Sullivan, Cornelius H. "Rethinking Computer Systems Architecture." *Computerworld Extra* (November 17, 1982): 5–9.

Wetherbe, James C., and Gordon B. Davis. "Developing a Long-range Information Architecture." *Proceedings of the National Computer Conference, 1983*. Pp. 261–269.

KEY TERMS

enterprise model	information architecture	strategic information
form	information model	planning
function		

REVIEW QUESTIONS

1. Define an information architecture.
2. Explain the two views of information architecture. How do they differ?
3. What is the difference between proactive and reactive planning?
4. The composite view of information architecture incorporates both the strategic planning and technology facilities views. Explain how each is used in the composite view.
5. An important aspect of the composite view is that the organization drives the information architecture. Why is this important?
6. Describe the enterprise and information model concepts. Why is it important to consider both in information architecture?
7. Which should be developed first—the enterprise model or the information model? Why?

8. Setting the project boundaries should be one of the first considerations. Why?

9. Explain the importance of identifying the business function prior to identifying the organization structure.

10. How does the composition of the enterprise and information teams differ?

11. Describe the first step in developing the information model. How does this step differ from the same step for the enterprise model?

12. Software, hardware, and data inventories are conducted when the information system structure is identified. What information is captured for each inventory?

13. Explain how the information model and enterprise model are combined to develop the information structure.

14. List several internal and external reasons for differences between the enterprise and information models.

15. Why might an organization's goals be reexamined as a result of enterprise and information model analysis?

16. How can corporate culture hinder or help the analysis process?

17. Would you expect a centralized business to function more efficiently with a centralized or decentralized information system? Why?

18. Explain the importance of centralized purchasing of information system resources.

19. Why is it necessary to redocument the enterprise and information models after developing the information architecture?

CASE The information systems at Maclean Industries have grown by bits and pieces over the years. Often, new portions of the overall information system were added without serious consideration of the effects on other parts of the system. Activities or resources used in one part of Maclean's overall information system were duplicated needlessly by other portions. As it turns out, many departments were also using different hardware and software. This led to costly and time-consuming efforts by the MIS department to support the disparate systems. In addition, the information systems in some departments are not supplying users with information in a form that allows them to function most efficiently. The information systems costs at Maclean have increased so much in the last few years that management can no longer afford to overlook them.

DISCUSSION QUESTIONS

1. Would the development of an information architecture help Maclean solve its problems? Explain.

2. Outline the general concerns Maclean would have in developing (a) an enterprise model and (b) an information model.

CHAPTER 10

Information Management

CHAPTER OUTLINE

THE COMPONENTS OF INFORMATION RESOURCE MANAGEMENT

DEVELOPING INFORMATION MANAGEMENT POLICIES

CHAPTER OBJECTIVES

- To demonstrate the need for information management and to point out why information management is an important component of information literacy.
- To describe the theory of information resource management and the components which comprise it.
- To suggest what should be included in information management policies.
- To describe the establishment of information management policies at State University.

INTRODUCTION

Part of information literacy is knowing how to work with information regardless of the form it takes or the means by which it is processed. This involves understanding the activities associated with the input, storage, processing, and communication of information and the choice of appropriate tools in a given situation. Another part of information literacy is the ability to identify, gain access to, manipulate, and effectively use the information necessary for one's job. A third part of information literacy is the ability to critically evaluate the quality of information, to know when information is incorrect, inaccurate, or incomplete. This is the concern of information management: ensuring that information is available, accurate, and in a useful format. But how does this occur?

We know from Chapter 2 that management is defined as the directing of human and material resources toward the achievement of some predetermined goal. If we apply this definition to the present context, **information management** can be defined as

> the establishment of procedures for directing an organization's hardware, software, data, and people toward the goal of producing and maintaining the types of information needed by its users.

Managing information in this fashion requires a very good understanding of the kinds of information being used in an organization. It requires distinguishing information storage and retrieval goals from decision support goals. It also requires the ability to apply managerial activities such as planning, coordinating, and controlling to information processing. Finally, it requires an understanding of information properties such as integrity, completeness, and relevance. Just as with general management, information management should be carried out at three levels: strategic planning, managerial control, and operational control. Information management occurs in varying degrees in all organizations. However, it is not always done in an organized fashion and based on sound principles. To assist in the process of developing information management policies, we can draw upon the concepts present in the theory of **information resource management (IRM)**.

The Information Resource Management Concept

The information resource management theory, which has emerged over the past fifteen years, provides useful insights regarding the management of information. The use of this theory fits well with the Systems Approach being used in this book. If an organization is a system and a system is composed of resources, information should indeed be thought of as a valuable resource. IRM advocates a management approach based on maintaining a distinction between the information itself and the technology that manipulates it. The underlying premise of IRM is that information is a significant organizational resource in much the same way that people, machines, and capital are considered corporate resources. Therefore, like other resources, information should receive concerted management attention. Since the purpose of this chapter is to consider what should be included in the establishment of information management policies, we can look to the concept of information resource management to provide us with the means for accomplishing this goal. Let us discuss the fundamental concepts implied in the term IRM.

Information Is Distinct from the Technology

Until the advent of the computer and advanced communication technology, information and the media through which it was processed and stored were inextricably linked. We used to manage information indirectly through the control of technology. For example, a book and the information in it were considered to be one and the same. Therefore, by setting up mechanisms for the orderly storage and retrieval of books, we assumed we were controlling the storage and retrieval of information as well.

Today's technology, however, has forced us to alter that view. For example, the widespread use of photocopy machines has forced libraries to realize that controlling the dissemination of books and periodicals does not necessarily control the dissemination of the information contained in them. There is another way in which new technology has compelled us to recognize the distinction between managing technology and managing information. New technology has made it easy to represent the same information in a variety of forms. The same statistics, for example, can be expressed in either numeric or graphic form. Video technology offers organizations another option for the dissemination of information. Because of the number of technological alternatives available, it is important to see that information is distinct from the various technologies that manipulate it. Thus, we have come to recognize that information is an organizational resource in its own right.

Information Is Valuable

Because of our ability to manipulate, store, and move vast quantities of information very quickly, the importance of the information resource has grown in organizations. This is especially notable in the case of financial transactions. Think of all the settings in which information replaces money. When we go to a store, we can pay cash for a purchase, but we also have several other options. We can write a check. This is a piece of paper containing *information* about the amount of money to be withdrawn from an account. But at the bank, there isn't really a stack of bills set aside with someone's name on it. When a check is processed, *information* about the amount of money assigned to that account is changed. If we use a credit card to make the purchase, *information* about the amount of the purchase is recorded. Later, a statement representing the amount we owe is sent to us. In all these activities, *information about money*, rather than actual currency, is being collected, processed, stored, and communicated.

Information is valuable in other ways as well. To a university, information has financial value in a different sense. Consider a university's alumni file. Among other things, it represents a potential source of donations. If this list were to disappear, so too would a source of revenue. For the university bookstore and library, information is valuable in still another way. Providing information in the form of books is the reason they exist. Their goal is to ensure an adequate supply of appropriate books for students and faculty. The greater the demand for these books, the more valuable this information becomes to these organizations.

It is for all these reasons that we can say that information is increasingly being recognized both as a valuable resource and as a corporate asset. An example of information as a resource would be market information on consumer preferences for soft drinks. An example of information as a corporate asset would be the formula for Coke.

A Different Approach to Managing Information Is Needed

Why has the notion of information resource management become popular today? There are two primary reasons. First, as pointed out in Chapter 1, America and many other societies have become "information societies." This means that most people's work is actually information or knowledge work. Consider for a moment the organizations used as examples throughout this book — a bank, a university, and a small business. In each one, information processing plays a significant role and is an activity in which many personnel may be engaged. Therefore, since information handling has become such an important aspect of most work, it is understandable that more attention should be paid to its management.

The second reason information is being given so much attention is related to recent technological developments. The existence of small, inexpensive, and easy-to-use information technology such as the personal computer makes sophisticated information processing available to everyone in an organization. This means that people without any specialized training can do their own computerized information processing tasks. Previously, these tasks would have been performed by computer professionals with considerable formal education and experience working with computers. For organizations, this means that management approaches which had been based on the assumption of limited access to a central facility by knowledgeable individuals must change to reflect this new group of users.

The recognition that information is a distinct resource whose use involves the majority of most people's efforts presents a strong argument for reexamining existing approaches to managing information. These observations suggest that this entity — information — is important enough to be managed in and of itself.

Issues for Consideration in Managing Information

The process of understanding what is meant by information resource management is actually the process of answering a few fundamental questions about managing information.

What Does It Mean to "Manage Information"?

How can we distinguish between the technology and the information in the management process? What gets managed? How do we apply the managerial activities of planning, organizing, staffing, coordinating, and controlling to information?

What Is the Role of End Users in the Information Management Process?

It is one thing to manage information when it is stored centrally in a large corporate computer. It is quite another thing to attempt to manage the information that is processed and stored in individual offices via personal computers. Should end users help develop management policies? Should they be held personally accountable for the quality control of the information they produce and use? How can this be accomplished?

What Information Should Be Managed?

Perhaps it is impossible to try to formally manage all the information that exists in an organization. Maybe information management doesn't necessarily mean centralized management. Perhaps a distinction should be made between "corporate" and "individual" information.

How Will Information Management Change in the Future?

Not only do we need to complete the process of constructing useful information management approaches for today, but we also need to look ahead to the future and think about what information management should mean in light of the technologies that will be in use.

THE COMPONENTS OF INFORMATION RESOURCE MANAGEMENT

An interesting observation about the information processing field is that the theory of information resource management was developed independently in three separate disciplines and in both the public and private sectors with little cross-fertilization occurring among them.[1] These three disciplines are database management, records management, and data processing management. When taken together, however, these different views about IRM result in a complete set of components which should be incorporated into information management policies. The following sections trace the evolution of IRM to show how these components emerged and how they can work together to provide a comprehensive approach to the management of the information resource.

Database Management

The **database management** approach to IRM grew out of computer science, a discipline primarily concerned with data that would be used by the mainframe computer. In the beginning, the management concerns were all technical in nature. Because the immediate database management problems were the technical ones associated with database development and operations, the primary qualifications for personnel performing this function were technical as well. However, as the use of databases and database management systems grew, there was a gradual shift in perspective regarding data management. Database management systems came to be recognized as only one part of the management of data. The other part, described by the terms database administration, data administration, data management, and data resource management, was to focus on the coordination and control of an organization's data so that it could be a true organizational resource.

As database usage grew and became more integrated, issues arose such as the ownership of data and software and the maintenance of data security and integrity. Those personnel concerned with the technical aspects of data management became database administrators. Those concerned with administrative aspects became data administrators. The job of the database administrator included defining the rules that control the database and determining the manner in which the data would be stored. The scope of responsibility was the creation, design, and use of databases.

The domain of data administration became the establishment and enforcement of policies and procedures for managing the company's data as a corporate resource. Emphasis was placed on **data sharing** and on issues related to maintaining a **global view** of the corporate data. Sometimes the term *information resource management* was used to describe this top-level management function. Identifying IRM as a management function (like that of the corporate controller) rather than a technical one was an attempt to elevate data administration above its technical roots.

This view of information resource management addresses questions such as: What information is most crucial to the success of the company? How can the quality, timeliness, reliability, consistency, and accuracy of the information be improved? And how can data redundancy be reduced? IRM has been defined in this context as

> whatever policy, action, or procedure concerning information which management establishes to serve the overall current and future needs of the enterprise. Such policies, etc., would include considerations of availability, timeliness, accuracy, integrity, privacy, security, auditability, ownership, use, and cost effectiveness.[2]

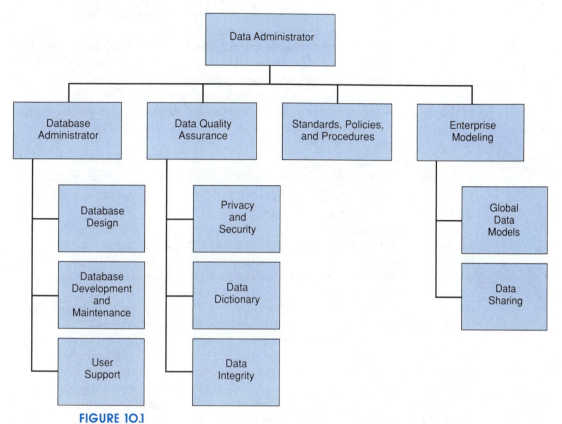

FIGURE 10.1

An organization chart reflecting the database management view of IRM

The IRM function from the database management perspective can be summarized as follows: to maintain the quality, integrity, and accessibility of that portion of an organization's data that resides in the central mainframe's database. It is therefore concerned with machine-readable data only. The notions of standards development and enforcement reflect the emphasis placed on control. An organization chart depicting the database management view of IRM is shown in Figure 10.1.

Records Management

The **records management** concept of IRM has its origins in library science, records management, administrative management, and other fields concerned with the effective storage, retrieval, and utilization of documents in organizations. This area was the first to actually use the term *information resource management* to describe a coherent and global approach to managing information.

The public sector played a leading role in the development of this view of information resource management. The Commission on Federal Paperwork was established in 1974 in response to growing federal information reporting requirements and the resulting burden placed on both government agencies and private-sector organizations. The commission produced a number of documents recommending ways to minimize this paperwork burden. In addition, the work of the commission contributed to the enactment of the **Paperwork Reduction Act** in 1980.[3] This legislation provides a framework for the implementation of information resource management.

THE COMMISSION ON FEDERAL PAPERWORK

The goals of IRM, as reflected in the Paperwork Reduction Act, fall into seven major categories:[4]

1. *Paperwork Reduction*: To oversee agencies' information collection requests, to issue guidance on the exercise of paperwork controls, and to propose changes in legislation to remove impediments to achieving these ends. It also meant facilitating sharing in information collection, the development of the Federal Information Locator System, and the establishment of central collection agencies. Finally, standards were to be set for retention, maintenance, and disposal of records.

2. *Data Processing and Telecommunications*: To create policies to more effectively acquire and utilize computer and telecommunications resources. This involved establishing procedures to promote the use of computers and telecommunication technology in government agencies. It also involved creating and enforcing standards governing equipment acquisition and use.

3. *Statistics*: To develop long-range plans for improved performance of federal statistical activities and to develop and coordinate government-wide statistical policies.

4. *Records Management*: To correct the deficiencies in existing records management practices and to coordinate records management policies with other information resource management functions addressed in the Act. A related objective was to develop standards for record retention requirements levied on the private sector and state and local governments.

5. *Information Sharing and Disclosure*: To ensure that information resource management practices associated with governmental data sharing did not violate privacy rights. Policy guidance on disclosure of information, confidentiality, and security of information would be available. To enhance general management practice in this area, it recommended that legislation be proposed which would remove the inconsistencies regarding privacy, confidentiality, and disclosure of information.

6. *Information Policy and Oversight*: To create a strong, central management function responsible for the development of uniform and consistent information policies. To ensure success in this endeavor, the

agencies charged with carrying out such policies were therefore to be given guidance in developing and implementing information management procedures.

7. *Organization Development and Administration*: To establish and fund the Office of Information and Regulatory Affairs, which would oversee the implementation of this Act.

A definition of information resource management was provided by the Paperwork Commission in its charge to each federal agency to

> systematically inventory its major information systems and periodically review its information management activities, including planning, budgeting, organizing, directing, training, promoting, controlling, and other managerial activities involving the collection, use, and dissemination of information.

In its review of the Paperwork Reduction Act, the General Accounting Office defined information resource management as

> a concept for integrating and focusing a variety of activities on managing information throughout the life cycle — from collection or creation through final disposal — and in each segment of it in furtherance of program and agency objectives. It involves managing data and information in such a way that program and agency managers are able to obtain and use information efficiently, effectively, and economically.

During this time, individuals in the private sector were also exploring more realistic approaches to records management in light of the growing problem of information proliferation. The focus was on eliminating redundant document processing activities and facilitating the user's access to and value received from information.

While the database management arena intended to achieve a global view of the data through such technological means as data dictionaries, the records management approach saw the need for a person or organizational function to achieve this end. Specifically, it called for a high-level manager, called a **chief information officer (CIO)**, who would provide the comprehensive oversight necessary to facilitate the coordination and sharing of documents that was required if the paperwork burden was to be reduced.

The responsibility of records management ranges from manually produced documents in the organization to computer-generated records and the software designed to facilitate their access and use. In order for an organization to gain control of its expanding volume of documents, information specialists were needed. Individuals performing this function would be responsible for the acquisition and dissemination of information and decision making regarding what information to discard and when. Some people have also suggested that records management should be responsible for the integration of functions such as data processing, publications, and printing. According to this view, the information manager should direct and control all aspects of information handling: data processing and storage, data file activities, records management, and data archives.

Originally, the term *information resource management* only referred to the management of information in document form. However, with the increasing use of computers for document processing activities, the term began to take on broader interpretations. This was a recognition that information management required a holistic approach which would bring together organizationally disparate information-handling activities such as computing and communicating, data and word processing, internal and external databases, and corporate and personal information. Evidence of this trend is present in integrated office automation products currently available.

The same evolutionary process evident in the database management arena can be observed in records management. Beginning with the physical control of documents and the development of isolated data processing, telecommunications, and office automation systems, organizations have moved toward integrating both technology and data. In doing so, the function of information resource management from the records management perspective has focused on reducing paperwork, document sharing, and records retention policies. An organization chart reflecting the records management view of IRM is shown in Figure 10.2.

Data Processing Management

The **data processing management** perspective on IRM emerged from the fields of business administration and management information systems (MIS). It was concerned with improving the data processing function to better support corporate decision making. As with the other perspectives, the concept of IRM within the MIS community was the result of an evolution in management thinking. This can be seen in two frameworks which describe the history and development of data processing. Both reflect the gradual progression of management practice toward information resource management.

The first is the computer "generations" framework. (See the appendix for a complete discussion of computer generations.) Along with significant technological advances, the generations also reflect the changing perspectives about information, technology, and their interactions. During the first generation, the focus was on using the computer to perform calculations. The second generation acknowledged the distinction between the information processing needs of scientists and those of business. The third generation focused on the integration of data (databases), technology (remote access), and software (the applications portfolio) to provide managers with the comprehensive view needed for management decision making. The fourth generation expanded on that theme by emphasizing the provision of a better quality of information, not just to senior managers, but to all users in the organization. Following the introduction of the personal computer and "user-friendly" software, which together made computer use more accessible to nontechnical per-

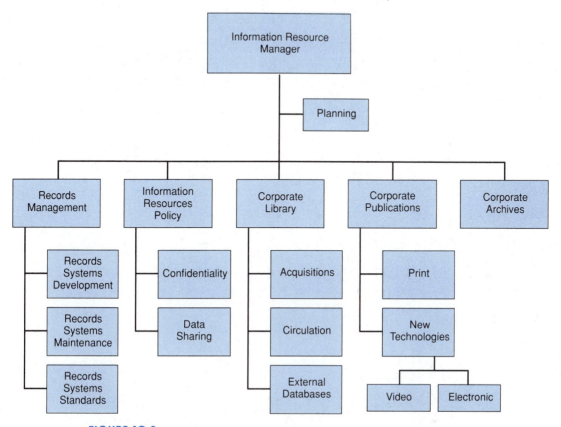

FIGURE 10.2

An organization chart reflecting the records management view of IRM

sonnel, there was a dramatic increase in computer use throughout the organization. At this time it became abundantly clear to top management that the costs associated with corporate information processing were becoming a major budget item. It was during this period that the notions of "managing information," "corporate information systems planning," "strategic planning for information processing," and other synonyms for IRM began to be used.

The other framework which reflects the progression toward information resource management is **Nolan's Stage Theory**,[5] which describes the evolution of information systems planning in an organization. Based on data collected from several firms, Nolan identified a consistent progression through which the data processing management function moved. Figure 10.3 depicts these stages.

The earliest stages are concerned with the actual use of the technology. The first stage, initiation, describes the process of introducing and encouraging use of the new technology. Particular individuals or units of the organization serve as "champions" or role models by demonstrating the uses of

Growth Processes	Stage I: Initiation	Stage II: Contagion	Stage III: Control	Stage IV: Integration	Stage V: Data Administration	Stage VI: Maturity
Applications Portfolio	Functional cost reduction applications	Proliferation	Upgrade documentation and restructuring of existing applications	Retrofitting existing applications using database technology	Integration of applications	Application integration "mirroring" information flows
DP Organization	Specialization for technical learning	User-oriented programmers	Middle management	Establish computer utility and user account teams	Data administration	Data resource management
DP Planning and Control	Lax	More lax	Formalized planning and control	Tailored planning and control systems	Shared data and common systems	Data resource strategic planning
User Awareness	"Hands off"	Superficially enthusiastic	Arbitrarily held accountable	Accountability learning	Effectively accountable	Acceptance of joint user and data processing accountability
Level of DP expenditures	**Stage I: Initiation**	**Stage II: Contagion**	**Stage III: Control**	**Stage IV: Integration**	**Stage V: Data Administration**	**Stage VI: Maturity**

Transition Point

FIGURE 10.3
Nolan's Stage Theory

computers. The next stage, contagion, is characterized by the widespread adoption of the technology. This is done in the absence of accompanying management procedures.

The next stages are concerned with better management of the information processing function. The third stage, control, results from the recognition that the computing resource requires the same management attention as other corporate resources. At this stage, standards and other procedures are adopted to promote greater consistency. The fourth stage, integration, brings information processing into the planning process. The concern is with fitting individual information processing applications into a management framework in order to support both decision making and transaction processing.

The final stages extend the management of information processing by focusing on the management of the information. During the fifth stage, data administration, database technology is utilized to develop shared applications across functional areas. In this stage, information managers implement the features of the database management view of IRM. Data is considered to be distinct from particular technology and applications which use it. For the first time, information is recognized as a separate corporate resource. The last stage, maturity, extends the database management view of IRM by relating corporate information to corporate planning. In this final phase, a data management function has been established, and most significantly, the information system applications "mirror" the information flows in the organization. That is, a planning function is developed to relate information and its use to the activities and goals of the organization. Achieving this requires the same strategic planning for information as is required for other resources in the company. This notion is equivalent to the **information architecture** concept described in Chapter 9.

The use of the term *information resource management* in the data processing management context represents a recognition that *all* information, not just *management* information, needs the attention of management. Emphasizing the need for formal planning, the terms "information policy," "corporate information policy," and "information systems plan" have also been used. Information is seen not only as a resource but also as an asset and as a competitive or strategic weapon. As pointed out in Chapter 9, a global view of the corporate data can be created through the development of an information architecture.

Business Systems Planning (BSP),[6] a technique developed by IBM, grew out of the systems development domain. It is a set of guidelines for the achievement of IRM, though that term is not actually used. The BSP approach is to develop an overall understanding of the business and then establish a priority for implementing information systems to support those business goals. This top-down approach begins by identifying business processes and moves on to identify and associate data classes and systems with those business processes. It also includes the review of existing information systems management, the definition of the information architecture, and the development of an action plan. A key objective of the BSP approach is a close fit between the business goals (and information flows) and the systems developed to support them. This is equivalent to Nolan's final stage, in which the applications mirror corporate information flows. Another important aspect of BSP is the assumption that data is a valuable corporate resource. The significant contribution of BSP to this view of IRM is the emphasis on top-down systems planning and bottom-up systems implementation. This approach, consistent with the information architecture concept discussed in Chapter 9, helps to ensure a fit between corporate objectives and the information systems to support them. Figure 10.4 is an illustration of Business Systems Planning.

From the MIS point of view, IRM generally refers to a combination of data processing management, corporate planning, and database management. What is absent is the management of documents. IRM is typically defined as a formal approach to data design and management, or a way to promote the direct, active management of corporate data to make it work for the company. Unlike the database management approach, which may or may not involve users, this view of IRM has the implied goal of relevance. Therefore, meeting users' needs becomes as important as the efficient storage and retrieval of the data.

The main goals of this view of IRM are as follows:

1. Establishing appropriate fiscal measures of information value
2. Strategic planning for information processing systems so that a coherent approach to satisfying corporate information needs can exist
3. Responding to the needs of all users
4. Managing information processing from a business rather than a technical perspective

An important component of this view of IRM is raising the senior MIS management position to the level of other senior managers such as the chief financial officer (CFO). The titles information resource manager and chief information officer have been used to describe this position. The role of the CIO is to bridge the gap between corporate planning and information processing. Whereas the chief executive officer (CEO) sets the goals and performance measures for the firm and the CFO is responsible for the financial stability of the firm, the CIO is responsible for developing an information plan which articulates the success factors at all levels of the organization. This person should possess a combination of technical and business expertise and should be seen by others as a general rather than a technical manager.

Ensuring the availability, quality, and integration of the firm's data is a major goal of the CIO. An additional goal includes changing people's attitudes about the benefits of data processing. Typically, benefits are seen from a short-term perspective, such as cost displacement or return on investment. IRM, on the other hand, attempts to measure benefits as long-term improvement of competitive advantage and opportunity fulfillment. A typical organization chart of a company which reflects the data processing view of IRM is shown in Figure 10.5.

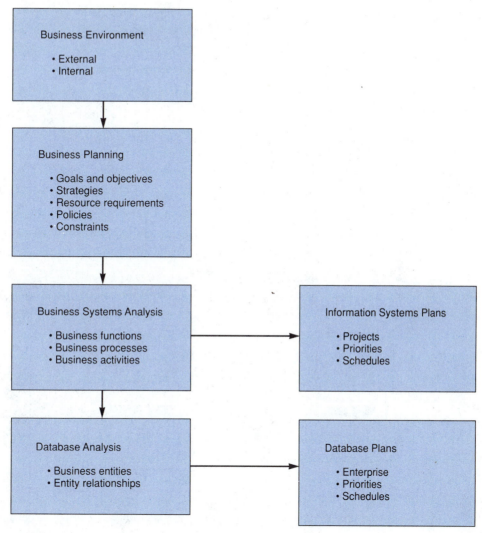

FIGURE 10.4
Business Systems Planning

The responsibilities of a CIO according to the MIS perspective can be summarized as follows:

- Ensuring system integration and impartial service
- Keeping abreast of technological developments which may benefit the organization
- Establishing information processing, access, and dissemination policies
- Possessing the authority and responsibility for the development and maintenance of MIS operations
- Ensuring data confidentiality, security, and retention

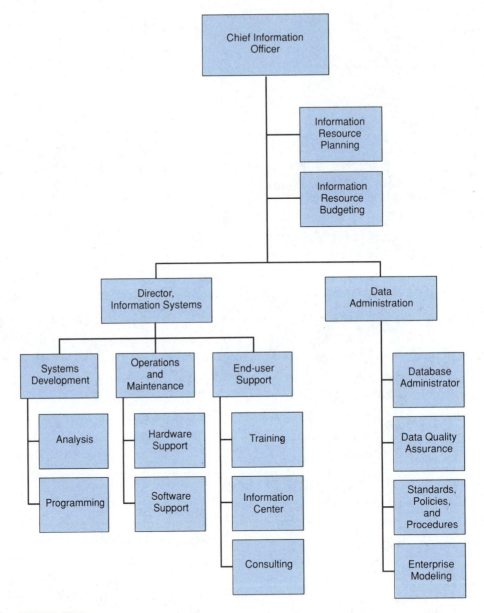

FIGURE 10.5

An organization chart reflecting the data processing management view of IRM

Figure 10.6 summarizes the key goals of each of the three views of IRM just discussed and the methods used for attaining them.

Despite the logic of the arguments in favor of IRM and the identifiable benefits that can be gained by using it, few organizations can say they have

FIGURE 10.6
Summary of three approaches to IRM

IRM Perspective	IRM Goals	Methods for Achieving Goals
Database Management	Maintain global view of data (reduce redundancy) Ensure data integrity and accessibility (maintain value) Enforce data ownership and accountability (assign responsibility)	Data dictionaries Database management systems Data administrator Centralized data access Standards
Records Management	Reduce paperwork Document retention and disposal Coordinate and share documents Protect confidentiality	Chief information officer Paperwork Reduction Act
Data Processing Management	Information flows mirror organizational structures Formal information systems planning Relate information policies to corporate policies Treat information systems as a strategic resource Determine fiscal measures of information value	Chief information officer Information architecture Business Systems Planning Corporate information systems policy

completely implemented the concept. Critics have called IRM just another name for data processing and simply a way for data processing departments to increase their power base. Even IRM's proponents have identified some significant barriers that must be overcome. In order to attain the "global" view of the data or information, disciplines traditionally viewed as quite distinct from one another must work together. Thus, IRM has to broaden its base beyond the data processing department to include all areas of corporate information handling. IRM must also overcome resistance, which can arise on two counts. First, changes in existing procedures and practices can be seen as threatening to some people. Second, if senior managers do not really understand IRM, they may see it as just another attempt by data processing to increase its budget. Many MIS managers themselves do not understand the concept. This confusion often contributes to their lack of motivation to use IRM. Finally, new accounting tools are needed to assess the true costs and value of information processing.

The Convergence of Approaches

By examining the origins and evolution of the concept of information resource management, we come to some interesting conclusions. First, we can observe that the need was recognized independently in three distinct information processing disciplines: database management, records management, and management information systems. Further, we can note that the recognition of the need to consciously manage information in a fashion that is distinct from the management of the technology resulted in three separate approaches: the management of databases, the management of documents, and the management of corporate data processing. In most cases, however, these approaches addressed only a part of the information that needs to be managed in an organization.

Despite the fragmented history of IRM, there is also evidence of a convergence of thinking about this concept. This convergent view of IRM brings together the various disciplines, technologies, and information types into a single management structure. Three classic books exemplify this movement toward a central, coherent view.

In 1979 Forest Horton published *Information Resources Management: Concepts and Cases*.[7] He was one of the first people to actually use the term IRM. His views grew out of the records management perspective—in particular, from his work with the Commission on Federal Paperwork. His book starts with the information explosion and the growing recognition of the need to harness this abundant resource. Given the exponential growth of information, he notes that the problem of information overload is as great as the lack of information. He calls for an interdisciplinary approach which focuses on the information, the uses, and the users irrespective of the particular information-handling technologies. His information management approach is based heavily on the use of such accounting and budgeting techniques as cost accounting and management by objectives.

William Synnott and William Gruber approached IRM from the perspective of MIS management in their 1981 book *Information Resource Management: Opportunities and Strategies for the 1980's*.[8] They cite problems inherent in the current management of information processing as the rationale for moving to IRM. They see information resource management as a natural progression from data processing management. A key theme in their approach is the chief information officer who would centralize information management efforts. They provide a series of strategies regarding the various information-handling components in the organization.

Combining his work on the stage theory with his work in data administration, Richard Nolan presented a third convergent approach to information resource management. The central theme of his book *Managing the Data Resource*,[9] published in 1982, is the shift that has occurred in management thinking from managing computers to managing data. His emphasis is on understanding the nature and characteristics of this resource to achieve the goals of more efficient data utilization, exploitation of its full potential, and integration with other corporate resources. He acknowledges that the data resource pervades the entire organization and thus should be an object of concern to units beyond the data processing department.

The convergent view of IRM is a response to the failure of a single disciplinary perspective to satisfy all the information management needs of a corporation. However, by drawing from the contributions of the three separate approaches, a management strategy can be created which deals with all the information in the organization. Database management techniques provide recommendations for the coordination and control of machine-readable data. Records management techniques provide insights into the effective collection, retention, and utilization of documents. Data processing management provides a policy structure for implementing information management policies throughout the organization. In light of the pervasiveness of computer-based information processing and new techniques for document management such as hypertext, the convergent view of information management stands out as the only viable management alternative.

The following definition of IRM is representative of the convergent view and is depicted in Figure 10.7:

> IRM is a synthesis of several approaches that have been demonstrated to be useful in managing information. It combines general management (resource handling), computer systems management, library science, and policy making and planning approaches.[10]

The convergent view of IRM reflects several assumptions. First, information is assumed to be a valuable corporate asset that can be used as a strategic weapon to gain competitive advantage for the firm. It is a recognition that information has financial value. Second, resource management techniques employed for other corporate resources should apply to the information resource as well. These include understanding the nature and special characteristics of this resource, establishing a management function to conserve and efficiently utilize it towards achieving an identifiable payoff, understanding the organizational implications of its use, and merging information management policies with other corporate policies. Third, the focus of attention is the information, not the technology. Corporate goals and the resulting information needs should determine how the technology is used. Fourth, the user plays a critical role in the success of IRM. This implies shifting the focus from an input, efficiency, and short-term orientation to concern with output, effectiveness, and long-term gains. Finally, it is assumed that achieving IRM is an evolutionary process incorporating organizational learning and positive experiences.

The application of the convergent view of IRM to the development of information management policies suggests three major goals. These goals address the data, the management function, and integration. First, there should be a global view of the corporate data which incorporates both database systems and documents. The management of this data should be oriented toward the achievement of organizational goals and objectives before individual, oper-

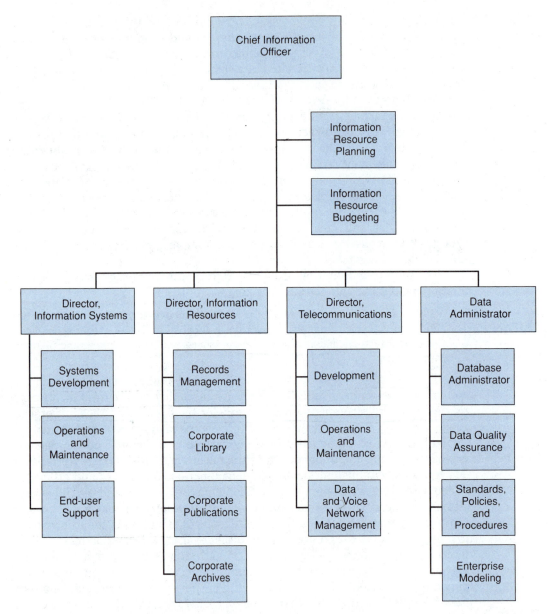

FIGURE 10.7
An organization chart reflecting the convergent view of IRM

ational concerns. Quality assurance, including cost accountability and integrity, should be achieved. Second, the management function should be positioned at a high level within the management structure, with the senior official (CIO) functioning as a senior corporate planner. This person should possess both technological and administrative skills. This management function should balance control, coordination, and centralization in a realistic fashion. Finally, both the data and the information-handling technologies and functions should be integrated. This involves reconciling the needs of various groups of providers and users of these tools.

As with the previous perspectives on IRM, the convergent view also has problems which must be overcome. A significant barrier is the lack of a method for assigning value to information, particularly financial value. Alternative cost/benefit measures to return on investment, cost displacement, and other short-term justifications are therefore needed. In order to move IRM from a logically appealing theory to a practical tool, policies based on IRM must reflect control in the form of workable standards and guidelines and include periodic review and adjustment. Because of the organizational changes that are inherent and the political threats that IRM might represent, the task of overcoming resistance must be taken seriously. As more of the work force engages in knowledge work, the ultimate justification for IRM will rest on its ability to enhance worker productivity. This, in turn, requires the development of meaningful measures of productivity in the value-added rather than the labor-displacement sense, as well as the development of controls over information proliferation in an end-user computing environment.

IRM in the Future: End-User Management

In the future, the success of information management approaches based on IRM will increasingly depend upon an organization's ability to shift its management focus from the information professionals to the growing body of end users. With an increased number of database users, the issues associated with data integrity become more serious. There are now many more people involved with data storage and retrieval, because database management systems allow users to have access to data without requiring them to know much about how or where the data is stored. As a result, control in an end-user environment is much more difficult to achieve. The objective of future information management policies will be to achieve the benefits of end-user computing without losing the level of consistency and integrity that information managers have worked so hard to establish.

The information processing domain of the future will be a distributed one in which the technology, data, and operational procedures will, to some degree, be under the direct control of end users. In this type of information processing environment, what are the most significant issues for the success of IRM-based management policies? There are five:

1. *Measuring productivity*. Traditional measures used for cost justification of computerization are not appropriate in an end-user context in which the goal is the improvement of white-collar productivity. Better measures of productivity are therefore needed if real benefits are to be demonstrated to top management.

2. *Determining the appropriate mix of control, coordination, and decentralization.* A balance must be maintained between individual control of information processing (as the term "personal computer" suggests) and a level of centralization needed to achieve some of the goals of IRM. Control issues center on establishing and enforcing (1) hardware and software standards; (2) data quality assurance given the potential for human error; and (3) security techniques to prevent improper use of the data.

3. *Accountability.* What should accompany increased user control is increased user accountability. This is, in fact, one vehicle for quality assurance in situations where end users download data from the corporate mainframe computer to their personal computers. One way of accomplishing this is for the CIO to function as an "information controller" who plans and allocates resources and to whom the end user is accountable for the use of those resources.

4. *Providing appropriate access.* The expanded set of resources available for information access is both a benefit and a potential problem. The ability to present information in various forms (e.g., graphic versus numeric) and the alternative technologies in existence for doing so (e.g., electronic versus video) require that criteria for assessing the tradeoffs be established. Given the end user's ability to create personal databases, the information manager must also work with end users to ensure that duplicate files neither undercut the goals of data sharing nor result in data inconsistency. With the ability to create and access numerous external databases comes a growing problem of information overload. Mechanisms are needed to help the user manage data and filter extraneous data.

5. *New management roles.* End users are becoming more involved in information-handling tasks traditionally assigned to information professionals. Thus, the end user will increasingly be the individual responsible for carrying out the objectives of IRM at the operational level. The information manager must therefore place increasing emphasis on user education and support.

DEVELOPING INFORMATION MANAGEMENT POLICIES

The previous discussion of IRM has provided us with several important issues to keep in mind when formulating information management policies. The next task is to consider how they are incorporated into the actual development of these policies. Clearly, it is important to maintain an interdisciplinary perspective. That is, we should incorporate the perspectives about information management that were found in the three separate disciplines. From database management, we should include the principles of coordination and control of computerized data to facilitate integration and sharing. This also involves developing and maintaining a global or organization-wide perspective on the data. From the records management perspective, we should include policies to cover the treatment of data and documents throughout their life cycle, from collection to storage and use to disposal. This also includes having policies about who should have access to certain types of information. From data processing management we should integrate proposed information policies into the existing corporate policy structure. We should also utilize the existing information processing infrastructure to do this and alter it where necessary. These policies should relate to and be carried out by all people in the organization.

Information management policies should reflect our recognition that information is a valuable resource and that there is a growing dependence on it. To the extent that an organization is engaged in knowledge work, information can be thought of as the cohesive element in the organization. These policies should be able to incorporate new technologies as well as new uses of existing technologies. Finally, they should facilitate satisfying the users' need for information, whether for purposes of access, analysis, or action. Since information is an individual phenomenon, it is the individual who ultimately determines whether the data has meaning and is useful. As a result, it is crucial to have user involvement in the development, use, and evaluation of information systems and in the establishment of the policies which will manage them.

Those whose job it is to develop and implement information policies spend a long time learning how to do this. Obviously, it cannot all be learned by reading a single chapter. The purpose of this chapter is simply to highlight some of the key elements that should be included in information management policies. This knowledge will enable one to more effectively interact with those whose primary job is to formulate policies, and be able to consider some issues that should be addressed when departmental and personal information processing systems are being developed.

An effective and complete information management policy incorporates all the resources of the information system: the technology (hardware and software), the data, and the personnel. In essence, information management is a part of the procedures resource of the information system. Thus, an information system is not complete until the information management element is established. The following sections describe some of the features that should be present in information policies.

Managing the Data

Managing the data means two things: treating it as a valuable resource and ensuring that it has a certain level of quality.

Treating Data as a Resource

One element of treating data as a resource is assigning objective value to the data. This includes noting that some data has more value than other data. Value is given to a resource in accordance with the demand for it. In the case of information, the more crucial it is to the objectives of the organization, the more valuable it is. Value is also given to information based on its cost. Cost can be assigned to information according to the cost of acquiring it in the first place or replacing it if it were destroyed. For all these reasons, an organization's data should be classified according to how critical it is to the existence of the organization.

For a business, the accounts receivable data would be more critical than the inventory file, since it represents *actual* as opposed to *potential* dollars and since the inventory data can be recreated by examining the inventory. For the same reason, an up-to-date record of the activity of customer accounts at a bank is more critical than a file of customer telephone numbers.

Another aspect of treating data as a resource is incorporating all of the organization's data into a management structure. This doesn't necessarily mean that a single person or department is responsible for all the data. Rather, it means that there should be consistency across the various units that acquire, process, store, and disseminate it. In the database tradition, this is referred to as maintaining a global view of the data.

For example, if a university library knows that the student addresses are collected and stored by another unit of the university, and that it has access to this information, it will not have to collect and store this data again. Part of maintaining a global view means having common data definitions and ways of storing data. For example, suppose the social security number is used as the student identification number at State University. If this fact is made known, offices which deal with student employees will not have to collect and enter the social security number a second time.

Having a number of different computers at the university which use common data demonstrates the need to manage the data in a fashion that is distinct from the management of the technology. The bookstore may have its own minicomputer managed by bookstore personnel. However, it may use registration data that is stored in another computer. The management of the data, therefore, needs to involve both the bookstore and the registrar's office. The management of the specific computers, however, would be the responsibility of each individual unit.

Managing all of the information in an organization also means managing it no matter what form it takes. Some data, such as financial data, is numeric and may be stored in the central computer. Other data may be textual and stored in a personal computer in someone's office. Other data may not be stored in a computer at all. Some data will be valuable to all units in the organization and should be viewed as corporate data. An example would be bank customer account data. Other information should be treated as personal data since it will only be useful to one or a few individuals. A bank executive's calendar would be an example since it is only used by that person and his or her secretary.

Managing all of the information does not necessarily mean that one person is in charge of all the data in an organization. What it means is that consistent procedures should be in place to address all these types of information. For example, a faculty member's course materials may be developed using a computer to create and store them. While it may not be necessary to have someone else oversee how this person uses the computer, it is important to make sure that the user understands the importance of keeping backup copies of the material.

The final aspect of treating data as a resource is to have policies that cover the data and documents throughout their life cycle. A frequent problem encountered by information system users is that data is not kept up to date. When an information system is developed, procedures are set up to cover the collection and input of data into the computer. Sometimes, however, procedures to ensure that this information is kept current aren't as well established. In some cases, only minor difficulties arise, such as a letter being sent to the wrong address. However, if a personnel file is not kept current and the amount of a pay raise has not been recorded, the consequences can be much more serious.

Part of the problem with managing information comes from the fact that there is so much of it around. In the face of information proliferation, it is often difficult to separate what is useful from what is irrelevant. Not only should there be procedures governing the collection and updating of data, but there should also be procedures for disposing of data when it is no longer needed. Because of the computer's ability to store vast quantities of data in little space, this element of information management is often overlooked.

Data Quality Assurance

Ultimately, information is used to support some activity, whether it is decision making about where a course will be taught or the efficient storage and retrieval of designs for a new product. To be of value, information must have a certain level of quality. In earlier chapters the properties of information were discussed (see Chapters 2 and 6). These properties are timeliness, accuracy, integrity, reliability, consistency, conciseness, completeness, and relevance. Effective information management policies will ensure that the information exhibits all these properties. When this is the case, the user can have confidence in the information. Sometimes it is the lack of confidence in the information that causes people to create duplicate files and databases. On the other hand, if users do have confidence in the data, redundant collection, processing, and storage practices can be eliminated.

Security One set of policies related to data quality assurance is concerned with data protection. **Data protection** includes developing security procedures. **Security** refers to procedures governing the use of information processing resources to ensure that the data will not be lost, damaged, or misused. Security procedures relate not only to the data but to the people who will be using it. There are a number of reasons to protect data. Important data must be protected against both intended and unintended destruction, dissemination, and manipulation. Many times, organizations don't think about security until something catastrophic happens. Many times, organizations forget that bad things can happen unintentionally.

One problem that a university has to protect itself against is hacking. **Hackers** are people who enjoy exploring the capabilities and weaknesses of computers. There have been numerous incidences of hackers breaking into computer systems and tampering with important data "just for the fun of it." Security policies must be in place to prevent this where possible, to recover from it when necessary, and to deal with those who perpetrate such acts.

In other organizations, the security threat may be more serious. Because of the nature of their information, banks must have well-developed security programs. Part of the reason they do is that laws governing their fiscal responsibility to clients require it. A related reason is that since this information is financial, there would be more incentive to tamper with it. Again, provisions governing prevention and recovery must be established.

Another fairly recent security threat has come about because of the growing number of computer users. If these people don't understand the need for data protection, they can unintentionally damage or lose their data. Suppose Paul Bunyan, the owner of Wooden Wonders, doesn't know anything about computer security when he begins to use a computer to manage his business. He is enthused about the prospect of storing everything on floppy disks instead of on paper filed in cabinets. Then, suppose one day while he is updating his customer list, the lights in the office start to flicker. A mole out in the yard has started to eat away at the underground electric wires. Perhaps the electricity doesn't quite go off, but the current fluctuates. Since computers run on electricity, a drop in current will cause incorrect data signals to be produced. If Paul has not made provisions for copying this data, he will be unpleasantly surprised to learn that some of it is incorrect and some of it is missing. As more and more people use computers, the potential for unintended destruction of data is a growing concern.

Data protection policies fall into three categories: preventive, detective, and corrective procedures. **Preventive procedures** are put in place to anticipate problems and plan for them. The most important preventive procedure is making **backup** copies of data and software. These extra copies should be stored in a different location. **Off-site storage** is used so that if something happens to the computer facility, the data will not be lost. The use of backups and off-site storage procedures helps to guard against unintended destruction of the data. But it is also important to protect against *intended* destruction, manipulation, or dissemination of the data. **Passwords** are used to identify legitimate users of a multi-user system. Before an individual can gain access to the data, he or she must enter a valid password. To prevent unauthorized use of these passwords, they should not be disseminated to other people and should be changed frequently. It is also a good idea to avoid using a password that another person might easily guess, such as one's name.

Another preventive procedure for guarding against unauthorized use of an information system is **separation of duties**. Chapter 3 made a distinction between accounting and non-accounting information systems. Accounting systems are those which deal with the financial data of the company. Individuals working with these systems should be prevented from having complete access to them. That is, the person who develops the software should not be the same one who operates the system. For example, the person who develops the payroll system should not be the one who produces the weekly paychecks. Having more than one person involved in these systems reduces the possibility of embezzlement and fraud.

Detective procedures enable information processing managers to become aware of actual or potential problems with the data. Most computer timesharing facilities will allow a user only a limited number of attempts to sign onto the computer. This procedure is put in place so that someone attempting to illegally gain access to the computer can be stopped. In addition, security software can be used to keep track of which data a given user is accessing. If illegal activities are detected, this monitoring procedure can assist management in identifying the perpetrators.

Corrective procedures are used to help the organization recover from a problem once it has occurred. One procedure for recovering from intended abuse of the data would be to establish and enforce sanctions for unauthorized use of the computing facilities. At a university, students who gain unauthorized access may be prohibited from using the computer for a period of time or may be prohibited indefinitely. Organizations must also develop corrective procedures relating to unintended abuses of the data. **Disaster recovery** plans should be developed to cope with situations such as fires, floods, or electricity outages. For example, a bank could make arrangements with another bank to use its computer if something were to happen to its own facilities.

Managing the Technology

The fact that data is given serious management attention does not diminish the importance of managing the technology. The two aspects of technology that must be managed are the hardware and the software resources of the information system.

Before the days of end-user computing, managing the technology was much easier. There weren't as many people using the computer, those who did were computer professionals, and the technology wasn't diffused throughout the organization. There also weren't as many technological options to choose from. Today, managing the technology means developing policies and procedures that take into account the current types, uses, and users of technology.

Standards

A very important part of managing the technology today is the development and enforcement of **standards**. Not all kinds of computer equipment are compatible. Software that runs on one computer will not necessarily run on another. Therefore, if people are going to work together on writing projects, it is much easier if they use the same word processing software. When personal computers were first introduced, it was common for organizations to have a variety of incompatible computers. One reason for this was that the MIS department often did not have management responsibility for these computers. Another reason was that end users often didn't *tell* the MIS department that they had personal computers. After a period of confusion and incompatibility, most organizations now have standards governing the types of computers and software that will be used. Sometimes the technology must be purchased through the MIS department. In other cases, the desired equipment must be approved by the MIS department before it can be purchased. These are some options for implementing standards.

In determining the type and extent of standards it is important to be aware of the pros and cons involved. The advantages of standards are financial and managerial. Economies of scale in purchasing equipment can be realized if all users acquire the same hardware and software. From a management perspective, it is easier to support and train users when they all work with the same products. Against these benefits, however, must be considered the drawbacks. The standard hardware and/or software may not be that which the users prefer. This may result in lowered use, or a reduction in productivity, or worse, in users acquiring nonstandard (and nonsupported) technology anyway. One problem with the establishment of organization-wide standards is that they are sometimes determined without users' input.

Thus, while it is important to have standards, it is also important that the people who will be using the technology have some input into decisions that will affect the way they will process information. The ideal situation is to have a standards group composed of both end users and computer professionals. The end users can have the chance to state their needs, and the computer professionals can provide the broader perspective of the ramifications of decisions on the rest of the organization. For example, the bookstore may want to purchase certain software to help it keep track of its inventory. However, if it intends to use course registration data, and the software which manages this data is incompatible with the proposed software, perhaps another choice should be made.

Integration

More and more, people in organizations want to share data that might be stored in various computers. Allowing for this requires that the technology be purchased, used, and managed with this goal in mind. Part of this goal is achieved through standards. But once compatible equipment is purchased, ensuring continued ability to share data requires that people adhere to policies which facilitate coordination. For example, if a number of offices are going to use course registration data (student records, facilities management, bookstore, personnel), there must be certain procedures governing the use of that data. Concerns might include who can update this information and when it should be done. Thus, the policy might state that this information can be updated only at a time when people aren't trying to use it. At a bank the users need to know whether the data they are accessing is current as of yesterday, last week, or last month.

Because computers can be connected, there are a variety of ways that data can be processed and stored. Will the central mainframe computer be used? Should the information be processed in a departmental minicomputer? Perhaps it should be done on a personal computer located in someone's office? Will this data be stored on floppy or hard disks? Should microfilm be used? Should certain documents be stored in the computer at all? When several groups will be using this data, policies answering these kinds of questions must be in place.

Managing the People

Managing the people means establishing policies that state how data will be used and by whom. It also involves determining who has responsibility for what data. Finally, it means relating information management policies to other management policies in the organization.

How Data Will Be Used

Policies governing the collection, storage, retrieval, use, and communication of information should be in existence. They should also be consistent. They should govern the legitimate personnel for various operations on the data. Establishing policies in this regard represents the attempt to maintain a balance between two competing interests: the desire to share data and the need to provide privacy and security.

Promoting sharing means ensuring the availability of and accessibility to data by authorized users. Availability means that the data should be in the proper form and of a level of quality that enables users to have confidence in it. Accessibility refers to facilitating the user's ability to obtain that data. This would include both the storage and retrieval methods and the design of interfaces which are matched to the technological sophistication of the intended users.

Like security, privacy is another component of data protection. **Privacy** is the inherent right to keep one's affairs from public disclosure. When this notion is applied to information, it refers to an individual's or organization's right to keep certain information from public view. Protecting confidentiality is one way of ensuring privacy. **Confidentiality** means that information about an individual would not be disclosed without that person's consent. In an effort to eliminate redundant data collection, processing, and storage, organizations promote data sharing across departmental units. This is a good practice, but it should not occur in an uncontrolled fashion. Having the technological means to share data doesn't necessarily mean the data *should* be shared. In precomputer days, a level of privacy existed by virtue of the inefficiencies of storing data in file cabinets in many different locations. The goal today is to maintain the same level of privacy in the presence of technology that facilitates data sharing.

For example, we have pointed out several times in the book that many different units of a university have the need for student information. Based on this observation, the university would seem like a natural place to promote data sharing. Also, if we have compatible hardware and software, this sharing can be accomplished relatively easily. But it would be wrong to open up all student information to any unit of the university. Perhaps the identification number, name, address, and telephone number can be shared. But other information such as course grades should be made more confidential. Not only is this common sense, but there are also certain privacy laws to which organizations must conform.

The Respective Roles of Information System Personnel

In both the management and the actual use of information processing, two groups of people are involved: end users and information professionals. As end users take on more and more of the actual information processing activities, it is natural to expect them to take on more responsibility for what they do. This is also a requirement given the fact that some information processing is carried out on personal or minicomputers in departments or individual offices. End users have to be held accountable for their use of data. This means that the organization must determine what the appropriate use of the data is and must monitor users to make sure they are using it in the proper fashion. For example, there have been big news stories about people who used spreadsheet programs incorrectly, with very severe consequences for their organizations. End users have to be held accountable for using the appropriate and most current data and using the software for the purposes for which it was developed.

Another aspect of responsibility is ownership. If more than one unit of the organization uses the data, who owns it? There are several possibilities. A central unit of the organization could "own" it. Or the office that originally collects it could "own" it. Or the office that uses it the most could be the owner. For example, the student records office would probably "own" student information. While other units such as the library could have access to some of that information, the library would be subject to the procedures established and enforced by the student records office.

A number of information professionals contribute to providing information for an organization. Systems analysts and programmers are two groups involved with the design and development of information systems (see Chapter 8). Another group which is involved sometimes has the label information specialist. These people usually work with documents, whether or not they are stored in the computer. Their job is to oversee the document life cycle: the acquisition, storage, access, dissemination, and disposal of documents. Personnel in a library fulfill this role. As more and more information is stored in computer-readable form, the importance of this position grows.

Along with the concept of information resource management has evolved the role of chief information officer. This individual has greater responsibility than the typical MIS manager. The CIO has ultimate responsibility for all information processing in the organization. It is the CIO's job to make sure that adequate information management policies are established and enforced. An important component of this is making sure that the policies respond to real needs and that they can actually be achieved. As was pointed out in the case of the Paperwork Reduction Act, sufficient guidance must be given to the units responsible for carrying out these policies. It is the CIO's responsibility to see that the information management policies are realistic.

Information Policies and the Rest of the Organization

The final aspect of managing people is relating information management policies to the rest of the organization's policies. Just as overall strategic planning for the organization must be done, so too should strategic planning for information processing. These strategic plans should be consistent with the overall business goals of the organization. Also, at this level, the approach needs to be holistic. That is, all information flows and forms should be taken into account. Finally, just as information resource management evolved, so too should organizational information policy making. As technology and user skills change, policies governing the use of information and technology must adapt to changing circumstances.

EXAMPLE: DEVELOPING AN INFORMATION MANAGEMENT POLICY AT STATE UNIVERSITY

To see how an organization might go about creating or revising its information management policies, let us consider the approach to information management taken at State University. This approach shows how the development of an information architecture can help to relate information processing to organizational goals, incorporates the three different views of information resource management, and illustrates how information management policies can address the management of data, technology, and people.

Background

Over the past eight years, several changes have occurred with respect to information processing at State University. As a result of these changes, the central administration decided that it was time to take a serious look at the computing and information processing situation. Since 1984, personal computers have proliferated throughout the university. Individual schools have purchased these computers and accompanying software. In 1986, the university made an attempt at control when it formulated a policy about standard hardware and software. Consequently, it determined that only IBM-compatible computers would be used. This meant that if a person or school decided to purchase another kind of computer, the computing center would not provide support in terms of advice on equipment purchases, repairs and maintenance, or training. The university also decided on the use of standard software. WORDWRITE was chosen for word processing and XBASE was chosen as the standard database software. University personnel had little involvement in the decision-making process and some were unhappy with the choices. However, there was no mechanism in place for recommending changes or giving feedback. Consequently, some people decided to purchase their own hardware and software. One problem which resulted was that the software was not compatible with that used in other units of the university. Further, when these people encountered hardware problems, they were on their own; they could not go to the computing personnel for help.

At this same time, there was another situation which caused the central administration to take a closer look at the computing situation. The university was in the process of building a new library. This library was long overdue. The current library had no technological support such as an on-line card catalog or access to bibliographic databases. The university had made a commitment to bringing the new library into the twenty-first century by incorporating many of these types of technological support.

As a result of these and other forces, the president of the university commissioned a task force to undertake a complete review of the information processing framework at State University. This review process was to result in policy recommendations regarding the implementation of new technology and the ongoing management of information processing. This task force was made up of administrators, faculty, students, and alumni. After two years of work, the task force had completed its charge—in time for the opening of the new library. The following sections describe how they went about examining the situation, the procedures involved in developing information policy recommendations, and the final results of their efforts.

Procedures for Creating an Information Management Policy

Developing the Information Architecture
The first activity of the task force was to examine the organizational structure of the university and the current information processing framework. The purpose of doing so was to learn the extent to which the current facilities, management structure, and policies supported the information processing needs of the university. Since there would also be

new information processing demands stemming from the new library services, the task force also wanted to learn whether the existing framework was capable of incorporating these new forms of information access, processing, and storage. With the move to greater library automation and the proliferation of personal computers, the task force wanted to address all forms of data and all types of information technology in the resulting policies.

The Enterprise Model Developing the enterprise model involved documenting and examining the major activities carried out by the different units of the university. The focus was on those units engaged in information processing activities, such as computer facilities in offices, libraries, and data processing centers. In conjunction with this effort, a series of functional organization charts were assembled. A number of these already existed. Sometimes they existed but were not up to date. In other cases, they had to be developed from scratch. The organization charts included both high-level charts showing the overall structure of the university and low-level charts showing, in detail, the structures of the various units of the university. The high-level organization chart shown in Figure 10.8 indicates the distribution of responsibility for various types of information processing in the university. Figure 10.9 is a detailed organization chart showing responsibility for information processing in one unit, the School of Business.

Upon examination of the enterprise model, it was clear that responsibility for information processing was quite decentralized. In fact, each of the four university vice-presidents had responsibility for some form of information processing. The Academic Computing Center maintained several minicomputers under the Vice-President for Academic Affairs. The Director of Administrative Computing reported to the controller, who was under the Vice-President for Finance. The library was under the domain of the Vice-President for Administration. Also reporting to this person was the Director of Operations, who was responsible for telecommunications. Finally, the Vice-President for Public Relations was responsible for three separate departments, each of which was heavily involved in information processing: the Alumni Office, which maintained an extensive alumni file; the Publications Office; and the University Archives. In addition, each school had its own information processing structure. For example, there was an individual at the School of Business who was responsible for personal computers used by the faculty and for the computing facility used by business students. Another individual was responsible for support services, which included the word processing center. In other schools, it was even more complex. For example, both the School of Law and the School of Engineering maintained their own libraries. There was little interaction between these libraries and the main university library.

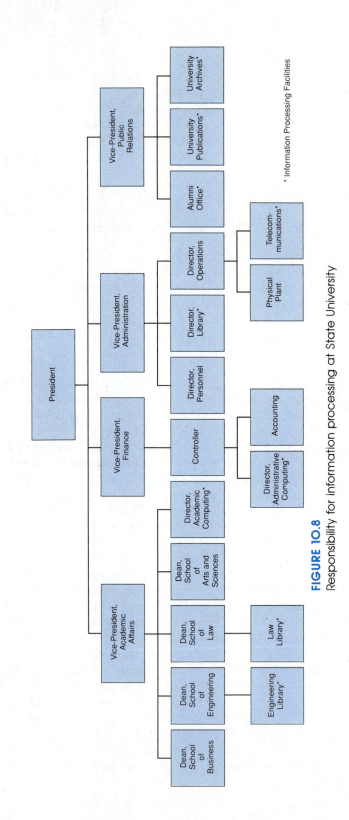

FIGURE 10.8

Responsibility for information processing at State University

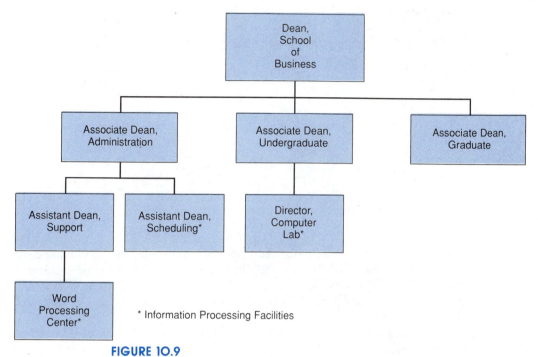

FIGURE 10.9

Responsibility for information processing in School of Business

With so many different units engaging in information processing and management, the task force was certain that there was overlap and inconsistency. They knew that some of this would become apparent when they developed the information model.

The Information Model The purpose of the information model was to document the information processing resources that existed in the university and the degree of interaction among them. This involved compiling an inventory of hardware and software currently in use, collections of documents (such as those in libraries and archives), and data (such as student and alumni files). Figures 10.10 and 10.11 show parts of the hardware and software inventories that resulted.

Another aspect of developing the information model was to identify those individuals in the institution who had responsibility for information processing activities and information management. This was drawn from the organization charts developed as part of the enterprise model as shown in Figures 10.8 and 10.9.

Examination of the information model revealed both duplication of effort and lack of resource sharing. Several examples point this out. An obvious area of duplication of effort was in the libraries. Since both the

FIGURE 10.10

Hardware inventory

Computer Manufacturer	Model	Quantity
IBM	PC	250
IBM	PC/AT	250
IBM	PS/2	100
Compaq	286	50
AT&T	6300	50
Apple	Macintosh	100
Wang	OIS	1
DEC	VAX 11/780	6

Engineering and Law Schools had their own libraries, they also had to hire a staff of librarians to acquire and catalog books, keep the card catalog up to date, manage the book circulation file, and provide reference services. These personnel duplicated activities already being performed by the main library.

Lack of data and personnel sharing was observed upon examination of the Administrative and Academic Computing Departments. Each maintained its own computing center completely separate from the other. Each was also using the same type of computer hardware, but since the facilities were administratively unconnected, there was no sharing of personnel, equipment, or expertise. Consequently, each had its own programming and operations group and each purchased its own maintenance contract from the computer vendor. There was no formal communication between the two computing centers regarding common problems and workable solutions. Hence, each spent needless time working on issues that the other center had successfully resolved.

In addition, lack of procedural, personnel, and data resource sharing was evident upon examination of the management of personal computing in units like the School of Business. This situation resulted from the way in which end-user computing came into being at the university. Because the Academic Computing Center had always been large-computer-oriented, it was slow to accept personal computers. Consequently, many more student labs on campus provided access to the large minicomputers than contained personal computers. As a result, individual departments and schools in the university began to purchase their own personal computers. When the School of Business wanted to start teaching MIS courses using personal computers, it found that there were not sufficient facilities to support student use. Therefore, it established its own personal computer lab and hired personnel to manage it. The Academic Computing Center has refused to get involved in any way in these labs. When problems arise which the

FIGURE 10.11

Software inventory

Software/Language	Hardware
WORDWRITE	IBM/Compaq/AT&T
WordPerfect	IBM/Compaq/AT&T
WordStar 2000	IBM/Compaq/AT&T
Microsoft Word	IBM/Compaq/AT&T
	Macintosh
MacWrite	Macintosh
MacPaint	Macintosh
MacDraw	Macintosh
XBASE	IBM/Compaq/AT&T
dBASE III PLUS	IBM/Compaq/AT&T
R:Base 5000	IBM/Compaq/AT&T
Lotus 1-2-3	IBM/Compaq/AT&T
VP Planner	IBM/Compaq/AT&T
TWIN	IBM/Compaq/AT&T
IFPS	VAX
SPSS	VAX
Minitab	VAX
C	VAX
FORTRAN	VAX
COBOL	VAX
BASIC	VAX
Ada	VAX
RDB	VAX
INGRESS	VAX

personnel cannot resolve, they are forced to go to outside sources—vendors or consultants—for assistance. The task force found that this process was most inefficient, considering the technical expertise that existed in the Academic Computing Center.

Inefficiencies existed in administrative offices as well. Once the faculty and students at the School of Business began to use personal computers, the Dean's Office decided to use them as well. Several computers were purchased for uses such as developing faculty teaching schedules and making classroom assignments. A problem noted by the task force was that the information generated from these computers was not integrated with that produced by the central administration. Therefore, scheduling, room assignments, and other data had to be manually communicated to personnel in the Facilities Department, which reported to the Vice-President for Administration. Quite often, inaccurate information was communicated to the Facilities Office. This resulted in vacant rooms not being assigned to classes or more than one class being assigned to the same room.

A final example demonstrates the inefficiencies caused by the lack of technology sharing. Some faculty in the School of Arts and Sciences had requested the purchase of computer hardware and software which would support computer-aided design. However, they were not able to convince the dean of the school that such a request was justified, because the equipment would be used infrequently and only by a small number of students and faculty. As a result, the courses and research projects that depended on this technology were not developed. In the course of examining the information model, the task force learned that the School of Engineering already had such equipment. They observed that with better communication and the development of policies regarding technology sharing, those students and faculty who needed this equipment for their work could have access to it.

The Information Architecture   The task force intended to provide three products as a result of their efforts. One would be guidelines for the development of information management policies. The second would be recommendations for management restructuring. The third would be a new information architecture which would reflect the proper deployment of information system resources in the university. The architecture which resulted from an analysis of the enterprise and information models was described in a document which showed the planned information processing and management configuration and contained diagrams reflecting the interconnections among hardware, software, and data. Action plans for the accomplishment of this new configuration were then developed and assigned priorities for implementation.

A New Management Structure   Once the information architecture was developed, the task force moved on to their second charge: recommending changes to the existing management structure in order to facilitate the achievement of the architecture's goals. As a result of the information architecture process and considerable research into approaches to information management, the task force identified three perspectives they thought should be reflected in the new management structure.

First, some organizational unit should be responsible for maintaining a global view of the university's data, documents, and technology. While they acknowledged that centralizing every facet of information processing was unrealistic, they nevertheless saw the need for better coordination and sharing. In their view, this could only be achieved if some person or some department *knew* about the existence of such resources.

Second, in order to achieve this global view, they saw the need to bring many of the information processing units together under a single executive. They therefore recommended that the president establish the position of Vice-President for Information Resources. The Directors of the

Libraries, Academic Computing, and Administrative Computing would report to this person. One additional department would be established: the Department of Data Administration. This new management structure is shown in Figure 10.12.

Third, because of the way information processing had evolved at the university, especially in the area of personal computing, the task force saw the need to maintain some degree of end-user autonomy. Therefore, smaller information processing facilities would still be under the domain of the individual units which had created them. An example is end-user computing in the School of Business. The personal computing lab would still be operated and managed by the School of Business, but the task force recommended that its director also have dotted-line reporting responsibility

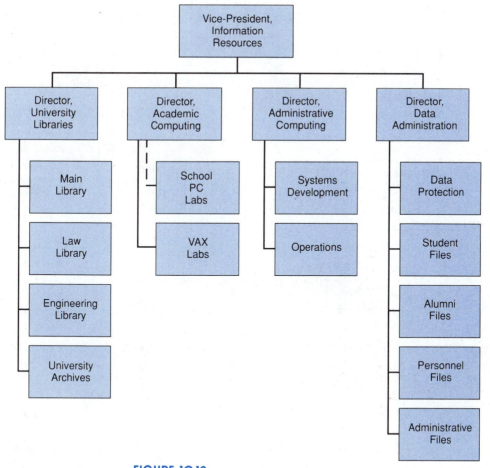

FIGURE 10.12
New information management structure

to the Director of the Academic Computing Center. Their rationale was that the School of Business knew its own information processing needs and had done a good job in satisfying them. But to reduce duplication of effort and to promote the sharing of resources, these smaller facilities needed to work more closely with personnel in the Academic Computing Center. The same situation applied to the Dean's Office. The individual responsible for administrative computing in the School of Business would have a dotted-line reporting relationship with the director of the Administrative Computing Center. This aspect of the management structure is shown in Figure 10.13.

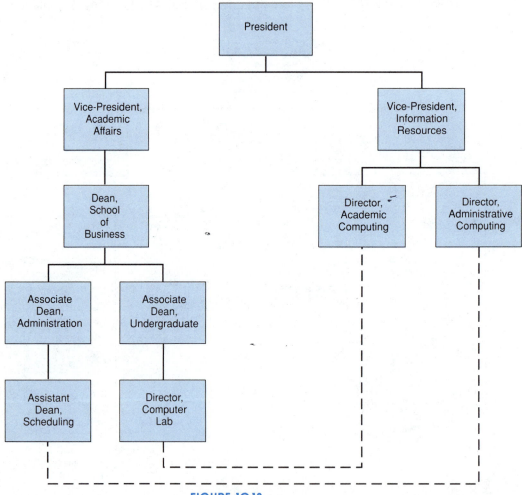

FIGURE 10.13
Joint reporting relationships

Components of the Information Management Policy

Having developed the information architecture and a new management structure to support it, the task force was now ready to complete their final charge: to develop recommendations for the creation of information policies. The objective of such policies was the effective management of information and information system resources at the university. To facilitate this effort, the task force developed a set of policy guidelines. Once approved, these guidelines would represent the university's goals in information management. The guidelines were organized into three categories: managing data, managing technology, and managing people. The following is the document produced by the task force which outlines the guidelines that should be followed in developing information management policies at the university.

GUIDELINES FOR THE DEVELOPMENT OF INFORMATION MANAGEMENT POLICIES AT STATE UNIVERSITY

Managing Data

The Data Resource

Managing data as a resource means developing policies which reflect an acknowledgment that information is a valuable resource to the university. One aspect is, therefore, assigning value to the data. For example, the Administrative Computing Center needs to assign value to its files based on such criteria as the cost to university operations if the data were missing, the cost of recreating the data (collecting and entering it), and the cost to the university's strategic mission if the data were missing. An example would be losing a file containing names of prospective alumni donors.

A second aspect of treating data as a valuable resource is maintaining a global view of the data. A global view of student records could be accomplished in several ways. The university could maintain a centralized database of all student records. An alternative would be for each school to maintain its own student records, but for lines of communication to be established among the schools and between each school and the registrar. These lines of communication could be implemented through both procedural and technological means. An example of procedures is the use of a common data dictionary which would maintain a current set of data definitions describing the data in student records. Better communication could also be accomplished through the use of telecommunications technology to link these individual databases together. A compromise would be to maintain two databases. A central database of student information would be the joint responsibility of the data administrator and the registrar. This database would contain data which is common across all students in the university, such as name, permanent address, school, and year of graduation. Each of the schools could maintain its own student database containing data relevant only to that school. Such data might include the student's major, advisor's name, and class standing. Once again, communication between the schools and the registrar could be maintained through procedural and technological means.

A third aspect of the data resource would be to establish data retention and disposal policies. With the computer's ability to easily collect and store data comes the potential for information overload. For this reason, policies are needed to indicate when data should be archived for long-term storage and when certain data is no longer needed. For example, the alumni file currently has no provisions for removing the names of alumni who have died. While it is important for historical purposes to maintain this data in archives, it is not necessary to keep these names in the active alumni file.

Considering the amount of data that exists at the university, it is important to maintain a realistic scope for the management of data. One way of doing so is to make a distinction between personal and corporate data. Corporate data is that which is needed by various units of the organization and is important to its ongoing operations. Ownership and responsibility for corporate data should be established by information managers at the university. Personal data is that which is used by an individual in doing his or her job. Examples are project management and calendar data and correspondence. In the case of personal data, the individual is responsible for establishing and carrying out information management procedures. Such procedures would govern collection, use, storage, and backup activities.

Data Quality Assurance

Data quality assurance is achieved through procedures relating to data access and use as well as those governing end-user education and support. Both kinds of procedures are needed to ensure that the university can have confidence in the integrity of the data being produced from the computers.

Data protection is accomplished through security procedures which govern access to information processing resources. Such procedures should be preventive, detective, and corrective. Preventive procedures are put into place to prevent security violations. An example would be the requirement of passwords to gain access to time-shared computer facilities. Detective procedures are implemented to determine when security violations are occurring. An example would be recording attempts to access a computer account without the correct password. In some cases corrective action is needed, as a result of either intended or unintended threats to the data. Corrective procedures governing intended threats might include the establishment of sanctions for computer hackers who alter or destroy other people's data. Corrective procedures governing unintended threats should include the establishment of disaster recovery procedures. This means developing plans for maintaining computer operations and protecting the data when some disaster such as a flood, hurricane, or power outage occurs.

Education and user support are an important part of data quality assurance, because many times data is damaged or destroyed unintentionally. Training programs should be established for all types of users: computer operations personnel, students, faculty, staff, and administrators. There should be mechanisms for new members of the university community to learn about using the computer facilities. There should also be provisions for training people when new facilities become available. For example, if an office switches from using a mainframe computer to using personal computers, training classes should be established. Since not all user problems can be anticipated in advance, procedures for providing ongoing user support should also be established. User consultants should be available through help centers and/or telephone hot lines.

Managing Technology

Standards

While it is important to maintain personal computer hardware and software standards, it appears that certain changes in the existing policy are needed. The current standards had been established with little input from the end users of the technology. As a result, some were unhappy with the decision but used the standard equipment anyway. Others who were unhappy decided to purchase their own hardware or software. There were two problems with this latter approach. First, no one in the university was on hand to support this nonstandard technology. Second, compatibility across units of the university was more difficult to achieve when different software or hardware was being used.

Four main benefits are derived from adherence to standards. First, the university could qualify for vendor discounts based on large-volume purchases of hardware and software. Second, computer center personnel could be available to provide user training and technical support when needed. Third, various units of the university would be better able to share data if common software were used. Finally, greater integration of computing into coursework could be facilitated if all students learned to use the same software. If instructors could assume that students knew how to use a common set of software tools, courses could be planned accordingly. This applies particularly to word processing, spreadsheet, database, and statistical software.

To achieve the benefits of standards while at the same time responding to some of the issues raised by end users, the policy on setting standards should be revised. The current standards should be reviewed to see if they are still appropriate. In the hardware arena, this means determining whether adhering to a policy of only using IBM-compatible personal computers is still appropriate. In the software arena, it means reexamining the policy of using WORDWRITE for word processing and XBASE for database applications. A mechanism for incorporating user views into the hardware and software selection process should also be instituted. Finally, there should be a mechanism for collecting user feedback so that as new technology becomes available and needs change, users can influence the decision-making process.

When a unit of the university has needs which might warrant the acquisition of nonstandard hardware or software, it should inform some oversight body. This should be done for two reasons. First, there may be another part of the university with similar needs. The proliferation of different technology could be reduced if both units acquired the same technology. Second, maintaining an up-to-date inventory of hardware and software would minimize confusion and maximize the opportunity for providing support.

Integration

Another goal of managing the technology is to facilitate greater integration of the information system resources. As already indicated, the integration of hardware and software can be greatly facilitated by the use of standards. The integration of data can be achieved through both technological and procedural means. Two areas that should be given immediate attention are networking data from individual schools with that of the central administration and linking faculty offices with the technology to be available in the new library.

Networking the school offices with central administration offices would overcome some of the difficulties that have been identified with regard to scheduling and maintaining student records. Computers used in the individual schools should be connected via telecommunications to the main university computer. Data files should be able to be uploaded from a school's personal computer to the mainframe. Likewise, an administrator in a dean's office should be able to access the mainframe database when needed. However, procedures governing access to data should be put in place to ensure that only authorized individuals can gain access to this data.

Part of the plan when designing the new library was to facilitate faculty members' access to the library resources. This can be achieved by enabling faculty members to access the on-line card catalog and periodical listing in the library from their offices. The library should also consider enabling faculty members to access bibliographic databases as well. To achieve these forms of integration, it is important that sufficient telecommunications capability be available. This includes providing all faculty members with access to terminals, modems, and communication lines.

Managing People

The final part of these policy guidelines involves recommendations about the management of personnel associated with the information systems. At State University, this means *everyone* at the university. These policies should relate to the appropriate use of university data, the structure of responsibility for the information system resources, provisions for providing user education and support, and the relationship between the information policies and overall university policies.

Appropriate Use of Data

One part of data protection was addressed in the recommendations about data quality assurance. Preventive, detective, and corrective security measures are needed to ensure the integrity of the data. Another part of data protection, however, is determining who should have access to that data and how it should be used. For this reason, current policies about privacy and confidentiality of personal data should be reviewed and, if necessary, altered. These policies should clearly state an individual's privacy rights in given circumstances and how this confidential data can and cannot be used by the university. In reviewing these policies, the units involved should consult with the university legal staff to ensure adherence to current privacy laws. In addition, there should be clear statements regarding which university personnel should have access to this data and under what circumstances.

Responsibility Structure

According to the new management structure, the office of the Vice-President for Information Resources will maintain oversight responsibility for all information processing at the university. Some of this will occur directly by having libraries, Academic Computing, Administrative Computing, and Data Administration report to this administrator. However, some offices and schools will also maintain their own information processing facilities. These units must work with relevant parts of the central administration to establish appropriate delineation of responsibility. While the Vice-President for Information Resources will be responsible for maintaining a global perspective on information processing at the university and will be directly responsible for the information processing areas cited earlier, individual units of the university will be responsible for carrying out policies on the operational level and for providing ongoing feedback to the vice-president.

Education and Support

It is crucial that adequate user education be available and be supplemented by support. The directors of the libraries, Academic Computing, and Administrative Computing are responsible for ensuring that users in each of their areas be provided with adequate training on hardware and software and that technical and operational support be available. This can be accomplished in different ways. Since the library system is more centralized, common training sessions in the use of library technologies can be developed. Since the different schools may have individual needs, the Director of Academic Computing may choose to provide training in decentralized fashion through the individual schools. That is, individual schools may conduct their own training for staff and faculty and may provide students with hands-on training through courses.

Information Policies and University Policies

One goal of developing the information architecture was to learn about the fit between the information processing infrastructure and the management structure of the university. Unless the flows of information are consistent with the management structure, the information processing resources will not be supporting organizational activities to the fullest extent. At State University, it is important to remember that the management structure is highly distributed. That is, the central administration is responsible for the overall direction of the university, while the individual schools are responsible for the way in which this movement occurs. In this regard, the individual schools retain a considerable degree of autonomy. While several recommendations from this task force have been to consolidate operations and responsibilities, this does not mean that the individual schools should lose their autonomy either in overall management or in information processing. The information policy which should result from these guidelines is intended to be consistent with the overall management structure of the university. That is, the Vice-President for Information Resources is responsible for the global view of information processing, for maintaining a current inventory of hardware, software, and data, and for facilitating integration where appropriate. The individual units of the university are responsible for their own information processing activities and should have the opportunity to influence information policy changes when needed. For this to occur, the lines of communication should always be kept open and the information processing infrastructure should constantly be reviewed.

Conclusion

At the conclusion of their efforts, the task force presented a final report to the university president and the preceding guidelines were distributed throughout the university. After considerable discussion involving students, faculty, staff, and administrators, the new management structure and a final form of the guidelines were approved. These guidelines represented a blueprint for information processing at State University. They provided a basis for the development of specific information management policies and the delineation of responsibility for carrying them out.

SUMMARY

Information literacy is more than just the ability to manipulate tools. It is also the ability to influence the functions of data collection, processing, and storage so as to guarantee the quality and integrity of the information that results. The theory of information resource management provides an underlying conceptual base for the development of information management policies.

If information is recognized as a resource which has significant value for an organization, it must be managed in the same way that other organizational resources are managed. In developing information management policies, an organization should place emphasis on the information itself rather than the technologies that are in place for processing, storing, and disseminating the information. In this process, people play a critical role, because it is the user who is the ultimate judge of the value of information.

Information resource management has evolved from three separate disciplines. Taken together, these views of IRM provide a rich set of components which should be integrated in the development of organizational information management policies. The database management perspective focuses on the use and management of software tools to maintain a global view of the corporate data which resides in the mainframe computer. Centralized data administration has historically been the mechanism for ensuring data integrity. The records management view is concerned with methods of paperwork reduction such as document retention, disposal, and sharing policies. But such policies must be tempered by concern about confidentiality and appropriate access. The data processing management view is directed at strategic planning for information systems. Toward this end, techniques such as creating an information architecture, Business Systems Planning, and establishing a chief information officer help an organization relate information policies to overall corporate goals.

Since an information system is composed of hardware, software, data, procedures, and personnel, creating an information management policy is the process of establishing guidelines governing the data, technology, and people associated with the system. Managing the data involves assigning value to the information resource and developing data protection procedures that will support data quality assurance. Procedures related to managing the technology include the development of hardware and software standards and the creation of plans to facilitate the integration of technology. Managing people involves establishing policies related to the appropriate use of the data; the roles to be carried out by both systems professionals and end users with respect to information processing; and the relationship between information policies and other corporate policies.

CHAPTER NOTES

1. Eileen M. Trauth, "The Evolution of Information Resource Management," *Information and Management* 16 (1989): 257–268.
2. Alan Goldfine, ed., *Database Directions: Information Resource Management—Strategies and Tools* (Washington, DC: U.S. Department of Commerce, National Bureau of Standards Special Publication 500-92, September 1982): ix.
3. *Paperwork Reduction Act of 1980*, 44 USC 35.
4. U.S. General Accounting Office, *Comptroller General's Report to the Chairman, Committee on Government Operations, House of Representatives: Implementing the Paperwork Reduction Act: Some Progress But Many Problems Remain* (Washington, DC: Government Printing Office, 1983): 48–56.
5. Richard Nolan, "Managing the Crisis in Data Processing," *Harvard Business Review* (March-April 1979): 115–126.
6. *Business Systems Planning—Information Systems Planning Guide* (White Plains, NY: International Business Machines, Publication No. GE20-0527-1, 1975).
7. F. W. Horton, *Information Resources Management: Concepts and Cases* (Cleveland, OH: Association for Systems Management, 1979).
8. William Synnott and William Gruber, *Information Resource Management: Opportunities and Strategies for the 1980's* (New York: John Wiley and Sons, 1981).
9. Richard Nolan, *Managing the Data Resource Function*, 2d ed. (New York: West Publishing Co., 1982).
10. C. Wood, "The IRM Perspective," *Computerworld in Depth* (July 20, 1985): 12.

ADDITIONAL REFERENCES

Horton, Forest W. *How to Harness Information Resources: A Systems Approach.* Cleveland, OH: Association for Systems Management, 1974.
Hussain, Donna, and K. M. Hussain. *Information Resource Management.* Homewood, IL: Richard D. Irwin, 1984.

Marchand, Donald A., and Forest W. Horton. *Infotrends: Profiting from Your Information Resources*. New York: John Wiley and Sons, 1986.

The Privacy Protection Study Commission. *Personal Privacy in an Information Society*. Washington, DC: U.S. Government Printing Office, July 1977.

Trauth, Eileen M. "A Research-Oriented Perspective on Information Management." *Journal of Systems Management* (July 1984): 12–17.

_____. "Information Resource Management." In *Encyclopedia of Library and Information Science* 43, ed. Allen Kent. New York: Marcel Dekker, 1988.

KEY TERMS

backup
Business Systems Planning (BSP)
chief information officer (CIO)
confidentiality
corrective procedures
database management
data processing management
data protection

data sharing
detective procedures
disaster recovery
global view
hackers
information architecture
information management
information resource management (IRM)
Nolan's Stage Theory
off-site storage

Paperwork Reduction Act
passwords
preventive procedures
privacy
records management
security
separation of duties
standards

REVIEW QUESTIONS

1. What is meant by the term *information resource management*?
2. What are the two primary reasons information resource management has become popular?
3. Discuss the database management approach to IRM.
4. Explain the difference between a database administrator and a data administrator.
5. What influences did the Paperwork Reduction Act have on the development of IRM theory?
6. What has been the focus of IRM from the perspective of records management?
7. Discuss the computer generation framework as a description of the data processing management perspective on IRM.
8. What is Nolan's Stage Theory?
9. Explain the role of a chief information officer.
10. Compare the definitions of IRM according to the database management, records management, and data processing management views.
11. Explain the convergent view of IRM. Why did it develop? What are its main goals?
12. The convergent view of IRM has problems to overcome. Discuss a few of these problems.
13. Discuss the significant issues for the success of IRM-based information management.
14. In implementing IRM, what does it mean to manage data? to manage technology? to manage people?

15. What are the two main aspects of managing data?
16. Explain several aspects of treating data as a resource.
17. What is data quality assurance?
18. Explain the importance of security in assuring data quality.
19. Briefly describe the three categories of data protection policies.
20. Why are technology standards important?
21. What is meant by integration when discussing IRM policy?
22. Explain the importance of privacy as a component of data protection.
23. Why is end-user accountability important?

CASE

When Mary Tyson was hired by Paul Bunyan, one of her objectives was to determine ways in which information technology could help to make Wooden Wonders run more efficiently and effectively. Four areas of the company she identified were product design, advertising, client records, and accounting. She has begun the process of considering hardware and software which will assist with the processing, storage, and use of this data. However, she is also aware that proper procedures must be put into place for the management of this data.

Mary knows that many companies do not consider information management policies until after computer-based information systems are already in operation. These organizations must then spend considerable time developing, and in some cases changing, procedures. In her view, Wooden Wonders has the opportunity to do it correctly the first time. Therefore, she would like to develop an information management policy for Wooden Wonders which will ensure that information is available, accurate, and in a useful format.

DISCUSSION QUESTIONS

1. How should Mary go about developing this information policy?
2. What features of the management of data, technology, and people should be included in her plan?
3. How can she ensure that the information policy is consistent with the overall management policy at Wooden Wonders?

APPENDIX

Information Technology

INTRODUCTION

An important question to ask before beginning an overview of information technology is, How much do I need to know? Clearly, a computer or systems professional—one who will make a career of configuring hardware, developing systems, and writing software—needs to know a considerable amount about computer and communication technology. But what about the rest of us? How much do we need to know and why?

The answer is clear, although the exact amount of knowledge required isn't. The answer is that one should know enough to be an *informed consumer*. The analogy was made in Chapter 1 between the knowledge needed to own and use an automobile and the knowledge needed to use a computer. Most people are primarily interested in cars as transportation. The mechanics of the car are secondary. However, to ensure that their transportation needs will be met, they must be able to ask the right questions and understand the answers. This requires a certain amount of knowledge about the internal workings of an automobile. Similarly, end users need to know enough to satisfy their information processing needs. They meet these needs either by purchasing the technology themselves or by negotiating with someone else to do it.

The material in this appendix is an overview of the technology concepts with which an end user should be familiar. It is divided into five major sections: computer hardware, communication hardware, computer software, programming languages, and information processing generations. Each chapter in the book refers the reader to the material from this appendix that is applicable to that particular chapter. Thus, readers can either study the entire appendix at one time or refer to it a section at a time as required by the chapter they are currently reading.

I. COMPUTER HARDWARE

Overview

Computer Architecture
The computer is made up of four components: the central processing unit, input devices, output devices, and storage devices. This configuration is shown in Figure A.1.

Representing Data in the Computer

Binary Representation A language such as English uses fifty to sixty symbols. These include the twenty-six letters of the alphabet in both uppercase and lowercase, the ten numerals, and special characters like the asterisk, the comma, the semicolon, and the period. The code used to represent data in the

FIGURE A.1

Architecture of the computer

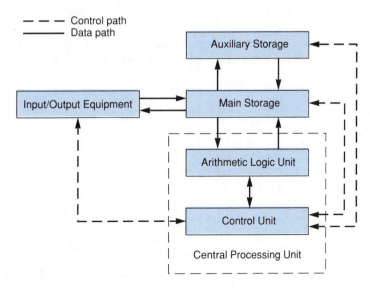

computer, however, uses only two symbols: 0 and 1. It is therefore called *binary code*. Letters, numbers, and special characters are all represented in the computer as combinations of zeros and ones. These symbols are called *bits*, for binary digit. A bit is the physical representation of data in the computer. Characters like the letter "A" are made up of combinations of bits. A combination of bits which represents a character or number is referred to as a *byte*. A byte is the smallest unit that can be located and moved about in the computer. In early computers a byte consisted of four bits; today most bytes contain eight bits.

To translate numbers and letters into bits, some conversion rule is needed. Numbers are converted by using the rules of number systems. We use the decimal number system in our daily lives. That is, we use ten different numerals to represent quantities. Since the computer uses only two numbers, that number system is referred to as the *binary system*. Figure A.2 shows decimal numbers and the equivalent numbers in the binary system.

While there is a natural way to convert decimal numbers into binary numbers, there is no automatic way to convert letters into binary form. Therefore, conversion codes had to be established. The earliest code was called a 4-bit BCD (Binary Coded Decimal) code; that is, it used four bits to represent a character or byte. If we examine all the possible ways that four zeros and ones could be combined, we find that with a 4-bit code there are 2^4, or sixteen, possible combinations of characters. It was soon recognized that this was not enough to represent all the characters that we normally use, so the 6-bit BCD code was developed. This code used six bits to represent a byte, allowing for 2^6, or sixty-four, possible combinations. This was an improvement, but once again, this code would not allow for representing all the data that was needed,

FIGURE A.2

Decimal, binary, octal, and hexadecimal representation

Decimal	Binary	Octal	Hexadecimal	Decimal	Binary	Octal	Hexadecimal
0	0	0	00	50	110010	62	32
1	1	1	01	51	110011	63	33
2	10	2	02	52	110100	64	34
3	11	3	03	53	110101	65	35
4	100	4	04	54	110110	66	36
5	101	5	05	55	110111	67	37
6	110	6	06	56	111000	70	38
7	111	7	07	57	111001	71	39
8	1000	10	08	58	111010	72	3A
9	1001	11	09	59	111011	73	3B
10	1010	12	0A	60	111100	74	3C
11	1011	13	0B	61	111101	75	3D
12	1100	14	0C	62	111110	76	3E
13	1101	15	0D	63	111111	77	3F
14	1110	16	0E	64	1000000	100	40
15	1111	17	0F	65	1000001	101	41
16	10000	20	10	66	1000010	102	42
17	10001	21	11	67	1000011	103	43
18	10010	22	12	68	1000100	104	44
19	10011	23	13	69	1000101	105	45
20	10100	24	14	70	1000110	106	46
21	10101	25	15	71	1000111	107	47
22	10110	26	16	72	1001000	110	48
23	10111	27	17	73	1001001	111	49
24	11000	30	18	74	1001010	112	4A
25	11001	31	19	75	1001011	113	4B
26	11010	32	1A	76	1001100	114	4C
27	11011	33	1B	77	1001101	115	4D
28	11100	34	1C	78	1001110	116	4E
29	11101	35	1D	79	1001111	117	4F
30	11110	36	1E	80	1010000	120	50
31	11111	37	1F	81	1010001	121	51
32	100000	40	20	82	1010010	122	52
33	100001	41	21	83	1010011	123	53
34	100010	42	22	84	1010100	124	54
35	100011	43	23	85	1010101	125	55
36	100100	44	24	86	1010110	126	56
37	100101	45	25	87	1010111	127	57
38	100110	46	26	88	1011000	130	58
39	100111	47	27	89	1011001	131	59
40	101000	50	28	90	1011010	132	5A
41	101001	51	29	91	1011011	133	5B
42	101010	52	2A	92	1011100	134	5C
43	101011	53	2B	93	1011101	135	5D
44	101100	54	2C	94	1011110	136	5E
45	101101	55	2D	95	1011111	137	5F
46	101110	56	2E	96	1100000	140	60
47	101111	57	2F	97	1100001	141	61
48	110000	60	30	98	1100010	142	62
49	110001	61	31	99	1100011	143	63

such as both uppercase and lowercase letters. The code used today is an 8-bit code which allows for 2^8, or 256, different combinations. This code allows us to represent the full range of symbols that we normally use to communicate.

There are two different codes in use today to convert characters into binary form. The EBCDIC (Extended Binary Coded Decimal Interchange) code, developed by IBM, is used for large computers made by IBM and other computers which are similarly constructed (referred to as "IBM-compatible"). The ASCII (American Standard Code for Information Interchange) code, developed by the American National Standards Institute, is used for personal computers (including IBM computers) and large computers which are "non-IBM-compatible." Each of these codes has a different way of converting characters into binary form. Figure A.3 shows the way each code represents data in binary form.

Octal and Hexadecimal Representation The output from the computer is normally translated from its binary form into decimal numbers and English characters before it is displayed. However, there are certain situations which require a programmer to see the binary form of the data, such as when some problem occurs with the hardware or the software. Also, some computer languages require the programmer to express commands in binary form. Since it takes eight bits to represent each character, the output can be very lengthy and difficult to read. For this reason, a shortcut is used. When it is necessary to see the output in binary form, it is actually printed out using either the octal or the hexadecimal number system. The *octal* number system (base 8) uses eight numbers: 0–7. The *hexadecimal* number system uses sixteen characters: the numbers 0–9 and the letters A–F. The reason octal and hexadecimal numbers are used is that both are based on powers of two ($8 = 2^3$ and $16 = 2^4$). This makes the translation between binary and either octal or hexadecimal much easier than the translation between binary and decimal. Figure A.2 shows additional decimal numbers represented in binary, octal, and hexadecimal forms.

Computer Measures Because the binary number system is the basic unit for representing data in the computer, the numbers used in the measurement of computer features are all powers of two. Figure A.4 is a list of the numbers commonly used and what they are used to measure.

The Central Processing Unit

The processing activity of the computer is carried out by a device called the *central processing unit*, or *CPU*. This unit can be thought of as the "brain" of the computer. It has three parts: the control unit, the arithmetic logic unit, and

FIGURE A.3

ASCII and EBCDIC codes

Symbol	ASCII	EBCDIC	Symbol	ASCII	EBCDIC
(space)	0100000	01000000	N	1001110	11010101
!	0100001	01011010	O	1001111	11010110
"	0100010	01111111	P	1010000	11010111
#	0100011	01111011	Q	1010001	11011000
$	0100100	01011011	R	1010010	11011001
%	0100101	01101100	S	1010011	11100010
&	0100110	01010000	T	1010100	11100011
'	0100111	01111101	U	1010101	11100100
(	0101000	01001101	V	1010110	11100101
)	0101001	01011101	W	1010111	11100110
*	0101010	01011100	X	1011000	11100111
+	0101011	01001110	Y	1011001	11101000
,	0101100	01101011	Z	1011010	11101001
−	0101101	01100000	[	1011011	01001010
.	0101110	01001011	\	1011100	
/	0101111	01100001	]	1011101	01011010
0	0110000	11110000	^	1011110	
1	0110001	11110001	__	1011111	
2	0110010	11110010	a	1100001	10000001
3	0110011	11110011	b	1100010	10000010
4	0110100	11110100	c	1100011	10000011
5	0110101	11110101	d	1100100	10000100
6	0110110	11110110	e	1100101	10000101
7	0110111	11110111	f	1100110	10000110
8	0111000	11111000	g	1100111	10000111
9	0111001	11111001	h	1101000	10001000
:	0111010	01111010	i	1101001	10001001
;	0111011	01011110	j	1101010	10010001
<	0111100	01001100	k	1101011	10010010
=	0111101	01111110	l	1101100	10010011
>	0111110	01101110	m	1101101	10010100
?	0111111	01101111	n	1101110	10010101
@	1000000	01111100	o	1101111	10010110
A	1000001	11000001	p	1110000	10010111
B	1000010	11000010	q	1110001	10011000
C	1000011	11000011	r	1110010	10011001
D	1000100	11000100	s	1110011	10100010
E	1000101	11000101	t	1110100	10100011
F	1000110	11000110	u	1110101	10100100
G	1000111	11000111	v	1110110	10100101
H	1001000	11001000	w	1110111	10100110
I	1001001	11001001	x	1111000	10100111
J	1001010	11010001	y	1111001	10101000
K	1001011	11010010	z	1111010	10101001
L	1001100	11010011	{	1111011	
M	1001101	11010100	}	1111101	

Note: Blanks in EBCDIC column mean symbol is not represented in EBCDIC code.

FIGURE A.4
Binary numbers commonly used in measurement

$2^1 = 2$:	the number of symbols in the binary alphabet.
$2^2 = 4$:	the number of bits used to represent characters in a 4-bit code, historically the first code.
$2^3 = 8$:	octal, the size of a byte, the instruction size in the first personal computers, and the number of bits used to represent characters in the current codes.
$2^4 = 16$:	hexadecimal, the instruction size in modern personal computers and early minicomputers, and the number of different characters that could be represented by the 4-bit code.
$2^5 = 32$:	the instruction size in supermicrocomputers, modern minicomputers and mainframe computers.
$2^6 = 64$:	the number of different characters that could be represented by the 6-bit (BCD) code, and 64K bytes was the primary memory capacity in the first personal computers.
$2^7 = 128$:	128K bytes is the primary memory capacity in older personal computers and the size of memory increments that can be added to the primary memory of personal computers.
$2^8 = 256$:	the number of different characters that can be represented by the current 8-bit (EBCDIC and ASCII) codes, and 256K bytes is the primary memory capacity in some personal computers.
$2^9 = 512$:	512K bytes or 1/2 megabyte is the primary memory capacity of many personal computers.
$2^{10} = 1,024 = K$:	the amount of primary memory in personal computers and the capacity of some floppy disks is measured in kilobytes.
$2^{20} = 1,048,576 = M$:	the amount of primary memory in supermicrocomputers, minicomputers, and mainframe computers and the capacity of hard disks and some floppy disks is measured in megabytes.
$2^{30} = 1,073,741,824 = G$:	the capacity of large disk packs and other secondary storage devices such as optical disks is measured in gigabytes.

the primary or main memory. Each of these parts is made up of storage locations, called *registers*, into which the data and instructions are placed before and after processing is done. These registers can be thought of as mailboxes, each of which has an address. Figure A.5 is a diagram of a CPU.

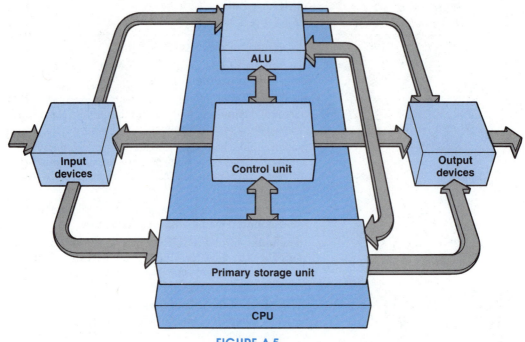

FIGURE A.5
Schematic of a CPU

CPU Architecture

Control Unit The *control unit* functions as the central switchboard or manager of the CPU. It fetches an instruction from the primary memory and analyzes it to determine what actions need to be taken. This is the first of two phases of operation of the CPU. It is called the *instruction cycle*.

Arithmetic Logic Unit The *arithmetic logic unit*, or *ALU*, is the worker of the CPU — that portion of the CPU responsible for carrying out calculations and logical comparisons. The arithmetic operations include addition, subtraction, multiplication, and division. The logical comparisons are performed to compare two pieces of data and determine if they are equal or if one is greater than the other. All of the processing activities of the computer can be reduced to those two activities. The ALU accesses the necessary data from the primary memory, places it into the registers, performs the operations, and then returns the result to the main memory. These activities constitute phase two of the CPU operation, called the *execution cycle*. One machine cycle is required to perform the instruction cycle, and one or more machine cycles are required to perform the execution cycle. Figure A.6 demonstrates the way two numbers are added together. In the instruction cycle, the instruc-

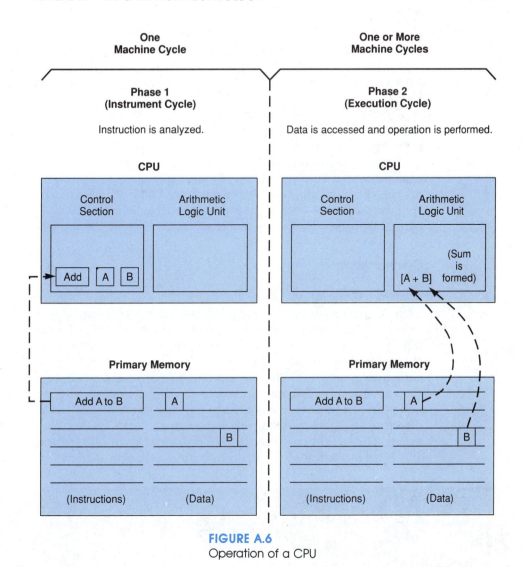

FIGURE A.6
Operation of a CPU

tion "ADD A to B and place in C" is retrieved by the control unit, which identifies the instruction ADD. In the execution cycle, the values stored in locations A and B are placed into the registers of the ALU and added together, and the result is returned to the primary memory and stored in location C.

Primary Memory *Primary* or *main memory* is where data and program instructions wait to be interpreted and executed. This memory is temporary; it holds data and instructions before, during, and after execution. When data and instructions are entered into the computer, they are first placed in the primary memory. From there, the control unit fetches and oversees the execution of each instruction. When the data is needed for calculations or comparisons, it is taken from the primary memory and sent to the ALU. Once the calculations have been performed, the result is sent back to the primary memory.

Primary memory is divided into a series of locations, each of which has a unique address. The size of these locations is known as the *word size* of the computer. A word is the amount of data which can be moved from the primary memory to the ALU in a single operation. The first personal computers were capable of transferring only one byte—eight bits—at a time; these machines are called 8-bit computers. Today, personal computers are capable of transferring two or four bytes at a time and are therefore called 16-bit and 32-bit machines, respectively. Figure A.7 is an illustration of the primary memory.

CPU Hardware

Hardware Generations Over the years, there have been significant advances in the use of technology to carry out the functions of the CPU. Each advance marks the onset of a new generation of computers, and so far there have been four generations of computers. Both the basic components of the CPU and the underlying component of primary memory have changed with each new computer generation. The earliest technology used for primary memory was the vacuum tube. Second- and early third-generation computers used magnetic core. In this technology, tiny core rings were magnetized in a clockwise direction to represent a one and in a counterclockwise direction to represent a zero. Thus, eight core rings would represent eight bits of data, or one byte. The representation of data through magnetic core is shown in Figure A.8.

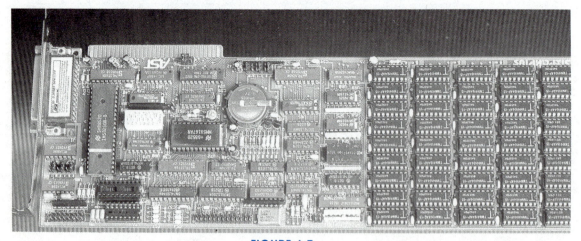

FIGURE A.7
Primary memory

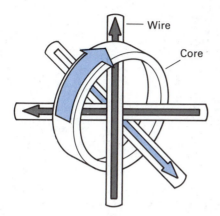

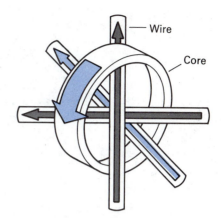

(a) When current passes through the wires in opposite directions, the core is magnetized in a clockwise direction indicating an "on" (1) condition.

(b) When current passes through the wires in the same direction, the core is magnetized in a counterclockwise direction indicating an "off" (0) condition.

FIGURE A.8
Core memory

Late third-generation computers used integrated circuits (ICs) to represent data. With integrated circuits, the flow of current rather than the magnetization of core is used to represent bits in the computer. As the process of miniaturization improved, many integrated circuits could be placed in the space of one circuit. This has resulted in very large scale integrated (VLSI) circuits. With VLSI, several hundred transistors can be etched on a single silicon chip and several chips are then placed on a circuit board. Very large scale integration marked the beginning of the fourth generation of computers.

Semiconductor Chip A *semiconductor chip* is the basic building block of today's computers. A single semiconductor chip can hold hundreds of thousands of integrated circuits. These chips are used to hold both data and instructions within the computer. Figure A.9 is a photograph of a semiconductor chip.

RAM and ROM The CPU is made up of two kinds of semiconductor chips. The *RAM* (random access memory) chip is used for the primary memory, where the data and program instructions are temporarily stored. The data and instructions stored in this chip exist only as long as there is a continuous flow of current. The *ROM* (read only memory) chip is where underlying computer instructions are stored. These instructions are permanently embedded in the chip. They can be accessed and used but not changed by the user. There are three different types of ROM. They differ in the way the instruc-

FIGURE A.9
Semiconductor chip

tions are encoded on the chip and whether or not the instructions can be erased. The instructions in the ROM are etched on the chip during the manufacturing process. *PROM* (programmable read only memory) chips are programmed by the chip manufacturer using a special chip programming language. The instructions on *EPROM* (erasable programmable read only memory) chips can be erased by placing the chip under a special light. ROM chips are used for such instructions as input and output commands. Since the programs or software is permanently embedded into the chip, ROM chips are also referred to as *firmware*.

Microprocessor The CPU of a microcomputer is called a *microprocessor*. Since the microprocessor contains the entire CPU — the control unit and the arithmetic logic unit — it is sometimes referred to as a "computer on a chip." Microprocessors are small and inexpensive enough to be incorporated into other machines as well, including devices such as computer terminals, refrigerators, microwave ovens, and automobiles. These processors differ in their speed, the number of instructions they can process, and the amount of primary memory they can address. Common microprocessors are the INTEL 8088, which is used in the IBM PC; the INTEL 80286, used in the IBM AT; and the INTEL 80386, used in the Compaq 386 computer.

Motherboard The chips that make up the CPU are mounted on circuit boards and inserted into slots at the back of the computer. The CPU and the other components of the microcomputer are connected together by a *motherboard*. In Figure A.10, the entire CPU is included on the motherboard.

Expansion Slots There are also spaces available to connect other boards to the motherboard. One board supports the monitor, and another allows the computer to be connected to a printer and disk drive. Other useful features can also be added to the computer. Examples might be adding more primary memory or graphics and communication capabilities. The spaces into which additional circuit boards would be inserted are called *expansion slots*. The

FIGURE A.10
Motherboard

number of expansion slots determines the expandability of the computer. Figure A.11 shows the expansion slots at the back of a computer.

Characteristics of Computers

Not only are there many different manufacturers of computers today, there are also many different classifications of computers. Before the advent of the semiconductor chip, computers could be classified according to their size. Today there are very small computers which are more powerful than ones many times greater in size. Therefore, other means of classifying computers must be used as well. Computers are typically classified according to capacity, speed, cost, and reliability.

Capacity The capacity of the computer can refer to one of several measures. It can refer to the amount of data that the primary memory (RAM) can contain. Typical capacities of today's microcomputers would be 640 kilobytes or several megabytes (1,000 bytes) of memory. A given software package re-

Expansion slots

FIGURE A.11
Expansion slots *(photo courtesy of IBM Corporation)*

quires a minimum amount of primary memory to operate. In a setting in which more than one user is sharing a minicomputer or mainframe computer, the amount of primary memory will determine the number of programs that can reside in it.

Capacity can also refer to the data word size. As explained earlier, word size refers to the number of bits which can be fetched during a single execution cycle. The larger the word size, the more bits can be fetched. Larger word size is generally associated with faster processing speed.

Finally, capacity can refer to the expandability of the computer. This would mean the upper limit on the amount of primary memory that could be added to the computer. It could also mean the maximum number of *peripherals* or input and output devices that could be attached to the computer. This upper limit in a PC is determined by the number of expansion slots on the computer.

Speed The CPUs of computers differ with respect to their speed or the amount of time it takes to process an instruction. These time periods are measured in seconds, *milliseconds* (thousandths of a second), *microseconds* (millionths of a second), *nanoseconds* (billionths of a second), and *picoseconds* (trillionths of a second). The speed of first-generation computers was measured in milliseconds. The speed of a second-generation computer was measured in microseconds. Third-generation computers measure speed in nanoseconds. Today's fourth-generation computers measure speed in picoseconds.

The timing of the CPU is controlled by the *cycle clock*, or simply the clock. The clock of the computer continuously beats at uniform intervals. The speed of the clock is measured in millions of beats per second, or megahertz (MHz). Typical clock speeds of a personal computer would be 12, 16, or 20 megahertz. For example, a 20-MHz computer has a clock that beats 20 million times a second. Since the operations in the machine need to be synchronized, the continuous beating of the clock provides the basis for this synchronization. The number of beats required to perform a machine cycle varies. The amount of time required to perform both the instruction and the execution phases of the CPU is referred to as a *machine cycle*. The amount of time (i.e., the number of clock beats) needed to process an instruction varies with the complexity of the instruction.

The speed of a given computer is measured by the number of instructions that can be carried out in some time period. A standard measurement of a million instructions per second (*MIPS*) has come to be used. Computer manufacturers rate their computers in MIPS and publish these speeds. However, the testing and rating of MIPS is not standard across manufacturers. Therefore, this measure can be used to determine the comparative speeds of computers within a single family (e.g., the IBM 3090 series), but it may not give an accurate assessment of computers made by different vendors. Users may need to run their own sample programs to test how the different computers will perform in their own environment. Special programs are available for use in rating the relative performance of different computers. The speed of the computer combined with its data word size will give an indication of the power of the computer.

Cost The cost of computer hardware has been steadily decreasing. In the 1970s, a single large computer could outperform several small ones, although the cost would be the same. The situation has changed with the advent of the personal computer, however. Several personal computers now have more power than a comparably priced large computer.

Reliability Machines differ in terms of their reliability, as measured by the time between machine failures — the time when the computer doesn't work right or doesn't work at all. A *fault-tolerant* computer is one designed to maximize the times between errors or system failures so as to ensure high reliability. Fault-tolerant computers are able to detect and correct errors. This can be accomplished by having more than one CPU perform the same task. In this way, if one CPU malfunctions, another is available to continue the processing task. In some circumstances one CPU will "check" another. This is the case with NASA's Space Shuttle. Several computers are involved, all of which must be in agreement in order for an activity to proceed.

Classification of Computers Computers can be categorized into four basic classes: supercomputers, mainframes, microcomputers, and minicomputers.

The first computers were *mainframe computers*. Throughout the 1950s and most of the 1960s, all computers could be classified as mainframes. Today, mainframes are large, powerful machines which are capable of supporting several hundred diverse users and a high volume of information processing tasks. An organization would ordinarily need only one mainframe computer. The primary memory capacity of a mainframe would be measured in megabytes, or millions of bytes. Figure A.12 is a photograph of a mainframe computer.

Minicomputers are so named because they were introduced as "mini-mainframe" computers. They were intended to be smaller, slower, and less costly while retaining the multi-user and general-purpose capabilities of mainframes. Minicomputers are smaller than mainframes in actual size, maximum amount of primary memory, number and types of peripheral devices that can be used, and number of users that can be supported.

The first commercial minicomputer was the PDP-8, produced by Digital Equipment Corporation in 1968. The early minicomputers were 16-bit ma-

FIGURE A.12
Mainframe computer *(photo courtesy of AccuRay Corp.)*

chines. In 1977 Digital introduced the VAX 11/70 computer. With its 32-bit data word, this machine introduced a new class of computers—*superminicomputers*, or *superminis*. Most minicomputers in use today fall into the category of supermini. When minicomputers are distributed throughout an organization, they are sometimes referred to as *departmental computers*. Departmental computers are often connected to the other computers in the organization so that data and other system resources can be shared. Figure A.13 shows a minicomputer.

A *microcomputer* is the smallest computer in size but is not necessarily the least powerful. The first microcomputer was the Altair 8800, introduced in 1975. Other names for the microcomputer include *personal computer* (PC), *work station*, *home computer*, *laptop computer*, and *portable computer*. The major attraction of microcomputers is that they are inexpensive. A basic microcomputer configuration, which includes the CPU, keyboard, and monitor, will range from under $1,000 to a few thousand dollars. Microcomputers are also expandable. Additional primary memory or increased functionality to allow computer graphics can be provided by installing boards containing the necessary chips in the expansion slots of the computer.

The first microcomputers were certainly less powerful than minicomputers or mainframe computers. However, today there is a new class of

FIGURE A.13
Minicomputer *(photo courtesy of Hewlett-Packard Co.)*

microcomputer called a *supermicrocomputer*, or *supermicro*. These machines have performance levels comparable to those of many minicomputers and mainframes of the early 1970s. They have a 32-bit word length and can support more than one user. The DEC Microvax computer, introduced in 1983, is an example of a supermicro. Figure A.14 is a photograph of a microcomputer.

A *supercomputer* is a very large mainframe computer whose primary activity is carrying out sophisticated and complex calculations. It can process large amounts of data very rapidly, in part because of the size of the data word. Whereas the word size of a microcomputer is 8, 16, or 32 bits and that of a minicomputer and mainframe is 32 bits, the word size of a supercomputer is 64 bits. This means that the CPU can process twice as much data as a mainframe in a given execution cycle. Supercomputers can process more than twenty million computations a second. Although the first supercomputer, the Cray-1, was introduced in 1976, it has only been in the last few years that this type of computer has come into widespread use. Before this, a limited number of supercomputers were produced for such industries as defense and aerospace. Figure A.15 is a photograph of a supercomputer.

Figure A.16 shows a comparison of the classes of computers according to their characteristics.

A summary of this discussion of computers is provided in Figure A.17, which shows the characteristics of classes of computers according to computer generation.

FIGURE A.14
Microcomputer

FIGURE A.15
Supercomputer *(photo courtesy of Los Alamos National Laboratory)*

Input Devices

Instructions and data can be entered into the computer in several forms. Some involve typing the text at a keyboard; others involve manipulating symbols or sound. Some forms of input require the data to be prepared first; others allow the data to be entered directly. Chapter 4 considers the circumstances in which the different methods of input would be appropriate. The types of input devices associated with each of these methods of input are described in this section.

Off-line Mode

Off-line means that the device is not in direct contact with the computer. The off-line mode of input is the mode in which the data capture device is not directly connected to the CPU. Some preparation of the input must occur before it is actually entered. There are two types of off-line devices: unit record equipment and key-to-tape or key-to-disk.

Unit Record Equipment The first method of input was to transfer the instructions and data to *punched cards*. This method of input is still in use today. Several devices are used for the preparation and entry of data in this mode. The *keypunch* machine is used to punch holes in the card. Certain

FIGURE A.16

Comparison of computer classes

Example	Microcomputer				
	Microprocessor Chip	Data Word Length*	Clock Speed	RAM	Cost**
IBM PC and XT	INTEL 8088	16	4 MHz	640 KB	<$2,000
IBM AT	INTEL 80286	24	8 MHz+	640KB–7MB	$2,000–$7,000
IBM PS/2 MODEL 80***	INTEL 80386	32	16 MHz+	1–16 MB	>$5,000

*The number of bits transferred from main memory in a single machine cycle.
**Cost of the average configuration.
***Supermicro.

Example	Minicomputer*				
	Machine Cycle Time	RAM	MIPS	Channels	Cost
VAX-11/780	290 nsec	1–64 MB	1.06	1–8	$145,000+
VAX 8650**	55 nsec	4–68 MB	6.8	1–12	$475,000+

*32-bit word.
**Supermini.

Example	Mainframe				
	Machine Cycle Time	RAM	MIPS	Channels	Cost
IBM 3081/GX	24 nsec	16–64 MB	12.5	10–24	$2.5 million+ (16MB)
IBM 3090/400	52.7	64–128 MB	52.7	64–90	$9.3 million+ (128MB)

Example	Supercomputer				
	RAM	MIPS	MFlops*	Number of Processors	Cost
Cray-2	256 MB	1,200	1000	4	$8.5–$16 million
NCUBE	512 MB**	2,000	500	1024***	$1.5 million+

*Millions of floating-point operations.
**512 KB per processor time, 124 processors.
***Hypercube structure.

holes correspond to certain numbers, letters, and special characters. A picture of a punched card is shown in Figure A.18.

Once the cards are punched, they are then processed by a machine called a *verifier*. This machine is similar to a keypunch machine, except that holes are not punched again. The purpose of the verifier is to identify any mistakes the

FIGURE A.17

Characteristics of computers by generation

	Generation			
	First	**Second**	**Third**	**Fourth**
	Mainframe	**Mainframe**	**Mainframe**	**Mainframe**
Date	1951–59	1959–64	1964–75	1975–88
Example	Univac I (1951)	IBM 7090 (1960) [**Mini:** DEC PDP-1 (1960)]	IBM 360 (1965) [**Mini:** DEC PDP-8 (1965)]	IBM 308x (1981) [**Mini:** DEC PDP-11/78 (1981)]
RAM Component	Vacuum tubes	Transistors	Integrated circuits	VLSI
Secondary Storage	Magnetic tape	Plus magnetic disk	Same as second	Same as second
Time per Operation	0.1–1 msec	1–10 μsec	0.1–1 μsec	0.025–0.1 μsec
Programming Language	Machine language	Assembler language, FORTRAN, COBOL	BASIC, PL/1	Fourth-generation languages, Focus, ORACLE

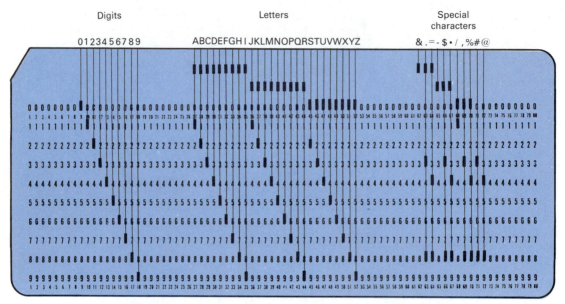

FIGURE A.18
Punched card (*courtesy of International Business Machines Corp.*)

keypunch operator may have made. If the operator of the verifier finds a mistake, the document from which the data is taken must be examined. The data from these punched cards is then input into the computer by means of a *card reader*. Unlike the keypunch machine and verifier, the card reader is an on-line device. This equipment is referred to as *unit record equipment* because all the data about one person or one item is punched on a single card. Figure A.19 shows some unit record equipment.

Key-to-Tape/Disk An alternative method of off-line input is to key the data onto magnetic tapes or disks before entering it into the computer. Instead of being transferred to punched cards for verification before input, the data is transferred to tape or disk and then verified. Figure A.20 shows a key-to-disk configuration.

On-line Mode

On-line means that the device is directly connected to the CPU. With the on-line mode of data entry, the data is entered directly into the computer. The *terminal* is the device used for on-line input. A terminal has a keyboard for typing the data and a display device which shows what has been entered. The terminal is then connected by some communication device to the CPU. There are two types of display devices: softcopy and hardcopy terminals.

Hardcopy Terminal A *hardcopy* terminal displays the data on paper. These terminals are also referred to as *printing terminals*.

FIGURE A.19
Keypunch machine *(photo courtesy of IBM Corporation)*

Softcopy Terminal A *softcopy* terminal displays the data on a screen which resembles a television screen. This screen is called a CRT (c̲athode r̲ay t̲ube) or a VDT (v̲ideo d̲isplay t̲ube). A basic softcopy terminal is simply used for inputting data into the computer. This type of terminal is also called a *dumb terminal*. Some terminals, called *smart* or *intelligent terminals*, have a limited amount of processing and storage capacity. Figure A.21 shows a softcopy terminal.

In retail establishments, terminals are replacing cash registers. These terminals not only compute the amount of the sale but also transmit that data to the computer. These are called POS or *point-o̲f-s̲ale* terminals. Figure A.22(a) shows a POS terminal; Figure A.22(b) highlights the scanner component that reads the UPC bar code.

Input Aids Certain input aids are also available for use with terminals. These devices facilitate interaction with the computer and speed up the process of data entry.

In the process of entering data, the user often has a set of activities from which to choose. Most programs are developed so that the user can select the desired activity by striking one of several special keys on the keyboard called

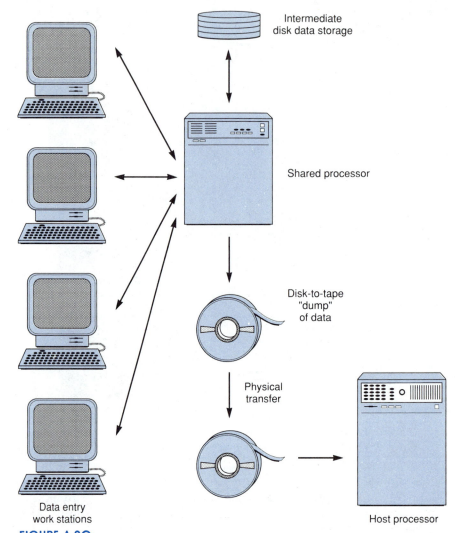

FIGURE A.20
Off-line key-to-disk data entry process

function keys. Function keys enable a user to execute a command by depressing a single key. A given software package will assign its own meaning to the function keys. For example, depressing the F1 function key while using a word processing program might be a signal to the software that the user needs help. Often, a *template* defining the meaning of each function key is provided to assist the user. Figure A.23 shows a keyboard with function keys.

The user can also be aided in the selection and execution of the desired activity by being provided with a *menu*, or list of alternatives. One way to select the desired activity is to point to the menu item by using the *cursor keys*

FIGURE A.21
Softcopy terminal

on the keyboard. The cursor keys have directional arrows on them. Depressing the keys will cause a pointer — the cursor — to move up, down, left, or right on the screen. Another way of moving the cursor is to use a *mouse*, a small, box-like device attached by a wire to the computer. It enables the user to move the cursor about on the screen. If the mouse is rolled over a flat surface, the cursor moves to the same relative position on the screen. Figure A.24 shows a mouse.

Entering data can also be facilitated by the use of symbols. *Icons* are pictures which stand for some activity. The Apple Macintosh computer was one of the first computers to employ icons in its software. Typically, a row of icons appears at the top of the screen. Instead of entering a command from the keyboard, the user could use a mouse to move the cursor to one of the icons which are displayed. For example, a user wanting to delete some material could use the mouse to move the cursor to the icon of a trash can, which indicates "deletion." By pressing a button on the mouse, the user executes the command. Icons and the mouse are especially useful for people who do not know how or are physically unable to type. Figure A.25 shows a computer with icons on the screen.

Input to the computer can also be aided by the use of touch screens and light pens. A *touch screen* is a special type of video tube which allows the user to indicate the desired activity by touching a part of the screen. The computer senses the part of the screen which the individual has touched and then executes that command. The *light pen* is used in similar fashion. The pen is placed against the screen at the desired alternative. These pens can also be used to write or sketch on the screen, thereby providing a "picture" of the input. Figure A.26 shows a touch screen and a light pen.

The most common methods of on-line input involve using text or symbols for input. However, a user may also communicate with the computer through sound input. Computers using a voice input device are able to recognize spoken commands, although the vocabulary is usually quite limited. A second way

(a) Point-of-sale terminal (photo courtesy of Albertson's Inc.). (b) POS terminal's scanning component, with laser beams that encircle an item and read its bar code *(photo courtesy of ICL, Inc.).*

(a)

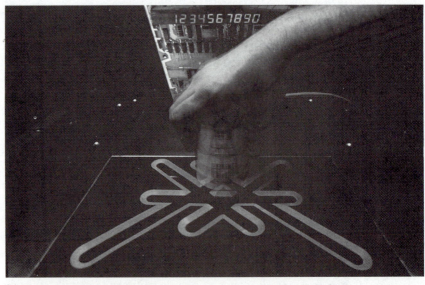

(b)

FIGURE A.23
Keyboard

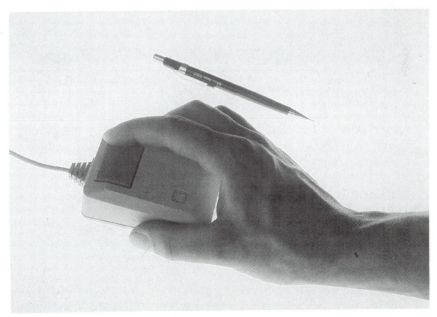

FIGURE A.24
Mouse

that sound is used as input is in the use of the touch-tone telephone. A series of *harmonics* (i.e., touch-tone digits) will stand for some data or a certain command to be executed.

Machine-readable Mode

With this type of data input, there is no need to key the data from the keyboard because the document which contains the data can be "read" by the computer. There are several types of *machine-readable* devices in use today.

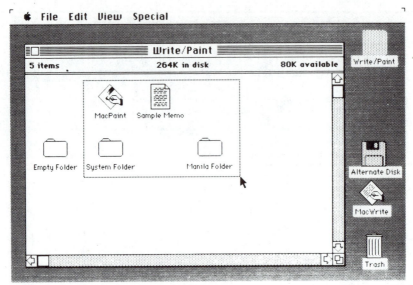

FIGURE A.25
Icons *(photo courtesy of Apple Computer, Inc.)*

Bar Code   A *bar code* is a pattern of lines read by a scanning device. It is used in grocery stores to increase efficiency and to produce more detailed receipts. Figure A.27(a) shows a bar code.

Optical Character Recognition   An *optical character recognition (OCR)* device reads preprinted or handwritten characters. OCR devices can read either a single character or an entire page at a time. These devices are especially useful when large volumes of printed data need to be entered into the computer. Figure A.27(b) shows an OCR device.

Magnetic-Ink Character Recognition   *Magnetic-ink character recognition (MICR)* devices can interpret characters which are written in a special magnetic ink. This method of input was developed by the banking industry to speed up the processing of checks. An advantage of MICR is that the account number at the bottom of the check is readable by humans as well as computers. Figure A.28(a) shows a magnetic-ink character set; Figure A.28(b) shows a sample check using magnetic-ink characters.

Mark-Sense Reader   The source document associated with a *mark-sense reader* has a collection of circles and bars which someone then fills in (typically with a No. 2 pencil). The mark-sense reader is programmed to recognize the specific marks placed on the source document. This type of source document is used to record answers to objective tests such as the Scholastic Ap-

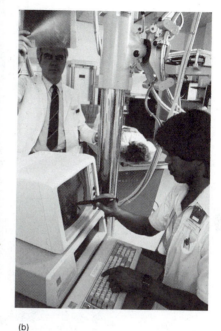

(a)   (b)

FIGURE A.26

(a) Touch screen *(photo courtesy of Hewlett-Packard Co.)*. (b) Light pen *(photo courtesy of Travenol Laboratories, Inc.)*

titude Test (SAT) or the Graduate Management Admissions Test (GMAT). Figure A.29 shows a mark-sense sheet.

Output Devices

The forms in which data can be output from the computer resemble the forms in which it can be input: on paper, on screen, with special devices, and through sound.

Hardcopy Output

Hardcopy refers to output that is printed on paper. Devices which provide hardcopy output are called printers. There are many types of printers, differing with respect to their speed, method of printing, and quality of output. Speed is based on two factors: the amount printed at one time and the speed with which it is printed. Three alternative devices exist. Character printers such as a dot matrix printer or a daisy wheel printer print one character at a

FIGURE A.27
(a) Bar code. (b) OCR device
(courtesy Intermec Corp.)

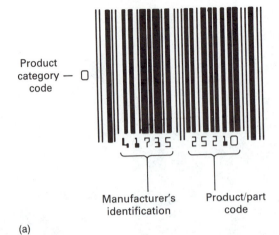

Product
category —
code

⊔⌐735 2521⌐

Manufacturer's   Product/part
identification   code

(a)

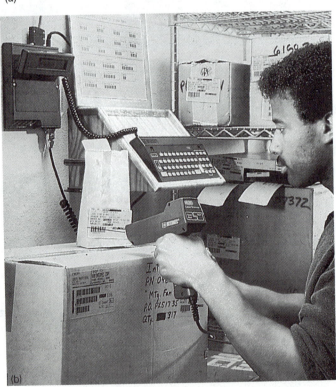

(b)

time. Line printers such as a chain printer print a line at a time. Page printers
such as a laser printer print a page at a time.

    The two methods by which these printers produce output on paper are
impact and nonimpact. In an impact printer, a ribbon is used and charac-
ters/images are formed as the imprinting mechanism strikes the paper through

FIGURE A.28
(a) Magnetic-ink character set.
(b) Sample check with account number encoded in magnetic ink

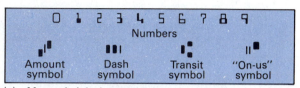

(a) Magnetic-ink character set

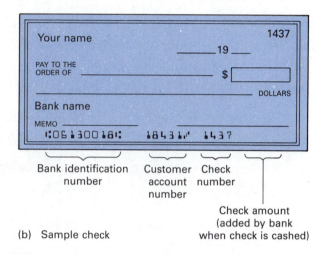

(b) Sample check

a ribbon. This is the way characters are printed on a typewriter. In a nonimpact printer, neither ribbons nor imprinting mechanisms are used. Instead, the image is formed by other means such as heating treated paper or using photographic techniques.

The quality of output is simply how good the output looks. High-quality output looks as if it were professionally typeset. Letter-quality output is as good as that produced by a traditional typewriter, with continuous lines in the characters, true descenders (i.e., the tail of the "y" goes below the line), subscripts, and superscripts. Draft quality is very legible but not very pretty. Between draft and letter quality is near letter quality (NLQ). In Figure A.30 printers are classified according to the three dimensions: speed, method of printing, and quality of output.

Printing Mechanisms Printers can be categorized as either impact or nonimpact printers. An *impact printer* is one which produces the output by physically making a mark on the paper. This can be done in one of two ways. Output from a *full-character* printer resembles that from a typewriter. A device commonly used to make the impact on the page is a *daisy wheel*, shown in Figure A.31.

The second type of impact printer is a dot matrix printer. The marks are made on the page through little rods which are activated. The letters are at-

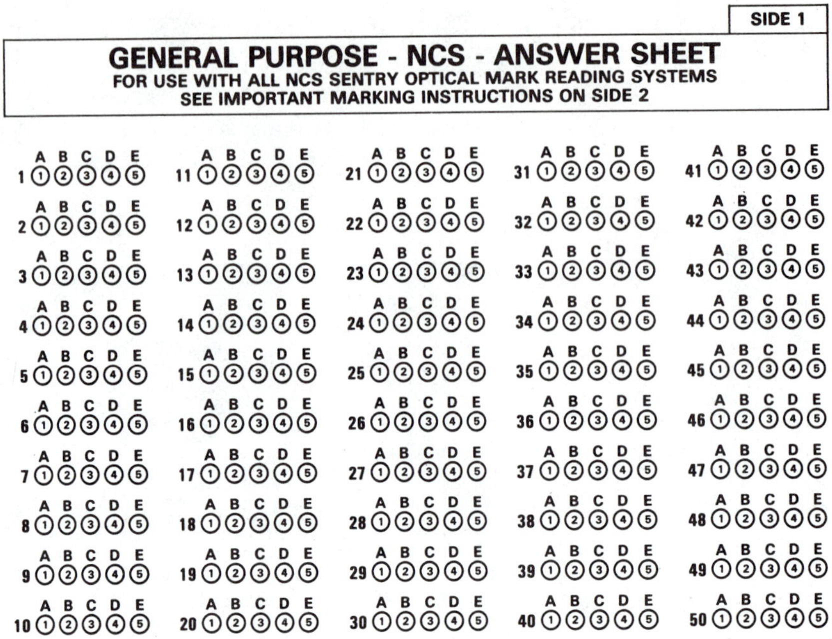

FIGURE A.29

Mark-sense sheet (*NCS General Purpose Answer Sheet reprinted courtesy National Computer Systems, Inc.* © 1977)

tached to a chain. Figure A.32 shows how characters are formed by a dot matrix printer.

Nonimpact printers produce print by means other than striking the page. An *ink-jet printer* produces output with little sprays of ink. It can be used to

FIGURE A.30

Classification of output devices/printers

Type	Character Transfer	Type of Printing	Speed	Quality
Character	Impact	Dot matrix	20–200 CPS	Low to NLQ
		Daisy wheel		Letter quality
	Nonimpact	Dot matrix	80–500 CPS	Low to medium
Line printer	Impact	Dot matrix	150–600 LPM	Low to medium
		Drum	300–2000 LPM	Low to medium
		Chain	300–2000 LPM	Low to medium
Page	Nonimpact	Laser	5–100 PPM	Very high
		Ink jet	12–120 PPM	Very high

FIGURE A.31
Daisy wheel

produce complicated characters such as those in the Hebrew or Chinese alphabet. The common types of nonimpact printers today are the *thermal* and the *laser printer*. With a thermal printer, treated paper is used with a print head that uses heat to darken the paper. Usually, a dot matrix form of the character is produced. Thermal printing is not always the method of choice, because the treated paper is relatively expensive, and it is apt to darken over time or when exposed to any kind of heat, such as the heat of a car in the summer. The laser printer is a very popular type of nonimpact printer. It uses an electrophotographic approach similar to that used in photocopiers to produce a printed page of output.

FIGURE A.32
How a dot matrix printer forms letters

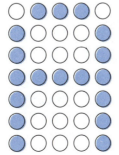
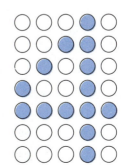

Character-at-a-time Printer This is another name for a hardcopy terminal. The print mechanism is much like that of a typewriter. Since characters are printed one at a time, it can be a slow form of printer. The output can be produced in either full-character or dot matrix form.

Line-at-a-time Printer This type of printer is also referred to as a *line printer*. It prints an entire line of data at a time, making it much faster than a character printer. The output is produced in impact form by a print chain with 132 print heads on it. Figure A.33 shows a line printer.

Page Printer The fastest type of printer is the page printer. A very popular type of page printer is a laser printer. Another method of printing a page at a time is the ink-jet method. Figure A.34 shows a laser page printer.

Softcopy Output

Softcopy output is that which is produced on the CRT. It is temporary, either because it will later be transferred to hardcopy form or because it will no longer be needed. This would be the case for text that is reviewed in draft form on the screen before the final version is printed on paper. An example of softcopy output was shown in Figure A.25.

Other Forms of Output

Punched Card Output is sometimes produced on punched cards so that it can later be input into the computer, thereby saving time during input. When this is the case, the output is referred to as a *turnaround document*. For example, suppose a telephone bill is produced on a punched card. The card contains the client's name, telephone number, and account number and the amount of the bill. The client is instructed to return the punched card along

FIGURE A.33
Line printer

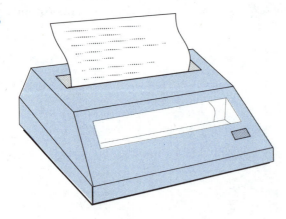

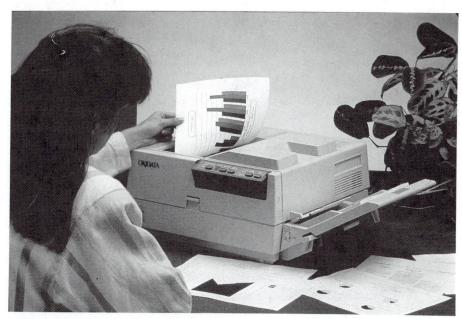

FIGURE A.34
Laser printer *(photo courtesy of Okidata, an Oki America company)*

with the payment. The only other data that the input personnel need to add to the card is the amount of the payment actually received. A punched card was shown in Figure A.18.

Plotter　A *plotter* is an output device that produces line drawings using automatically controlled pen(s). If multiple pens are used, the plotter can draw in multiple colors. Two types of plotters are shown in Figure A.35.

Photographic Output　*Computer output microform (COM)* uses photography to produce the output. The output on the screen is photographed and reduced to a very compact form. It is transferred to either a roll of film (*microfilm*) or a single sheet of film (*microfiche*). This is done to save space when storing data for archival purposes. A microform reader is then needed to magnify the output when a person needs to read this data. Another type of photographic output is computer animation and 35-mm slides.

Voice Output　A *voice output* device "speaks" the output to the user. A *voice synthesizer* with a limited vocabulary translates the output from binary form to human words. Voice output devices are used for telephone directory assistance, for providing output for the blind, and in some children's toys.

(a)

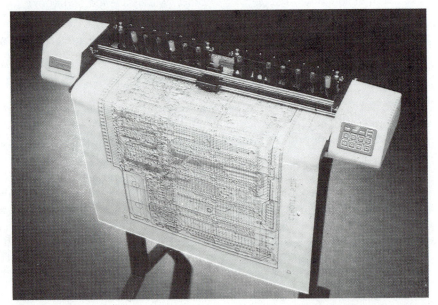

(b)

FIGURE A.35

(a) Desktop plotter. (b) Large plotter for images in greater detail *(photos courtesy of Houston Instrument)*

Storage Devices

Along with the type of storage present in the CPU, there is an additional type of storage associated with the computer, called *secondary storage* or *auxiliary storage*. There are two main reasons for having secondary storage. The first is that the primary storage has limited capacity. A personal computer, for example, may have a limit of 640K bytes of primary storage. Therefore, there has to be a means of storing additional data. The second reason is that the primary storage is *volatile*, meaning that it is highly changeable. Since data in the primary storage is represented by the flow of current, when the current is shut off (i.e., when the computer is shut off) the data stored in the CPU disappears. Therefore, there has to be a means of storing data and programs for later use. The secondary storage devices serve both of these purposes.

Magnetic Tape

Magnetic tape is a sequential storage device. It stores characters one after another in the form of magnetized spots. The presence of a magnetized spot indicates a *1* and the absence of a spot indicates a *0*. For certain data on the tape to be found, the tape must be read from the beginning. Magnetic tapes come in both reel-to-reel and cassette form. These types of magnetic tapes are shown in Figure A.36.

A tape contains nine tracks which run the length of the tape. One bit of data is stored on each track. Thus, one character or byte is stored, in either the ASCII or EBCDIC code, in column form across the tracks. Figure A.37 shows a tape with bits stored on the tracks.

Parity Since a byte contains eight bits, the last track on the tape is used to store a bit called a *parity bit*. The parity bit is used to determine if there are any errors in the data stored. Depending on the type of computer, parity is set either to even or to odd. Even parity means that the sum of the bits is always an even number; odd parity means that the sum of the bits is always an odd number. The parity bit is assigned to the ninth track in the following fashion. If the sum of the eight bits which represent a given character is an even number and the computer is set to odd parity, the last bit will be a *1* so that the sum will be an odd number. Then, if something happened when the data was being stored and an incorrect bit was stored, the sum would be even, indicating an error in the data. The type of parity is encoded at the beginning of the tape before it is first used. Magnetic tape is used for sequential processing (see Chapter 6 for a discussion of sequential processing) and for archival or backup storage.

Density Magnetic tapes differ in their capacity or *density*. Density refers to how tightly compacted the columns of bytes are on the tape. It is measured in *bytes per inch (BPI)*. The higher the density, the more data can be encoded

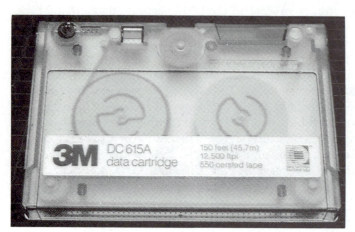

(a)

(b)

(c)

FIGURE A.36

Data storage media: (a) Cassette tape. (b) Magnetic reel-to-reel *(photo courtesy of BASF Corp. Information Systems).* (c) Magnetic reel-to-reel tape mounted on tape drives *(photo courtesy of Boise Cascade Corp.)*

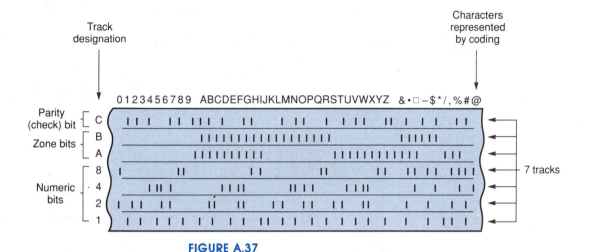

FIGURE A.37
Section of tape showing BCD coding

on the tape. High-density tapes are 6250 BPI (characters per inch of tape), but they can also be written at a lower density such as 1800 BPI.

Blocking A *tape drive*, a device which reads and writes data on a tape, does not rotate continuously. Therefore, when data is written on a tape, a blank space of one half inch is left to provide skid room so that no data will be read while the tape drive is getting up to speed. This blank space is called an *interblock gap (IBG)*, because the data between two of these blank spaces is referred to as a block. One *block of data* is transferred in a single input/output operation. A block of data is also called a *physical record*. In an unblocked file, the physical record is equal to a logical record.

As an example, consider an employee record consisting of 450 characters. On a tape written as 1800 BPI, this record takes up one quarter inch and the gap takes up one half inch. A tape written in this manner would have more blank space than data written on it! To rectify this situation, more data needs to be put into a single block. In blocking, more than one user record or *logical record* is placed into a single block. The number of logical records per block is called the *blocking factor*. In Figure A.38, the blocking factor is five.

Advantages and Disadvantages Magnetic tape is an inexpensive method of storing large amounts of data. Also, because of the way data on tape is processed, there is built-in security. Since a tape is read in sequential fashion, when data on a tape is to be changed, a new tape containing the new as well as the unchanged data must be created. Because of this, there is built-in backup. If something happens to the new tape, the data can be recreated from the previous tapes. Chapter 6 discusses the method of processing data

FIGURE A.38
Unblocked and blocked tape
section

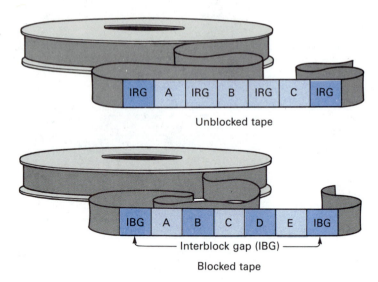

Unblocked tape

Blocked tape

on tape. Another form of protection occurs in the form of a protection ring, a ring that must be on the tape in order for it to be written. This protects a tape from being inadvertently changed. Also, because tapes are portable, they can be removed from the tape drive and put in a secure location or used on another computer.

There are certain drawbacks to using tape, however. Tapes can only be used for sequential/batch processing. This means that one cannot directly access a certain portion of data, but must go through all the previous data in order to locate the desired data. In addition, as with anything stored in magnetic form, tape is vulnerable to environmental factors. Dust, heat, and magnets can damage the data. Tapes also require off-line processing. That is, they cannot be the medium of choice in conjunction with interactive computer use. Finally, tapes transfer data into and out of the CPU at a much slower rate than other secondary storage devices.

Magnetic Disk

Magnetic disk is a direct-access storage device. As with tape, the bits are stored in the form of magnetized spots on tracks. However, rather than being stored *across* eight tracks, a byte of data on a disk is stored *along* a single track. Therefore, the data is stored in concentric circles around the disk. Each track holds the same amount of data. Magnetic disks have varying numbers of tracks, depending upon the size of the disk. The data is stored in such a way that once the physical location of the data is known, that data can be accessed directly without traversing any intervening data. In order for the data to be located, therefore, an address must be assigned to the data. Some information related to disk storage is illustrated in Figure A.39.

FIGURE A.39

Disk storage: (a) Diskette divided into tracks and sectors. (b) Floppy disk (3½ inch) *(photo courtesy of Amdek Corp.).* (c) Floppy disk drive *(photo courtesy of Franklin Computer Corp.).* (d) Operator inserting floppy disk into disk drive unit *(photo courtesy of Verbatim Corp.)*

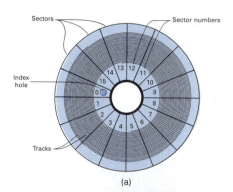

(a)

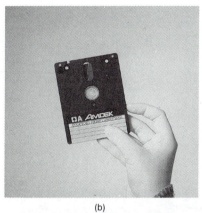

(b)

(c)

(d)

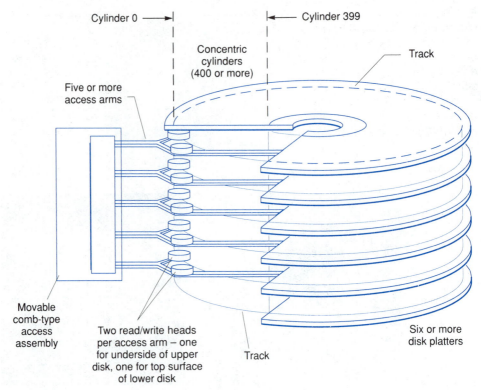

Cylinder 0 ——→| |←—— Cylinder 399

Concentric cylinders (400 or more)

Track

Five or more access arms

Movable comb-type access assembly

Two read/write heads per access arm – one for underside of upper disk, one for top surface of lower disk

Track

Six or more disk platters

FIGURE A.40
Disk pack with read/write heads

Parts of a Disk For the data to be directly located, there must be an address containing the exact physical location of the data. Therefore, a disk is organized into several parts. A device called a *disk pack* contains several disks or *platters*. Each disk has two sides, or *surfaces*, on which data can be stored. Each surface is partitioned into pie-shaped wedges called *sectors*. The address of a piece of data, therefore, is indicated in terms of the specific platter, surface, sector, and track on which the data is stored. When common data is stored on the same track of several platters in a disk pack, it is said to be stored on a *cylinder*. Figure A.40 shows a disk pack with read/write heads.

Types of Disks There are several different types of magnetic disks. Mainframes and minicomputers use hard disks that are usually 14 inches in diameter. These may either be individual disks or come in a disk pack containing several disks. These disks are mounted on a device called a disk drive. There are also disks called *Winchester disks* which come encapsulated with their own read/write heads. In PCs, Winchesters have a single disk. An example is shown in Figure A.41.

FIGURE A.41
Fixed Winchester disk with case removed to show hard disk and read/write head (*photo courtesy of Seagate*)

FIGURE A.42
Floppy diskette jacket

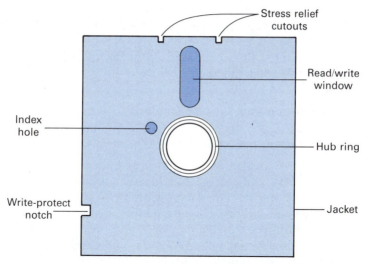

In addition to hard disks, there are also *floppy disks*, or *diskettes*, which are removable as well. Floppy disks are much less expensive than hard disks. The earliest diskettes were 8 inches in diameter. Today, the common size of a diskette is either 5-1/4 or 3-1/2 inches. The IBM PC uses 5-1/4-inch diskettes, while the Apple Macintosh and the IBM PS/2 use 3-1/2-inch diskettes. Figure A.42 shows a 5-1/4-inch diskette jacket in greater detail.

Accessing Data on a Disk It takes a certain amount of time for the read/write head of the disk drive to move across the disk to the correct track. This is referred to as the *seek time* of disk access. It also takes some time for the disk to rotate to the position where the read/write head is located. This is referred to as *rotational delay*. Therefore, the overall time that it takes to transfer data from a disk to the CPU is made up of the seek time, the rotational delay, and the time it takes to actually move the data from the secondary storage device.

Advantages and Disadvantages The main advantage of disk storage is that it allows for direct access to data. Therefore, any setting in which the user would like to call up a specific piece of data and view it on the screen would require the use of disks. Disks are also required for databases. They can be used for sequential storage and indexed sequential processing as well. Since the desired data can be located directly, disk storage provides fast access to the data. The cost of disk storage has declined with the availability of high-capacity disks for personal computers. This makes them an affordable medium for storage.

A major disadvantage of disk storage is that it provides no built-in backup. When data is to be changed, the old data is simply replaced by the new. This is unlike updating data on tape, which requires a new tape to be created. Therefore, special procedures regarding backup need to be established when disks are used for storage.

Figure A.43 is a comparison of the characteristics of the different kinds of magnetic disks available today.

Other Secondary Storage Devices

While magnetic tape and magnetic disk are the most common forms of secondary storage, other media are also currently in use.

Optical Disk An *optical disk* is another device for direct-access storage. It uses light energy and a laser beam for reading and writing data on the disk. Its optical properties allow for a much higher recording density than its magnetic counterparts. A 12-inch-diameter optical disk has a storage capacity of 2,000 million bytes, or 2 gigabytes (billion bytes). This type of technology is often used for storing vast amounts of data, such as an encyclopedia or the Bible. An optical disk is also less vulnerable to the environment and is usually coated in plastic so that people can handle it freely. Once data is stored on an optical disk, it is in read-only mode. This means data can be read off the disk but new data cannot be added to it, because the data is "burned" onto the disk. An optical disk is removable, has high storage capacity, and is very reliable. There are two kinds of optical disk devices: those which can only read data and those which can write data once and then read it many times. These latter devices are referred to as *WORM* (write once read many) drives. Soon there will be optical disks that can be written on multiple times.

Recently, optical disks have become available for use with personal computers. These are compact disks (CDs) similar to those used to hold music in digital form. However, these CDs use a different coding scheme from that used for music. Since the user can read this data but cannot write to these disks,

FIGURE A.43

Comparisons of disks

Multiple-platter Hard Disks (Mainframe)				
Name	Average Access Time*	Transfer Rate	Size	Capacity
IBM 3360J	12.0 + 8.3 = 20.3	6 MB/sec	14 in.	2.5 GB**
IBM 3360	16.0 + 8.3 = 24.3	3 MB/sec	14 in.	1.3 GB
IBM 3350	25.0 + 8.4 = 33.4	1.2 MB/sec	14 in.	317.5 MB
IBM 3340	25.0 + 10.1 = 35.1	88.5 KB/sec	14 in.	34 MB
IBM 3330 II	30.0 + 8.4 = 38.4	806 KB/sec	14 in.	200 MB
IBM 3330 I	30.0 + 8.4 = 38.4	806 KB/sec	14 in.	100 MB

*Average seek time plus rotational delay in msec.
**Gigabytes (billions of bytes).

Other Technology				
Name	Average Access Time	Transfer Rate	Size	Capacity
CD-ROM	--	--	4.75 in.	500 MB
Optical disk	--	--	12 in.	2 GB

Microcomputers (Hard Disk)				
Name	Average Access Time	Transfer Rate	Size	Capacity
IBM XT	85	610 KB/sec	5.25 in.	20 MB
MFM	30–85	610 KB/sec	5.25 in. or smaller	20–80 MB
RLL	28 or 40	10.00 KB/sec	5.25 in. or smaller	20–144 MB
SCSI	15–20	--	--	--
ESDI	15–20	--	5.25 in. or smaller	60–700 MB

Microcomputers (Floppy Disk)				
Name	Average Access Time	Transfer Rate	Size	Capacity
Double density	150.0 + 80.0 = 230	31 KB/sec	5.25 in.	360 KB
High density	65.0 + 50.0 = 115	--	5.25 in.	1.2 MB
Rigid	90	--	3.5 in.	800 KB
Rigid high	--	--	3.5 in.	1.44 MB

they are called CD-ROMs. A 4-3/4-inch diameter CD-ROM can hold 500 mega-bytes of data.

Optical disk technology is currently very expensive, although prices continue to drop. Devices that can both write and read optical disks are more expensive than devices that can read only. However, they are still more

FIGURE A.44
Optical disk

expensive than floppy disk drives. Optical disks currently cost about $12 for 1MB of storage. Figure A.44 shows an optical disk.

Bubble Memory Bubble memory is a technology which provides a nonvolatile memory which can be used for both primary and secondary storage. Bubble memory is a type of solid state chip on which magnetic bubbles are formed in a thin film of garnet. A bubble is a point that can be polarized. The presence of polarization indicates a *1* and the absence a *0*. Invented by Bell Labs in 1971, bubble memory was originally expected to replace semiconductors. This has not occurred, primarily because of the performance and price breakthroughs of semiconductors. Bubble memory is particularly suited to applications that require durability because of its tolerance of hostile elements such as heat and dust. It is also compact and lightweight and has low power requirements. Widespread use of bubble memory has never materialized. Figure A.45 shows bubble memory.

Mass/Archival Storage Devices A mass storage device is a device used for long-term, archival storage as well as backup for magnetic tapes and disks. It has very large capacity and low storage costs. In comparison with magnetic tapes and disks, it has a larger capacity and is cheaper but has much longer access times. An example is the IBM 3850 Mass Storage System, shown in Figure A.46, which uses honeycomblike cells to store tape data cartridges and has a capacity of almost 500 gigabytes. A mechanical arm retrieves the cartridge containing the desired data in about ten seconds. This is much quicker than traditional off-line tape storage, whose access time is operator-dependent because the tape has to be physically mounted on the tape drive before it can be read.

FIGURE A.45
Bubble memory *(photo courtesy of Bell Laboratories)*

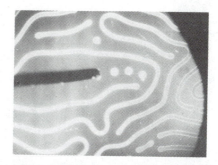

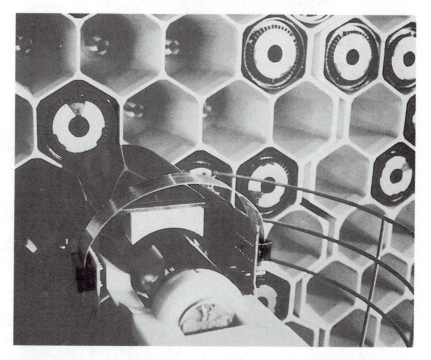

FIGURE A.46
IBM 3850 Mass Storage System *(photo courtesy of International Business Machines Corp.)*

II. COMMUNICATION HARDWARE

Overview

The communication process involves the act of sending a *message* from a *source* to a *destination* through some *channel*. This process is depicted in Figure A.47.

This model applies to all forms of communication, from human conversation to television broadcasts to data transmission through computer networks.

FIGURE A.47
The basic model of communication

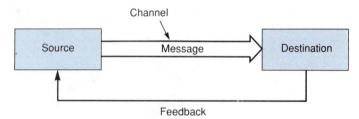

Chapter 7 describes the types of data communication networks in use today. This section describes the technology employed in these networks to move a message from its source to its destination through some channel.

Source

A *source* is the point of origin of a message. When the purpose of the communication is to transmit data to be processed, the source serves as the input device to a computer in some remote location. Four common devices are used as sources for data transmission: a terminal, a computer, a card reader, and a telephone.

Terminal

A terminal consists of a keyboard, screen, or printer and some communication media. The data entered at the keyboard is then sent to the computer through some communication link. Figures A.21 and A.22 show two different types of terminals.

Computer

A computer can be the source of data transmission in one of two ways. When a personal computer is used to transmit data to a mainframe or minicomputer, it is functioning as a terminal. In this case, a board containing certain chips to facilitate communication must be inserted into an expansion slot at the back of the computer. One also needs to have communication software, which enables the personal computer to behave like, or *emulate*, a terminal.

When the output from one computer is being sent to another computer in a network, the first computer is also functioning as a source. All sizes of computers—microcomputers, minicomputers, and mainframe computers—can function as sources of data transmission within a network. Figure 7.5 in Chapter 7 shows different types of networks.

Card Reader

The card reader can function as the source when punched cards are used as the input medium. If the data on punched cards is being sent to a computer from a remote site, the card reader device along with other communication technology becomes part of a *remote job entry (RJE)* station.

Telephone

The telephone is a common device used as a means of human communication, but it can also be used as a source for data transmission. The tones produced by a touch-tone telephone can transmit signals to some computers. For example, some mutual fund companies have systems that allow their customers to request the closing price of a fund by entering the code number of the fund. Some banks enable customers to dial a certain telephone number and then key in an account number to receive the current balance of that account.

Destination

The *destination* refers to the receiver of a message. In data communication the destination is most often a computer. In some cases, however, the destination might be a terminal. This would occur when information which is requested is sent to a user's terminal. The computer can play several roles in serving as the destination for data transmission.

Host Computer

The *host computer* is the computer which processes the input data which has been sent from the source devices. A host may be connected to many terminals in remote locations, or it may be the computer in a network which receives data from other computers for further processing or delivery to some user.

Front-End Processor

The destination computer must not only process the data but must also cope with some network traffic management issues. For that reason, in some networks there is a separate computer — usually a minicomputer — which contains the communication software and is dedicated to managing the communication traffic to and from the host computer. This computer is called a *front-end processor*, because the data is first received by it before being sent to the host for processing. Figure A.48 shows the host computer and front-end processor in a network.

Local Area Network Server

The personal computers and other devices in a local area network (LAN) often need to share software and data. One option is to store this software and data on one or more centralized secondary storage devices. A *LAN server* is the computer in the LAN which facilitates the provision, security, and privacy of this shared software and data by being a central focus point for all requests. The server validates the request, records it if necessary, accesses the requested material, and initiates transmission to the requester. In this role, the server is

FIGURE A.48
Computer network

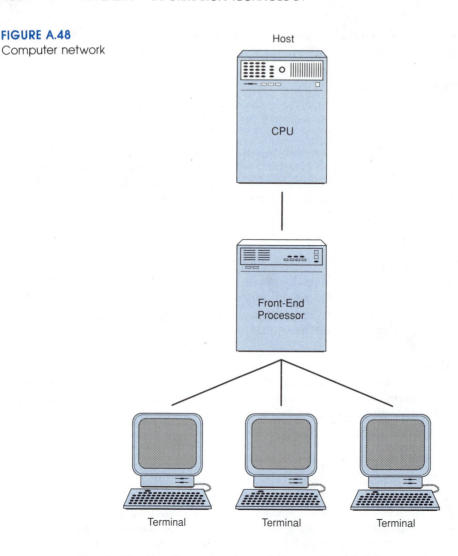

the destination for requests and the source of data sent to another personal computer.

Message

Types of Messages

A *message* refers to the content or meaning of what is being transmitted. There are three basic types of messages which are sent in communication. Voice communication refers to the transmission of words spoken by a human. This can be either direct, as in a face-to-face conversation, or mediated, as in a telephone conversation. Another type of message is a picture such as the video sent for a television program. The *message* in a computer network is the data being sent for processing or being shared with a computer at another site. When a message is transmitted, its signal or representation can be in one of two forms — analog or digital.

Forms of Messages

Analog Transmission Voice and video signals are inherently waveforms. In a face-to-face conversation, voices travel through the air as sound waves. When a television station transmits a show to a person's home, it is sending waves which carry both the sound and the picture. Both of these are examples of *analog* transmission, because the data is sent in the form of an analog signal or wave. Figure A.49 is an example of an analog signal.

A wave has certain properties. *Amplitude* refers to the height of the wave, and *phase* refers to the portion of the wave cycle transmitted in a given time period. *Frequency* is the number of complete wave cycles transmitted per unit of time. Higher frequencies are usually associated with faster data transmission. A vast number of analog signals are transmitted over the airways. These signals must remain separate and not interfere with each other in order to be understood by their receivers. A football fan does not want to be watching the Super Bowl on television and have the program change without warning to another program, have the picture distorted by another transmission, or have the picture (video) of the football game with the sound of another program or a radio station. To remedy this situation, each station is assigned its own unique carrier frequency. These frequencies are spaced sufficiently far apart that no interference should occur within a particular geographic area. Each type of transmission (e.g., radio, television, CB radio) is assigned a spectrum of frequencies by the Federal Communications Commission (FCC). A television station assigned to Channel 4 is not transmitting at a frequency of four waves per second but at some rate that the FCC has assigned to Channel 4. Figure A.50 shows the frequency spectrum.

Digital Transmission The alternative method for sending messages is in the form of electronic pulses representing a collection of zeros and ones, or bits. This newer form is referred to as *digital* transmission because a digital signal is being sent. Unlike voice and image data, computer data must be in bi-

FIGURE A.49
Analog transmission

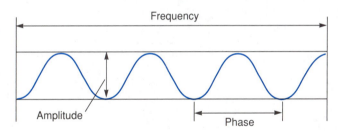

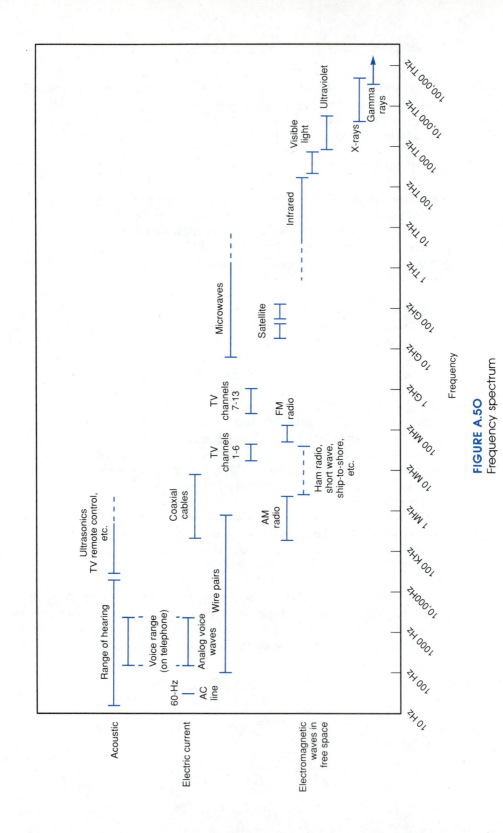

FIGURE A.50
Frequency spectrum

nary form in order to be processed by the computer. Therefore, messages generated by a computer or a terminal are in digital rather than analog form. Computers can send and receive only digital signals. Digital signals can be transmitted at various speeds. The speed at which data is sent is expressed in *bits per second (BPS)*. Speeds for sending data from a terminal to a computer include 300, 1200, 2400, 4800, and 9600 BPS.

Modems Telephone lines are the most common means of data transmission over any distance. However, since telephone systems were set up to carry voice communication, messages were expected to be in analog form. In most cases, if one wants to transmit data to a computer over telephone lines, he or she must contend with the fact that the source and destination send/receive digital signals and that the means of transmission — the telephone line — can only accommodate an analog signal. For example, a person who has a terminal at home may want to display the current stock market activity using the Dow Jones News Retrieval Service. Or a bank teller may want to process transactions on savings and checking accounts at a branch office even though the computer with the account information is located in the main office many miles away.

To handle situations in which a digital signal needs to be sent in analog form, the digital signal must be converted to analog for transmission over the channel and then converted back to digital form so it can be understood by the receiver. The communication interface tool that accomplishes this task is the *modem*. Modem is a short name for modulator/demodulator. *Modulation* is the process of converting a signal from digital to analog form and *demodulation* is the reverse process. Modems connect both digital devices (i.e., the terminal and the computer) to the telephone system. A modem may be either internal or external to the digital device. A common external modem is an acoustic coupler, which connects the digital device with the telephone system through the telephone handset. An internal modem is one which carries out the modulation/demodulation process within the computer itself. In this case, the necessary chips would be placed on a board to be inserted in one of the expansion slots in the back of the computer. Modems are classified according to the transmission rates that they can handle, which are usually 300, 1200, or 2400 BPS. Figure A.51 shows computer-to-computer communication with a modem.

Not all transmission media require analog signals. Digital telephone lines now exist. In the following section, various channels for communication will be discussed. Among them are those which provide for digital transmission. The advantage of these channels is that no signal conversion is necessary before data transmission can occur.

Channel

A *communication channel* is the medium through which a message is sent. Therefore, communication channels are also referred to as *transmission media*.

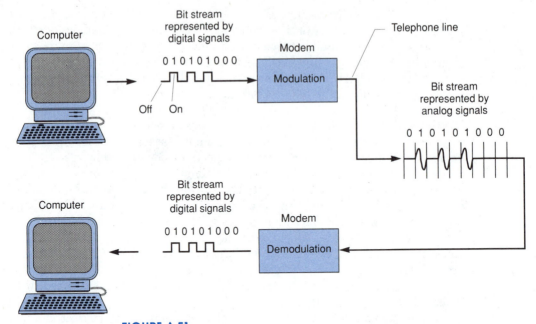

FIGURE A.51
Using modems to send and receive a digital message

Channel Types

Bounded Media Bounded media employ wires to form a physical connection between source and destination. There are three types of wires: twisted pairs, coaxial cables, and fiber optics.

Twisted pair wires consist of two copper wires which are intertwined. They are bundled together in multi-pair cables for convenience in handling and economic packaging. They are used for telephone lines. Twisted pair wires can be used to transmit both voice and computer data. In most circumstances, it is necessary to use a modem to transmit computer data over telephone lines.

Coaxial cables offer the capability of packaging multiple wires together. They have a central conductor resembling a single fat wire and an outer ground cylinder to complete the electrical circuit. Cables often include additional material such as a shield to protect the conductors from the environment. Coaxial cables first gained widespread use for transmitting television signals. *Community antenna television (CATV)* was used to bring television signals to remote or hilly areas which could not be reached by conventional broadcast. Coaxial cable therefore has the capability of transmitting video, voice, and computer data. As a result, when used for data transmission, it has much greater capacity, faster transmission speed, and better quality than twisted pair wires in a cable of equivalent diameter.

Fiber optics refers to the transmission of signals as light pulses through glass strands. The glass fiber provides a significant reduction in weight and volume over the equivalent capacity wire. Fiber optics offers many advantages. The "wires" are thinner. There is less resistance because there are fewer physical impurities in glass than in wire to cause interference. The fibers are currently able to transmit data at a rate of billions of bits per second. A final advantage of fiber optics is that the data can be transmitted in digital form. Therefore, when it is used for computer data transmission, no signal conversion between analog and digital is necessary. A disadvantage is that fiber-optic wires are difficult to connect. Fiber-optics technology is just beginning to be put in place.

Figure A.52 shows types of bounded transmission media.

Unbounded Media Unbounded media refer to means by which the airwaves are used to connect the source and the destination to transmit messages. Messages can be sent as radio waves in the forms of broadcast, microwave, or satellite transmission.

Broadcast waves are at the lowest end of the frequency spectrum. This is the transmission method used by television stations. The waves have a total frequency range of 500,000 to 108,000,000 cycles per second. One cycle is referred to as a hertz. Thus, a wave with a frequency of a hundred million cycles per second is referred to as a 100-megahertz (MHz) signal. In some countries, broadcast waves are used to transmit data in the form of videotext. Videotext is a means of transmitting pages of data such as the newspaper,

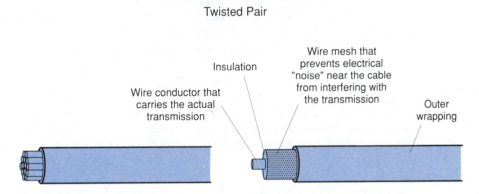

Twisted Pair

Coaxial Cables

FIGURE A.52
Transmission media

catalog information, or airline schedules. Videotext is described in further detail in Chapter 7.

Microwave transmission is carried out at rates of up to 45 million bits per second (MBPS). The microwave bandwidth can support voice-grade transmissions, television images, and high-speed data links. One problem with the use of microwave is its inherent susceptibility to interference from other signals in the air called *noise*. Even at short distances, such as ten or more feet, noise can be a problem if many other signals are present. Therefore, only a small amount of data is usually carried directly over the airwaves without further enhancement. Another problem is that waves travel in straight lines (line-of-sight transmission), and the earth is curved. Unless the transmitter and receiver are in each other's "line of sight," the message will go out into space and will not reach its destination. For this reason, microwave relay stations are set up to amplify messages and keep them close to the curvature of the earth. In this manner, a message which must travel 100 miles is sent from the source to a series of microwave relays until it eventually arrives at the destination. Figure A.53 shows a microwave relay.

Satellite transmission is a special type of microwave transmission used for longer distances such as across a country when line-of-sight transmission is not possible. The message is sent from the source to a satellite and then to the destination. Satellites transmit from ground to satellite at one frequency and from satellite to ground at another frequency. To be effective, satellites must remain stationary relative to a certain position on earth 22,300 miles away, in what is called a geosynchronous orbit. Only three satellites are required to provide communications all over the world. The transmission rate for satellites is commonly 50 MBPS.

Despite the advantages of satellite transmission, there are some drawbacks as well. Transmission delays can result because of the distances the messages must travel, even though the signal travels at the speed of light. Also, because of its position relative to the sun, the satellite may be periodically unavailable. In addition, there can be security problems since anyone with the necessary equipment can receive the transmission. Figure A.53 shows satellite transmission.

Channel Characteristics

As just discussed, there are a variety of channels or transmission media from which to choose in sending a message. These media differ with respect to several characteristics, the most important of which are bandwidth and directionality.

Bandwidth The term *bandwidth* is used to refer both to the capacity of the channel and to the portion of the frequency spectrum used to transmit the message. The bandwidth of a channel will influence the speed at which data can move through it. There are three classifications of transmission bandwidths: narrowband, voice-grade, and broadband.

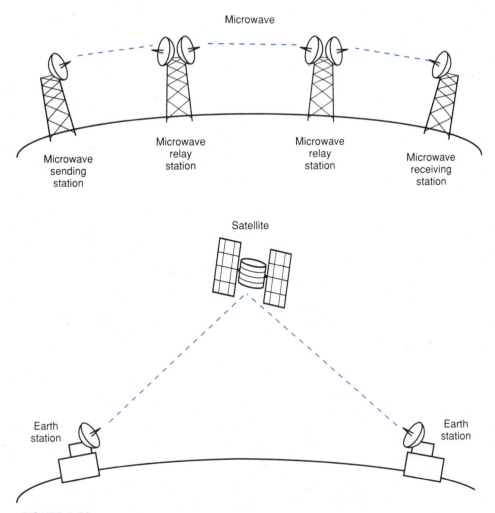

FIGURE A.53
Data transmission through the air—microwave and satellite

Narrowband channels have the lowest capacity. Typically, the channel capacity of a narrowband channel is 5 to 30 characters per second. Narrowband communication over analog media requires the use of coded data. These channels are typically used for telegraph transmission.

Voice-grade channels are those that were designed to transmit voice communication. They can carry more than 1,000 characters per second. Twisted pair wires used for telephones are the most common example of voice-grade channels. They can be used for both computer and voice data. The speed of these lines is often expressed by the baud rate. *Baud* refers to the number of signals sent per second. In parallel transmission, eight bits are sent at once. Therefore, an entire byte or character is sent at one time. In serial transmission, bits are sent in a stream, one at a time. Therefore, depending on whether one is sending in serial or parallel, the baud rate would refer to either the number of *bytes* sent per second or the number of *bits* sent per second. Typical baud rates for voice-grade lines are 300, 1200, or 2400.

Broadband channels are those which include multiple, parallel channels over the same media and can accommodate all types of messages. They are so versatile because they were designed to transmit video, which requires the largest channel capacity. Broadband channels can transmit more than 100,000 characters per second. Some organizations are choosing to install broadband networks which will carry voice, video, and computer data on the same lines. Coaxial cable, fiber optics, radio, microwave, and satellite can all support broadband channels.

Directionality   The second important characteristic of communication channels is the direction in which the message moves. There are three direction alternatives: simplex, half-duplex, and full-duplex. Examples of these, with a road as an analogy, are shown in Figure A.54.

In *simplex* communication, the channel is analogous to a one-way road, which allows traffic to move in only one direction. The message can only travel from source to destination and *not* vice versa. An example of simplex communication is the AP and UPI wire services, which provide news information to newspapers, radio stations, and television stations. This data is transmitted from the source to the destinations, but the receivers cannot send anything back to the source.

In *half-duplex* communication, the channel is similar to a single-lane bridge. Cars can only travel in one direction at a given time. A message can travel from source to destination or vice versa, but two messages cannot be sent in both directions simultaneously. Short-wave radios, intercoms, and CB radios employ half-duplex communication.

In *full-duplex* communication, the channel is like a conventional road with traffic traveling simultaneously in both directions. Full-duplex communication between terminal and computer greatly speeds up the processing activity.

Channel Enhancers
Earlier in this section, front-end processors were described as computers responsible for traffic management tasks. The following is a description of some of the activities that these front-end processors carry out.

Multiplexors   *Multiplexors* are used to map groups of lower-speed data so that they can be sent simultaneously over a higher-speed channel. In this way, the channel can be used more efficiently. Multiplexing is achieved by dividing the total transmission capacity of a shared channel into smaller portions called subchannels which can be used by individual devices. Each

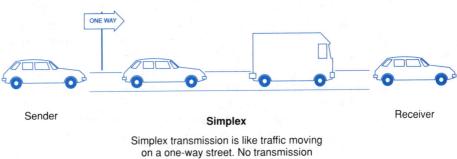

Sender Simplex Receiver

Simplex

Simplex transmission is like traffic moving
on a one-way street. No transmission
in the wrong direction is allowed.

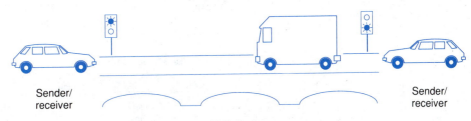

Sender/
receiver

Sender/
receiver

Half-duplex

Half-duplex transmission is like traffic moving
on a bridge wide enough to allow only one car
across at a time. When no cars are on the bridge
in the left-to-right direction, transmission may
proceed in the right-to-left direction.

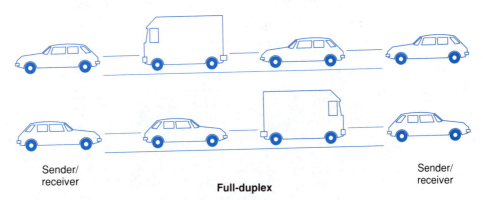

Sender/
receiver

Sender/
receiver

Full-duplex

Full-duplex transmission is like
conventional traffic moving both left-to-right
and right-to-left simultaneously.

FIGURE A.54
Traffic analogy for data transmission alternatives

subchannel operates independently. The two most common types of multiplexing are time-division and frequency-division multiplexing.

In *time-division multiplexing*, the time available for transmission is broken into pieces called slots. Different devices are each assigned a slot. The multiplexor takes the incoming message, delays it, and places it into an assigned time slot. During a given time slot, a subchannel uses the entire bandwidth. Various schemes are used to assign devices to time slots.

In *frequency-division multiplexing*, the total bandwidth (i.e., the spectrum of frequencies that can be handled by the transmission media) is divided into subchannels, by assigning each one a different frequency range. This is how FM radio stations are assigned frequencies. The multiplexor takes the simultaneous traffic from the subchannels and transmits each in its own frequency

Time-Division Multiplexing, Baseband Technology

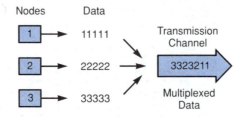

Frequency-Division Multiplexing, Baseband Technology

Stations Sharing One Channel

One Physical Cable

Many Frequency Channels

Stations with Unique Dedicated Channels

FIGURE A.55
Multiplexing techniques

range, with the total using the whole bandwidth. At the receiving end, the signal must then be redivided into its subchannel frequency components.

Figure A.55 shows these two forms of multiplexing.

Concentrators *Concentrators* are computers which are used to move data through channels more efficiently. Concentrators take advantage of the spaces between transmissions to fill in data from other devices. This allows more devices to share a given channel than we would think the capacity would handle. For example, a concentrator might be used when data is to be collected from several local sites and then sent to a remote computer for processing. Low-speed lines such as regular telephone lines might be used to connect several terminals to a central location. Then the concentrator would group this data together and send it over a higher-speed channel to its destination. The advantage of using a concentrator is that cheaper, low-speed lines can be used to connect the terminals to the central site where communication volume might be low or intermittent. Then an expensive, high-speed line would be used to connect the concentrator with the destination computer where the volume is high and continuous. Figure A.56 shows a network configuration employing a multiplexor as a concentrator.

Message Switching *Message switching* refers to the dynamic routing of messages given the traffic on certain lines. That is, if one route is being heavily utilized, a message can be sent along another route to its destination. An analogy to message switching is listening to the helicopter report on the radio, learning of a traffic jam on one's normal route home, and deciding to take an alternate route. One form of message switching is called message *store-and-forward*, in which the message is held for a while before it is sent on to the destination. Sometimes messages do not need to be received immediately after being sent. For example, a message created on Wednesday informing all users of a week-end computer shutdown may not need to be delivered until the next morning. In this case, the message can be stored and transmitted at a later time when traffic is light. This allows for better management of the flow of messages in a network and permits the transmission of low-priority messages at times when the network is underutilized.

Amplification As pointed out in the discussion of microwave transmission, signals sent through the airwaves often need some assistance to reach their destination. The electrical signals coming out of a computer cannot generate signals strong enough to travel any distance without being drowned out by noise. Therefore *repeaters* are needed to make the signal strong again when it is being sent over a distance. In addition, signals are sent in a straight line. Since the earth is curved, relay stations are needed to receive the signal and send it in another straight line to the next relay station until the ultimate destination is reached. Figure A.53 shows a microwave relay station.

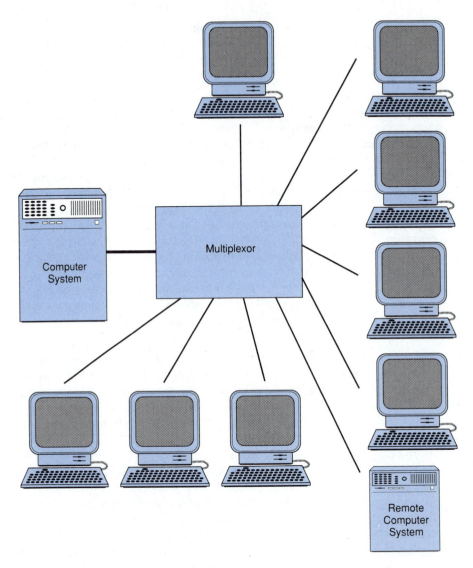

FIGURE A.56
Network with a multiplexor

III. COMPUTER SOFTWARE

Overview

Computer software refers to the procedures which govern the behavior of the hardware. The software instructs the computer in how to carry out certain activities. Software can be divided into two major categories: application software and system software. *Application software* is used to solve a specific business problem. An accounting program is an example of application software. This software can be developed by the personnel within the using organization or purchased from a commercial software company. *System software*, on the other hand, is more general in its intended and potential use. System software is not usually written by a business but by a computer vendor or an organization specializing in software development.

Each type of software provides a different function, but both are needed to successfully use the computer. The relationship between system software, application software, and computer hardware is shown in Figure A.57.

System Software

The objective of system software is to facilitate the use of the computer by managing the CPU and other devices associated with the computer. It provides general management functions such as managing the primary memory, carry-

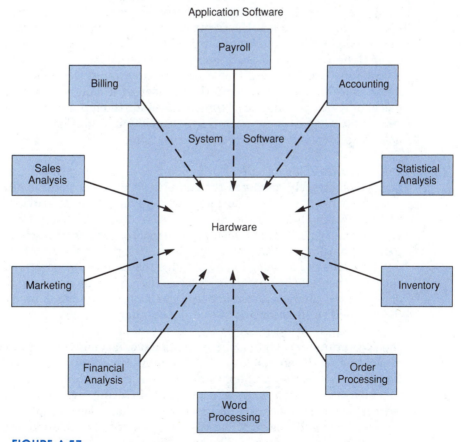

FIGURE A.57
Relationship between hardware, system software, and application software

ing out storage and retrieval from secondary storage, carrying out communication activities, and providing the correct application development environment. System software includes the operating system, language translators, data management software, and data communications software.

Operating Systems

The *operating system* controls the overall operation of the computer. It manages the computer resources so that they are used effectively. These resource management activities include managing the primary and secondary memory and coordinating the input, process, and output activities. Every computer has an operating system. Common operating systems for personal computers are *DOS* (<u>d</u>isk <u>o</u>perating <u>s</u>ystem), *OS/2, CP/M* (<u>c</u>ontrol <u>p</u>rogram for <u>m</u>icrocomputers), and *UNIX*.

Stacked Job Processing The first type of operating system did not provide for interactive processing. A user simply submitted a complete job and then waited for its turn to be processed. Often, a group of jobs to be completed would be assembled and then processed sequentially. This is referred to as *stacked job processing*. Users often had to wait quite a while before their jobs would be run and the output produced. Stacked job processing was used during the first and second computer generations. In today's interactive mode, jobs can be submitted from multiple input sources and processed much more quickly. The time that a user of a modern computer waits is based only on the amount of time it takes for the job itself to run. The "wait time" until the job is submitted has been eliminated. Figure A.58 shows the activities involved in stacked job processing.

The Executive The *executive* or *supervisor* is that part of the operating system which directly manages the computer's resources and is always stored in primary memory when the computer is in operation. It provides such functions as loading (moving data and programs from secondary storage into primary memory), selecting which job to execute, handling program errors, and printing output. In PCs the supervisor is stored in the ROM.

A *command language* is a language that allows the user to interact with the supervisor of the operating system. It enables the user to sign on or gain access to the computer, execute a program or utility, or call up a *directory* or list of the files the user has stored in secondary storage.

Multiprogramming Operating systems have varying degrees of complexity, depending on the complexity of the computer configuration they must manage. The greater the complexity of the operating system, the more computer resources it takes up. That is, a complex operating system will require more primary memory space and processing time than a less complex one. One factor which contributes significantly to complexity is the number of users the computer system supports. The operating systems of most PCs support only

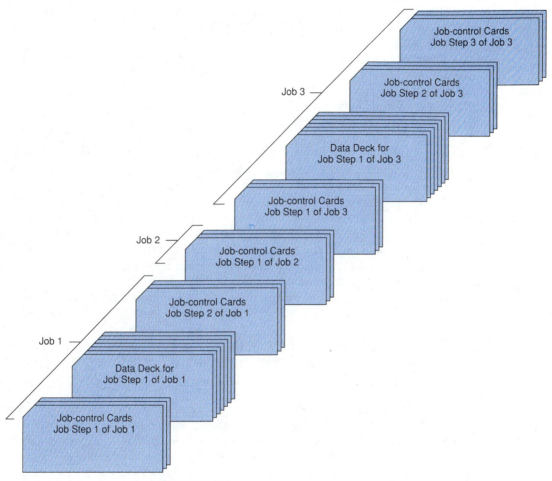

FIGURE A.58
Sample input decks for stacked job processing

a single user at a time and, therefore, do not have to coordinate the ownership of separate users' files or manage the interaction between users. Sharing in this sense occurs when users take turns on the machine. Such sharing is, then, accomplished by the use of procedures established by the users or systems support personnel. However, when a system supports multiple users who are signed on to the computer at the same time, the operating system must coordinate the transfer of control between the jobs of the various users and ownership and access to users' files.

The rationale for having more than one user of a computer is to more efficiently utilize the CPU by taking advantage of the speed with which it accomplishes tasks. When the computer is executing a job, both the program(s) and data are in the primary memory. When that job is completed, the computer has to wait to execute the next job until the appropriate data and programs are loaded into primary memory. The CPU of a single-user computer is idle during this waiting period. To remedy this inefficiency, more than one program and corresponding data can be stored in main memory by means of a *multiprogramming* operating system. Primary memory is split into partitions and each is able to store a different job. In some systems, primary memory is divided into equal-size partitions. Usually, more jobs can be stored in main memory with variable partitions, but the operating system is more complex. The use of these partitions allows the computer to instantaneously switch between the various users' jobs when the execution of one is stopped. A job stops when it terminates either normally or abnormally (e.g., an error occurs) or requires additional data.

Jobs in primary memory are executed in *round-robin* priority fashion until they terminate. This means that one job is executed, then the next, and so on, in an order based on their priority and when they entered main memory. This method improves the overall throughput of the jobs through the system. However, it may increase the elapsed time taken to execute a specific job, because a very lengthy job could tie up the system if executed for a long time without interruption. The number of jobs in main memory depends on the size of main memory, the size of the jobs, and the memory partitioning scheme that is employed.

All mainframe computers have multiprogramming operating systems. Many minicomputers and supermicrocomputers have multiprogramming capability as well.

Multitasking A task is an element of a job. In most microcomputers, a user can run only one task at a time. For example, the computer cannot run one program while printing output from another. *Multitasking* operating systems allow more than one task to be active at a time. To facilitate this, the *windowing* capability allows the components of more than one task to be displayed on the screen at once. Windowing is a function that allows the user to divide the screen into several areas. Each area or window can display a different task so that the user can move between them. For example, a user may be using a word processing language and find out that some data is needed from a spreadsheet. In a multitasking environment, the user can jump directly from the word processing program to the spreadsheet program. In a non-multitasking environment, the user would have to exit the word processing program, return to the operating system, and call up the spreadsheet program to get the desired information. Then the user would have to reverse the process to get back into the word processing program. In a multitasking environment, both word processing and spreadsheet programs can be active at the same time.

Job Scheduling A job is selected for processing based on a number of schemes. One selection technique is to process jobs in the order in which they are submitted for execution. This is referred to as *first in first out (FIFO)*. In this scheme, all jobs have equal priority. Other selection algorithms are based on the assumption that jobs have differing priorities. Priority assignment may be based on a variety of factors, and the specific factors and their relative weights would depend on the needs of the organization. Factors may include the user's position in the company, the part of the organization in which the user works, and the resources required to complete the job.

Time Sharing A *time-sharing* operating system extends a multiprogramming environment by interrupting a job's execution after a prespecified amount of CPU time has been utilized. This amount of CPU time is referred to as a *time slice*. Thus, a job is executed until it terminates, requires data or another routine, or exhausts its time slice. When execution of one job is interrupted, the next job is immediately started. Jobs are executed in a round-robin fashion until termination occurs, and then another job is loaded into main memory. The advantage of time sharing is that a long job is prevented from dominating the computer's resources; this improves overall job throughput. With a time-sharing operating system, more jobs can be accommodated, especially those involving interactive processing, because the computer can be processing another job while the user is typing at the keyboard.

Virtual Storage Primary memory is not infinite. In a multiprogramming and time-sharing environment, several different jobs are to be placed in the main memory. Sometimes, however, an entire job will not fit into the available memory partition. In this case, the job cannot be executed until a later time when a partition of sufficient size can be created or unless the program is divided up into smaller portions. Since users do not want to have the burden of dividing their programs and data into pieces that will fit in main memory, virtual storage was developed.

In a computing environment which has *virtual storage*, the primary memory appears to be infinite, because the operating system divides the job into pieces and moves these pieces in and out of main memory in a manner that facilitates execution. The parts of the job that are not currently needed are moved temporarily to disk storage. Doing this gives the users the impression that they have *virtually unlimited* memory. The major disadvantage of virtual storage is that it takes time to move the pieces in and out of main memory. When this movement gets excessive, the system performance can degrade and the computer system is said to be *thrashing*. In most cases, however, the impact of virtual storage on performance is transparent to the user. It relieves the user from having to make a given job fit into the computer's memory. Virtual storage is available on all large computers (supercomputers, mainframe computers, minicomputers), as well as on supermicrocomputers.

Family of Computers A *family of computers* is a series of computers based on the same hardware architecture. A single operating system is designed to support a family with upward compatibility between its members. That is, a program which runs on one computer in the family will run on any larger machine in the family. The first major family of computers was the IBM 360 series, which introduced the architecture for the general-purpose computer.

In addition to hardware families defined by a single manufacturer, there are families based on the ability to run the same operating system. These are machines that are called *compatibles*. Such families are widespread in the microcomputer environment but have existed in the mainframe arena as well — for example, Amdahl's series of machines developed as a compatible alternative to the IBM 370 series. Microcomputer families are based on the underlying CPU chip which is used and their ability to run the same operating system and applications. Microcomputer operating systems that run on a series of machines are CP/M, UNIX, and DOS. An application that runs on an IBM PC under a version of DOS should be portable to other DOS-based computers, such as those produced by WYSE, Leading Edge, or Tandy.

Input/Output Management   A computer system performs three major functions: input, processing, and output. The operating system helps in the execution of these three functions by managing the resources which perform them. It also establishes the connections between the CPU and input/output devices such as the printer, terminal, and disk drives. In a personal computer environment, this connection is established by instructions located in the ROM which are called the *BIOS* — the basic input-output system.

In the first generation, the computer could only control and concentrate on one of these functions at a time. That is, the computer could not simultaneously perform input, processing, and output activities. This had an adverse effect on throughput. To remedy the situation, operating systems were designed to incorporate an *input-output control system (IOCS)* which could simultaneously control these activities. The use of IOCS dramatically improved throughput. The IOCS was incorporated into the operating systems of second-generation computers.

Many computer jobs generate output that needs to be printed. Since the printing activity is much slower than processing, it can constrain the system's throughput. For example, a job that is being processed stops execution when output needs to be printed. A second job then begins execution and continues until it requires the printer. But the second job cannot commence printing if the previous job is still printing and therefore cannot continue executing. In such a situation, when the computer is not efficiently utilizing its CPU because it is waiting for input or output, it is said to be *input/output (I/O) bound*. An I/O bound computer does not fully use its most expensive resource, the CPU. This situation was remedied when operating systems began to provide the *spooling* (simultaneous peripheral operation on-line) capability. With spooling, the outputs of jobs are moved out of the primary memory and temporarily stored on a secondary storage device while waiting for the printing resources to be available. The job can then continue processing. Spooling can also be used for input. Spooling allows the computer to perform input or output functions at higher speeds than the normal, slower speeds of the peripheral equipment. To maximize throughput, the output is printed according to a priority scheme other than first in first out (FIFO). For example, the smallest output tasks might be performed before larger ones.

Other Types of System Software

System software facilitates the use of the computer, manages the computer resources, and provides common utilities to the user community. While the operating system is the most important type of system software, there are other types which provide special functions.

Program Translator A computer can only understand machine code—that is, the binary form of the computer program. Therefore, when a user develops a program in a language like COBOL or BASIC, it must be converted into machine code before the computer can execute it. The program written in COBOL or BASIC is called the *source program*, and the machine-code version is called the *object program*. A *program translator* is system software which will translate a program written in a specific language into machine code. There are two types of program translators used to translate these kinds of programs.

A *compiler* translates the entire source program first and then executes the object program. This is a two-step process. If this program is to be run many times, the object program version will be stored so that the user need only execute the object program. This will save time because the program will not have to be translated each time it is run. A disadvantage of a compiler is that the programmer does not receive immediate feedback about errors in the program. If there is a problem with the program, the errors will not be detected until the compiler translates and then attempts to execute it. Programs written in COBOL normally use compilers for translation.

An *interpreter*, on the other hand, translates and executes only a portion of the source program at a time. This process is then repeated until the execution of the whole program is complete. The main advantage of using an interpreter is that it provides the user with immediate feedback. If there is a problem with the program, the programmer is notified immediately and will not have to wait until the entire program is translated and execution is attempted. The disadvantage of using interpreters is that the program must be translated from the source program to the object program every time it is executed. If the program is to be run frequently, a considerable amount of time could be wasted. Interpreters are especially useful for languages like BASIC which are used to teach people how to program, because the student receives immediate feedback.

Editor An *editor* is a program for creating and modifying files. Before a program can be run, the data and instructions must be entered into the computer. The editor is used for this purpose. It has commands for adding, deleting, and saving data much like those in a word processing program. The file that is created may either contain data or be a program. Editors simplify program development by providing an easy-to-use facility for program creation and modification.

Graphics Software   Graphics software enables a user to present information in graphical form, such as a pie chart, bar chart, or graph, instead of presenting it in tabular or prose form. It allows the user to input the data which will be the basis of the graphics. It also allows the user to specify the parameters for the graphic output.

Data Management Software   *Database management systems (DBMS)* are described in Chapter 6 as a method of data storage and retrieval and reporting. They provide a language for defining the data to be stored, for manipulating that data, and for retrieving it. They also provide utilities for security, privacy, and backup.

Data Communication Software   Data communication software is necessary for carrying out data communication activities. For example, if one wanted to use a personal computer to access data stored in another computer, he or she would need to have data communication software loaded in the computer to carry out that task. Data communication hardware is described earlier in the appendix; Chapter 7 provides a detailed discussion of the activities involved in data communication.

IV. PROGRAMMING LANGUAGES

The reason for using computers is to accomplish the kinds of tasks that are carried out by application software. It is application software which supports record-keeping or decision-making needs of a company. The programs which are part of business information systems are examples of application software. Chapter 4 discusses the role of programming languages in a computer-based information system and highlights a few popular languages. It is the purpose of this section to discuss in greater depth the variety of programming languages that are available for developing application software. Programming languages can be classified into low-level languages and high-level languages. They reflect five generations of software improvements.

Low-Level Languages

Low-level languages are those which are tied directly to the particular hardware features of a given computer. They were the first programming languages available, and considerable knowledge about computer hardware was required to use them to write programs.

Machine Language

The first language available to programmers required them to write programs in the language of the computer—that is, binary. These are called *machine languages*. Machine language is the only language directly understandable by the computer. In machine language the programmer must specify the instructions through the use of a binary code and must reference data by naming its actual storage location. Machine languages are *first-generation languages*. Figure A.59 shows an example of a program written in machine language.

Machine languages are *machine family dependent*. That is, a machine-language program will only work on one family of computers. It cannot be removed to another kind of computer for execution.

One advantage of using machine language is that since programs are already expressed in binary form, they do not require any further processing (such as language translation) before execution. This saves both processing time and the space in primary memory needed to hold the program translator software. In addition, if machine language is used correctly, the programmer

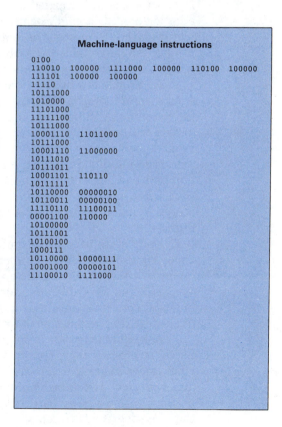

FIGURE A.59

Machine-language instructions and assembler code (mnemonics) for a program to compute and print out the result of 2 times 4

has a considerable amount of operational control and can ensure the efficient utilization of computer resources.

However, there are also many disadvantages of using machine language. Programming in machine language is extremely tedious. The programmer must learn the binary form of all the commands and must keep track of the locations in which the data is stored. This requires the programmer to have detailed knowledge of the hardware. Since both the program itself and the output from the program are expressed as a series of zeros and ones, it is extremely difficult to detect and correct errors or to make changes to the program. In addition, it would be very difficult for someone unfamiliar with the program to understand what the program is about.

Assembly Language

Assembly language is symbolic machine language. It represents the second generation of computer software and is referred to as a *second-generation language*. To make the programming task easier, mnemonics are used to represent the operations to be carried out. For example, ADD might be used to express addition and SUB might be used to express subtraction. To free the programmer from the requirement of remembering the physical location of the data, assembly language added the ability to assign symbolic names to the actual storage locations. The symbolic address of some data is called a *variable*.

A variable is a memory location whose value may be changed during the execution of a program. There are two basic types of data that can be stored in the computer through the use of variables—numeric and character. The type of data will determine the amount of space required for storage. Therefore, the variable name must indicate what type of data is stored in that location. *Numeric variables* hold numbers that are involved in arithmetic expressions. Only numbers can be stored in numeric variables. *Character variables* contain data that is not involved in arithmetic expressions. Examples of data that can be stored in a character variable are a name, an address, and a social security number.

Each statement in assembly language represents one line of machine code. Figure A.59 shows an example of a program written in assembly language, with its machine-code equivalent.

Since an assembly-language program is not expressed in binary form, it must be converted into machine code before it is processed. This is accomplished by a program translator called an *assembler*.

Assembly language is only slightly easier to use than machine language. Since programs are written in symbolic rather than binary form, it is somewhat easier to use, correct errors, and make changes, but it is still a rather tedious process. Like machine language, it is machine dependent and is only portable within a given hardware family. Assembly-language programs provide the same degree of efficiency and control for the very experienced and capable programmer as those written in machine language.

High-Level Languages

High-level programming languages were developed to facilitate the programming process. These languages represented an improvement on earlier programming languages by making them easier to learn and use and making it easier to read and correct programs. There are many different types of high-level languages, classified by significant improvements which place them in one of three software generations. The category of high-level languages includes third-, fourth-, and fifth-generation languages. They can also be classified by their intended use such as business or scientific, and general purpose or special purpose.

Third-Generation Languages

Third-generation languages are structured and are called procedural programming languages. A program written in a *third-generation language* is called a source program. Before it can be used it must be converted into binary form. This form of a program is called an object program. One statement in a high-level programming language is usually represented as several statements in machine code. The software which accomplishes this translation is either a compiler or an interpreter. This process was discussed earlier, in the section on system software. Figure A.60 shows a BASIC program that computes the sum and average of ten numbers inputted by the user.

There is a tradeoff involved in using a high-level language. On the one hand, it is much easier to develop and use programs. However, the programmer loses some control over how the program will actually be executed, because many of these decisions are handled by the program translator. On balance, though, programming is much faster with a high-level than with a low-level language. Standard versions exist for many programming languages. The standard version is a form of a language which is approved by the *National Bureau of Standards*, and the standard form is called the *ANSI (American National Standards Institute)* version. The existence of a standard version of

```
10   REM COMPUTE SUM AND AVERAGE OF 10 NUMBERS
20   LET SUM = 0
30   FOR I = 1 TO 10
40     INPUT N(I)
50     LET SUM = SUM + N(I)
60   NEXT I
70   LET AVG = SUM / 10
80   PRINT "SUM = ",SUM
90   PRINT "AVERAGE = ",AVG
999  END
```

FIGURE A.60
BASIC program to compute the sum and average of ten numbers entered by the user

a programming language means that it will be compatible with a variety of computers. This in turn provides a degree of portability. A program is *portable* when the same source program can be used on more than one computer. The following is a discussion of some of the most common third-generation languages.

FORTRAN (formula translator), the oldest of the general-purpose scientific programming languages, was designed to allow scientists and engineers to write programs in mathematical form. It was first introduced on second-generation scientific computers in 1957. Today it is available on all sizes of computers from all manufacturers. Although it was developed for scientific use, the current version, FORTRAN 77, is suitable for solving both business and scientific problems. Statements in FORTRAN are easy to read and easy to learn. While it provides the mathematical precision necessary for arithmetic operations, the input and output operations are more cumbersome than those of some newer languages. In addition, the length of variable names is more restricted and, therefore, less descriptive than in some other languages. Finally, the manipulation of character data can be difficult.

COBOL (common business oriented language) was designed in 1959 as a general-purpose business language to be used on second-generation computers. Over half of all business programs in use today have been written in COBOL. Programs in COBOL are expected to be portable and easy to maintain. The language was designed to facilitate the manipulation of large amounts of input and output data. The statements of the language are English-like to enhance readability. However, this results in programs which are very wordy and usually longer than an equivalent program written in some other language. Figure A.61 shows a COBOL program equivalent to the BASIC program in Figure A.60. COBOL is available on a variety of types and sizes of computers.

To make the text of the program resemble something written in English, a COBOL program is divided into a series of divisions:

Identification division—identifies the programmer and the purpose of the program

Environment division—identifies the hardware environment in which the program will operate

Data division—defines the data to be used in the program

Procedure division—describes the processing activities to be carried out

COBOL is more portable than most other languages since the U.S. government played a large part in the development and standardization of the language. In fact, the major motivation for the development of COBOL was to have a common language to support government data processing needs.

Since COBOL programs are quite lengthy, the language is difficult to learn and takes several years to master. The process of writing and correcting a COBOL program is also lengthy. The syntax is very rigid and requires the programmer to be painstakingly aware of details such as spacing. COBOL is geared more to batch processing than to interactive applications.

BASIC (beginner's all-purpose symbolic instruction code) was designed as a general-purpose interactive programming language which would be easy to learn and use. Made available for general use in 1964, BASIC was initially intended for teaching students how to program. It was designed with a minimum of restrictions and conventions governing activities such as input and output. Its scope of applicability has greatly increased with its widespread availability and use on microcomputers. It is currently the most common programming language used on microcomputers.

BASIC is easy to learn and simple to use for several reasons. One is that there are relatively few commands and their meaning is generally pretty clear (e.g., PRINT). It is also a conversational language. That is, it uses an interpreter which gives immediate feedback to the programmer about errors. Today, it is used for both business and mathematical applications. One significant drawback of BASIC is the lack of standardization across the various versions. Therefore, a version of BASIC that will work on an Apple computer will be different from the version used on an IBM computer. Figure A.60 shows a BASIC program.

PASCAL (named after the French mathematician Blaise Pascal) is a powerful general-purpose programming language developed by Nicklaus Wirth in the early 1970s. It has the simplicity in formula specification of FORTRAN, with COBOL's ability to operate on complex data structures. PASCAL is a block-structured language. That is, its programs are composed of a series of blocks or subprograms. The main program describes the control flow between the blocks. PASCAL supports a complex control structure and lends itself to structured programming. Because programs are logically structured into blocks, they are easier to maintain. PASCAL has only a few different types of statements. In addition, the terse nature of the language means that PASCAL programs are not self-documenting, or not easily read, except by the original programmer. PASCAL is primarily used as an alternative to FORTRAN. It does not have widespread use in business. Figure A.62 shows a PASCAL program equivalent to the BASIC and COBOL programs in Figures A.60 and A.61.

Ada (named after Lady Augusta Ada Byron, a computing pioneer along with Charles Babbage in the nineteenth century) was developed in response to a 1974 U.S. Department of Defense decision that COBOL would not satisfy its future computing needs and that a new general-purpose programming language would be needed. A standard version of Ada was developed and approved in the early 1980s. Ada was intended to reduce development and operation costs and improve the reliability of programs. The intent was to have programs running as efficiently as possible. For a combination of reasons, Ada is not widely used for business applications. One reason is the current large investment of most companies in COBOL programs. Another is the high cost of

```
IDENTIFICATION DIVISION.
PROGRAM-ID.        AVERAGES.
AUTHOR.            DEB KNUDSEN.
DATE-COMPILED.
ENVIRONMENT DIVISION.
CONFIGURATION SECTION.
    SOURCE-COMPUTER. HP-3000.
    OBJECT-COMPUTER. HP-3000.
INPUT-OUTPUT SECTION.
FILE-CONTROL.
    SELECT NUMBER-FILE ASSIGN TO "NUMFILE".
    SELECT REPORT-FILE ASSIGN TO "PRINT,UR,A,LP(CCTL)".
DATA DIVISION.
FILE SECTION.
FD  NUMBER-FILE
    LABEL RECORDS ARE STANDARD
    DATA RECORD IS NUMBER-REC.
01  NUMBER-REC                     PIC S9(7)V99.
FD  REPORT-FILE
    LABEL RECORDS ARE STANDARD
    DATA RECORD IS REPORT-REC.
01  REPORT-REC                     PIC X(100).

WORKING-STORAGE SECTION.
01  END-OF-NUMBER-FILE-FLAG        PIC X(3) VALUE SPACES.
    88  END-OF-NUMBER-FILE                  VALUE "YES".
01  SUM-OF-NUMBERS                 PIC S9(7)V99.
01  AVERAGE-OF-NUMBERS             PIC S9(7)V99.
01  NUMBER-OF-NUMBERS              PIC 9(5).

01  WS-REPORT-REC.
    05  FILLER                     PIC X(2)   VALUE SPACES.
    05  FILLER                     PIC X(17)  VALUE
                                   "Sum of Numbers = ".
    05  WS-SUM-OF-NUMBERS          PIC Z,ZZZ,ZZZ.99-.
    05  FILLER                     PIC X(3)   VALUE SPACES.
    05  FILLER                     PIC X(15)  VALUE
                                   "# of Numbers = ".
    05  WS-NUMBER-OF-NUMBERS       PIC ZZZZ9.
    05  FILLER                     PIC X(3)   VALUE SPACES.
    05  FILLER                     PIC X(21)  VALUE
                                   "Average of Numbers = ".
    05  WS-AVERAGE-OF-NUMBERS      PIC Z,ZZZ,ZZZ.99-.
    05  FILLER                     PIC X(8)   VALUE SPACES.
```

FIGURE A.61
COBOL program to compute the sum and average of ten numbers entered by the user

```
PROCEDURE DIVISION.

100-MAIN-PROGRAM.
    OPEN INPUT  NUMBER-FILE
         OUTPUT REPORT-FILE.
    MOVE SPACES TO REPORT-REC.
    MOVE ZEROS TO SUM-OF-NUMBERS.
    MOVE ZEROS TO AVERAGE-OF-NUMBERS.
    MOVE ZEROS TO NUMBER-OF-NUMBERS.

    READ NUMBER-FILE
      AT END MOVE "YES" TO END-OF-NUMBER-FILE-FLAG.

    IF END-OF-NUMBER-FILE
      NEXT SENTENCE
    ELSE
      PERFORM 200-PROCESS-NUMBER-FILE
        UNTIL END-OF-NUMBER-FILE.

    PERFORM 300-COMPUTE-AVERAGE.

    PERFORM 400-PRINT-RESULTS.

    CLOSE NUMBER-FILE
          REPORT-FILE.

    STOP RUN.

200-PROCESS-NUMBER-FILE.
    ADD 1 TO NUMBER-OF-NUMBERS.
    ADD NUMBER-REC TO SUM-OF-NUMBERS.

    READ NUMBER-FILE
      AT END MOVE "YES" TO END-OF-NUMBER-FILE-FLAG.

300-COMPUTE-AVERAGE.
    DIVIDE SUM-OF-NUMBERS BY NUMBER-OF-NUMBERS
      GIVING AVERAGE-OF-NUMBERS.

400-PRINT-RESULTS.
    MOVE SUM-OF-NUMBERS TO WS-SUM-OF-NUMBERS.
    MOVE NUMBER-OF-NUMBERS TO WS-NUMBER-OF-NUMBERS.
    MOVE AVERAGE-OF-NUMBERS TO WS-AVERAGE-OF-NUMBERS.

WRITE REPORT-REC FROM WS-REPORT-REC.
```

FIGURE A.61 *(continued)*

```pascal
PROGRAM average(input, output);
{ Compute the sum and average of ten numbers }
VAR num, sum, avg : real;
    i : integer;

BEGIN
    sum:=0.0;
    FOR i := 1 TO 10 DO
    BEGIN
      read(num);
      sum:=sum + num;
    END;
    avg:=sum/10;
    writeln('Sum =',sum);
    writeln('Average =',avg);
END.
```

FIGURE A.62

PASCAL program to compute the sum and average of ten numbers entered by the user

using Ada. A final reason is that Ada is difficult to learn. Therefore, its applicability to non-government systems is usually restricted to large, complex applications.

C, which was developed by Bell Labs in the mid-1970s, is a language used to develop system software. This language provides the ease of use of a high-level language while giving the programmer the direct access to the hardware that is available with low-level languages. C allows the programmer to have the same direct control of the hardware that is available with assembly language. At the same time, it possesses the characteristics of a high-level language such as control of data structures and powerful commands that enable quicker pro-

```c
#include <stdio.h>

main ()
    {
        int i, num;
        float sum;

        printf("Enter numbers \n");
        sum = 0;
        for (i = 0; i < 10; i++)
          {
              scanf("%d",&num);
              sum = sum + num;
          }
        printf("Sum = %3.1f\n",sum);
        printf("Average = %3.1f\n",sum / 10.0);
    }
```

FIGURE A.63

C program to compute the sum and average of ten numbers entered by the user

gram development. One must be a skilled programmer to use and understand a C program. Figure A.63 shows a C program equivalent to the BASIC, COBOL, and PASCAL programs in Figures A.60–A.62.

Figure A.64 presents a comparison of some third-generation languages. It shows the different ways that common functions are expressed in these different languages.

Fourth-Generation Languages

Fourth-generation languages (4GLs) are also referred to as *nonprocedural languages* and *problem-oriented languages*, because these languages focus on the results or *problem* to be solved rather than the *procedure* for doing so. These languages can be used by non-programmers because they are easy to use. They are also used by programmers because they improve productivity. Since 4GLs allow the user to concentrate on *what* needs to be done rather than *how* it is accomplished, they tend to be more limited in applicability than third-generation languages.

A fourth-generation language has been described as a high-level language that provides an integrated syntax for data definition, data management, and data analysis. It can yield productivity gains of ten times that of COBOL and can be learned in much less time.[1] Fourth-generation languages are not languages in the same sense as first-, second-, or third-generation languages. Rather, a 4GL can be thought of as a template or tool that enables the user to carry out some processing function more easily. The most common functions carried out by 4GLs are report generation, data storage and retrieval, spreadsheet use, and statistics. The general processing commands exist; the user has only to enter the specific data. This orientation represents one significant difference between fourth and other generations of languages: they are special-purpose languages. One significant difference between third- and fourth-generation languages is that, whereas third-generation languages are *general purpose*, fourth-generation languages are *special purpose*. This means that, whereas a 3GL can accomplish a wide variety of processing tasks, the range of processing tasks a 4GL can accomplish is more restricted. There is a definite and limited set of processing activities that the language can carry out.

RPG (report program generator), developed in 1969, was the first nonprocedural language. While its development came during the third generation of languages, its features are similar to those of today's fourth-generation languages. It was different from any existing languages in that it was designed to be report-oriented rather than procedure-oriented. RPG was developed to be used by businesses to process data, use and update files, and generate reports. Its primary market was small businesses using small minicomputers. As such, it was designed to be easy and quickly learned by non-programmers.

RPG programs are coded by filling out several forms:

- the file layout description;
- the input description;

FIGURE A.64
Comparison of third-generation languages

Instructions	Higher-Level Languages		
	BASIC	**FORTRAN**	**COBOL**
Move	LET A = 5	A = 5	MOVE 5 TO A.
Arithmetic	LET A = B*C	A = B*C	MULTIPLY B BY C GIVING A.
Comparison	IF A = 5 GOTO 10	IF (A.EQ.5) GO TO 10	IF A = 5 GO TO MAIN-JOB.
Control	GOTO 10 STOP	GO TO 10 STOP	GO TO MAIN-JOB. STOP RUN.
Loops	FOR J = 1 TO 5 ⋮ NEXT J	DO 20 J=1,5 ⋮ 20 CONTINUE	PERFORM MAIN-JOB 5 TIMES. or PERFORM MAIN-JOB VARYING J FROM 1 BY 1 UNTIL J>5.
Read	READ A,B,C ⋮ DATA 5,9,−2	READ(5,30) A,B,C 30 FORMAT(3I5)	READ CARD-FILE AT END. GO TO END-OF-JOB.
Write	PRINT A,B,C	WRITE(6,15) A,B,C 15 FORMAT('1',3I5)	WRITE PRINT-LINE AFTER ADVANCING 1 LINE.

- the output description, including the layout of reports and screens; and
- the calculations that must be performed to produce outputs from the input.

The data from these forms is then input from the keyboard. There are three major drawbacks of RPG. First, it has limited capabilities and is available on a limited number of computers. Second, care must be taken when filling out the forms. Finally, there is no standard version of RPG and, consequently, it has little portability.

In addition to the form of computer interaction present in languages like RPG, fourth-generation languages provide several other means of invoking information processing and retrieval activities. The use of a *query language* enables a user to request information by expressing a few simple commands. This is useful for a non-programmer who simply wishes to view or retrieve some data. A fourth-generation language which has a query language would also have a form of the language which more closely resembles third-generation languages. This is referred to as the *command language*. Using a command language gives a programmer or skilled user more control over the retrieval or processing activities and, therefore, a greater range of options.

A 4GL which demonstrates these features is *Focus*. Focus is one of the oldest fourth-generation languages, initially developed for IBM mainframe

FIGURE A.64 (continued)

Data	Higher-Level Languages		
	BASIC	**FORTRAN**	**COBOL**
Variable names	Single letter or letter number (e.g., A, A1)	6 characters (e.g., FUN, FUN2)	30 characters; hyphen OK (e.g., MAIN-LINE-ROUTINE)
Data types	A = number A$ = string All numbers real	I-N = integer Others = real number Other variable types can be implicitly declared.	PIC 999 = number PIC AAA = alpha PIC XXX = either
Data length	1 word	1 word	Length of picture: PIC XX = 2 bytes PIC X(20) = 20 bytes
Arrays	DIM A(15)	DIMENSION A(15)	A OCCURS 15 TIMES PIC 99.
Labels	Line numbers (e.g., 10)	Line numbers (e.g., 10)	Paragraph names (e.g., MAIN-LINE-ROUTINE)
Comments	REM(ARK)	C in column 1	* in column 7
Data values	READ, ASSIGNMENT	DATA A/5/	A PIC 9 VALUE 5
Messages	PRINT "Hello"	PRINT 5 5 FORMAT(' Hello')	DISPLAY "Hello"

computers and now available for IBM and IBM-compatible personal computers. The special purpose of this language is data management. That is, Focus facilitates the storage and retrieval of data within an information system. In addition to providing both query and command language forms of interaction, Focus is also able to interact with programs written in third-generation languages such as COBOL, and with statistical languages.

Another method for interaction with a 4GL is the use of a menu. A menu enables a user to select the desired processing activities from a range of alternatives. Lotus 1-2-3 is an example of a 4GL which employs this method of communicating commands to the computer. Because Lotus is a tool for spreadsheet development, its processing capabilities are limited to those related to this application. Lotus 1-2-3 is designed to enable the user to enter data and formulas and is capable of providing a range of options for formatting the resulting output. Microsoft's EXCEL, another spreadsheet product, and financial modeling tools such as IFPS are other examples of this type of fourth-generation language.

In fourth-generation languages designed to carry out statistical operations work, the user enters the commands specifying the particular statistical processing to be carried out and then supplies the necessary data. The language relieves the user of the tedious task of typing in all the statistical formulas. It also gives the user a simplified way of specifying the desired form of the output.

Fifth-Generation Languages

A *fifth-generation language* is one which incorporates artificial intelligence into its design, operation, or outputs. *Artificial intelligence (AI)* means that the activity, if performed by a person, would require human intelligence. There are two ways in which AI can be involved with a programming language.

One is that the output of the program can be an artificial intelligence application. That is, the language may be used to develop such artificial intelligence products as expert systems or robots. Languages such as *LISP* (list processing language) and *PROLOG* are the most popular languages used to develop artificial intelligence applications. Such languages provide the means to define the rules and knowledge base required for these very sophisticated applications.

The term is also used to describe languages which incorporate AI into their features. A language such as INTELLECT incorporates artificial intelligence in the form of natural language. *Natural language* means that the user can enter English-like commands to describe the activities to be carried out. Thus, users do not have to learn the special commands of a programming language. They can use their own "natural language." This enables users to be immediately productive with the use of the software. In addition to accepting English-like statements, some fifth-generation languages provide a collection of menus and windows which allow the users to select the appropriate activities to be carried out. There can be some problems with the interpretation of English statements, however. They may be ambiguous, resulting in the wrong answer or requiring the system to ask the user questions to clarify the request. To avoid these problems, natural languages require a dictionary in order to understand the vocabulary of the user. They must also have a collection of data from which the desired data can be selected. Therefore, before a natural language can be effectively used, the appropriate dictionary and database must exist.

V. INFORMATION PROCESSING GENERATIONS

A computer-based information system is composed of five resources: hardware, software, data, procedures, and people. Upon closer examination, we can note that each resource has undergone considerable change over the past four decades. When a significant advancement occurs, it signals the beginning of a new generation. The hardware and software generations were described earlier in this appendix. While it is commonplace to apply the notion of generations to hardware and software, we can also observe significant advances in the data, personnel, and procedures resources. The following is an overview of the data and personnel/procedures generations.

Data Generations

Chapter 6 considers data storage and retrieval concepts in greater detail. The purpose of this section is to review the advancements in methods of storage and retrieval, which is what is meant by the term *data generation*.

During the 1950s, in the *first data generation*, each computer program operated on a specific data set. The data was stored on sequential devices such as punched cards or magnetic tape. This made the process of responding to an inquiry very difficult. The only way to answer a question about a specific account, for example, was to look sequentially through long listings of computer output.

The *second data generation* represented a significant improvement in the way data could be accessed. The introduction of magnetic disk storage in the 1960s provided the capability for direct access to data. Using random and indexed files, a user could respond to a specific query. A given data set, however, was still only used by a single program.

The advent of databases in the 1970s ushered in the *third data generation*. With a database, data could be shared across applications. This meant that a common data set could be used by many different computer programs. This data was *physically* integrated, which means that the database was stored at one location. In the late 1970s, as integrated databases came into widespread use, organizations also began to recognize the importance of developing controls so that the integrity of the data could be guaranteed.

Two significant advances in data storage and retrieval during the 1980s have brought about the *fourth data generation*. Since the first databases were physically integrated, this meant that all of the data had to be stored in a single location. It also meant that the computer and storage devices involved had to have considerable storage capacity. The result was that databases were only available on large computers—mainframes and large minicomputers. In the 1980s, the capability of *logical* integration of data in a database became available. This means that an entire database does not have to reside in a single location. It can be *distributed* across several computers by utilizing data communication technology.

The other significant advance in the fourth data generation is that databases are now available on all sizes of computers. Therefore, the owner of a small business who has a single personal computer has access to the same shared data capabilities as the president of a large corporation. Databases are fast becoming the most common method of data storage and retrieval.

User Generations

Personnel refers to the people who are involved in the development, use, and management of information systems. The term *procedures* refers to the organizational practices related to the use of information systems by those personnel. For this reason, both personnel and procedures are implied in the concept of *user generations*.

The *first-generation users* were scientists and engineers who used the computer to perform complex calculations. Since early computers required interaction through machine or assembly language, only highly skilled individuals could carry out this task. These engineers were both the developers and the clients of the systems that were developed. That is, they developed and wrote the programs and were also the users of the output. For this reason, procedures were very informal. Since a scientist knew his or her own processing needs, formal procedures for identifying system requirements were not used. When change was called for, the person simply made whatever alterations were necessary for that particular application.

With the development of high-level languages such as FORTRAN and COBOL, computer use became available to more individuals and the need for programming skill grew. Therefore, along with the development of these languages came the advent of *second-generation users* — computer scientists educated specifically to design and use software tools. Despite the greater ease of using high-level languages, a considerable amount of skill was needed to successfully develop and use computer software. Since computer programmers were now developing systems for others to use, more formal procedures were established. System development methodologies were established and carefully followed. People who wanted changes made to their programs had to submit formal requests and wait their turn on the priority list. These computer programmers were also the computer operators. That is, when someone in an organization requested some information, it had to be provided by the computer programmers.

One problem with second-generation users was that, while they were very knowledgeable about the computer, they were often less knowledgeable about business practices. Therefore, a new group of users — MIS professionals — emerged as the *third-generation users*. Management information systems personnel were educated about both computers and business so that they could better understand the needs of the those requesting information systems support. These personnel also developed software using third-generation languages. To respond more effectively to the need for information to support management decision making, MIS personnel devoted a greater amount of time to understanding system requirements. Today, virtually all businesses of sufficient size have a data processing or management information systems department. This department is responsible for establishing and executing procedures governing the development and use of information systems and the use of data in their organizations.

The significant advance marked by the *fourth-generation users* is the fact that for the first time in the history of computing, individuals are able to design, use, and manage information systems without having considerable education about computers. These users are referred to as *end users*. End users are

	1950	1960	1970	1980	1990
HARDWARE **Mainframe**	*1st generation* (1951-58) Vacuum tubes	*2nd generation* (1959-63) Transistors	*3rd generation* (1964-75) Integrated circuits	*4th generation* (1975-88) Very large scale integration	*5th generation* (1990-) Artificial intelligence
PC				*1st generation* 8-bit (1975-81) Apple II, TRS-80 *2nd generation* 16-bit (1981-) IBM-PC	*3rd generation* 32-bit (1985-) IBM-PS/2 MOD. 80 Microvax, Macintosh II
SOFTWARE **Programming Languages**	*Low-level* *1st generation* Machine *2nd generation* Assembler *High-level Early 3rd generation* FORTRAN, COBOL	*3rd generation* PL/1, BASIC	*Early 4th generation* PASCAL, RPG (1969)	*Very high level* *4th generation* Spreadsheets: Visicalc (1979) Lotus 1-2-3 Problem-oriented languages: Focus, ORACLE, dBase	*5th generation* (Use artificial intelligence) INTELLECT Integrated tools: Symphony, Framework
Information Systems	Transaction (1953-) Processing Systems		Management (1965-) Information System	Decision (1975-) Support System Expert Systems (late 1970s-)	
DATA	*1st generation* Non-integrated data: Sequential tape files	*2nd generation* Non-integrated data: Disk files (direct access capability)	*3rd generation* Integrated data: Databases	*4th generation* Logically integrated data: Distributed databases	
USERS	*1st generation* Scientists and engineers	*2nd generation* Computer scientists *3rd generation* MIS professionals		*4th generation* End users	

FIGURE A.65

The relationship between hardware, software, data, and user generations

individuals who work in some business area outside the MIS department. Their role has moved from a passive one to an active one. There are several reasons why these individuals are now directly involved in computing activities. One reason is that computers are now much more accessible. The declining cost of technology and the ease of using fourth-generation software make it easier to own and operate a personal computer. Another reason is that many business personnel found it inefficient to go through an intermediary—a computer programmer or MIS specialist—in order to have their needs satisfied.

The presence of a new class of users has been accompanied by a greater emphasis on procedures. Since there are now many more computer users in an organization, and since many of these persons have not been formally educated about computers, new procedures have to be established. Many users now have to function as information system managers. Therefore, they have to be concerned with procedures governing backup, access to data, verification of input and processing activities, and acquisition of compatible technology. In recent years, MIS departments have placed a much greater emphasis on the development of end-user computing policies.

The relationship among the hardware, software, data, and user generations is depicted in Figure A.65.

APPENDIX NOTE

1. Gerald D. Cohen, President of Information Builders, Inc., presentation to the Boston Chapter of the Society for Information Management, March 1987.

GLOSSARY

acceptance test   The evaluation of a new system with respect to usability and consistency with the requirements document.

access system   A system used to facilitate the users' access to information. There are two kinds of access systems: record-keeping and transaction processing systems.

accuracy   The correctness of information.

action system   A system whose goal is to access some data, analyze it to reach a decision, and then carry out some activity.

Ada   A powerful structured programming language developed as an alternative to COBOL.

adaptive approach   A decision-making approach used in circumstances of uncertainty in which neither the goal nor the strategies are completely understood; the decision maker must constantly collect feedback about actions taken and make alterations in behavior as a result.

algorithm   A step-by-step rule or procedure to be followed in order to solve a problem or accomplish a task.

amplitude   The height of an analog wave.

analog (signal)   A signal in wave form, such as a sound wave.

analysis system   A system which assists decision makers by analyzing data needed to support their decisions.

ANSI   American National Standards Institute; standards organization of the U.S. government.

ANSI/SPARC data model   A multi-level collection of data models that reflects the external model (user's view), the conceptual model (DBMS-independent global view), the internal model (DBMS-dependent global view), and the physical model (where data actually exists on a secondary storage device); developed by the American National Standards Institute/Standards Planning and Requirements Committee.

application A computer program designed to carry out a particular task; also called *software subsystem*.

application development The process of designing, developing, and implementing an application system.

application software Software used to solve a specific business problem.

applications portfolio The complete set of application systems that exist in an organization.

application system A system consisting of hardware, software, data, procedures, and people that is designed to solve a specific business problem; commonly thought to be synonymous with *application software*.

arc A path that allows for the movement of data from one node to another in a network.

arithmetic logic unit That portion of the CPU which is responsible for carrying out calculations and logical comparisons.

artificial intelligence (AI) An activity performed by a computer that if performed by a person would require human intelligence; includes techniques such as heuristic reasoning, learning, and natural language.

assembler A program translator which converts assembly language into machine code.

assembly language A symbolic machine language that uses mnemonics to represent the operations to be carried out. It is the second-generation programming language.

audit trail A list of events that have occurred which can be reviewed later to show what has occurred and when it has occurred, thus allowing others to verify those events.

automated business system An action system used to collect, store, retrieve, and analyze data, then make a business decision and act on it.

automated manufacturing system A computer-based action system used to convert general product designs into detailed manufacturing specifications.

automated teller machine (ATM) An interactive device that allows customers to access a bank's computer and complete transactions, such as cash withdrawals. It is a common means of electronic funds transfer.

auxiliary storage A place for permanent storage of data; also called *secondary storage*.

backup An extra copy of data or software.

bandwidth The total capacity of the channel; the portion of the frequency spectrum that is used to transmit the message.

bar code A pattern of lines read by a scanning device.

baseband transmission A signaling alternative for transmission in a LAN in which all data is transmitted at the same frequency.

BASIC A third-generation programming language originally developed to teach students the concepts of programming; allows the user to concentrate on the programming logic without having to worry about complex input and output commands and other "overhead" statements. It is a general-purpose interactive programming language which is easy to use and learn.

basic non-voice service A type of communication service a company can offer; refers to the use of the computer but only to assist in the transmission of a signal.

batch processing   A method of processing in which a group of data (called a batch) is collected for later processing. The data is then entered into the computer at once, in a batch, then processed. Batch processing provides low costs per transaction processed.

baud   The number of signals sent per second.

binary code   The code used to represent data in the computer; uses only two symbols, 0 and 1.

binary system   A number system that uses only the numbers 0 and 1.

BIOS   The basic input-output system. In a PC, instructions are located in the RAM which establish the connections between the CPU and input/output devices such as the printer, terminal, and disk drives.

bit   *B*inary dig*it;* the physical representation of data in the computer.

bits per second (BPS)   The unit of speed at which digital data is transmitted.

bottom-up design   A design strategy in which the lowest level of system resources is identified first, followed by successive layers of aggregation until the whole system is described.

boundary   The line that defines the scope of a system and specifies what is inside and what is outside the system.

broadband channels   Channels which include multiple, parallel channels over the same media and can accommodate all types of messages.

broadband transmission   A signaling alternative for transmission in a LAN in which the bandwidth of the coaxial cable is divided into a distinct number of communication channels, each of which supports a particular function having its own frequency.

broadcast waves   Waves at the lowest end of the frequency spectrum; the signal is simultaneously transmitted to many destinations.

bus network   A network similar to a ring network, except that the ends of the channel in a bus network are not connected.

Business Systems Planning (BSP)   A technique developed by IBM to develop an overall understanding of the business and then establish a priority for implementing information systems to support those business goals.

bypass   A technique used by an organization that does not wish to be connected to the local telephone company; the organization can be its own telephone company.

byte   A combination of bits which represents a character or number, usually 8 bits.

bytes per inch (BPI)   A measure of density of a storage medium.

C   A programming language used to develop system software.

card reader   An on-line device used to read data from a punched card.

central processing unit (CPU)   The processing hardware of the computer. It is the device which carries out the processing activity of the computer. The CPU is composed of three parts: the control unit, the arithmetic logic unit, and the primary or main memory.

channel   The medium through which a message is sent; also called *communication channel.*

character variables   Variables which contain alphanumeric data that is not involved in arithmetic expressions.

chief information officer (CIO)   A high-level manager who provides the comprehensive oversight necessary to facilitate the coordination and sharing of information.

client   The person who is served by an information system; also called the *user*.

coaxial cable   A transmission medium that has greater carrying capacity, wider bandwidth, and less susceptibility to noise than twisted pairs. Capable of transmitting video, voice, and computer data.

COBOL   A third-generation programming language designed for general-purpose business applications; the structure of the commands resembles English grammar to enhance readability.

CODASYL   Specifications for DBMSs based on the network model; developed by the COmmon DAta SYstems Language committee of the National Bureau of Standards.

co-development   An approach to system development in which the end-user department develops the information system in conjunction with the MIS department of the organization.

cognition   The act of knowing something.

cognitive style   The manner in which the input, process, and output activities of human information processing are carried out.

collisions   Interference that results when messages bump into each other while traveling through a network.

command language   A language that facilitates the user's interaction with the computer and software packages.

common carrier   A regulated entity, such as AT&T, US Sprint, or MCI, which provides its users with access to communication channels.

communication channel   The medium through which a message is transmitted.

Community Antenna Television (CATV)   A coaxial cable system used to bring television signals to remote or hilly areas which could not be reached by conventional broadcast; also, a TV system that provides a greater number of channels.

compatibility   The ability of different devices to communicate with each other.

compatibles   Computer families with the ability to run the same operating system.

compiler   A program translator that translates an entire source program first into a complete object program, and then enables one to execute the object program.

completeness   The state of having enough information to carry out a task.

components   The functions or activities performed by a system to achieve its goals.

computer-aided software engineering (CASE)   A collection of tools which facilitate accomplishing the spectrum of tasks involved in the systems life cycle, from systems analysis through development to maintenance.

computer-based information system (CBIS)   An information system containing the following five resources or parts that work together to produce information: hardware, software, data, procedures, and people.

computer literacy   The ability to turn naturally to the computer for problem solving; includes an understanding of the structure and operations of the computer as well as knowledge of how to use software packages.

computer network A collection of computer hardware and software, terminals, and the interconnecting links, plus the communication software which enables data to be communicated through the network.

computer output microform (COM) A technique that uses photography to produce output and reduce it to a very compact form. Examples are microfilm and microfiche.

concentrators Computers used to move data through channels more effectively by taking advantage of spaces between transmissions to fill in data from other devices. The utilization of channels is increased by allowing multiple devices to share the channels.

conceptual design Translates the requirements stated in the system proposal into an overall model of the system; also called *logical design*.

conceptual view A model of the total data environment; it is independent of a given DBMS.

conciseness The quality of having no more information than what is needed to carry out a task.

concurrency controls Controls used to maintain data accuracy when multiple users access and update the same database at the same time.

confidentiality The assurance that information about an individual will not be disclosed without that person's consent.

consistency The quality that related groups of information are not contradictory.

constraints Factors in the environment that influence the system and that the system cannot change.

contextual cues Signs that enable the listener to piece together what a signal probably means even if a clear pattern cannot be recognized.

control unit The part of the CPU that functions as the central switchboard or manager of the CPU.

conversion The process of moving from the existing to the new system.

corrective procedures Procedures used to help the organization recover from a problem once it has occurred.

coupled systems Systems in which the output from one system can be used as input to another system.

CP/M (control program for microcomputers) A common type of operating system for 8-bit personal computers developed by Digital Research.

cursor keys Computer terminal keys used to move a pointer, called the cursor, up, down, left, or right on the screen.

cybernetics A theory that proposes that any entity requires feedback on its progress as it moves toward its goal.

cycle clock The device that controls the timing of the CPU.

cylinder The same track over several platters of a disk.

daisy wheel The component of a printing device commonly used to make the impact on the page to produce full-character output.

data The raw material out of which information is formed.

data administration   The organization which establishes and enforces the policies and procedures for managing the company's data as a corporate resource; involves the collection, storage, and dissemination of data as a globally administered and standardized resource; often called *information resource management*.

database   A collection of interrelated and integrated sets of data (files) used by many applications.

database administration   A technical function which performs database design and development, provides education on database technology, provides support to users in operational data-management-related activities, and may provide technical support for data administration.

database management   A discipline concerned with managing all aspects of a database.

database management systems (DBMS)   Software that facilitates data storage, retrieval, and reporting.

data communication   The transmission of data from some sending device to a computer.

data definition/data description language (DDL)   A language which provides the user with the means for creating and changing the data definitions of a database.

data dependence   The need to change a program if the data file it is using has been changed.

data dictionary   The collection of all the organization's meta-data (i.e., data about data); describes the data in terms of data item names, synonyms for that data item, the kind of data stored in that data item, its location, applications which use it, and the organizational unit responsible for it.

data division   The third division of a COBOL program; defines the data to be used in the program.

data flow   The movement of data into and out of each process in a system; part of a data flow diagram.

data flow diagram (DFD)   A graphical representation of the activities of a system that enables the analyst to identify the different categories of data that are involved in the system.

data generation   The methods of storing and retrieving data.

data item   The smallest meaningful unit of data which is used by a computer; also referred to as *data element* or *data field*.

data manipulation language (DML)   A component of a DBMS which provides the capabilities for locating, retrieving, storing, and reporting the data in the database.

data model   An abstract description of the data in an organization; defines the rules for linking the data items of a database together.

data network   The hardware, software, and protocols required to support the desired network activities.

data processing management   A management perspective concerned with improving the data processing function to better support corporate decision making.

data protection   Procedures to ensure that data will not be lost, damaged, or misused.

data sharing   The use of the same data file or database by more than one user or application.

data store   A repository for the data which is a part of the system; part of a data flow diagram.

data structure   The underlying structure of a database defined in the internal model and implemented in the physical data organization.

debit card   A card similar to a credit card, except that debit-card funds are electronically tranferred from the buyer's account to the seller's account.

debugging   The process of determining and correcting errors in a computer program.

decision making   The application of problem-solving skills to the analysis of alternative courses of action and to the ultimate choice among them.

decision support system (DSS)   A system whose purpose is to help someone with the analysis of alternative courses of action in a decision-making setting.

decision table   A type of documentation used to outline a set of conditions which may be encountered and to indicate what actions should be performed for each condition.

density   The measurement of how tightly compacted the columns of bytes are on the tape; measured in BPI (bytes per inch).

departmental computers   Minicomputers or supermicrocomputers that are distributed throughout an organization, serving departmental/organizational units.

departmental information system   An information system used to support the operations of a department.

designer   An individual responsible for understanding the type of information system that is reflected in the goal. The designer must select and sometimes develop the appropriate hardware and software resources; make sure the appropriate data resources are collected and stored in a fashion that will enable them to be transformed into information; ensure that the system works properly; and establish procedures governing the use and maintenance of the system.

design walkthrough   A step-by-step review of a system design, including the input and output layouts, the processing logic, and the procedures regarding use of the system.

destination   The part of the communication process that receives a message.

detailed design   The design stage which specifies exactly how the hardware, software, and data will work together to provide the desired information.

detective procedures   Procedures that enable information processing managers to become aware of actual or potential problems with the data.

digital transmission   A method of sending messages in the form of electronic pulses representing a collection of zeros and ones, or bits.

direct conversion   A conversion method in which the existing system is no longer used once the new system is operational.

direct file   A file in which records can be accessed directly by use of the record key.

directory   A list of files which the user has stored in secondary storage.

disaster recovery procedures   Corrective procedures developed to cope with unintended abuses of the data such as fires, floods, or electricity outages.

diskette   A flexible, removable storage medium.

disk pack   A device which contains several disks.

distributed database   A database that is stored across several computers by utilizing data communication technology.

distributed data processing   A method of data processing in which a number of computers are involved in the information processing function.

DOS (disk operating system)   A common type of operating system for a personal computer.

dumb terminal   A terminal that can be used only for inputting data into the computer or receiving data from the computer.

editor   A program for creating and modifying files.

egoless programming   Programming that is the result of a team rather than an individual effort; facilitates the sharing of ideas by promoting a cooperative atmosphere and capitalizes on the different strengths of the programmers.

electronic bulletin board   A computerized database accessible to many users for posting and retrieving messages.

electronic data interchange (EDI)   A form of communication between organizations which enables the automatic exchange of business information between a company and its suppliers, customers, partners, or others outside the company.

electronic funds transfer (EFT)   The movement of money (funds) by a computerized system; for example, a business can pay employee salaries by transferring funds directly to employee checking accounts.

electronic mail   A computerized record-keeping system for the electronic delivery of textual messages from one computer to another.

emulate   To behave like.

end user   An individual who interacts directly with computer technology to obtain or manipulate information.

end-user computing (EUC)   The active involvement of end users in design and development of information systems as well as in the analysis and implementation phases; also refers to the direct use of computer-based technology by non-information systems personnel in the course of doing some other job.

enhanced services (or *enhanced non-voice services*)   Services such as access to an established network, enhancements to provide better protection for data, and the availability of specific applications such as electronic mail, teleconferencing, and access to commercial databases in addition to just providing a communication channel.

enhancement   The process of improving the signal or the physical form of a message.

enterprise model   A description of the organization or environment within which the information systems exist.

environment   What is outside the system.

environment division   The second division of a COBOL program. It identifies the hardware environment in which the program will operate.

EPROM   Erasable programmable read only memory; a type of ROM chip that can be erased by placing the chip under a special light.

Ethernet   A standard for baseband LAN transmission.

execution cycle   The second phase of CPU operation; involves the ALU accessing the necessary data from primary memory, placing it inside the registers, performing the operations, and then returning the result to the main memory.

execution error   An error that occurs while a program is running (executing).

executive   The part of the operating system which directly manages the computer's resources. It is always stored in primary memory when the computer is in operation.

executive information system (EIS)   A type of information system intended to be used by high-level managers, executives, etc., to assist in decision making.

expansion slots   The spaces available to connect other boards to the motherboard to expand the capabilities of the computer.

expert system   A system used to assist with unstructured decision making by guiding the behavior of an individual in a decision-making task which normally requires considerable experience and knowledge in some subject; also called *knowledge-based system*.

external entity   Some person or organizational unit in the environment of the information system which either provides input data or receives output information; part of a data flow diagram.

external memory   A memory aid used to enhance the memory and problem-solving skills of humans.

external view   The user's view of the database; sometimes called the *subschema*.

extract database   A copy of an entire set of data or a copy of that portion of the data a particular user needs to obtain; ensures that a user won't accidentally damage the original data.

family of computers   A series of computers based on the same hardware architecture.

fault-tolerant computer   A computer designed to maximize the times between errors or system failures so as to ensure high reliability.

feature analysis   The first step in the process of pattern recognition; involves identifying and classifying the important features of a signal into a recognizable pattern.

feedback   A verification that a message was received. Information on an entity's progress as it moves towards its goal.

feeling type   A method of information processing that tends to personalize the situation and base conclusions on feelings and personal values.

fiber optics   Signals sent as light pulses through glass strands.

fifth-generation language   A language which incorporates artificial intelligence into its design, operation, or output.

firmware   Another name for ROM chips.

first in first out (FIFO)   A job scheduling technique which processes jobs in the order in which they are submitted; with FIFO, all jobs have equal priority.

first-generation language   See *machine language*.

first-generation users   Scientists and engineers who used the computer to solve complex calculations.

fixed disk   A hard disk which is a permanent part of the computer and cannot be removed.

floppy disk   A flexible, removable storage medium; also called *diskette*.

Focus   A fourth-generation language designed for data management.

form   The structure of the organization or system.

form filling   A type of question-and-answer interaction in which the user is presented with a display screen and is instructed to provide the necessary information.

FORTRAN   One of the oldest general-purpose scientific programming languages.

fourth-generation language   A language which focuses on the results or problems to be solved rather than the procedure for doing so.

fourth-generation users   Individuals who are able to design, use, and manage information systems without having considerable education about computers; also called *end users*.

frequency-division multiplexing   A method of multiplexing which divides the bandwidth into subchannels by assigning each a different frequency range; used in broadband networks.

front-end processor   The computer which first receives the data before it is sent to the host for processing.

full-duplex   Describes a communication channel capable of simultaneous two-way communication.

full-character output   Output resembling that from a typewriter.

function   The flow of information or work in a system.

function keys   Special keys that enable a user to execute a command by depressing a single key.

general-purpose programming language   A language capable of accomplishing a wide variety of processing tasks.

General Systems Theory   A theory developed to help scientists consider the behavior of wholes; focuses on the purpose of the system, not just the observed behavior of its parts, with an eye to understanding the interaction of those parts.

global environment   The environment that falls outside of the organization.

global view (of data)   A consistent view of data across an organization.

hackers   People who enjoy exploring the capabilities and weaknesses of computers and who use their skills to gain access to other computer systems.

half-duplex   Describes a communication channel capable of two-way communication, though data cannot be transmitted in both directions simultaneously.

hardcopy   Output that is printed on paper.

hardware   The computer itself, as well as the technology used to acquire, store, and communicate data.

hardware interface   Those characteristics of the input and output devices which interact with the human sensorimotor system.

harmonics   The sounds produced by pressing the keys on a touch-tone telephone.

help   An interface facility capable of responding to a wide range of user questions.

heuristics The "rules of thumb" that rely upon individuals' considerable knowledge of the subject matter, their judgment, and their experience.

hexadecimal number system A number system that uses sixteen characters: 0-9 and the letters A-F; also called the *base 16 number system*.

hierarchical data model The oldest of the three data models, in which the data items are linked like the branches of a tree; the relationships between records are always one-to-many.

hierarchical network A communication network organized in a tree-like structure similar to a company's organization chart; transmission between nodes goes up and down the hierarchy.

home computer See *microcomputer*.

host computer The computer which processes the input data which has been sent from the source devices. A computer that has the technical capability to transmit data through a network.

host language A type of data manipulation language used by professional programmers consisting of statements used to augment an existing programming language like COBOL, FORTRAN, or PL/1.

human-computer interface The common boundary of the technological and the human subsystems that joins these two subsystems together to create an information system.

human information processing The activities of perception, cognition, and response which humans use to carry out the input, process, and output activities of information processing.

hypertext A document retrieval system for text documents; enhances a conventional access system by making retrieving and using information much easier for the end user.

icon A graphic symbol which represents an activity to be carried out by the computer.

identification division The first division of a COBOL program. It identifies the programmer and the purpose of the program.

impact printer A printer which produces the output by physically making a mark on the paper.

imperfect information The unavailability of the complete information needed to support the choice of a strategy.

indexed sequential access method (ISAM) An access method which allows records to be accessed either sequentially or directly.

indexed sequential file A file in which records can be accessed either sequentially or directly.

inference engine The component of an expert system that stores the rules used by an expert system to make decisions.

information Processed data which is perceived to be meaningful or useful.

information architecture The model by which one understands what is involved in creating an information processing environment that will enable the efficient and effective functioning of one or more systems.

information center An organizational unit where end users can go to use certain software or to get training or assistance in software use or system development.

information-intensive society   A society in which most people are concerned with the production and use of information or the production and use of information technology.

information literacy   The ability to acquire, process, use, and communicate the right information.

information management   A discipline concerned with ensuring that information is available, accurate, and in a useful format.

information model   A description of the information system resources in the organization.

information overload   Having so much information that it is difficult to determine what is useful and what is not.

information policy   A policy that recognizes that all information, not just management information, needs the attention of management and formal planning, because information is seen not only as a resource but also as an asset and as a competitive or strategic weapon.

information resource management (IRM)   A theory which states that information is a significant organizational resource in much the same way that people, machines, and capital are considered corporate resources and should therefore, like other resources, receive concerted management attention.

information system   The computers, programs, data, people, and procedures used to produce and use information.

information systems professional   An individual who specializes in working with information systems.

information theory   A well-developed body of knowledge that has had a significant influence on the field of information processing.

informed consumer   An individual with sufficient information to make a decision.

ink-jet printer   A printer that produces output by little sprays of ink.

input   The system function that involves collecting data from the environment, putting it into a form understandable to the system, and entering it into the system.

input/output bound   Referring to a state in which the computer is not efficiently utilizing its CPU because it is waiting for input or output.

input-output control system (IOCS)   Software which simultaneously controls input, processing, and output activities.

instruction cycle   The first phase of operation of the CPU; involves fetching an instruction from the primary memory and analyzing it to determine what actions need to be taken.

integrated services digital network (ISDN)   An international standard developed for digital networks that will be able to accommodate voice, data, video, and other types of messages.

integrity   The property that the overall quality (accuracy, timeliness, reliability, consistency, completeness, conciseness, and relevance) of the information can be relied on.

intelligent terminal   A terminal with a limited amount of processing and storage capacity.

interblock gap (IBG)   A blank space between two blocks of data on a secondary storage device.

interface   The boundary between the environment and the information system. A link between the resources and components of a system.

intermediary   An expert in the use of a command language and the information stored in a computer.

internal view (model)   The conceptual view constrained by a specific DBMS; also called the *physical database structure*.

interorganizational system   An action system in which the action taken involves interacting with the information system of another company.

interpreter   A program translator that translates and executes only a portion of the source program at a time.

intuitive approach   A holistic or global data gathering approach that involves receiving input from several sources at once and placing heavy emphasis on the influence of context in the interpretation of the input data.

key   A special set of data used to arrange records in some order and to locate a specific record in a file or database.

keypunch machine   The machine used to punch holes in a card to represent data.

knowledge   The outcome of learning; results from the increasingly complex network built up through the assimilation of information.

knowledge base   The component of an expert system that contains the knowledge necessary to assist in decision making in a particular domain.

knowledge-based system   See *expert system*.

knowledge engineer   A person who works with the expert to identify the way decisions are reached and the knowledge needed to reach them.

language   A tool which provides the labels necessary to turn experiences and events into concepts so that they can be stored in memory.

laptop computer   A lightweight microcomputer intended to be portable.

laser printer   A printer that uses an electrophotographic approach similar to that used in photocopiers in order to produce a printed page of output.

learning   The accumulation of concepts and the establishment of connections among them; one of the purposes of human information processing.

leased line   A communication line leased from a common carrier for the exclusive use of the lessee.

light pen   A device placed against the computer screen at a desired alternative to select that feature or used to write/sketch on the screen.

line printer   A printer that prints an entire line of data at a time; also called *line-at-a-time printer*.

LISP   A programming language used to develop artificial intelligence applications.

local area network (LAN)   A network in which the geographical scope is limited to a single building or cluster of buildings which are close together, such as those on a college campus.

local environment   The environment that falls within the organization.

logic error An error that occurs when the program runs but does not produce the correct results.

logical data independence A state that exists when the conceptual view of data is changed and the external views are still valid.

logical integration The condition that an entire database does not have to reside in a single location but appears to be whole to the user.

logical view The conceptual and internal views of a database.

long-term memory Memory that stores the concept or meaning behind the words that were heard, not the sounds of the words themselves.

low-level language A language which is tied directly to the particular hardware features of a given computer; refers to first- and second-generation programming languages.

machine cycle The amount of time required to perform both the instruction and the execution phases of the CPU.

machine family dependent Referring to a program that will only work on one family of computers.

machine language A language that requires the programmer to specify instructions through the use of a binary code and reference data by naming its actual storage location; the only language directly understandable by the computer.

machine-readable document A source document understandable to both people and computers; for example, account numbers on checks printed using magnetic ink.

magnetic disk A direct-access storage device.

magnetic-ink character recognition (MICR) The interpretation of characters which are written in a special magnetic ink and formed according to a specific pattern.

magnetic tape A sequential storage medium which is available in both reel-to-reel and cassette form.

mainframe computers Large, powerful machines which are capable of supporting several hundred diverse users and a high volume of information processing tasks.

main memory See *primary memory*.

maintenance The adaptation of a system to suit new requirements such as new laws, regulations, reporting requirements, and industry competition; the last phase of the formal systems life cycle.

management information system (MIS) An information system that provides information for management decision making by integrating and synthesizing data generated from business operations.

managerial control The process by which managers ensure that resources are obtained and used effectively and efficiently to accomplish the organization's objectives.

mark-sense reader A device programmed to recognize the specific marks placed on the source document.

master file A file containing the collection of all related record occurrences, each with correct and current data.

menu A list of options presented to the user which aids in the selection and execution of a desired activity.

message   The data that travels between the source and the destination; in a computer network, the data which is sent for processing or is being shared with a computer at another site.

message switching   The dynamic routing of messages given the traffic on certain lines.

meta-data   Data about data.

metropolitan area network (MAN)   A network in which the geographical scope covers offices at different sites within a city or metropolitan area.

microcomputer   The smallest computer in size; not necessarily the least powerful.

microfiche   A single sheet of film used to store data for archival purposes.

microfilm   A roll of film used to store data for archival purposes.

microprocessor   The CPU of a microcomputer.

microsecond   A millionth of a second.

microwave   A type of data transmission that uses the airwaves and is carried out at a rate of up to 45 million bits per second.

millisecond   A thousandth of a second.

minicomputer   A computer intended to be smaller, slower, and less costly while retaining the multi-user and general-purpose capabilities of mainframes.

modem   A communication interface tool which accomplishes the task of converting a digital signal to an analog signal and vice versa.

module   An individual programming task assigned to a programmer.

monopoly   A company or business with no competitors in a single industry.

motherboard   The circuit board on which the CPU and other components are mounted.

mouse   A small box-like device attached by a wire to the computer which enables the user to move the cursor about on the screen.

multiplexor   A device capable of mapping groups of lower-speed data to be sent simultaneously over a higher-speed channel.

multiprogramming system   A system which allows more than one program and corresponding data to be stored in main memory.

multitasking system   An operating system which allows more than one task to be active at a time.

nanosecond   A billionth of a second.

narrowband channel   The channel with the lowest capacity, 5 to 30 characters per second.

National Bureau of Standards (NBS)   The standards organization of the U.S. government; renamed the National Institute of Standards and Technology.

natural language   A programming language that allows a user to enter English-like commands in order to describe the activities to be carried out.

natural-language processing   A method of processing in which the user's input to the system is provided in the form of answers to questions posed by the expert system in English or some other human language.

network data model A data model developed as an alternative to the hierarchical model; allows for the definition of associations between records that may be one-to-one, one-to-many, or many-to-many.

network server A dominant node in a LAN that stores and manages centralized software and data and may coordinate LAN activities.

node A point in a network which can send or receive data and which can do local processing.

noise Variations introduced into a signal from some source other than the sender.

Nolan's Stage Theory A theory that describes the evolution of information systems planning in an organization.

non-accounting systems Systems that are not involved with financial data.

nonimpact printer A printer that produces print by means other than striking the page.

nonprocedural language See *fourth-generation language*.

nonrational approach A decision-making approach which suggests that people do not always behave in a logical, rational fashion.

nonverbal communication Signals such as tone of voice and "body language" (gestures, posture, and eye movements) that add meaning to verbal data.

numeric variables Variables which contain numbers and are used in arithmetic expressions.

object program The machine-code version of a program.

octal number system A number system that uses eight numbers: 0–7; also called the *base 8 number system*.

office information system/office automation system A system that automates traditional office processes such as word processing and electronic mail through the integration of computer and communication systems.

off-line Referring to a device that is not in direct contact (i.e., connected) with the computer.

off-site storage The process of making backup copies of data and software and storing them in a different location.

on-line Referring to a device that is in direct contact with the computer.

on-line documentation A complete version of the written documentation (of a system or software package) that is available through the help facility.

Open Systems Interconnection (OSI) model A standard developed by the International Standards Organization which describes the interactions required of systems that wish to communicate with other systems; consists of seven layers.

operating system Software that controls the overall operation of the computer.

operational control The process of ensuring that specific tasks are carried out effectively and efficiently and communicating feedback about the success of doing so.

operational control system See *transaction processing system*.

optical character recognition (OCR) The interpretation of preprinted or handwritten characters that are formed in a specific pattern.

optical disk A direct-access storage device that uses light energy and a laser beam for reading and writing data on the disk; a common type is CD-ROM.

organizational constraints Factors influencing a system such as the type of information, the organizational structure, and the type of individuals to be taken into account.

organizational information system An information system designed to serve an entire organization.

organizational interface The people, procedures, or data positioned between the user and the technology to facilitate the interaction between the two.

OS/2 A common type of operating system for a personal computer developed for the IBM PS/2 family of PCs.

output The products, services, or other effects produced by a system. The communication of the results of processing in a format understandable to the person using that information.

pages A method of dividing primary memory into equal-size partitions.

Paperwork Reduction Act Legislation that provides a framework for the implementation of information resource management.

parallel conversion A conversion method in which both the existing system and the new system are operating at the same time.

parity bit An extra bit used to determine if there are any errors in the data stored.

PASCAL A powerful general-purpose programming language; PASCAL programs are composed of a series of blocks or subprograms.

password A personal code used to identify legitimate users of a multi-user system; used in conjunction with a user identification number.

path The series of arcs that a message takes through a network to get from source to destination.

pattern recognition The process that involves taking the auditory input which arrives at the ear and converting it into a recognizable message.

perception The sensing and pattern-recognition activities performed on input data.

perfect information The availability of sufficient information to enable one to select the most appropriate strategy for attaining a desired goal.

peripherals The input, output, and storage devices that are attached to a computer.

personal computer (PC) See *microcomputer*.

personal information system An information system designed to serve an individual.

phase The portion of a wave cycle transmitted in a given time period.

phased-in conversion A conversion method in which the new hardware and software are implemented gradually so that the impact of this change on the organization is minimized.

phonemes The basic units of speech; the unique sounds in a language which, when combined in certain ways, result in meaningful spoken words.

physical data independence A state that exists when the physical or internal view of data can be changed without requiring a corresponding change in the conceptual view.

physical integration The storage of data in a database at one location.

physical record   A block of data transferred in one input/output operation.

physical view   The view of data that depicts the actual storage of data on a secondary storage device.

picosecond   A trillionth of a second.

pilot conversion   A conversion method in which the new system is implemented in parts for one group of users at a time.

platter   Another term for *disk*.

point-of-sale terminal   A terminal that computes the amount of a sale and transmits that data to a computer.

political approach   The decision-making approach in circumstances in which the goal is identified but imperfect information exists.

portable   Referring to a program which can be used on more than one computer.

portable computer   See *microcomputer* and *laptop computer*.

post-implementation audit   An evaluation of a system performed after the system has been in operation for a period of time; a review of the properties such as timeliness, response time, and quality of output.

post-industrial society   See *information-intensive society*.

preparation   Addresses the concerns involved with the people, procedures, and resources of the information system.

preventive procedures   Procedures put in place to anticipate problems and plan for them.

primary key   A key whose value is unique and whose value is always known; the key used the most; consists of one or more data items.

primary memory   Temporary memory that holds data and instructions before, during, and after execution; part of the CPU, primary memory provides very fast direct access.

printing terminal   A terminal that displays output as hardcopy.

privacy   The inherent right to keep one's personal affairs from public disclosure.

private branch exchange (PBX)   An inexpensive alternative for integrated voice and data communication which can use standard telephone wires as a single transmission medium for both voice and data.

problem   What is to be solved.

problem-oriented language   See *fourth-generation language*.

problem solving   Behavior directed toward the achievement of a goal.

procedure   The method used to solve a problem; instructs the individual and the organization as to their roles in obtaining information; the organizational practice related to the use of information systems by those personnel.

procedure division   The fourth division of a COBOL program; describes the processing activities to be carried out.

process   The activities by which inputs are transformed into outputs.

process control system   A system used to monitor the manufacturing process and adjust it as circumstances require.

program   A series of detailed instructions which must be carried out by the computer in order to solve a problem; written in a language understandable to a computer.

program flowchart   A graphical presentation of the logic or procedures required to carry out an algorithm.

program generator   Software that enables a program to be generated in a particular programming language directly from pseudocode or other user-oriented specifications.

programmer   The individual who focuses on turning the algorithm into a form the computer can read; this person designs and develops a computer program.

programming language   A highly structured method of communication with the computer.

program module   See *module*.

program specification   The logic of the computer software, or what it is that the programs are supposed to do.

program trading   An automated business system used in the stock market to store data on the behavior of certain stocks and, based on programmed rules, make a decision about buying or selling stocks, and then execute a buy/sell decision.

program translator   System software which will translate a program written in a specific language into machine code; two types are compiler and translator.

project team   A development team made up of representative users and the systems professionals responsible for developing the system.

PROLOG   A programming language used to develop artificial intelligence applications.

PROM   Programmable read only memory; a type of ROM chip that is programmed by the chip manufacturer using a special chip programming language.

prompt   In human communication, a nonverbal signal used to indicate that it is the other person's turn to speak. In human-computer communication, a visual signal used to tell the user that it is time to enter some data and also indicates the position on the screen where the data should be entered.

protocol   The "rules of communication" which describe how communication is carried out within a layer; must be agreed upon by the participants in order for communication to succeed.

pseudocode   A prose-oriented technique using structured natural language (such as English) to outline the steps involved in carrying out an algorithm.

punched cards   Cards in which punched holes were used to represent instructions and data.

purpose   A system's goal, or reason for existing.

query language   A language that allows a user to request information by expressing a few simple commands. Software that allows an end user to create databases and retrieve data necessary to answer a question.

question-and-answer   A type of dialogue approach in which the user is presented with a question that appears on the screen, and responds using either a regular keyboard or function keys.

RAM Random access memory; a type of semiconductor chip used for the primary memory to temporarily store data and program instructions; the data and instructions stored in this chip exist only as long as there is a continuous flow of current. Data waits in RAM to be transferred to the CPU.

rational approach A decision-making approach that views decision making as a logical sequence of steps; assumes that the goal can be clearly identified, that sufficient information exists to enable one to select the most appropriate strategy for attaining that goal, and that, given the goal and the strategy, the decision maker will automatically follow that strategy.

record/record type A collection of related data items which describe a single entity.

record-keeping system A system whose goal is the efficient storage and retrieval of data.

record occurrence An individual record that contains the values for each of the data items that have been collected and stored.

records management The discipline which is concerned with the effective storage, retrieval, and utilization of documents in organizations.

redundancy Repetition; exists in language so that if some words are missed in communication, the listener has other chances to figure out what the message means; occurs when the same piece of data is stored in more than one file.

registers Storage locations inside the CPU into which the data and instructions are temporarily placed before and after processing is done.

regulatory constraint A type of constraint which comes from the global environment; specifically, public policy which has an impact on communication decisions.

related systems See *coupled systems*.

relational data model A data model based on simple flat files called tables.

relevance The quality that the information is meaningful and useful for the purposes for which it was produced.

reliability The assurance that the same result will always occur if the same data and procedures are used.

repeaters Stations which boost a signal and send it to the next station in the path.

report writer A facility that simplifies and expedites the presentation of the data from the database.

resources The means by which the purpose of a system is achieved; the raw materials, or the inputs that are transformed into outputs.

response time The amount of time between a user's request for information and its provision.

restart/recovery The feature of a backup facility that brings a file or database back into a usable state after a failure.

ring network A network in which the nodes are arranged in a circle; data flows among nodes by moving in one direction around the ring.

robot A computer-based tool which combines artificial intelligence with physical mobility in a programmable computer designed to move material, parts, tools, or specialized devices through a series of motions to perform a variety of tasks.

ROM Read only memory; a type of semiconductor chip in which underlying computer instructions are permanently embedded. They can be accessed and used but cannot be changed by the user.

root The node containing the dominant computer from which all the other nodes branch off. Also, the top record in a hierarchical database.

rotational delay The period of time for the disk to rotate the desired data to the position where the read/write head is located.

round robin A means of executing jobs in order based on priority and the time they entered main memory.

RPG (report program generator) The first nonprocedural language developed to be report-oriented rather than procedure-oriented.

satellite transmission A special type of microwave transmission used for longer distances, such as across a country, and when line-of-sight transmission is not possible. The message is transmitted from the source to a communications satellite in a geosynchronous orbit and then down to the destination.

schema The complete database. Also, a description of the complete logical database structure.

secondary keys Keys used in addition to the primary key.

secondary storage device A permanent storage medium for data; usually magnetic tape or magnetic or optical disk.

second-generation language See *assembly language*.

second-generation users Computer scientists who were educated specifically to design and use software tools.

sectors The pie-shaped wedges that are used to logically partition each disk surface.

security The procedures governing the use of information processing resources to ensure that the data will not be lost, damaged, or misused.

seek time The amount of time it takes for the read/write head to move across the disk to the correct track where the desired data is stored.

segmentation A method of dividing primary memory into different-size partitions.

semiconductor chip The basic building block of computers which is used to hold both data and instructions within the computer; a single chip can hold hundreds of thousands of integrated circuits.

sensing The reception of auditory signals by the ear. The detail-oriented data gathering approach in which attention during input tends to be focused on a single source, such as spoken words only; emphasizes literal interpretation.

separation of duties A preventive procedure for guarding against unauthorized use of an information system which states that individuals working with a system should be prevented from having complete access to the system; that is, the person who develops the software should not be the same one who operates the system.

sequential file A file in which each record is arranged in sequence according to its primary key, in either ascending or descending order.

service bureau A company which specializes in doing data processing for others.

short-term memory   Memory that stores a meaningful representation of auditory signals; data is stored there for a very short time, and the capacity of the short-term memory is also limited.

signal   The physical form of a message.

simplex   Describing a one-way communication channel. Data can be sent from a source to a destination but the receiving end cannot send anything back to the source.

smart terminal   See *intelligent terminal.*

softcopy (output)   A temporary copy of ouput. Data displayed on a computer screen.

software   A program or set of instructions that tells the computer how to accept and manipulate the data in order to turn it into information; also called *computer program.*

software interface   The features incorporated into the software that enable users to interact with the computer and the software.

source   The point of origin of a message.

source document   A document, typically paper, which contains the data from a transaction; for example, a receipt from a credit-card purchase.

source program   A program written in a high-level programming language.

special-purpose programming language   A programming language with restricted abilities that focuses on a specific information processing task.

speech analysis   The task of identifying and classifying the important features of a sequence of words into a recognizable pattern.

spooling (*s*imultaneous *p*eripheral *o*peration *o*n-*l*ine)   A technique that allows the computer to perform input or output functions at higher speeds than the normal, slower speeds of the peripheral equipment; the input or output data is held temporarily on disk to wait for processing or printing.

stacked job processing   A processing method which assembles a group of jobs and processes them sequentially.

standards   Constraints imposed by the current technological environment. Rules governing the types of computers and software that can be used.

star network   A communication network topology in which all nodes are connected only to the dominant (central) computer. All messages between nodes must go through the central computer.

steering committee   A high-level committee which authorizes the system development effort to get under way and conducts the final evaluation which concludes the project.

store-and-forward   A form of message switching where the message is held for a while before it is sent on to the destination.

strategic information planning   A process that involves using an information architecture as a way of planning for the development of information systems; emphasizes long-range planning, the integration of systems, the flows of data among them, and the use of information systems to gain competitive advantage for the organization.

strategic planning   A process that involves establishing the goal of the information system; that is, determining the type of information it will produce.

structure chart   A chart used to graphically represent the component parts of a system in a hierarchical form.

structured decisions   Decisions which occur when all the components of a decision are understood and all the necessary information is available for carrying it out.

structured systems analysis (SSA)   A top-down system analysis technique in which the system is systematically partitioned into a collection of subsystems which are in turn hierarchically decomposed into their resources and components.

structured walkthrough   A preliminary review of the developers' work by a small group of interested individuals, such as members of the programming team, members of other related teams, and representative users; the purpose is to detect errors and problems.

suboptimization   The achievement of subsystem goals at the expense of the overall system goal.

subschema   An external view of a database which may be a subset of the schema or comprise the complete schema.

subsystem   An individual resource that possesses all the properties of a system and is viewed as a system itself or as part of a larger system.

supercomputer   A very large mainframe computer whose primary activity is carrying out sophisticated and complex calculations.

supermicrocomputer   A microcomputer that has a performance level comparable to that of many minicomputers; it has a 32-bit word length and can support more than one user; also called *supermicro*.

superminicomputer   A minicomputer with 32-bit word length; also called *supermini*.

supervisor   See *executive*.

switched lines   Regular telephone lines that when not being used for data communication can be used for voice.

synergy   The quality that the whole is greater than the sum of its parts. For systems, this means that the effect of all subsystems working together is even greater than the combination of the individual effects of each subsystem.

syntax   The specific rules of grammar that must be followed when using a programming language.

syntax error   An error that occurs when the program is not written according to the rules of the programming language.

system   A collection of resources that work together to achieve a goal.

system proposal   A formal document produced at the end of the analysis phase which states the plan for moving from the present state to the desired state.

system requirements   The changes that must be made to achieve the information system's goal. Also, a description of a new information system.

system software   Software which facilitates the use of the computer by managing the CPU and other devices associated with the computer. Also, the software interface between the user or application software and the computer.

systems analyst   An individual who defines the information processing needs of a system, business, department, or person.

Systems Approach   A model that takes the theories about systems that were used in engineering and the sciences and applies them to business settings and business problems.

systems development life cycle   A formal methodology for decomposing the systems development process into a series of phases with supporting techniques.

tape drive   A device which reads and writes data on a magnetic tape.

technological constraint   A type of constraint imposed by the technology.

telecommunication network   A computer network that is concerned with transmitting data over a distance.

teleconferencing   A method that utilizes communication technology to enable people to hold meetings electronically.

template   A device defining the meaning of each function key; it is provided to assist the user.

terminal   A combination of a display screen and keyboard for inputting data into a computer and viewing the results of processing.

thermal printer   A printer utilizing treated paper with a print head that uses heat to darken the paper to form output.

thinking type   An information processing approach that uses logical analysis to form a conclusion.

third-generation language   A procedural programming language.

third-generation users   Management information systems personnel who were educated in both computers and business so that they could better understand the needs of those requesting information systems support.

thrashing   The excessive movement of program pieces in and out of memory such that the system performance is degraded.

time-division multiplexing   A method of multiplexing by which available transmission time is broken into slots; jobs are assigned to these time slots.

timeliness   Having information in time to be able to use it.

time-sharing system   An operating system which creates a multiprogramming environment by interrupting a job's execution after a prespecified amount of CPU time has been utilized.

time slice   The amount of time allotted in a time-sharing system.

top-down design   A design approach that describes the system resources at the level of the whole system and then proceeds to describe it in successive layers of detail.

topology   The arrangement of nodes in a network.

touch screen   A special type of video tube which allows the user to indicate the desired activity by touching a part of the screen.

transaction   A business event such as a bank deposit or credit-card charge.

transaction file   A file that contains the data from transactions which will then be used to update the records in a master file.

transaction processing   Using the data in a transaction file to update a master file or database.

transaction processing system   An access system used to record, process, and manage data about everyday business activities.

transborder data flow (TDF)   The movement of data through transnational communication networks for the purpose of storage, processing, and retrieval by a computer.

transmission medium   A communication channel.

tuple   A unique row, or record occurrence, in a two-dimensional table (e.g., a relation).

turnaround document   Output that is produced on punched cards so that it can later be input into the computer and thereby save time during input.

twisted pair wires   Two copper wires which are intertwined; used to transmit both voice and computer data.

UNIX   A powerful type of operating system of a personal computer that can handle multiple users.

unstructured decisions   Decisions which have no preestablished decision procedures.

usability   The capability, in terms of human functioning, of being used easily and effectively by a specified group of users to accomplish a specified range of tasks within a specific context.

user   The person who is served by the information system.

user-friendly   Referring to software that is geared to the end user and which incorporates features such as setup instructions that do not assume extensive knowledge of computers, "help" routines built into the software to assist users who get stuck, and commands that are presented through menus so that the user doesn't have to remember a lot of commands.

user generation   A stage in the development of the people who interact with computers and information systems and the procedures by which they do so.

user view   The perspective of the person who will be using the data in a database; also called *external view*.

value-added network (VAN)   A network in which a vendor provides all the related hardware, software, and protocols as well as the transmission line.

variable   The symbolic name or address of a data element.

verifier   A machine used to identify any mistakes that the keypunch operator may have made.

videotext   A record-keeping system that utilizes communication technology.

virtual storage   An operating system capability that divides a job into pieces and moves these pieces in and out of main memory in a manner that facilitates the execution of the job and makes primary memory appear to be infinite.

voice-grade channels   Channels designed to transmit voice communication.

voice input   Spoken natural language accepted by the computer as input.

voice output   Human speech output produced by the computer using a voice synthesizer.

voice recognition   The ability of the computer to accept spoken natural language as input.

voice service   A communications service that a company can provide; refers to the transmission of human telephone conversation.

voice synthesizer   A device that translates the output from binary form to human words.

volatile   Highly changeable, as is the primary storage of a personal computer. Also refers to storage that can hold data only when the electrical power is switched on.

wide area network (WAN)   A network that connects parts of an organization which are spread across a wide geographical area, such as a company with offices throughout the United States.

Winchester disk   A disk which is encapsulated with its own read/write heads.

window   A partition of the computer screen that enables a user to work with more than one process at the same time.

windowing   A function that allows the user to divide the screen into several areas at once.

word size   The amount of data which can be moved from the primary memory to the ALU in a single operation.

work station   See *microcomputer*.

WORM   Write once read many; a type of optical disk which is capable of being written only once though it may be read many times.

INDEX